JEWISHNESS
and BEYOND

STUDIES IN HUNGARIAN HISTORY
László Borhi, editor

JEWISHNESS
and BEYOND

Jewish Conversions in Hungary 1825–1914

MIKLÓS KONRÁD

Translated by Jason Vincz and the author

INDIANA UNIVERSITY PRESS

This book is a publication of

Indiana University Press
Office of Scholarly Publishing
Herman B Wells Library 350
1320 East 10th Street
Bloomington, Indiana 47405 USA

iupress.org

Translation funded by the László Tetmajer Fund of the Hungarian
Studies Program, Department of Central Eurasian Studies,
Indiana University Bloomington.

© 2024 by Miklós Konrád for original text
© 2024 by Department of Central Eurasian Studies, Indiana
University for translation

All rights reserved
No part of this book may be reproduced or utilized in any form or by
any means, electronic or mechanical, including photocopying and
recording, or by any information storage and retrieval system,
without permission in writing from the publisher.

First printing 2024

Library of Congress Cataloging-in-Publication Data

Names: Konrád, Miklós, author. | Vincz, Jason, translator.
Title: Jewishness and beyond : Jewish conversions in Hungary 1825-1914 /
  Miklós Konrád ; translated by Jason Vincz and Miklós Konrád.
Other titles: Zsidóságon innen és túl. English
Description: Bloomington, Indiana : Indiana University Press, [2024] |
  Series: Studies in Hungarian history | Includes bibliographical
  references and index.
Identifiers: LCCN 2023054855 (print) | LCCN 2023054856 (ebook) | ISBN
  9780253070500 (hardback) | ISBN 9780253070517 (paperback) | ISBN
  9780253070524 (ebook)
Subjects: LCSH: Jews—Hungary—History—19th century. |
  Jews—Hungary—History—20th century. | Christian converts from
  Judaism—Hungary—History—19th century. | Christian converts from
  Judaism—Hungary—History—20th century. | BISAC: HISTORY / Europe /
  Austria & Hungary | RELIGION / Religious Intolerance, Persecution &
  Conflict
Classification: LCC DS135.H9 K64513 2024 (print) | LCC DS135.H9 (ebook) |
  DDC 943.9/004924009034—dc23/eng/20240325
LC record available at https://lccn.loc.gov/2023054855
LC ebook record available at https://lccn.loc.gov/2023054856

This book is dedicated to Orsi, János, and Ábel.

CONTENTS

Acknowledgments ix
Note on Names and Statistical Figures xi
Abbreviations xiii

Introduction 1

1. The Historical Context of the Conversions of
   Hungarian Jews 9

2. Numbers of Conversions, Chronological Patterns,
   and Social Reactions 109

3. Profiles of Hungarian Jewish Converts 158

4. Paths to Conversion—Portraits 196

5. After Conversion 302

   Afterword 377

   Bibliography 381
   Index 419

ACKNOWLEDGMENTS

I would like to thank Pál Fodor and Antal Molnár, the directors of the Institute of History of the Research Centre for the Humanities in Budapest, for their trust and patience. It gives me great pleasure to be able to express my gratitude to Judit Klement, Zsejke Nagy, Anikó Prepuk, Clara Royer, Éva Somogyi, Zsuzsanna Toronyi, Orsolya Völgyesi, András Cieger, Zoltán Fónagy, Gábor Gyáni, Viktor Karády, Michael Miller, Peter Reich, Michael Silber, and Gábor Schweitzer. Special thanks to László Borhi, without whom this book would not have been possible, and to Jason Vincz for his translation.

NOTE ON NAMES AND STATISTICAL FIGURES

In the case of place names, I have given in parentheses the current names of places that are no longer in Hungary since the Treaty of Trianon (1920), as well as the country in which they are located today—for example, Pozsony (Bratislava, Slovakia).

I have used Hungarian forms of the first names of Jews who were born in or immigrated to Hungary (e.g., Lipót Löw instead of Leopold Löw).

The national figures for the Jewish population up to 1850 exclude Transylvania, the Partium, and the Military Frontier. The statistics from the period of the Dual Monarchy (1867–1918) refer only to Hungary in its strict sense—that is, they do not apply to Croatia, Slavonia, or the *corpus separatum* of Fiume (Rijeka, Croatia), even though these regions were legally part of the Kingdom of Hungary. Census data for the years 1869, 1880, and 1890 refer to the civilian population while those for 1900 and 1910 refer to both the civilian and military populations.

The italicized portions of quoted texts appear in this form in the original unless I have indicated otherwise in an endnote.

ABBREVIATIONS

BFL: Budapest Főváros Levéltára (Budapest City Archives)

ICB: Israelite Congregation of Buda

ICP: Israelite Congregation of Pest

MNL OL: Magyar Nemzeti Levéltár Országos Levéltára (National Archives of Hungary)

MRPE: Ministry of Religion and Public Education

MTA KIK Kt: Magyar Tudományos Akadémia Könyvtár és Információs Központ, Kézirattár (Library and Information Centre of the Hungarian Academy of Sciences, Manuscript Department)

MZsML: Magyar Zsidó Múzeum és Levéltár (Hungarian Jewish Museum and Archives)

OSZK PK: Országos Széchényi Könyvtár, Plakát- és Kisnyomtatványtár (National Széchényi Library, Poster and Small Print Library Department)

OSZK Kt: Országos Széchényi Könyvtár, Kézirattár (National Széchényi Library, Manuscript Department)

JEWISHNESS *and* BEYOND

Introduction

"If there is a people on this earth that might turn inward upon itself at the turn of the century, it is certainly the Jewish people, for in the century which has now drawn to a close, it has gone through a transformation unparalleled in the history of the nations, and for which there exists only one precedent in its own past: the Alexandrian Era."[1] These were the opening lines of Lajos Blau's introduction to the first twentieth-century issue of the *Magyar-Zsidó Szemle* (*Hungarian-Jewish Review*), the only Jewish scholarly journal published in Hungarian. In addition to serving as the editor of the *Szemle*, Blau (1861–1936) also taught at the Rabbinical Seminary of Budapest (of which he would become the director in 1913). He concluded this summary of the changes that had taken place since the late eighteenth century with an appraisal of his own era. Blau was not particularly worried by the antisemitism of the period; though he acknowledged the proliferation of "racial theories," he did not consider them to be any more dangerous than the religious fanaticism of earlier eras. Like most members of the bourgeois society of his day, Blau put his faith in progress and thus believed that while antisemitism might slow the advance of the Enlightenment, it could not stop it. What troubled him most about the future of Europe's emancipated Jewry was its "internal disarray." And here Blau's optimism turned to gloom: commitment to ancestral heritage had given way to indifference, and piety had turned to "religious infidelity." The nineteenth century, the scholarly rabbi concluded, could rightly be called "the century of conversion to Christianity."[2]

There is no doubt that during this period, the Jewish communities of Western and Central Europe, emancipated after struggles of varying duration and intensity,[3] had undergone a dramatic transformation. In Hungary, an ever-increasing proportion of the country's Jewish population—which had been growing at a dizzying pace, from 126,620 in 1805 to 911,227 in 1910—was abandoning the world of tradition. Most gave up speaking Yiddish—some switched immediately to Hungarian, though many more would switch to German first. They attended public elementary schools instead of the cheder and universities instead of the yeshiva; they frequented cafés rather than the shul and read newspapers rather than prayer books; many chose not to identify any longer as Jews, instead referring to themselves as Hungarian citizens of the Israelite faith. And though it is impossible to know precisely how many, it is clear that over the course of the nineteenth century, several tens of thousands of Hungarian Jews left their community and converted to one Christian denomination or another.

In the centuries prior to the era of emancipation, a decision of this sort represented a fundamental break. In choosing to be baptized and crossing over into the Christian world, converts uprooted themselves from a Jewish community that differed from the majority society not only in its religious beliefs but also in its origins, legal status, self-definition, culture, language, and lifestyle. This constituted an enormous shift in these converts' lives, even if their new coreligionists were skeptical of their motives and disinclined to accept them socially.[4] The impact of conversion was steadily diminished by the European Enlightenment and its Jewish analog, the *Haskalah*, as well as rationalist reinterpretations of Christianity and Judaism, secularization, and the resulting reduction in the social and cultural distance that separated Jews from Christians.[5]

Though the number of conversions fluctuated significantly, their growth beginning in the Reform Era (1825–48) may nevertheless seem paradoxical. The paradox is not that ever-increasing numbers of Jews were changing their religious affiliation in an era when religion itself was playing a smaller and smaller role in people's lives, as Christian expectations and Jewish self-justifications converged on the notion that conversion was not so much an embrace of the Christian faith as an espousal of European culture associated with Christianity and/or an entrée into Hungarian society. The paradox lies in the simultaneity of this increase in conversions and the diminution of the disadvantages associated with belonging to the Jewish community. The ostensible weight of these disadvantages declined significantly with the

INTRODUCTION 3

emancipation of Hungary's Jews in 1867 and the elevation of Judaism to equal status with the country's Christian denominations in 1895. Despite the fact that Law XXXVIII of 1790 ("*De Judaeis*") had led to modest improvements in the lives of Hungary's Jews,[6] abandoning the Jewish faith at the beginning of the nineteenth century still meant liberation from a pariah community whose members were prevented from settling in certain areas, barred from particular occupations, and subjected to special taxes. By the turn of the twentieth century, however, Hungary's Jews could no longer be described as pariahs.

On a theoretical level, liberal nationalists—whose ideology was dominant among Hungary's political and cultural elites from the Reform Era to the collapse of the Dual Monarchy at the end of World War I—were entirely accepting of Jews. Hungary's ruling classes' interests motivated them to be inclusive, as ethnic Hungarians were a minority population in their own country up to the end of the nineteenth century, and Magyarization was much more likely to succeed among Germans and Jews, who were scattered among the Hungarian populace, than among Romanians and Slovaks, who tended to live together in relatively homogeneous territorial blocs and were then in the midst of their own national awakenings. Given the pioneering roles Jews had played in the country's economic modernization, it is no surprise that Hungary's liberal-nationalist elites advocated Jewish emancipation, then took pains to safeguard Jews' equal rights after 1867. Hungary's ruling classes promoted Magyarization among the country's Jews, promising that it would make them full members of the Hungarian nation, equal in value to any Christian. By Magyarizing themselves in language, culture, and sensibilities, Jews would become as Hungarian as anyone else, differing from their fellow citizens only in their religion. While there were thus conditions attached to their recognition as Hungarians and their acceptance into Hungarian society, abandoning their faith and becoming Christians were certainly not among them.

The question thus arises: how can one explain the fact that Hungarian Jews converted to Christianity at much higher rates in the early decades of the twentieth century than they had a century earlier? As was the case elsewhere in Europe, these conversions did not overwhelm Hungary's Jewish community or pose a demographic threat to its existence. However, if one takes into account that the number of conversions among Hungarian Jews (which had been insignificant up to the Reform Era) rose to nearly five hundred per year in the first decade of the twentieth century—and if one takes into consideration the fact that by the time of the First World War, a significant proportion of Hungary's Jewish elite, including those who had distinguished themselves in the country's economic, political, and cultural spheres, were now *former* coreligionists of their fellow Jews—it becomes clear that conversion is one of the central issues in the modern history of Hungarian Jewry and crucial to any analysis of the coexistence of Jewish and Christian Hungarians.

While the Zionist-inspired school of historiography rejected the possibility that the Jewish people could live harmoniously in the diaspora, asserted that Jews' efforts to gain acceptance in the societies of other nationalities were necessarily doomed to failure, and suggested that such aspirations inevitably led to self-abnegation,[7] the historians whose views have become dominant in recent decades maintain that most European Jews overcame the challenges that arose in the course of their acculturation and integration and managed to find a viable, if delicate, balance between a redefined sense of Jewishness and their new commitments, which made it possible for them to preserve their distinctiveness, cohesion, and collective identity. That is, they acculturated without losing their sense of Jewish selfhood.[8] Historians who have adopted this optimistic view of Jewish integration into Christian societies are understandably less inclined to engage in thorough examinations of Jews who could not find—or were unwilling to maintain—a balance of this sort.[9] According to Todd Endelman, these researchers went too far in the other direction: "Historians who highlighted the vitality of diaspora Jewish life tended to ignore or minimize evidence regarding the weakening of Jewish ties and the toll that radical assimilation took."[10]

Hungarian Jews have been omitted from most of these historiographical debates, and thus there is no newly dominant historical perspective on their lives, nor any previous course to correct. There are, however, telling sources. The notion of writing this book occurred to me when I realized that at the turn of the twentieth century, Lajos Blau and his contemporaries—other rabbis and the authors and editors of Jewish newspapers and almanacs, to whom I shall refer hereafter as *Neolog intellectuals*, or the *Neolog intelligentsia*—regarded the speed with which Neolog Jews were abandoning their faith and their communities to be a phenomenon of dramatic proportions and considered the growing number of conversions within their own circles to be an issue of primary importance. It goes without saying that these authors were not objective, nor did they strive to be. At the same time, they knew much more about the Jewish society of their era than we ever will. I thus set about writing the first monograph on Jewish conversions in Hungary between the Reform Era

INTRODUCTION 5

and the First World War out of a conviction that it would provide us with a more precise understanding of the receptiveness and inclusivity of Hungarian Christian society and a more nuanced appreciation of the dilemmas Jewish men and women faced in the course of their integration into this society—not just those who abandoned their faith but those who remained faithful to their religion and community as well.

This book covers a period of nearly a century. With regard to its chronological boundaries, the starting point is self-evident. Conversions become a significant phenomenon during the Reform Era, which was characterized by efforts to create a modern, bourgeois Hungary; this is when the issue of Hungarian Jews' adoption of Christianity surfaced as part of the emerging discourse surrounding the present and future of Jewish integration into Christian society. The upheavals of the 1848 Revolution brought the Reform Era to a close and triggered the first wave of conversions among the Jews of Hungary. The First World War, along with the revolutions that followed it, would open a new chapter in the relationship between Hungary's Christians and Jews.

In the five chapters of this book, I have attempted to provide answers to the following sets of questions:

The historical context of these conversions. What general factors might have motivated Hungarian Jews to abandon their faith and join a Christian denomination? This question can be divided into two parts. First, how did conversion become a conceivable option for an ever-greater number of Jews? Second, what were the chief motives of those Jews who actually chose to convert?

Numbers of conversions, chronological patterns, cyclical factors, and social reactions. What do the numbers tell us? How many Hungarian Jews converted? More precisely, given that national statistics were not recorded until 1896, how many of the Jews of Pest seem to have converted prior to that year? How significant were these numbers by Central European standards? Which periods were characterized by the largest and smallest numbers of Jewish conversions and why? What sorts of period-specific factors might have driven Jews to join Christian denominations, and how should one interpret the intermittent nature of the growth in these waves of conversion? How did the Hungarian public react to Jews who converted, and how did their Jewish and Christian contemporaries' perceptions of them evolve?

6 JEWISHNESS AND BEYOND

The demographic profile of these converts. Who converted? Were certain strata of the Jewish population overrepresented among the converts? Which social and cultural classes were marked by the greatest numbers of conversions, and how did these proportions change over time?

Paths to conversion. Historical investigations of the causes of conversion generally cite the cases of specific individuals exemplifying particular reasons for abandoning Judaism and adopting the Christian faith. This practice excludes converts for whom the sources do not identify unequivocal motives and thus often results in reductive accounts of individuals' generally complex rationales. More importantly, it fails to provide enough space for meaningful discussions of the subjects themselves. Ultimately, though, the history of the conversion of the Jews is nothing more than the stories of the Jews who converted. The only way to lend substance to this history is to create individualized portraits of those converts. Where were they born, into what sorts of environments and families? How were they raised? Where did their lives take them? What were their dreams for the future? And why did they convert? Even if this sort of anecdotal evidence is insufficient as a basis for drawing general conclusions about the masses of converts, such portraits may enable us to shed some light on certain features and patterns that characterized conversions among members of the Jewish upper class and especially the Jewish intelligentsia, and on changes that typified the progress of the nineteenth century.

The aftermath of conversion. Stories of conversion never ended with a baptism. Did converting help these Jews achieve their goals? To what extent did they consider their conversions to be "successful"? In a society that would continue to consider them more or less Jewish, converts could not simply erase their pasts. How did they relate to their former Jewish lives? Finally, how did unconverted Jews relate to their former coreligionists, to family members, friends, and colleagues who had left the fold?

Notes

1. [Lajos Blau], "A letűnő évszázad," *Magyar-Zsidó Szemle* 17, no. 1 (1900): 1.
2. Ibid., 4.
3. David Sorkin, *Jewish Emancipation: A History across Five Centuries* (Princeton, NJ / Oxford, UK: Princeton University Press, 2019), 61–256.

INTRODUCTION

4. Todd M. Endelman, *Radical Assimilation in English Jewish History, 1656–1945* (Bloomington/Indianapolis: Indiana University Press, 1990), 20; id., "Memories of Jewishness: Jewish Converts and Their Jewish Pasts," in *Jewish History and Jewish Memory: Essays in Honor of Yosef Hayim Yerushalmi*, ed. Elisheva Carlebach, John M. Efron, and David N. Myers (Hanover, NH: University Press of New England / Brandeis University Press, 1998), 31; Elisheva Carlebach, *Divided Souls: Converts from Judaism in Germany, 1500–1750* (New Haven, CT / London: Yale University Press, 2001), 2–3, 42–45; Lauren Fogle, "Between Christianity and Judaism: The Identity of Converted Jews in Medieval London," *Essays in Medieval Studies* 22, no. 1 (2006): 108.

5. Jacob Katz, *Out of the Ghetto: The Social Background of Jewish Emancipation, 1770–1870* (Cambridge, MA: Harvard University Press, 1973), 109–10, 113–14.

6. The text of this law is available at https://net.jogtar.hu/ezer-ev-torvenyei. In the interest of avoiding an unnecessary profusion of footnotes, all subsequent unfootnoted discussions of Hungarian laws (and citations from their text) will refer to this website.

7. For an example of this outlook, see David Vital, *A People Apart: A Political History of the Jews in Europe 1789–1939* (Oxford, UK / New York: Oxford University Press, 1999).

8. Ismar Schorsch, *Jewish Reactions to German Anti-Semitism, 1870–1914* (New York: Columbia University Press; Philadelphia: Jewish Publication Society of America, 1972); Marion Kaplan, "Tradition and Transition: The Acculturation, Assimilation and Integration of Jews in Imperial Germany—A Gender Analysis," *Leo Baeck Institute Year Book* 27 (1982): 3–35; id., *The Making of the Jewish Middle Class: Women, Family, and Identity in Imperial Germany* (New York / Oxford, UK: Oxford University Press, 1991); Phyllis Cohen Albert, "Ethnicity and Jewish Solidarity in Nineteenth-Century France," in *Mystics, Philosophers, and Politicians: Essays in Jewish Intellectual History in Honor of Alexander Altmann*, ed. Jehuda Reinharz and Daniel Swetschinski (Durham, NC: Duke University Press, 1982), 249–74; Marsha L. Rozenblit, *The Jews of Vienna, 1867–1914: Assimilation and Identity* (Albany: State University of New York Press, 1983); id., *Reconstructing a National Identity: The Jews of Habsburg Austria during World War I* (Oxford, UK / New York: Oxford University Press, 2001). For a critical evaluation of this historiographical trend, see Paula E. Hyman, "The Ideological Transformation of Modern Jewish Historiography," in *The State of Jewish Studies*, ed. Shaye J. D. Cohen and Edward L. Greenstein (Detroit, MI: Wayne State University Press, 1990), 143–57; Todd M. Endelman, "Response," in Cohen and Greenstein, *The State of Jewish Studies*, 158–64; id., "The Legitimization of the Diaspora Experience in Recent Jewish Historiography," *Modern Judaism* 11, no. 2 (1991): 195–209.

8 JEWISHNESS AND BEYOND

9. Between 1770 and 1799, roughly 7 percent of Berlin's Jews converted to Christianity. Of the 3,493 Jews who lived in the city in 1812, the same proportion eventually abandoned their faith. Among the economic elite of Berlin's Jews, however, the percentage of converts was many times higher. Taking all this into consideration, it is noteworthy that in his book about the "transformation" of Germany's Jews in this era, David Sorkin devoted a total of ten lines to the issue of conversion, which he considered insignificant because it did not threaten the "continued existence" of urban Jewish communities. See David Sorkin, *The Transformation of German Jewry, 1780–1840* (Oxford, UK / New York: Oxford University Press, 1987), 111. For conversions in Berlin, see Deborah Hertz, "Seductive Conversion in Berlin, 1770–1809," in *Jewish Apostasy in the Modern World*, ed. Todd M. Endelman (New York / London: Holmes & Meier, 1987), 48–82; id., *Jewish High Society in Old Regime Berlin* (New Haven, CT / London: Yale University Press, 1988), 204–50; Steven M. Lowenstein, *The Berlin Jewish Community: Enlightenment, Family, and Crisis, 1770–1830* (New York / Oxford, UK: Oxford University Press, 1994), 120–33.

10. Todd M. Endelman, *Leaving the Jewish Fold: Conversion and Radical Assimilation in Modern Jewish History* (Princeton, NJ / Oxford, UK: Princeton University Press, 2015), 14.

1

The Historical Context of the Conversions of Hungarian Jews

Mózes Ullmann, one of the preeminent Jewish entrepreneurs and wholesalers of the Reform Era, converted to Roman Catholicism in Vienna on March 1, 1825.[1] His younger brother, the produce merchant Gábriel (Gábor) Ullmann, did not abandon the Jewish faith; as an active member—and later president—of the Jewish community of Pest in the 1820s and 1830s, he played an important role in introducing certain moderate religious reforms and modernizing the congregation's organizational structure.[2]

We could assemble a long list of similar examples. Conversion was a personal decision that cannot be fully explained by the changes that affected the Jewish community as a whole, nor by a given individual's family background, upbringing, career choices, financial circumstances, or social connections. Many nineteenth-century Hungarian Jews grew up in secularized families or distanced themselves from Judaism and Jewish traditions, and yet, despite the occupational disadvantages associated with their denominational status and the insults and injuries they suffered in their attempts to integrate into Christian society, they did not abandon the Jewish faith. There were also Jews whose decisions to convert remain incomprehensible, even in light of the typical motivating factors I will introduce below.

I do not intend to discount the significance of the general trends driving the steady increase in the number of conversions in the nineteenth century. In this chapter, I will attempt to chart these trends in order to identify the forces that might have motivated increasing numbers of Hungarian Jews to convert to one or another of the various Christian denominations.

The Dwindling Forces of Social Cohesion

In countries like England and France, where the majority societies expressed relatively little opposition to the integration of their Jewish population, conversion remained a rare phenomenon even among Jews who had distanced themselves from Judaism.[3] However, in countries where social and political antisemitism was more intense (such as those of Central Europe), acculturated and secularized Jews were much more inclined toward apostasy than their predominantly orthodox coreligionists in Russia, vanishingly small proportions of whom converted even though they were much more likely to suffer the effects of antisemitism.[4]

Although the act of distancing oneself from Judaism did not in itself lead to conversion, it was a fundamental and necessary precondition. Religious Jews did not choose to become Christians. Jewish secularization was accompanied by a proportional increase in the pool of potential converts because the more or less complete disappearance of a Jew's religious ties eliminated the emotional impediments that precluded the option of baptism. Thus, one must first determine the size and sociocultural profile of the group of Jews who would have considered conversion during the period under discussion. How large was this segment of the Hungarian Jewish population by the time of the First World War, and who were they?

I concur with historians and social scientists who reject "secularization theory" insofar as I do not regard secularization as an inevitable concomitant of modernization, nor as a linear process that necessarily and universally resulted from modernization.[5] At the same time, it cannot be ignored that secularization was among the fundamental processes that characterized the transformation of Central and Western European Jewry in the modern era. Historians have devoted surprisingly little attention to this subject. To the best of my knowledge, no one has published a comprehensive examination of the changes in nineteenth-century European Jews' attitudes toward religious commandments and rituals, nor even a study of such changes in the Jewish population of a single country in this period.[6] Scholars who focus on modern Jewish identity barely mention the subject,[7] although as Todd Endelman has emphasized, synagogue attendance, dietary restrictions, rest on the Sabbath, observance of the High Holidays, and ceremonies practiced within the family have historically been the fundamental markers of Jewish distinctiveness.[8] One reason why contemporary historians have so conspicuously neglected

Jewish secularization in the modern era may be precisely this rampant decline in religiosity, which raises doubts about these historians' claims that acculturated Jews managed to maintain attachments to their communities and their own Jewish identity.[9]

The decline in religiosity among the Jews of Hungary was not a continuous process nor a general phenomenon. Up to the end of the 1860s, Hungary's established Jewish community was regularly augmented by massive influxes of Jewish immigrants from Galicia, most of whom were strictly observant.[10] Furthermore, while the antisemitic crisis of the first half of the 1880s intensified certain individuals' desires to liberate themselves from their Jewish status, it also filled the synagogues again—temporarily. Secularization had almost no effect on the ultra-Orthodox Jews—many of them Hasidic—of Hungary's northeastern counties (known in Yiddish as the Unterland) or on the more moderate rabbinical Orthodoxy of the country's northwestern counties (the Oberland), although its impact on the Orthodox communities of western Hungary and the country's larger cities was more significant. By the turn of the century, the Orthodox Jewish press was regularly complaining about the declining piety of the young Jews who attended gymnasia and public secondary schools for sciences and modern languages (reáliskolák, modeled after Austrian Realschulen).[11] By 1910, these publications were repeatedly printing complaints about the growing number of Jews within Orthodox communities who failed to protect "the sanctity of the Sabbath."[12] It is clear, however, that while the process of secularization did affect some of Hungary's Orthodox Jews, a significant minority of the country's Jewish population, particularly the ultra-Orthodox Jews of the Unterland, remained fully faithful to their ancient religious traditions throughout the period under discussion.

The Jews of Germany had more or less abandoned their traditional lifestyles by the 1830s. In Hungary, traditional Jewish culture persisted in practically untouched form until the 1820s,[13] when the first signs that conscientiousness in religious matters had begun to slacken became apparent. In 1825, delegations representing the Jewish communities of thirteen counties gathered in Pozsony (Bratislava, Slovakia) to elect a committee to present a petition for Jewish civil rights to the Hungarian Diet, which had convened in the city. In the summer of 1826, the president of the Jewish community of Veszprém, Arje Löb Rapoch, presented this committee with a draft of the community-organization regulations he hoped government authorities would impose on the country's Jewish communities. Nothing came of this plan, but it is striking that the third and fourth points of this proposal would have prohibited Jewish communities from employing cantors, prayer leaders, *shochetim*, or teachers who were not devout (*gottesfürchtig*), suggesting Rapoch had encountered— or at least heard of—such people.[14] In 1828, the rabbi of the Jewish community of Szeged, Hirs Bak, asked the city council to require Jewish merchants to keep their shops closed on Saturdays and religious holidays.[15] In 1831, Simon Oppenheimer, the rabbinical judge (*dayan*) of Pest, submitted a complaint to the city's Jewish community council because local grocers and tobacconists were keeping their shops open on Shabbat and holidays.[16] Nevertheless, these sorts of cases were still isolated incidents. Moreover, Jewish communities could usually count on the support of local authorities in dealing with violators of religious commandments, which made it possible to take (temporarily) effective action against them.[17]

The 1840s represented a turning point. As a result of Act XXIX of 1840 (*"Concerning the Jews"*), which permitted Jews to take up residence anywhere in Hungary (including its royal free cities and excepting only its mining towns), many new urban Jewish communities were established and grew to significant proportions. This law also provided Jews with new opportunities in commerce, industry, and intellectual careers. However, urban life and expansion of the professional opportunities open to them made it more difficult for many Jews to fulfill their religious obligations.[18]

Forming social relationships with Christians also increased the difficulty of complying with Jewish religious laws. For example, acceptance into a so-called casino or social club in Pest or one of Hungary's provincial cities made one more likely to violate Jewish dietary restrictions at least occasionally.[19] Like entrepreneurs, members of the modern Jewish intellectual class emerging at the time also had trouble reconciling religious obligations with the new aspirations awakened by these new opportunities. "Our conceptions of secular affairs have changed fundamentally," wrote the Pápa physician Samu Pserhofer in the only published issue of the first Hungarian-language Jewish periodical, *Magyar Zsinagóga (Hungarian Synagogue)*, published in 1847 by the eminent Reform rabbi Lipót Löw. Pserhofer wrote in the name of those who wanted to involve themselves in "all the causes and tasks of life," compete with their fellow citizens on the "field of honor," and contribute to "every national endeavor." All these ambitions would take a toll on religious life: "Countless times every day, we contradict the edicts of ritual with our deeds."[20]

Pserhofer was convinced that even if he had violated numerous religious commandments, he had done so with "healthy" intentions. Others, like Pserhofer's fellow physician Elias Oesterreicher of Pest, were horrified by this state of affairs. In his 1842 book, Oesterreicher indignantly noted that young people were growing up "without religion, without morals," and without "ever hearing the word of God"—that is, without attending synagogue.[21] In a travel guide published that same year, the converted Orientalist Mayer Bonaventura estimated that a third of the Jews of Buda and Pest were no longer serious about celebrating Shabbat or observing dietary restrictions.[22] The abandonment of traditional religious practices was not limited to Pest. On several occasions in the late 1830s and early 1840s, married women appeared in the synagogue in Makó without wigs, their own hair visible under their headscarves.[23] On the eve of the 1848 revolution, their contemporaries took it for granted that employees of commercial enterprises in Pest would work on Saturday and rest on Sunday.[24] Such behavior was implicitly encouraged by lay leaders of certain Jewish communities, who sometimes disregarded these religious prescriptions themselves. Violating the commandments of the faith had previously resulted in excommunication, but by the 1840s, Jews who disregarded religious laws in their private lives could still be members of their communities and even assume leadership roles.[25]

At the same time, one should not exaggerate the significance of these changes. According to József Schweitzer, religious life in Pécs was still "completely conservative" before 1848.[26] As Michael Silber has noted, Mayer Bonaventura's 1842 estimate suggests that two-thirds of the Jews of Buda and Pest were still strictly observant. Given that the Jews of Pest were the vanguard of social change within the broader community, a significantly higher proportion of Hungary's Jews might still have been Orthodox at that time.[27] Thus, despite these changes, an overwhelming majority of Hungary's Jews would continue to live in the world of tradition until Hungary's feudal society was dismantled in the wake of the Revolution of 1848.

Thanks to Hungary's Orthodox Jews, traditional religious life continued to flourish in Hungary in the 1850s,[28] yet Michael Silber has drawn the following conclusion about the Jews of Pest in this period: "the rise in the numbers of Jews who worked on the Sabbath and the drop in kosher meat consumption in the fifties indicated that a substantial segment of the Jewish population was altogether indifferent to any religious practice or worship."[29] Several sources confirm that the demand for kosher meat decreased.[30]

14 JEWISHNESS AND BEYOND

Decisions to forego everyday synagogue attendance and celebrations of Shabbat would become widespread in Hungary in the 1850s and 1860s, and this phenomenon was not limited to wealthier and/or more educated Jews. According to an official report written in 1851, the thirteen Jewish places of worship in operation in Pest at that time could not provide enough seating for the faithful during the High Holidays, which raises a question that answers itself: Where were the faithful for the rest of the year?[31] According to an 1861 article published in the weekly *Magyar Izraelita* (*Hungarian Israelite*), it was "common knowledge" that the synagogues and prayer houses of Pest could not accommodate all the Jews who wanted to attend worship services on the High Holidays.[32] Indirectly, this also shows that the practice of going to the temple only on the High Holidays, a custom characteristic of Neolog Jewish life, became widespread in the Hungarian capital during this period.

The most important factor in the decline of traditional piety in the long term proved to be the educational reform the neo-absolutist government imposed on Hungary's Jewish communities in the 1850s, though its effects were not felt until the 1860s. In hopes of preparing Jews to participate in the modernization of Hungary, reining in the process of Magyarization to which they had been subjected since the 1840s, and keeping Jews in the German-speaking cultural sphere, Austrian imperial minister Leo Thun-Hohenstein issued a decree in 1851 ordering Jewish communities to replace their cheders with German-language elementary schools using state-mandated teaching materials. The number of these Jewish elementary schools rose from thirty to three hundred in one decade. According to Jacob Katz, these institutions "brought about a gradual and quiet cultural revolution.... An entire generation arose that did not know the atmosphere of the cheder, saturated as it was with the values of an intimate Jewish tradition."[33]

From the perspective of instilling religious sentiments in the younger generations, it was an unfortunate coincidence that—according to an 1864 article in the *Magyar Izraelita*—until the 1840s, "in most communities, almost every Jewish father provided his sons with instruction not only in the Holy Scriptures, but in the Talmud as well," whereas by the 1860s, educational institutions had assumed the task of providing religious instruction to children.[34] Another recurrent theme in the periodicals of this era was the degree to which religious education in schools would exert an influence on the souls of Jewish children if their parents did not provide them with a religious upbringing at home. The author of an 1863 article in the *Magyar Izraelita* summarized an opinion that would be repeated ceaselessly in subsequent decades: "Where parental support is lacking, the builder labors in vain."[35]

In 1867, after nearly three decades of recurrent parliamentary debate, the Jews of Hungary were finally granted emancipation. On December 27 of that year, emperor of Austria and king of Hungary Franz Joseph gave royal sanction to Act XVII of 1867 ("On the equality of the Israelites with regard to civil and political rights").[36] The law extended equal rights to Jews but not to Judaism, which would be elevated to "received" status—made equal with Christian denominations—only when the king approved Act XLII of 1895, the so-called Reception Law, on October 16 of that year.[37] A year after the passage of the emancipation law of 1867, representatives of Israelite communities in Hungary and Transylvania convened a national assembly. Their main objective was to regulate the operations of Jewish communities and their schools and to establish an intermediary body to ensure communication between these communities and the state. This Universal Assembly, known more commonly as the Jewish Congress, met from December 10, 1868, to February 23, 1869, and led to an organizational schism among Hungary's Jews. The majority of the Orthodox representatives withdrew from the assembly before its conclusion. On June 14, 1869, Franz Joseph approved the organizational statutes adopted at the assembly, though the regulations would be binding only on "congressional"—that is, Neolog—congregations. The Orthodox camp launched a pressure campaign, attempting to capitalize on Hungarian parliamentarians' commitment to the inviolability of the principle of religious liberty, and on March 18, 1870, as a result of their zealous lobbying effort, the National Assembly instructed József Eötvös, the minister of religion and public education, to suspend the implementation of the "congressional" statutes on the grounds that they violated Orthodox Jews' beliefs and thus could not be imposed on them. On October 22, 1871, Franz Joseph approved a second set of statutes pertaining to Orthodox communities and their national organization. Eötvös's successor as minister of religion and public education, Tivadar Pauler, issued an edict on November 15, 1871, making these statutes public.[38]

Though their proportion continuously declined, a majority of Hungary's Jews would continue to belong to Orthodox communities throughout the period under discussion.[39] However, as I have noted, organizational affiliation and actual religious behavior are two different things. In any case, it would appear that the majority of Hungarian Jews still adhered to the central tenets of the faith at the time of emancipation. According to the anonymous author of a reformist pamphlet published in 1867, wherever Jews lived under the authority of Orthodox rabbis—and in the author's estimation, the latter made up nine-tenths of Hungary's rabbinate—"the education of the people is at the same lowly level as it was among their forefathers. . . . Since those days, they have not changed a hair's breadth, neither in lifestyle, nor in customs, nor in their rituals."[40] Even so, the debates at the Jewish Congress demonstrate that representatives of both camps, Neolog and Orthodox, were worried about increasing indifference to the sanctity of the Sabbath, which suggests that the pamphlet's author was exaggerating.[41]

The observance of Shabbat was still commonplace in certain Neolog milieux. The fictionalized autobiography of Tamás Kóbor suggests that in the 1870s, Shabbat was still a natural part of Jewish social life in the predominantly Neolog Terézváros district of Pest, and that its solemnity pervaded the atmosphere of the entire neighborhood.[42] Significantly, these aspects of Kóbor's recollections applied only to the poor Jews of the district. It is perhaps symbolic that Rabbi Márk Handler of Aszód, in a January 1868 thanksgiving service on the occasion of the emancipation, used the first Hungarian-language sermon of his life to express gratitude for equal rights, but then immediately added, "Let us not imagine, my honored brethren, that we should express our thanks by relinquishing our devotion to our ancestral faith, by abandoning certain laws under the pretext of enlightenment, [or] by failing to observe the Sabbath and our holidays."[43] A Rosh Hashanah sermon delivered by Rabbi Sámuel Kohn of Pest the following year confirms that some of the city's Jews went to synagogue only for the High Holidays. Kohn opened his remarks to the Israelite Congregation of Pest (ICP) by saying, "We have all come here—even those who are not in the habit of visiting this house of the Lord all year round."[44]

Rabbi Kohn's reproach had no effect. Sermons, pamphlets, the few Jewish periodicals of the era, and other writings produced in subsequent decades were unanimous in opining that enthusiastic Magyarization and the rapidly increasing affluence of the Jewish middle class that formed in the years following the emancipation had been accompanied by a large-scale desertion of religious tradition, indifference to the life of the community, and the utter neglect of religious education in schools. In his 1874 New Year's sermon, Sámuel Kohn deplored the "passive indifference of the largest part" of his coreligionists, with a particular emphasis on his concern that "the young do not care about the holy affairs of their religion and their denomination."[45] The author of an

1877 article in *Der Ungarische Israelit* castigated his Jewish contemporaries for believing that "the more irreligious we show ourselves to be, the sooner the nations will recognize us as being like themselves."[46] Late-1870s jokes about the secularization of acculturating Jews presented the observance of Shabbat, for example, as an "Orthodox" custom.[47]

Another novelty of the 1870s was a prayer book for young Jews that indicated precisely which prayers should be said on which occasions, an indication that this book's authors believed published guides needed to provide children with the sort of religious instruction they would previously have received from their parents.[48] The Jewish religious-instruction manuals of the period clearly tailored their arguments to a generation that was already abandoning its religious traditions. Izrael Singer taught religion at the status quo ante community elementary school in Sátoraljaújhely and at the town's Catholic gymnasium; his 1876 religious manual "for Israelite youth" began with the following question: "Does a person really need religion?"[49]

The rapid secularization of Neolog Jews became a constant topic of debate in the growing number of Jewish periodicals published in Hungary beginning in the 1880s. Several of these periodicals were established precisely to combat Jews' alienation from their community. Neolog intellectuals occasionally expressed hope that a secular form of Jewish identity might emerge in the wake of the apparently unstoppable process of secularization.[50] Even Rabbi Lajos Blau, the scholarly editor of the *Magyar-Zsidó Szemle*, recognized that "alongside religious indifference, there also exists a bond that connects individuals to our circles: [our] shared past, shared suffering, [and] shared origins."[51] Even so, Neolog intellectuals would remain convinced that in the end, "without the Torah, there is no Jewry."[52] Although numerous lay members of the Neolog intelligentsia obeyed only a subset of the faith's commandments, many still rejected the idea that some sort of abstract piety divested of religious practice would prove capable of preserving Jews' connections to their Jewishness.[53]

By the 1880s, the writers at these Jewish periodicals took the Jewish bourgeoisie's near-total disregard for the commandments of the faith as a fait accompli. I use the word *bourgeoisie* because even though these authors usually voiced their complaints in general terms, their primary concern was the decline in religiosity among members of the Jewish middle and upper classes. As a family doctor in the village of Bakonyszombathely wrote in 1888, "A genuine rarity among us is the intelligent [i.e., educated] Jew who, in satisfying the demands of his civilian occupation, wonders when and how he shall honor the obligations arising from his Jewish faith."[54] The authors of these Jewish periodicals were particularly pessimistic about youth. In 1885, instructor Vilmos Radó of the State Teachers' Training Institute claimed that one could not find more than "a few religious elements or traces of childhood religious impressions" in the souls of the younger generation.[55] In 1887, a law student from Nagyvárad observed that "the majority of the young Jews [at the university] are ashamed to be Jewish."[56]

The Neolog intelligentsia were convinced that the source of the problem was the failure of Jewish parents to provide their children with religious instruction at home. In 1885, Ilona Goldziher of Budapest—niece of Orientalist Ignác Goldziher—wrote that Jewish children were indifferent to their faith and its observances primarily because Jewish families had "completely erased religious upbringing from their list of obligations."[57] Izor Léva, a teacher at the Jewish elementary school in Bácstopolya (Bačko Topola, Serbia), expressed himself in similar terms four years later: "The children's religious and moral sentiments are hardly nourished or indulged at home; indeed, for the most part, there is no longer any room for religious life in the family."[58]

The contents of an 1882 newsletter ICP authorities sent to parents whose children attended the community's schools suggest that the organization's leaders shared these concerns: "It is not possible for education to produce satisfactory results unless the education provided by the school is effectively promoted and supplemented by the parents at home. . . . Please take every opportunity to draw your children's attention to the importance of religious instruction and the great significance you attach to it. This is the unavoidable religious duty that every Jewish parent . . . must fulfill."[59] It would seem the members of the Jewish middle and upper classes of Budapest considered this obligation to be a pointless burden. Speaking at a meeting of Budapest's Jewish religious instructors on February 13, 1890, Fülöp Csukási lamented that parents "feel a horrible aversion to Hebrew letters." After relating a few anecdotes about certain bankers' wives' and lawyers' objections to having their children educated in matters of religion, Csukási emphasized that these people "were not individual exceptions, but the voices and archetypes of the intellectual masses representing the uppermost stratum of our religious community."[60]

There may have been Jews who did not consider it necessary to teach their children Hebrew yet took care in their own way to provide them with some sort of religious education at home. A small number of personal remembrances from this period offer a more complex picture than this deluge of complaints from the Neolog intelligentsia, but the accounts do not provide evidence of the sort of emotionally intense religious upbringing that would have been capable of exerting an influence on children's souls. Born in 1870 and raised in Budapest by a well-to-do ophthalmologist, Tekla Vidor recalled that her upbringing "consisted exclusively of encouragement to live a moral life."[61] Kornél Preisich was born in 1869 near Szolnok and grew up in that city, where his father, Adolf, was a prosperous produce and wine wholesaler. Kornél and his four siblings had to pray in the mornings and evenings, and their parents celebrated the High Holidays, on which occasions the children were taken to the synagogue. Even so, Kornél limited his characterization of the religious atmosphere in his wealthy family to the following comment: "In our home, we never lived an intimate religious life."[62]

The wave of antisemitism that swept through Hungary beginning in the early 1880s, particularly following the Tiszaeszlár blood libel affair (1882–83), temporarily halted the decline in religious sentiments among the country's Jews. In October of 1883, the Jewish weekly *Egyenlőség* (*Equality*) joyfully reported that in comparison to the High Holidays of previous years, "the faithful flocked to the synagogue in disproportionally great numbers."[63] The burst of religious zeal proved ephemeral, and according to rabbinical student Mátyás Enyedi, it hardly affected the younger generation at all. Like others, Enyedi assigned responsibility for this situation to parents: "If [a Jewish child] does not see the practice of religion in his parents' home, how else should he be inspired by the holy concepts of our religion?"[64]

By the late 1880s, Neolog periodicals had largely given up lamenting that the faithful had quit attending synagogue every day and instead expressed joy that they came out for the High Holidays.[65] It is clear that large numbers of Budapest's Jews still visited synagogues and temporary prayer houses during the High Holidays in the 1890s. However, the Neolog intelligentsia would declare this phenomenon to be misleading with increasing frequency beginning in the 1890s. In 1894, the physician Izor Glass of Budapest wrote, "I would say it is characteristic of the overwhelming majority of our more distinguished ladies that if they decide to visit the synagogue once or twice a year, they inevitably make this trip with great elegance, but without a prayer book."[66] In a letter submitted to the Neolog weekly *A Jövő* (*The Future*) in 1898, "a modern lady" declared that many observed the holiest day of the Jewish year, Yom Kippur, only because "*bon ton*" required them to do so.[67]

Skepticism about the actual religious sentiments of middle-class Jews who filled the Neolog synagogues during the High Holidays was accompanied by dismissive attitudes toward the manner in which they were presumed to behave at home. The author of an 1890 article published in *Egyenlőség* asserted that "in most cases, children do not experience religious practice at home; they do not [experience] Shabbat or the holidays; they do not hear the words of the prayers—nothing that might remind them of their faith and religion."[68] By the 1890s, the Neolog intelligentsia was certain that Shabbat had long since disappeared from "the salons and the better houses" and was observed "only in impoverished hovels."[69] These complaints would pile up as the years passed. Fewer and fewer Jewish parents, particularly in Budapest, hosted bar mitzvah ceremonies for their thirteen-year-old sons;[70] according to other accounts, they did so only "sporadically."[71] By 1897, minor holidays were generally observed only in villages, as "urban office-clerk life" had "mostly" put an end to them in the cities.[72] This observation also applied to household rituals, which Veszprém's chief rabbi, Arnold Kiss (who would go on to serve as the chief rabbi of Buda from 1901), said Jewish families abandoned as soon as they began to climb the social ladder.[73] Writing under the pseudonym Sándor Komáromi in 1894, *Egyenlőség*'s assistant editor Samu Haber asserted that "we have reached the point where the teaching of religion, in almost every manifestation, in form and in spirit, requires a school."[74] This was a particularly bitter pill for the Neolog intelligentsia, uniformly convinced that religious education in schools was doomed to fail if parents did not model appropriate behavior for their children.

It is important to note that the decline in religious practice did not entail rejection of the basic rituals that signified membership in the community. In the jurisdiction of the ICP (i.e., districts IV through IX in Budapest), only 2.3 percent of Jewish parents failed to have their newborn boys circumcised in 1896 and only 2.1 percent in 1897. In the latter year (two years after the 1895 authorization of civil marriages), 95 percent of Jewish couples who married in civil ceremonies in the Budapest districts of the ICP also wed at the synagogue.[75]

The worries of the Neolog intelligentsia did not abate in the decade and a half preceding the First World War—on the contrary. As Lajos Blau noted in the *Magyar-Zsidó Szemle* at the dawn of the twentieth century, "It is a general complaint that the old piety has disappeared, that religious life is vanishing from the family, that the synagogues are deserted."[76] Over the years, the

CONTEXT OF THE CONVERSIONS OF HUNGARIAN JEWS   21

ceaseless complaints of the Jewish press had changed only in tone: some writers allowed themselves angry outbursts while others expressed bitter resignation. Whether the writers were discussing Christian governesses who "make the Jewish children who are entrusted into their care hate the religion of the Jews, of which there is otherwise no trace in the house,"[77] or high school students, "most of whom are not taught religion at home,"[78] or wealthy Jews whose homes lacked even "a single little nook into which the Torah could fit or be wedged,"[79] there are two striking aspects of these complaints. First, the Neolog intelligentsia continued to see no difference between public piety (on display in synagogues and prayer houses) and private practice (exhibited at home and in family life), as they considered the lack of the latter to be as flagrant as the former. Second, as was the case in the 1880s, the worries pertained primarily to members of the Jewish middle and upper classes.

In the case of the upper bourgeoisie, all evidence suggests the fears were warranted. Of course, there were members of the Jewish economic elite who did not strictly comply with the majority of the commandments of the faith but were nonetheless religious in their own way. Zsigmond Kornfeld, who served as a board member, chief executive, and later president of the Hungarian General Credit Bank, prayed at the Dohány Street Synagogue during the High Holidays, attended services at the Rumbach Street Synagogue (built for the more conservative members of the ICP),[80] participated in Passover seders, and fasted on Yom Kippur.[81] At the same time, Kornfeld characterized Jews who observed Shabbat as "Orthodox" and held his bank's managerial meetings on Saturday afternoons. Indeed, as the vice president of the ICP, Kornfeld advocated the formal elimination of dietary laws, given that—as he explained to another of the community's leaders—"in school, the children are taught that it is forbidden to eat *treif*, but at home the children eat *treif*."[82]

Alongside Kornfeld, one should also mention Manfréd Weiss, Hungary's largest taxpayer at the time of the First World War.[83] Founder of the Csepel Steel and Metal Works, Weiss spent decades as a member of both the ICP's representative council and the board of the Chevra Kadisha of Pest, then took a seat on the steering committee of the Rabbinical Seminary of Budapest in 1913. During the High Holidays, Weiss spent the entire day praying at the synagogue. Every year on the anniversary of his parents' deaths, he went to say kaddish at a small prayer house on Vasvári Pál Street that formally operated under the authority of the ICP but was actually Orthodox. Weiss also provided regular financial support to the yeshiva in Hunfalva (Huncovce, Slovakia), which was renowned among Orthodox believers throughout Europe. According to *Egyenlőség*, Weiss paid annual visits to Sámuel Rosenberg, the Hunfalva rabbi who served as the yeshiva's head.[84] When Weiss was granted the title of baron in 1918, even the Zionist *Zsidó Szemle* (*Jewish Review*), which tended to disparage the Jewish haute bourgeoisie, noted that he was "in his own way a good Jew."[85]

Even so, Zsigmond Kornfeld and Manfréd Weiss were exceptional even among the members of the Jewish upper classes who participated in religious life. Looking back on the early years of the twentieth century from the vantage point of 1919, rabbi and historian Béla Bernstein claimed that the leaders of the Jewish community were "generally irreligious" and accepted their positions simply for "the superficial honor."[86] Mózes Richtmann was even more emphatic in a 1912 article: "It is awfully ridiculous that if certain 'good' Jews were to abandon the faith tomorrow, they would not have to change a thing about their current lifestyles."[87]

By the turn of the century, most of "Lipótváros" (used increasingly as a metonym for the capital city's Jewish haute bourgeoisie and upper-middle class) was avoiding active participation in Jewish community life. As the son of one of the managing directors of the Hungarian General Credit Bank, the philosopher György Lukács was intimately acquainted with this milieu and used one short sentence in his memoir to summarize its inhabitants' general attitude toward Judaism: "Lipótváros families were totally indifferent to questions of religion."[88] The rabbi of the Lipótváros Prayer House Association (established in 1905) recalled that the name of this Budapest district had "become a concept" at the turn of the century, and that Lipótváros was "utterly identified with indifference to the formalities of the faith." The rabbi spoke from experience: within two years of its founding, his 360-member association had to hire five employees to ensure the presence of the *minyan*, or ten-man quorum, required for public worship services.[89]

ICP statistics confirm that Lipótváros families were more indifferent to Judaism than their poorer coreligionists. The Neolog community operated Hebrew schools for elementary school students and Talmud-Torah schools for the students at *Bürgerschulen*, *Realschulen*, and gymnasia so that Jewish parents could provide their sons with a more thorough theological education than they would receive from the materials mandated for their religion courses. In 1913, 2.9 percent of the male Jewish students at Lipótváros' Bürgerschulen and high schools attended Talmud-Torah schools; this figure among the Jewish students of Terézváros was 13.2 percent.[90]

We know little about the religious lives of Budapest's Jewish petty bourgeoisie. The aforementioned statistics suggest that members of this social class were more attached to their religion than were wealthier Jews. However, by the turn of the century, it would seem that middle- and upper-class parents were not the only ones who were failing to familiarize their children with religious rituals at home, as evidenced by the fact that in 1904, the ICP began requiring Jewish fourth graders in all the Budapest districts under its jurisdiction to attend weekly religious services and do an hour of "liturgical exercises," requirements that had previously applied only to high school students. Bernát Munkácsi, who had served as superintendent of the community's schools since 1890, wrote that the objective of this measure was to "provide the pupils at boys' elementary schools with *practical* knowledge of traditional religious services as well."[91]

In his 1911 book *Out of the Ghetto*, Tamás Kóbor described the Sabbath atmosphere in the poor Jewish streets of the Terézváros of his childhood and continued, "Now Saturday is no longer holy; the people, the girls are at work."[92] By the 1900s, Neolog publications had given up calling their coreligionists to account for failing to observe Shabbat, expressing little more than a general sorrow that "Saturday is now—alas—a day of rest only for the few."[93]

One set of religious practices on which rich and poor Hungarian Jews agreed was the observance of the High Holidays. A number of sources, including Raymond Recouly (the political editor of the French daily *Le Figaro*), Wickham Steed (the Vienna correspondent for *The Times* of London), the liberal newspaper *Pesti Hírlap* (*Pest Journal*), the antisemite Kálmán Weszprémy, contemporaneous reports in the daily paper of the antisemitic People's Party, and the memoirs of Budapest Jews all agree that a festive atmosphere pervaded Budapest during the Jewish High Holidays; the city's stock exchange and most of its shops were closed, and local theaters, cafés, and other entertainment venues were practically empty on such occasions.[94] According to a 1905 article in *Egyenlőség*, there were 150 Neolog and Orthodox sites in Budapest—synagogues, prayer houses belonging to various Jewish associations, and privately operated auxiliary prayer houses—where Jews could attend Rosh Hashanah services that year.[95]

Occasions like these continued to provide the Jewish press with "incontrovertible evidence" that the Jewish community still pulsed with "ancestral vigor,"[96] though pessimism was dominant by that time. In 1904, *Egyenlőség* journalist Miklós Hajdu wrote, "[Jewish people] have almost codified the perverse practice of seeking out the house of God twice a year, at the time of the new year and on the day of atonement, and then with this, all Jewishness comes to an end."[97] The behavior of Jews who attended synagogue only on holidays intensified these journalists' disillusionment. According to the author of a 1904 article in *Egyenlőség*, "The ladies, if they happen to be at the temple, do not pray, but chatter away like they are at some kind of party. . . . Even during the most heart-rending prayers, they will discuss how expensive cucumbers are this year."[98] Such behavior must not have been exceptional; the newspaper of Buda's Neolog community regularly reminded its readers during the High Holidays that "chatting in the synagogue was strictly prohibited," as was "reading secular books or newspapers" during prayers.[99] This represented the best-case scenario, considering the complaints of the religious press that many Jews, particularly professionals, did not even attend High Holiday services. In 1909, *Egyenlőség* wrote, "How often have we seen a Jewish lawyer fail to make an issue of it and sit down *sans gêne* to negotiate on the day of Yom Kippur."[100]

Another new development of the first decade of the twentieth century was the proliferation of complaints about the Neolog Jews of Hungary's provincial cities. Anna Lőwy, a teacher at the Jewish elementary school in Pécs, was indignant that parents "have already forgotten so much about the prohibitions of religious matters that their children, who attend Jewish school, for the ten o'clock snack to be consumed on the premises of this Jewish school, get ham from home."[101] According to Chief Rabbi Ede Neumann of Nagykanizsa, the heads of local households worked on Saturdays, and most celebrated only Rosh Hashanah and Yom Kippur.[102] Samu Bródy, the headmaster of the Jewish community school in Gyula, sarcastically suggested that an excess of modesty was the reason his coreligionists appeared at synagogue "as rarely as possible."[103] The autobiography of writer Béla Zsolt (born in 1895 in Komárom) offers insights into the religious practices of his middle-class family. Bródy's father, a lawyer and later the director of a savings bank, took him to the synagogue only on Yom Kippur; his family did not keep a kosher kitchen and slaughtered pigs. As Zsolt wrote, "At home, hardly anything reminded us of our Jewishness."[104] In the much smaller town of Albertirsa in Pest County, local Jews still attended Shabbat services, though according to Rabbi Zsigmond Büchler, they did so "reluctantly, grudgingly."[105] Arthur Linksz, who grew up in the Veszprém County town of Devecser, recalled in his memoir that only one or two local Jewish families observed Shabbat.[106]

Finally, I should add a word about Jewish villagers. It is an accepted fact that secularization was primarily an urban phenomenon, and thus this process presumably affected Jews in Budapest more than Jews in smaller provincial cities, and Jews in smaller provincial cities more than Jews in villages. For Hungarian Jews of the first decade of the twentieth century, this assumption lacks any empirical proof, though it was certainly true of the Jewish villagers in the Orthodox-dominated regions of Hungary. Even so, religious life in the village was marked by difficulties of its own. Lavoslav Schick, a Croatian Zionist who lived in Hungary for a couple of years around the turn of the century, estimated that a Jewish community needed at least one hundred people to be able to hold regular religious services, ensure that their children received religious education, and support the requisite religious institutions. In 1900, 23.9 percent of Hungary's Jewish population lived in municipalities with fewer than one hundred Jews. According to Schick, "Jewish religious life was lively even in the really small communities" of the predominantly Orthodox-inhabited counties of northern Hungary, but he was considerably more pessimistic about communities in other parts of the country where Jewish populations had dwindled to a few individuals.[107]

Jewish newspapers barely mentioned village Jews. Like Schick, rabbi Ede Neumann was convinced that the situation of rural (Neolog) Jews had reached a critical state by 1913: "They see a rabbi only on the occasion of a wedding or a funeral and not always even then. They hold religious services only where they live in greater numbers, but even there very rarely, mostly only for the autumn holidays, when they hire some itinerant artist to perform the prayers. . . . The difficulties encountered in maintaining a ritually observant household are well-known." Neumann believed the religious education of children was the first to suffer from this deplorable situation:

> They do not care about it at all. It is pure luck if a few fathers teach their children to recognize the Hebrew alphabet or a few families band together to engage someone to serve as *shochet*, a prayer leader, or a so-called religious instructor for their children. That is the most fortunate situation. Let us not speak of the value of this instruction. We owe a debt of gratitude for it, because it bears witness to the goodwill and selflessness of these believers. In its results it is perhaps somewhat better than nothing. In most cases, there is simply nothing. The children go to the village school where their classmates of other faiths are provided with intensive religious education, while they are completely abandoned.[108]

26   JEWISHNESS AND BEYOND

In summation, by the period preceding the First World War, a majority of Hungary's urban Neolog Jews, particularly those in Budapest, had begun to disregard most of the commandments of the faith. Their public religious practice had dwindled to more or less obligatory participation in services marking the major spring and fall holidays. At home, within their families, they generally celebrated only the High Holidays and all but neglected Shabbat, at least in terms of avoiding work. Their incidental decisions to retain certain religious customs— partly complying with dietary restrictions, for instance—may have resulted from inner religious convictions, though these practices seem more likely to have been preserved as elements of a kind of Jewish bourgeois decorum. Secularization exerted an increasing influence on the Jewish middle class and haute bourgeoisie. A large majority of the latter classes had become almost totally indifferent to religion or were so from the beginning, having grown up in families where customs and sentiments associated with Judaism had largely died out. In these circles, relationships with the faith were essentially formal.

This synopsis glosses over many nuances and blurs numerous distinctions— ignoring the differences between men and women, for example. According to the school of historical thought that has become dominant in recent decades, women of the acculturated European Jewish middle classes distanced themselves from the faith more slowly and to a lesser degree than men. Scholars of this school contend that since middle-class culture restricted women's activities to maternal and domestic roles, it was easier for them to comply with religious prescriptions associated with home and family life, while their husbands' social and professional lives made it more difficult for them to fulfill the religious obligations imposed on Jewish men.[109]

The situation in Hungary was no different. Male members of Hungary's bourgeois society of the time were generally convinced that the vocation of middle-class women was limited to performing maternal and conjugal duties. Such was also the Jewish ideal regarding women's obligations. As a wife, a Jewish woman's mission was to smooth away "the worry-plowed furrows" and "care-filled wrinkles" on the forehead of a husband who had exhausted himself on the battlefield of life,[110] to observe religious laws pertaining to the home in her role as the "priestess of the house" and keeper of the "family sanctuary,"[111] and to make sure that her children were raised in the faith[112]— something her husband, "whom life had called onto the world's stage," could no longer ensure.[113]

Another similarity between Hungary, the United States, England, France, and Germany[114] was that rabbis and contributors to Jewish periodicals in all those countries held prominent (middle-class) women responsible for the increasing impiety of the younger generations. Their argumentation was based on an "unassailable" premise: if young Jews were no longer identifying as Jewish, the root cause must be a flawed family upbringing. If younger generations were not attached to their Jewishness, it was because they had not been taught to feel affection for it as children. Since intimate bonds of this sort developed primarily in the context of the religious upbringing the young received from their mothers in the home, logically Jewish mothers were to blame for the failure of their children to develop such associations. As literary critic Károly Sebestyén wrote in 1896, "The family is a woman's sphere of authority. Her reign there is absolute; whatever she does is of her own doing and whatever she neglects, this negligence weighs upon her soul!"[115] According to these accusations, women paid more attention to fashion than to the prayer book and cared more about winning the favor of Christians than about managing their own households. Women were thus assigned primary responsibility not only for the flawed upbringing of the younger generations but for the general disintegration of middle-class Jewish identity. In the words of the philosopher Menyhért Palágyi, "She goads us to ape foreign models; she causes many to be ashamed of their Jewish nature and [causes] the great decline in Jewish self-esteem."[116]

Regarding the piety of Jewish women, the opinions of Jewish men of the period fundamentally contradict modern-day historians' assumptions. Paula Hyman has suggested that the criticism of Jewish communal leaders was an unconscious attempt to deflect blame: "By focusing on the failings of Jewish mothers as transmitters of Jewish culture to their children, communal leaders were able to project on women their own guilt over their inability to set limits to assimilation."[117] Like Marion Kaplan, Paula Hyman based her conclusions primarily on the memoirs of Jewish women. In the Hungarian Jewish context, however, there are hardly any women's autobiographies from the period that offer detailed descriptions of their family lives, specifically of the domestic roles their mothers played or their own conjugal roles. In any case, the proposition that Jewish women's religious sentiments were fading faster than Jewish men's is difficult to reconcile with the fact that the most successful Neolog publication of the Dualist period—by far—was Arnold Kiss's 1898 prayer book for Jewish women, *Mírjam*. A true bestseller, it had

28 JEWISHNESS AND BEYOND

gone through twenty-two print runs by 1910, thirty print runs by 1914, and fifty print runs by 1918.[118]

Even so, one aspect of Paula Hyman's argumentation does not apply to conditions in Hungary. As Hyman wrote, "In my survey of the nineteenth-century Jewish press of England, France, Germany, and the United States, and of public Jewish pronouncements, I have found no references specifically to fathers' responsibilities for the education of their children or for the inculcation of a Jewish identity nor blame of fathers for the defection of their children from the Jewish community."[119] This was not the case in Hungary. There is no doubt that the most prevalent—one might even say official—thesis in the period was that Jewish women were to blame for their children's increasing indifference to religion. However, the theory that women were exclusively responsible was contradicted by innumerable written accounts that did not distinguish between men and women and simply reproached "parents" for neglecting their duty to provide their children with a religious upbringing. Finally, though it was rare, there were male authors who explicitly and exclusively castigated Jewish men for these failures. As Miksa Szabolcsi, one of the most prominent members of the Neolog community and editor in chief of *Egyenlőség*, wrote in an 1892 piece about a Jewish apostate entitled "Apák vétke (The Sin of the Fathers)," "Your sons, if they are unfaithful to the heritage of Israel, if they casually cast aside their religion for a job or on a whim: *they are not to blame, but you!*"[120] In a 1901 trial sermon delivered at the request of the Jewish community of Buda, Bertalan Edelstein—whom the congregation subsequently chose as its rabbi—also condemned Jewish men for their religious indifference, which he said was causing them to raise a "crooked" generation.[121] Likewise, in a 1911 sermon, Chief Rabbi Arnold Kiss of Buda criticized Jewish men for spending their free time in cafés rather than at home introducing their children to the beauty of Judaism.[122]

Religious ritual and sentiment, of course, were not the only ways in which Jews maintained a connection to their Jewishness. The examples of József Bánóczi and József Vészi demonstrate that even editors of Jewish periodicals and active participants in the operations of Jewish community associations could limit their religious practice to (perfunctory) observance of the High Holidays.[123] Many who had completely abandoned the practice of religion still proclaimed themselves to be "good Jews"—and here I am not thinking only of individuals for whom Jewish identity was expressed in the struggles for emancipation and the legal reception of the Jewish faith, or in the battle against antisemitism.[124] The son of the poet József Kiss recalled that his father "lived a secular life; he did not go to temple and did not fast, but in one of the last things he wrote (the arrangements he made in the event of his death), he declared that he had always been a good Jew and wanted a simple burial in accordance with Jewish morals, without pomp."[125] Sándor Bródy (one of Hungary's most successful writers around the turn of the century) did not know the basics of or care a whit about religion yet fought more than one duel in his youth because someone had disparaged Jews in his presence.[126]

In addition to religious faith, another significant emotional impediment to abandoning the Jewish community was a sense of belonging, nourished by common origins and a common history. Among members of the secularized urban Jewish bourgeoisie, these affinities may have been further reinforced by the fact that they tended to work in the same professional circles, live in the same neighborhoods, socialize among themselves, and marry each other. But by the turn of the century, Jewish converts were also part of this social milieu. Compared to religious attachments, secular (non-Zionist) forms of Jewish identity were relatively minor obstacles to the conversion of religiously indifferent Jews for whom the formal act of baptism would do relatively little to alter their Jewish identity. Secularization was thus the chief factor in the gradual increase in the number of Jews who contemplated conversion over the course of the nineteenth century, for while indifference to religion did not necessarily lead to conversion, a committed religious identity precluded even the thought of conversion.

Besides secularization, Hungarian Jews' emergence from closed communities and increasingly frequent contact with members of the broader Christian society also increased the likelihood that they would consider conversion. Given the significant urbanization of the Hungarian Jewish population, which exceeded that of any other denominational community in nineteenth-century Hungary,[127] and the professional and social polarization of this urban population beginning during the Reform Era and reaching significant proportions in the first few decades after the 1867 emancipation,[128] retentive forces were much weaker among Jews who left the smaller communities where they had been born and blended into the urban masses, and among Jews who chose occupations other than their fathers', thereby positioning themselves in largely non-Jewish professional and social circles. Even so, I have not come across a single case in which a Hungarian Jew converted because he moved from his native village to Budapest and abandoned a commercial occupation for a liberal profession or employment with the state; because he began to associate primarily with Christians and grew indifferent to the Jewish community and Jewish culture; or because being Jewish no longer meant anything to him—and yet continued to be a religious Jew. The only common trait among Jews who chose to convert was not indifference to their "Jewishness" but indifference to their religion.

By the first decade of the twentieth century, secularization had removed the fundamental obstacle to conversion for almost all of the Jewish haute bourgeoisie, most of the Jewish middle class, and segments of the Jewish petty bourgeoisie and rural population. However, as I have noted, lack of religious upbringing or lack of faith was not in itself sufficient to lead to conversion. Secularization merely created the psychological conditions necessary for conversion; actual decisions to convert were motivated by a combination of other factors.

The Allure of Conversion

I have, for the most part, limited the chronological framework of this etiology of conversion to the age of the Austro-Hungarian Dual Monarchy (1867–1918). Legal restrictions on Hungarian Jews had been gradually loosened from the end of the eighteenth century, but up until the emancipation of 1867, converts enjoyed an obvious and immediate set of guaranteed advantages. Numerous Jews were subsequently induced to convert by a desire to circumvent the one remaining legal constraint: the prohibition of Jewish-Christian intermarriage, which remained in force until 1895. Other than this restriction, the emancipation law of 1867 declared Jews to be "equally entitled to exercise all the civil and political rights" enjoyed by their Christian compatriots, and thus in theory, the Jewish religion would no longer constitute a legal obstacle or impediment.

In European countries where Jews were emancipated, rates of conversion among similarly secularized and acculturated Jewish populations varied according to Christian societies' attitudes toward them. The more tolerant a society was of Jewish otherness, the fewer obstacles it placed in the way of Jews' professional advancement and social integration—that is, the fewer the potential advantages of joining a Christian denomination, the less inclined Jews were to convert. Conversely, the greater the prejudice against Jews, and the more the members of a given Christian society doubted that Jews could genuinely belong to their nation, the more inclined Jews were to convert.[129]

On the basis of its numbers of Jewish converts to Christianity, which I will examine in the following chapter, Hungary ranked somewhere in the middle of the European hierarchy of inclusion; its Christians were less accepting of Jews than those of England or France and less resistant to Jews than the Christians in Germany or other parts of the Habsburg Empire.

In and of itself, the close correlation between conversion rates and majority societies' attitudes toward Jewish otherness suggests that secular considerations motivated Jewish conversions. As was the case elsewhere in Central Europe, Hungarians of this era firmly believed that most Jews who converted were not driven to do so by their religious beliefs. In 1903, Count Miklós Zay wrote, "Given the enlightened tendencies of our day, it is extraordinarily rare for a Jewish person to change his faith out of a deep and genuine religious conviction."[130] Zay's opinion was shared by Neolog intellectuals, joke writers,[131] and, in some cases, Christian clergymen.[132] There were certainly converts whose religious convictions motivated them to join Christian congregations. Even so, I believe the unanimous opinions of historians who study conversions of Western and Central European Jews are valid for Hungarian Jews as well: only an insignificant proportion converted because they considered the Christian faith to be truer than their own.[133] This is not to suggest that conversions were motivated exclusively by opportunistic considerations. Some felt closer to Christianity for reasons unconnected to pragmatic concerns while others understood conversion to be a symbolic gesture signifying identification with a given nation or with European (Christian) culture. Nevertheless, as Todd Endelman has emphasized, even in instances like these, it is difficult to imagine that the decisions were unaffected by opportunistic considerations; whatever their self-justifications, converts had to be aware that a change of religion would put them in a more favorable social position.[134]

In the following section, I will attempt to gauge the degree to which Christian Hungarians expected their Jewish compatriots to join a Christian denomination in exchange for recognition as "genuine" Hungarians, or as a condition of professional advancement or social acceptance. That is, to what extent were Jews pressured to convert? In other words, what advantages might they have hoped to gain by becoming Christians?

Becoming Hungarian

During the Reform Era and again in the 1860s, some Hungarian liberals recommended making Jewish emancipation contingent on certain preconditions, such as reform of the Jewish religion and a certain level of acculturation, while others advocated granting civil rights only to Jews whom they judged to have cast aside their presumed moral corruption.[135] When Hungarian revolutionaries unanimously passed an emancipation law at the National Assembly of Szeged on July 28, 1849 (it was never enforced as a result of Hungary's defeat in the 1848–49 War of Independence), they simultaneously ordered the Interior Ministry to convene an assembly of rabbis and elected representatives so that the Jews could reform their "articles of faith" and proclaim them publicly.[136]

By the time the Austro-Hungarian Monarchy was officially established in 1867, these sorts of explicit infringements of the principle of religious liberty had disappeared from the discourse of Hungary's liberal political elite, who attached no conditions to the equal rights guaranteed by the 1867 emancipation law. These legislators emancipated Jews in the hope that they would become Hungarians in language and culture, not in exchange for their having done so. In fact, most Hungarian Jews still did not speak Hungarian in 1867.[137] And while Jews were certainly expected to acculturate, in reality they faced no general "assimilationist pressure." In 1871, when the Hungarian government recognized the right of Orthodox Jewish communities to organize themselves and arrange their lives in accordance with the Jewish legal code known as the *Shulchan Aruch*, it was clear to everyone that Hungary's liberal-nationalist political elite had thereby guaranteed the preservation of a communal way of life that excluded the possibility of identifying primarily with the Hungarian nation.[138] In this respect, Hungary's turn-of-the-century political leaders were just as liberal as their 1867 predecessors. The Hungarian political elite of the Dualist era allowed Jews who so desired to continue living their lives in almost total isolation from Hungarian society and culture. The traditional world of the culturally isolated ultra-Orthodox Jews of the Unterland region would endure essentially undisturbed until the end of World War I.[139] The cost of this liberty was a renunciation of the possibility of social advancement, which did not interest ultra-Orthodox Jews anyway. Acculturation was obligatory only for those Jews who hoped to become part of the majority society and climb its social ladder.

From the Reform Era to the collapse of the Dual Monarchy, the chief objective of Hungary's political elite was to increase the proportion of ethnic Hungarians within the kingdom's population, only about 43 percent in the early 1840s.[140] In concrete terms, this meant increasing the number of people

CONTEXT OF THE CONVERSIONS OF HUNGARIAN JEWS   33

who declared Hungarian to be their mother tongue on the national census. According to Ignác Romsics, "By the beginning of the 19th century, the language-based concept of nation had become the axiomatic, fundamental principle of the new Hungarian nationalism."[141] Though there were Hungarian leaders—notably Count István Széchenyi—who rejected this notion, a large majority of the era's political elite considered language to be the chief criterion of national affiliation.[142] Thus, linguistic Magyarization was the most important of the expectations facing Hungary's Jews. As poet and natural scientist Péter Vajda warned Jews in 1840, "Do not be neglectful of Magyarization; this is the one thing your new homeland urgently asks of you."[143]

A large majority of Hungary's Jews satisfied expectations with regard to linguistic Magyarization: between 1880 and 1910, the proportion of the kingdom's "Israelites" who declared their mother tongue to be Hungarian rose from 56.3 to 76.9 percent; in Budapest, the figure rose from 59.1 to 90.1 percent.[144] The linguistic Magyarization of the country's Jews produced the desired result, increasing the proportion of Hungarian citizens who declared their mother tongue to be Hungarian to an absolute majority of 51.4 percent by 1900. Without Jews, the proportion would not have risen to 51 percent until the eve of the First World War. Hungary's political elite—rhetorically, at least—rewarded Jews for their efforts to master the Hungarian language and their commitment to the Hungarian concept of the state by declaring them fully Hungarian. In 1903, an interview with former prime minister Dezső Bánffy (1895–99) appeared in the weekly *Jövendő* (*Future*) after he accepted the presidency of the Lipótváros Casino, which was regarded as a bastion of Jewish upper-class society; Bánffy addressed "the Jewish question" in the following terms: "I love and respect every denomination and race in this country if they aspire to the unification of all Hungarians or at least do not work against it. With regard to Jews, I make no exception. And why would I? How could I? . . . In this country, it is folly to dwell on origins and investigate so-called racial Hungarianness. Whoever is with us, is us."[145]

Thus, in theory, any Jew who learned to speak Hungarian became a Hungarian. In his analysis of the 1890 census, József Jekelfalussy—the director of the National Hungarian Royal Statistical Office—reported that "Jews in Hungarian-speaking counties have, as it were, completely blended into our nation," by which he meant that the bulk of the Jewish inhabitants of these counties had declared themselves to be native speakers of Hungarian.[146] In ethnic and religious terms, Hungary was the most diverse country in Europe, and thus the principles of Hungarian liberal nationalism that developed during the Reform Era and remained dominant among the country's political elite up to the collapse of the Dual Monarchy necessarily included openness and inclusion.

At the same time, Hungarian liberal nationalists—like all the era's nationalists—aspired to homogeneity and thus expected total cultural identification from Jews, along with the greatest possible reduction of their otherness.[147] In 1889, an author who had signed a previous submission to *Egyenlőség* as "a true friend of the Jews" (and whom the paper identified on this occasion as "one of the outstanding men of public life") was quite clear on this point: "We again draw the Jews' attention to the fact that it is in their own interest to refrain from any [expression of] particularity and to strive with all their strength not to distinguish themselves from the country's other inhabitants in any way, not even in the most trifling superficiality."[148] In 1900, the popular liberal journalist Béla Tóth expressed himself in similarly unambiguous terms: "Hungarianness is the only force that will erase all the alien traits from the essence of our Jewish brethren. Indeed, this is the ultimate goal. . . . Let everything that might suggest that the Jew is but a newcomer here disappear. Perish all foreignness, whether in thought, name, word, custom, or letter."[149]

According to János Gyurgyák, Hungary's liberal political elite "did not itself know precisely what it meant by assimilation," though he added, "of course, primarily it wanted complete absorption."[150] If we understand Gyurgyák to have meant that Hungary's liberal leaders never specified the extent of the acculturation they expected from the country's Jews, then his assertions were accurate—and in this respect, the Hungarian case was not unique.[151] The question is whether the Hungarians who urged Jews to become as Hungarian as possible believed that they could not truly do so unless they became Christians. Many presumably did—but not all. In his 1871 monograph on the history of the city of Debrecen, István Szűcs voiced the expectation that Jews become loyal children of the homeland in "body and soul" and adapt themselves to the "language, character, and customs" of the Hungarian nation. Yet Szűcs did not demand that Jews convert—on the contrary, he considered selfless dedication to their faith to be one of the most conspicuous virtues of the Jewish "race."[152] Not even the aforementioned Béla Tóth linked the Magyarization of the Jews to conversion; in 1899, he sharply criticized social circles "which [unbaptized] Jews, through some strange accident, are not able to enter."[153]

CONTEXT OF THE CONVERSIONS OF HUNGARIAN JEWS   35

Though very few members of the political elite publicly addressed the issue of assimilation, most of those who did rejected demands that Jews convert as a condition of full integration. The rejections themselves demonstrate that such demands were made. Among the most notable of those who spoke out was the reform politician József Eötvös, who served as minister of religion and public education in the Batthyány government in 1848 and the Andrássy government from 1867 to 1871. On March 31, 1840, in the upper chamber of the Hungarian Diet, Eötvös delivered a speech in defense of the unconditional emancipation of the Jews, following Christian Wilhelm Dohm in refuting the notion of Jewish moral corruption by citing Jews' loyalty to their religion and their admirable unwillingness to convert to Christianity out of opportunistic self-interest. This speech was published in expanded form as a study the following year.[154] As a devout Catholic, Eötvös was convinced that the Jews' mission had been fulfilled with the coming of Jesus Christ and that their path would naturally lead them to Christianity. Conversion to Christianity, however, was not desirable unless it was based on genuine faith, and therefore only by means of exemplary behavior could Christians hasten the coming of this long-awaited moment.[155] As a pious Catholic, Eötvös hoped that Jews would convert, but as a liberal politician who embraced—and struggled for the implementation of—the principle of religious liberty, he unreservedly condemned worldly inducements or any kind of pressure that might inspire insincere conversions to Christianity.

Whether out of inner conviction or because the liberal "political correctness" of the era demanded it, numerous politicians declared that they did not consider conversion to be a condition of emancipation or of Jews' acceptance as Hungarians. In 1839, the young intellectual and future education minister Ágoston Trefort wrote, "If they want to become our fellow citizens, they must cast aside their current Jewishness," though he immediately added, "Let it not be said that we hereby demand the repudiation of their religion."[156] At a district assembly of the lower chamber of the Hungarian Diet on September 7, 1844, the future justice minister Sebő Vukovics said it was unacceptable to expect Jews to abandon their religion, "which in times of persecution was their only consolation," in order to receive civil rights.[157] Fifty years later, on October 20, 1894, Géza Pap, the rapporteur of the Hungarian parliament's public education committee, criticized opponents of the legal "reception" of the Jewish religion, who, instead of advocating the expansion of civil rights, saw conversion to Christianity as the solution: "It has been said, for example,

36   JEWISHNESS AND BEYOND

that they have the ability to integrate into Hungarian society because they have the option to convert. However, honored house, the principle asserted here is one of religious immorality. Because what is thus demanded? That someone relinquish his religious convictions and the force of his belief for material and worldly profit."[158]

In discussions with Jewish delegations, some politicians emphasized that calls for Magyarization should not entail the expectation that Jews convert. During an 1894 speaking tour of Hungary following his return from abroad, Ferenc Kossuth—son of the exiled statesman Lajos Kossuth—told a delegation from the Jewish community of Mindszent, "It is with joy as a liberal and pride as a Hungarian that I note the fusion of Hungarian Jewry and the nation. May you continue to be one, without liberals and Hungarians demanding that you abandon your faith."[159]

There were politicians who publicly advocated conversion, but those who permitted themselves to issue explicit appeals were generally second- and third-tier parliamentarians—and, not incidentally, devout Christians. Such were Aladár Molnár, who began his career as a pastor of the Reformed Church; the independent parliamentary representative and Roman Catholic priest Benedek Göndöcs; and Chaplain István Vajay.[160] In the spring of 1895, during the third debate on the legislative proposal that would later that year make Judaism one of Hungary's "received" religions, Vajay recommended that Jews emulate the original Hungarian settlers of the Carpathian Basin, who had preserved their state by integrating themselves into Christendom: "Let our Jewish fellow citizens take this as an example and proceed in this direction on the threshold of the celebration of our thousand-year existence [here]."[161]

High-profile politicians expressed themselves more cautiously. On November 22, 1890, Moderate Opposition leader Albert Apponyi also used a parliamentary speech to make reference to the Hungarians' medieval-era conversion. He argued that adoption of Christianity had resulted in the moral elevation of the Hungarian nation and said, "According to the testimony of history, that which applies to the one, applies to the other." Given that Jews' morality was rather fragile, "it would indeed be of great benefit to Jewry if it were to be integrated into the Christian faith."[162] On October 8, 1894, during the first of the upper chamber's debates on the legislative proposal to make Judaism a received religion, Count Nándor Zichy—future president of the anti-liberal Catholic People's Party that would form three months later—justified his rejection of the bill by saying that his Christian faith prevented him from

CONTEXT OF THE CONVERSIONS OF HUNGARIAN JEWS   37

supporting any measure that would permit Christians to convert to Judaism. Nevertheless, he added, "There is no obstacle to their absorption into the body of the nation and their coming closer to us by blending into Christendom."[163] It is not a coincidence that all the representatives who urged Jews to convert did so from the opposition benches.

We do not have enough information to be able to draw conclusions about the opinions influential politicians and intellectuals of the era expressed on the subject of conversion in the course of private conversations. In 1873, Gyula Andrássy— foreign minister of the Austro-Hungarian Monarchy and former prime minister of Hungary (1867–71)—purportedly made the following comments to Lajos Dóczi, a (then unconverted) Jewish official in his press department: "I can hardly find an expression forceful enough to describe the practice of certain Jews who convert to Christianity once they have fought their way to a prominent position. It is a slap in the face to their religion. . . . It should be the moral obligation of precisely these Jews to stand by their faith at all costs."[164] We do not know whether Andrássy actually made such a statement or expressed himself in precisely these terms. In any case, the Jewish historian Henrik Marczali described another incident involving Andrássy that corroborates the foregoing portrayal. In the autumn of 1886, the elderly Andrássy asked Marczali to organize and publish some of his speeches. Other obligations prevented Marczali from accepting Andrássy's offer, so he recommended his student Béla Lederer: "The only problem with him, I said, is he's a Jew. Has he converted? asked Andrássy. No! I answered. All the better! said Andrássy, and took his speeches to Lederer, who did a brilliant job."[165]

Unlike Andrássy, Ágoston Trefort—by far the longest-serving minister of religion and public education in the Dualist era—expressed unequivocal support for the conversion of Jews in the course of private conversations. In the aforementioned 1839 article, Trefort said Jews could "cast aside their Jewishness" without abandoning their faith, but as minister of religion and public education (from 1872 until his death in 1888) he was generally unwilling to appoint Jews to high school or university teaching positions unless they converted to Christianity. Although several autobiographical works and countless contemporaneous newspaper articles mentioned Trefort's discriminatory employment policies and support for conversion (which I will discuss in greater detail below), the sources say nothing about the longtime cabinet minister's motives—with one exception. The journalist and high school teacher Iván Szigetvári claimed Trefort was concerned about the prospects of

38 JEWISHNESS AND BEYOND

Christian instructors: "Once he even told a university teacher: If I have one Jewish teacher appointed today, in 20 years there will be no Christian teachers at the universities."[166]

Trefort never publicly advocated conversion and condemned antisemitism on several occasions, but he clearly felt a certain antipathy toward Jews. Others who considered conversion to be a meaningless formal gesture may actually have recommended it out of sympathy for their Jewish acquaintances. Proposals of this sort arose from a pragmatic recognition of the social disadvantages associated with Jewish religious status. The bank director Simon Krausz—born in 1873 in Budapest—recalled that during his youth, the most distinguished customer at his father's coal shop was the city's chief prosecutor: "Sándor Kozma was kind to us and constantly advised my poor mother to convert to Christianity. He—one of the most liberal leading figures of the 1880s—recommended it because in his opinion, it was 'a pity to send children forth into life's harsh struggle with such a heavy burden.'"[167] After completing his university studies in 1882, the linguist and ethnologist Bernát Munkácsi attempted unsuccessfully to find a high school teaching position; in 1925, he wrote that his Christian friends thought his religion hurt his prospects and had regularly recommended conversion "as a natural, simple requirement." Munkácsi remarked that these classmates "simply could not understand why switching religions was such a big deal."[168]

It is quite possible that some of the Christian intellectuals who did not attach any particular significance to conversion were simply indifferent to the whole issue. In 1885, the historian Dávid Angyal discussed his decision to convert to Christianity with his mentor, the eminent literary historian Pál Gyulai, whose periodical, the *Budapesti Szemle* (*Budapest Review*), had been publishing Angyal's work for years. Gyulai endorsed Angyal's decision, though he had never encouraged his young colleague to convert and did not care which denomination he chose.[169]

Other than their relative rarity, the most conspicuous attribute of the opinions Christian intellectuals published on the subject of conversion was their genre distribution: whereas the great majority of authors of pamphlets and newspaper articles encouraged Jews to convert, novelists and poets were almost unanimous in rejecting the measure.

Born into a family of serfs, to a Croat father and Slovak mother in 1799, writer and revolutionary parliamentary representative Mihály Táncsics (who Magyarized his name in 1848) published the didactic novel *Pazardi* in 1836, and while the book itself may be a work of fiction, the open letter with which it begins is a polemic. Addressing himself to "our unjustly persecuted and irrationally despised neighbors of the Jewish faith," Táncsics regretted that he lacked the power to help the Jewish people and could not do more than provide them with the following advice: "The age of evangelism has passed, though I would nevertheless advise you to wash your heads so that you might adapt yourselves to the greater part of civil society and enjoy its benefits. . . . Happy days will soon arrive, once every Jew shares equally in the protection of the law and can make use of his natural rights, though most regrettably, it falls to you to wait."[170] Táncsics did not provide any answers to thorny questions like how Jews would be able to enjoy the coming emancipation if they had already converted or why it would be necessary to provide these no longer Jewish citizens with equal rights in the first place.

In an article published in 1840, agricultural engineer János Udvardy Cserna—a member of the Hungarian Academy of Sciences—expressed himself less amicably. Although Udvardy Cserna acknowledged Jews' industriousness, he suggested that emancipation was undesirable as the Jewish faith was incompatible with "Christian morality" and taught Jews to love only their coreligionists. "The Jew" could "never amalgamate himself" into the Christian middle class, and if he were to be emancipated, "with his cunning morals," Christians would be plunged into servitude. Udvardy Cserna concluded, "As long as the Jew does not convert to the Christian religion, he cannot be a citizen with equal rights in a Christian country."[171] Udvardy Cserna's article is a textbook example of the Enlightenment-era turn in interpretations of Jewish conversions to Christianity: the emphasis shifted from the theological truth of the Christian religion to its moral superiority.

Where Udvardy Cserna objected to the morality of the Jewish religion, the author of another 1843 publication—a pamphlet by Dr. G. J.—based his rejection of Jewish emancipation on Jewish messianism. Ever since God had dispersed the "Jewish nation" for their sins, the Jews' only wish had been for the Messiah to take them back to the Land of Canaan, and so it was utterly senseless to expect them to regard the country where they lived as their homeland or its inhabitants—with whom they would not even eat—as their compatriots. According to Dr. G. J., Jews and Christians would never merge into "one nation," leaving only one solution: preserving "the prevalent custom" of requiring Jews who yearned for civil rights "to relinquish the Jewish religion and be Christians." The doctor waved off the notion that Jews were changing with the changing of the times. They were not changing, and if they did, "then they were no longer Jews."[172]

In a May 1844 article published in *Pesti Hírlap* (still edited by Lajos Kossuth at the time), lawyer, writer, and translator Gábor Fábián categorized himself as a "friend" of emancipation, though he had little sympathy for Jews. Unlike those who believed emancipation alone would be sufficient inducement for Jews to blend into the Hungarian nation, Fábián declared that unconditional emancipation would not be enough to break down the existing social barriers. Without Jewish-Christian mixed marriages, it would be "utterly impossible for the national element to absorb the Jewish element," and only the introduction of such marriages could bring about the "desired assimilation": "If we remove this obstacle . . . the law of physical attraction dictates that the larger element will ultimately engulf and dissolve within itself the smaller one."[173] Unlike the previously cited authors, Fábián did not openly advocate conversion, and yet he clearly hoped that the otherwise impeccably liberal reform he championed would result in the complete disappearance of Hungarian Jewry. In terms of their final outcomes, there was therefore no difference between the two positions.

Between 1850 and 1880, with the exception of a few press reports expressing approval for individual instances of conversion, there is no evidence that Hungary's Christian intelligentsia publicly advocated the conversion of Jews. It is hardly a coincidence that there were very few outward manifestations of antisemitism in Hungary in this era, up to the mid-1870s, at least. In keeping with the spirit of this period, lawyer Soma Vereby of Pest denounced demands that Jews convert in an 1858 pamphlet published on the occasion of the construction of the Dohány Street Synagogue in Budapest. Arguing against opponents of emancipation "who reproach Jews for not renouncing their religion," Vereby approvingly cited the response of an imaginary Jew: "So you want us to abandon [the faith] for which we have suffered and endured for a thousand years?"[174]

Nevertheless, Kálmán Mikszáth, the great master of Hungarian critical-realist prose, endorsed the conversion of Jews in an 1881 article, presenting his emancipated compatriots' adoption of Christianity as the logical outcome of the process by which they were becoming Hungarian. The views Mikszáth expressed on the subject of Jews exhibited a remarkable degree of variability around the year 1880. In an 1879 article, he suggested the process of Magyarization was essentially complete among the Jews of Szeged.[175] Yet in an

CONTEXT OF THE CONVERSIONS OF HUNGARIAN JEWS   41

anonymous 1880 pamphlet, Mikszáth expressed himself in more pessimistic terms: "In the whole of Hungary, Szeged is the place where Jews are best integrated with Christians and Hungarians, and yet—a sad indicator for the future—they constitute a separate caste; their customs, thinking, and life-ways are distinct."[176] The article in which Mikszáth advocated conversion thus represents only *one* of the diverse viewpoints he expressed in his journalistic output of this period. In a sketch published in the September 24, 1881 issue of the *Pesti Hírlap,* he wrote:

> I have a rash proposition. For the second time in a week, it would seem that a Hungarian Jewish family has converted to Christianity. The papers recently reported the conversion of a journalist, then that the esteemed translator of *Numa Roumestan* had made a Christian of himself, on which account I congratulate him much more than for his rendering of *Numa Roumestan.* Under these circumstances, I propose that as [we have done] for Magyarizations of names, we should launch a *'permanent column'* for conversions to Christianity. Because there is something to the saying, 'In for an inch, in for a mile.' To go with a Hungarian name, one must adopt the Hungarians' religion: Catholicism or Calvinism (in extreme cases, the Lutheran faith is not bad either).[177]

The liberal Mikszáth's convivial—one might say jocular—tone concealed a fundamentally anti-liberal idea: if the religion of "the Hungarians" was limited to Christian denominations, then Jews who remained loyal to their faith could not (truly) become Hungarians.

In a pamphlet published that same year, the retired chief prosecutor of Hódmezővásárhely, Béla Matók, suggested the "Jewish question" could be resolved if Christians and Jews recognized each other's virtues and worked together to remove all obstacles "that separate us." It would not have been surprising if Matók had subsequently identified conversion of Jews as the best means of breaking down these barriers. Instead, he opened a section entitled "What Must We Therefore Do?" by writing, "What is demanded by the Jewish question currently on the agenda? Abandoning the faith? I do not think so, nor could it be so, as I consider contempt for the freedom of human thought and will to be one of the greatest mistakes."[178] The author of an anonymous 1894 pamphlet, however, asserted that conversion of Jews—more precisely, educated Jews—was the only permanent solution to the "Jewish question." This writer, described in a contemporaneous journal article as an aristocrat, predicts that if Jews do not commit themselves to conversion, "I and all of us . . . will consider Jews to be aliens in our society, not Hungarians."[179]

In the aforementioned 1903 article by Miklós Zay, the count expressed his ongoing support for the liberal notion of integration without conversion: "I believe that enlightened people with patriotic sentiments cannot feel enthusiasm for conversions. . . . In our circumstances, we must eliminate even the appearance that conversion is one of the prerequisites of integration."[180] None of the authors cited in the following paragraphs espoused this view. In a 1910 study of the gentry, Győző Concha articulated demands that Jews convert and did so in a manner reflective of neoconservative nationalist thought that emerged in the mid-1890s. Concha was an eminent jurist and political scientist, a member of the Hungarian Academy of Sciences, and the former (and future) dean of the law school and political science department at the University of Sciences of Budapest. His idea of gentry was not an antisemitic class dreaming of a noble past but rather a Hungarian version of the English gentry, inspired by the latter's perceived work ethic. Concha offered "wealthy Jews" a place within this as-yet undeveloped gentry—with two conditions. First, the "leading role" would be reserved for noble-born owners of medium-size estates; Jews would have to content themselves with the task of providing these "leaders" with practical virtues they lacked. Secondly, Jews would have to become Christians. Concha did not openly call on Jews to convert but made it clear that the future elite of the Hungarian middle class would have to be Christian; therefore, Jews would also have to be Christians to occupy a (subordinate) position in this class.[181]

Among the novel phenomena of the 1910s was that some Christian members of the progressive liberal intelligentsia—a significant proportion of which consisted of Jews or converted Jews—began to advocate conversion. In 1913, Zoltán Szász contradicted the assertions of Jewish newspapers by declaring that conversion was not a betrayal because "nobody chooses" his or her religion, so abandoning it was not a disavowal of a previous conviction but "sublime self-liberation," or at least "the entirely legitimate act of an adult individual." Conversion could not be regarded as an unprincipled act even if it was a calculated one; in a society where Jewishness entailed social disadvantages, the adoption of Christianity was "a very human deed," a wisely pragmatic "act of adaptation." Szász concluded that it would be to the benefit of all, and to Jews themselves in particular, if through conversion, "the most unjust of the barriers that divide people from one another would collapse into nothingness."[182]

CONTEXT OF THE CONVERSIONS OF HUNGARIAN JEWS   43

As a final observation on these attitudes, I should note that during the First World War, more and more Hungarians—regardless of political orientation— advocated conversion as a solution to the "Jewish question." In his 1917 book *A zsidók útja* (*The Journey of the Jews*), bourgeois-radical writer, jurist, and university professor Péter Ágoston declared that "host peoples" who had emancipated the Jews could rightfully expect them to "disappear within them," asserting that this was "a Jewish interest as well, because as long as they do not disappear, there will always be a Jewish question."[183] Polemical press responses to the controversial book prompted Oszkár Jászi—the bourgeois-radical leader whose Jewish parents had baptized him as a child—to conduct a survey on the "Jewish question" in the pages of *Huszadik Század* (*Twentieth Century*), the sociological monthly he edited. Many of the Christian intellectuals who discussed Ágoston's book in the daily press and numerous respondents to this survey—including bourgeois-radical jurist Dezső Buday, liberal journalist Kálmán Porzsolt, and the aforementioned Győző Concha—endorsed conversion as a solution.[184]

As I have noted, unlike most newspaper articles and pamphlets, Christian literary works generally presented conversion of Jews in a negative light, as an unprincipled act, and lauded the selfless virtue of fidelity to the ancestral faith. A glaring example of the disparities between genres is Mihály Táncsics' aforementioned didactic novel *Pazardi*. Whereas Táncsics encouraged Jews to convert to Christianity in the open letter at the beginning of this novel, he also presented one of the book's main characters, the faithful Jew Izsák Perger, as a model of civic virtue for the entire Hungarian nation.[185]

The most consistent condemnation of conversion appeared in the works of Mór Jókai, the most popular Hungarian writer of the nineteenth century. From his first literary creation, the 1843 drama *A zsidó fiú* (*The Jewish Boy*), to his turn-of-the-century novels, Jókai never changed his view of conversion: self-sacrificing loyalty to one's faith was an exalted virtue while conversion demonstrated a lack of character, and calls for conversion were dishonorable.[186] In Jókai's 1903 novel *A mi lengyelünk* (*Our Man from Poland*), which takes place during the 1848–49 war of independence and the subsequent period of neoabsolutism known as the Bach era (1851–58), it becomes clear only in the final pages of the book that the protagonist, Negrotin, is Jewish. When Natália, the woman who loves him, discovers Negrotin's origins and asks him to convert so as to be able to marry her, he refuses on the following grounds: "Jehovah forgives every sin that a man commits in his life, except one, apostasy.... He who can disavow his God can disavow his beloved, and his homeland, too."[187] Not only is the Jew who abandons his faith an unprincipled person, he is a potential traitor as well, and thus a bad Hungarian. Jókai lived up to the principles he articulated in his books: when he married his second wife, Jewish actress Bella Nagy, in 1899, he did not ask her to convert to Christianity and indeed she did not.[188]

In his 1861 drama *A zsidók Magyarhonban* (*Jews in the Hungarian Homeland*), István Szentkirályi likewise portrayed conversion as a breach of faith that defined the character of the convert as well. When the young landowner in the story, which also takes place during the 1848–49 Hungarian Revolution and War of Independence, asks a wealthy Jewish leaseholder for the hand of his daughter, the latter responds, "If my daughter renounces her ancestral faith for the sake of a man of another religion, I will strike her with the thunderbolts of fatherly malediction until the end of my life." But the young landowner does not want his beloved to convert—on the contrary: "I assure you that I would overcome by force my love for your daughter if she were to break faith with her religion and her father." All these characters hope the revolution will bring about emancipation, and with it the possibility of civil—interfaith—marriage. After the failure of the war of independence, the young landowner sees only one solution to their dilemma: emigration to America, where he can marry his beloved "as a woman who is true to her faith."[189]

Sándor Lukácsy, whose folk plays were quite popular in their day, wrote an 1875 piece entitled *A zsidó honvéd* (*A Jewish Soldier in the Hungarian Army*), a trope that would crystallize into a literary *topos* in this era: the Jewish soldier who is accepted into the Hungarian nation as a result of his participation in the 1848–49 war of independence. Soldiers Dávid and Iczig are the good Jews whose primary ambition, as they declare, is "to Magyarize themselves in language, heart, and deed." The bad Jew is the banker Steinberger, who attempts to persuade his daughter to convert to Christianity so that he might offer her hand to a young baron and gratify his own ambitions by basking in the glow of a baronial coronet.[190]

In the rare literary works where Christian writers presented conversion as a positive phenomenon, they justified it as a sacrifice on the altar of love. Elek Benedek, one of the pioneers of Hungarian children's literature, depicted it this way in a novel "for young girls" published in 1896. Weisz, a Jewish widower who owns a sewing workshop, falls in love with Katalin, a seamstress born into an impoverished noble family and now in his employ. Weisz asks

Katalin to marry him; she declines because she does not love him. Weisz asks her why not:

"Because I am a Jew?"

"No, no!"

"Don't deny it, Katalin. That's the real reason. I will abandon my faith for you!"

"I do not accept this great sacrifice! I know how much you [people] cling to your religion. . . ."

"That's true," said Weisz, his face now glum.

"That's true. . . . But for you I would make even this sacrifice."[191]

Elek Benedek's wife, Mirjám Fischer, made the sacrifice, adopting her husband's Reformed faith and the Christian name Mária before their 1884 marriage.[192]

In Christian Hungarian society, churches represented the stratum that believed conversion was an obvious part of the future of the country's Jews. The historical Christian perspective on this subject is well-known: the divine promise to the people of Israel had been fulfilled with the coming of Jesus Christ and thus the Jews would be led inevitably to accept the New Covenant that superseded the Mosaic Covenant. Though the survival of the Jews as Jews, languishing in their dispersion, still served a divine purpose as a living symbol of the triumph of Christianity, over the centuries the Christian churches continually made efforts of varying intensity to convert them.

This official ecclesiastical perspective was still in effect in the era under discussion here, though the spirit of the age did put its stamp on perceptions of Jewish conversion. On the one hand, some clergymen were so suspicious of converts' sincerity that they regarded conversion as undesirable. On the other hand, beginning in the 1880s, theological justifications for conversion would sometimes be supplanted by explicitly secular, "nationalist" rationales. The author of an 1895 article in the Catholic weekly *Magyar Szemle* (*Hungarian Review*) declared, "As long as the Jews remain Jews, all their Hungarianness is just external gloss!" Jews needed to understand that only by means of conversion could they become "genuine members of the Christian Hungarian nation."[193]

Whenever possible, Christian clergymen—with a few previously noted exceptions—attempted throughout the period in question here to convert the Jews who lived in their milieus, though the meager number of published attempts to convince Jews of the truth of Christian doctrine suggests that proselytizing activity was not particularly intense around the turn of the century.[194] Up to the 1860s, the Catholic periodical *Religio*—first published in 1841 and known until 1849 as *Religio és Nevelés (Religion and Education)*—regularly produced reports on cases of conversion, most of which took place in provincial Hungary. The authors of these reports, often the parish priests who baptized the converts, never failed to emphasize that the new members of their churches had adopted Christianity out of genuine religious conviction.[195] Protestants saw as evidence of sincerity the fact that converts chose their denomination instead of Catholicism because—as a Reformed pastor wrote in 1896—"there is no earthly glitter, pomp, [or] material advantage" in a Protestant church.[196] In reality, however, Christian clergymen did not always concern themselves with converts' sincerity, as is suggested by a 1905 book on the legal aspects of conversion written by canon and university professor Ferenc Hanuy for the Catholic clergy. According to Hanuy, conversion to Christianity was valid even if "the person to be baptized was influenced by worldly motives, such as, for example: the hope of material gain, patronage, or honor." Even so, Hanuy did emphatically remind his readers that using conversion "merely to achieve numerical growth for the Church is not permitted."[197]

In addition to Christian clergymen, antisemites—for lack of a better alternative—frequently advocated conversion, though with strong reservations. Antisemites' endorsement of such a "solution" to the "Jewish question" may seem paradoxical, since modern antisemites have had difficulty renouncing the notion that "the problem with Jews is not the religion, but the race"—as antisemitic university students chanted during demonstrations in Pest in the 1880s and the first decade of the 1900s.[198] Győző Istóczy's stance on the issue might be described as more nuanced, insofar as he at least historicized the question. In a speech Istóczy delivered to the National Assembly on January 22, 1883, the leader of Hungary's antisemitic movement said, "Before 1867 and even more so before 1848, converted Jews were united with our society heart and soul, without reservation, mostly because Jews anathematized and disowned the so-called *meshumads*, for which reason converted Jews also repudiated their racial kin." However, Istóczy cautioned, the rising power of Jewry was drawing converted Jews back to their former community, and thus converts served as advanced Jewish outposts in Christian circles to which "Jews of the Jewish faith still have no access."[199] In a pamphlet published before Hungary's 1887 parliamentary elections, the Independent Antisemitic Party, led by the journalist Gyula Verhovay, made no exceptions: "The fiendish racial character of the Jews is most evident among those Jews who assume the Christian religion. There is no difference between the convert and the actual Jew."[200] There is abundant evidence that racial theories permeated the opinions of antisemitic members of the *Ecclesia militans*, as evidenced by its newspapers, such as the Catholic weekly *Esztergom*, founded by the future bishop of Székesfehérvár, Ottokár Prohászka. The author of a 1908 article in *Esztergom* lamented that "Hungary got so Jewified that they have wormed their way into leading roles even in our Catholic public affairs and the writing of our newspaper—if not Jews in the strict sense of the word, at least converted Jews," and as "centuries of experience show, the Semitic spirit lingers in [their] offspring for three or four generations."[201]

Nevertheless, most antisemites considered conversion a possible solution to the "Jewish question," alongside other options such as the repeal of emancipation or expulsion. Some advocated conversion because their genuine Christian faith did not permit them to base their antisemitism on racial considerations; these included the Catholic parish priest Ignác Zimándy, who served as a parliamentary representative of the National Antisemitic Party from 1884 to 1887,[202] and Jesuit priest Béla Bangha, a chief ideologue of the militant Catholicism of the 1910s. Though Bangha produced a lengthy analysis of the "'racial' characteristics of degenerate Jewry," he also believed that there could be Jews who were "genuinely touched by Christianity."[203] Even if they were skeptical of the power of conversion to transform Jews, most antisemites who supported conversion did so because they considered it the most realistic of the possible solutions; if it did not achieve results immediately, it could do so over the course of several generations.[204]

In the decades between the Reform Era and the outbreak of the First World War, Jews often heard that their emancipation and social acceptance entailed certain conditions, though conversion was not among them. At the same time, they also frequently heard that they should adopt the religion of the majority in the interest of achieving legal equality or recognition as Hungarians. Many members of the traditional political elite and Christian intelligentsia sincerely believed that their "Israelite compatriots" could become "good Hungarians" even if they maintained their faith. Many remained committed to the liberal principle of religious tolerance, which excluded the possibility of requiring conversion. In my estimation, however, in addition to the numerous Hungarians who considered conversion of Jews to be expressly desirable and even necessary, a significant number of Christians—even if they did not consider

48   JEWISHNESS AND BEYOND

the adoption of Christianity to be a sine qua non condition of becoming Hungarian—felt that Christian Hungarians were more Hungarian than Jews. This feeling led them to welcome conversion from a national perspective, even if they did not openly encourage it.

Professional Discrimination

From the emergence of political antisemitism in the mid-1870s until the end of the Dualist era, Hungarian governments consistently and emphatically condemned all forms of antisemitism. In the summer of 1911, Prime Minister Károly Khuen-Héderváry expressed his pride that "Hungarian liberalism has never permitted the gloomy guest of recent decades, antisemitism, to find its feet," and emphasized the need to avoid even the impression that "the Hungarian government might endorse or tolerate such denominational tendencies."[205]

The anonymous author of an article in the monthly *Hitközségi Szemle* (*Congregational Review*) responded to Prime Minister Khuen-Héderváry's assertion by saying, "Large problems cannot be remedied with words, only with deeds." This author—presumably rabbi Gyula Weiszburg, the editor of the *Hitközségi Szemle* and general secretary of the ICP—claimed the prime minister's actions did not match his rhetoric:

> The prime minister speaks about antisemitism in vain if, within his sphere of authority, he does nothing to prevent the possibility of its unfaltering persistence in institutions. ... If young Jewish teachers continue to be asked for baptismal certificates if they want to get a job ... if the directors of the Hungarian Royal Post Office continue to advise candidates for promotion to abandon the Jewish faith, in short, if antisemitism continues to be cultivated, officially and to a much greater degree unofficially, and they find it so natural that even though they encounter it everywhere, they are not scandalized by it.[206]

Hungarian Jews began to assume roles in public administration even before they were granted equal rights—that is, while Hungarian law theoretically did not allow them to do so. Jews had been appointed medical officers of a couple of counties by the 1840s. In the 1850s and 1860s, Jews were chosen to serve as county or municipal physicians, municipal councilors, judicial assessors, and school-board members. In 1867, Prime Minister Gyula Andrássy appointed Jewish journalist Mór Ludasi (Ludassy) to serve as director of his press office even before the Jewish emancipation law took effect.[207] Officially, Jews were not guaranteed the right to occupy public office until the 1867 emancipation law entitled them to "exercise all the civil and political rights" enjoyed by their Christian compatriots.

Many historians have discussed discrimination encountered by Jews of the Dualist era when they applied for jobs with state, county, or municipal bureaucracies, the justice system, or public education.[208] Nathaniel Katzburg published a book in Hebrew in 1975 asserting that Hungarian public offices "hired great masses from the non-Jewish middle classes, but very few Jews."[209] According to Jehuda Don, George Magos, and Viktor Karády, Jews were not hired as public officials unless they converted, and if they did manage to get jobs as Jews, they would not rise above a certain rank unless they became Christians.[210] In his brief survey of the history of the Jews of Budapest, Károly Vörös characterized the years from 1873 to 1896 as follows: "In the intellectual professions, public offices—whether at the municipal, county, or ministerial level—were in practice entirely closed to Jews."[211] Even so, Tibor Hajdu has refuted this contention, suggesting that a shortage of educated young people in Hungary in the 1870s and 1880s made it possible for Jews with appropriate diplomas to "achieve success almost without restriction."[212] Hajdu attributed the diminution of the flow of Jews into public administration in the latter half of the first decade of the 1900s to the saturation of this employment sector.[213] Gábor Gyáni has noted that discrimination of the late Dualist era did not affect Jews specifically but the bourgeoisie in general, as was the case in England and Germany.[214]

National statistics indicate that in 1910, the proportion of Jews working in certain segments of the public sector exceeded their share of the overall population, though it remained lower in other segments. Jews constituted 4.99 percent of Hungary's 1910 population but 5.53 percent of its state officials, 5.81 percent of its municipal bureaucrats, 6.9 percent of its judicial functionaries, and 6.24 percent of its high school teachers. Meanwhile, Jews made up only 2.44 percent of Hungary's county officials, 4.08 percent of its judges, 1.21 percent of its prosecutors, and 4.26 percent of its college instructors and university professors. Between 1890 and 1910, the proportion of Jews among Hungary's state, municipal, and county officials and its high schoolteachers rose continually. The proportion of Jews among judicial officials rose between 1890 and 1900, then dropped between 1900 and 1910. From 1900 to 1910, relevant censuses show a drop in the proportions of Jews working as university professors.[215] Of the 467 teachers appointed to full and associate professorships at Hungarian universities through the Dualist era, 22—or 4.71 percent—were affiliated with the Jewish religion when they were hired, which corresponds roughly to the proportion of citizens of the Jewish faith within Hungary's overall population in that period.[216]

A different picture emerges if we compare the proportion of Jewish public sector employees with the percentages of Jewish students at high schools and institutions of higher learning that trained them for upper-level positions in this sector, as the former lagged far below the latter. In 1910, 22 percent of Hungary's high school and *Realschule* students and 29.6 percent of the students at its institutions of higher learning professed the Jewish faith; in the second semester of the 1909–10 academic year, 32.2 percent of the students in the department of law and political sciences at the University of Sciences of Budapest declared themselves to be Jews.[217] These are the numbers to which we should compare the percentage of Jews who worked as public servants, rather than to their proportion of the overall population.

In and of itself, the considerable disparity between these proportions does not constitute evidence of discrimination. A significant number of Jews who graduated from secondary schools and universities did not seek employment in the civil service. Some were reluctant to leave familiar environments to work in a predominantly Christian milieu. Others were discouraged because public service would require them to desecrate the sabbath and make it nearly impossible for them to observe Jewish High Holidays.[218] Public sector employment may nevertheless have been more attractive than a career in the private sector, as both expected their personnel to embody a certain middle-class lifestyle and dress appropriately, while the private sector paid lower wages and offered less stability. In addition, private sector careers were considered less prestigious than those in public service, which, in the words of journalist Mihály Pásztor, entailed "rank, authority, and power."[219]

Even if the discrepancies in education and employment figures are not evidence of discrimination against Jews per se, it is unlikely that solely individual preferences motivated an overwhelming majority of Hungary's Jewish high school and university graduates to accept jobs outside the public sector. The most obvious evidence that citizens of the Jewish faith were specifically targeted for discrimination in the Dualist era is the fact that immediately or shortly after converting to Christianity, individuals were usually appointed to public sector positions for which they had not been hired as Jews.

CONTEXT OF THE CONVERSIONS OF HUNGARIAN JEWS 51

As the Hungarian government consistently rejected the charge that Jews had to convert to be appointed to public sector (in particular, teaching) positions,[220] researchers who investigate anti-Jewish discrimination must augment the indirect evidence provided by statistical data with opinions and observations of people who experienced the era. Jewish accounts suggest the years immediately following the Austro-Hungarian Compromise and emancipation of 1867 were auspicious. In 1882, Albert Sturm wrote the following reflection on Boldizsár Horvát, the Andrássy government's justice minister from 1867 to 1871: "The Bódi Horvát democrats were looking all over for Jewish jurists to serve on the court of appeals and the supreme court; they looked everywhere for such Jews because they wanted them to embody the exalted doctrine of equality."[221] As the Andrássy government's minister of religion and public education, József Eötvös provided many young Jews (one was Ignác Goldziher) with state scholarships to study abroad.[222]

After his death in 1871, Eötvös was briefly succeeded by Tivadar Pauler, but Ágoston Trefort would oversee the Ministry of Religion and Public Education (MRPE) from September 4, 1872 until he died on August 22, 1888. Neither Pauler nor Trefort would continue their predecessor's policies. Pauler's well-known aversion to Jews manifested itself in his behavior as justice minister around the time of the Tiszaeszlár blood libel[223] and also surfaced in his writings.[224] As for Trefort, in 1839 and again in an 1862 presentation to the Hungarian Academy of Sciences, he recommended limiting emancipation to Jews whose morals were sufficiently consistent with those of Christian society.[225] In 1862, Trefort expanded on this view of emancipation, opining that Jews generally possessed a "weak sense of honor."[226] Though Trefort had begun to advocate emancipation without conditions by April of 1867,[227] he would continue to exhibit an ambivalent attitude toward Jews throughout his seventeen-year tenure in charge of the MRPE. In a decree issued in 1878, the minister attributed the excessively long schooldays at certain Jewish public elementaries to the "selfishness of parents who are engaged in profiteering throughout the entire day."[228] In an 1884 campaign speech delivered in Pozsony, Trefort declared that in dealing with antisemitism, the government's task was to defend Jews, but also to disseminate "among uneducated Jews the type of culture that represents the most effective antidote to antisemitism."[229] The implicit logic of this argument suggests that antisemitism was at least partly provoked by "uneducated" Jews who had yet to transcend their state of moral degeneracy. Press reports and contemporaries' memoirs unanimously

JEWISHNESS AND BEYOND

indicate that Trefort put considerable pressure on Jewish teaching applicants to convert to Christianity in exchange for an appointment. After Trefort died in 1888, Ignác Goldziher wrote in his diary that "he was the Antiochus Epiphanes of Hungarian Jewry, the priest of evil who dragged dozens of young Jews to the baptismal font."[230]

We have no direct proof Trefort actually required—*expressis verbis*—Jews who sought teaching positions to show a baptismal certificate in exchange for an appointment, though his contemporaries recalled that Trefort's ministry was very unlikely to hire Jews who did not convert. After completing his university studies in 1879, Dávid Angyal attempted without success to find a high school teaching position. His memoirs would attribute the lack of success to the Jewish religion he abandoned a few years later.[231] Statistics indirectly confirm the historian's memories: in 1890, two years after Trefort's death, only 47 (2.17 percent) of Hungary's 2,165 high school teachers were of the Jewish faith, a tiny fraction in comparison with the Jewish cohort studying at its institutions of higher learning (27.8 percent).[232]

Neolog Jewish periodicals of the 1880s, and the weekly *Egyenlőség* (which first appeared in November 1882) above all, continually published complaints about discrimination against Jews. In December 1882, Albert Sturm deplored hiring practices at state bureaucracies and government ministries as well as public offices in counties and municipalities, including Budapest. In Sturm's estimation, the situation was bleakest for Jewish candidates seeking high school teaching positions: Trefort was unwilling to appoint them to state schools, and Budapest's municipal schools avoided Jewish applicants, even those "with the best qualifications, [if] they lack the malleability to cease being Jews ad hoc." These unfortunates' only remaining option was to take a job as a teacher at a Jewish elementary school.[233]

The most frequent targets of criticism formulated in these periodicals were the policies of Pauler and, above all, Trefort. In the summer of 1884, the author of an article in *Egyenlőség* wrote, "Mr. Trefort plays a genuinely missionary role. Teachers of the Jewish faith have repeatedly said that they cannot be appointed because of their religion and that they have been prodded and harassed until one or two of them converted, on Mr. Trefort's explicit advice, to the Roman Catholic faith."[234] *Egyenlőség* asserted there were no (unconverted) Jews among the full professors at the University of Sciences of Budapest "because Minister Trefort hopes thereby to preserve the Catholic character of the Budapest university."[235] In the first volume of the scholarly journal *Magyar-Zsidó Szemle*, coeditor József Bánóczi advised young Jews to abandon their efforts to find public sector jobs and instead pursue careers in commerce or the liberal professions.[236] The much more combative writers at *Egyenlőség* refused to reconcile themselves to the situation, keeping the issue on their agenda and attacking Trefort repeatedly. "We demand," wrote *Egyenlőség*'s staff in March 1886, "that when the issue of appointments comes up, that the government not recognize any religious difference and not pass over Jews merely because they are Jews."[237]

The 1890s brought unequivocal change. The liberal atmosphere in the era of the so-called church policy reforms manifested itself in the employment of Jewish teachers at public schools.[238] When Trefort died in September 1888, Albin Csáky took over the MRPE, and within six months *Egyenlőség* was reporting, "Under the new minister, the era of proselytism and conversion-at-all-costs at the ministry of religious affairs has come to an end."[239] On October 28, 1889, during the parliamentary finance committee's discussions of the MRPE budget, Independence Party representative Ignác Helfy asked Albin Csáky to clarify "the rumors and statements that appear rather frequently in the press indicating that there is particularly great zeal for conversion at the ministry of education." If someone had the credentials necessary to assume a certain post, Helfy protested, "then the faith into which he was born cannot be an obstacle to obtaining it." *Egyenlőség* printed Csáky's response in bold type: "I assure the honorable representative that the stance he just articulated is my stance as well; that is, with regard to conversion, the ministry under my direction will avoid anything that could even be compared to pressure."[240] And indeed, criticism of the MRPE's secondary school appointment policies essentially disappeared from the Neolog Jewish press beginning in the early 1890s.

Nevertheless, the Jewish press was increasingly embittered that the University of Sciences of Budapest had no Jewish full professors. In June 1890, parliamentary representative Sándor Ullmann of the governing Liberal Party published a pseudonymous outburst in *Egyenlőség*: Hungarian liberalism "has one principle to which it steadfastly adheres, which it is unwilling to yield, and this is that no Jew can obtain a regular professorship at the University of Budapest."[241] Three months later, another article in *Egyenlőség* complained there were Jewish university rectors in openly antisemitic Germany, but "in liberal Hungary, the smirking demon of pedantry stands at the gates of the university with a crucifix and drives away even the most praiseworthy if they are not Christian."[242]

The year 1894 produced a breakthrough in this area. The faculty of the University of Budapest ranked the Jewish jurist Gusztáv Schwarz (from 1912, Szászy-Schwarz) first among the six applicants for a position at the institution's department of Roman law, which had been vacated the previous year. Breaking the long-standing taboo, József Eötvös's son Loránd, who had taken over the MRPE in June 1894, advised Hungary's King Franz Joseph to approve Schwarz's nomination, which he did on September 1 of that year. Gusztáv Schwarz became the first unconverted Jew appointed to a regular, non-honorary teaching position at the University of Budapest.[243] Shortly thereafter, the university's humanities department named its first Jewish full professor. In 1878 (at the age of twenty-two), Henrik Marczali had begun teaching medieval and modern history as an assistant professor at the university. In 1879, the humanities faculty nominated Marczali for a promotion to the rank of associate professor.[244] "However," Marczali wrote in his memoirs, "my appointment depended on factors completely unrelated to my work or the positive opinion of the faculty." Marczali said, "The conversion campaign began" under the leadership of Vilmos Fraknói, the canon of Nagyvárad (and future titular bishop of Arbe), and Archbishop (and cardinal) Lajos Haynald of Kalocsa. "As Fraknói put it: if I relent, they will bring me the professorship on a silver platter." Nevertheless, Marczali was not willing to convert—not so much out of a commitment to his Jewishness as out of pride.[245] And though the university's faculty would have supported Marczali's appointment, Trefort quashed the initiative.[246] Finally, on December 19, 1894, a two-thirds majority of the humanities faculty of the University of Budapest recommended Marczali for a position in the department of Hungarian history that had been vacant for two years. Gyula Wlassics, who had replaced Loránd Eötvös as head of the MRPE in January 1895, forwarded this proposal—along with a warm endorsement of his own—to the king, who approved Marczali's appointment on March 5 of that year.[247]

In the 1890s, complaints about discrimination against Jews vanished almost completely from the Jewish press. Another shift occurred around the turn of the century, unquestionably linked to a resurgence of antisemitism in Hungary's political and social lives, along with the rise of neoconservative ideology and the agrarian movement. Both of the latter manifested themselves in the government formed by Prime Minister Kálmán Széll in 1899.[248] As Egyenlőség's senior political editor Sándor Fleischmann wrote in April 1900, "For the first time in years, one again hears about the influence of

CONTEXT OF THE CONVERSIONS OF HUNGARIAN JEWS 55

baptismal certificates on certain civil rights. There are once again offices in which the question of a baptismal certificate is settled before the question of qualifications."[249] A couple of months later, Tamás Kóbor, who wrote many of *Egyenlőség*'s editorials at the time, expressed himself in much sharper terms: "This country is not a religious state, but only those of the Christian faith can lay claim to office. No one persecutes us, but if we want to live, they ask us for a baptismal certificate."[250] A Zionist pamphlet published in 1900 described the impossibility of Jews' finding jobs in county administrative offices.[251] A 1901 piece in *Egyenlőség* denounced the discriminatory policies of the ministries, particularly the ministries of agriculture and justice.[252] Two years later, *Egyenlőség* responded to intensifying complaints about so-called "Jewish expansion" into the liberal professions by emphasizing that this phenomenon was the product of discrimination against Jews in the public sector—that is, if more Jews were employed in state, county, and municipal administration, fewer would turn to the liberal professions.[253]

Egyenlőség hardly discussed the hopeless situation in the counties, nor the complicated local circumstances that affected municipal administration, focusing instead on discrimination in state-level appointments, which reflected government policies designed to pressure Jews into converting. Complaints about these pressures were more or less constant from the turn of the century to the outbreak of the First World War. In November 1904, Chief Rabbi Bernát Singer of Szabadka (Subotica, Serbia) wrote, "It is a regrettable fact that the state authority is one of the most zealous fighters for conversion."[254] In 1908, Chief Rabbi Mátyás Eisler of Kolozsvár went further, declaring, "We know that the state openly rewards conversion, because those who are not fit to occupy or manage a particular office solely because they are Jewish immediately become fit once they are no longer Jews."[255] These complaints did not vary with the passing of time or changes in government. According to *Egyenlőség*, discrimination against Jews was increasingly an unwritten rule: "In every Hungarian state office, almost without exception, lurks an antisemitism which does not manifest itself in scorn for Jews, but rather in tacit agreements not to let them in. Then there are places where this has created a kind of implicit custom, such that no one would even think that a functionary of the Jewish faith could find a position there, like someone of another religion might."[256]

On the subject of education, a total of four Jewish scholars were appointed to full professorships at the University of Sciences of Budapest between the turn of the century and the outbreak of the First World War. It is questionable whether this is evidence of the liberalism of the era or rather a sign that these Jewish scholars' outstanding merits made it impossible to maintain the decades-old practice of shunning them. In 1874, philosopher Bernát Alexander and his childhood friend József Bánóczi returned to Hungary after spending six years studying at universities in London, Paris, Berlin, Göttingen, Leipzig, and Vienna. In 1919, Alexander recalled that they had hoped to find work as assistant professors when they returned from abroad, "but we were soon disillusioned. We found out there was no way we could get into the university [of Budapest]—that no one had got in there—unless we got baptized. Later, attempts of this sort were also made by Trefort, the hero of liberalism."[257] In 1876, Alexander began teaching at the state *Realschule* in the fifth district of Budapest. He was appointed lecturer on the history of philosophy at the University of Budapest in 1878 and finally became an associate professor at the university in 1895. At the end of the customary three-year probationary period in 1898, the university's faculty voted against promoting Alexander to the rank of full professor and did so again in 1900.[258] Their official reason for doing so was that Alexander also worked as a journalist, though no one took this argument seriously. Elek Benedek was indignant: "Let's speak frankly. They voted against Bernát Alexander because he is *Jewish*."[259] Finally, in 1904, Alexander's patron and supporter Albert Berzeviczy, then minister of religion and public education, promoted him to a full professorship despite the faculty's opposition.[260]

Ignác Goldziher (born in 1850, as was Bernát Alexander) was habilitated in 1871, thereby becoming Hungary's first assistant professor of the Jewish faith. Then, in 1873, Religion and Public Education Minister Trefort appointed Catholic priest and Orientalist Péter Hatala chairman of the department of Semitic philology at the University of Budapest—even though Hatala was unfamiliar with the Arabic language and literature, and former education minister József Eötvös had promised the position to Goldziher. Over the years, Goldziher was offered professorships at universities in Cambridge, Strasbourg, Heidelberg, Vienna, Prague, Königsberg, Halle, and Breslau, though patriotism and a desire to be near his family would keep him in Budapest. Only after Hatala's retirement in 1905 did Goldziher earn his full professorship and take over as the chair of the department of Semitic philology. The preeminent Orientalist of his era thus taught at the University of Budapest without pay for thirty-four years while earning his living as general secretary of the Israelite Congregation of Pest, a job he truly hated.[261] Though Bernát Alexander and Ignác Goldziher were both eventually appointed to full professorships at the University of Budapest, they would undoubtedly have obtained these positions decades earlier had they converted to Christianity.[262]

Statistics indicate that the number and proportion of Jewish secondary school teachers in Hungary continued to grow in the first decade of the twentieth century. As I have mentioned, there were 47 Jewish high school teachers in the country in 1890, rising to 94 by 1900 and 246 (including 6 women) by 1910. In proportional terms, Jews went from 2.17 percent of Hungary's high school teachers in 1890 to 3.42 percent in 1900 and 6.24 percent in 1910 (6.37 percent including women).[263] This data contrasts with other statistics that provide unambiguous, albeit indirect, evidence of discrimination against Jews: in 1910, when 6.24 percent of Hungary's high school teachers were Jewish, Jews made up more than 50 percent of the country's private instructors and tutors. It is unlikely that the 532 Hungarian Jews who worked as private instructors and tutors in 1910 took this uncertain career path as their first choice, given the much greater security and prestige enjoyed by high school teachers.[264] The seeming paradox of the data demonstrating that the number and proportion of Jewish high school teachers rose between 1890 and 1910, and the conviction of many contemporaneous observers that anti-Jewish hiring practices were an indisputable reality is attributable to two factors. First, the indisputable discrimination at state-run institutions does not necessarily show up in these statistics, which did not distinguish between Jewish high school teachers at state secondary schools and those employed by municipalities. Given the famously liberal employment policies István Bárczy pursued as mayor of Budapest (1906–18), the proportion of Jewish teachers at municipal secondary schools may have been significantly greater than at state secondary schools. Secondly, contemporaneous observers were not primarily concerned with the number of Jews hired but rather with the role discrimination played in keeping Jews from being appointed or promoted, as well as the pressure they faced to convert if they wanted to further their careers. None of this could be tracked by means of statistical data.

In early 1906, *Egyenlőség* published a denunciation of the division of the MRPE that oversaw Hungary's high schools: "The former circumstances reappeared two or three years ago. Institutions of the state do not hire any Jewish teachers, or [do so] only in very rare cases, under pressure from the highest-ranking connections." The author lamented that recent Jewish graduates who applied at Department V of the MRPE faced a new tactic: they were told there were no high school teaching vacancies, which was true as "teachers from Catholic religious schools are transferred into the positions that open up at state schools—which the education ministry has the right to do." Unable to secure positions, Jewish graduates became private tutors, "but those who cannot find even a preceptorship, who cannot do anything else to earn their daily bread, they indeed—slowly, quietly, under the pressure of the circumstances—convert. And then immediately there is a position, a vacancy."[265]

A few weeks later, Sándor Barkóczy succeeded Ödön Boncz as director of Department V, taking responsibility for Hungary's high schools. The staff at *Egyenlőség* hoped Barkóczy would break with his predecessor's policies but were disappointed. Barkóczy, known to his contemporaries as "the black baron," was an old soldier of the *Ecclesia militans*. In 1903, in the interest of mobilizing bureaucrats and intellectuals, he had cofounded the far-right Congregation of Lords—the most influential of the associations organized under the aegis of the Marian Congregations.[266] Shortly after his appointment, at the 1906 general assembly of the National High School Teachers' Association, Barkóczy declared, "Character formation and the guidance of the will cannot occur properly unless all public education is placed on a foundation of religious morality. However, in referring to a foundation of religious morality, I do not mean . . . some kind of dogmatic distortion of religion, but true and correctly interpreted Christianity alone"—that is, Catholicism.[267] Barkóczy's statement caused a scandal. At the Hungarian parliament, Albert Apponyi, the minister of religion and public education, distanced himself from Barkóczy, specifying that "state education, by its very nature, cannot be of a religious character."[268] Despite this statement, the Marian Congregations would exert an ever-greater influence over public education, particularly high schools, over the course of Apponyi's ministry.[269] Many observers attributed the Congregations' growing influence to Apponyi himself,[270] though other factors must have been at play, given that this state of affairs did not change when Apponyi left office with the dissolution of the so-called coalition government in 1910. In his diary, literary historian and translator Marcell Benedek, the son of Elek Benedek, observed, "The dark clerical spirit spreads through the secondary school like an ink-stain on a white table cloth." Benedek, who was teaching at a state high school in Budapest at the time, continued, "Our poor principal, who has always been a liberal, never lets a faculty meeting pass without imploring us: let us teach on the basis of religious morality."[271]

CONTEXT OF THE CONVERSIONS OF HUNGARIAN JEWS   59

In *Egyenlőség*'s reports of concrete instances of discrimination and the Marian Congregations' undiminished influence over public education under the National Labor Party governments,[272] writers frequently repeated the line "You do not need a diploma here, but a baptismal certificate."[273]

Under pressure from the National High School Teachers' Association, the MRPE transferred Barkóczy to another position in January of 1912,[274] at which point the frequency of Jewish press complaints about the ministry decreased, though they did not disappear entirely. Due to the Neolog intelligentsia's increasing resentment toward Hungary's traditional political elite and their growing disillusionment with István Tisza's policies, the complaints intensified. On the eve of the First World War, a young Jewish candidate for a high school teaching position committed suicide after being told that he would not be hired without a baptismal certificate. Discussing this incident in a lead article for *Egyenlőség*, a young lawyer named Sándor Mezei (Mezey) struck an unprecedentedly bitter note: "The state, by making it possible and easy for you and your companions to study, encouraged and committed you to a career, the support of which promised you prosperity, but instead of prosperity handed you a bullet simply because you are a Jew—for no other reason, simply because you are a Jew. And yet not only for that reason: but because you did not become an apostate."[275]

Though almost all the reports cited above are from the Jewish press, one should note that in the decade and a half before the First World War, other contemporary periodicals, including the bourgeois-radical *Huszadik Század*, the liberal *Pesti Hírlap* and *Pesti Napló*, and *Alkotmány* (*Constitution*) of the Catholic People's Party, treated anti-Jewish discrimination in the public sphere as a given.[276] A 1911 article in *Alkotmány* invoked such discrimination as support for the daily's petition to the education minister requesting that Jews be admitted to university in numbers that corresponded to their proportion of the overall population. The official mouthpiece of the Catholic People's Party argued that this *numerus clausus* would put an end to the hypocrisy of admitting Jewish students to universities' humanities departments and then not permitting them to teach children in schools.[277]

In summary, from the Austro-Hungarian Compromise of 1867 to the collapse of the Dual Monarchy in 1918, only an exceptionally small number of Hungarian citizens of the Jewish faith were able to find jobs in county-level public administration, which still functioned as a kind of feudalistic society. In Hungary's centralized state administration, justice system, state-run public utilities, municipal offices, and public education system, anti-Jewish discrimination varied chronologically and geographically: in certain periods (the years following the 1867 Compromise or the 1890s) and in certain locales (such as Budapest), discrimination against Jews subsided or essentially disappeared, while at other times (the 1870s and 1880s, or the period following the turn of the century) it intensified. For Jews seeking public sector jobs, conversion was sometimes an explicit prerequisite for employment and openly discussed as such in private conversations. Though it was more of a tacit condition in other cases, complying unquestionably improved one's chances of being hired. The same was true of public sector promotions: affiliation with the Jewish religion was not necessarily an obstacle to advancement, but progress up the ladder was facilitated and accelerated by conversion.

Further research will be required to draw sharper distinctions between the various factors that gave rise to anti-Jewish discrimination in Hungary in the period under discussion. When Ágoston Trefort, the minister of religion and public education, decided in 1879 to make conversion a condition of Henrik Marczali's promotion to an associate professorship, he may have been motivated by political considerations, whereas social antisemitism may have prompted the faculty of the University of Budapest to oppose Bernát Alexander's promotion to the rank of full professor. Social antisemitism may also have been behind the classified advertisements in provincial newspapers where municipal officials explicitly sought "Christian" physicians for their communities and districts. Classified ads of this sort were most common in the first decade of the twentieth century, though they were published in the 1890s as well—in a period when Jewish press complaints about government policy and state administrative offices had almost vanished.[278]

The discrimination that afflicted Hungarian Jews who wished to pursue public sector careers was not unique to Hungary. It is hardly surprising that such discrimination was milder in more liberal and democratic societies. In the half century leading up to the First World War, there was significantly less discrimination against Jews in England and France than there was in Germany, Austria, or Hungary.[279] But while in the Austrian territories the only expectations of Jews were acculturation and loyalty to the supranational Austrian state and the Monarchy, political elites in Hungary and particularly Germany demanded that their Jewish citizens assimilate by identifying fully with the national concept that prevailed in these countries.[280] There were, however, significant differences between Hungary and Germany. In the

CONTEXT OF THE CONVERSIONS OF HUNGARIAN JEWS 61

German Reich (and particularly in Prussia), political authorities, the conservative party, and prominent university professors openly acknowledged the existence of discrimination against Jews and declared it legitimate on the basis of the principle of the "Christian state."[281] The Hungarian government, on the other hand, officially denied the existence of anti-Jewish discrimination. As long as the "implicit customs" *Egyenlőség* attributed to certain public offices were formally disavowed, hope was preserved that discriminatory hiring practices would eventually disappear.

Anticipation of change may have been reinforced by the fact that a few Jewish political officials rose to positions of power within Hungary's governing elite in the final years of the Dualist era. While Ignác Einhorn (alias Ede Horn) was appointed state secretary for commercial affairs seven months before his death in 1875, only in the 1910s would another Hungarian Jewish politician secure a similarly influential position, though several would then do so in the period around World War One. Ferenc Heltai served as the mayor of Budapest from February of 1913 until his death in August of that year; Lipót Vadász was appointed state secretary for judicial affairs in Prime Minister István Tisza's second cabinet (1913–17); and Vilmos Vázsonyi was a minister of justice and minister without portfolio (in charge of voting rights) in Prime Minister Móric Esterházy's government (1917) and during Sándor Wekerle's third term as prime minister (1917–18). Regardless of these officials' personal merits, their appointments were symbolic gestures, indications that the Hungarian government hoped to secure the political support of the Jewish middle class. As evidenced by the reactions of the staff of *Egyenlőség*, these gestures produced their intended results. As embittered as they were by discrimination, these journalists were an equally enthusiastic audience for any sign of hope that the Jewish faith might no longer limit their prospects. When Ferenc Heltai was nominated (and later elected) to serve as mayor of Budapest, the city became the third European capital (after London and Rome) to have a Jewish mayor. In a 1913 feature on Heltai's election, Arnold Kiss saw Heltai's appointment as evidence that "in our sweet homeland . . . genuine merit can be the only determining factor, and when the finest civic honor is conferred, [one is] indifferent to the fact that the man who has received this glittering distinction adheres with indomitable strength of character to the faith of his forefathers."[282] A week later, *Egyenlőség* published a report on the thirty-eighth general assembly of the Philological Society; after listening to Gusztáv Heinrich pay tribute to the late literary historian Ignác Kont—who, Heinrich noted, had emigrated to France because his Jewishness had prevented him from finding even a high school teaching position in Hungary—the general assembly of the Philological Society elected its new thirty-member board. The author of the article asked, bitterly and rhetorically, "Would you believe they elected not a single Jew to this board? Do you think so? Because if you think so, you got it right. Not a single one. Eulogies are another matter. Would the Jewish gentleman like a eulogy? That he can get."[283] And it was not just the Neolog intelligentsia—many other Jews presumably vacillated between similarly turbulent feelings of hope and bitterness. But while hope sustains the spirit, it does not put bread on the table; thus, conversion was undoubtedly a great temptation for Jews who wanted to find jobs in the public sector. In addition, and perhaps more importantly, the inevitably symbolic nature of anti-Jewish discrimination in the public sector sent an indirect message to the whole of Jewish society, convincing Jews with aspirations in other domains that it was more rewarding to be a Christian in Hungary than a Jew.

Neolog intellectuals were also highly sensitive to anti-Jewish discrimination in the public sphere because they expected more of the country's political authorities—who declared themselves to be liberals right up to the collapse of the Dual Monarchy—than they did of the society at large. This presumably explains why Jewish periodicals essentially ignored private sector discrimination against Jews, attributing it very little significance. In an 1897 issue of *Egyenlőség*, Adolf Soltész referred to job advertisements that explicitly requested Christian applicants by saying, "A person smiles, but cannot easily understand such absurdities."[284]

Beginning in the 1880s, hundreds of such help wanted ads were published in national newspapers and gazettes specializing in employment notices. Though this observation is based on a survey of only two daily newspapers— the *Pesti Hírlap* and *Budapesti Hírlap* (*Budapest News*)—and the weekly *Országos Pályázati Közlöny* (*National Application Gazette*, first published in 1902), the trend seems clear: the number of job postings specifically requesting Christian applicants increased slightly over time. Most of these help wanted ads were on behalf of retail enterprises seeking salesmen and saleswomen, cashiers, and assistants in fashion boutiques, textile shops, grocery stores, leather shops, cosmetics stores, pharmacies, hardware stores, lumber suppliers, tool shops, and tobacconists.[285] Also sought were office workers for companies and factories of various sizes;[286] artisans for tailors, sewing workshops, and upholstery workshops;[287] bartenders, hostesses, and head waitresses for restaurants;[288] and machinists, managers, accountants, and trainees for agricultural operations.[289] As the years passed, the only notable changes in these Christian-only job postings were that fashion boutiques were partially supplanted by department stores[290] and that employers specified new types of skills, such as "electro-technical" proficiency.[291] There was little change in the number of ads seeking Christian physicians to work at health spas, factories, and sanatoria,[292] nor in law offices' calls for Christian law students and law school graduates who had yet to pass the bar exam.[293]

We cannot be sure that all the employers who published these job postings were Christians. One cannot exclude the possibility that Jewish merchants wanted to hire Christian sales staff to serve their Christian customers. Nor is it clear that the designation *Christian* always meant *not Jewish*, though if employers wanted to hire people who were members of their own denomination, why did they not say so specifically? This did occur occasionally. It is also possible that employers' use of the generic designation *Christian* did not reflect an antipathy to Jews so much as a desire to work alongside salespeople and apprentices with whom they felt greater cultural affinity.

These job postings may thus have been motivated by a variety of intentions. If many of these calls for Christian applicants surely reflected an employer's antipathy to Jews, in other instances that concern was secondary and the *Christian* stipulation can be attributed to other more "understandable" considerations. Even so, the intent behind limiting applications to Christians did nothing to change the fact that doing so was discriminatory. For decades on end, Jews who looked for jobs in the classified ads were forced to recognize they were persona non grata at many workplaces in many parts of Hungary and that, even in the private sector, their chances of finding work would be limited unless they converted to Christianity.

Discrimination could not prevent a Jew with appropriate qualifications from setting up shop in one of the liberal professions. The religious identity of a physician or lawyer could, however, influence his potential clientele. According to the memoirs of writer Sándor Márai, born in Kassa in 1900, the prejudices of middle-class Hungarian Christians did not influence their choice of physicians in this period of "good-natured" antisemitism.[294] In contrast, and though not explicitly regarding the situation of Jewish doctors, *Egyenlőség*'s assistant editor Sándor Komáromi wrote an article in 1905 expressing his concern that many Jewish students at Hungary's colleges and universities would not be able to earn a respectable living; it was obvious to Komáromi that Christians avoided Jewish professionals and patronized them only when forced to do so. Komáromi described the consequences of these students' predicament in dramatic terms: "Those Jewish youths who are educated and unable to find success naturally come into conflict with themselves, and their first thought is that their faith stands in the way of their prosperity. And because they want to rise at all costs, the first ballast they toss from the airship of their lives is religion."[295]

More research will be required to determine whether the experiences of Hungarian Jewish professionals around the turn of the century are more accurately represented by Márai's recollections or by Komáromi's contemporaneous observations. This much is clear: job postings published in the last decade of the nineteenth century and the first decade of the twentieth indicate that some Hungarian lawyers sought Christians to take over their law offices or join them in opening a firm[296] and that certain presumably middle-class families appealed to Christian physicians to open private practices in their communities.[297]

Finally, liberal Hungarian Christians clearly agreed with their Jewish contemporaries that an affiliation with the Jewish faith was an obstacle to professional success in the public sector and in general. As Zoltán Szász wrote in the bourgeois-radical periodical *Világ* (*World*) in 1912, "Although there is no legal difference between Jewish and non-Jewish citizens . . . it is nevertheless undeniable that our governmental and social conditions are still such that in most fields, with an equal expenditure of energy, a Christian will go farther than a Jew."[298] As noted, Szász advocated conversion as the solution to this problem, reinforcing Sándor Komáromi's contention that ambitious young Jewish graduates were impelled to abandon their faith. In any case, the discrimination Hungarian Jews faced in the public sector and the prejudice they encountered in the private sphere were powerful incentives to abandon the Jewish religion in the late nineteenth and early twentieth centuries.

Social Acceptance

The writer Kálmán Mikszáth posed the following question in an article featured in the *Szegedi Napló* (*Szeged Journal*) in October of 1880: "What can the Hungarian nation legally and equitably ask of the Jews?" In summarizing his opinions, Mikszáth identified the Hungarian nation's legitimate expectations of the Jews but did not ignore Hungarians' obligations to their Jewish compatriots: "Thus while Jews must commit themselves to approximating cultured

Hungarian society in its culture, social concepts, and customs, this society must in return embrace the Jew, easing and facilitating his integration."[299] In a speech in Nagyvárad three years later, Prime Minister Kálmán Tisza declared that social amalgamation was a two-way street, urging Jews not to respond to antisemitism by "withdrawing bitterly" and Christians to "tighten the bonds of social coexistence without regard to differences of faith and race."[300]

Though Christian politicians and intellectuals placed greater emphasis on Jews' obligations to Hungarian society, Jews' integration necessarily depended on the openness of their Christian compatriots. The program of bourgeois transformation articulated during the Reform Era included demands for dismantling what contemporaries called *social barriers*. Removal of the obstacles impeding the integration of Jews—who were destined to strengthen the Hungarian nation—was theoretically an integral element of this initiative.

It is worth asking how much was actually done to break down these barriers and how willing Hungarian Christians were to associate with Jews and accept them into their social circles, homes, and families. If Hungarian Christian society was unreceptive, could Jews overcome resistance by converting? What were the potential social benefits of conversion? Given the insufficient quantity of sources describing the social circumstances of the Jewish petty bourgeoisie and working class, this investigation will be limited to the Jewish middle and upper classes.

At the turn of the twentieth century, Christians constituted a minority of Hungary's eight hundred to one thousand haut bourgeois families. Most of the Christian members of this class, which emerged in Hungary in the first half of the nineteenth century, were descendants of the German-speaking families who immigrated from Austria, Germany, and Switzerland.[301] Thus, in the age of nationalism, for the Jews who made up most of Hungary's financial and industrial haute bourgeoisie, the only *Hungarian* milieu into which to integrate themselves was the country's hereditary aristocracy or the upper strata of untitled nobility, which contemporaries increasingly referred to as the "gentry" or the "historical middle class."[302] The first subject of inquiry here is the extent to which the Hungarian Jewish haute bourgeoisie was characterized by efforts to find acceptance among the families and social circles affiliated with these strata.

Contemporaneous observers were essentially unanimous in believing that integration was the most ardent desire of every wealthy Hungarian Jew. In the short stories of the Reform Era, the primary characteristic of the affluent

Jew—almost always an antagonistic figure—was greed.[303] In the 1850s and 1860s, this motif was slowly supplanted by the stereotype of the nouveau riche Jew who craved the approval of the magnates.[304] Beginning in the 1880s, Hungarian Christian novelists depicted upper-class Jews as "new nobles" who had transformed themselves into landowners uniformly driven by the hope that old noble or aristocratic families would accept them if they converted to Christianity, or at least embrace their children if they were baptized.[305] Literature published around the turn of the century did not significantly alter this image, and thus the Jewish parvenu who apes the magnates and nobles in hopes of currying favor with them crystallized into a topos.[306]

Jewish writers' portrayals of the haute bourgeoisie were even more unflattering. By the 1860s, their depictions of nouveau riche Jews were accompanied by charges that this stratum was responsible for the antisemitism of Hungarian society, which affected the Jewish middle class and intelligentsia most. In a story Bertalan Ormody published in 1866, the root cause of antisemitism is wealthy Jews' worship of the "idol of money,"[307] while in Ferenc Molnár's first novel, *Az éhes város* (*The Hungry City*), published in 1901, it is their fawning over members of the aristocracy and gentry.[308]

The accusation was not confined to works of fiction. In a campaign speech delivered in January of 1905, Vilmos Vázsonyi, leader of the Democratic Party (which depended on the votes of the Jewish petty bourgeoisie of Pest), expressed an identical opinion: "Why the 'vanity fair' up there in that class I refer to as 'the social Riviera?' Don't they realize that we, the poor working Jews who struggle from dawn to dusk for our families, must endure the revulsion aroused by their futile yearning?"[309] In the 1890s, Neolog intellectuals would also begin to condemn haut bourgeois Jews for their "urge to rub shoulders," which drove them to appoint aristocrats to serve on the boards of their banks, and for the idleness of the sons of wealth who internalized only the negative characteristics of the traditional elite they "cozied up to": snobbery and extravagance.[310]

For decades, historians uncritically accepted the suppositions expressed during the era in question and repeated that wealthy Hungarian Jews desperately attempted to integrate themselves into the social circles of the hereditary aristocracy and the nobility.[311] In a 1983 article, historian László Varga expressed doubt that such efforts were widespread and pointed out that contrary to conventional beliefs, conversion to Christianity did not become "general" among the Jewish upper class; intermarriage between this class and

CONTEXT OF THE CONVERSIONS OF HUNGARIAN JEWS   67

the traditional Hungarian elite did not assume "mass proportions"; the over-whelming majority of ennobled Jews were awarded their titles in recognition of genuine economic merit; and their purchases of land were motivated by rational economic considerations, "not assimilation." Varga thus condemned as "fundamentally" exaggerated the notion that the Jewish upper class of the era was characterized by attempts to "wedge itself" into "the traditional ruling class."[312] In a study published a couple of years later, Viktor Karády expressed himself even more resolutely: with its "archaic lifestyle" and diminishing eco-nomic power, the elite of noble origin "obviously" could not have been the "medium of integration" for the Jewish upper class; "staying in an alliance with this elite was expedient as long as it remained in power, but to undertake an assimilationist 'identification' with it would have been suicidal."[313]

Given our current understanding, it is impossible to determine the precise extent of efforts members of the Jewish upper class made in seeking accep-tance within social circles and families of the traditional elite. As noted, litera-ture and journalism of the period were almost uniform in asserting that such striving characterized this class. Anecdotes from the period also feature the cliché of the haut bourgeois Jew yearning for the company of old noble fami-lies.[314] The cliché appears in some memoirs[315] while others contradict such a depiction of the upper class. In her fictionalized autobiography, poet and artist Anna Lesznai described her maternal grandfather, József Deutsch—en-nobled and granted the *praedicatum* "hatvani" in 1879—as a merchant who scorned the nobility and was proud of his bourgeois (and Jewish) origins.[316] The philosopher György Lukács's father, the banker József Lukács (who had also been granted a noble title), consciously and cautiously avoided the ap-pearance of "fawning."[317]

In the Dualist era, gravitation toward the traditional elite was more com-mon among members of the second and third generations who were born into wealth than among the fathers and grandfathers who earned these fortunes. The trend is most conspicuous in cases of intermarriage. Yet, when the scions of upper-class Jewish families married members of the traditional elite, it did not necessarily signify a renunciation of their fathers' ambitions, since the selection of spouses in these circles was less a question of love than a strategic decision intended to consolidate the family's position. When children of the upper class married into families of aristocratic or noble origin, it was at least as much a reflection of the will of the fathers as it was of the sons or, especially, daughters. There were significant numbers of haut bourgeois dynasties in which the most illustrious member or titular head of the family continued to adhere to the Jewish faith while at least one other member married into the traditional Hungarian elite.[318]

In any case, the Jewish spouse-to-be always converted before the ceremony—with one known exception, though that couple eventually converted to Christianity as well. Such conversions were, of course, legally unavoidable before the civil marriage law (XXXI of 1894) took effect on October 1, 1895. Until that date, Hungarian law did not permit conversion to Judaism, so a Jew could not legally marry a Christian without first converting. These conversions often took place just before the wedding. On January 9, 1882, Pál Ordódy de Ordód and Alsólieszkó Jr., son of the minister of public works and transportation Pál Ordódy, married Ilka Ehrenfeld, daughter of landowner Antal Ehrenfeld. According to a notice in the *Pesti Hírlap*, "the bride was baptized the day before."[319]

Once civil marriage was introduced in 1895, Hungarian Jews were no longer obliged to convert in order to marry Christians. However, the possibility of a civil ceremony did not change anything for members of the Jewish upper class who married into the aristocracy or the highest stratum of the "historical middle class." The one possible exception was Melánia Blaskovich of the aristocratic Ebeczki Blaskovich family, who not only agreed to marry the Jewish Hermann Königswarter in 1887 but also converted to Judaism at the behest of her father-in-law, Baron Moritz von Königswarter. She was, however, to join her husband in converting to Christianity when the elder Königswarter died.[320] And so we do not know of a single instance in which a man or woman from the upper echelons of Hungarian society identifying with the values of the aristocracy or the gentry married an unconverted Jew. Even after the introduction of civil marriage, Jews who wanted to marry members of these social circles took for granted the obligation to convert to Christianity.

The next line of inquiry is to determine Hungarian Jews' chances of being accepted into the social circles associated with the aristocracy and the "historical middle class," and to ascertain whether converting to Christianity improved the likelihood of their acceptance.

Jews and members of the traditional Hungarian elite started to form social—that is, extra-professional—relationships during the Reform Era, when liberal ideas were ascendant and a relatively broad class of capital-rich Jewish merchants and entrepreneurs began to establish itself. In an 1831 book recounting a tour of Hungary, August Ellrich of Berlin could still write that "one encounters many wealthy Jews in Hungary," though "the Hungarian" is not really willing to sit at a Jew's table.[321] In 1833, Ferenc Pulszky's amateur numismatist uncle invited an educated, passionate coin collector—the son of a wealthy Jewish merchant—on a study trip to Italy. Pulszky's father, however, objected to this invitation: "My father was ashamed; he could not suppress his aversion to Jews, whom he considered a more ignoble race, nor could he understand how his brother-in-law could associate with Holländer."[322] Even so, some Hungarian casinos and social organizations did begin to admit Jewish members in the 1830s and 1840s, and as historian Michael Silber has suggested, Hungary's nobles were more receptive of Jews than its predominantly German-speaking urban burghers were.[323]

Beginning in the 1850s and 1860s, boardrooms of joint-stock companies would become important sites for social interaction between male members of the Jewish upper class and noble families, particularly aristocrats.[324] These contacts were limited to narrow, formal parameters, and it is quite possible that certain aristocrats did not particularly relish them. Nevertheless, from the years following Hungary's defeat in the 1848–49 war of independence to the late 1870s, the trend was clear: the (more) liberal members of the aristocracy and especially the nobility were increasingly accepting of Jews, a development consistent with what contemporaneous observers described as the general philosemitism of Hungarian Christian society at the time. In the 1850s and 1860s, according to Dávid Kóhn of Gyula, "even if they did not have political rights, Jews' social situation in Hungary was better, more favorable than it had ever been."[325] In the spirit of the "social fusion" that would serve the interests of the homeland, many casinos and social organizations opened their doors to Jewish applicants in the 1860s.[326] Symbolic expressions of this atmosphere of acceptance included the formation of the Equality Circle in the spring of 1867, shortly before the legal emancipation of Hungary's Jews in December of that year. The objective of the Circle, founded at the initiative of the mayor of Pest, was to promote amicable relations between Jews and Christians. The revolutionary general György Klapka, recently returned from exile, served as the Equality Circle's first president, with ICP Secretary Ignác Barnay as his vice president. Within a short period after its founding, the Circle had 600 members, including 250 Jews.[327]

The 1870s were marked by the emergence of a class of rural Jewish landowners whose wealth, lifestyles, and (recently granted) noble titles made them potential associates of local elites. In 1872, physician Mór Moscovitz

70   JEWISHNESS AND BEYOND

(ennobled in 1867) purchased an estate in Zemplén County, where his son Géza (Geyza), an enthusiástic hunter and equestrian, took up residence and began socializing with the families of local aristocrats and landed nobles.[328] According to the autobiography of Vilmos Vázsonyi's wife, Margit Szalkay, her father, Jakab Schwartz, who owned land in Mátészalka, "maintained close friendships with the most influential upper-class families," in part due to his being the district president of the Liberal Party and hosting election preparations at his house.[329]

According to contemporary observers, in the 1880s, rising political antisemitism began to impede social integration of Hungary's Jews. In 1880, steadfastly liberal politician Ferenc Pulszky asserted that traditional propertied classes were increasingly hostile to the new landowners who settled among them: "We revile Jews if they get rich, accept them into our circles only in exceptional cases, and are then annoyed if they leave the country that has granted them civil—but only rarely social—equality."[330]

According to *Egyenlőség*, Hungarian antisemitism first became perceptible when the process of Jewish social integration derailed. In 1883, a journalist lamented the passing of the atmosphere of the 1870s: "Jews were accepted everywhere, as members of casinos and clubs; the finest sense of concord prevailed in social circles or on the occasion of a ball, etc. . . . Today there is a certain chill everywhere, a capriciousness in temperament, proposals from every side to remove Jews from casinos; across the country, Jews are excluded from elite balls, nor are they invited in as organizers."[331] Others, like the anonymous author of a pamphlet published in the mid-1880s, believed the emergence of political antisemitism did not exacerbate what was already an adverse set of circumstances: "Hatred and distrust of Jews have always existed, they were just dormant. . . . The difference between the current and prior situations is that there is now open declaration of that which previously lay dormant or manifested itself only in social relations."[332]

In 1886, an anonymous author intimately acquainted with "Budapest society"—that is, the social circumstances of the capital's Christian elite—published a book that painted a rather dismal picture of the social integration of the Jewish upper class. The only Jewish men this liberal-minded author mentioned in the chapter entitled "The Financial World" had long since converted to Christianity—with the sole exception of the banker Mór Wahrmann. In 1869, Wahrmann had become the first Jewish representative elected to the Hungarian National Assembly. Yet, as the anonymous author put it,

CONTEXT OF THE CONVERSIONS OF HUNGARIAN JEWS   71

"aristocratic gentlemen are very glad to attend his luncheons and soirées, though inviting him is not really on the agenda."[333]

Jewish journalists thought they detected a certain improvement beginning in the late 1880s.[334] Their optimism was fed by the obvious symbolism of cabinet ministers' and their wives' appearing at meetings of the Israelite Women's Association of Pest during the contentious period leading to church policy reforms.[335] Yet in 1896, the year after the triumph of these reforms, the editor in chief of *Egyenlőség* reported that the process of social integration had once again come to a halt: "This year in particular, our Christian brethren are making sure that Jewish people do not dance, or at least do not dance *with them*. [In the fourteen years] since the outbreak of the Tiszaeszlár epidemic, there have not been as many Jew-free balls in Budapest as in this year alone."[336]

And when the process of integration stalled out—and political antisemitism came back to life—in the late 1890s, the phenomena proved to be long-lasting. From then until 1914, *Egyenlőség*'s discussions of social acceptance of the Jewish elite were characterized less by optimism than by bitterness. In early 1902, news surfaced that former prime minister Sándor Wekerle's organizing committee for the annual lawyers' ball, one of Hungary's most elegant Carnival celebrations, produced a 1,500-person guest list without a single Jew on it. *Egyenlőség*'s staff saw this incident as the reflection of a general trend: "Let us also take note of this so that we might, when the occasion arises, rub it in the faces of the doubting Thomases who do not want to know about the shameful spread of the plague of social antisemitism, which is much more dangerous than official antisemitism."[337]

The authors of generalizations like these did not strive for nuance, nor did they try to determine which stratum of the Christian social elite was less accepting of upper-class Jews—the aristocracy? Or the upper echelons of the gentry? The aforementioned Géza Moscovitz maintained close relationships with several aristocratic families,[338] though his charismatic personality made him something of an exception in this regard. Moreover, if one believes the claims his daughter made in her fictionalized autobiography, certain local aristocrats were reluctant to accept Moscovitz's lunch invitations and did so only in order to be able to coordinate their approaches to county affairs.[339]

Most magnates did not even go so far. When the Prince of Wales—the future King Edward VII of the United Kingdom—visited Hungary in the 1890s, he stayed with a Jewish banker who organized a hunting trip in the prince's honor and allowed Edward to invite the guests. Count Mihály Károlyi, future prime minister and president of Hungary, recalled that the prince's invitees included "my stepmother's older brother Miklós Pálffy, who nevertheless rejected the prince's invitation, saying that he would not set foot in the house of a Jew."[340]

If certain magnates were occasionally willing to grace wealthy Jews' homes with their presence, the converse was practically never the case—as evidenced by reports in *Szalon Újság* (*Salon News*), published from late 1900 to 1913. Produced "exclusively for aristocratic society," one of *Szalon Újság's* stated objectives was to provide readers with comprehensive reports on "the inner life of aristocratic society" and "salon life."[341] Over the course of its thirteen-year existence, the paper's lists of guests at weddings, soirées, and receptions included only about a dozen converted Jews (or children of converted Jews), yet this significantly exceeded the number of unconverted Jews it mentioned, which amounted to a total of one—the aforementioned Géza Moscovitz, who attended the wedding of Prince János Liechtenstein and Countess Maricza Andrássy in 1906.[342]

A handful of memoirs suggest that the upper echelons of the "historical middle class" were somewhat more receptive, at least in certain provincial cities like Nagyvárad. Recalling her childhood friend Adél Brüll, Mrs. Dezső Fehér said that in the 1890s "our circles ascertained with a mixture of wonder and envy that the 'genteel' society of [Nagyvárad] had accepted the beautiful Adél Brüll and her parents. Adél and her parents were invited to big, exclusive Carnival celebrations."[343] And though none of Nagyvárad's approximately forty Jewish attorneys received an invitation to the local lawyers' ball in 1901,[344] the Jewish writer Ernő Ligeti also highlighted the openness of the city's Christian elite in his accounts of the early decades of the twentieth century there: "Ferenc Miskolczi, the stern lord-lieutenant of the county . . . sat down to play cards with Samu Kepes or other Israelites without any awkwardness."[345]

This issue was further complicated by the fact that in turn-of-the-century Hungary, there were social barriers other than those along the Jewish-Christian divide. In addition to the almost insurmountable walls separating aristocrats from the lesser nobility,[346] social exclusion among these classes targeted not only Jews but anyone without noble origin.[347] In the 1890s, when figures like Jenő Rákosi, editor in chief of the *Budapesti Hírlap* (*Budapest News*), and the famous writer Ferenc Herczeg—both of whom were of middle-class Danube Swabian origin—articulated concerns that the strata of Budapest society. they believed to be destined to draw closer together were avoiding doing so, they defined these strata according to overlapping social, professional, and religious categories.[348]

This raises the question: were wealthy Jews who sought social acceptance among aristocrats or the upper strata of the "historical middle class" distinctly disadvantaged by their religious identity, in addition to their bourgeois origins and professions? For contemporary observers, the answer was obvious. According to Count Miklós Zay, "Over the years, substantial wealth accumulated in the hands of Hungary's Jews; they purchased livestock and estates; countless urban dwellings were built with their money, and with material ascent came the desire for social ascent. For wealthy and distinguished Jews, there is only one open road to further ascent: abandoning the faith of their fathers and converting to Christianity."[349] A decade later, novelist Sándor Bródy assessed the situation of the Jewish upper class: "It has no room to develop, and if it does move, it will at best grow out of itself."[350]

Judaism was clearly a handicap (and conversion an advantage) in joining the National Casino, the Countrywide Casino, and the Park Klub, admittance to which depended on a vote of the membership. Count István Széchenyi established the National Casino in 1827. The Countrywide Casino was founded in 1883 at the initiative of parliamentary secretary Arisztid Dessewffy. Membership of the National Casino rose from 45 in 1827 to roughly 750 by the turn of the century, while the Countrywide Casino grew from 352 members in 1883 to nearly 2,000 by 1910. Neither club's bylaws mentioned Judaism as an obstacle to admission. Count Széchenyi articulated his objectives in founding the National Casino during its inaugural assembly on June 10, 1827: "Our homeland, too, should have the sort of distinctive and resplendent gathering place where the more important, prominent, and better educated, clever and discerning men of every class of society can come together for friendly conversation."[351] Thus when he founded the National Casino, Széchenyi himself was not "thinking of segregating social strata, but rather of commingling them within certain bounds."[352] This intention was reflected in the paragraph on membership conditions in the first detailed set of bylaws the National Casino drew up in 1878: "Any honorable and independent man of unimpeachable character and cultured deportment may be a member of the National Casino."[353]

The committee coordinating the founding of the Countrywide Casino publicized its intentions in these terms: "Its objective is to provide the middle class of Hungarian society with a gathering place that, in addition to providing

74 JEWISHNESS AND BEYOND

social entertainment, will serve to promote contemplation and the exchange of ideas in the public interest."[354] According to the casino's founding charter, its membership could include "any honorable, patriotic, and independent man of cultured deportment, unrestricted capacity for action, and unimpeachable character and reputation."[355]

Contemporaneous observers tended to refer to the National Casino as the *Magnate Casino* and the Countrywide Casino as the *Gentry Casino* and to regard them as meeting places for members of these social strata. However, the designation *Magnate Casino* excluded a significant portion of the National Casino's membership. Beáta Nagy's research indicates that throughout the period from its 1827 founding to 1941, almost half the casino's members were not aristocrats.[356] According to the calculations of historian Gabriella Eőry, state, county, municipal, and judicial officials made up 44.8 percent of the Countrywide Casino's membership in 1883 and 52.4 percent of its members in 1913; over the course of this same 30-year period, the proportion of landowners among the casino's membership decreased from 20.5 to 14.9 percent, the share of lawyers and other intellectuals dropped from 25.7 to 17.8 percent, and the proportion of those who worked in industry, commerce, and credit rose from 3.8 to 6.9 percent.[357]

Despite the principles enshrined in its bylaws, the National Casino would admit Jewish members only for a short period in the 1860s and early 1870s (with one exception). In 1832, the casino rejected the application of Mór János (formerly Mózes) Ullmann, who had converted to Catholicism seven years earlier, and denied membership to the still-unconverted Sámuel Wodianer in 1837.[358] In the 1840s, however, the National Casino admitted four baptized Jews as well as a Jewish physician: the recently converted (and thus now successful) Sámuel Wodianer in 1841; Bernát Ferenc Weisz in 1844; Sámuel's son Albert Wodianer Sr. in 1845; Bernát Ullmann in 1847; and finally, the casino's first Jewish member, Mór Moscovitz, in 1848.[359] Given that he had been the family doctor and confidant of future prime minister Gyula Andrássy since the 1830s, Dr. Moscovitz—who died a Jew—almost certainly had the Andrássy family to thank for his admission to the casino.[360] Moscovitz's case was an outlier, as the casino would not admit another Jew until 1860 (ophthalmologist and future head of the ICP Ignác Hirschler). It did accept six converted Jews in the intervening twelve-year period—two more Wodianers, two Ullmanns (who took the name Szitányi in 1867), and two Koppélys (who changed their name to Harkányi that same year).[361] Hirschler's admission

CONTEXT OF THE CONVERSIONS OF HUNGARIAN JEWS   75

was obviously related to the reawakening of Hungarian political life in the period following publication of the October Diploma of 1860. It inaugurated a uniquely liberal era in the history of the National Casino. By 1872, eight more Jewish men had been admitted.[362] This was an extraordinary development, even if the casino accepted a slightly higher number of converted Jews (ten) in this same period. However, that which the father had begun, the son unintentionally brought to an end: after admitting Mór Moscovitz's son Géza in 1872, the National Casino would accept only converted Jews (and, increasingly, their descendants)—who, according to my calculations, amounted to a total of fifteen people up to 1918.[363] When Géza Moscovitz died in 1913, the National Casino—which over the years had admitted ten unconverted Jews and thirty-five converts or people of Jewish origin—was now, at least in religious terms, "Jew-free."

The case of the Countrywide Casino is much simpler. As contemporaneous observers frequently complained, it never admitted a single member of the Jewish faith,[364] though it did accept converted Jews and men of Jewish origin. By the end of 1883, the Countrywide Casino had 632 members, a politically heterogeneous group ranging from staunch liberals like Dezső Szilágyi and Sándor Kozma to committed antisemites Géza Ónody and Iván Simonyi. It also included at least eight people who had converted from Judaism or were of Jewish origin.[365] In 1913, the last peaceful year of the Dualist era, the casino had 2,036 members; an estimated 36 were converted Jews or of Jewish origin.[366]

Budapest's third most prestigious social club was the Park Klub, which, unlike the aforementioned casinos, admitted women. The opulently furnished club opened its doors in April of 1895.[367] Baron Béla Atzél's ambition in founding the Park Klub was to bring together members of aristocratic families with wealthier, better educated members of the lesser nobility.[368] In practice, however, the Park Klub became an almost purely aristocratic club. Within a couple of years of its founding, very few of its members were untitled nobles.[369] The Park Klub's Jewish membership statistics are unambiguous: in 1900 and 1910, it included at least twenty converted Jews (or individuals of Jewish origin) but not a single person of the Jewish faith in 1900. The only Jewish member on its rolls in 1914 was Baron Alfonso Rothschild of the Viennese Rothschilds, who joined in 1907.[370]

To summarize: while in certain periods and for certain individuals Jewish religious status was no obstacle to social interaction, neighborly relations, or even friendships with members of the traditional Hungarian elite, it essentially eliminated the possibility of genuine social integration. Considering that aristocrats and high-ranking members of the "historical middle class" did not, as a rule, marry unconverted Jews, and taking into account the procedures the National Casino, Countrywide Casino, and Park Klub used to select their members, one can state that while conversion did not guarantee a Jew's acceptance into these circles, it was an unavoidable condition of integration.

It is unclear whether middle-class Jews, who far outnumbered the Jewish haute bourgeoisie, felt any desire to socialize with non-Jewish Hungarians whose lifestyle, education, and financial circumstances were similar to their own. *Per definitionem*, this question pertains only to the Dualist era, because it was only in the 1870s that the Jewish middle class came into being as an acculturated social stratum with the cultural attributes associated with middle-class status. The question is complicated by the fact that the Jewish middle class encompassed strata that lived and worked in disparate social environments: well-to-do merchants, entrepreneurs, and bank officials spent most of their professional lives among their coreligionists; practitioners of the liberal professions and intellectuals operated in mixed Jewish-Christian environments; and Jewish civil servants formed a tiny minority in their overwhelmingly Christian workplaces.

The Jewish press frequently repeated accusations that many members of the Jewish bourgeoisie cast aside their self-respect and slavishly humbled themselves in their efforts to "rub shoulders" with middle-class Christians, just as their upper-class Jewish counterparts tried to curry favor with the Christian elite.[371] While Ferenc Molnár's aforementioned 1901 novel suggests the younger generations of bourgeois Budapest Jews did make hopeless efforts to "rub shoulders" with middle-class Christians,[372] the notion is not supported by the recollections of the pediatrician Kornél Preisich or writer Sándor Márai, nor by a letter the young Béla Bartók wrote to his mother. In his autobiographical notes, Preisich—a Jew who joined the Reformed Church in the early 1900s—mentioned in passing that his father, produce and wine wholesaler Adolf Preisich, who settled in Szolnok in 1879, had nothing more than polite acquaintances among the members of the city's "influential" Christian families. There was nothing to indicate that the elder Preisich aspired to form closer relationships with the latter.[373] In the early years of the twentieth century, the young Bartók was convinced the main reason "no Christian person was ever to be seen" in the Budapest homes of the bourgeois

CONTEXT OF THE CONVERSIONS OF HUNGARIAN JEWS

Jewish families whose children he taught piano was that these families were standoffish in their dealings with Christians.[374] In his memoirs, Márai—born in 1900—recalled that during his childhood in Kassa, the Jews with whom his family shared a house, a well-to-do insurance agent and his wife, "lived largely in seclusion, arrogantly; they did not seek the acquaintance of their fellow tenants. In the limited sphere of social interaction, the man was courteous and indifferent."[375]

Thus, compared to upper-class Jews, those of the middle class seem to have been less interested in finding acceptance in the social circles and families of their Christian counterparts. Within the Jewish bourgeoisie, one might surmise, such ambitions were less prevalent among merchants, more prevalent among liberal professionals, and most common among state-, county-, and municipal-level civil servants. Once again, the questions are: to what degree did affiliation with the Jewish religion impede acceptance into Christian middle-class society, and to what degree did conversion to Christianity facilitate it?

Before the introduction of civil marriage in 1895, Jews of all social classes had to convert before marrying Christians. In a pamphlet published in 1868, physician Mór Frieder of Beregszász declared such conversions were especially common among those "whose enlightenment and education might have made them an honor and an asset to their coreligionists and their faith"—that is, members of the educated middle class.[376] Given the lack of empirical research and the paucity of contemporaneous expressions of opinion on the inclination of middle-class Hungarian Christians to marry unconverted Jews following the introduction of civil marriage, we are limited to speculation. Among Christians, willingness to marry a Jew was presumably greater among merchants and employees of private firms than among licensed professionals, greater among Hungarians of middle-class origin than among those of noble origin, and in all likelihood insignificant among civil servants, whose mentalities tended to conform most closely to those of the traditional elite. In general, even after the introduction of civil marriage, the overwhelming majority of middle-class Christians were unlikely to marry a Jew unless he or she converted first. At the very least the future partner would have been urged to convert.

Historians' assessments of social relations between middle-class Hungarian Jews and Christians in this period are essentially unanimous. Péter Gunst concluded that turn-of-the-century "civil servants of noble origin had hardly any social contact with private-sector employees of Jewish origin"[377] while Gábor Gyáni asserted that "as a result not only of their origins, but also of their identity, the genteel middle class, most of whom came from former noble-landowner families and had in some cases earned their livelihoods from public offices for several generations, kept their distance from the generally first-generation Jewish intelligentsia and entrepreneurial middle class."[378] Gunst and Gyáni omitted possible regional differences from their analyses, but sources suggest social intermingling with Jews was more common in provincial cities than in Budapest, while social exclusion of Jews was more prevalent in the capital city.

In 1883 in Nyíregyháza, the site of the Tiszaeszlár blood libel trial, Ilona Gömöry—the daughter of the city's prison warden—befriended another girl at her middle school, the daughter of a prosperous Jewish wheat merchant. According to the memoir of Ilona's younger brother János, the Jewish girl's father regularly visited the Lutheran Gömöry family's home, where he sought—and found—refuge from the bitterness of antisemitism.[379] In the 1890s, lawyer and future mayor of Zalaegerszeg József Keresztury, son of a smallholder of noble origin, associated primarily with Jews. As his son, writer and poet Dezső Keresztury, wrote in his autobiography, "Among the letters my father wrote to his fiancée in Gulács, there is a passage with a fairly detailed discussion of the gossip that my father's best friends were Jews. My father wrote about this in the enlightened spirit of the age: he could not really have done otherwise, given that the intellectual stratum on which he relied in his urban-development initiatives was composed of a fairly substantial proportion of Jews."[380] Every afternoon in the early years of the twentieth century, in front of the statue of General György Klapka in Komárom, Béla Zsolt's bank director father met the city's mayor and the proprietors of a Christian savings bank. After lingering for a few minutes of conversation at the statue, the entire crew withdrew to a nearby beer garden, where "they began drinking beer and talking politics, and a profusion of familiar anecdotes flowed from their mouths. My father always did the talking on serious subjects because he was the man from Pest; he read the Viennese, and often the Parisian papers as well."[381]

Other sources report a contradictory set of experiences. In a diary entry dated January 18, 1890, Samu Leopold Jr., a student at the Economics Academy of Mosonmagyaróvár from 1889 to 1891, wrote, "Today the white hats (gentry) are hosting a ball to which—Jews not having been elected to the organizing committee—we are not going."[382] Four years later, a liberal Christian writer at the *Hevesvármegyei Hírlap* (*Heves County News*) expressed outrage over his experience at an amateur theatrical performance in Eger: "Jewish spectators took up half the theater, and the other half was empty. In the entire viewing public, there were hardly 8 or 10 Christian men, and not a single Christian lady! And what was the reason for this? Only that this theatrical performance was staged by an amateur company composed of Jews."[383] What the *Hevesvármegyei Hírlap* denounced as "an assault on the democratic and liberal orientation of the 19th century"[384] writer János Kodolányi took as a given. In 1909, Kodolányi's father, a Catholic of noble origin, was transferred to Baranya County in southern Hungary to work as a chief forester based in the village of Vajszló. The Kodolányi family hosted the village's notary and Catholic parish priest and occasionally Reformed pastors and local leaseholders. In his autobiography, Kodolányi noted that "if the lessor was a Jew, he could of course not count on social contact."[385] Recalling his youth in pre-WWI Kassa, Sándor Márai, whose family of lawyers was of Zipser German origin, offered a more nuanced and empathetic account of the Jewish middle class, characterizing their treatment as a paradoxical mixture of "tacit exclusion and polite toleration": "It was proper to mingle with Jews at official social celebrations. . . . Casual and 'equal' fraternization took place at gatherings and official sites. . . . Still, did Jews and Christians really live together within a single class? No, just alongside one another." According to Márai, even if Christian families "rhapsodized" about their Jewish physicians, "they did not use the [informal pronoun] *te* with him, nor did they invite him to dinner, even by accident."[386]

Memoirs seem to corroborate the contention that Budapest's middle-class Christians were less accepting of Jews than were their counterparts in provincial cities and towns. With the exception of the artistic and literary worlds, all the relevant evidence I have uncovered suggests as much. The daughter of firewood wholesaler Vilmos Schlesinger, Ilona Harmos, who grew up in Pest in the 1890s, was made to feel like an outcast by her first independent social experiences. The Schlesingers, like many Budapest families, spent their summer months in a village outside the city. Harmos, who had converted to Catholicism by the time she wrote her autobiography, noted that "genteel non-Jews" looked down on the Jews who summered alongside them, and their children avoided Jewish children. When Ilona was twelve, her parents enrolled her in the third year of secondary school, but her experiences there were no better. Christian girls at school addressed each other using their first names and the informal pronoun *te* but called Ilona by her family name—if they talked to her at all.[387] As the obstetrician and gynecologist (and later psychiatrist) István Kulcsár put it in his autobiography, "When I was a child, in the liberal era, Christian society exhibited a dual morality toward Jews. Officially, in the press and at school, it embraced its Jewish fellow citizens, telling them 'you are a Hungarian, too,' but in social life it was cool and withdrawn." Kulcsár, who left the faith for the Reformed Church in 1920 at the age of nineteen, was fully aware of these social circumstances when he entered secondary school in the early 1910s: "I was familiar with the duality of society's behavior and accepted it as fact. Only thus can I explain my lack of resentment that my middle-class Christian classmates did not invite me to their parents' homes and only proletarian Christians have continued to be my pals."[388]

Literary accounts of turn-of-the-century Budapest also suggest middle-class Christians tried to maintain the barriers separating them from their Jewish fellow citizens. In a 1918 novel set at the turn of the century, Andor Gábor provides brief descriptions of the various Budapest families his Christian protagonist visits. He encounters "mixed" company at the studio apartment of the painter György Cserna; other than our main character, however, everyone at the home of the rich Jew Gotthelf is Jewish; the Tagányi residence, meanwhile, is frequented "exclusively by the bureaucrat-gentry." In the latter milieu, "they could not even imagine the sort of Jew with whom it might be possible to associate outside the office."[389]

Sources discussing social contact between bourgeois Jews and middle-class Christians—or, much more frequently, the lack thereof, resulting from Christians' rejections of Jews—generally do not mention whether a Jew's conversion to Christianity might have facilitated such relationships. Considering that conversion eased the exclusionary tendencies of the traditional elite, it could not have been otherwise in the Christian middle-class circles that imitated this stratum. All things considered, I am of the opinion that in the Dualist era, every stratum of the Christian middle class, with the possible exception of the bohemian art world, was more accepting of Jews who converted to Christianity than of Jews who did not. Though this may not have been the primary motivation for middle-class Jews who converted, it was certainly a contributing factor.

On October 8, 1894, minister of religion and public education Albin Csáky first presented the Hungarian House of Lords with the legislative proposal that was to elevate Judaism to the status of "received religion." The provision of the proposed law that elicited the most vehement opposition was its legalization of conversions to Judaism. Csáky defended the proposal by trying to assure his audience of its theoretical nature, suggesting that the possibility of converting to Judaism out of "financial interest" could be "almost completely" excluded and that it was "scarcely imaginable" that "social advantages" would prompt anyone to become a Jew: "I believe that all of us understand that no one is really going to secure himself any social advantages by converting to the Jewish faith." According to the proceedings of the House of Lords, Csáky's audience greeted his statement with "spirited laughter and amusement."[390] Neolog intellectuals accepted the truth of Csáky's observation as well—though with bitterness rather than mirth. As Gyula Weiszburg, general secretary of the Israelite Congregation of Pest put it in 1912, "That the equality of Jews is in fact a lie, and that they have never even begun to take it seriously, particularly in its finer, more idealistic demands, is neither a new nor a bold assertion; from the prime minister to the last village night-watchman, from the Jewish member of the House of Lords to the most abundantly side-locked *chevra shamash*, everybody knows this."[391] Of course, for the Neolog intelligentsia, the solution was not conversion but perseverance and further struggle. But not everyone was so determined. The disadvantages associated with the Jewish faith, along with aspirations to secure certain benefits (whether financial or social) may have prompted any number of religiously indifferent Jews to consider adopting another religion, one that might improve their chances of success in a variety of spheres, including their social lives.

Conversion as Escape

Being recognized as a Hungarian, being accepted socially, getting a job, getting married—the motivations for conversion that I have discussed thus far have involved concrete objectives. However, conversion may have also functioned as a form of escape—an act inspired by a desire to be liberated from the stigma of Jewishness. The enduring contradiction between theoretical equality and actual social practice (which Jews and their liberal Christian contemporaries regularly highlighted beginning in the 1880s),[392] the profound belief in the notion of Jewish inferiority permeating a wide swathe of Christian society, and even minor indications of contempt for Jews could all serve as sufficient grounds for a person to try to escape this stigma by converting to Christianity.[393]

The objective disadvantages of belonging to the Jewish faith were significantly less troublesome at the turn of the century than a hundred years earlier.

Even so, psychological vulnerability to antisemitism intensified with increasing secularization and acculturation. Premodern Jews tended to believe that antisemitism was part of the plan God had formulated for his people; they had been exiled from the Holy Land as punishment for their sins and would, in accordance with the will of the Creator, languish under the oppression of non-Jews until the coming of the Messiah.[394] Jews who were indifferent to Christian society and culture and regarded hostility to Jews as natural may have suffered from antisemitism, but it did not wound them psychologically. Thus, in turn-of-the-twentieth-century Hungary, injuries Orthodox Jews suffered as a result of their religious affiliation were unlikely to reduce them to a state of spiritual shock. However, such offenses may have been deeply scarring for secularized Jews who considered themselves Hungarian and were thus less emotionally equipped to handle manifestations of antisemitism. Over the course of the nineteenth century, these wounds, along with secularizing Jews' fraying connections to their religion and community, may have driven increasing numbers of individuals to liberate themselves from their status as Jews.

The most obvious evidence that conversion served as a means of escape is the increase in the number of Jews who became Christians during periods of surging antisemitism. Nevertheless, as sensitivities to anti-Jewish prejudice intensified in conjunction with the processes of secularization and acculturation, outbursts of antisemitism would not even have been necessary to induce ever-larger numbers of Jews to consider converting, given that their increasingly tenuous connections to the Jewish faith and the associated community made their "Jewishness" not just a painful stigma but an increasingly senseless and incomprehensible absurdity.

Watching the multitudes of passersby from the window of a café in Pest, the protagonist of Ernő Szép's autobiographical novel *Lila akác* (*Purple Acacia*), a young bank clerk, wonders, "Why am I banished from among them?" This interior monologue, like the rest of Szép's narrative, is addressed to one of his friends, a Christian physician. The brooding sentiments to which Szép gave voice were presumably common among young Hungarian Neolog Jews around the turn of the century:

> Something I was ashamed to think of always occurred to me there—that I'm a Jew. . . . How the pain and astonishment crashed in on me! "Jew," I said, so only the window pane could hear it, I said so I could believe there really is such a word, and I began not to understand what it is at all: a Jew.

I'm a Jew? How am I a Jew? What is that? Am I yellow or green or blue or
what? I'm the same skin color as the Hungarians. Whose idea was it that
I should be a Jew here? Honest to God, I had no intention of being a Jew
when I was born. This stupid surprise awaited me here in this world when
I disembarked. Here, I have to be a Jew. Why? On the inside, when I don't
think about it, I'm absolutely not a Jew. . . . You see, this is a serious thing,
because for you Christians it doesn't happen that when nothing hurts and
you have no annoyances or worries, there is still something wrong with you
that can ruin your mood. It's a kind of shadow that's still there for us even
in the sunlight. Look into the dark eyes of the Jews, no matter how bright it
is, there is sorrow in their eyes. Even if I had no cause to be gloomy, I always
had one cause. . . . My entire life has had one *gêne*; an obstacle awaits me if I
want to want to make a run at the world. If I raise my head, it's like I'm about
to bang it on the ceiling.[395]

Szép's fictionalized alter ego rejected the notion of abandoning the Jewish
faith, not because he disapproved of doing so but because he did not believe it
would liberate him from the stigma of Jewishness. Still, he frequently yearned
for a *non*-Jewish existence: "I was often seized by such blind envy when I
looked at my classmates Prédl and Leszner and Sprung; how calmly they filed
their nails with these German names, because they're original Christians;
how easy it is for them, they don't even know!"[396] Like the protagonist of
Purple Acacia, the majority of Pest's young Jewish private sector employees
held fast to the religion into which they had been born. However, some did
convert, and even in cases where concrete ambitions played a role in their
decisions, a desire to escape their Jewishness and a longing for a *non*-Jewish
existence may have been the deciding factors—even when they knew that
converting would not make them "genuine" Christians.

Notes

1. Anna L. Staudacher, *Jüdische Konvertiten in Wien 1782–1868*, vol. 2 (Frankfurt am Main: Peter Lang, 2002), 506. My use of the word *Catholic* in this text will always signify the Roman—rather than the Greek—Catholic Church.

2. Zsigmond Groszmann, "A pesti zsidóság vezetői," in *Emlékkönyv dr. Kiss Arnold budai vezető főrabbi hetvenedik születésnapjára*, ed. Mihály Guttmann, Simon Hevesi, and Sámuel Lőwinger (Budapest: Lőwinger, 1939), 52; Michael K. Silber, "Ullmann Family," in *The YIVO Encyclopedia of Jews in Eastern Europe*, vols.

84   JEWISHNESS AND BEYOND

1–2, ed. Gershon David Hundert (New Haven/London: Yale University Press, 2008), http://www.yivoencyclopedia.org/article.aspx/Ullmann_Family.

3. Michael R. Marrus, *Les Juifs de France à l'époque de l'affaire Dreyfus* (Bruxelles: Editions Complexe, 1985), 79–81; Todd M. Endelman, "The Social and Political Context of Conversion in Germany and England, 1870–1914," in *Jewish Apostasy in the Modern World*, ed. id., 86–87, 93–95; id., *Radical Assimilation in English Jewish History, 1656–1945*, 80; Paula E. Hyman, *The Jews of Modern France* (Berkeley/Los Angeles/London: University of California Press, 1998), 57, 64; Philippe-Éfraïm Landau, "Se convertir à Paris au XIXᵉ siècle," *Archives Juives* 35, no. 1 (2002): 27–43.

4. Michael Stanislawski, "Jewish Apostasy in Russia: A Tentative Typology," in *Jewish Apostasy in the Modern World*, ed. Todd M. Endelman, 189–205; Todd M. Endelman, "Conversion as a Response to Antisemitism in Modern Jewish History," in *Living with Antisemitism: Modern Jewish Responses*, ed. Jehuda Reinharz (Hanover, NH/London: University Press of New England, 1987), 73–74.

5. Hans Blumenberg, *Säkularisierung und Selbstbehauptung* (Frankfurt am Main: Suhrkamp, 1974); Hugh McLeod, *Secularisation in Western Europe, 1848–1914* (Basingstoke, UK: Macmillan Press, 2000), 1–12.

6. For the eighteenth century, see Shmuel Feiner, *The Origins of Jewish Secularization in Eighteenth-Century Europe*, trans. Chaya Naor (Philadelphia/Oxford, UK: University of Pennsylvania Press, 2011).

7. Studies of acculturated Jewish women constitute a partial exception to this assertion; these accounts suggest that Jewish women, unlike their increasingly impious male counterparts, worked to preserve religious traditions in their homes and family lives. See Kaplan, "Tradition and Transition," 3–35; id., *The Making of the Jewish Middle Class*, 64–84; Paula E. Hyman, *Gender and Assimilation in Modern Jewish History: The Roles and Representation of Women* (Seattle/London: University of Washington Press, 1995), 10–49.

8. Endelman, "The Legitimization of the Diaspora Experience in Recent Jewish Historiography," 201.

9. Ibid., 202.

10. László Varga, "Zsidó bevándorlás Magyarországon," in *Zsidóság a dualizmus kori Magyarországon: Siker és válság*, ed. id. (Budapest: Pannonica Kiadó/Habsburg Történeti Intézet, 2005), 11–30.

11. Májer Rosenzweig, "A tanév elején," *Zsidó Híradó*, August 29, 1895, 2–3; "Pedagógus: Tanév előtt," *Zsidó Híradó*, August 24, 1899, 2–3; "Pedagógus: Tanév végén," *Zsidó Híradó*, June 28, 1900, 1–2.

12. V. G., "A szombat szentsége," *Magyar Zsidó*, March 5, 1909, 2–3. These protests demonstrate that belonging to an Orthodox community did not necessarily make a person religious. Since all Jews were required to join a Jewish community in

CONTEXT OF THE CONVERSIONS OF HUNGARIAN JEWS   85

their place of residence, many secularized Jews were classified as Orthodox simply because the Orthodox congregation was the only available choice where they lived. Jacob Katz estimated that at the turn of the century, roughly a third of Hungary's Jews could have been considered Orthodox, "at least to the extent that in the eyes of the observer, their Jewishness was clearly apparent in their outward religious behavior." This is a significantly lower proportion than the 52.2 percent of Hungarian Jews who were recorded as members of the country's Orthodox communities in 1900. Jacob Katz, "The Identity of Post-Emancipatory Hungarian Jewry," in *A Social and Economic History of Central European Jewry*, ed. Yehuda Don and Victor Karady (New Brunswick, NJ/London: Transaction, 1990), 20; Gyula Zeke, "Szakadás után . . . Adalékok a magyarországi zsidóság felekezeti irányzatainak társadalomtörténetéhez (1868–1949)," in *Hét évtized a hazai zsidóság életében*, vol. 1, ed. Ferenc L. Lendvai, Anikó Sohár, and Pál Horváth (Budapest: MTA Filozófiai Intézet, 1990), 145–61.

13. Michael Silber, "The Historical Experience of German Jewry and Its Impact on Haskalah and Reform in Hungary," in *Toward Modernity: The European Jewish Model*, ed. Jacob Katz (New Brunswick, NJ/Oxford, UK: Transaction, 1987), 130–32.

14. Leopold Löw, *Der jüdische Kongress in Ungarn, historisch beleuchtet: Beitrag zur Rechts-, Religions- und Kulturgeschichte* (Pest: Verlag von L. Aigner, 1871), 95.

15. Immánuel Löw and Zsigmond Kulinyi, *A szegedi zsidók 1785-től 1885-ig* (Szeged: Szegedi Zsidó Hitközség, 1885), 164.

16. Sándor Büchler, *A zsidók története Budapesten a legrégibb időktől 1867-ig* (Budapest: Izraelita Magyar Irodalmi Társulat, 1901), 400.

17. Silber, "Historical Experience of German Jewry," 133.

18. Jacob Katz, *A House Divided: Orthodoxy and Schism in Nineteenth-Century Central European Jewry*, trans. Ziporah Brody (Hanover, NH/London: University Press of New England, 1998), 43–44.

19. Ibid., 44. For an analysis of the casino as a vehicle for social integration, see Michael K. Silber, "The Entrance of Jews into Hungarian Society in the *Vormärz*: The Case of the 'Casinos,'" in *Assimilation and Community: The Jews in Nineteenth-Century Europe*, ed. Jonathan Frankel and Steven J. Zipperstein (Cambridge, UK/ New York: Cambridge University Press, 1992), 284–323.

20. Dr. Samu Pserhofer, "Egy izraelita atya igénytelen észrevételei a gyermekek hitbeli neveléséről," *A Magyar Zsinagóga*, first issue, 1847, 72.

21. Elias Oesterreicher, *Der Jude in Ungarn wie er war, wie er ist und wie er seyn wird* (Pesth: Trattner-Károlyi, 1842), 57.

22. Silber, "Historical Experience of German Jewry," 134.

23. Zsolt Urbancsok, "A Pulitzer család stratégiái a 18–19. században," in *Hagyományláncolat és modernitás*, ed. Norbert Glässer and András Zima (Szeged:

86 JEWISHNESS AND BEYOND

Néprajzi és Kulturális Antropológiai Tanszék, 2014), 130–131; Katalin Fenyves, "Jákob háza Magyarországon: A zsidó női vallásosság alakulása a 19. Században," in *Hagyományláncolat és modernitás*, ed. Glässer and Zima, 265–67.

24. Michael K. Silber, "The Social Composition of the Pest Radical Reform Society (Genossenschaft für Reform im Judenthum), 1848–1852," *Jewish Social Studies* 1, no. 3 (1995): 116.

25. Katz, *A House Divided*, 45.

26. József Schweitzer, *A pécsi izraelita hitközség története* (Budapest: A Magyar Izraeliták Országos Képviseletének Kiadása, 1966), 33.

27. Silber, "Historical Experience of German Jewry," 134.

28. Michael K. Silber, "Hungary before 1918," in *The YIVO Encyclopedia of Jews in Eastern Europe*, ed. Gershon David Hundert, 1:777. In the case of Silber's thirteen-page article, I provide the page number of the printed version. For the other articles published in the *Yivo Encyclopedia*, I refer only to their internet addresses.

29. Silber, "Social Composition," 115.

30. Zsigmond Groszmann, "A pesti zsidó gyülekezet alkotmányának története," in *Emlékkönyv dr. Hevesi Simon pesti vezető főrabbinak, papi működése negyvenedik évfordulójára*, ed. Mihály Guttmann, Sámuel Lőwinger, Ferenc Hevesi, and Dénes Friedmann (Budapest: Neuwald Illés, 1934), 148; Béla Bernstein, "A zsidók története Vasmegyében (1912–1915)," in *Bernstein Béla emlékkönyv*, ed. Ibolya Mózer (Szombathely: BDTF Történelem Tanszéke, 1998), 126–27; Jenő Zsoldos, ed., *1848–1849 a magyar zsidóság életében* (Budapest: Múlt és Jövő, 1998), 221–23; Schweitzer, *A pécsi izraelita hitközség története*, 28; László Harsányi, *A szentesi izraelita hitközség története* (Budapest: MIOK, 1970), 52; Katz, *A House Divided*, 44.

31. Silber, "Social Composition," 113, 115.

32. "Pesti izr. hitközség közgyűlése 1863. évi január 6-án," *Magyar Izraelita*, January 9, 1863, 10.

33. Katz, *A House Divided*, 37.

34. Bak Ignác, "A népiskola és a vallástan," *Magyar Izraelita*, February 5, 1864, 42.

35. X . . ., "Az izr. népiskolának és különösen a mintafőtanodának feladata Magyarhonban, VI," *Magyar Izraelita*, June 25, 1863, 226–27.

36. Géza Komoróczy, *A zsidók története Magyarországon*, vol. 2, *1849-től a jelenkorig* (Pozsony: Kalligram, 2012), 89–95; Miklós Konrád, "Egyenjogúsítás feltételekkel: A feltételes zsidóemancipáció eszméjének diadala és bukása," *Múlt és Jövő* 28, no. 3 (2017): 28–35.

37. Anikó Prepuk, "Miért éppen a recepció? Az izraelita vallás egyenjogúsítása az 1890-es években," in *Emlékkönyv L. Nagy Zsuzsa 70. Születésnapjára*, ed. János Angi and János Barta (Debrecen: Multiplex Media/DUP, 2000), 263–281.

38. Katz, *A House Divided*, 31–233; Nathaniel Katzburg, "The Jewish Congress of Hungary, 1868–1869," in *Hungarian-Jewish Studies*, vol. 2, ed. Randolph L. Braham (New York: World Federation of Hungarian Jews, 1969), 1–33.

39. According to Gyula Zeke's calculations, in 1880, 56.1 percent of Hungary's Jews were members of Ortodox communities, 38.2 percent of Neolog communities, and 5.7 percent of status quo ante congregations; the latter communities were not formally subordinated to any organizational hierarchy. In 1910, Ortodox communities made up 51.9 percent of Hungary's Jewish popuation, Neolog communities 43.1 percent, and status quo ante congregations 5.0 percent. See Zeke, "Szakadás után," 152.

40. Egy hitrokon, *A zsidók reformátiója* (Pest: Heckenast Gusztáv, 1867), 16, 26.

41. Katz, *A House Divided*, 142.

42. Tamás Kóbor, *Ki a ghettóból*, vol. 1 (Budapest: Franklin-Társulat, 1911), 14, 19–21, 36–37, 108–13.

43. Márk Handler, "Szónoklat," in *Jubiláris emlékmű Handler Márk tatai rabbi 40 éves hivatali jubileuma alkalmából*, ed. Simon Hevesi (Handler) lugosi rabbi (Lugos: Handler Rudolf, 1904), 24–25.

44. Sámuel Kohn, "Újévünk intése," in *Zsinagógai szónoklatok* (Budapest: Rosenberg Testvérek, 1875), 3.

45. Sámuel Kohn, "Az Istenben való öröm a mi erősségünk," in *Zsinagógai szónoklatok*, 23–24.

46. Aladár Komlós, *A magyar zsidóság irodalmi tevékenysége a XIX. században* (1940–1942) (Budapest/Jerusalem: Múlt és Jövő, 2008), 117–18.

47. [Adolf Ágai], *Abrincs! 150 jordány vicz Seiffensteiner Salamontul* (Budapest: Athenaeum, 1879), 98.

48. "Könyvismertetés," *Izraelita Lapok*, September 10, 1874, 6.

49. Izrael Singer, *Vallástan az izraelita ifjúság számára* (Budapest/Sátoraljaújhely: Klein Alfréd Könyvkiadása, 1876), 4.

50. Sándor Berényi, "Még néhány szó az új nemzedékről," *Magyar-Zsidó Szemle* 5, no. 5 (1888): 303–05; Mór Mezei, "Dr. Hirschler Ignácz," *Egyenlőség*, November 13, 1891, 2.

51. [Lajos Blau], "Önbírálat," *Magyar-Zsidó Szemle* 20, no. 3 (1903): 202.

52. Miksa Szabolcsi, "A reczepczió megszavazása után," *Egyenlőség*, June 29, 1894, 4.

53. Miksa Szabolcsi, "A hitehagyás és a nevelőnőképző," *Egyenlőség*, April 28, 1901, 3.

54. Károly Stadler, "A zsidó közművelődési egyesület," *Magyar-Zsidó Szemle* 5, no. 1 (1888): 48.

55. Vilmos Radó, "A zsidó népiskolák, II," *Magyar-Zsidó Szemle* 2, no. 3 (1885): 200.

56. Ármin Auspitz, "Miért nem vallásos az új nemzedék?" *Magyar-Zsidó Szemle* 4, no. 7 (1887): 432.

57. Ilona Goldziher, "A hitoktatás a leányiskolában," *Magyar-Zsidó Szemle* 2, no. 1 (1885): 63.

58. Izor Lévai, "A hitoktatás és a felekezeti iskola," *Magyar-Zsidó Szemle* 6, no. 6 (1889): 371.

59. "A pesti izr. hitközség," *Szombati Újság*, December 2, 1882, 386.

60. Fülöp Csukási, "A héber nyelvoktatás jelentősége, I," *Magyar-Zsidó Szemle* 7, no. 3 (1890): 184–85.

61. Vidor Tekla visszaemlékezései [Tekla Vidor's memoirs], Budapest Történeti Múzeum Kiscelli Múzeum, Térkép-, kézirat- és nyomtatványtár. Typewritten manuscript. Ltsz. 87.40.1.

62. Kornél Preisich, "Önéletrajzi jegyzeteiből," in *Évkönyv 1983/84*, ed. Sándor Scheiber, (Budapest: MIOK, 1984), 260–74, quote from 268.

63. K. L., "A magas ünnepek," *Egyenlőség*, October 7, 1883, 6.

64. Mátyás Enyedi, "Ifjúságunk s a zsidóság," *Magyar-Zsidó Szemle* 4, no. 3 (1887): 164.

65. "Elfogyott minden jegy," *Egyenlőség*, September 29, 1889, 8; "Az istentisztelet a lefolyt peszach-ünnep alatt," *Egyenlőség*, April 18, 1890, 4.

66. Izor Glass Sr., "Előkelő asszonyaink," *Egyenlőség*, January 26, 1894, 9.

67. Egy modern asszony, "Válasz az előbbi levélre," *A Jövő*, January 14, 1898, 4.

68. "Üdvös újítás az ifjúsági istentisztelet körül," *Egyenlőség*, December 19, 1890, 4.

69. "Levelek egy modern zsidó anyához, II," *Egyenlőség*, January 9, 1891, 3.

70. "Barmiczva," *Egyenlőség*, July 14, 1893, 10–11.

71. "Barmiczva-Rothschild," *Egyenlőség*, March 21, 1897, 10.

72. Egy modern asszony, "Divat—a vallásban," *A Jövő*, December 31, 1897, 2.

73. Arnold Kiss, "Karácsony," *Egyenlőség*, December 27, 1896, 2.

74. Samu Haber, "Ifjúsági istentisztelet," *Egyenlőség*, June 8, 1894, 4.

75. Ármin Frisch, "Az egyházpolitika jegyében," in *Évkönyv 1899*, ed. Vilmos Bacher and József Bánóczi (Budapest: IMIT, 1899), 203–09.

76. Lajos Blau, "Vallásunk jelenéről és jövőjéről," in *Évkönyv 1900*, ed. József Bánóczi (Budapest: IMIT, 1900), 166–67.

77. Szabolcsi, "A hitehagyás és a nevelőnőképző," 3.

78. Béla Bernstein, "Az ifjúsági istentiszteletek," *Egyenlőség*, December 7, 1902, 3.

79. Arnold Kiss, "Sóvuósz," *A Budai Izraelita Hitközség Értesítője* 5, no. 5–6 (1914): 3.

80. "Róshasono," *Egyenlőség*, October 8, 1905, 9.

81. József Radnóti, *Kornfeld Zsigmond* (Budapest: Szerző kiadása, [1931]), 96.

CONTEXT OF THE CONVERSIONS OF HUNGARIAN JEWS   89

82. Ibid., 111; Károly Halmos, "Kornfeld Zsigmond, az emancipált 'állambankár,'" in *Sokszínű kapitalizmus: Pályaképek a magyar tőkés fejlődés aranykorából*, ed. Marcell Sebők (Budapest: HVG Könyvek, 2004), 159; Gusztáv G. Ehrlich, "Ötven éve dolgozom," in *Zsidó évkönyv az 5688. bibliai évre*, ed. Vilmos Kecskeméti (Budapest: n.p., 1927–28), 245.

83. László Varga, "Egy finánctőkés karrier: A Weiss-család és Weiss Manfréd," *Történelmi Szemle* 26, no. 1 (1983): 57.

84. Ernő Ballagi, "Báró Weiss Manfréd," *Egyenlőség*, December 30, 1922, 2; "A szemináriumi vezérlő bizottság," *Múlt és Jövő* 3, no. 9–10 (1913): 433–34; Nándor Székely, "Ezüst kandeláberek között," *Múlt és Jövő*, December 29, 1922, 3–4.

85. "Két új báró," *Zsidó Szemle*, October 18, 1918, 9.

86. Béla Bernstein, "Intelligenciánk és a zsidóság," *Múlt és Jövő* [after November 22], 1919, 2. Banned by the Republic of Councils, the journal *Múlt és Jövő* reappeared in the form of a weekly paper on October 3, 1919; from that first issue until January of 1920, the paper's pages were not dated.

87. Mózes Richtmann, "A legújabb vallásbölcseleti kísérlet," *Hitközségi Szemle* 3, no. 7–8 (1912): 173.

88. György Lukács, *Megélt gondolkodás: Életrajz magnószalagon* (Budapest: Magvető, 1989), 88.

89. Sámuel Weisz, *A Budapest-Lipótvárosi imaházegyesület (előbb Lipótvárosi Talmudtóra-Egyesület) 25 éves története* (Budapest: Jakab-Nyomda, 1930), 3, 5.

90. Bernát Munkácsi, *A Pesti Izraelita Hitközség oktatásügyének értesítője az 1912–13. iskolaévre* (Budapest: Breitner Károly, 1912), 60–81.

91. Bernát Munkácsi, *A Pesti Izraelita Hitközség oktatásügyének értesítője az 1904/905. iskolaévre* (Budapest: Kállai Ármin, 1904), 120–21.

92. Kóbor, *Ki a ghettóból*, 1:37.

93. "Istentiszteletünk," *Magyar Izrael* 2, no. 2 (1909): 27.

94. Raymond Recouly, *Le pays magyar* (Paris: Félix Alcan, 1903), 112; Henry Wickham Steed, *The Habsburg Monarchy* (London: Constable, 1913), 168–69; "Zsidóünnepek," *Pesti Hírlap*, September 12, 1912, 11; Kálmán Weszprémy Jr., *A Magyarországi zsidók statisztikája* (Debreczen: Debreczen Sz. Kir. Város Könyvnyomda-Vállalata, 1907), 114; "A demokrata Budapest," *Alkotmány*, January 22, 1909, 1; Frigyes Brámer, "Zsidó élet Pesten a század elején," in Sándor Scheiber, ed., *Évkönyv 1977/78* (Budapest: MIOK, 1978), 93.

95. "Főünnepi imahelyek," *Egyenlőség*, September 24, 1905, 14–15; "Róshasono," 8–9.

96. Jakab Steinherz, "A zsidó katonák és a főünnepek," *Egyenlőség*, November 2, 1902, 5.

97. Miklós Hajdu, "Új erőforrások," *Egyenlőség*, November 27, 1904, 4.

98. "A templomi ájtatosság," *Egyenlőség*, October 2, 1904, 8.

99. "Templomi rend," *A Budai Izraelita Hitközség Értesítője* 5, no. 5–6 (1914): 6–7.

100. Ármin Steiner, "Zsidó ünnep a bíróság előtt," *Egyenlőség*, February 14, 1909, 6.

101. Anna Lőwy, "Szülői értekezletek," *Magyar-Zsidó Tanítók Lapja*, April 15, 1903, 4–5.

102. Ede Neumann, *A nagykanizsai izr. hitközség hitoktatási intézményei az 1909–1910. tanévben* (Nagykanizsa: Krausz és Farkas, 1910), 5–6.

103. Samu Brody, "A zsidó hitközség élete," in *Emlékezések* (Gyula: Corvina nyomda, 1903), 14.

104. Béla Zsolt, *Villámcsapás (Schwarz András önéletrajza)* (Budapest: Pantheon [1937]), 76–77.

105. Zsigmond Büchler, *Gondolatok és ötletek* (Kunszentmiklós: Schwarcz Lipót, 1910), 16.

106. Arthur Linksz, *Harc a harmadik halállal: Ifjúkorom Magyarországon* (Budapest: Magvető, 1990), 40, 43, 113–14.

107. Lavoslav Schick, "A magyar zsidók statisztikájához," *Egyenlőség*, January 10, 1904, 4.

108. Ede Neumann, *A nagykanizsai izr. hitközség hitoktatási intézményei az 1912–1913. tanévben* (Nagykanizsa: Gutenberg-Nyomda, 1913), 3–4.

109. Kaplan, "Tradition and Transition"; id., *The Making of the Jewish Middle Class*, 64–84; Hyman, *Gender and Assimilation in Modern Jewish History*, 10–49.

110. Márk Handler, *A nő áldásdús befolyása: Szónoklat* (Budapest: Burián Mór, 1881), 3; Gyula Fischer and Gábor Weisz, *Rachel: Imák zsidó nők számára* (Budapest: Schwarz Ignácz, 1908), 160.

111. Schmiedl, "Vallástani kézikönyveink," *Izraelita Hitközségi és Iskolai Lap*, July 25, 1873, 3; Simon Hevesi, *Vallástani előkészítő a konfirmáns leányok számára* (Budapest: Lampel R., 1914), 31.

112. M. Kayserling, *Zsidó nők a történelem, az irodalom és a művészet terén*, vol. 1 (Budapest: Révai Testvérek, 1883), 15.

113. Zsigmond Kúti, "Leányaink nevelése," *Izr. Tanügyi Értesítő* 22, no. 4 (1897): 95.

114. Paula E. Hyman, "The Modern Jewish Family: Image and Reality," in *The Jewish Family: Metaphor and Memory*, ed. David Kraemer (New York/Oxford, UK: Oxford University Press, 1989), 188–89; Kaplan, *Making of the Jewish Middle Class*, 64; Hyman, *Gender and Assimilation*, 47.

115. Sebestyén Károly, "Zsidó nőképző," *Egyenlőség*, January 3, 1896, 7.

116. Menyhért Palágyi, "A zsidó nő a közművelődésben," *Egyenlőség*, October 2, 1891, supplement, 5.

CONTEXT OF THE CONVERSIONS OF HUNGARIAN JEWS 91

117. Hyman, "Modern Jewish Family," 190. See also id., *Gender and Assimilation*, 48.

118. Arnold Kiss, *Mirjam: Imádságok zsidó nők számára* (Veszprém: Köves és Boros kiadása, [1898]).

119. Hyman, *Gender and Assimilation*, 47.

120. Miksa Szabolcsi, "Apák vétke," *Egyenlőség*, September 16, 1892, 6.

121. Bertalan Edelstein, "Áldás és átok: Próbabeszéd, 1901. augusztus 10.," in *Zsinagógai beszédek* (Budapest: Szerző kiadása, 1906), 6–7.

122. "Részletek dr. Kiss Arnold főrabbi újévi beszédéből," *A Budai Izraelita Hitközség Értesítője* 2, no. 11 (1911): 12.

123. Regarding Vészi, see "Vészi József," *Egyenlőség*, August 3, 1884, 7; Géza Sárosi, "Vészi József," *Egyenlőség*, August 6, 1899, supplement, 1–2; Ágnes Széchenyi, "Vészi József, a műhelyteremtő és dinasztiaalapító (1858–1940)," *Budapesti Negyed* 16, no. 2 (2008): 243–71. Concerning Bánóczi, see Zoltán Ferenczi, "A megrendszabályozott tanítójelölt," *Ungarische Wochenschrift*, March 21, 1902, 2–3; Bernát Alexander, "Bánóczi József," in *Emlékkönyv Bánóczi Józsefnek születése hetvenedik évfordulójára, 1919. július 4.* (Budapest: Franklin-Társulat nyomdája, 1919), 11–13; id., "Bánóczi József életéből," *Egyenlőség*, December 4, 1926, 6; Ilona Benoschofsky, "Bánóczi József—levelezése tükrében," in Scheiber, *Évkönyv 1977/78*, 23, 25–26.

124. Ignaz Hirschler, *(Autobiographisches Fragment)* (Budapest: Druck von Max M. Pollak & Comp., 1891), 21–22; Mezei, "Dr. Hirschler Ignácz," 2.

125. Jenő Sándor Kiss, "Bevezetés," in József Kiss, *Legendák a nagyapámról* (Budapest: Kiadják Kiss József gyermekei, 1916), 15–16.

126. Sándor Bródy, "Zsidókról," *Fehér Könyv* 2, no. 3 (1915): 85; Secundus [József Patai], "A hosszú napkor elpusztult Jeruzsálem," *Múlt és Jövő* 2, no. 9 (1912): 422; Sándor Feleki, "Zsidó magyar írók és tudósok, XXII, Bródy Sándor," *Egyenlőség*, May 1, 1891, 12.

127. In 1869, 29.5 percent of Hungary's Jewish population lived in cities, whereas 50.85 percent of the country's Jews were city dwellers by 1910. The Jewish proportion of Hungary's overall urban population rose from 8.3 percent to 12.4 percent in this period. László Sebők, ed., *Az 1869. évi népszámlálás vallási adatai* ([Budapest]: TLA Teleki László Intézet/KSH Népszámlálás/KSH Levéltár, 2005), 276–77; *Magyar Statisztikai Közlemények*, new series, vol. 27 (Budapest: Athenaeum, 1909), tables, 98–99; *Magyar Statisztikai Közlemények*, new series, vol. 64 (Budapest: Athenaeum, 1920), 100–02, 110–11.

128. László Katus, "The Occupational Structure of Hungarian Jewry in the Eighteenth and Twentieth Centuries," in Michael K. Silber, *Jews in the Hungarian Economy 1760–1945: Studies Dedicated to Moshe Carmilly-Weinberger on his Eightieth Birthday* (Jerusalem: The Magnet Press/The Hebrew University, 1992), 92–105.

129. Endelman, "Conversion as a Response to Antisemitism," 61–66; id., "Social and Political Context of Conversion," 102.

130. Miklós Zay, "Zsidók a társadalomban," *Huszadik Század* 4, no. 12 (1903): 960.

131. I will discuss Neolog intellectuals' opinions of conversion and converted Jews in greater detail below. For more on these jokes, see [Ágai], *Abrincs!*, 30; *Drukk! Humorisztikus naptár az 1882-ik ordenáré esztendőre* (Budapest: Athenaeum, [1882]), 14, 125; Miksa Bródy, Kornél Tábori, and Szomaházy István, *Börzehumor* (Budapest: Vidám Könyvtár, [1912]), 37; Endre Kubán, *Kósere Snókesz: Zsidó adomák* (Budapest: Biró Aibert, [1912]), 11.

132. "A modern zsidóságról," *Religio* no. 33 (1st Half 1881): 259; Károly Huszár, *A keresztények legyenek-e zsidók?* (Budapest: Bagó Márton és Fia, 1884); Imre Szabó, "A budapesti reformátusság lelki rajza," in *Íme, a magvető kiméne vetni* (Budapest: n.p., 1928), 13.

133. Carl Cohen, "The Road to Conversion," *Leo Baeck Institute Year Book* 6 (1961): 279; Jacob Katz, "Judaism and Christianity Against the Background of Modern Secularism," in *Jewish Emancipation and Self-Emancipation* (Philadelphia/New York/Jerusalem: The Jewish Publication Society, 1986), 37–38; id., "Identity of Post-Emancipatory Hungarian Jewry," 14; Endelman, "Social and Political Context of Conversion," 83–84; id., "Conversion as a Response to Antisemitism," 75; id., *Leaving the Jewish Fold*, 11; Amos Elon, *The Pity of it All: A Portrait of German Jews* (London: Allen Lane, 2003), 82.

134. Endelman, "Social and Political Context of Conversion," 93; id., *Leaving the Jewish Fold*, 11.

135. Konrád, "Egyenjogúsítás feltételekkel"; id., "Jewish Emancipation as a Compromise," in *The Creation of the Austro-Hungarian Monarchy: A Hungarian Perspective*, ed. Gábor Gyáni (New York/London: Routledge, 2022), 229–56.

136. Zsoldos, *1848–1849 a magyar zsidóság életében*, 260–64. For the background and context of the revolutionary emancipation law, see Ambrus Miskolczy, *A zsidóemancipáció Magyarországon 1849-ben* (Budapest: Múlt és Jövő, 1999).

137. Comprehensive linguistic statistics concerning Hungarian Jews were not recorded until the census of 1880, when 56.3 percent of the country's Jewish population declared Hungarian to be their "mother tongue." Thirteen years earlier, the proportion of native speakers of Hungarian among the country's Jews was almost certainly under 50 percent.

138. Order number 26.915, issued by the Ministry of Religion and Public Education on November 15, 1871, legally recognized the bylaws of the *Autonomous Orthodox Jewish Denomination of Hungary and Transylvania*; cited in Árpád Zeller, *A magyar egyházpolitika 1847–1894*, vol. 1 (Budapest: Boruth E., 1894), 976–88.

139. Nathaniel Katzburg, "Assimilation in Hungary During the Nineteenth Century: Orthodox Positions," in *Jewish Assimilation in Modern Times*, ed. Bela

CONTEXT OF THE CONVERSIONS OF HUNGARIAN JEWS 93

Vago (Boulder, CO: Westview, 1981), 51; Katz, "Identity of Post-Emancipatory Hungarian Jewry," 22–25.

140. This percentage applies to the territory of the Kingdom of Hungary (including Transylvania but excluding Croatia and the Military Frontier). See Tamás Dobszay and Zoltán Fónagy, "A rendi társadalom utolsó évtizedei," in *Magyarország története a 19. Században*, ed. András Gergely (Budapest: Osiris, 2003), 81.

141. Ignác Romsics, "Nemzet és állam a modern magyar történelemben," in *Magyarország helye a 20. századi Európában*, ed. Pál Pritz (Budapest: Magyar Történelmi Társulat, 2002), 9.

142. Gábor Gyáni, "Etnicitás és akkulturáció a századfordulós Budapesten," *Regio* 6, no. 1–2 (1995): 104.

143. Péter Vajda, "Előszó," in Móritz Bloch, *A zsidókról* (Pest: Trattner-Károlyi, 1840), XIX.

144. Gyula Zeke, "Statisztikai mellékletek," in Lendvai, Sohár, and Horváth, *Hét évtized a hazai zsidóság életében*, 1:190.

145. "Beszélgetés Bánffy Báróval," *Jövendő*, March 15, 1903, 5.

146. *Magyar Statisztikai Közlemények*, new series, vol. 1 (Budapest: Pesti Könyvnyomda, 1893), 149.

147. András Kovács, "Az asszimilációs dilemma," *Világosság* 29, no. 8–9 (1988): 607–08; János Gyurgyák, *A zsidókérdés Magyarországon: Politikai eszmetörténet* (Budapest: Osiris, 2001), 276.

148. A zsidók egy igaz barátja, "Egy őszinte szó," *Egyenlőség*, August 5, 1888, 1–3; "Újabb tanács," *Egyenlőség*, February 10, 1889, 10.

149. Béla Tóth, "Elég-e?" *Pesti Hírlap*, October 21, 1900, 3.

150. Gyurgyák, *A zsidókérdés Magyarországon*, 18–19.

151. Peter Pulzer, *Jews and the German State: The Political History of a Minority, 1848–1933* (Detroit, MI: Wayne State University Press, 2003), 33; Todd Endelman, "Jewish Self-Identification and West European Categories of Belonging," in *Religion or Ethnicity? Jewish Identities in Evolution*, ed. Zvi Gitelman (New Brunswick, NJ/London: Rutgers University Press, 2009), 108–09.

152. István Szűcs, *Szabad királyi Debreczen város történelme*, vol. 3 (Debreczen: A Város Könyvnyomdája, 1871), 1065, 1067.

153. Béla Tóth, "Gentryskedés," *Pesti Hírlap*, August 13, 1899, 2–3.

154. Christian Wilhelm Dohm, *Über die bürgerliche Verbesserung der Juden* (Berlin und Stettin: bei Friedrich Nicolai, 1781), 92–94; József Eötvös, *A zsidók emancipációja* (1841) (Budapest: Magvető, 1981), 25, 29–30.

155. Eötvös, *A zsidók emancipációja*, 60. On several later occasions, Eötvös would reconfirm his conviction that Jews would inevitably be drawn toward the adoption of Christian principles and moral doctrine. See id., *Vallomások és gondolatok* (Budapest: Magyar Helikon, 1977), 438–39, 583–84.

156. Ágoston Trefort, "Az oroszbirodalomban 1835-b. hozott zsidókat illető törvény," *Themis* no. 3 (1839): 40.

157. Ferencz Kovács, ed., *Az 1843/44-ik évi magyar országgyűlési alsó tábla kerületi üléseinek naplója*, vol. 6 (Budapest: Franklin-Társulat, 1894), 11.

158. *Képviselőházi napló, 1892–1897*, vol. 20 (Budapest: Pesti Könyvnyomda, 1894), 113.

159. "Kossuth Ferencz a mindszenti zsinagógában," *Egyenlőség*, November 16, 1894, 4.

160. *Képviselőházi napló, 1878–1881*, vol. 10 (Budapest: Pesti Könyvnyomda, 1880), 393; *Képviselőházi napló, 1881–1884*, vol. 13 (Budapest: Pesti Könyvnyomda, 1883), 159.

161. *Képviselőházi napló, 1892–1897*, vol. 25 (Budapest: Pesti Könyvnyomda, 1895), 97.

162. *Képviselőházi napló, 1887–1892*, vol. 20 (Budapest: Pesti Könyvnyomda, 1890), 89.

163. *Főrendiházi napló, 1892–1897*, vol. 4 (Budapest: Pesti Könyvnyomda, 1895), 88.

164. "Andrássy gróf és a zsidóság," *Egyenlőség*, February 23, 1890, 2–3.

165. Jenő Molnár, "A mi nagyjaink: Marczali Henrik," *Egyenlőség*, June 16, 1923, 5.

166. Rutilus [Iván Szigetvári], "A mi szabadelvűségünk," *Élet*, April 1, 1894, 242.

167. Simon Krausz, *A pénzember: Egy magyar bankár élettörténete* (1937) (Budapest: Kossuth, 1991), 9.

168. Bernát Munkácsi, "Pályám kezdete," *Izr. Tanügyi Értesítő* 50, no. 1–3 (1925): 18.

169. Dávid Angyal, *Emlékezések* (1943), ed. Lóránt Czigány (London: Szepsi Csombor Kör, 1971), 84–85.

170. Mihál Stancsics, *Pazardi* (Kolozsvár: Barra Gábor, 1836), 3, 5–8.

171. Udvardy [János Cserna], "A zsidókról gazdasági tekintetben," *Ismertető Összművészetben, Gazdaságban és Kereskedésben*, May 31, 1840, 687–95.

172. G. J., *Némelly igénytelen nézetek, vallásilag véve, a magyarhoni zsidók meghonosítása ügyében* (Kőszeg: Reichard Károly, 1843).

173. Gábor Fábián, "Zsidó-emancipatio," *Pesti Hírlap*, May 5, 1844, 299–300.

174. Soma Vereby, *A zsidókról és ezeréves szenvedéseikről* (Bécs: Manz Nyomda, 1858), 26.

175. Kálmán Mikszáth, "A szegedi zsidók," in *Cikkek és karcolatok*, vol. 7, *1879*, ed. József Nacsády (Budapest: Akadémiai, 1968), 73.

176. Kálmán Mikszáth, "Tisza Lajos és udvara Szegeden: Fény- és árnyképek" (1880), in *Cikkek és karcolatok*, vol. 10, *1880–1881*, ed. József Nacsády and Gyula Bisztray (Budapest: Akadémiai, 1970), 89–90.

CONTEXT OF THE CONVERSIONS OF HUNGARIAN JEWS 95

177. Kálmán Mikszáth, "A nemzet szaporodása," in *Cikkek és karcolatok*, vol. 12, *1881. augusztus–december*, ed. Gyula Bisztray (Budapest: Akadémiai, 1971), 62–63. Alphonse Daudet's novel *Numa Roumestan* was translated by Jakab Béla Fái, who converted to Catholicism in May 1881.

178. Béla Matók, *A Zsidó Kérdés, Nro. 2* (Budapest: Kocsi Sándor, 1881), 5, 91.

179. *Új kormány* (Budapest: Singer és Wolfner, 1894), 40.

180. Zay, "Zsidók a társadalomban," 961.

181. Győző Concha, "A gentry," *Budapesti Szemle* 142, no. 401 (1910): 181, 194–97.

182. Zoltán Szász, "Zsidó antiszemitizmus," *Pesti Hírlap*, September 6, 1913, 3.

183. Péter Ágoston, *A zsidók útja* (Nagyvárad: Nagyváradi Társadalomtudományi Társaság, 1917), 286–87.

184. *A zsidókérdés Magyarországon: A Huszadik Század körkérdése* (Budapest: A Társadalomtudományi Társaság Kiadása, 1917), 70–71, 83–84; Zsolt [Kálmán Porzsolt], "Esti levél: Áttérés," *Pesti Hírlap*, April 1, 1917, 8–9.

185. Stancsics, *Pazardi*.

186. See Béla Bernstein, *Jókai és a zsidók: Zsidó vonatkozások és alakok összes műveiből* (Budapest: "Garai" Irodalmi és Nyomdai R.–T., 1925), 10–13; György Révész, *A zsidó Jókai regényeiben* (Nyíregyháza: Szerző kiadása, 1940), esp. 42–43. For more on Jókai's general attitude toward Jews, see Howard Lupovitch, "Ordinary People, Ordinary Jews: Mór Jókai as Magyar Philosemite," in *Philosemitism in History*, ed. Jonathan Karp and Adam Sutcliffe (Cambridge, UK: Cambridge University Press, 2011), 128–145.

187. Mór Jókai, *A mi lengyelünk* (1903) (Budapest: Akadémiai, 1969), 434.

188. Béla Kempelen, *Magyar zsidó családok*, vols. 1–3 (Budapest: Makkabi, 1999), 2: 28–29.

189. István Szentkirályi, *A zsidók Magyarhonban* (Pest: Gyurian József, 1861), 40–41, 86.

190. Ármin Kecskeméti, "A 'zsidó' a magyar színműirodalomban," *Magyar-Zsidó Szemle* 13, no. 3 (1896): 215–16.

191. Elek Benedek, *Katalin* (Budapest: Athenaeum, 1896), 245.

192. Elek Benedek, *Édes anyaföldem! Egy nép s egy ember története*, vol. 2 (Budapest: Pantheon, 1920), 26–27; "Esküvő," *Budapesti Hírlap*, July 30, 1884, 5; Dénes Lengyel, *Benedek Elek* (Budapest: Gondolat, 1974), 47–48.

193. Zeph [József Winkler], "Felekezeti irodalom," *Magyar Szemle*, January 20, 1895, 26.

194. See, for instance, Béla Tóthfalussy, *A keresztény és a zsidó vallás összehasonlítása* (Budapest: Athenaeum, 1900); A. S., *Zsidó vagyok-e én? Párbeszéd egy névleges és egy tényleges zsidó között* (Budapest: Vallásos Iratokat Terjesztő Társulat, 1901); Bonifácz Platz, *Katholikus levelek egy megtérő nőhöz* (Budapest: Szent-István-Társulat,

1902); Alfonz szerzetes, *Tévelygő Izráel vagy a zsidók felvilágosítása a szentírás alapján* (Szatmár: A "Pázmány-sajtó" nyomása, 1904).

195. See, for instance, the following (otherwise untitled) new items that appeared in this publication's column "Ecclesiastical Reports": *Religio és Nevelés*, no. 19 (2nd Half 1843): 150–51; no. 12 (1st Half 1845): 97–98; *Religio*, no. 8 (1st Half 1855): 61; no. 24 (2nd Half 1862): 189; no. 34 (1st Half 1866): 270–71.

196. Zsigmond Szabó, "Művelt zsidónak az ev. ref. egyházba áttérése alkalmával követett eljárás," *Dunántúli Protestáns Lap* 7, no. 42 (1896): 670.

197. Ferencz Hanuy, *A vallásváltoztatás az egyházjog és a magyar államjog szerint* (Pécs: Taisz József, 1905), 86.

198. Emil Grósz, *Ötven év munkában* (Budapest: Királyi Magyar Egyetemi Nyomda, 1939), 17–18; József Patai, *Herzl* (Budapest: A »Pro Palesztina« kiadása, [1932]), 249.

199. Győző Istóczy, *Országgyűlési beszédei, indítványai és törvényjavaslatai, 1872–1896* (Budapest: Buschmann F., 1904), 145.

200. Gerzson Szendrey and József Gareis, eds., *A függetlenségi és 48-as antiszemitapárt alapja és létjoga Magyarországon* (Budapest: Buschmann F., 1887), 17.

201. "Zsidó méreg," *Esztergom*, January 5, 1908, 7.

202. [Ignác Zimándy], *Mi tett engem antiszemitává?* (Budapest: "Hunyadi Mátyás" Könyvnyomdai Intézet, 1886), 33–34, 50.

203. Béla Bangha, *A kereszténység és a zsidók* (Budapest: Mária Kongregáció, 1912), 12, 27.

204. Ödön Farkas, *A zsidó kérdés Magyarországon* (Budapest: Aigner Lajos, 1881), 55; Gedeon [Rezső Kupár], "Keresztény hegemónia," in *A zsidókérdés Magyarországon* (Budapest: Szent Gellért Könyvnyomda, 1898), 8; Géza Petrássevich, *Magyarország és a zsidóság* (Budapest: Szent Gellért Könyvnyomda, 1899), 204; Egy jogász és egy bölcsész, *Kereszt, zsidó, vallás* (Budapest: Stephaneum, 1900), 24.

205. "A sztropkói eset a miniszterelnök előtt," *Egyenlőség*, August 20, 1911, 1–2.

206. "A miniszterelnök utálja az antiszemitizmust," *Hitközségi Szemle* 2, no. 9 (1911): 291–92.

207. Zsigmond Groszmann, *A magyar zsidók V. Ferdinánd alatt (1835–1848)* (Budapest: Egyenlőség, 1916), 23; id., *A magyar zsidók a XIX. század közepén (1849–1870)* (Budapest: Egyenlőség, 1917), 19, 44–45; Lajos Venetianer, *A magyar zsidóság története a honfoglalástól a világháború kitöréséig* (Budapest: Fővárosi Nyomda, 1922), 253.

208. Thus far, there has been only one published empirical study of discrimination against Jewish Hungarians, a biographical database of Jews (and individuals of Jewish origin) who taught at Hungarian universities between 1848 and 1944; see Gábor I. Kovács, ed., *Diszkrimináció, emancipáció—asszimiláció, diszkrimináció:*

CONTEXT OF THE CONVERSIONS OF HUNGARIAN JEWS   97

Magyarországi egyetemi tanárok életrajzi adattára 1848–1944, vol. 1, *Zsidó és zsidó származású egyetemi tanárok* (Budapest: ELTE Eötvös, 2012).

209. Nathaniel Katzburg, *Fejezetek az újkori zsidó történelemből Magyarországon* (Budapest: MTA Judaisztikai Kutatócsoport/Osiris, 1999), 149.

210. Victor Karady and István Kemény, "Les Juifs dans la structure des classes en Hongrie," *Actes de la Recherche en Sciences Sociales* 22, no. 1 (1978): 58; Viktor Karády, "Asszimiláció és társadalmi krízis," in *Zsidóság, modernizáció, polgárosodás: Tanulmányok* ([Budapest]: Cserépfalvi, 1997), 132; Yehuda Don and George Magos, "The Demographic Development of Hungarian Jewry," *Jewish Social Studies* 45, no. 3–4 (1983): 193.

211. Károly Vörös, "A budapesti zsidóság két forradalom között, 1849–1918," *Kortárs* 30, no. 12 (1986): 109.

212. Tibor Hajdu, "A diplomások létszámnövekedésének szerepe az antiszemitizmus alakulásában," in *A holokauszt Magyarországon európai perspektívában*, ed. Judit Molnár (Budapest: Balassi, 2005), 55.

213. Tibor Hajdu, "Az értelmiség számszerű gyarapodásának következményei az első világháború előtt és után," *Valóság* 23, no. 7 (1980): 27.

214. Gábor Gyáni, "Polgárosodás mint zsidó identitás," *BUKSZ* 9, no. 3 (1997): 273.

215. *Magyar Statisztikai Közlemények*, new series, vol. 16 (Budapest: Athenaeum, 1906); *Magyar Statisztikai Közlemények*, new series, vol. 56 (Budapest: Pesti Könyvnyomda, 1915). These figures apply only to men.

216. Kovács, *Diszkrimináció, emancipáció*, 161. The proportion of Jews in the overall Hungarian population was 3.99 percent in 1869, 4.54 percent in 1880, 4.67 percent in 1890, 4.94 percent in 1900, and 4.99 percent in 1910.

217. Zeke, "Statisztikai mellékletek," 191; *Magyar Statisztikai Évkönyv*, new series, vol. 18, *1910* (Budapest: Athenaeum, 1911), 385, 387.

218. Joél Halévy, "Zsidók az állam szolgálatában," *Jövőnk*, October 31, 1919, 4.

219. Zsombor Bódy, *Egy társadalmi osztály születése: A magántisztviselők társadalomtörténete 1890–1938* (Budapest: L'Harmattan, 2003), 93–106; Mihály Pásztor, *Cifra nyomorúság: Adatok a modern Budapestről* (Budapest: Nap Nyomda RT., [1909]), 44.

220. See, for instance, *Képviselőházi napló, 1892–1897*, vol. 3 (Budapest: Pesti Könyvnyomda, 1892), 376, 400–01.

221. Albert Sturm, "A mit zsidó tolakodásnak neveznek," *Egyenlőség*, December 10, 1882, 3.

222. Komlós, *A magyar zsidóság irodalmi tevékenysége a XIX. században*, 170; József Eötvös, *Levelek* ([Budapest]: Magyar Helikon, 1976), 569.

223. Ignác Acsády, "Pauler Tivadar és tanácsadói," *Egyenlőség*, December 10, 1882, 1–2; "Pauler válasza Mezei Ernő interpellatiójára," *Szombati Újság*, December

98   JEWISHNESS AND BEYOND

2, 1882, 385; "A mit a statisztika beszél," *Egyenlőség*, November 23, 1884, 3–4; Judit Kubinszky, *A politikai antiszemitizmus Magyarországon 1875–1890* (Budapest: Kossuth, 1976), 113, 119, 165–66.

224. Péter Gunst, *Marczali Henrik* (Budapest: Akadémiai, 1983), 70–71.

225. Trefort, "Az oroszbirodalomban 1835-b. hozott zsidókat illető törvény"; id., "A társadalom tudománya és Riehl munkái," *Budapesti Szemle* 16, no. 53 (1862): 303.

226. Trefort, "A társadalom tudománya és Riehl munkái," 303. For Lipót Löw's reaction, see Leopold Löw, "Die ungarischen Juden vor dem Forum der ung. Akademie," *Ben Chananja*, December 19, 1862, supplement, 425–30.

227. "Vegyes hírek," *Magyar Izraelita*, April 25, 1867, 31.

228. *Magyarországi rendeletek tára 1878* (Budapest: M. Kir. Belügyministerium, 1878), 772.

229. Ágoston Trefort, "A pozsonyi I. választókerületben 1884. június 22. tartott beszéd," in *Beszédek és levelek* (Budapest: Méhner Vilmos, 1888), 148–49.

230. Ignác Goldziher, *Napló* (Budapest: Magvető, 1984), 136.

231. Angyal, *Emlékezések*, 68.

232. *Magyar Statisztikai Közlemények*, new series, 16: 234–35; Zeke, "Statisztikai mellékletek," 191.

233. Sturm, "A mit zsidó tolakodásnak neveznek," 2–4.

234. "Trefort úr mint hittérítő," *Egyenlőség*, July 6, 1884, 6–7.

235. Fejér, "Zsidók az egyetemen," *Egyenlőség*, August 3, 1884, 5.

236. József Bánóczi, "A zsidó tanárok," *Magyar-Zsidó Szemle* 1, no. 8 (1884): 510, 512.

237. G., "Kik magyarosodnak?" *Egyenlőség*, March 7, 1886, 2.

238. The Hungarian ecclesiastical laws of 1894–95, which amounted to a separation of church and state, introduced civil marriage and state recordkeeping, regulated the religious identity of children of confessionally mixed marriages, legally recognized the Jewish faith as one of the Kingdom's "received" denominations, legalized conversion to Judaism, and permitted disaffiliation from any religious organization.

239. Béla Feleki, "Jogviszonyaink tekintettel az áttértek gyermekeire," *Egyenlőség*, March 24, 1889, 3.

240. "Zsidó ügyek az országgyűlési pénzügyi bizottság ülésében," *Egyenlőség*, November 3, 1889, 1.

241. Liberalis [Sándor Ullmann], "Fayer László és Marczali Henrik," *Egyenlőség*, June 6, 1890, 1–2.

242. "Dr. Marczali Henrik," *Egyenlőség*, September 5, 1890, 5–6. In Germany, the first full professor of the Jewish faith was the mathematician Moritz Abraham Stern, who was appointed to a position at the University of Göttingen in 1859. See Ernest Hamburger, *Juden im öffentlichen Leben Deutschlands: Regierungsmitglieder, Beamte*

CONTEXT OF THE CONVERSIONS OF HUNGARIAN JEWS 99

und Parlamentarier in der monarchischen Zeit, 1848–1914 (Tübingen: Mohr Siebeck, 1968), 55. The first full professor of the Jewish faith at the University of Vienna was the historian Max Büdinger, appointed in 1872. Peter Pulzer, "Legal Equality and Public Life," in *German-Jewish History in Modern Times*, vol. 3, *Integration in Dispute 1871–1918*, ed. Michael A. Meyer (New York: Columbia University Press, 1997), 157.

243. Kovács, *Diszkrimináció, emancipáció*, 137.

244. Sándor Feleki, "Zsidó magyar írók és tudósok, X, Dr. Marczali Henrik," *Egyenlőség*, January 2, 1891, 11; Henrik Marczali, *Emlékeim* (Budapest: Múlt és Jövő, 2000), 121.

245. Marczali, *Emlékeim*, 121–22; [id.], "Marczali Henrik," in [Sándor Nádas], *Ki volt mi volt: 99 önéletrajz: Magyar selfmademanek* (Budapest: Pesti Futár Kiadása, 1928), 78; [id.], "Hogy lettem én egyetemi tanár," in *Zsidó évkönyv az 5689. bibliai évre*, ed. Vilmos Kecskeméti (Budapest: n.p., 1928–29), 129–30.

246. Kovács, *Diszkrimináció, emancipáció*, 100.

247. Marczali, *Emlékeim*, 176; Kovács, *Diszkrimináció, emancipáció*, 100.

248. Miklós Szabó, *Az újkonzervativizmus és a jobboldali radikalizmus története (1867–1918)* (Budapest: Új Mandátum, 2003).

249. Sándor Fleischmann, "Aggodalmak," *Egyenlőség*, April 29, 1900, 2.

250. Tamás Kóbor, "Modern makabeusok," *Egyenlőség*, December 16, 1900, 1–2.

251. Ábrahám Éber, *A zsidó nép és a sionizmus* (Győr: Gross Testvérek, 1900), 22–23.

252. Tamás Kóbor, "'Az mindegy,'" *Egyenlőség*, February 10, 1901, 2.

253. Sándor Komáromi, "'Fölösleges emberek,'" *Egyenlőség*, January 4, 1903, 3.

254. Bernát Singer, "A kitérések, II," *Egyenlőség*, November 13, 1904, 4.

255. Mátyás Eisler, "A magyar zsidók emancipációja," in *Évkönyv 1908*, ed. József Bánóczi (Budapest: IMIT, 1908), 310–11.

256. "Glosszák a hétről," *Egyenlőség*, September 10, 1911, 4.

257. Alexander, "Bánóczi József," 28.

258. András Gergely, *Az Eötvös Loránd Tudományegyetem filozófiai tanszékének története 1867–1918* (Budapest: n.p., 1976), 16–17.

259. Elek Benedek, "Alexander Bernát," *Nemzeti Iskola*, February 17, 1900, 1.

260. Gergely, *Az Eötvös Loránd Tudományegyetem filozófiai tanszékének története*, 17; Kovács, *Diszkrimináció, emancipáció*, 26–27.

261. "Goldziher," *Egyenlőség*, September 8, 1889, 5; Róbert Simon, *Goldziher Ignác: Vázlatok az emberről és a tudósról* (Budapest: Osiris, 2000), 60–70; Kovács, *Diszkrimináció, emancipáció*, 60–61.

262. Bernát Alexander and Ignác Goldziher's Jewish colleagues among the full professors on the faculty at the University of Budapest included the legal scholar László Fayer (appointed in 1900) and the Assyriologist and Egyptologist Ede Mahler (appointed in April of 1914).

263. *Magyar Statisztikai Közlemények*, new series, 16: 234–35; *Magyar Statisztikai Közlemények*, new series, 56: 648.

264. *Magyar Statisztikai Közlemények*, new series, 56: 761.

265. "A kultuszminisztérium V. ügyosztálya," *Egyenlőség*, February 25, 1906, 1–2.

266. Miklós Szabó, "Középosztály és új konzervativizmus," in *Politikai kultúra Magyarországon 1896–1986: Válogatott tanulmányok* (Budapest: Medvetánc, 1989), 185–88.

267. Lajos Tomcsányi, *Báró Barkóczy Sándor D^R*. (Budapest: n.p., 1925), 21–22; Bernát Heller, "Kármán Mór, 1843–1915," in *Évkönyv 1916*, ed. József Bánóczi (Budapest: IMIT, 1916), 279.

268. *Képviselőházi napló, 1906–1911*, vol. 1 (Budapest: Athenaeum, 1906), 301.

269. Zoltán Zigány, "A felekezeti szellem erősödése a közoktatásban," *Huszadik Század* 9, no. 7 (1908): 1–14; Péter Nagy, *Szabó Dezső* (Budapest: Akadémiai, 1964), 51–57.

270. Lajos Návay, *Politikai jegyzetei (1910–1912)*, ed. János Gilicze and Zoltán Vígh (Békéscsaba/Szeged: Csongrád Megyei Levéltár, 1988), 116–17.

271. Marcell Benedek, *Naplómat olvasom* (Budapest: Szépirodalmi, 1965), 195.

272. Led by István Tisza, the National Labor Party won a decisive victory in the 1910 parliamentary elections; Tisza would serve as Hungary's prime minister from 1913 to 1917.

273. "Glosszák a hétről," *Egyenlőség*, October 6, 1909, 3.

274. Endre Ady, *Összes prózai művei*, vol. 10, ed. József Láng and Erzsébet Vezér (Budapest: Akadémiai, 1973), 426, 511; Miklós Hajdu, *Konfesszionális vizeken* (Budapest: A Páholy sajátja, 1912), 7–10.

275. Idem [Sándor Mezei], "Beszélgetés egy halottal," *Egyenlőség*, July 26, 1914, 1–2.

276. Várdai, "A zsidó államtitkár," *Huszadik Század* 14, no. 5 (1913): 627; "Mikor a pályázó zsidó," *Pesti Hírlap*, March 28, 1905, 10; "Hittérítés—kenyérrel," *Pesti Napló*, December 9, 1910, 4; J. M., "A Tanáregyesület ügyéhez," *Alkotmány*, November 1, 1911, 2.

277. J. M., "A Tanáregyesület ügyéhez," 2.

278. *Pesti Hírlap*, August 1, 1890, 15. *Budapesti Hírlap*, May 11, 1894, 18; November 21, 1895, 20; February 12, 1898, 24; July 20, 1899, 17; April 5, 1900, 19; October 6, 1903, 22; January 17, 1907, 26; October 8, 1907, 30; December 15, 1907, 29; January 16, 1908, 27; June 18, 1908, 30; July 12, 1908, 29; April 25, 1909, 27.

279. Todd M. Endelman, *The Jews of Britain, 1656 to 2000* (Berkeley/Los Angeles/London: University of California Press, 2002), 103–04, 164, 257; Pierre Birnbaum, *Les fous de la République: Histoire politique des Juifs d'État de Gambetta à Vichy* (Paris: Seuil, 2000); Ernest Hamburger, "Jews in Public Service under the German

Monarchy," *Leo Baeck Institute Year Book* 9 (1964): 206–38; id., *Juden im öffentlichen Leben Deutschlands*, 31–100; John W. Boyer, "Karl Lueger and the Viennese Jews," *Leo Baeck Institute Year Book* 26 (1981): 128–29; Robert S. Wistrich, *The Jews of Vienna in the Age of Franz Joseph* (Oxford, UK: Oxford University Press, 1989), 173–74; Pulzer, *Jews and the German State*, 44–68, 85–120; id., "Legal Equality and Public Life," 154–62.

280. H. D. Schmidt, "The Terms of Emancipation 1781–1812: The Public Debate in Germany and Its Effect on the Mentality and Ideas of German Jewry," *Leo Baeck Institute Year Book* 1 (1956): 28–47; William O. McCagg Jr., *A History of Habsburg Jews, 1670–1918* (Bloomington/Indianapolis: Indiana University Press, 1989), 100; Marsha L. Rozenblit, "The Jews of Germany and Austria: A Comparative Perspective," in *Austrians and Jews in the Twentieth Century: From Franz Joseph to Waldheim*, ed. Robert S. Wistrich (New York: St. Martin's Press, 1992), 1–18.

281. Uriel Tal, *Christians and Jews in Germany: Religion, Politics, and Ideology in the Second Reich, 1870–1914* (Ithaca, NY/London: Cornell University Press, 1975), 136–37, 140–42; Chris Clark, "The 'Christian' State and the 'Jewish Citizen' in Nineteenth-Century Prussia," in *Protestants, Catholics and Jews in Germany, 1800–1914*, ed. Helmut Walser Smith (Oxford, UK/New York: Berg, 2001), 83–84.

282. Arnold Kiss, "Heltai Ferenc," *Egyenlőség*, February 16, 1913, 1.

283. "Glosszák a hétről," *Egyenlőség*, February 23, 1913, 3–4.

284. Adolf Soltész, "A zsidóság a társadalomban, I," *Egyenlőség*, January 31, 1897, 4.

285. *Budapesti Hírlap*, April 18, 1885, 8; April 14, 1886, 4; January 18, 1887, 12; January 18, 1890, 12; February 23, 1890, 15; September 4, 1897, 18; January 11, 1900, 17; August 28, 1903, 17; September 10, 1903, 24; August 28, 1903, 18; September 3, 1907, 31; September 15, 1907, 30; January 28, 1913, 31; *Országos Pályázati Közlöny*, February 8, 1902, 6; March 15, 1902, 5; July 7, 1906, 4.

286. *Budapesti Hírlap*, January 14, 1890, 14; August 4, 1897, 16; January 5, 1900, 16; February 9, 1900, 18; August 23, 1903, 30; September 7, 1907, 26; September 15, 1907, 30; December 10, 1907, 30. *Országos Pályázati Közlöny*, March 15, 1902, 4–5; April 5, 1902, 5–6; May 3, 1902, 8; June 2, 1906, 1.

287. *Budapesti Hírlap*, January 11, 1900, 17; January 27, 1900, 18; September 15, 1907, 30.

288. *Budapesti Hírlap*, February 9, 1900, 17; September 17, 1913, 20.

289. *Országos Pályázati Közlöny*, February 1, 1902, 4; March 15, 1902, 4; May 3, 1902, 6; May 5, 1906, 3. *Budapesti Hírlap*, January 25, 1913, 31.

290. *Budapesti Hírlap*, September 3, 1907, 31.

291. *Budapesti Hírlap*, January 25, 1913, 31.

292. *Pesti Hírlap*, October 25, 1893, 24; March 14, 1912, 28. *Budapesti Hírlap*, April 8, 1894, 22; March 28, 1908, 26.

102   JEWISHNESS AND BEYOND

293. *Budapesti Hírlap*, April 23, 1895, 16; October 3, 1896, 16; January 25, 1902, 18; December 24, 1904, 22; October 28, 1909, 31.

294. Sándor Márai, *Egy polgár vallomásai (1934–1935/1940)* ([Budapest]: Helikon, 2013), 227.

295. Sándor Komáromi, "Helycsere!" *Egyenlőség*, September 3, 1905, 1–2.

296. *Pesti Hírlap*, October 28, 1891, 16; *Budapesti Hírlap*, December 29, 1905, 22; January 27, 1906, 22; February 23, 1907, 27.

297. *Budapesti Hírlap*, January 21, 1898, 16; February 27, 1898, 20; September 6, 1903, 27.

298. Zoltán Szász, "Pénzemberek," *Világ*, March 24, 1912, 33.

299. [Kálmán Mikszáth], "Istóczy tizenkét röpirata," *Szegedi Napló*, October 17, 1880, 1.

300. "Tisza Nagyváradon," *Budapesti Hírlap*, September 20, 1883, 4.

301. Péter Hanák, "Magyarország társadalma a századforduló idején," in *Magyarország története 1890–1918*, vol. 1, ed. id. (Budapest: Akadémiai, 1978), 446.

302. For a discussion of the evolving meaning of the concept *gentry* in the Hungarian social imagination, see György Kövér, "Magyarország társadalomtörténete a reformkortól az első világháborúig," in Gábor Gyáni and György Kövér, *Magyarország társadalomtörténete a reformkortól a második világháborúig* (Budapest: Osiris, 2006), 165–66.

303. Anna Szalai, "Bevezető," in *Házalók, árendások, kocsmárosok, uzsorások: Zsidóábrázolás a reformkori prózában*, ed. id. (Budapest: Osiris, 2002), 7–97.

304. J. Zs. [Jenő Zsoldos], "Zsidó a magyar regényirodalomban," in *Zsidó Lexikon*, ed. Péter Ujvári (Budapest: A Zsidó Lexikon kiadása, 1929), 985.

305. See Kornél Ábrányi Jr., *Régi és új nemesek* (Budapest: Athenaeum, 1881); Gergely Csiky, "Az Atlasz család (1890)," in *Századvég*, vol. 1, ed. Anna Szalai (Budapest: Szépirodalmi, 1984), 361–560.

306. Ferenc Herczeg, *Andor és András* (1903) (Budapest: Singer és Wolfner, 1925), 47–48.

307. Bertalan Ormody, "Zsidó aristokrátia," *Regélő*, July 31, 1866, 68–69.

308. Ferenc Molnár, *Az éhes város* (1901) (Budapest: Pesti Szalon Könyvek, 1993), 235–40.

309. Vilmos Vázsonyi, *Beszédei és írásai*, vol. 1, ed. Hugó Csergő and József Balassa (Budapest: Az Országos Vázsonyi-Emlékbizottság kiadása, 1927), 296.

310. Lajos Palágyi, "Osztálykülönbségek," *Egyenlőség*, January 12, 1890, 2; "Glosszák a hétről," *Egyenlőség*, April 3, 1910, 4; Ferenc Székely, "Két levél," in *Évkönyv 1897*, ed. Vilmos Bacher and József Bánóczi (Budapest: IMIT, 1897), 83.

311. See, for instance, Ernő Lakatos, *A magyar politikai vezetőréteg 1848–1918* (Budapest: Szerző kiadása, 1942), 73; Emma Lederer, *A magyar társadalom*

kialakulása a honfoglalástól 1918-ig ([Budapest]: Népszava, [1947]), 169–70; William O. McCagg Jr., *Jewish Nobles and Geniuses in Modern Hungary* (Boulder: East European Quarterly, 1972); Péter Hanák, "Vázlatok a századelő magyar társadalmáról," in *Magyarország a Monarchiában: Tanulmányok* (Budapest: Gondolat, 1975), 358.

312. László Varga, "A hazai nagyburzsoázia történetéből," *Valóság* 26, no. 3 (1983): 79. György Ránki used similar argumentation in asserting that McCagg's theory of the feudalization of the Hungarian bourgeoisie "has to be re-examined in a fundamental way." György Ránki, "The Development of the Hungarian Middle Class: Some East-West Comparisons," in *Bourgeois Society in Nineteenth-Century Europe*, ed. Jürgen Kocka and Allen Mitchell (Oxford, UK/Providence, RI: Berg, 1993), 446.

313. Viktor Karády, "Zsidó identitás és asszimiláció Magyarországon," in *Zsidóság, modernizáció, polgárosodás*, 40–41.

314. Aurél Förster, *Anekdoták*, vol. 1 (Budapest: "Stádium" Sajtóvállalat RT. Kiadása, 1925), 192–93.

315. Hilda Bauer, *Emlékeim: Levelek Lukácshoz* (Budapest: MTA Filozófiai Intézet/Lukács Archívum, 1985), 44.

316. Anna Lesznai, *Kezdetben volt a kert*, vol. 1 (Budapest: Szépirodalmi, 1966), 129–30.

317. Erzsébet Vezér, "A mindennapi élet története: Beszélgetés Popperné Lukács Máriával," *Kritika*, no. 6 (1985): 28.

318. This was the case in a number of families of ennobled Jews, including the (dirsztai) Dirsztays, the (baranyavári) Ullmanns, the (végvári) Neumans, the (tornyai) Schosbergers, the (gyulafalvi and bogdányi) Groedels, the (szászbereki) Kohners, the (csetei) Herzogs, the Wahrmanns, the Madarasy-Becks, the Hatvany-Deutsches, the (gelsei and beliscsei) Guttmanns, and the (erényi) Ullmanns. See Kempelen, *Magyar zsidó családok*, 1: 87, 96, 105, 112–13, 131, 134–35, 138, 140; 2: 27, 38, 63–64, 141; 3: 94.

319. "Eljegyzések és esküvők," *Pesti Napló*, January 11, 1882, 4.

320. I will discuss Hermann Königswarter and his wife in greater detail in chapter 4.

321. August Ellrich, *Die Ungarn wie sie sind* (Berlin: Vereins-Buchhandlung, 1831), 205.

322. Ferenc Pulszky, *Életem és korom* (1880–1882), vol. 1 (Budapest: Franklin-Társulat, 1884), 35.

323. Silber, "The Entrance of Jews into Hungarian Society."

324. Péter Busbach, *Egy viharos emberöltő. Korrajz*, vol. 2 (Budapest: Kilián Frigyes, 1899), 34; Károly Vörös, "Pest-Budától Budapestig 1849–1873," in *Budapest története a márciusi forradalomtól az őszirózsás forradalomig*, ed. id. (Budapest: Akadémiai, 1978), 225.

104   JEWISHNESS AND BEYOND

325. Dávid Kóhn, *Hatvan év múltán: Visszaemlékezések* (Gyula: Dobay János, 1936), 214–15.

326. "Levelezések: Aradi zsidó-ügyek," *Magyar Izraelita*, March 7, 1862, 83; Imre Csetényi, "A hatvanas évek és a zsidóság," in *Tanulmányok a zsidó tudomány köréből Dr. Guttmann Mihály emlékére*, ed. Sámuel Lőwinger (Budapest: Neuwald Illés, 1946), 103; Edit Kerecsényi, "Nagykanizsa társadalma és egyleti élete 1900 táján," in *Zalai Gyűjtemény 21: Közlemények Zala megye közgyűjteményeinek kutatásaiból 1984–1985*, ed. Alajos Degré and Imre Halász (Zalaegerszeg, Hungary: Zala Megyei Levéltár, 1985), 109; Csilla B. Horváth, "A pécsi kereskedők szerepe a helyi polgári társas élet szervezésében," in *Struktúra és városkép: A polgári társadalom a Dunántúlon a dualizmus korában*, ed. Péter G. Tóth (Veszprém: Laczkó Dezső Múzeum, 2002), 445–46.

327. Pál Tenczer, "Sváb rabbi jóslata Falk Miksáról," *Egyenlőség*, June 5, 1898, 3; François Fejtö, *Hongrois et Juifs: Histoire millénaire d'un couple singulier (1000–1997)* (Paris: Éditions Balland, 1997), 99.

328. Erzsébet Vezér, *Lesznai Anna élete* (Budapest: Kossuth, 1979), 9–12.

329. Vilmosné Vázsonyi, *Az én uram* (Budapest: Genius, [1931]), 8.

330. Ferencz Pulszky, "A zsidókról," *Pesti Napló*, July 25, 1880, 1.

331. Iván Horváth, "A zsidók s a magyar társadalom," *Egyenlőség*, February 18, 1883, 3–4.

332. [Egy zsidó], *A zsidókérdés* (Budapest: Wilckens és Waidl, [1884/1885]), 3–4.

333. *A budapesti társaság* (Budapest: Pallas, 1886), 452.

334. Antroposz, "Visszapillantás," *Egyenlőség*, January 6, 1889, 1.

335. Sz. [Miksa Szabolcsi], "Egy darab reczepczió in praxi," *Egyenlőség*, February 8, 1895, 10–11.

336. Miksa Szabolcsi, "Két irány," *Egyenlőség*, February 14, 1896, 6.

337. "Hazug demokráczia," *Egyenlőség*, January 26, 1902, 10.

338. Lajos Hatvany, *Levelei*, sel. and ed. Lajosné Hatvany and István Rozsics (Budapest: Szépirodalmi, 1985), 285.

339. Lesznai, *Kezdetben volt a kert*, 1: 148.

340. Mihály Károlyi, *Hit, illúziók nélkül* (Budapest: Magvető/Szépirodalmi, 1977), 38.

341. "A 'Szalon Újság'-ról: Még néhány tájékoztató szó," *Szalon Újság*, December, 1900, 1.

342. "Andrássy-Liechtenstein nász," *Szalon Újság*, September 15, 1906, 6.

343. Zsófia Dénes, *Akkor a hársak épp szerettek . . . Legendaoszlató emlékezések és dokumentumok Ady Endre váradi életéről* (Budapest: Gondolat, 1983), 108.

344. Endre Ady, "Napló. Pecsétek és egyebek" (*Szabadság*, January 9, 1901), in *Összes prózai művei*, vol. 1, comp. Gyula Földessy (Budapest: Akadémiai, 1955), 414.

CONTEXT OF THE CONVERSIONS OF HUNGARIAN JEWS   105

345. Ernő Ligeti, "Emőd Tamás," in *Ararát: Magyar zsidó évkönyv az 1944. Évre,* ed. Aladár Komlós (Budapest: Országos Izr. Leányárvaház, 1944), 59.

346. Mihályné Károlyi, *Együtt a forradalomban* (Budapest: Európa, 1978), 131; Tamás Dobszay and Zoltán Fónagy, "Magyarország társadalma a 19. század második felében," in Gergely, *Magyarország története a 19. században,* 436.

347. *A budapesti társaság,* 451; "Gentry," *Országos Gentry-Közlöny,* June 2, 1889, 1; Géza Czirbusz, *Magyarország a XX. évszáz* [sic] *elején: Föld- és néprajzi, nemzetgazdasági és társadalomtudományi szempontból* (Temesvár: Pollatsek, 1902), 409; Győző Münstermann, *A középosztály önvédelme* (Kolozsvár: Ajtai K. Albert, 1904), 16.

348. Jenő Rákosi, "Budapest városrészei," in *Az Osztrák–Magyar Monarchia írásban és képben,* vol. 9, *Magyarország III. kötete* (Budapest: Magyar Királyi Állami Nyomda, 1893), 191–92; Ferencz Herczeg, "Zsúrok és zsúr-látogatók," in *A mulató Budapest,* ed. Henrik Lenkei (Budapest: Singer és Wolfner, 1896), 117.

349. Zay, "Zsidók a társadalomban," 960.

350. Sándor Bródy, "Tímár Liza" (1914), in *Színház* (Budapest: Szépirodalmi, 1964), 392.

351. *A Nemzeti Casinó szabályai és tagjainak névsora 1901* (Budapest: Franklin-Társulat Nyomdája, 1902), 1. The casino's yearbooks (which were published under several titles starting in 1828, and which I examined from the first issue up to 1918) will be referred to hereafter as *A nemzeti kaszinó évkönyve* (*Yearbook of the National Casino*).

352. Gábor Gyáni, "Magyarország társadalomtörténete a Horthy-korban," in Gyáni and Kövér, *Magyarország társadalomtörténete a reformkortól a második világháborúig,* 230–31.

353. *A nemzeti kaszinó évkönyve 1878,* 56–57. Up to 1878, the National Casino's yearbooks had little to say about its conditions of membership. The 1829 yearbook noted that in conferring memberships, "Birth and faith are not taken into account," though this clarification does not appear in any other edition. See *A nemzeti kaszinó évkönyve 1829,* 41.

354. Béla Novák, "Fővárosi kaszinók a 19. században," *Budapesti Negyed* 12, no. 4 (2004): 98–99.

355. Gabriella Eőry, "Az Országos Kaszinó és a középosztály," in *Zsombékok: Középosztályok és iskoláztatás Magyarországon a 19. század elejétől a 20. század közepéig,* ed. György Kövér (Budapest: Századvég, 2006), 322, 324.

356. Beáta Nagy, "Az elit társasélete a klubok, kaszinók keretében," in *Rendi társadalom—Polgári társadalom 1: Társadalomtörténeti módszerek és forrástípusok,* ed. László Á. Varga (Salgótarján: Nógrád Megyei Levéltár, 1987), 69.

357. Eőry, "Az Országos Kaszinó és a középosztály," 338.

358. István Széchenyi, *Naplói*, vol. 4, *(1830–1836)*, ed. Gyula Viszota (Budapest: Magyar Történelmi Társulat, 1934), 241; id., *Naplói*, vol. 5, *(1836–1843)*, ed. Gyula Viszota (Budapest: Magyar Történelmi Társulat, 1937), 122.

359. *A nemzeti kaszinó évkönyve 1841*, 54; *A nemzeti kaszinó évkönyve 1844*, 55; *A nemzeti kaszinó évkönyve 1845*, 55; *A nemzeti kaszinó évkönyve 1847*, 53; *A nemzeti kaszinó évkönyve 1848*, 34.

360. Groszmann, *A magyar zsidók a XIX. század közepén*, 46; Vezér, *Lesznai Anna élete*, 9–10.

361. *A nemzeti kaszinó évkönyve 1860*, 15.

362. These eight Jewish members were Jakab Lányi (admitted in 1861), Henrik Lévay (1862), Soma Rothfeld (1867), Hermann Todesco (1870), Miksa Brüll (1870), Frigyes Schey (1870), Mór Wahrmann (1870), and Géza Moscovitz (1872).

363. I limited my examination of the descendants of these converts to the paternal branches of their family trees.

364. Mór Szatmári, *Közszellemünk fogyatkozásai* (Budapest: Werbőczy Nyomda, 1898), 24; Zay, "Zsidók a társadalomban," 962; Gyula Vigyázó, *A magyar zsidóság és a keresztény társadalom* (n.p.: Szerző kiadása, 1908), 15–16.

365. *Az Országos Kaszinó évi jelentése az 1883-ik évről* (Budapest: Athenaeum, 1884).

366. *Az Országos Kaszinó évkönyve 1913* (Budapest: n.p., 1914).

367. "Park-Club," *Szalon Újság*, April 30, 1905, 5–6.

368. Pál Hoitsy, *Régi magyar alakok: A letűnt nemzedék férfiai* (Budapest: Légrády Testvérek Kiadása, [1923]), 69; József Bölöny, "Klubélet a magyar fővárosban, 1827–1944," *História* 15, no. 2 (1993): 11.

369. "A klubélet Budapesten," *Az Újság*, December 25, 1910, 130–31.

370. *A Park Club évkönyve 1900* (Budapest: Hornyánszky Viktor, 1901); *A Park Club évkönyve 1914* (Budapest: Hornyánszky Viktor, 1915).

371. M., "Becsüljük meg önmagunkat, III," *Egyenlőség*, October 31, 1886, 1–2; Spectator, "Hamis modernség," *A Jövő*, May 20, 1898, 1–2; J. K., Dr., "A Magas Tátra," *Szombati Újság*, May 4, 1906, 1.

372. Molnár, *Az éhes város*, 6.

373. Preisich, "Önéletrajzi jegyzeteiből," 269.

374. Béla Bartók, *Családi levelei*, ed. Béla Bartók Jr. (Budapest: Zeneműkiadó, 1981), 49. For a discussion of the young Bartók's anti-Jewish sentiments, see Judit Frigyesi, *Béla Bartók and Turn-of-the-Century Budapest* (Berkeley/Los Angeles/London: University of California Press, 1998), 83–84.

375. Márai, *Egy polgár vallomásai (1934–1935/1940)*, 15, 18.

376. Mór Frieder, *A magyar zsidók egyenjogosítása 1867-dik évben* (Pest: Hornyánszky és Träger, 1868), 20.

CONTEXT OF THE CONVERSIONS OF HUNGARIAN JEWS   107

377. Péter Gunst, "A polgári társadalom kiformálódása," in *Polgárosodás és szabadság: Magyarország a XIX. Században*, ed. János Veliky (Budapest: Nemzeti Tankönyvkiadó, 1999), 252.

378. Gábor Gyáni, "Budapest története 1873–1945," in Vera Bácskai, Gábor Gyáni, and András Kubinyi, *Budapest története a kezdetektől 1945-ig* (Budapest: Budapest Főváros Levéltára, 2000), 166–67.

379. János Gömöry, *Emlékeim egy letűnt világról* (Budapest: Szépirodalmi, 1964), 58.

380. Dezső Keresztury, *Emlékezéseim: Szülőföldeim* (Budapest: Argumentum, 1993), 39.

381. Zsolt, *Villámcsapás*, 58.

382. Ernő Csekő, "Pályatöredékek a századfordulóról: Leopold Samu és Guttmann Irén (Lys-Noir)," *Múlt és Jövő*, new series, 22, no. 2 (2011): 74.

383. "A Harmadik ok," *Hevesvármegyei Hírlap*, May 23, 1894, 1.

384. Ibid.

385. János Kodolányi, *Süllyedő világ*, vol. 1 (Budapest: Athenaeum, [1940]), 169.

386. Márai, *Egy polgár vallomásai (1934–1935/1940)*, 227–28.

387. Dezsőné Kosztolányi Ilona Harmos, "Burokban születtem: Ifjúkori memoár," in *Burokban születtem: Memoár, novellák, portrék* (Budapest: Noran, 2003), 116, 123.

388. Balázs Körmendi [István Kulcsár], *Zsidó gyónás (1942–1943)* (Budapest: Interart, 1990), 58–59.

389. Andor Gábor, *Doktor Senki* (1918) (Budapest: Szépirodalmi, 1982), 139–40.

390. *Főrendiházi napló, 1892–1897*, 4: 94–95.

391. Gyula Weiszburg, "Jogfosztás rendszerrel," *Hitközségi Szemle* 3, no. 9 (1912): 189.

392. "Egyenjogúsítás nálunk és—máshol," *Egyenlőség*, February 4, 1883, 2; Kornél Ábrányi Jr., *Nemzeti ideál* (Budapest: Légrády Testvérek, 1898), 38; Lajos Báttaszéki, *A vérvád* (Budapest: Orsz. Központi Községi Nyomda, 1900), 50; Zay, "Zsidók a társadalomban," 967; Ernő Mezei, "Negyvenéves forduló," *Egyenlőség*, December 29, 1907, 6; Eisler, "A magyar zsidók emancipációja," 310–11; "A zsidók és a főrendiház," *Egyenlőség*, June 23, 1912, 1–2.

393. Numerous Christian authors noted the persistence of prejudices against emancipated Jews in the Dualist era; see, for example, Ábrányi Jr., *Régi és új nemesek*, 44; Lajos Joób, "A polgári házasság történeti megvilágításban," *Budapesti Szemle* 75, no. 201 (1893): 368; Rutilus [Szigetvári], "A mi szabadelvűségünk," 238–42; Kodolányi, *Süllyedő világ*, 1: 86. Of course, Jews also wrote about these prejudices but in a considerably more embittered tone. See Verus [Jenő Vázsonyi], "Emléklap az orosz zsidókért," *Egyenlőség*, August 14, 1891, 1–2; Ignácz Weisz, *A*

108 JEWISHNESS AND BEYOND

zsidók és a nemzetiségek (Brassó: A "Brassó" Könyvnyomdája, 1894), 38–39; Tamás Kóbor, "Le a zsidókkal!," *Egyenlőség*, May 5, 1901, 1; Bertalan Edelstein, "Kétség és remény," in *Zsinagógai beszédek*, 22–23; Bernát Krausz, *A zsidóság egyesülése: Két felekezet-e a zsidóság?* (Gyöngyös: Szerző kiadása, 1908), 5; Bernát Alexander, "Zsidó problémák," in *Magyar zsidó almanach*, vol. 1, ed. József Patai (Budapest: Magyar Zsidó Almanach, 1911), 186–87.

394. Ben Halpern, "Reactions to Antisemitism in Modern Jewish History," in Reinharz, *Living with Antisemitism*, 4–6.

395. Ernő Szép, *Lila ákác* (1919) (Budapest: Szépirodalmi, 1976), 50–51, 53–54.

396. Ibid., 57.

2

Numbers of Conversions, Chronological Patterns, and Social Reactions

In the period from the Reform Era to the outbreak of the First World War, the conversion of Jews was not an issue of primary importance to Hungarian Christians. Hungary's Neolog Jewish press, however, was portraying conversion as a problem of the highest order by the turn of the century, an increasingly dramatic symptom of an internal crisis more threatening to Hungarian Jewry than antisemitism.

The numbers and proportions of Hungarian Jews who converted would fluctuate significantly between the Reform Era and the First World War, though both sets of figures rose gradually over the course of this period. How significant was this increase in Hungary compared to the rest of Central Europe? What cyclical factors might have led increasing numbers of Hungarian Jews to convert? How should one interpret the spikes in conversions recorded between the Reform Era and the First World War? Finally, how did perceptions of the significance of conversions change over time? This chapter is a summary of my efforts to find answers to these questions and to gauge the broader social impact of the relevant statistical data.

Statistics are the primary tool for evaluating the significance of these conversions. Unfortunately, we lack geographically comprehensive official data for the period under discussion. The National Hungarian Royal Statistical Office (founded in 1867 and known as the Hungarian Royal Central Statistical Office starting in 1896) began compiling and publishing data on conversions to and from Judaism in 1896, when the Hungarian parliament enacted the ecclesiastical laws introducing state recordkeeping procedures, elevated

Judaism to the status of "received religion" and made it legal to convert to Judaism. National data allowing us to track conversions of Hungarian Jews from year to year does not exist prior to 1896.

There are two historical estimates of the number of Hungarian Jews who converted to Christianity during the period in question. In a study published in 1899, German missionary Johann de le Roi estimated that a worldwide total of 224,000 Jews had converted to a Christian denomination in the nineteenth century.[1] Though historians who deal with this issue often refer to de le Roi's data, they routinely emphasize its unreliability.[2] For countries without official data, de le Roi relied on incomplete church statistics and unreliable numbers published by Protestant missions. Using data from the foregoing and purely speculative methods that varied from country to country, de le Roi calculated overall numbers of nineteenth-century Jewish converts. He concluded that a total of 8,000 Hungarian Jews converted to Catholicism, 2,056 converted to a Protestant denomination, and 200 Austro-Hungarian Jews converted to Eastern Orthodoxy, though the latter figure is not specific to Hungary.[3] Another estimate was produced by genealogist Béla Kempelen, who asserted the following in the second volume of his three-volume work *Magyar zsidó és zsidó eredetű családok* (*Hungarian Jewish Families and Families of Hungarian Jewish Origin*, published between 1937 and 1939): "we can put the number of conversions in our homeland during the . . . half century from 1867 to 1919 at 20,000."[4] There is no evidence to suggest that de le Roi's calculations are even approximately accurate. On the basis of my research, Kempelen's estimate seems closer to the truth.

The Legal Regulation of Conversion

Before examining the quantitative data, it is important to survey the legal environment in which the conversions took place. Before the implementation of the ecclesiastical laws of 1896, the Hungarian state did not gather data on Jewish conversions because the lack of comprehensive rules governing conversion between Judaism and Christianity made it impossible to do so. The question did not even come up before the 1867 emancipation of Hungarian Jewry. The lack of regulation between 1867 and 1895 resulted from Judaism's unique legal status. The 1867 emancipation law provided Jews with equal rights on an individual basis but said nothing about the Jewish religion itself. Simply *tolerated* until 1867, the Jewish religion acquired the status of *recognized* denomination after the emancipation law.[5] However, the legal inequality of the *recognized* Jewish religion and the *received* Christian denominations excluded the possibility of regulating conversions between them. As the legal framework of the Dual Monarchy was based on the principle of equality under the law, it would have been unimaginable to invoke any other principle than that of reciprocity in regulating the conversion of Jewish and Christian Hungarians, who were equal in terms of individual rights.

This legal inequality disappeared with the enactment of the ecclesiastical laws. Before them, Jewish conversions had been accompanied by a fair amount of legal chaos. On April 26, 1893, in his justification for the legislative proposal to elevate Judaism to received status, minister of religion and public education Albin Csáky said it was precisely this legal disarray that necessitated regulating conversions between Judaism and Christianity: "Until now, the procedure to be followed in converting from the Israelite faith to one of the lawfully received Christian denominations has not been legally regulated at all. There exist certain relevant but older and thus mostly obsolete royal decrees from the end of the past century, but these being largely unfamiliar to the ministering clergy, the actual state of affairs to this day is that an Israelite individual can be baptized at any time without any further conditions."[6]

Not only had the decrees Csáky mentioned been forgotten, but they had only partially regulated conversions from the Jewish faith. Most dealt exclusively with baptisms of children. On June 17, 1762, Empress Maria Theresa issued a decree prohibiting the baptism of Jewish children without the permission of their parents or guardian.[7] The prohibition was not enforced, so Maria Theresa published an edict on April 21, 1775, forbidding midwives from baptizing newborns against their parents' wishes.[8] Midwives continued to baptize Jewish newborns without parental authorization, leading Emperor Joseph II to issue a decree on July 9, 1787, making such action a crime punishable by six months in prison and a fine of one thousand ducats.[9] However, Emperor Joseph's decree also failed to put an end to illegal baptisms. At the session of the Hungarian Diet which convened in June of 1790, "the community of Jews living in Hungary" submitted a nine-point petition listing their grievances in Latin, beginning with a request that they be free to practice their religion and not be forced to convert to Christianity.[10]

It is important to emphasize that the legal requirements for conversion from one Christian denomination to another were not put into their final, relatively precise form until the passage of Act LIII of 1868 (*"on the reciprocity of the lawfully received Christian denominations*"). Section one of the law definitively enshrined the freedom of members of received religions to switch denominations. The rules detailing the process of conversion would be applied to Jews beginning in 1895 and stay in effect up to the collapse of the Dual Monarchy.[11]

In addition to the total lack of state regulation governing the baptism of adult Jews until the 1890s, the most striking aspect of conversion was its unidirectionality. Jews could convert to Christianity, but Christians could not convert to Judaism. Although it was illegal until the passage of Act XLIII of 1895 (*"on the free exercise of religion"*), some Hungarians did enter the Jewish religion prior to this date. Before emancipation, most of them were probably former Jews who had converted to Christianity and then decided to return to the fold. That this sometimes occurred is suggested by a decree dated February 18, 1762, making reversion to the Jewish faith punishable by up to two years in prison.[12] After Jews were granted equal rights, there seems to have been a slight uptick in the number of conversions to Judaism. Between 1867 and 1895, Hungarian papers published roughly a dozen stories about young Christian men and women who converted to Judaism because they wanted to marry Jewish brides or grooms who were presumably unwilling to leave the fold. These articles sometimes noted Hungarian law did not allow conversions to Judaism, though in most cases these occurrences were presented as interesting bits of trivia, without commentary. It would appear that most of the reporters were simply unaware of the illegal nature of these conversions.[13]

Some Hungarians converted to Judaism in the Austrian half of the Dual Monarchy, where such conversions were legalized on May 25, 1868.[14] Most of those converts were people who wanted to marry a Jewish spouse and live their married lives as Jews in the Hungarian half of the monarchy. Under Hungarian law, marriages of this sort (and the children resulting from them) were illegitimate, although in an 1880 article advocating the introduction of civil marriage, Ferenc Pulszky suggested that authorities took no action against them. To the best of Pulszky's knowledge, there were "nearly 100" such couples living in Budapest alone.[15]

Prior to the adoption of the ecclesiastical laws that ultimately settled the issue, the Hungarian government did make one other effort to regulate at least part of the procedure governing Jews' conversions to Christianity. On February 16, 1890, minister of religion and public education Albin Csáky issued a decree in response to a practice the Jewish press had denounced on several occasions. As Csáky wrote in justifying this decree: "We have repeatedly seen cases in which Israelites who had converted to some Christian denomination—that is, who were baptized—later presented themselves as Israelites again, using original birth certificates obtained from the Israelite registrar to deceive certain rabbis and Israelite congregations. . . . It has even happened that such individuals then marry in accordance with the Israelite rite on the basis of such birth certificates."[16] Such practices were made possible because section three of Act LIII of 1868—requiring individuals who intended to convert to report their plans to the pastor of their congregation on two occasions—did not pertain to Jews since Judaism was not among Hungary's received religions. In other words, there was no formal requirement that Jews exit the Jewish religion before joining a Christian denomination. The registrars of the relevant Jewish congregations were not officially notified of conversions and therefore could not record them.[17]

Csáky's 1890 decree did not oblige potential converts to report their intentions, though it did theoretically solve the problem that had prompted him to issue it. The order required ministering clergy to adhere to the following procedure in baptizing Jews: first, ministers and priests were obliged to require Jews who wanted to convert to submit an authentic Jewish birth certificate. After the baptism, the clergyman was to record that the ceremony had taken place, along with its location and date, on the Jewish birth certificate. He was then to forward the document to the deputy county lord-lieutenant (*alispán*) or to the mayor of the municipality where the registrar of the relevant Jewish congregation had originally filed it. Local authorities were to forward the modified birth certificate to the appropriate Jewish registrar, who was required to record the new baptismal data in his own register of births and certify that he had done so on the original birth certificate. The Jewish registrar would return it to the local authorities, who were to send it back to the clergyman who performed the baptism. Only after receiving the original birth certificate from the Jewish congregation's registrar was a priest or minister authorized to issue a baptismal certificate to the newly converted Christian.[18]

After several years of intense political struggle, the ecclesiastical laws of 1894 and 1895 finally regulated conversions to and from the Jewish religion, using the same procedure that governed received Christian denominations. Ultimately, the following laws would regulate the conversions of Hungarian Jews: sections 3–5 and 8 of Act XXXII of 1894 (*"on the religion of children"*) extended the provisions of section 14 of Act LIII of 1868 to Jews while sections 5 and 22 of Act XLIII of 1895 (*"on the free exercise of religion"*) extended

114 JEWISHNESS AND BEYOND

the provisions of sections 1–8 of Act LIII of 1868 to Hungarians of the Jewish faith. Sections 23–30 of Act XLIII of 1895 made it possible to declare oneself unaffiliated with any religion—that is, to become *konfessionslos*.

The most important phases of the conversion process were laid out in sections 3–7 of Act LIII of 1868. Section three: "Those who wish to convert, be they members of whichever church, shall declare their intention to do so before a clergyman of their own congregation in the presence of two witnesses of their choice. At least 14 days but no more than 30 days after making this first declaration, they shall again, in the presence of these same or other witnesses of their choice, before a clergyman of their own congregation, state that they continue to intend to convert." Section four: "Prospective converts must request separate unstamped documentation of their first and second declarations from the clergyman before whom they expressed their intent to convert." Section five: "In the event that the clergyman, for whatever reason, does not issue the requested documentation, the witnesses who were present should provide separate unstamped documentation of the statements made on both occasions." Section six: "When the prospective convert presents the documentation thus acquired to a clergyman of the denomination [he or she] intends to join, the given church is thereby fully authorized to embrace [him or her]." Section seven: "The clergyman to whom the convert has presented this documentation, thus with whom the transition has come to an end, is obliged to notify the minister of the congregation to which the convert previously belonged."

Applying the provisions of Act LIII of 1868 to Jews—that is, requiring them to notify their congregation's rabbi of their intention to convert before they could be baptized—addressed a complaint that had persisted in Jewish circles for a long time. On January 8, 1896, the Ministries of Religion and Public Education, Interior, and Justice issued a joint decree on the implementation of Act XLIII of 1895, emphasizing that individuals who had not "formally" withdrawn from their congregations were to be regarded as members of their previous religion even if they had joined another denomination.[19]

The conversion of children was clarified as well. Section 14 of Act LIII of 1868 stipulated that children under seven would automatically convert when their parents did, girls adopting the new religion of their mother, boys that of their father. According to section 2 of the law, only individuals who had reached the age of eighteen could decide independently to convert, though married women under eighteen could also switch religions. Excepting married women, children between seven and eighteen whose parents were of the same religion were prohibited from converting. Converted parents with children between seven and eighteen were oddly required to continue raising them in the religion they had abandoned and to enroll them in religion classes teaching the tenets of that faith.[20]

Parliamentary regulations governed every phase of the conversion process, though they did not comprehensively define the administrative obligations of the clergy. Section seven of Act LIII of 1868 required pastors who oversaw conversions to keep the leader of the convert's former congregation informed, though it did not stipulate what the latter was to do with the information. The aforementioned decree issued by Albin Csáky in 1890 required registrars of Jewish congregations to record all known conversions in their communities' registers, but when the conversion-related provisions of Act LIII of 1868 were applied to members of the Jewish faith, this edict was effectively nullified.[21] The registration requirement would continue to apply to residents born before October 1, 1895, as section 93 of Act XXXIII of 1894 (*"on state record-keeping"*) required religious communities to maintain the birth, marriage, and death records created prior to the introduction of state record-keeping procedures on October 1, 1895, and stipulated that extracts derived from records created on or before September 30 of that year would continue to serve as valid public documents. Thus, as was the case with any modification to a vital record, when someone born before October 1, 1895 switched religions, the change was to be recorded in the relevant denominational registry, which, of course, could not be done until the baptizing pastor informed the appropriate Jewish registrar of the conversion.[22] As an 1898 MRPE resolution specified, Jewish converts who had reached the age of 18 could now prove the legitimacy of their conversions and status as new Christians with two official public documents: a baptismal certificate and an original birth certificate "in which a conversion (change of religion) has been recorded."[23] However, as I will discuss below, most of the conversions were not legally recorded as a result of the negligence or misconduct by Christian clergymen.

Applying the relevant legal provisions to conversions of Jews did a great deal to resolve the prior bureaucratic tangle. Nevertheless, Zsigmond Groszmann, director of the rabbinical office of the Israelite Congregation of Pest, criticized the regulations on several occasions. For instance, section three of Act LIII of 1868 required potential converts to report their intentions to "a clergyman of their own congregation." However, this text lacked precision: did it mean the congregation the prospective convert belonged to at birth, where he or she had been registered? Or did it mean the congregation where he or she currently lived, with which he or she was thus obliged to affiliate? Most prospective converts—correctly, in Groszmann's view—interpreted this reference to their "own" religious community to mean the one in the area where they lived.[24]

Another of Groszmann's objections pertained to the reporting of an intention to convert. Section three of Act LIII of 1868 did not say whether an individual declaring an intention to convert was required to provide personal information corroborated by official documents. Groszmann wrote: "Of what should this withdrawal announcement consist? The intention of the law can only be that the clergyman record the convert's personal data, with which he can establish this person's identity." Even if Jews who reported an intention to convert provided such data, the rabbi had no way of verifying its accuracy.[25]

These criticisms of conversion procedures applied to theoretical cases in which prospective converts and the clergymen who supervised their conversions both complied with the relevant law. In practice, clergymen disregarded certain regulations, while prospective converts and clergymen both ignored other provisions of the law.

The problems began with the declaration of an intention to convert, which some converts simply skipped and were thus baptized without first reporting to the rabbi who served as registrar for the congregation where they lived or were born. Of course, this could not happen unless the baptizing clergyman also failed to comply with the law and baptized the convert without requiring him or her to produce the documentation issued by the rabbi or the two witnesses before whom he or she had expressed an intention to convert. Jewish newspapers alleged that clergymen frequently failed to satisfy this obligation.[26] The target of *Egyenlőség*'s most frequent and most vehement criticism was the "persistent lawbreaker" Béla Tóthfalussy, parish priest of Budapest's Erzsébetváros district from 1894 until his death in 1904.[27] After his death, Miksa Szabolcsi of *Egyenlőség* wrote that "Tóthfalussy converted several hundred Jews without their having reported to the rabbinate in advance and without him having informed the rabbinate of their baptism, as the law requires."[28]

Jews who were baptized without reporting an intention to convert were able to enjoy the benefits of Christian status, which they could, if necessary, prove with official baptismal certificates, while continuing to present themselves as Jews in their dealings with their former coreligionists, who had not been officially notified of their conversion. They could also, if necessary, verify their Jewishness with official birth certificates, since their conversion to Christianity had not been recorded in these communities' birth registers.

Jewish newspapers publicized secret conversions only in particularly scandalous instances. One such case was a wedding at the Rumbach Street Synagogue, which the ICP reserved for its more conservative members. The wedding involved a convert and a Jewish woman whose father would not have given the union his blessing had he known his daughter's fiancé left the fold. *Egyenlőség* reported the incident not only to expose the turpitude of the convert but also to defend Rabbi Mózes Feldmann, who had officiated the ceremony in good faith: "How could the Jewish priest have known that the man he was uniting in marriage was a Roman Catholic when he, having been baptized by Béla Tóthfalussy, presented himself to the rabbi as a Jew, and when his papers, which were in order, said nothing of his disaffiliation?"[29]

We do not know how many converts abandoned the Jewish faith without declaring their intention to do so. In 1896, the annual reports of the ICP began including statistics on former members who had announced their conversions to congregation's rabbinate, but in every edition from 1910 onward, the ICP's rabbinical office declared itself unable to determine "whether others had converted to another faith without ever informing us of their intention to disaffiliate."[30] In 1903, Chief Rabbi Arnold Kiss of Buda asserted, "In countless instances, a renegade avoids" rabbis.[31] And as noted above, Miksa Szabolcsi would soon allege that Béla Tóthfalussy had illegally baptized several hundred Jews.

An even bigger problem, one that reopened old wounds, was the practice of baptizing Jewish children between the ages of seven and eighteen. As Miksa Szabolcsi emphasized, such children could not legally convert "even at their parents' request," excepting married women.[32] Examples cited by Jewish journalists demonstrate that clergymen of every Christian denomination performed illegal baptisms, though the majority who did so were Catholic.[33] The prevalence of the practice is reflected by the fact that in 1903, Bernát Munkácsi, superintendent of the ICP's schools, sent a circular letter to the community's religious instructors urging them to "report cases of unlawful disaffiliation among their students to the office of the congregation's school superintendent without delay."[34] In 1911, Mór Fényes, the ICP's assistant rabbi and supervisor of religious instruction, estimated that "several hundred" Jewish minors had been illegally baptized since 1895.[35]

Finally, Jewish publications frequently complained that despite the obligation articulated in section 7 of Act LIII of 1868, Christian clergymen who baptized Jews often neglected to inform the rabbis of the congregations to which these converts formerly belonged. Even if someone duly reported an intention to disaffiliate, until a rabbi received official notification of the subsequent baptism, he could not record the conversion in his congregation's birth register, nor would he know whether this person had actually converted or merely announced an intention to do so, then failed for some reason to follow through.

The failure to report conversions was a general practice among Christian pastors in Budapest and presumably elsewhere as well. According to the 1908 report issued by the ICP, pastoral offices in Budapest reported Jewish baptisms "only exceptionally."[36] My analysis of the disaffiliation records of the rabbinical office of the ICP paints a more precise picture. Every time the rabbinate was notified of a baptism, it was entered in the "notes" column of the congregation's disaffiliation records, along with precise notation indicating the relevant parish or pastoral office. In the years 1897, 1903, and 1907, a total of 573 people notified the rabbinical office of the ICP that they intended to convert to Christianity (meaning they did not intend to remain unaffiliated), yet the ICP received only 24 notifications of baptism in this period, accounting for just 4.2 percent of their congregants who announced an intention to convert.[37]

The state's legal regulation of conversion was not perfect. Certain requirements were unclear or insufficiently detailed, though the possible consequences of these flaws affected society even beyond the Jewish community. The application of the laws was another matter. In many cases, Christian clergymen ignored the legal provisions that applied to conversions of Jews, and courts failed to punish these systematic violations of the law. Even though baptizing children between the ages of seven and eighteen was punishable by law, no Hungarian court ever convicted a Christian clergyman for having baptized Jewish minors. Thus, as in other areas of life, the 1895 laws granted members of Jewish congregations full legal equality with their Christian compatriots, but the laws regulating conversion were applied in a way that rendered this equality theoretical at best.

Chronological Patterns and Reactions to Conversion

Numbers of Conversions and Chronological Patterns up to 1895

Given the lack of official statistical data pertaining to the whole of Hungary, one could theoretically calculate the number of Hungarian Jews who converted before 1896 by surveying the baptismal records of the country's Catholic

CONVERSIONS, CHRONOLOGICAL PATTERNS, AND REACTIONS   119

parishes and Protestant congregations. Though this information has been preserved on microfilm at the Hungarian National Archives, an investigation of this sort would require several researchers to invest years' worth of labor. Historical research on the subject has been limited to two chronologically and geographically circumscribed studies: László Marjanucz's analysis of the baptismal records of the Catholic parish of downtown Szeged, where 17 Jews were baptized between 1871 and 1886,[38] and Árpád Welker's much broader examination of the baptismal records of the Protestant congregations of Pest from 1800 to 1895 (with the exception of one small German Reformed congregation that began keeping separate records in the 1870s). Welker's research on Pest's Kálvin Square Reformed congregation, Deák Square Lutheran congregation, and Unitarian congregation shows the first Jewish convert was baptized there in 1824, and these congregations registered 1,087 Jewish converts between 1824 and 1895. The number more or less accounts for all the Jews who joined Protestant churches in Pest in the nineteenth century.[39] I have supplemented Welker's research by analyzing the baptismal records of the Roman Catholic parish of Szentistvánváros (Lipótváros) for the years 1840 through 1895, which indicate that another 269 Jews were baptized there over the course of this 56-year period.[40]

How significant are the numbers? We might compare Pest's data with the number of conversions recorded in another major Central European city during the same period. Berlin is a more appropriate analog than Vienna since authorities in the latter limited Jewish settlement up until the 1848 revolution. There were at most 4,000 Jews living in Vienna in 1847, whereas Berlin's Jewish population in 1848 was 9,600, and Pest's was 14,280.[41] A precise comparison would require us to know the number of converted Jews living in Pest in this period. Lacking such data, we shall take the denominational preferences of Jews who converted in Pest around the turn of the century and project them backward onto the previous era. I must emphasize that this calculation will provide us with only an approximate breakdown. The denominational composition of the Christian population of Pest changed considerably over the course of the nineteenth century, as the proportion of Protestants, who had previously been kept out of the city, grew significantly relative to the Catholic population. Catholics made up 96 percent of Pest's population in the late eighteenth century. This proportion fell to 87.5 percent in 1813, 75.3 percent in 1850, 68.3 percent in 1870, and 56.7 percent in 1910.[42] It is conceivable that more of Pest's Jews converted to Catholicism than to a Protestant denomination in the first half of the nineteenth century because of the privileges the Catholic Church enjoyed until 1848. Official statistics did not record the denominational affiliations of Jews who converted to Christianity in Pest until 1931, at which point authorities began publishing data for the whole of Budapest. In 1896, the ICP's annual reports began recording the numbers of converts who left the community, without specifying the denominations they joined. I have therefore limited myself to an analysis of the data in the ICP's disaffiliation reports for the years 1897, 1903, and 1907. Over the course of these three years, 29.7 percent of the Jews who withdrew from the ICP indicated that they intended to join the Reformed, Lutheran, or Unitarian Church.[43] Assuming that a similar percentage of Pest's baptized Jews joined Protestant denominations between 1824 and 1895 (when an estimated 1,087 Jews converted to Protestantism), we may estimate that roughly 2,572 of Pest's Jews converted to Catholicism during the period, to make a total of 3,659. Given that Protestants made up a much smaller percentage of Pest's population in the first half of the nineteenth century than in the early years of the twentieth, it is likely that fewer of the city's Jewish converts chose to join a Protestant congregation in this earlier period, so the actual number of converts was probably larger.

In any case, the previous estimate makes it possible to approximate the proportion of Pest's Jews who converted in this period. A total of 6,371 Jews converted in Berlin between 1800 and 1895.[44] The absolute number and relative proportion of Jewish converts there were both substantially greater than in Pest, as Berlin's Jewish population grew from 3,300 in 1800 to 94,391 in 1895, while Budapest's Jewish population increased from 1,464 in 1804 to 157,059 in 1900.[45] In addition, the data on Berlin's converts pertains only to those who joined a Protestant denomination.

Another significant issue is the change over time in the number of baptized Jews. Not a single Jew joined any of Pest's Protestant congregations between 1800 and 1823. The first such baptism took place in 1824, with no further conversions to Protestantism among Pest's Jews between 1825 and 1830. The number of Jews who joined Pest's Protestant congregations would remain insignificant in the 1830s and early 1840s, fluctuating between one and five per year. The first major increase in the number of Jews who joined one of Pest's Protestant churches occurred in 1842 and 1843; the total rose to nearly thirty in the latter year. Árpád Welker attributed this first relatively minor wave of conversion, limited to the Reformed denomination, to the activity of the Scottish Mission, which proselytized the city's Jews under the auspices of the Budapest Reformed Church starting in 1841.[46] Conversions to Protestantism among the Jews of Pest dropped back to single digits in 1845 and 1846, though it rose dramatically thereafter. In 1848, sixty of Pest's Jews converted to a Protestant denomination, and from that date until 1895, 1891 was the only year in which more than sixty Jews joined Pest's Protestant congregations. Among members of the ICP who announced an intention to disaffiliate in the years 1897, 1903, and 1907, an annual average of roughly fifty-six indicated that they would join a Protestant congregation.[47]

The average number of Jews baptized annually in the Catholic parish of Lipótváros in Pest was low and stable from 1840 to 1847—roughly three per year, for a total of twenty-three in this period. The year of the revolution saw a jump in the number of conversions there too: in 1848, twenty-six Jews were baptized in the Catholic parish of Lipótváros,[48] more than in any year up to 1895. Strikingly, even in absolute terms, there were years in the 1880s and 1890s when fewer Jews converted than in 1848. Taking into account the fact that the Jewish population of Pest rose more than thirteenfold between 1848 and 1910, the proportion of Jews who converted there in 1848 was much greater than in any other year between 1800 and 1914.[49]

Welker attributed the 1848 wave of conversions to that spring's antisemitic riots and the "nationalist fervor" ignited by the revolution.[50] Antisemitic agitation was recorded in more than thirty Hungarian towns in the month and a half following the March 15 outbreak of the revolution. The turmoil, together with the explosion of revolutionary patriotic fervor, may well have intensified Jews' desire to convert in order to escape the Jewish stigma and/or blend in with the Hungarian revolutionaries. In my opinion, decisions to convert at that time may also have been motivated by a loss of hope, insofar as Jews had expected that the revolution would lead to emancipation, but numerous signs quickly disabused them of this notion.[51] This sudden jump in conversions can thus be explained as a product of the interaction of several distinct factors with mutually reinforcing effects: patriotic ardor sparked by the revolution; anti-Jewish demonstrations; the omission of Jews from the equal-rights provisions of the revolutionary government's April Laws; growing the fear, anger, and frustration among Jews as their emancipation was put off; and finally, the intoxicating experience of the revolution itself.

The wave of conversions abated in 1849. The number of Jews who joined one of Pest's Protestant congregations between 1850 and 1881 was insignificant: an average of just under five per year did so in the 1850s, with five to ten joining each year in the 1860s and around ten per year in the 1870s. In the Catholic parish of Lipótváros, thirty-two Jews converted per year on average in the 1850s, fourteen in the 1860s, and twenty-five in the 1870s.[52] Given that the Jewish population of Pest increased fourfold between 1850 and 1880, the proportion of converts to Christianity declined sharply in this period. The foregoing supports the hard data and estimates of the numbers of English, Polish, and German Jews who converted to Christianity (particularly in Warsaw and Berlin) in various periods of the nineteenth century. Increasing acculturation was not necessarily accompanied by growth in the numbers of Jews who became Christians.[53]

The number of Jews who converted to Protestantism in Pest exhibited another spectacular increase in 1882 while the number of Jews who converted to Catholicism in the parish of Lipótváros began to rise more moderately in 1881. Only a portion of this growth can be explained by the increasing antisemitism of Hungarian public and political life, which became apparent in the mid-1870s as a result of the parliamentary activities of Győző Istóczy and intensified in the early 1880s, particularly following the Tiszaeszlár blood libel affair in the spring of 1882.[54] Hungary's antisemitic crisis culminated in anti-Jewish riots in the autumn of 1883. The National Antisemitic Party, formed in October of 1883, achieved less success than was expected in Hungary's 1884 parliamentary elections, then very quickly faded into obscurity. Several reasons were responsible: there was as yet no consistent demand for the party's message; Hungary's political elite, still faithful to the principles of liberalism, took decisive action; and internal divisions rapidly undermined the cohesion of the party. It had been established jointly by so-called "48-ers" and "67-ers," opponents and supporters of the 1867 Compromise with Austria, who disagreed on Hungary's most fundamental political questions—with the exception of antisemitism.[55] In September of 1885, the author of a piece in Egyenlőség remarked with satisfaction, "No longer are the antisemites ranting, but rather only—whispering. And very little of this whispering reaches the greater public."[56] By the summer of 1886, the newspaper that was the era's most sensitive seismograph of Hungarian antisemitism had finally calmed down: "The antisemitic movement . . . is disappearing. Before long, it will be completely extinguished."[57] Notwithstanding, the number of Jews who reported to Protestant pastoral offices in Pest to convert rose continually from 1882 to 1886. The number of converts who joined Pest's Reformed Church peaked at forty-one in 1885, and the total number of Jews who joined all the

CONVERSIONS, CHRONOLOGICAL PATTERNS, AND REACTIONS   123

city's Protestant congregations reached a high of nearly sixty in 1886. Data from the parish of Lipótváros are also evidence that the number of Jews who converted to Catholicism continued to rise even after the antisemitic crisis petered out—seven did so in 1882, and five each in 1883 and 1884, but thirteen did so in 1885 and another twelve in 1886.[58]

Árpád Welker has argued convincingly that this measured increase in conversions in a period of declining antisemitism can be attributed to the failure to introduce so-called partial civil marriage (meaning marriage between a Christian and a Jew). Civil marriages between Christians and Jews were approved as part of the emancipation legislation passed by the Hungarian National Assembly on July 28, 1849, but the failure of the revolution meant Act IX of 1849 never took effect.[59] As Act LIII of 1868 established reciprocity between received Christian denominations only, this legislation did not authorize marriages between Jews and Christians either. In October of 1881, the government of Prime Minister Kálmán Tisza sent the House of Representatives a legislative proposal calling for the legalization of civil marriages between Jews and Christians. Between November of 1883 and January of 1884, this proposal was debated and approved by the House of Representatives, rejected twice by the House of Lords, then withdrawn.[60] According to Welker, the continued growth in the number of conversions after 1884 was a result of the fact that "there existed a significant group of [people] who planned to marry after the expected passage of the marriage-rights law, then converted after 1884 as a result of its failure."[61]

A unique aspect of the dynamics of conversion in the 1880s was that after this wave of conversions subsided after 1886, the numbers did not drop off as drastically as they had in the two years after the Hungarian revolution of 1848–49. The number of Jews joining Pest's Protestant congregations fell to a low of just over thirty in 1888, still triple the number of baptisms these congregations had recorded in 1881, the year before conversions began to rise. More than fifty of Pest's Jews converted to Protestantism the following year, and this number would continue to exhibit moderate growth up to 1895. Meanwhile, the number of conversions to Catholicism in the parish of Lipótváros did not drop even temporarily; except for the years 1894 and 1895, the annual number of Jews baptized there was consistently higher than in the early 1880s.

What might explain this phenomenon? Despite the appearance of a small number of wealthy Jewish merchants and an even smaller number of Jewish intellectuals in the Reform Era, the majority of Hungary's Jews continued

124 JEWISHNESS AND BEYOND

to live in a world of tradition, at least partly because the state refrained from interfering in the internal affairs of the Hungarian Jewish community in the half-century following the death of Emperor Joseph II.[62] Most of Hungary's Jews continued to speak Yiddish and exhibit a fundamental indifference to non-Jewish culture. The cultural modernization of the broad mass of Hungarian Jewish society—including the urban Jewish bourgeoisie that emerged as a result of Hungary's mid-century economic boom—took place in the 1850s. The mass Magyarization of the country's Jews began only in the 1860s, particularly in the wake of the 1867 emancipation. Even if social historian Károly Vörös was correct in concluding that Budapest's Jews had attained a "bourgeois and petty bourgeois lifestyle and standard of living" by 1873 (when Buda, Óbuda, and Pest were unified), it would not have been until the late 1880s that social and cultural changes affecting them produced sizeable circles of Jews who might have considered the option of conversion to Christianity.[63] Around the turn of the century, the average age of Jews who announced an intention to disaffiliate from the ICP was roughly twenty-eight. If we assume this was also the case a generation earlier, then Hungarian Jews who converted in the latter half of the 1880s were born in the late 1850s and early 1860s and came of age in the post-emancipation years, characterized by indifference to Jewish affairs, disorganization and stagnation in Hungary's Jewish congregations, and general disregard for religious instruction.[64] At the same time, this was the generation in which increasing numbers of Jews were abandoning the occupations of their merchant fathers and the overwhelmingly Jewish professional and social environments that went with them. The generation of Jews that emerged by the 1880s was composed of a growing number of intellectuals, licensed professionals, clerks, university students, and university graduates at the beginning of their careers whose slackening connections to Jewishness decreased their community's retentive force, while intensifying interactions with a Christian society that harbored ambivalent feelings toward Jews heightened the seductive power of conversion. I would suggest the steady increase in the number of Hungarian Jews who chose to convert was a product of the combined influence of all these factors.

I will conclude this examination of pre-1895 chronological patterns in conversions among Hungarian Jews with an attempt to resolve an apparent paradox. Antisemitism had essentially disappeared from the Hungarian political arena by the 1890s.[65] Yet in the period between 1824 and 1895, the number of Jews who converted to Protestant denominations in Pest peaked at sixty-seven in 1891—significantly more than in 1886, when the largest wave of conversions in the 1880s occurred.[66] And while only twenty-three Jews were baptized in the Catholic parish of Lipótváros between 1881 and 1884 (the most "successful" years of Hungary's antisemitic movement), an average of just under six per year, fifty-seven Jews were baptized there between 1889 and 1892, an annual average of more than fourteen.[67] If we accept the premise that the rate of conversion was a reliable indicator of the degree to which Jews were satisfied with their circumstances, then this seemingly paradoxical rise in conversions in the liberal atmosphere of the early 1890s suggests that despite the theoretical ascendancy of liberalism, an increasing numbers of Pest's Jews no longer believed it was possible to accomplish their goals in Hungary while remaining Jewish.

Nineteenth-Century Reactions to Conversion

Another way to track chronological patterns in Jewish conversions is to examine societal responses to them. Doing so may help compensate for the lack of comprehensive data from the period prior to 1895. How much attention did Hungarians—Christian and Jewish—pay to their Jewish compatriots' conversions, and how much significance did they attribute to the phenomenon?

In an 1840 book about her travels in Hungary, English writer Julia Pardoe noted that among the wealthiest members of the country's Jewish community, "many families had already converted to Christianity," yet Hungarian Christians hardly seem to have taken note of Jews' conversions in the 1840s.[68] The most important liberal daily of the era, the *Pesti Hírlap*, did not inform its readers of the conversions of prominent Jewish merchants and intellectuals of the day, with the exception of Sámuel Wodianer's.[69] The Scottish Mission achieved its most notable success when Izrael Saphir and his family converted in 1843; unlike the poor Jews who made up most of the Mission's converts, Saphir was a reputable wool merchant and one of the leaders of Pest's Jewish community.[70] His conversion was not mentioned in the *Pesti Hírlap*. The newspaper also failed to report the unprecedented increase in the number of Jews who converted at the Scottish Mission in 1843, presumably as a result of the influence of the Saphir family's conversion. Pest's newspapers did not evince much interest in 1848, when there was a dramatic increase in the number of conversions, though a few did note the sudden rise in conversions among wealthy Jewish merchants.[71]

126   JEWISHNESS AND BEYOND

Jewish observers who discussed the issue included Chief Rabbi Löw Schwab of Pest, who advocated emancipation in an 1840 pamphlet featuring two lines on the subject of conversion: Rabbi Schwab expressed his hope that "the true patriot" would not expect Jews to convert as a theoretical means of "nationalization."[72] According to a Scottish Mission document published much later, the baptism of Izrael Saphir and his family caused consternation among the Jews of Pest, who even circulated a pamphlet attacking the mission at the time.[73] With a few short-lived exceptions, there were no Jewish papers in Hungary at that time,[74] and the chief sources of news about Hungarian Jewish events were thus Jewish papers printed in Germany, above all the *Allgemeine Zeitung des Judenthums*, first published in Leipzig in 1837. In 1843 and 1844, the *Allgemeine Zeitung* published a few articles criticizing the activities of the Scottish Mission, but rather than focusing on the Mission's effectiveness, these reports tended to condemn rabbis who allowed missionaries to raid their synagogues and Jewish elementary schools or to praise Chief Rabbi Löw Schwab for his commendable resistance.[75] The *Allgemeine Zeitung* published only one report of any length on the conversion of a prominent Hungarian Jew in this period, an article on the 1843 conversion of the linguist Móric Bloch (known as Mór Ballagi from 1848 onward), written by the aforementioned Rabbi Lipót Löw.[76] The reaction was not surprising: Móric Bloch was, alongside Lipót Löw, the most renowned representative of Hungarian Jews' struggle for legal equality, and his "apostasy" assumed a symbolic character. In truth, however, Löw's immediate motivation for writing the article was not Bloch's conversion but an open letter from Pastor József Székács of the Lutheran Church of Pest, criticizing Jews for expressing revulsion on the occasion of Bloch's conversion. Székács suggested their hostile reaction was a sign that Jews were still not ready for equal civil rights.[77] Written sources from this period—like the religious instruction manual Löw Schwab published in 1846 or the pro-emancipation pamphlet issued by the Zagreb book dealer Lipót Hartmán in the summer of 1848—rarely contained more than a few lines on conversion and generally criticized the act itself, rather than individual converts.[78] Even so, in another pamphlet published in 1848, the year of the revolution and its accompanying wave of conversions, the otherwise unknown Sándor Herczfeld explicitly and rather mercilessly castigated individual converts: "But you baptized Jews, who wanted to liberate your miserable lives with a baptism, should dig yourselves a great pit, lie down in it, and lament your cowardly lives there, because you cannot believe that clever Hungarians do not know

CONVERSIONS, CHRONOLOGICAL PATTERNS, AND REACTIONS 127

that whoever switches his God and his religion out of fear will also betray his Homeland out of fear."[79]

Hardly anything was written on the subject of conversion in the decade following Hungary's defeat in the 1848–49 war of independence, the presumable reason being not the paralysis of Hungarian intellectual life that characterized this period but rather the fact that conversions dropped to a minimum. The exceptional nature of conversions in this period is suggested by the story of a Jewish doctor, his wife, and their four children joining the Catholic Church in Mezőkövesd in 1855, with the archbishop of Eger traveling fifteen kilometers to the market town to perform the baptism himself. Attendees included the president of the Borsod County Court, all the way from Miskolc (fifty kilometers away), the personnel of the local district magistrate's office, and parishioners from neighboring communities, all of whom crowded into the church.[80]

After a few faltering attempts in the 1840s, the Hungarian-language Jewish press finally took flight in the 1860s. The Pest weekly *Magyar Izraelita*, which was published intermittently from 1861 to 1868, occasionally printed articles about "Jewish mothers" who were happy not to be identified as Jews, and essays investigating the reasons and possible remedies for the "deterioration of religion" and the "decline of Jewry," but over the course of its seven-year existence, this periodical never once broached the subject of conversion.[81]

The national press rarely mentioned baptisms of Jews in the 1870s, either. Daily newspapers occasionally reported the conversions of individual Jews, especially if they were particularly newsworthy, as was the case with a Budapest family of seven who were baptized in 1879. According to the *Fővárosi Lapok* (*The Capital City Pages*), "The public interest elicited by this case testifies to the fact that these days the Christianization of an entire Jewish family is not an everyday occurrence."[82] Writer Elek Benedek expressed a similar opinion in his memoirs. Benedek moved to Budapest after finishing high school in 1877. Describing Budapest at that time, Benedek briefly mentioned the city's Jews and noted in passing that "converted Jews are as rare as a white raven."[83] Benedek's Jewish contemporaries had even less to say about conversion in this period, focusing almost exclusively on the 1868–69 Jewish Congress that led to the schism in Hungary's Jewish community. The issue did not come up in the 1875 *Zsidó évkönyv* (*Jewish Yearbook*), which featured a representative sampling of the priorities of Neolog intellectuals. We find no references to conversion in the 1870s speeches of rabbis Sámuel Kohn and Immánuel Löw, the latter of whom served as chief rabbi of Szeged beginning in 1878.[84]

128   JEWISHNESS AND BEYOND

The situation changed in the 1880s. An increasing number of Hungarian Jewish newspapers began to examine the subject of conversion with greater frequency—though it was still not an issue of primary importance. Yet it was during this same period that the supposed alienation of Jews from their religion and community became the foremost concern of Neolog intellectuals. It was this period of growing anti-Jewish sentiment that occasioned the first expressions of apprehension that the weakening of Jewish consciousness was an even greater threat to the future of Jewry than antisemitism. According to the lead editorial in the first issue of *Szombati Újság* (*Saturday News*), which appeared in Budapest in 1882 and 1883, "A unique phenomenon has appeared in our larger cities and threatens our existence more than all the burning stakes of the inquisition and all the deceptions of the false prophets: Jewish youths are ashamed of their religion and call it a virtue if the Jew in them is not recognized. Jews are the greatest enemies of Jewry; the sons of Shem are the most embittered antisemites."[85] Surprisingly (and significantly), the author said nothing at all about conversions.

The anonymous author of a pamphlet published in the autumn of 1882 urged Jews who were indifferent to their religion to convert to Protestantism, describing the conversion of "educated Jews" as the solution to the "Jewish question."[86] According to the weekly *Somogy* (named for the county in southwestern Hungary), the pamphlet's author was a Budapest law student named Gyula Fekete, who converted to Protestantism along with an acquaintance from his hometown of Kaposvár. *Somogy* reported that their conversion "had caused a great sensation" there.[87] Regardless of whether Gyula Fekete actually wrote the pamphlet, the conversion of the law student and his acquaintance was considered an extraordinary incident in his home city. *Egyenlőség* mentioned the same pamphlet without exploring the identity of its author or attributing any particular significance to its subject, nor connecting it to the increasing numbers of conversions being recorded at that time.[88] Even so, *Egyenlőség* did note the increasing frequency of conversions among Jews in the period. According to an article it published in October of 1884, "religious conversions have been on the agenda for some time," though the author of the piece stated that conversion was not the problem of the Jews and essentially refused to discuss the issue: "It does not concern us if someone converts from the Jewish religion to another religion."[89] Of course, conversion was of great concern to *Egyenlőség*'s staff, who continually complained that Jews' faith prevented them from getting jobs in the public sector.

These scattered reports give the impression that *Egyenlőség*'s writers did not really know how to approach the subject of conversion in the 1880s. They mentioned the issue with increasing frequency, but it seemed to irritate them more than it worried them. Other Jewish periodicals expressed even less concern. The *Magyar-Zsidó Ifjúság Lapja* (*The Journal of Hungarian-Jewish Youth*, published in Budapest between 1885 and 1887) was founded with the expressed intention of reinforcing young educated Jews' ties to their religion and their community,[90] yet it never mentioned the subject of conversion.

Even in the late 1880s and early 1890s, *Egyenlőség*'s writers were not sure how much significance to attribute to conversions. In 1889, poet Lajos Palágyi expressed his certainty that as a result of antisemitism, "the number of conversions was greater in the last decade than in the preceding decades."[91] Taking a different line, in 1891 (when more Jews joined Protestant congregations in Pest than in any other year between 1800 and 1895), engineer and economist Jenő Vázsonyi, elder brother of the prominent liberal politician Vilmos Vázsonyi, wrote that given the potential social benefits of conversion, "it is astonishing that the number of baptisms is proportionally so small."[92]

Thus, up to 1895, Hungary's Neolog intelligentsia did not consider conversion an issue of dramatic proportions. The most widely circulated daily papers also generally ignored the issue, including the wave of conversions that took place in the mid-1880s. When these publications did discuss the baptisms of certain Jews or Jewish families, the news continued to appear in brief reports that failed to place the conversions in their broader social context. Editors' chief criterion for deciding whether to print the story of a particular conversion was its newsworthiness. The conversion of an entire family, a wealthy landowner, or the director of a theater; a deaf-mute girl who converted for her deaf-mute fiancé, a young woman who was shot in the head by a jealous army lieutenant just a few months after converting in order to marry him—these news items were interesting enough to merit a couple of lines in the press.[93]

Numbers of Conversions and Chronological Patterns from 1896 to 1914

According to annual data published in the Hungarian statistical yearbook, 8,452 of Hungary's Jews (not counting those of Croatia-Slavonia) converted to one of the Christian denominations between 1896 and 1914. Given that another 418 Jews disaffiliated without converting to another religion, a total of 8,870 Hungarian Jews abandoned the Jewish faith in this period. Between 1897 and 1914, 496 converts and 105 of the Jews who had simply disaffiliated would return to the Jewish fold, thus the "net loss" to the Jewish community in this period was 8,269 individuals.[94]

Given that official statistics did not include children under seven whose parents chose to switch religions, the actual number of converts was larger than the total recorded by the Hungarian Royal Central Statistical Office. According to the spirit of the law, children under seven had not actually converted but merely *followed* their parents into their new faith. How many might have done so? In 1896, the ICP began reporting the number of its members who announced an intention to leave the congregation, and in 1898 it started including the number of children under seven who left the community with their parents. Including these children in the tally increased the overall number of converts by 7.16 percent.[95] If we assume the same percentage applied to the entire population of Hungarian Jews who converted between 1896 and 1914, as many as 605 children under the age of seven might have switched religions, bringing the number of Hungarian Jews who were baptized in this period to 9,057 and the total number of Jews who abandoned their faith to 9,475.

Is it possible that the number of Hungarian Jews baptized between 1896 and 1914 was even higher? The Hungarian Royal Central Statistical Office compiled its annual conversion data using information it received from Christian clergymen. Each pastoral office was expected to complete an annual questionnaire on the subject of conversion and submit it to the statistical office. The questionnaires asked ecclesiastical officials to record the numbers of men and women who had converted to the given faith, to identify the religions from which they had converted, and to note how many had converted back to their previous religion.[96] The statistical office did not—and could not—verify the accuracy of the data it received from Christian clergymen; doing so would have required an army of bureaucrats to review the annual baptismal records of approximately 11,000 pastoral offices.[97] Thus, strictly speaking, early twentieth-century Hungary's official statistics do not reflect the actual numbers of Jews who converted to Christianity but the numbers of conversions Christian clergymen reported to the statistical office. Might they have included illegal baptisms on the questionnaires they submitted to the statistical office? Such "crimes" were never investigated, so they could—and, as far as I can tell, often did—report such conversions. To the extent illegal conversions went unrecorded, however, official statistics may have significantly underreported the actual number of Hungarian Jews who converted in this period. Without any evidence to substantiate this supposition, I consider my previous calculations

CONVERSIONS, CHRONOLOGICAL PATTERNS, AND REACTIONS   131

(9,057 converts and a total of 9,457 Jews who disaffiliated from the faith) to be roughly accurate.

Is this number high or low? Historians who appraise conversion numbers from a demographic perspective—including Jehuda Don and George Magos, Todd Endelman, and Viktor Karády—tend to regard it as low.[98] Other historians emphasize the significance of the social standing of the Jews who converted. According to Jacob Katz, conversions, like mixed marriages, alarmed Hungary's Jewish community because "[they] occurred in economically and intellectually advanced circles, thus causing a conspicuous qualitative loss beyond the numerical significance."[99] Michael Silber arrived at a similar conclusion: "While conversion was the choice of only a small percentage, it took a great toll among the cultural and economic elites. It was an indicator of Hungarian society's incapacity to tolerate truly Jewish difference and the failure of contemporary Judaism and Hungarian Jewry to be attractive enough to retain its most talented sons and daughters."[100]

Several historians have compared Hungarian conversion statistics to neighboring countries' data, and the results are clear: Hungary's numbers were relatively low in the years around the turn of the century.[101] One out of every 927 Czech Jews converted between 1901 and 1903, and one out of every 1,100 German Jews did so in the early years of the twentieth century, while only one of out every 1,885 Hungarian Jews did so in 1900.[102] However, the validity of such comparisons is called into question by several contradictory and incommensurable factors. For instance, while Hungarian children between the ages of seven and eighteen (with the exception of married women) were not permitted to convert, Austria's so-called *Interkonfessionelles Gesetz* (approved on May 25, 1868) prohibited conversions among children between the ages of seven and fourteen.[103] And while Hungarian and Austrian children under the age of seven automatically followed their parents in converting to a new religion and were thus not counted in conversion data, this practice applied in Germany to children under the age of fourteen.[104] Since German conversion data was tabulated only for Jews who joined Protestant churches, there are no comprehensive statistics for German Jews who converted to Catholicism, though it has been estimated that one-third of Germany's Jewish converts became Catholics.[105] Comparisons between Hungarian and German conversion statistics are further distorted because an 1876 amendment to Germany's 1873 *Kirchenaustrittsgesetz* made it possible for Jews to withdraw from their religious community while retaining an affiliation with the Jewish

132   JEWISHNESS AND BEYOND

faith. Thus, those who wished to create symbolic distance between themselves and the Jewish community could do so by adopting an officially intermediate status that did not exist in Hungary.[106]

The comparisons are also warped by Hungary's Jewish population having a much greater proportion of Orthodox Jews—who might be described as largely immune to the temptation to convert—than Germany's. In Jacob Katz's estimation, at the turn of the century, a third of Hungary's Jews could have been categorized as Orthodox "at least to the extent that in the eyes of the observer their Jewishness was clearly apparent in their outward religious behavior"[107] while Orthodox Jews made up at most 15 percent of Germany's Jewish population at that time.[108] Moreover, German neo-Orthodoxy was much less strict than the ultra-Orthodox Jewry of northeastern Hungary or even the more moderate Orthodox Jews of northwestern Hungary.[109]

Given that the vast majority of Hungary's Orthodox Jews lived in the provinces, a more appropriate basis for international comparison would be the conversion statistics for the Jewish populations of Budapest and the capitals of the surrounding countries. In Berlin, one out of every 600 Jews *converted* annually between 1892 and 1901 while 1 out of every 640 did so between 1902 and 1908.[110] In Prague, one out of every 433 Jews *disavowed Judaism* between 1898 and 1902 (this proportion includes converts and people who chose to remain unaffiliated).[111] In Vienna, 1 out of every 263 Jews *converted* in 1900 while 1 out of every 232 Jews *disavowed Judaism*.[112] I have calculated these ratios for the Jewish population of Budapest using data from the annual reports of the Israelite Congregation of Pest (ICP) and the lists of Jewish disaffiliates from the Israelite Congregation of Buda (ICB), which the latter began publishing in late 1911. In 1900, the Jewish population of Pest's districts IV–IX, which were under the jurisdiction of the ICP, was 155,288.[113] Members of the Budapest Autonomous Orthodox Israelite Congregation (founded in 1870) should be subtracted from this number because its apostates, if there were any, had to report their disaffiliation to their own authorities. However, the Orthodox Congregation did not publish official membership statistics, so we do not know its exact size. A comparison of the numbers of births registered by the Orthodox Congregation and the ICP in the years 1886–89, 1892–94, and 1896–97 suggests that Budapest's Orthodox community may have comprised as many as 5,000 individuals at the turn of the century.[114] Subtracting this number from the Jewish population of districts IV–IX yields a total of 150,288 Neolog Jews living under the jurisdiction of the ICP at the turn of the century. Given that 148 Jewish adults informed the ICP of their intention to disaffiliate in 1900, the overall ratio would be 1 apostate for every 1,015 Jews in Pest.[115] In 1901, the number of disaffiliates registered by the ICP jumped to 194 adults. Comparing this number to the estimated population of Neolog Jews living in districts under the jurisdiction of the ICP yields disaffiliation ratios of 1 out of every 775 adults.[116]

In Buda, the ICB began to publish monthly disaffiliation reports in December of 1911, making public the names of the Neolog Jewish residents of districts I and II who declared their intention to withdraw from the community. In the three-year period from 1912 to 1914, the ICB listed 72 adult disaffiliates, an annual average of 24. The 1910 Jewish population of districts I and II was 9,436, so the ICB's average annual disaffiliation ratio in this period was roughly one out of every 393 Jews.[117] Combining the ICB's numbers with the annual average of 246 adult Jews who disaffiliated from the ICP in this period produces an average annual ratio of 1 apostate for every 704 members of Budapest's Jewish communities in the three-year period from 1912 to 1914.[118] Given that more than 93 percent of Budapest's Jewish population belonged to the ICB or ICP, this number could serve as a reasonable approximation for the entire city.[119] It should be noted, however, that Budapest's actual disaffiliation ratio was almost certainly higher, as the ICB and ICP could not record the disaffiliations of converts who were baptized without fulfilling their legal obligation to report their intentions to their congregations.

In addition to local factors that may have motivated Jewish residents of major Central European cities to convert, there is another circumstance that limits the validity of comparisons of conversion data in Budapest, Prague, and Vienna. Unlike Germany and Hungary, which introduced civil marriage (and thus legalized mixed marriages) in 1876 and 1895, respectively, Austria and its Hereditary Lands did not allow marriages between Jews and Christians. This legal impediment unquestionably led to significant increases in the numbers of conversions in Vienna and Prague.[120]

Nevertheless, it is striking that Jewish residents of Vienna were almost three times as likely to convert as Jewish residents of Pest, especially when one considers that, as Gerald Stourzh has pointed out, Vienna's conspicuously high conversion rate cannot be attributed solely to Austria's prohibition of Jewish-Christian marriages, as Prague's conversion rate was much lower even though mixed marriages were banned in Bohemia as well.[121] And although the conversion rate in the small Jewish community of Buda was exceeded only by that of the Jews of Vienna, the overall conversion rate of Budapest Jews was lower than that of Berlin Jews, even though the latter city's data did not include converts to Catholicism.

An examination of the conversion rates makes it clear that emancipated Jews were most likely to convert to Christianity in locales characterized by a combination of a considerable degree of acculturation and entrenched antisemitism.[122] Since there was no significant disparity in the level of acculturation of the Jewish population of Berlin, Prague, Vienna, and Budapest, the divergent conversion rates, as Peter Honigmann has pointed out, may have been a function of the varying intensity of antisemitism in these cities.[123] In other words, differences in the conversion rates between similarly acculturated Jewish communities were the most reliable indicator of the local intensity of antisemitism.[124] Historians have almost unanimously concluded that antisemitism was less intense in Hungary at the turn of the century than in Germany, Bohemia, or Austria.[125] In 1897, Theodor Herzl, the founder of modern political Zionism, described Hungary as "an oasis in the antisemitic world."[126] While this was surely an exaggeration, the fact that Budapest Jews' conversion rate was lower than that of the Jews of Berlin, Prague, or Vienna does corroborate historians' contention that Hungarian antisemitism was comparatively moderate.

As regards the evolution in the number of conversions between 1896 and 1914, the growth rate in the number of Hungarian Jews who converted to Christianity was higher than the growth rate of the Jewish population. If we compare the Jewish population of Hungary in 1900 and 1910 to the average numbers of Jewish converts per year from 1898 to 1902 and 1908 to 1912, we see that there was one convert for every 1,956 Hungarian Jews at the turn of the century and one convert for every 1,789 Hungarian Jews in 1910. Budapest was also characterized by increases of this sort. If we compare the Jewish population of the six districts of Budapest under the jurisdiction of the ICP in 1900 and 1910 (minus the estimated 5,000 Orthodox Jews who lived there) with the average number of adult Jews who announced their intention to disaffiliate from the ICP from 1898–1902 and 1908–12, we see that there was approximately 1 apostate for every 901 Jewish residents of Pest at the turn of the century and 1 for every 758 around 1910.

An annual breakdown of the national data shows that the absolute number of conversions among Hungarian Jews rose every year from 1896 to 1901, from 220 to 544. The number of conversions then stabilized from 1902 to 1914. The

1901 total of 544 converts was exceeded only once in this period—in 1909, when 545 Hungarian Jews converted to Christianity. From 1896 to 1914, an average of 445 Hungarian Jews converted each year, but subdividing this period into three five-year (and one four-year) segments shows continual growth in the annual conversion rate. The average number of Jewish converts per year from 1896 to 1900 was 321; this figure rose to 476 between 1901 and 1905, to 490 from 1906 to 1910, and to 505 from 1911 to 1914. Combining the statistics for Jews who converted to Christianity and those who declared themselves *konfessionslos* between 1896 and 1914, an average of 467 Hungarian Jews left Judaism per year in this period. The largest numbers did so in 1912 (574), 1909 (564), and 1901 (554). Broken down into the aforementioned intervals, the annual average rose from 334 in the period between 1896 and 1900 to 493 between 1901 and 1905, 514 between 1906 and 1910, and 541 between 1911 and 1914.

The number of Jews who informed the ICP of their intention to disaffiliate also increased steadily from 1896 to 1914. The growth spiked in the year 1901, though less dramatically in Pest than in the rest of Hungary. A total of 3,737 adults notified the ICP of their plans to disaffiliate over the course of this 19-year period, averaging just under 197 individuals per year, with a low of 120 in 1896 and a high of 249 in 1912. From 1896 to 1900, the annual average number of adults who told the ICP they were leaving Judaism was 141; this average rose to 192 in the period from 1901 to 1905, 226 from 1906 to 1910, and 234 from 1911 to 1914. Thus, in the period between the implementation of the 1895 ecclesiastical laws and the outbreak of the First World War, more and more Hungarian Jews left the fold, both in absolute numbers and as a proportion of the country's Jewish population.

What might explain this increase? The most obvious hypothesis would be rising antisemitism. While the Horthy era (1920–44) was marked by much greater hostility to Jews, there is no doubt that antisemitism and its effects on Hungarian Jews' lives intensified from the mid-1890s to the outbreak of World War I. After the enactment of the ecclesiastical laws, a new type of conservatism put old-school Hungarian liberals on the defensive. The birth of the Catholic People's Party, founded in January of 1895 as a protest against the ecclesiastical laws, marked the reemergence of an antisemitic party in Hungarian political life. Unlike Győző Istóczy's National Antisemitic Party, which had disintegrated by the late 1880s, the People's Party was represented in the National Assembly from 1896 until the collapse of the Dual Monarchy.

136   JEWISHNESS AND BEYOND

Though there were no openly antisemitic planks in the party's platform,[127] its parliamentary representatives and its official newspaper, *Alkotmány*, published a more or less continuous stream of anti-Jewish incitement.[128] And though the Catholic People's Party was never particularly influential on the national political stage, it did exercise some power as part of the governing coalition between 1906 and 1910.

In addition to the Catholic People's Party, Hungary's increasingly active Catholic political movement established numerous social organizations in the final decade of the Dualist era, notably the Catholic People's Alliance. This organization was founded in 1908 and had 285,000 members by the end of 1914, and while it was not officially antisemitic, its internal communications reflected explicit antipathy toward Jews.[129] The Marian Congregations, which the Hungarian province of the Jesuit Order had founded in hopes of creating a militant Catholic political elite, were increasingly influential among members of the Christian middle class.[130] Antisemitic ideas gained currency at Hungarian universities from the beginning of the twentieth century and at the Hungarian Academy of Sciences after 1905.[131] At least partly as a result of the activities of the Marian Congregations, Hungarian cultural life would be characterized by an increasingly open and vehement form of antisemitism that conflated Budapest with Jews, Jews with intellectuals, and intellectuals with social democracy, bourgeois-radical circles, and freemasonry.

As the economic power of the Jewish upper class came to rival that of the aristocracy by the 1890s, large landowners hoping to maintain their political influence and keep Jews from gaining further ground established the Hungarian Farmers' Association in 1896 on the model of the German *Bund der Landwirte*. The pressure group assumed considerable authority in the government of Prime Minister Kálmán Széll (1899–1903) and became a dominant force in Prime Minister Sándor Wekerle's coalition government (1906–10). Within the National Labor Party (which took over as the successor of the Liberal Party when István Tisza led it to overwhelming victory in Hungary's 1910 parliamentary elections), agrarians and their adversaries—members of the so-called mercantilist camp, many of whom were Jewish—established a delicate but functional equilibrium.[132] Even so, antisemitic overtones would continue to echo through the Hungarian political arena in the years before World War I, "palpably influencing the flavor and mood of debate" even at the Budapest general assembly,[133] which was otherwise dominated by the upper bourgeoisie, while parliamentary negotiations concerning the budget of the

Ministry of Religion and Public Education routinely devolved into verbal abuse of Jews.[134]

Can the rapid increase in conversions among Hungarian Jews from 1896 to 1901 be attributed to an intensification of antisemitism? It is true that Hungary's Jews were quickly disabused of their hopes that passage of the 1895 ecclesiastical laws and the inclusion of Judaism among Hungary's received religions had finally signaled their acceptance into Hungarian society.[135] It is also noteworthy that the number of Hungarian Jews who disaffiliated from their congregations jumped from 448 in 1900 to a peak of 554 in 1901, the year Catholic students and the Catholic People's Party organized antisemitic demonstrations at the University of Budapest and the agrarian movement almost took over the governing Liberal Party.

However, it is impossible to establish an explicit correlation between these cyclical increases in political antisemitism and conversions to Christianity. If we attribute the growth in the number of conversions in the period up to 1901 primarily to an increase in political antisemitism, we have to ask why conversions did not rise significantly between 1906 and 1910, when the governing coalition was dominated by the agrarian movement (and included the Catholic People's Party) and government policy was unambiguously more antagonistic to Jews than it had been around the turn of the century. In 1907 and 1908, when *Egyenlőség* characterized the Independence Party that dominated the House of Representatives as "anti-liberal and antisemitic dregs" and declared that the "terroristic, clericalist" policies of the Catholic People's Party had "become ipso facto the guiding principle within the coalition majority,"[136] fewer Hungarian Jews converted to Christianity than in the much more tranquil year of 1903.

Of course, antisemitism cannot be reduced to its manifestations in politics and public life. However, it is difficult to determine whether antisemitism caused Hungarian Jews more frequent problems in their everyday lives in the two decades before World War I than in previous eras. Numerous Hungarian-Jewish writers remembered these decades as an essentially peaceful period in which antisemitism did not play a significant role in their lives.[137] At the same time, many Hungarian Jews recalled suffering antisemitic insults and injuries—some minor, some significant and painful.[138] Among the factors that determined the frequency of such affronts was one's place of residence. In his home city of Kolozsvár, writer Ernő Ligeti suffered numerous indignities as a result of his Jewishness, but he had no unpleasant experiences of the sort in Nagyvárad, where he moved to work as a journalist in 1911.[139] This issue is further complicated by the fact that different individuals experienced manifestations of antisemitism in divergent ways. Some Jews shrugged off insults and reconciled themselves to the situation; others were unable to do so.[140]

Perhaps the most convincing evidence that antisemitism was an increasingly oppressive force in the lives of Hungarian Jews in the period from 1896 to 1914 was the growing bitterness and hopelessness expressed in the Jewish press, particularly *Egyenlőség*. One important sign was the near-total disappearance of emphatic declarations concerning the inevitable fraternal union of Christians and Jews. The pages of *Egyenlőség* had teemed with such expressions when Judaism was declared a received religion in the mid-1890s, and though there was a brief, enthusiastic outburst of language of this sort at the outset of World War I, it already had the sound of a bygone era.[141]

There is no doubt antisemitism was ultimately responsible for most conversions, since in societies free of anti-Jewish prejudice, Jews who drifted away from Judaism rarely bothered to formally renounce their faith and adopt the religion of the majority society. Nevertheless, it is possible that the primary factors in the growth of the conversion rate among Hungarian Jews in the two decades before World War I were not the gradual intensification of antisemitism and the increasingly frequent injuries and insults Jews suffered but rather their diminished capacity to endure antisemitism and an increasing inability to withstand the temptation to convert. As Jews became increasingly alienated from their community and religion, their inclination to convert may have intensified without any accompanying increase in the frequency and seriousness of the personal injuries they suffered as a result of antisemitism. At the 1903 general assembly of the Sixth Israelite Community District, Mór Mezei, the district's vice president (and future president of the Neolog National Jewish Bureau), expressed indignation not at those who had been prompted to abandon their faith by "situations arising from social pressure, obstacles to earning a living, or marriage" but at those whose conversions "had no discernable causes" except that "these individuals have lost all attachment to the traditions of their ancestors and to their own pasts."[142] In his first novel, *The Hungry City*, Ferenc Molnár depicted his protagonist, Pál Orsovai, as an utterly average Budapest bank official. Orsovai's Jewishness is not an obstacle to professional advancement; the greatest misfortune associated with his religious identity is that it keeps him from being admitted to certain rowing clubs. In Molnár's telling, this setback is essentially enough to convince his

CONVERSIONS, CHRONOLOGICAL PATTERNS, AND REACTIONS 139

main character to convert: "It was a little late—he was already 23 years old or so—but he thought it was never too late to leave an unpleasant religion."[143]

Turn-of-the-Century and Twentieth-Century Reactions to Conversion

I analyzed responses to Hungarian Jews' conversions to Christianity up to 1895 partly in the hope of compensating—impressionistically or anecdotally—for a lack of national statistical data on the subject. From 1896 onward, however, contemporaneous assessments of the significance of Jewish conversion could have been informed by the statistics that Hungarian officials had begun to compile. What conclusions might contemporaneous observers have drawn from these statistics? Strikingly, journalists of the national press, whether Jewish or Christian, drew no conclusions at all. I could not find a single instance in which a journalist used conversion statistics as the basis for any sort of reflection.

Antisemitic writers were not much different in this regard, insofar as they did occasionally mention rising numbers of conversions, but because of their essentialist perception of Jewishness, they did not attribute any significance to the increases. The best example is one of the first Hungarian works of the era to use statistical data as the explicit basis for a demonstration of Jewish "takeover." In his 1907 book *A Magyarországi zsidók statisztikája* (*Statistics on the Jews of Hungary*), Kálmán Weszprémy published conversion data from the period between 1896 and 1905, though in his commentary, he quickly specified that conversions did not actually reduce the number of Jews, since "they remain here among us."[144]

The general public may not have paid attention to the statistics, but Hungarians appear to have perceived conversion as a widespread phenomenon, as evidenced by jokes circulating around the turn of the century.[145] An early 1911 issue of the literary weekly *Élet* (*Life*, published for "Christian Hungarian families" beginning in 1909) featured a humorous sketch about the 1910 census in which a wisecracking census-taker asks Jews imaginary questions including "When will you convert to Christianity?"[146]

Beyond these sorts of generalizing jokes, the Hungarian public focused primarily on conversions of members of the Jewish upper class, which was thought to have been decimated by baptisms. As Ferenc Molnár wrote in a vignette published in 1911, "It was once obligatory to have a so-called 'cover Christian' at all parties in Lipótváros. But this has now come to an end, because now everywhere the hosts themselves are also . . . the hosts themselves are not . . . the hosts are no longer . . . that is to say, they, too, can do what a Christian does."[147] Daily papers regularly reported on conversions in upper-class circles, particularly if the ages, families, or public roles of the individuals involved made it possible to sensationalize these stories.

Unlike the national press (and in contrast to their own previously expressed attitudes on the subject), Neolog intellectuals began to attribute more and more significance to conversions and to follow the issue with growing alarm. Jewish publications, in particular *Egyenlőség*, began discussing conversions regularly in the latter half of the 1890s. The Neolog intelligentsia's growing concern was rooted partially in the belief that conversion had become exceptionally frequent among financial and intellectual elites.[148] However, they were even more worried by the statistically observable rise in the total number of conversions. Neolog journalists spent the 1900s expressing alarm over the growth in the number of "apostates" and dramatizing the significance of conversion. As Miksa Szabolcsi wrote in *Egyenlőség* in late 1901, "Over the last five years, i.e., since government reports began to register them, the number of conversions—beloved faithful of Israel!—has *doubled*. Nothing in this country has grown by 100 percent over the last five years, not even misery. Only conversions can boast of such a record."[149] In June of 1902, the growing volume of "breakage off the trunk of the Jewish faith" prompted the reclusive Hanover-born Rabbi Meyer Kayserling, who delivered German-language sermons at the Dohány Street Synagogue in Budapest, to publish an article in *Egyenlőség* on the causes of conversion and possible of methods of preventing it.[150] A few months later, Miksa Szabolcsi sounded a general alarm in his analysis of the losses Jewry had suffered as a result of conversions: "Thus the number of Jewish disaffiliates is continually rising and rising significantly. Just imagine: the loss of Jews was almost five times greater in 1901 than it was in 1896, when the government's report first publicized data on conversions."[151]

In the first five years of the twentieth century, Jewish publications delivered more and more alarming reports on disaffiliations from the Jewish faith, declaring that they were increasing "day by day," had reached "frightening proportions," were spreading "like an epidemic," and were cause for the "greatest concern."[152] In 1904 and 1905, Chief Rabbi Bernát Singer of Szabadka addressed the issue of conversion in a nine-part series published in *Egyenlőség*, opening his introductory article with a dramatic assessment of the state of affairs: "Perhaps one of the greatest of the many, many problems facing the Jews of our era is conversion. . . . Every year, substantial numbers of our coreligionists disavow our faith, which weighs on us like a constant nightmare. That we see danger in this is demonstrated by the fact that all the actors in the life of our denomination are intensely engaged in dealing with it. Overtly or obliquely, rabbis in the pulpit speak of it with the greatest frequency; religious instruction is largely dedicated to fortifying young people in advance against later temptations."[153]

Though Singer concluded his series of articles on an optimistic note, the Hungarian Jewish press would continue publishing reports on the incessant growth of the "apostate camp."[154] Their perceptions of conversion were sometimes divorced from reality. In a book published in 1904, a retired teacher from Sátoraljaújhely claimed that more Jews were baptized in Hungary than "in any country of Europe."[155] A year later, Miksa Schächter, a member of the ICP's representative body, asserted that in Hungary, "the number of conversions nearly counterbalances the number of births."[156] This claim primarily demonstrates Schächter's indignation: 459 individuals left the Jewish community in 1904, when it recorded 27,567 live births.[157]

It would seem, then, that the sense of alarm was general, though it should be noted that all of the periodicals I have cited were published in Budapest. Some of their authors were provincials, but the majority lived in Budapest. Hardly any publications affiliated with Neolog or status quo ante religious communities were published outside the city of Budapest in this period. The few that did appear in the provinces paid less attention to the issue of conversion, presumably because it did not seem like a phenomenon of "epidemic" proportions in these areas. In 1905 and 1906, *Szombati Újság* (*Saturday News*, initially published in Miskolc, then Debrecen) printed just five articles—including two brief notices—on the subject of conversion.

Alarmist reports on the numbers of Jewish conversions began to dwindle around 1905, perhaps because the growth in the conversion rate had begun to slow down around 1901. It is also possible that the stabilization of the conversion rate at an unprecedently high level—that is, the fact that apostasy had not abated despite all efforts to prevent it—may have engendered a kind of resignation or intensified a brand of forced optimism. In 1905, journalist and historian Ignác Acsády wrote, "The sickness of conversion is truly ravaging certain strata of Jewry like an epidemic," though he immediately added, "as the merciless persecutions of the centuries passed, so shall the peculiar fashion of the most recent times, the storm of apparently voluntary conversions."[158] Despite declarations of this sort, however, neither the anxiety nor

142 JEWISHNESS AND BEYOND

the pessimism dissipated. As assistant rabbi Mór Fényes, the ICP's supervisor of religious instruction, wrote in 1910, "Rabbis no longer do anything but serve as border guards against the renegades, and even this they do not do with much success."[159] One of the telling aspects of the bar mitzvah–style confirmation ceremonies the ICP arranged for adolescent girls in the early 1910s was the explicit goal of having them solemnly pledge to "cleave to the God of Israel with steadfast fidelity under all circumstances throughout their entire lives."[160]

Beyond the Numbers

I shall conclude this chapter by addressing a question that has come up repeatedly: how much significance should we attribute to the conversions of Hungarian Jews in the period bounded by the Reform Era and the First World War? As we have seen, the Hungarian public at the turn of the century was not particularly concerned with Jewish conversions. At any rate, it was much more interested in other issues, such as the question of nationalities or the question of the working class. On the other hand, the "epidemic" of apostasy was "like a constant nightmare" for Neolog intellectuals, who considered conversion a greater threat to the future of modern Jewry than almost anything else.

The available quantitative data indicate that the number of Hungarian Jews who abandoned their faith was insignificant until the 1840s and (with the exception of the wave of conversions in 1848) remained unambiguously low until the 1880s. The number of conversions then began to rise dramatically, though at a variable pace. Even so, from a demographic perspective, the losses the Jewish community suffered in this period could be characterized as minimal. The estimated 9,475 men, women, and children who left Judaism between 1896 and 1914 represented just over 1 percent of the total Hungarian Jewish population of 911,227 (recorded in 1910). Hungarian Jews' conversion rate was also lower than that of other Jewish populations in Central Europe. The proportion of converts in the overall Jewish population was smaller in Hungary than in Germany and lower in Budapest than in Berlin, Vienna, or Prague.

However, in and of themselves, statistics do not allow us to gauge the actual significance of such conversions. The quantitative data make it possible to do only one thing: compare numbers of converted and unconverted Jews. But the resulting ratios do not provide us with an accurate understanding of the scale of conversion, because for a significant proportion of the Jews who did not convert, abandoning the faith was not even an option. The genuine social impact of conversion cannot be assessed accurately unless the number of Jewish converts is compared to the number of Jews whose detachment from the Jewish faith and the Jewish community made it possible for them to entertain the idea of converting in the first place.[161] With few exceptions, the Orthodox Jews who made up at least a third of Hungary's Jewish population at the turn of the century would not even have considered converting. Nor would Jews who—even if they did not comply with all the commandments of the faith—lived in milieux steeped in Jewish tradition, such as the Neolog Jewish communities of Hungary's villages and small towns, most residents of which were culturally closer to the acculturated members of moderate Orthodox communities than to the Neolog Jews of Lipótváros. Considering that alienation from the Jewish faith did not in itself lead to conversion, the basis for comparison must be further narrowed to Jews for whom a decision to convert might have been triggered by some concrete objective—marriage, a job, a promotion, social acceptance—or a more confused desire. Without question, the conversion rate among Jews driven by motives like these was many times greater than among the overall Jewish population. If we examine the proportion of converts among those Hungarian Jews susceptible to the temptation of a baptismal certificate, we see that by the final decades of the Dualist era, conversion had become a significant feature of life among acculturated Jewry. As I will discuss in the following chapter, significant proportions of the Hungarian Jewish economic, political, and cultural elites—including majorities in certain circles—had abandoned the Jewish faith by the outbreak of the First World War. Conversion must therefore be considered one of the central questions in modern Hungarian Jewish history.

Finally, there is some question whether the significance of conversion can be gauged on the basis of the number of Hungarian Jews who actually converted before the outbreak of World War I. There were many who reached the banks of the Rubicon without yet crossing it. In advocating a significant increase in the congregation's community tax at a 1911 meeting of the board of the ICP, Gusztáv G. Ehrlich said it was common knowledge that the ICP's leaders "have refrained thus far from imposing adequate taxes because they are afraid of conversion."[162] Their fears were well founded. In 1910, after the death of wholesaler Lipót Heidelberg, the ICP raised the community tax for Heidelberg's son, the chemical manufacturer Tivadar Helvey, by three hundred crowns, at which point Helvey immediately converted to Christianity.[163]

144 JEWISHNESS AND BEYOND

Andor Hegedüs, the merchant father of writer Géza Hegedüs, did not abandon his faith, but when his son was born in 1912, he admitted to his wife that if it were not for his Orthodox Jewish relatives, he would gladly have converted to Catholicism with her and their children.[164]

Of course, one could argue that cases of Jews who considered converting but did not do so in the period under discussion are irrelevant. Their significance may be clearer in the light of Neolog Jews in the early twentieth century converting in unprecedented numbers. In the three years from 1918 to 1920, roughly 10,000 Hungarian Jews converted to Christianity, which as an absolute number and as a proportion of the overall population surpassed any previous wave of conversions. This unprecedented conversion crisis was evidence of an equally unprecedented surge in antisemitism.[165] But it is also an indication that in the last peaceful years of the Dual Monarchy, the number of Hungarian Jewish converts to Christianity was dwarfed by the number of Jews who rejected the idea of converting primarily because they lacked the compelling reason that would, within a few years, make them leave the Jewish fold.

Notes

1. Joh. de le Roi, *Judentaufen im 19. Jahrhundert: Ein statistischer Versuch* (Leipzig, Germany: J. C. Hinrichs'sche Buchhandlung, 1899), 49. This number did not include individuals who had disaffiliated from the Jewish faith without converting to another religion.

2. A. Menes, "The Conversion Movement in Prussia During the First Half of the 19th Century" (1939), in *YIVO Annual of Jewish Social Science*, vol. 6, ed. Koppel S. Pinson (New York: Yiddish Scientific Institute/YIVO, 1951), 191; Todd M. Endelman, "Introduction," in *Jewish Apostasy in the Modern World*, ed. id., 18–19; id., "Anti-Semitism and Apostasy in Nineteenth-Century France: A Response to Jonathan Helfand," *Jewish History* 5, no. 2 (1991): 59.

3. De le Roi, *Judentaufen im 19. Jahrhundert*, 31, 40, 45.

4. Kempelen, *Magyar zsidó családok*, 2: 83.

5. János Horváth, *A magyar királyság közjoga* (Budapest: Dobrowsky és Franke, 1894), 511–12; Kálmán Melichár, *Egyházi szervezet és vallásügyi igazgatás Magyarországon* (Budapest: Pallas, 1902), 29.

6. *Képviselőházi irományok, 1892–1897*, vol. 10 (Budapest: Pesti Könyvnyomda, 1893), 292.

CONVERSIONS, CHRONOLOGICAL PATTERNS, AND REACTIONS   145

7. Franciscus Xav. Linzbauer, *Codex sanitario-medicinalis Hungariae*, vol. 2 (Budae: Typis Caesareo-Regiae Scientiarum Universitatis, 1852), 387; Miksa Pollák, *A zsidók története Sopronban: A legrégibb időktől a mai napig* (Budapest: IMIT, 1896), 222.

8. Linzbauer, *Codex sanitario-medicinalis Hungariae*, 683–684; Henrik Marczali, "A magyarországi zsidók II. József korában," *Magyar-Zsidó Szemle* 1, no. 5 (1884): 354.

9. Franciscus Xav. Linzbauer, *Codex sanitario-medicinalis Hungariae*, vol. 3, sectio 1 (Budae: Typis Caesareo-Regiae Scientiarum Universitatis, 1853), 372; Zita Deáky, "Falusi és mezővárosi zsidó bábák Magyarországon (18–19. sz.)," in … *és hol a vidék zsidósága? … Történeti és néprajzi tanulmányok a falusi, mezővárosi zsidók és nemzsidók együttéléséről*, ed. Zita Deáky, Zsigmond Csoma, and Éva Vörös (Budapest: Centrál-Európa Alapítvány, 1994), 147–48.

10. Sándor Büchler, "De Judaeis," in Bánóczi, *Évkönyv 1900*, 294–95.

11. Margit Balogh and Jenő Gergely, *Egyházak az újkori Magyarországon 1790–1992: Kronológia* (Budapest: História/MTA Történettudományi Intézete, 1993), 16–18, 57, 90.

12. Marczali, "A magyarországi zsidók II. József korában," 354; Pollák, *A zsidók története Sopronban*, 223.

13. "Az aradi színháztársulatnál," *Vasárnapi Újság* 15, no. 9 (1868): 105; "Rövid hírek," *Fővárosi Lapok* 8, no. 9 (1871): 38; "Hymen," *Fővárosi Lapok* 12, no. 227 (1875): 1015; "Az ó-budai zsidótemplomban," *Fővárosi Lapok* 15, no. 134 (1878): 659; "Érvénytelen áttérés," *Fővárosi Lapok* 17, no. 167 (1880): 837; "Fővárosi hírek," *Fővárosi Lapok* 19, no. 4 (1882): 26; "Ábrahám," *Pesti Napló*, February 3, 1894, 4. For more examples, see David Ellenson, "On Conversion and Intermarriage: The Evidence of Nineteenth-Century Hungarian Orthodox Rabbinic Writings," in *Text and Context: Essays in Modern Jewish History and Historiography in Honor of Ismar Schorsch*, ed. Eli Lederhendler and Jack Wertheimer ([New York]: Jewish Theological Seminary, 2005), 321–46.

14. Rozenblit, *The Jews of Vienna, 1867–1914*, 232, note 12.

15. Pulszky, "A zsidókról," 2.

16. "Miniszteri rendelet keresztény vallásra áttért zsidók anyakönyvezése tárgyában," *Magyar-Zsidó Szemle* 7, no. 4 (1890): 252.

17. F. M. [Ferenc Mezey], "Szemle," *Magyar-Zsidó Szemle* 8, no. 5 (1891): 332–33.

18. "Miniszteri rendelet keresztény vallásra áttért zsidók anyakönyvezése tárgyában," 252.

19. *Hivatalos Közlöny*, January 15, 1896, 14–15.

20. In response to the enormous number of Jewish conversions taking place at that time, the MRPE modified this provision in 1920, allowing the children of

146 JEWISHNESS AND BEYOND

converts to follow their parents into their new faith automatically, regardless of their age. See István Madarász, *A vallásváltoztatás magyar közjogi szempontból* (Budapest: Szerző kiadása, 1938), 54–55.

21. Ibid., 33.

22. Zsigmond Groszmann, "Kitérések," *Magyar Izrael* 4, no. 7–8 (1911): 167–68.

23. *Hivatalos Közlöny*, April 15, 1898, 193–94.

24. Zsigmond Groszmann, "Az áttérési törvény hiányai," *Hitközségi Szemle* 2, no. 8 (1911): 253.

25. Ibid., 254.

26. Miksa Szabolcsi, "Meturgeman: Törvényszegés," *Egyenlőség*, April 12, 1903, 6. In a column entitled "Meturgeman" (the Aramaic word for *translator* or *interpreter*), *Egyenlőség*'s editor in chief published his responses to letters submitted to the paper. Groszmann, "Kitérések," 168.

27. Miksa Szabolcsi, "Hívek egylete," *Egyenlőség*, February 8, 1903, 1; "Följelentés," *Egyenlőség*, October 9, 1898, 10; Miksa Szabolcsi, "A csodaplébános," *Egyenlőség*, January 22, 1899, 8–9; id., "A fidélis Tóthfalusy," *Egyenlőség*, January 29, 1899, 7–8.

28. Miksa Szabolcsi, "Gondolatok a protestáns memorandum olvasásakor," *Egyenlőség*, October 23, 1904, 3.

29. Miksa Szabolcsi, "Meturgeman: Különös esetről," *Egyenlőség*, June 28, 1903, 8; id., Gondolatok a protestáns memorandum olvasásakor, 3.

30. *A Pesti izr. hitközség elöljáróságának jelentése az 1910-iki közigazgatási évről* (Budapest: n.p., 1911), 21.

31. Arnold Kiss, "Hívek egylete," *Egyenlőség*, February 22, 1903, 3.

32. Szabolcsi, "Meturgeman: Törvényszegés," 6.

33. Gy. W. [Gyula Weiszburg], "Protestáns lélekfogdosás," *A Jövő*, January 14, 1898, 2–3; Miksa Szabolcsi, "Újabb elkeresztelési eset," *Egyenlőség*, September 4, 1898, 7–8; id., "Meturgeman: Elkeresztelések," *Egyenlőség*, June 7, 1908, 4–5; "Elkeresztelés," *Egyenlőség*, August 14, 1910, 12; "Elkeresztelési eset és még valami," *Egyenlőség*, June 27, 1915, 42.

34. Munkácsi, *A Pesti Izraelita Hitközség oktatásügyének értesítője az 1904/905. iskolaévre*, 124.

35. Mór Fényes, "Vallásváltoztatás a középiskolai tanfolyam alatt," *Hitközségi Szemle* 2, no. 12 (1911): 349.

36. *A Pesti izr. hitközség elöljáróságának jelentése az 1907-iki közigazgatási évről* (Budapest: n.p., 1908), 17.

37. Kitérési és prozelita jegyzőkönyvek [Records of converts and proselytes]. Magyar Zsidó Múzeum és Levéltár (hereafter, MZsML), TB. B/67.

38. László Marjanucz, *A szegedi zsidó családok a 19. században* (Szeged, Hungary: Móra Ferenc Múzeum, 1988), 42.

CONVERSIONS, CHRONOLOGICAL PATTERNS, AND REACTIONS   147

39. Árpád Welker, "Zsidó betérések a protestáns felekezetekbe Pesten, 1895 előtt," *Korall* 8, no. 27 (May 2007): 97. Unless reference is made to another study by Welker cited below, the figures for the number of Jews who joined Protestant congregations in Pest before 1895 are in all cases taken from here, primarily from the figures on pages 99 and 102.

40. Szentistvánvárosi (Lipótvárosi) r. kath. plébánia, kereszteltek anyakönyve [Baptismal records of the Roman Catholic parish of Szentistvánváros (Lipótváros)]. Magyar Nemzeti Levéltár Országos Levéltára (hereafter, MNL OL), A61–A65.

41. For Viennese data, see Rozenblit, *The Jews of Vienna, 1867–1914*, 17. Concerning Berlin, see Stefi Jersch-Wenzel, "Population Shifts and Occupational Structure," in *German-Jewish History in Modern Times*, vol. 2, *Emancipation and Acculturation 1780–1871*, ed. Michael A. Meyer (New York: Columbia University Press, 1997), 57. For more on Pest, see József Kőrösi, "Buda és Ó-buda városa népességének évenkénti kimutatása 1813-tól 1857-ig," *Statisztikai Havi Füzetek* 9, no. 5 (1881): 136.

42. Vera Bácskai, "A pesti zsidóság a 19. század első felében," *Budapesti Negyed* 3, no. 2 (1995): 6; Kőrösi, "Buda és Ó-buda városa népességének évenkénti kimutatása 1813-tól 1857-ig," 136; *Budapest Székesfőváros Statisztikai Évkönyve*, vol. 1, *1894* (Budapest: Grill Károly, 1896), 55; *Budapest Székesfőváros Statisztikai és Közigazgatási Évkönyve*, vol. 11, *1909–1912* (Budapest: Budapest Székesfőváros Statisztikai Hivatala, 1914), tables, 41.

43. Kitérési és prozelita jegyzőkönyvek [Records of converts and proselytes]. MZsML, TB. B/67.

44. For the period from 1800 to 1874, see Deborah Hertz, *How Jews Became Germans: The History of Conversion and Assimilation in Berlin* (New Haven, CT/London: Yale University Press, 2007), 223; for the years 1875 to 1895, see N. Samter, *Judentaufen im neunzehnten Jahrhundert: Mit besonderer Berücksichtigung Preußens* (Berlin: M. Poppelauer, 1906), 146–47.

45. The data for Berlin comes from Jersch-Wenzel, "Population Shifts and Occupational Structure," 57; Monika Richarz, "Demographic Developments," in Meyer, *German-Jewish History in Modern Times*, 3: 31. The numbers for Pest are taken from Michael K. Silber, "Budapest," in Hundert, ed., *The YIVO Encyclopedia of Jews in Eastern Europe*, http://www.yivoencyclopedia.org/article.aspx/Budapest; *Budapest Székesfőváros Statisztikai Évkönyve*, vol. 4, *1899–1901* (Budapest: Grill Károly, 1904), 36.

46. Árpád Welker, "Vegyes házasságok és vallásváltások a Kálvin téri gyülekezetben a 19. században," in *Reformátusok Budapesten: Tanulmányok a magyar főváros reformátusságáról*, vol. 1, ed. László Kósa (Budapest: Argumentum/ELTE

148 JEWISHNESS AND BEYOND

BTK Művelődéstörténeti Tanszék, 2006), 152–53. For more on the Scottish Mission, see Ábrahám Kovács, *The History of the Free Church of Scotland's Mission to the Jews in Budapest and its Impact on the Reformed Church of Hungary 1841–1914* (Frankfurt am Main: Peter Lang, 2006).

47. Kitérési és prozelita jegyzőkönyvek [Records of converts and proselytes]. MZsML, TB. B/67.

48. Szentistvánvárosi (Lipótvárosi) r. kath. plébánia, kereszteltek anyakönyve [Baptismal records of the Roman Catholic parish of Szentistvánváros (Lipótváros)]. MNL OL, A61.

49. The number of Jews in Pest increased from 14,280 in 1848 to 188,937 in 1910.

50. Welker, "Zsidó betérések a protestáns felekezetekbe Pesten," 100–01.

51. For a discussion of Jewish participation in the revolution, see Béla Bernstein, *A negyvennyolcas magyar szabadságharc és a zsidók* (1898) (Budapest: Múlt és Jövő, 1998). For a description of this atmosphere of antisemitism and the frustration it created among Hungarian Jews, see I[gnaz] Einhorn, *Die Revolution und die Juden in Ungarn* (Leipzig, Germany: Carl Geibel, 1851); Zsoldos, *1848–1849 a magyar zsidóság életében*. For an overview of the antisemitic riots of the revolutionary period, see Gábor Kádár and Zoltán Vági, "Hosszú évszázad: Antiszemita erőszak Magyarországon, 1848–1956," in *A holokauszt Magyarországon hetven év múltán*, ed. Randolph L. Braham and András Kovács (Budapest: Múlt és Jövő, 2015), 79–83.

52. Szentistvánvárosi (Lipótvárosi) r. kath. plébánia, kereszteltek anyakönyve [Baptismal records of the Roman Catholic parish of Szentistvánváros (Lipótváros)]. MNL OL, A61–A64.

53. Menes, "The Conversion Movement in Prussia During the First Half of the 19th Century," 187–205; Peter Honigmann, "Jewish Conversions—A Measure of Assimilation? A Discussion of the Berlin Secession Statistics of 1770–1941," *Leo Baeck Institute Year Book* 34 (1989): 24; Endelman, *Radical Assimilation in English Jewish History*, 7; id., "Jewish Converts in Nineteenth-Century Warsaw: A Quantitative Analysis," *Jewish Social Studies* 4, no. 1 (1997): 35–38; Deborah Hertz, "The Troubling Dialectic Between Reform and Conversion in Biedermeier Berlin," in *Towards Normality? Acculturation and Modern German Jews*, ed. Rainer Liedtke and David Rechter (Tübingen: Mohr Siebeck, 2003), 116–17; Steven M. Lowenstein, "Jewish Intermarriage and Conversion in Germany and Austria," *Modern Judaism* 25, no. 1 (2005): 42.

54. For a social history of the Tiszaeszlár blood libel affair, see György Kövér, *A tiszaeszlári dráma: Társadalomtörténeti látószögek* (Budapest: Osiris, 2011). For discussions of the political antisemitism of this period, see Kubinszky, *A politikai antiszemitizmus Magyarországon 1875–1890*; Andrew Handler, *Blood Libel at Tiszaeszlár* (Boulder, CO: East European Monographs, 1980); Rolf Fischer, *Entwicklungsstufen des Antisemitismus in Ungarn, 1867–1939: Die Zerstörung der magyarisch-jüdischen*

CONVERSIONS, CHRONOLOGICAL PATTERNS, AND REACTIONS 149

Symbiose (München, Germany: Oldenbourg, 1988), 42–92; Zoltán Paksy, *Istóczy Győző és a magyar antiszemita mozgalom (1875–1892)* (Budapest: L'Harmattan, 2018).

55. Ferenc Pulszky, "Az antisemitismus válsága," *Pesti Hírlap,* July 12, 1885, 1; Dániel Szabó, "A magyar társadalom politikai szerveződése a dualizmus korában," *Történelmi Szemle* 34, no. 3–4 (1992): 200.

56. -f. m., "Az antiszemiták táborából," *Egyenlőség,* September 20, 1885, 3.

57. H–ky., "Kiábrándulás," *Egyenlőség,* August 29, 1886, 1.

58. Szentistvánvárosi (Lipótvárosi) r. kath. plébánia, kereszteltek anyakönyve [Baptismal records of the Roman Catholic parish of Szentistvánváros (Lipótváros)]. MNL OL, A64.

59. Zsoldos, *1848–1849 a magyar zsidóság életében,* 264.

60. Anikó Prepuk, "Kísérletek az izraeliták felekezeti jogainak szélesítésére az emancipáció után (1867–1892)," in *Zsidóság—tradicionalitás és modernitás: Tisztelgő kötet Karády Viktor 75. születésnapja alkalmából,* ed. Zsuzsanna Hanna Biró and Péter Tibor Nagy (Budapest: Wesley János Lelkészképző Főiskola, 2012), 48–50.

61. Welker, "Zsidó betérések a protestáns felekezetekbe Pesten," 103–04. For an analysis of Hungarian liberal-nationalist discourse concerning Christian-Jewish intermarriage, see Miklós Konrád, "Vegyes házasság és asszimiláció: Érvek a keresztény-zsidó házasság bevezetése mellett," *Történelmi Szemle* 63, no. 3 (2021): 483–94.

62. Silber, "The Historical Experience of German Jewry and Its Impact on Haskalah and Reform in Hungary," 112, 132–33.

63. Vörös, "A budapesti zsidóság két forradalom között," 103.

64. As far back as the 1860s, the Hungarian Jewish press had been publishing complaints about the anarchy stirring in the bosom of the congregation and a general indifference toward Jewish denominational affairs. See Pál Tencer, "Nálunk és másutt," *Magyar Izraelita,* June 25, 1863, 225; (Fmt.), "Quid consilii? II," *Magyar Izraelita,* July 10, 1863, 242. For a discussion of the period following the 1867 emancipation, see J. Rf. [Jakab Reif], *Kosmopolitismus és nationalismus, különös tekintettel a zsidóság jelenkori állására* (Budapest: Reach Zs. kiadása, 1875), 19–22; A szerkesztőség, "Halljad Izráel!," *Szombati Újság,* January 1, 1882, 1; Szántó [Eleázár], "Mi a teendő," *Egyenlőség,* March 18, 1883, 6–7; Zsigmond Groszmann, "Vallásoktatásunk," in Lőwinger, *Tanulmányok a zsidó tudomány köréből Dr. Guttmann Mihály emlékére,* 273–74; Goldziher, *Napló,* 115–16.

65. János Asbóth, *Társadalom-politikai beszédei* (Budapest: Szent-Gellért-Nyomda, 1898), 131; Albert Sturm, "Visszapillantás," *Egyenlőség,* December 29, 1889, 2; Jenő Horovicz, *A zsidók mint választók, vagy: a zsidók a politikában* (Besztercze: Szerző kiadása, 1892), 4, 6.

150   JEWISHNESS AND BEYOND

66. Welker, "Zsidó betérések a protestáns felekezetekbe Pesten," 99.

. 67. Szentistvánvárosi (Lipótvárosi) r. kath. plébánia, kereszteltek anyakönyve [Baptismal records of the Roman Catholic parish of Szentistvánváros (Lipótváros)]. MNL OL, A64 and A65.

68. Miss Pardoe, *The City of the Magyar, or Hungary and her Institutions in 1839–40*, vol. 3 (London: George Virtue, 1840), 301.

69. "Fővárosi újdonságok," *Pesti Hírlap*, March 3, 1841, 140.

70. For more on the Saphir family's conversion, see Gavin Carlyle, *"Mighty in the Scriptures": A Memoir of Adolph Saphir, D. D.* (London: John F. Shaw & Co., 1893), 15–40.

71. Zsoldos, *1848–1849 a magyar zsidóság életében*, 89, 129, 289.

72. Arszlán Schwab, *A zsidók: Fölvilágosító értekezés*, ed. and notes Móritz Bloch (Buda: Magyar Kir. Egyetem, 1840), 54–55.

73. Carlyle, *"Mighty in the Scriptures,"* 33, 37; "Pesth, 13 October," *Allgemeine Zeitung des Judenthums*, November 6, 1843, 673. I have not been able to find any evidence of this pamphlet's existence.

74. Anikó Prepuk, "Az izraelita hírlapirodalom kezdetei Magyarországon," in *Emlékkönyv ifj. Barta János 70. Születésnapjára*, ed. Imre Papp, János Angi, and László Pallai (Debrecen, Hungary: Debreceni Egyetem Történeti Intézete, 2010), 311–28.

75. Ein Ungar [Ábrahám Hochmuth], "Pesth, im Juni (Eingesandt.)," *Allgemeine Zeitung des Judenthums*, July 24, 1843, 444–46; . . . . . . e., "Pesth, 18. August (Privatmitth.)," *Allgemeine Zeitung des Judenthums*, September 11, 1843, 554–55; A. Liebemann, "Kandidat der Medizin: Pesth, 1. September (Privatmitth.)," *Allgemeine Zeitung des Judenthums*, September 18, 1843, 573–74; "Pest, 16. Juli (Privatmitth.)," *Allgemeine Zeitung des Judenthums*, July 29, 1844, 430–32.

76. Leopold Löw, "Sendschreiben an Herrn Dr. Jos. Szekács, Prediger der evang. Gemeinde zu Pesth," *Allgemeine Zeitung des Judenthums*, November 25, 1844, 681–90; republished in Leopold Löw, *Gesammelte Schriften*, vol. 4, ed. Immanuel Löw (Szegedin, Hungary: Ludwig Engel, 1898), 331–52.

77. Jos. Székács, evangel. Prediger zu Pesth, *Allgemeine Zeitung des Judenthums*, September 9, 1844, 521–22.

78. Arszlán Schwab, *Emlékeztetés a vallásban nyert oktatásra* (Buda: Magyar Kir. Egyetem, 1846), 14, 23; Lipót Hartmán, *Magyar zsidó, vagy: zsidó magyar?* (Pécs, Hungary: Lyceumi nyomda, 1848), 27.

79. Sándor Herczfeld, *Mi nem megyünk Amerikába, hanem itt fogunk maradni!* (Pest: Trattner-Károlyi, 1848), 7.

80. "Egyházi tudósítások," *Religio*, no. 15 (1st Half 1855): 116. Other conversions that took place in this period are discussed in Imre Csetényi, "Az ötvenes évek

CONVERSIONS, CHRONOLOGICAL PATTERNS, AND REACTIONS 151

sajtója és a zsidókérdés," in *Emlékkönyv néhai dr. Kohn Sámuel pesti főrabbi születésének századik évfordulójára*, ed. Sámuel Lőwinger (Budapest: Neuwald Illés, 1941), 93.

81. Zsófi Psherhofer, "Iskolai s nevelési ügy," *Magyar Izraelita*, April 11, 1861, 117; X . . ., "Az izr. népiskolának és különösen a mintafőtanodának feladata Magyarhonban, VI," *Magyar Izraelita*, June 25, 1863, 226–27.

82. "A ferencvárosi templom," *Fővárosi Lapok* 16, no. 98 (1879): 479.

83. Elek Benedek, *Édes anyaföldem! Egy nép s egy ember története*, vol. 1 (Budapest: Pantheon, 1920), 230.

84. József Kiss (Rudolf Szentesi), ed., *Zsidó évkönyv*, vol. 1, 5636 (1875–1876) (Budapest: Franklin-Társulat, 1875); Kohn, *Zsinagógai szónoklatok*, vol. 1; Immánuel Löw, *Beszédei 1874–1899* (Szeged, Hungary: Traub B. és Társa, 1900).

85. Gr., "Van-e szükségünk zsidó lapra?," *Szombati Újság*, January 14, 1882, 18.

86. Egy szabadelvű, *A zsidókérdés Magyarországon: Röpirat, melyben megbizonyíttatik, hogy a művelt zsidóknak áttérése valamelyik protestáns vallásra erkölcsileg igazolt és nagy politikai érdekek által sürgetett eljárás* (Budapest: Kókai Lajos, 1882).

87. "Röpirat az izraelita ügyben és kikeresztelkedések," *Somogy*, November 21, 1882, 3. I will return to the subject of this pamphlet's authorship below.

88. "A zsidókérdés Magyarországon," *Egyenlőség*, November 19, 1882, 11; Manó Brachfeld, "Egy szabadelvű titkos tanácsos," *Egyenlőség*, November 26, 1882, 4–5.

89. József Szigeti, "Prozelita-csinálás," *Egyenlőség*, October 5, 1884, 4.

90. Ben-Juda, "Felavatás," *A Magyar-Zsidó Ifjúság Lapja* 1, no. 1 (1885): 2.

91. Lajos Palágyi, "Zsidók a társaságban," *Egyenlőség*, November 17, 1889, 7.

92. Verus [Vázsonyi], "Emléklap az orosz zsidókért," 1.

93. "Vidéki hírek," *Fővárosi Lapok* 19, no. 287 (1882): 1792; "Kikeresztelkedés," *Fővárosi Lapok* 20, no. 210 (1883): 1342; "Kikeresztelkedett család," *Budapesti Hírlap*, December 23, 1883, 6; "Rövid hírek," *Budapesti Hírlap*, May 27, 1885, 6; "Vidéki hírek," *Fővárosi Lapok* 26, no. 317 (1889): 2352; "Kikeresztelkedés," *Pesti Hírlap*, May 26, 1891, 8; "Szerelmi dráma Komáromban," *Budapesti Hírlap*, August 30, 1891, 4; "Áttérés a zsidó vallásról a katholikusra," *Pesti Hírlap*, March 20, 1893, 5; "Áttért földesúr," *Pesti Hírlap*, November 29, 1893, 8; "Rövid hírek," *Pesti Napló*, August 30, 1895, 2.

94. For a yearly breakdown of the data for the years 1896–1914, see volumes 4–22 of the Central Statistical Office's *Magyar Statisztikai Évkönyv (Hungarian Statistical Yearbook)*; for a table summarizing these numbers, see Zeke, "Statisztikai mellékletek," 194–95.

95. See the annual reports of the ICP's community board, 1898–1914.

96. *Magyar Statisztikai Közlemények*, new series, vol. 36 (Budapest: Pesti Könyvnyomda, 1911), 424–32.

97. László Buday, *A m. kir. központi statisztikai hivatal adatgyűjtéseinek magyarázata* (Budapest: Országos Központi Községi Nyomda, 1901), 1.

98. Don and Magos, "The Demographic Development of Hungarian Jewry," 194; Endelman, "Conversion as a Response to Antisemitism in Modern Jewish History," 64; Viktor Karády, "Felekezeti státusz és iskolázási egyenlőtlenségek," in Miklós Lackó, ed., *A tudománytól a tömegkultúráig: Művelődéstörténeti tanulmányok 1890–1945* (Budapest: MTA Történettudományi Intézete, 1994), 136.

99. Katz, "The Identity of Post-Emancipatory Hungarian Jewry," 26.

100. Silber, "Hungary before 1918," 781.

101. William O. McCagg Jr., "Jewish Conversion in Hungary in Modern Times," in Endelman, *Jewish Apostasy in the Modern World*, 143; Viktor Karády, "'Magyar, zsidó és katolikus': Egy kitérési jegyzőkönyv margójára," *Korunk* 10, no. 7 (1999): 26.

102. See Endelman, "Conversion as a Response to Antisemitism in Modern Jewish History," 62; Michael Anthony Riff, "Assimilation and Conversion in Bohemia: Secession from the Jewish Community in Prague 1868–1917," *Leo Baeck Institute Year Book* 26 (1981): 79; Zeke, "Statisztikai mellékletek," 187, 194.

103. Rozenblit, *The Jews of Vienna, 1867–1914*, 232; Honigmann, "Jewish Conversions—A Measure of Assimilation?" 35.

104. Endelman, "The Social and Political Context of Conversion in Germany and England," 85; Arthur Ruppin, *The Jews of To-Day*, trans. Margery Bentwich (New York: Henry Holt and Company, 1913), 190.

105. Richarz, "Demographic Developments," 16.

106. Peter Honigmann, *Die Austritte aus der Jüdischen Gemeinde Berlin 1873–1941: Statistische Auswertung und historische Interpretation* (Frankfurt am Main: Peter Lang, 1988).

107. Katz, "The Identity of Post-Emancipatory Hungarian Jewry," 20.

108. Ruppin, *The Jews of To-Day*, 153; Kaplan, *The Making of the Jewish Middle Class*, 13, 69; Monika Richarz, "Jewish Women in the Family and Public Sphere," in Meyer, *German-Jewish History in Modern Times*, 3: 82.

109. For a social history of German Jewish orthodoxy, see Mordechai Breuer, *Jüdische Orthodoxie im Deutschen Reich 1871–1918: Die Sozialgeschichte einer religiösen Minderheit* (Frankfurt am Main: Jüdischer Verlag bei Athenäum, 1986); David Ellenson, "German Jewish Orthodoxy: Tradition in the Context of Culture," in *After Emancipation: Jewish Religious Responses to Modernity* (Cincinnati, OH: Hebrew Union College Press, 2004), 237–56.

110. Endelman, *Leaving the Jewish Fold*, 114.

111. Riff, "Assimilation and Conversion in Bohemia," 76, 78. These calculations are mine.

112. Rozenblit, *The Jews of Vienna, 1867–1914*, 132; Gerald Stourzh, "An Apogee of Conversions: Gustav Mahler, Karl Kraus, and fin de siècle Vienna," in *From*

CONVERSIONS, CHRONOLOGICAL PATTERNS, AND REACTIONS 153

Vienna to Chicago and Back: Essays on Intellectual History and Political Thought in Europe and America (Chicago/London: University of Chicago Press, 2007), 226.

113. *Budapest Székesfőváros Statisztikai Évkönyve*, vol. 4, *1899–1901*, 36.

114. Anikó Prepuk, "A területi átrétegződés vizsgálata Pest ortodox zsidó kereskedői között (1873–1895)," *Magyar Történeti Tanulmányok*, 21 (1988): 44; *Budapest Székesfőváros Statisztikai Évkönyve*, vol. 1, *1894*, 283; Frisch, "Az egyházpolitika jegyében," 203–04.

115. *A Pesti izr. hitközség elöljáróságának jelentése az 1901-iki közigazgatási évről* (Budapest: n.p., 1902), 20.

116. Ibid.

117. The disaffiliates' names were published in the *Budai Izraelita Hitközség Értesítője* (*Bulletin of the Israelite Congregation of Buda*) under the heading "Apostates."

118. See pages 21, 27, and 29–30 of annual reports issued by the board of ICP for the years 1912–14.

119. In addition to the Neolog congregations of Buda and Pest, there were two other Neolog congregations in the Hungarian capital (one in Óbuda and one in Kőbánya) as well as two Orthodox congregations (the aforementioned congregation of "Budapest"—meaning Pest—and a tiny congregation encompassing a portion of Óbuda, founded in 1875).

120. Stourzh, "An Apogee of Conversions: Gustav Mahler, Karl Kraus, and fin de siècle Vienna," 243–44; Rozenblit, *The Jews of Vienna, 1867–1914*, 128.

121. Stourzh, "An Apogee of Conversions: Gustav Mahler, Karl Kraus, and fin de siècle Vienna," 244–45.

122. Endelman, "Conversion as a Response to Antisemitism in Modern Jewish History," 73–74; id., *Radical Assimilation in English Jewish History*, 80; id., "Jewish Converts in Nineteenth-Century Warsaw," 51.

123. Honigmann, "Jewish Conversions—A Measure of Assimilation?" 4–5, 29–39.

124. Endelman, "Jewish Converts in Nineteenth-Century Warsaw," 52–53.

125. Peter Pulzer, *The Rise of Political Anti-Semitism in Germany and Austria: Revised Edition* (Cambridge, MA.: Harvard University Press, 1988), 141–42; Ezra Mendelsohn, *The Jews of East Central Europe between the World Wars* (Bloomington: Indiana University Press, 1983), 87–89, 93–94; Robert S. Wistrich, "Dilemmas of Assimilation in Central Europe," in *Between Redemption and Perdition: Modern Antisemitism and Jewish Identity* (London/New York: Routledge, 1990), 89–90; Rolf Fischer, "Anti-Semitism in Hungary 1882–1932," in *Hostages of Modernization: Studies on Modern Antisemitism*, ed. Herbert A. Strauss *1870–1933/39*, vol. 2, *Austria—Hungary—Poland—Russia* (Berlin/New York: Walter de Gruyter, 1993),

863; Hillel J. Kieval, "The Importance of Place: Comparative Aspects of the Ritual Murder Trial in Modern Central Europe," in *Comparing Jewish Societies*, ed. Todd M. Endelman (Ann Arbor: University of Michigan Press, 1997), 146–47.

126. Quoted by Fischer, "Anti-Semitism in Hungary 1882–1932," 863.

127. Gyula Mérei and Ferenc Pölöskei, *Magyarországi pártprogramok 1867–1919* (Budapest: ELTE Eötvös, 2003), 164–66; *Mit akar a néppárt?* (Budapest: Szent Gellért Könyvnyomda, 1895).

128. For calls to repeal the emancipation of Hungary's Jews and thinly veiled threats of a pogrom, see Antal Mócsy, "A zsidó-kérdésről," in *A zsidókérdés Magyarországon*, 9–12; Géza Petrássevich, "A zsidó vérvád," *Alkotmány*, May 7, 1902, 1–2; Ferenc Bonitz, "Az a nép," *Alkotmány*, February 11, 1906, 1–2; "A numerus clausus," *Alkotmány*, January 12, 1907, 1; Miklós Grieger, "A zsidó kolera," *Alkotmány*, October 2, 1910, 5; István Miklóssy, "Zsidóság a külföldön és nálunk," *Alkotmány*, September 17, 1911, 2–3; János Anka, "A zsidók Magyarországon," *Alkotmány*, April 12, 1914, 36–39. For more on the Catholic People's Party, see Dániel Szabó, *A Néppárt 1895–1914* (PhD diss., Budapest: 1983).

129. For more on the size of its membership, see *A Katholikus Népszövetség tíz éve, 1908–1918: A Katholikus Népszövetség elnökségének jelentése* (Budapest: Katholikus Népszövetség Kiadása, 1918), 15. For examples of the Alliance's antisemitism, see Miklós Zboray, "Tanuljunk összetartást," in *A Katholikus Népszövetség naptára 1911-re* (Budapest: Katholikus Népszövetség, 1910), 67–70; *Előadási anyagok gyűjteménye: Katholikus körök, egyesületek és szervezetek vezetőinek használatára*, vol. 1 (Budapest: Katholikus Népszövetség, 1912), 45, 147, 164–66, 168–69; "Népgyűlés Barkóczy mellett," *Budapesti Hírlap*, February 13, 1912, 8; *A katholikusok vagyoni helyzete Magyarországon* (Budapest: Katholikus Népszövetség, [1914]).

130. Szabó, "Középosztály és új konzervativizmus," 185–88.

131. Gunst, *Marczali Henrik*, 155–64; id., "Marczali Henrik (ami az emlékezésekből kimaradt)," in Marczali, *Emlékeim*, 329–35; Szabó, *Az újkonzervativizmus és a jobboldali radikalizmus története (1867–1918)*, 184–209.

132. Miklós Szabó, "Nemesi és polgári liberalizmus," in *Filozófia és kultúra: Írások a modern magyar művelődéstörténet köréből*, ed. Miklós Lackó (Budapest: MTA Történettudományi Intézete, 2001), 135–40. For a discussion of the chief organization of the mercantilist camp, see George Deák, *The Economy and Polity in Early Twentieth Century Hungary: The Role of the National Association of Industrialists* (Boulder, CO: Westview Press, 1990); id., "The Search for an Urban Alliance: The Politics of the National Association of Hungarian Industrialists [GYOSZ] before the First World War," in Silber, *Jews in the Hungarian Economy 1760–1945*, 210–24.

133. András Sipos, *Várospolitika és városigazgatás Budapesten 1890–1914* (Budapest: Budapest Főváros Levéltára, [1996]), 82.

CONVERSIONS, CHRONOLOGICAL PATTERNS, AND REACTIONS   155

134. Návay, *Politikai jegyzetei*, 115, 243.

135. For an expression of this disillusionment, see Béla Vajda, "Szabolcsi Miksa, 1857–1915," in Bánóczi, *Évkönyv 1916*, 211.

136. Spectator, "A függetlenségi párt züllése," *Egyenlőség*, January 13, 1907, 2; "Hozzászólás," *Egyenlőség*, September 13, 1908, 4.

137. Hugó Csergő, "A magyar zsidóság szerepe a századforduló szellemi életében," in *Zsidó írások…5701 szivanra*, comp. Sándor Wasserstrom (Budapest: Wasserstrom Sándor, 1941), 11–13; Géza Boros, *"Folik vagy nem folik?" Egy kupléénekes emlékei* (Budapest: Szerző kiadása, 1942), 80; Práger Miklós emlékei [Memoirs of Miklós Práger]. MZsML, XIX: Hagyaték; Linksz, *Harc a harmadik halállal*, 239; Jacob Katz, *With My Own Eyes: The Autobiography of an Historian* (Hanover, NH/ London: University Press of New England, 1995), 1–2.

138. Jakab Weltner, *Milljók egy miatt: Emlékek* (Budapest: Szerző kiadása, 1927), 24; Zsolt, *Villámcsapás*, 75–78, 130; Andor Endre Gelléri, *Egy önérzet története* (1957) (Budapest: Szépirodalmi, 1966), 140–41, 189–93; Brámer, "Zsidó élet Pesten a század elején," 94; János Hoffmann, *Ködkárpit: Egy zsidó polgár feljegyzései 1940–1944* (Szombathely: Szombathely Megyei Jogú Város, 2001), 40–41.

139. Ligeti, "Emőd Tamás," 59.

140. István Székács-Schönberger, *Egy zsidó polgár gyermekkora: Analitikus háttérrel* (Budapest: Múlt és Jövő, [2007]), 42; Lajos Nagy, *A lázadó ember* (1948) (Budapest: Magvető/Szépirodalmi, 1977), 348–49.

141. Miklós Konrád, "Jewish Perception of Antisemitism in Hungary before World War I," in *Jewish Studies at the Central European University*, vol. 4, 2003–2005, ed. András Kovács and Michael L. Miller (Budapest: Central European University, 2006), 177–90.

142. "A hatodik községkerület gyűlése," *Magyar-Zsidó Szemle* 20, no. 3 (1903): 239–40; "A községkerületi elnökök gyűlése," *Magyar-Zsidó Szemle* 20, no. 3 (1903): 223. In accordance with the regulations adopted at the Jewish Congress of 1868–69 (which, given the withdrawal of Orthodox Jews, applied only to Neolog congregations), Hungary's Jewish congregations were divided into twenty-six community districts. In principle, the National Bureau's tasks were limited to mediation between Neolog communities and the government. Over time, however, it gradually became Neolog Jews' central representative body and the Hungarian government's primary advisor on Jewish religious affairs. See *A magyar és erdélyhoni izraelitáknak 1868–69-dik évi egyetemes gyűlésén alkotott szabályzatok és hozott határozatok* (Pest: Pesti Könyvnyomda, 1869); Nathaniel Katzburg, "Problems of Organization within the Hungarian-Jewish Community during the Inter-War Period," in *Occident and Orient: A Tribute to the Memory of Alexander Scheiber*, ed. Robert Dán (Budapest/Leiden, Netherlands: Akadémiai/E. J. Brill, 1988), 267–68.

143. Molnár, *Az éhes város*, 13.

144. Weszprémy Jr., *A Magyarországi zsidók statisztikája*, 53.

145. Aladár Komlós, "Beszélgetések a zsidókérdésről," *Múlt és Jövő* 16, no. 3 (1926): 94.

146. "Mozgó képek," *Élet*, January 1, 1911, 26.

147. Ferenc Molnár, "A modern: Egy új pesti típus természetrajza," in *Hétágú síp: Tréfák, karcolatok, tárcák* (Budapest: Franklin-Társulat, 1911), 36–37.

148. Illés Adler, "A kitérések," *Egyenlőség*, November 23, 1902, 5; Bernát Singer, "A kitérések, IV," *Egyenlőség*, December 4, 1904, 4; Miksa Szabolcsi, "Meturgeman: A kitérők proskribálása," *Egyenlőség*, December 26, 1909, 4.

149. Miksa Szabolcsi, "Ébredjünk!," *Egyenlőség*, December 8, 1901, 1.

150. M. Kayserling, "Mit kell tennünk," *Egyenlőség*, June 1, 1902, supplement, 1.

151. Miksa Szabolcsi, "Tanulságok a kormány jelentéséből," *Egyenlőség*, November 2, 1902, 3.

152. Szabolcsi, "Hívek egylete," 1; "Társadalmi szemle," *Magyar-Zsidó Szemle* 20, no. 2 (1903): 114; Miksa Szabolcsi, "Téma: Levél egy íróbarátomhoz," *Egyenlőség*, October 2, 1904, 5; Izrael Singer, *Emlék-könyv 50 éves néptanítói és hittanári működésemből* (Sátoraljaújhely: Alexander Vilmos, 1904), 81.

153. Bernát Singer, "A kitérések, I," *Egyenlőség*, November 6, 1904, 3.

154. Bernát Singer, "A kitérések, IX," *Egyenlőség*, January 8, 1905, supplement, 1; Miklós Hajdu, "A lélekvásár," *Egyenlőség*, August 27, 1905, 1.

155. Singer, *Emlék-könyv 50 éves néptanítói és hittanári működésemből*, 81.

156. Miksa Schächter, "Az assimilatióról," in *Évkönyv 1905*, ed. József Bánóczi (Budapest: IMIT, 1905), 274.

157. Alajos Kovács, *A zsidóság térfoglalása Magyarországon* (Budapest: Szerző kiadása, 1922), 16.

158. Ignác Acsády, "Áttérések a múltban," in Bánóczi, *Évkönyv 1905*, 84.

159. Mór Fényes, "Hitoktatás és felekezeti mizériák," *Hitközségi Szemle* 1, no. 2 (1910): 28.

160. *A pesti izr. hitközség elöljáróságának jelentése az 1910-iki közigazgatási évről*, 7.

161. Honigmann, "Jewish Conversions—A Measure of Assimilation?" 26; Endelman, "The Legitimization of the Diaspora Experience in Recent Jewish Historiography," 204–05.

162. "Hitközségi kultuszadó," *Hitközségi Szemle* 2, no. 3 (1911): 144.

163. Secundus [József Patai], "Helvei és elvei," *Múlt és Jövő* 3, no. 4 (1913): 178. Helvey announced his disaffiliation at the congregation's rabbinical office in May of 1910. Kitérési és prozelita jegyzőkönyvek [Records of converts and proselytes]. MZsML, TB. B/67.

CONVERSIONS, CHRONOLOGICAL PATTERNS, AND REACTIONS 157

164. Géza Hegedüs, *Előjátékok egy önéletrajzhoz* (Budapest: Szépirodalmi, 1982), 260, 321.

165. The conversion rate began rising rapidly during WWI. In 1916, 463 Hungarian Jews converted to Christianity; the following year, 677 did so. There is no official data for 1918, but 7,146 Hungarian Jews converted in 1919 and another 1,925 in 1920. See Zeke, "Statisztikai mellékletek," 194. According to the data of the antisemitic statistician Alajos Kovács, 5,655 Jews converted in Budapest in 1919, followed by another 1,260 in 1920, for a two-year total of 6,915 individuals (3,976 men and 2,939 women). Kovács makes no mention of his sources for this information. Kovács, *A zsidóság térfoglalása Magyarországon*, 25.

3

Profiles of Hungarian Jewish Converts

Which socio-professional strata of Hungary's increasingly polarized Jewish society were most affected by conversions over the course of the nineteenth century? Who converted? Where? And to which denominations? With the exception of the turn-of-the-century disaffiliation records kept by the rabbinical office of the Israelite Congregation of Pest (which I will present at the end of this chapter), we have no reliable statistical data on the social status of Hungarian Jewish converts. Baptismal registers might provide us with data of this sort, but my research shows that the clergymen who maintained them were not consistent in recording information like converts' occupations, which they often omitted. Christian clergymen were somewhat more consistent in recording the occupations of converts' fathers. When children were baptized at their parents' behest, the parents' occupations are theoretically useful information. But with the available data, it is impossible to compile reliable occupational statistics even for the parents of baptized children. The most commonly specified parental occupation was *quaestor*, which generally meant livestock and produce dealer or occasionally wholesaler, and while *mercator* should have signified merchant or shopkeeper, Géza Eperjessy's research on fourteen Reform-Era Hungarian cities demonstrates that these designations were used to denote very heterogeneous groups of people.[1] In Hungarian-language registers, the term *kereskedő* (*merchant*) makes it definitely impossible to know whether the individual in question was a poor shopkeeper or a wealthy businessman.

I will begin this chapter by providing an overview of the social status of Hungarian Jewish converts to Christianity—particularly those who belonged

158

to the Jewish economic, political, and cultural elites—in the period from the Reform Era to World War I. I will then examine the gender breakdown and denominational distribution of converts on the basis of official statistics compiled in the period from 1896 to 1914. I will proceed to analyze the annual reports of the Israelite Congregation of Pest and data recorded by the Israelite Congregation of Buda in an attempt to determine the proportion of the overall population of Hungarian Jews who left the fold in Budapest. Finally, I will present a demographic profile of the Jews who disaffiliated in Pest around the turn of the century.

Conversions among the Jewish Elite

The European Enlightenment, the *Haskalah*, and the entry of Jews into Christian societies and cultural circles resulted in changes to the Ashkenazi communities of Central Europe, which manifested themselves in a new demographic profile of Jewish converts. From the early seventeenth to the mid-eighteenth century, converts were generally recruited from among marginal members of Jewish society, but as Jacob Katz noted, more important than the growing number of conversions (beginning in the 1770s) was that "the convert no longer stemmed from the margin of Jewish society, but from its very core. . . . The converts were from two leading groups, the rich and the intellectual."[2] Historians who study conversions among German Jews have arrived at the same conclusion.[3]

Historical studies of the Jews of eighteenth-century Hungary rarely discuss conversions, thus our knowledge of them is limited to a few isolated cases— not enough, in my view, to allow us even to hypothesize about patterns or tendencies.[4] Nevertheless, the rabbi and historian Mózes Richtmann considered the cases sufficient grounds for drawing a conclusion similar to Katz's in a 1912 study: "Before the emancipation, apostasy was disproportionately rare among those who could be reckoned with in terms of intellectual quality; converts came mostly from the lowest stratum of Jewry, from the rabble. This is also suggested by the sparse data on this subject that we find in the history of Hungarian Jewry. . . . What we see at the beginning of the 19th century is the same as what we saw at that century's end: wealthy Jews are the ones who abandon their ancestral faith."[5]

Richtmann's assertions require some clarification; the available information on the Hungarian Jewish converts of the Reform Era indicates that most of them came from one of two strata—many were, in fact, from wealthy merchant circles, and numerous others were intellectuals. In the first half of the nineteenth century, there were 142 Jewish merchants demonstrably involved in the wholesale trade in Pest.[6] Reliable information indicates that 10 of these Jewish wholesalers converted to Christianity by the end of 1848.[7] This is a significant proportion, representing 7 percent of Pest's verifiably Jewish wholesalers, and the actual number who converted in this period was certainly somewhat higher. An even larger proportion of the intelligentsia converted. By the time of the 1848 revolution, a narrow stratum of lay Jewish intellectuals had formed, consisting primarily of journalists and editors. There is definitive and presumably reliable information about the religious preferences of 35 of these Jewish intellectuals; 11 abandoned the Jewish faith by 1849, and another 2 did so somewhat later.[8]

We know even less about poor Jews who converted to Christianity in this period. In Zala County in 1830, in the presence of witnesses, a forty-three-year-old widowed beggar named József Salamon signed an agreement to transfer custody of his two-year-old daughter to Katalin Vargha, "in accordance with whose preference and will she should be raised as her own child in the true Christian Roman Catholic faith."[9] In 1844, the Catholic periodical *Religio és Nevelés* reported the conversions of the eighteen-year-old housemaid Francziska Klein in the village of Nágocs in Somogy County; the journeyman meat cutter Pál Stern in the village of Patak in Nógrád County; and a seventeen-year-old "Jewess" incarcerated in Eger. In 1846, the paper announced the baptism of a goldsmith from Zirc by the name of Propper.[10] Most of the Jews who converted as a result of the activities of the Scottish Mission (established in Pest in 1841) almost certainly belonged to the lower strata of Jewish society as well. The mission proudly and repeatedly alluded to the conversion of wool merchant Izrael Saphir and his family in 1843,[11] but successes of this sort may have been exceptional. As was the case in England, a majority of the Jews who converted at the Scottish Mission in Hungary were poor and thus receptive to the message of missionaries who provided them with free medical care and operated a free school for their children.[12] We do not know the precise number of Jews who were baptized at the Scottish Mission in Pest, as its published data are unreliable—for instance, the mission reported that thirty-one Jews converted to the Reformed faith in Pest in 1843 while the city's Reformed congregation recorded only twenty-three baptisms of Jews that year.[13]

PROFILES OF HUNGARIAN JEWISH CONVERTS   161

In other major Central European cities, such as Warsaw in the first half of the nineteenth century or Vienna between 1782 and 1868, the great majority of Jewish apostates were either of limited means or genuinely impoverished— artisans, apprentices, shopkeepers, day laborers, itinerant peddlers, and servants, as well as their illegitimate children.[14] Despite the different conditions of the Jewish population in the various Central European cities, it is likely that before 1848, poor Jews constituted the majority of converts in Pest, and probably continued to do so until the 1870s or 1880s. As we will see, though, the situation was demonstrably different around the turn of the century.

Jacob Katz estimated that in the Dualist era, conversion was most common among members of the Hungarian Jewish economic and cultural elite, and Michael Silber agreed that these circles suffered significant losses.[15] While Nathaniel Katzburg mentioned in passing that the number of conversions rose particularly "among the upper classes" in late nineteenth-century Hungary, Viktor Karády concluded that university students, licensed professionals, and artists were overrepresented among Hungary's turn-of-the-century Jewish converts.[16]

Somehow everyone has forgotten about the lower classes, even though it is possible that members of these strata formed a majority of the Hungarian Jews baptized in the early decades of the Dualist era. The parents of writer Frigyes Karinthy, members of the petty bourgeoisie, converted to Lutheranism in 1886.[17] Of the seventeen Jews baptized in the Catholic parish of downtown Szeged between 1871 and 1886, four were illegitimate children whose mothers were unlikely to have been members of the middle class. Antal Pollák converted because he promised to marry a Catholic woman whom he had presumably gotten pregnant; Géza Horváth did so to guarantee his appointment as a municipal notary. In 1877, Móric Mayer, safety inspector at a steam mill, joined his common-law wife's Catholic congregation after twenty-three years of cohabitation. In 1880, a police station employee by the name of Samu Pollák became a Christian; in 1883, a widow named Berta Gróf and her companion, a Catholic cobbler, requested their illegitimate child be baptized. Though the Jews who converted to Catholicism in Szeged in this period also included two lawyers, a doctor, a prosperous tenant farmer, a wealthy furniture dealer, and a factory owner (members of the middle and upper classes were thus overrepresented relative to their proportion of Szeged's Jewish population), the majority of the converts could not have been described as socially distinguished.[18]

162 JEWISHNESS AND BEYOND

Of the 136 Jews baptized at Kálvin Square Reformed Church in Budapest in the years 1873–75, 1884–85, and 1894–95, fifty-two married a member of the congregation within a month of converting. Twenty-one shared addresses with their future spouses when they were baptized—an indication they wanted to legitimize relationships that had existed for some time. Given that cohabitation was still inconceivable in middle-class milieux, the foregoing converts probably lived in modest circumstances.[19] In the 1870s and 1880s, people of modest means were the subjects of most marriage notices involving a bride or groom who had converted from Judaism. In 1876, a grocer's daughter from Pápa converted so she could marry a local musician. In 1882, a postal clerk from Nagykanizsa asked for the hand of Ilka Ditrichstein, who was planning to convert to Catholicism. In 1883 in Szenttamás, a village near Esztergom, the chief of police joined the Catholic Church one day and asked the cantor's daughter to marry him the next. In 1884, a set painter from the theater company in Kecskemét became a Catholic in order to wed his beloved. In 1889, an Esztergom County railway official got engaged to Irma Ehrenfeld, another Jewish bride who intended to be baptized.[20] Even though these conversions presumably had little to do with genuine religious conviction, no one involved—from the pastors who performed these baptisms to the journalists who reported on these engagements and marriages—seems to have expressed any moral reservations.

Despite the publication of dozens of announcements of this sort, the Hungarian public of the Dualist era still generally understood "converted Jew" to mean "rich Jew," presumably because the wealthier segments of Jewish society elicited the most interest and because the social visibility of members of the Jewish economic elite increased the significance of their conversions. In an 1883 speech to the upper chamber of the Hungarian parliament, Archbishop of Esztergom János Simor absurdly claimed that "almost every wealthy Israelite family" had converted to Christianity over the course of the previous half century.[21] At some point before 1914, in the notebook where he recorded his ideas for stories, writer Lajos Biró came up with a concise formulation of the cliché of the "natural" path Jewish families followed when they got rich: "Upwardly mobile Jewish family. They convert."[22] By the turn of the century, the figure of the (parvenu) Jew whose baptism was a natural concomitant of his enrichment had become a recurrent element of jokes and anecdotes printed in daily papers as well as songs and sketches performed in music halls.[23]

Neolog intellectuals fully concurred with this widespread public view. As ethnographer Adolf Strausz wrote in 1900, "Let's admit that we've been

PROFILES OF HUNGARIAN JEWISH CONVERTS 163

forsaken by precisely those families whose financial situation and social status could have made them the pride and protectors of Hungarians of the Jewish faith."[24] The only difference from general public opinion was that Jewish newspapers generally categorized Jewish cultural and economic elites together. In November of 1904, Chief Rabbi Bernát Singer of Szabadka complained, "We hear that this person and that person has bowed his head under baptismal water," adding without a shadow of a doubt, "We are losing a substantial proportion of the intellectual and financial aristocracy."[25] The complaints cropped up year after year; in 1912, the *Hitközségi Szemle* expressed certainty that "the process of defection in the upper strata of Jewry continues unabated."[26]

There is no question that the conversion rate among Hungary's Jewish financial elite was significantly higher than that of the country's overall Jewish population in the Dualist era. Even so, whatever contemporaneous observers may have suggested, conversions were far from a general phenomenon among wealthy Hungarian Jews. In 1893, Jews and individuals of Jewish origin owned fourteen of the Hungarian estates larger than 10,000 *hold* (roughly 5,700 hectares); the owners of three of these estates were children of converted parents or fathers. I have not been able to determine the religious affiliation of the owners of another, but of the thirteen owners of the other ten large estates, twelve remained with the Jewish faith, the only exception being the aforementioned Baron Albert Wodianer Sr., who converted in the Reform Era.[27] Historian László Varga noted that of the seven individuals he considered the most distinguished members of the second and third generations of the Jewish upper class, "the great generation of the haute bourgeoisie"—Sándor Hatvany-Deutsch, his cousin József Hatvany-Deutsch, Zsigmond Kornfeld, Adolf Ullmann, Manfréd Weiss, Leó Lánczy, and Henrik Fellner—only the latter two converted.[28] Lánczy did not make this decision himself: according to one of his great-grandchildren, Lánczy's father had him baptized into the Reformed Church when he was born in 1852.[29] Fellner, on the other hand, was still a member of the Hungarian Israelite Handicrafts and Public Education Association at the age of fifty-seven and thus could not have converted before the summer of 1916.[30] A fundamental difference between the Jewish wholesalers and entrepreneurs who emerged during the Reform Era and the Jewish haute bourgeoisie at the turn of the century was that the most prominent members of the former group—Mózes Ullmann, Sámuel Wodianer, Mór Wodianer, Fülöp Koppély, and Manó Kanitz—all abandoned their faith while none of the most distinguished

164 JEWISHNESS AND BEYOND

personalities associated with latter did so (not by 1914, anyway), presumably because members of the turn-of-the-century Jewish financial elite, unlike their predecessors, could pursue their entrepreneurial ambitions without being stopped by their religion. Most members of Budapest's Jewish haute bourgeoisie were included among the 12,822 names on the 1914 membership roll of Pest's Neolog *Chevra Kadisha*.[31]

It is impossible to determine the proportion of Hungary's upper-class Jewish families that converted by 1914. One might justifiably assume that conversion rates were highest within Jewish families that had—on paper, at least—joined the aristocracy by acquiring the title of baron. Between 1874 and 1918, the title was conferred on members of twenty-eight clans that were either Jewish or of Jewish origin. The heads of two of these clans—Adolf Kürschner (an unconverted Jew on whom the title was bestowed in 1910) and Oskar Adolf Rosenberg (a convert to Christianity who acquired the title in 1913)—were citizens of Austria. The founder of another clan, Rudolf Biedermann, who became a baron in 1902, was the child of a converted father and a mother of noble origin. The circumstances of the other twenty-five clans were relatively straightforward in that none of them was denominationally mixed—that is, none of them had both converted and unconverted families. When their members were granted their baronial titles, fifteen of these twenty-five clans were still of the Jewish faith, and the other ten were composed of converted families.[32] According to these figures, converts made up 40 percent of the clans whose members were granted aristocratic titles. But noble and aristocratic titles were conferred on individuals, not clans. Thus, if we consider all these families (all the men who were raised to the rank of baron along with their spouses and legitimate offspring), we see that the proportion of converts was significantly lower. Excluding the two Austrian citizens and the Christian-born Rudolf Biedermann, forty-five men born into the Jewish faith were granted the title of baron, thirty-two of whom were still affiliated with the Jewish religion at the time they received their title, leaving thirteen—or 28.9 percent—who had already converted to Christianity. If we consider only individuals whose fathers or relatives were or had been businessmen—that is, excluding the five men (Lajos Dóczi, Frigyes Korányi, Manó Herczel, Samu Hazai, and József Szterényi) raised to the rank of baron in recognition of their careers in the civil service, medicine, the military, and/ or politics—then the proportion of converts falls to nine out of forty, or 22.5 percent.[33] Regardless of the method we use to calculate this proportion, the majority of these men were of the Jewish faith when they became Hungarian barons. Of course, one could also conclude that even this conversion rate was exceedingly high.

In my estimation, however, conversions among upper-class Jewish families in the Dualist era were significant not only because their conversion rate was many times higher than that of the overall Hungarian Jewish population, but at least as much because there were hardly any such families in which all the members of the second, third, and (sometimes) fourth generations who came of age around the turn of the century still belonged to the Jewish faith. One exception was the Engel de Jánosi family, all of whose members were still affiliated with the Jewish faith in the early 1930s; the first conversions among them took place in the late 1930s and early 1940s.[34] The Neuschlosz family of industrialists and timber merchants was similar: from the early 1800s to 1914, only two of its thirty-three members are known to have abandoned the Jewish faith.[35] However, a great majority of Hungarian Jewish families had more members convert to Christianity. The daughters of the heads of these families were generally the most likely to abandon the Jewish faith and always did so in order to marry a Christian man. Such was the case with the only daughter of Vilmos Ormody, the three daughters of Ferenc Chorin Sr., and the daughters of Ödön Mauthner and József Botfai Hűvös, all of whom converted between 1897 and 1909.[36]

These young women's marriages clearly indicated that even if their parents remained within the Jewish community, their ties to it were fraying. In the interest of context, I should note that the revolutions that shook Hungary at the end of World War I were accompanied by an explosion of antisemitism that triggered an unprecedented wave of conversions, decimating the Jewish upper class. As early as 1917, Baron Marcell Madarassy-Beck and his family were informing the rabbinical office of the ICP of their intention to convert,[37] and Madarassy-Beck's nephew Gyula disaffiliated that same year.[38] The real surge took place in 1919. The many Jews who converted to Catholicism in Budapest that year included Baron Ödön Ullmann de Baranyavár and his wife on March 20;[39] Móricz Domony de Domony and his wife, Baroness Mária Kornfeld (the daughter of the late Zsigmond Kornfeld), on May 2;[40] and Ferenc Chorin Jr. and Baron Lajos Hatvany on May 30.[41] Baron István Ullmann de Baranyavár and his wife became Lutherans on June 1.[42] Baron Lajos Schosberger de Tornya and his wife joined the Catholic Church on August 9.[43] At some point that year, Elza Weiss (the daughter of Manfréd Weiss) adopted the Catholic faith of her husband, Alfréd Mauthner, who had converted before their marriage.[44] Baroness Stefánia Gutmann de Gelse and Belišće also converted to Catholicism in 1919; her husband (and cousin), Baron Arthur Gutmann de Gelse and Belišće, converted the following year.[45] Baron Mór Lipót Herzog de Csete and his wife, Janka Deutsch de Hatvan, converted to Catholicism in Ouchy, Switzerland, on April 13, 1920.[46] The last great wave of conversions was yet to come: between 1938 and 1942, 24,633 Hungarian Jews sought refuge in conversion.[47] According to an early 1938 article in *Egyenlőség*, "almost every" still-Jewish member of the Kohner family appeared en masse at the rabbinical office of the ICP to announce their conversions.[48] In the second (1938) of his three-volume genealogy, Béla Kempelen declared, "The 'more distinguished' Hungarian Jews have—with few exceptions—all already converted to the Christian faith."[49] Kempelen was not exaggerating: by the early 1940s, hardly any scions of the upper-class Jewish families of the Dualist era were still affiliated with the Jewish faith.

Conversion rates among Hungary's Jewish political elite were even higher than among the country's Jewish financial elite. While Christian candidates had almost no shot at winning a seat in Lipótváros, bastion of the Jewish upper class, an affiliation with the Jewish faith could be a serious political handicap elsewhere. An 1881 campaign poster produced in Szombathely featured an asterisk next to the "ambiguous" name of candidate Gyula Schwarcz, followed by a note: "Roman Catholic since birth."[50] In the Dunapataj district of Pest County in 1896, Mihály Földváry's political opponents attempted to discredit him with a campaign song identifying him as a Jew; Földváry, who eventually won the election, responded by circulating leaflets emphasizing that he was the descendant of an old noble family.[51] Presenting an opposing candidate as a Jew was a standard—and often effective—campaign ploy. When Independence Party candidate Lajos Halász (born into the Reformed Church) ran to represent the district of Kölesd in 1910, his opponents claimed he was a Jew. Halász flooded the district with copies of his birth certificate. His opponents responded by dispatching an elderly Jewish woman from Budapest, "Mrs. Fischer" (the German equivalent of Mrs. Halász), to go door to door encouraging the district's residents to vote for "her son."[52] This stratagem may not have been the deciding factor, but Halász was not elected to the legislature in 1910.

While Christianity was an electoral advantage in all but a few of Hungary's legislative districts, not every candidate who converted did so in order to win a seat in the assembly—though there were Jews who did.[53] Most Hungarian parliamentary representatives who converted in this era did so years before their initial election. Of the Hungarian parliamentary representatives elected in the Dualist era, sixty were of the Jewish faith when they were first elected while thirty-five had already converted; another nine had fathers (or parents) who had converted. Discounting the latter, converts made up 36.8 percent of the ninety-five Hungarian parliamentary representatives born into the Jewish faith.[54] Converts were predominant among Jewish-born members of the governing elite: by 1918, eight Hungarians of Jewish origin had served as state secretaries, six of whom were converts (Ede Horn and Lipót Vadász were the exceptions). Of four Hungarian government ministers of Jewish origin, three were converts (only minister of justice and minister without portfolio, Vilmos Vázsonyi, maintained an affiliation with the Jewish faith).[55]

The only group of Hungarian Jews with a conversion rate approaching that of the political elite was the cultural elite, meaning university professors and elected members of the Hungarian Academy of Sciences. I have already discussed the difficulties Jews faced in their efforts to find teaching positions at Hungarian universities, particularly the University of Budapest. In the Dualist era, a total of forty-eight individuals born into the Jewish faith were appointed to full or associate professorships at Hungarian universities. Twenty-six (or 54.2 percent) of these forty-eight professors converted to Christianity by the time they were hired, and twenty-two maintained their affiliation with the Jewish faith.[56] Of the fifty-four individuals of Jewish origin who were elected to the Hungarian Academy of Sciences between 1840 and 1917, forty-one were native Hungarians and thirteen were foreigners. Of the thirteen foreign members, ten were of the Jewish faith and three had converted; of the forty-one Hungarians of Jewish origin who were elected to the Academy, twenty-one had converted and twenty were still of the Jewish faith.[57] Whatever motives may have prompted them to switch religions, converts constituted a slight majority of the Hungarians of Jewish origin elected to the Hungarian Academy of Sciences from 1840 to 1917. Finally, apostasy was extremely common among progressive Jewish intellectuals who entered public life in the early twentieth century and were denied access to institutions of the cultural establishment they opposed anyway. It is an irony of fate that progressive intellectuals roundly condemned Jewish luminaries for their obsequious servility and attempts to "rub shoulders" with the traditional elite yet shared their propensity to convert.[58]

Gender Breakdown, Denominational Preferences, and Geographical Distribution

Though the Central Statistical Office began publishing data on conversions to and from Judaism in 1896, the information was limited to the annual number of Jews in the Kingdom of Hungary (excluding Croatia-Slavonia) who joined the Roman Catholic, Greek Catholic, Lutheran, Reformed, and Unitarian churches (and, starting in 1907, the Baptist Church, which the Hungarian state had officially recognized two years earlier). The only identifying information the Statistical Office provided was a gender breakdown. Between 1896 and 1914, 4,299 of the Hungarian Jews who converted to Christianity were men (50.9 percent), and 4,153 were women (49.1 percent). There was little variation in this distribution over the nineteen-year period. Broken down into the previously discussed intervals, these data show that women made up 48.6 percent of Hungary's Jewish converts from 1896 to 1900; 49.1 percent from 1901 to 1905; 49.5 percent from 1906 to 1910, and 49.2 percent from 1911 to 1914.[59] Unfortunately, we cannot compare this gender distribution to that of other Central European countries because no other government in the region compiled nationwide data of the sort.[60]

The ICP also published statistics on the gender distribution of members who announced an intention to convert. Its annual administrative reports indicate that 56.1 percent of intended disaffiliates were men and 43.9 percent were women between 1896 and 1914. However, the ICP's disaffiliation records (detailed below) show that the proportion of women among its converts was actually somewhat lower. Unlike the statistics published in the ICP's annual reports, limited to converts announcing their intentions in accordance with proper procedure, the congregation's disaffiliation records included everyone who indicated an intention to convert, even if they did so in irregular fashion, such as reporting once instead of twice. Of the ICP's members who announced an intention to disaffiliate in 1897, 1903, and 1907, a total of 40.3 percent were women—42.4 percent in 1897, 36.0 percent in 1903, and 44.0 percent in 1907.[61]

There were proportionally fewer women among the Jewish converts of Pest than among the overall population of Hungarian Jewish converts partly because women made up a smaller percentage of the Jewish population of Budapest than of the Jewish population of Hungary. In 1900, women constituted 47.8 percent of the Jewish population of the capital but 50.3 percent of the Jewish population of the country; in 1910, they made up 48.4 percent of the Jewish population of Budapest and 50.4 percent of the Jewish population nationwide.[62] Another explanation involves intermarriage between Jews and Christians. A woman's legally subordinate position meant a Jewish woman was less likely to withstand the pressure to convert applied by her Christian fiancé (or husband, or his family) than a Jewish man who married a Christian woman.[63] It is possible that the pressure was less intense in the more modern city of Budapest, so Jewish women living in the capital may have been less inclined to convert for a Christian fiancé than Jewish women in provincial Hungary.

The proportion of women among Jews who converted in Pest in the period in question corresponds roughly to the gender distribution recorded in Vienna, Berlin, and Prague. In Vienna, women constituted 43.6 percent of the Jews who converted in 1870; 44.5 percent in 1880; 44.0 percent in 1890; 43.6 percent in 1900, and 50.2 percent in 1910.[64] In Berlin, only a quarter of the Jews who converted between 1873 and 1906 were women, though their proportion rose to 37 percent in 1908 and 40 percent in 1912.[65] In Prague, the gender distribution of Jewish converts fluctuated significantly: women made up 64.9 percent of Jews who converted there from 1868 to 1882, but just 41.3 percent from 1883 to 1892; the figure rose to 50 percent from 1893 to 1897, fell to 36.8 percent from 1898 to 1912, and climbed back 50.2 percent from 1913 to 1917.[66]

Todd Endelman has attributed the generally lower proportion of women among Jewish converts of Central Europe's larger cities to the fact that women were relatively sheltered from the allure of conversion. As long as Jewish women were not motivated or compelled to join the workforce and remained at home as dependent wives, their social lives played out in much more Jewish milieux than their husbands', and thus they were less exposed to the temptations that led men to convert. Endelman concluded that the proportion of women among Jewish converts in Vienna was greater than in Berlin because women of the newer and less prosperous Jewish community of Vienna were more inclined to enter the labor market and thus more exposed to the temptations of conversion.[67] If this were the case, why was the proportion of women among Jewish converts in Pest lower than in Vienna, even though Jews of the former city were poorer than those of the latter? One probable answer is that antisemitism was less intense in Pest than in Vienna. Perhaps more importantly, by 1895, Jewish women in Pest—unlike those in

170 JEWISHNESS AND BEYOND

Vienna—were legally allowed to marry Christian men. Finally, the relatively modest rise in the proportion of women among Jewish converts of Pest (and Hungary in general) between 1896 and 1914 may have been a function of an extremely small increase in the number of wage earners among the country's Jewish women.[68]

In addition to absolute numbers and gender distributions, Hungarian authorities also published statistics on the denominations to which Jews converted. This may also shed some light on the motivation of the converts. The following is a representation of the denominational distribution of Hungary's non-Jewish population in 1900 and 1910:

Table 3.1 Denominations of the non-Jewish Population of Hungary in 1900 and 1910 (Percentage)

Church	1900	1910
Roman Catholic	51.2	51.9
Reformed	15.2	15.0
Eastern Orthodox	13.7	13.5
Greek Catholic	11.5	11.6
Lutheran	7.9	7.5
Unitarian	0.4	0.4
Other	0.1	0.1

The table below shows the denominations to which Hungarian Jewish men and women converted between 1896 and 1914:[69]

Table 3.2 Denominations to which Hungarian Jewish Men and Women Converted, 1896–1914 (Percentage)

Church	Men	Women	Men and Women
Roman Catholic	66.8	68.3	67.5
Reformed	23.2	20.3	21.8
Eastern Orthodox	0.4	1.5	0.9
Greek Catholic	1.5	1.8	1.6
Lutheran	6.9	7.4	7.1
Unitarian	1.1	0.6	0.9
Baptist	0.04	0.02	0.03
Total	100	100	100

The data in these tables indicate that the percentages of Jews who joined the Roman Catholic, Reformed, and Unitarian churches exceeded those denominations' proportions of the overall Hungarian population; the percentage of

PROFILES OF HUNGARIAN JEWISH CONVERTS

Jews who became Lutherans was slightly smaller than the Lutheran proportion of the population of Hungary; and the percentage of Jewish converts joining Eastern Orthodox and Greek Catholic churches was significantly smaller
than those denominations' proportions of the country's population.

Contemporaneous observers, from antisemites to Jewish journalists, were
uniformly convinced that converts chose particular Christian denominations
to advance their interests.[70] As Miksa Szabolcsi wrote in 1903, "Wherever
power, influence, and jobs are in the hands of Protestants, Jews generally
convert to the Protestant faith. . . . Here [in Hungary], a Catholic state, they
tend to promote their interests among the Catholics."[71] Historians have not
contradicted this assertion. According to Viktor Karády, "A convert's desti-
nation was determined primarily by the expected social benefit of switching denominations—the maximum of which was almost always offered by
the majority faith, Catholicism."[72] Nor could it have been a coincidence that
only tiny percentages of Hungarian Jewish converts chose to join the Eastern
Orthodox and Greek Catholic denominations—13.5 and 11.6 percent, respectively, of Hungary's population in 1910—given that these were the churches
with the lowest proportions of middle-class and ethnically Hungarian members.[73] Jewish converts to Protestantism were much more inclined to choose
the Reformed Church over the Lutheran Church, very likely because almost
all members of the former were ethnic Hungarians, as opposed to barely one-
third of the latter's.[74] Finally, it is striking that a large majority of Hungary's
upper-class converts—as indicated by the examples I cited earlier in this
chapter—chose to become Roman Catholics.

Unaffiliated status as formalized by sections 23–30 of Act XLIII of 1895 ("on
the free exercise of religion") was much less attractive to Hungarian Jews than
conversion. While Jewish disaffiliates constituted 7.2 percent of the 117,393
Hungarian citizens who switched religions between 1896 and 1914, they made
up only 1.3 percent of the 31,339 Hungarian citizens who declared themselves
konfessionslos in this period. Of the 8,870 Jews who abandoned Judaism over
the course of this nineteen-year interval, only 4.7 percent—345 men and 73
women—remained unaffiliated.[75] For the vast majority of Jews who abandoned their faith for pragmatic reasons, becoming konfessionslos would have
been an unnecessary risk. As former prime minister Dezső Bánffy wrote in
1903, "The religious-policy laws articulate the possibility of denominational
non-affiliation, but they do not promote it, nor do we promote it, because we
see in it no benefit in terms of religious morality or the national interest. It

could have a certain international—cosmopolitan—complexion."[76] An international, cosmopolitan complexion . . . hardly an attractive characterization for Jews who hoped that abandoning Judaism would increase their chances of success in Hungarian society.

The Central Statistical Office did not publish information on the geographical distribution of converts, though Christian pastoral offices' conversion reports went into minute detail. Since the turn of the twentieth century, when German and Austrian Jewish statisticians—most of them Zionists—published studies on the subject, the notion that Jewish conversion was primarily an urban phenomenon has become a cliché.[77] It is a logical assertion. Urban Jews were more secularized, more upwardly mobile, and thus more inclined to regard their religion as a potential obstacle; they were more likely to get involved in the sort of romantic relationships with Christians that could lead to conversion. Jews who migrated to the city were also less susceptible to the possible retentive force exerted by family members still living in the provinces. However, as Steven Lowenstein demonstrated in a study of German Jews, the assertions are only partially valid. The decisive factor was not so much whether Jews belonged to urban or rural communities but rather the degree to which these communities were rooted in Jewish tradition.[78]

Hungary's 1941 census—conducted after the implementation of the first and second of the country's antisemitic Jewish Laws and thus informed by "racial" logic—corroborates the thesis that urban Jews were overrepresented among the country's converts. However, it also indicates that conversions were concentrated in predominantly Neolog regions and were infrequent in Orthodox-inhabited rural areas and cities with traditionally Orthodox communities. Census participants were obliged to disclose whether any of their parents or grandparents had been born into the Jewish faith. Between 1938 and 1941, Hungary reacquired some of the Slovakian, Subcarpathian, Romanian, and Yugoslavian territories it had lost after World War I. As a result, Hungary's Jewish population rose to 725,007, also gaining 61,548 Christians and unaffiliated Hungarians whom the 1941 census identified as having at least one grandparent of the Jewish faith. The noted antisemitic statistician Alajos Kovács published a study of this census data in which he calculated the percentage of "Christians of Jewish blood" within the "Jewish" population (to ascertain, the total population of Hungarians of the Jewish faith or of Jewish origin) of each of Hungary's cities and counties. The percentage of

"Christians of Jewish blood" (those who had at least one grandparent born into the Jewish faith) was higher in the western and southwestern regions of Hungary where moderate Orthodoxy and Neolog Judaism were predominant, and much lower in the ultra-Orthodox strongholds of the northeastern part of the country. "Christians of Jewish blood" were proportionally most abundant in Pest County (14 percent), the Transdanubian counties of western Hungary, and the southern counties of the Great Hungarian Plain, and lowest in the Subcarpathian administrative districts of Ung, Bereg, and Máramaros in northeastern Hungary (0.2 percent on average). Hungarians of Jewish origin made up 7.8 percent of the country's urban population and 3.7 percent of its extra-urban population. Their proportions were significantly smaller in Orthodox regions. They made up 17.5 percent of the population of Budapest, 15.8 percent of the population of Szeged, and 13.3 percent of the population of Pécs. In the largely Orthodox northeast, they constituted only 4.5 percent of the population of Miskolc, 1.3 percent of the population of Ungvár (Uzhhorod, Ukraine), and 1.2 percent of the population of Szatmárnémeti. A total of 73.8 percent of Hungary's "Christians of Jewish blood" lived in cities, 61.6 percent of them in Budapest.[79]

Kovács's study does not provide data for the cities Hungary lost as a result of the 1920 Treaty of Trianon and did not reacquire between 1938 and 1941. Moreover, its percentages are somewhat misleading. For instance, in 1941, the Hungarian cities with the largest proportions of inhabitants with at least one Jewish-born grandparent were Budapest and Szeged, but the residents of the former included 37,931 "Christians of Jewish blood," while only 781 lived in the latter.

The disaffiliation data published in the annual reports of the Israelite Congregation of Pest and the monthly newsletter of the Israelite Congregation of Buda make it possible to gauge the proportion of the overall population of Hungarian Jewish converts made up by Jews who converted in Budapest. Between 1896 and 1914, 3,737 Jews legally informed the rabbinate of the ICP of their intention to disaffiliate; they accounted for 42.1 percent of the 8,870 Hungarian Jews who converted or declared themselves *konfessionslos* in this period. This percentage is roughly twice as large as the proportion of Hungary's Jews who lived in Budapest in 1900 (20.3 percent) and 1910 (22.3 percent). However, the actual number of Budapest Jews who converted was certainly higher. On the one hand, the ICP had no way to compile data for the several hundred adult Jews who converted without announcing their disaffiliation, nor could it track the similar number of minors between the ages of seven and eighteen who were illegally baptized. National statistics evidently included the former and probably the latter as well. Until 1906, the ICP did not officially record a conversion unless the individual in question reported his intentions to the congregation's rabbinate on two separate occasions. Thereafter, one announcement was enough. Finally, "only" 93.4 percent of the Jewish population of Budapest lived in districts under the ICP's jurisdiction in 1900, and 91.1 percent in 1910. Very few, if any, of the members of the Orthodox communities of Pest and Budaújlak converted to Christianity. Of the other three Neolog congregations in Budapest (Buda, Óbuda, and Kőbánya), only the Israelite Congregation of Buda (ICB) published disaffiliation data, starting only in late 1911. If we add together the 72 Jews who informed the ICB of their intention to disaffiliate between 1912 and 1914, the 693 Jews who told the ICP they intended to leave on two separate occasions in this three-year period, and half of the 89 Jews who made one such announcement to the ICP in this interval, we arrive at a total of 809.5 individuals—49.1 percent of the officially tallied 1,650 Hungarian Jews who converted or declared themselves unaffiliated between 1912 and 1914. If we include the adult Jewish residents of Budapest who converted without disaffiliating and the city's illegally baptized Jewish children, it seems likely that slightly more than half of the Hungarian Jews who abandoned their faith in this three-year period—and in the entire interval from 1896 to 1914—lived in Budapest.

The Disaffiliation Records of the Israelite Congregation of Pest

We have one historical source at our disposal that makes it possible to particularize the socio-professional profile of the Hungarian Jews who converted around the turn of the twentieth century: the disaffiliation records of the Israelite Congregation of Pest—more precisely, contemporaneous copies of some of their records. When section 22 of Act XLIII of 1895 (*"on the free exercise of religion"*) extended the terms of section 3 of Law LIII of 1868 to Hungarians of the Jewish faith, Jews who decided to convert were thereby required to inform their congregations' rabbis of their intentions in the presence of two witnesses on two separate occasions, the second coming at least fourteen but no more than thirty days after the first. Because the law no longer applied to denominational recordkeeping, it could not stipulate what these rabbis were supposed do with such announcements. Nevertheless, rabbis had an interest in keeping track of members who left their ranks. We do not know if smaller Hungarian Jewish communities—whose congregants were much less likely to convert than those of larger communities—kept records of this sort, but the ICP certainly did. The congregation's original disaffiliation records were lost, but in 2010, Zsuzsanna Toronyi, director of the Hungarian Jewish Museum and Archives, discovered contemporaneous copies of some of these records in a trove of documents hidden in the right tower of the Dohány Street Synagogue in Budapest. There were copies of all the reports prepared from 1896 to 1903 and in 1907, and for certain months of the years 1904–06, 1908, 1910, 1911, 1913, and 1917. The database for the present study consists of information from the ICP disaffiliation records dated 1897, 1903, and 1907.[80]

At the end of each month, a list labeled "disaffiliation report copy" was extracted from the ICP's original records, then certified and signed by rabbi Sámuel Kohn or the aforementioned Zsigmond Groszmann. The reports contained the following information: the name of the disaffiliate; his or her occupation, address, and place and date of birth; the names of his or her parents; the dates on which he or she reported an intention to disaffiliate; the denomination to which he or she intended to convert; and the names, addresses, and occupations of his or her witnesses. As I have noted, section 3 of Act LIII of 1868 did not require potential disaffiliates to report any personal data beyond their intention to leave their denomination. Yet in the three years' worth of data I examined for the purposes of this book, only two disaffiliates declined to provide personal information: forty-three-year-old Ármin Havas withheld the names of his parents and witnesses as well as the denomination to which he intended to convert; twenty-six-year-old Andor Holló also refused to identify his future denomination.

The truthfulness of this personal data is an even more important issue. Since disaffiliates were not obliged to authenticate their personal information by presenting the ICP with birth certificates, residency cards, or any other official documents, it is possible that certain individuals submitted inaccurate information by mistake—or intentionally. However, very few disaffiliates would have had reason to submit inaccurate information. Some Jews who planned to convert to Christianity may have told their rabbis that they intended to become *konfessionslos* in order to ease the moral burden of the step they were about to take. The four high school students who told the rabbinical office of the ICP that they were eighteen may have been younger and lied to circumvent the law prohibiting minors from converting. They could thus get themselves listed as Christians on their diplomas, shown to potential employers throughout their careers. Finally, some disaffiliates may have falsified their addresses. They may not have been residents of the districts of Pest under the congregation's jurisdiction (or lived in Budapest at all) but reported their disaffiliation in the capital to keep their coreligionists back home from finding out about their apostasy. Other than those three, I do not see any other reasons why potential disaffiliates might have falsified their personal data.

Regardless of any possible formal irregularities, the rabbinical office of the ICP recorded every disaffiliation on which it received official information, whether from the individual in question or from one of his or her relatives. The reports thus contain the personal data of individuals who did not disaffiliate in accordance with the law—largely Jews who reported their intentions once rather than twice. The ICP did not officially—and could not legally—recognize these individuals as disaffiliates but nevertheless recorded their names. We cannot exclude the possibility that some of these individuals reconsidered, but I have not removed them from the database. There were two male disaffiliates who failed to comply with the requirement that their second announcement take place more than fourteen and fewer than thirty days after the first. Another disaffiliate made his second announcement in a letter; four others reported their intentions to the rabbinate only by mail. I have included all these cases in my calculations. I did omit one individual—forty-seven-year-old pharmacist Adolf Glück, who apparently had difficulty making a decision but ultimately remained within the Jewish fold. On October 11, 1907, Glück announced his disaffiliation in accordance with the law. Three days later, he returned to the rabbinical office of the ICP to inform the congregation that he had decided not to convert. Two days after that, Glück returned again to report that he had changed his mind again, and asked the rabbinical office to reinstate his October 11 disaffiliation announcement. On October 25, he formally reaffirmed his intention to withdraw from the congregation, then on November 1, rescinded his disaffiliation announcements by mail.[81]

The number of individuals the ICP officially recognized as disaffiliates is thus smaller than the number listed in its records. The latter indicate that 125 individuals disaffiliated in 1897 (72 men and 53 women), 264 in 1903 (169 men and 95 women) and 232 in 1907 (130 men and 102 women) for a three-year total

PROFILES OF HUNGARIAN JEWISH CONVERTS 177

of 621 (371 men and 250 women). The last ten disaffiliation announcements in the 1897 report were not recorded on the usual form but on a page listing only the names of these disaffiliates and the denominations to which they intended to convert.

Group conversions. Most Jews who disaffiliated in groups did so with a spouse or other family member(s). The largest categories were siblings in 1897 and married couples in 1903 and 1907. In 1897, 32 (or 25.6 percent); in 1903, 48 (or 18.2 percent); then in 1907, 31 (or 13.4 percent) of the ICP's disaffiliates announced their intentions in groups.

Sometimes friends and acquaintances announced their intentions together. This was clearly the case when two or more disaffiliates made both of their required announcements on the same dates and in the presence of at least some of the same witnesses. There were no such instances in 1897, twelve in 1903, and just one in 1907, when twenty-five-year-old private-sector clerk Aladár Lévai and twenty-four-year-old journalist Jenő Kálmán announced their disaffiliation on the same dates using one another as witnesses.

Disaffiliates' witnesses. The number of individuals who brought relatives to serve as one or both of the witnesses to their announcements increased significantly over the course of the three years in question, from eight in 1897 to nineteen in 1903 and thirty in 1907.[82] Unfortunately, the ICP's records do not disclose these witnesses' denominational affiliations. In a few cases, at least one of the witnesses may have been a disaffiliate's boss or superior, as evidenced by an 1897 case involving the "owner of a laundry" who served as a witness for an "employee of a laundry." In other instances, the witnesses seem to have worked for the disaffiliates, such as the 1903 case where a proofreader served as witness for the owner of a printing house. Private sector clerk Emil Víg and café hostess Júlia Ripp each reported to the rabbinate in the company of two luggage porters, suggesting some disaffiliates simply hired witnesses. Much more often, witnesses had the same occupations as their disaffiliates and were presumably their colleagues. Witnesses frequently lived on the same street or even in the same building as the individual who announced his or her disaffiliation; they may have been acquaintances, future husbands or wives, or simply on hand and willing to do a favor.

Age. As Table 3 makes clear, a significant majority of Pest's turn-of-the-century Jewish converts, regardless of gender or occupation, decided to abandon the Jewish faith as young people.[83]

178 JEWISHNESS AND BEYOND

Table 3.3 Age and Gender of Disaffiliates from the ICP in 1897, 1903, and 1907 (Percentage)

| Age | 1897 | | | | 1903 | | | | 1907 | | | |
| | male | | female | | male | | female | | male | | female | |
	no.	%	no.	%	no.	%	no.	%	no.	%	no.	%
18–19	4	6.0	3	6.1	16	9.4	8	8.4	6	4.7	11	10.9
20–29	35	52.2	32	65.3	98	58.0	52	54.7	75	58.6	57	56.5
30–39	20	29.8	8	16.3	36	21.3	29	30.5	37	28.9	25	24.7
40–49	6	8.9	2	4.1	15	8.9	4	4.2	6	4.7	8	7.9
50–59	1	1.5	3	6.1	2	1.2	2	2.1	4	3.1	0	0
60 +	1	1.5	1	2.1	2	1.2	0	0	0	0	0	0
Total	67	100	49	100	169	100	95	100	128	100	101	100

The average age of the ICP's male disaffiliates was 29.3 years in 1897, 28.2 years in 1903, and 28.3 years in 1907; the average age of its female disaffiliates was 28.7 years, 28.2 years, and 28.0 years, respectively. Thus, the average age of disaffiliates decreased modestly over the period. The gender disparity was not significant. Most striking in these figures is the youth of the ICP's disaffiliates. Of the 609 Jews (with known birthdates) who informed the ICP of their intentions to abandon their faith in 1897, 1903, and 1907, 57.5 percent had yet to reach the age of 30, 82.8 percent were under the age of 40. Jewish converts in other large Central European cities also tended to be young. Michael Anthony Riff's research indicates that the majority of the Jewish men who converted in Prague from 1868 to 1917 were between the ages of 18 and 30.[84] In the period 1873–1906, 42 percent of Berlin's Jewish converts were under the age of 30, and another 31 percent were between 30 and 40.[85] Between 1870 and 1910, 39.9 percent of Vienna's male converts and 47.9 percent of its female converts were in their twenties while 28.5 percent and 26.7 percent, respectively, were in their thirties.[86] The percentage of converts under the age of 40 was thus lower in Berlin and Vienna than it was in Pest.

Whatever the reasons for converting, in most cases the choice was one of the strategic decisions of early adulthood. And while some were motivated by the desire to marry a Christian, the youth of the disaffiliates suggests that many of them converted not under the influence of injuries they had already suffered as a result of their religious affiliation but in the hope of avoiding such indignities in the future.

Occupation. Establishing the disaffiliates' occupations makes it possible to determine their social status. The ICP recorded the occupations of 364 of the 371 men who announced their disaffiliations over the three years in question.

PROFILES OF HUNGARIAN JEWISH CONVERTS

The rabbis who compiled the records did not attempt to divide the jobs into specific categories; they simply wrote down what the individual told them. As a result, we cannot determine whether the designation "clerk" applied to a public sector or private sector employee, for example. We don't know if the listed doctors and engineers worked for the state, for private companies, or as independent professionals. Wherever possible, I have clarified these situations using information in the *Budapesti czim- és lakjegyzék* (*Budapest Directory of Addresses and Residences*). The occupations of the aforementioned 364 men are as follows:

Table 3.4 Occupations of Male Disaffiliates from the ICP in 1897, 1903, and 1907 (Percentages)

Occupation	1897 n=67	1903 n=169	1907 n=128
Director of a Bank or Financial Institution, Industrialist, Entrepreneur	0	3.5	3.9
Man of Independent Means	3.0	3.0	0.8
Intellectual or Licensed Professional	22.4	23.1	32.0
Artist	7.4	4.1	1.6
Civil Servant	11.9	5.9	4.7
Private Sector Clerk	14.9	15.4	14.8
Civil Servant or Private Sector Clerk	4.5	2.4	0.8
Soldier	1.5	0.6	0.8
University or High School Student	4.5	16.0	17.2
Merchant	3.0	4.1	4.7
Junior Public Sector Official or Office Assistant	1.5	2.4	1.6
Support Staff in Artisanal, Industrial, Commercial, and Transportation Ventures (artisan's or merchant's assistant, shop clerk, laborer)	22.4	18.3	14.8
Other	3.0	1.2	2.3
Total	100	100	100

In many cases, it is impossible to determine a disaffiliate's social or financial status on the basis of the occupations listed above. A "merchant" might have been a man of modest means or a very wealthy person while a "director of a bank or financial institution" could have been a modest lender or the head of a huge bank. Similar uncertainties surround the category of "industrialist." Nor is it clear whether a "man of independent means" might have funded a petty bourgeois lifestyle by renting out an apartment or two. The category "artist" encompassed a diverse group of people: established or even famous figures who had achieved middle-class social status, such as sixty-one-year-old opera singer Fülöp Láng or thirty-two-year-old glass painter Miksa Róth; painters whose careers had just begun and whose social status was still uncertain (some would later become well-known, such as twenty-four-year-old painter Dezső Czigány); and finally, musicians and actors whose witnesses were housepainters, typesetters, or servants and were presumably members of the lower-middle class. For state, county, and city officials categorized as "civil servants," we cannot determine whether their salaries made them members of the middle class or the petty bourgeoisie. "Private sector clerk" might have applied to individuals whose salaries put them in the lower tier of the middle class or into the petty bourgeoisie.

Nevertheless, if one takes the men who were unambiguously members of the upper and middle classes—directors of financial institutions, industrialists, and members of the (vocational) intelligentsia, such as doctors, lawyers, engineers, architects, journalists, and high school teachers—and adds to them the individuals whose occupations indicate that they attempted to conform to upper and middle class cultural norms regardless of their financial status (elementary school teachers, civil servants, and private sector clerks), along with those whose cultural capital allowed them to aspire to such status (high school and university students), it becomes clear that a large and growing majority of male converts were at least potential members of the middle classes. Directors of banks and financial institutions, industrialists, entrepreneurs, intellectuals, civil servants, private sector clerks, and high school and university students made up 58.2 percent of all Hungarian Jewish men who converted in 1897, 66.3 percent of male converts in 1903, and 73.4 percent in 1907. As a corrective to compensate for the possibly mistaken inclusion of certain individuals in the middle class (such as elementary school teachers, who belonged there only in a cultural sense), I have omitted artists (some of whom were clearly members of the middle class) and merchants (some of whose witnesses' occupations suggest they were members of this class as well).

In most cases, members of the upper and middle classes were overrepresented among the ICP's Jewish disaffiliates while members of the lower social classes were always underrepresented. None of the men who disaffiliated from the ICP in 1897 was classified as director of a bank or financial institution, industrialist, or entrepreneur, and in 1903 only 3.5 percent of these individuals were included in such upper-class occupational categories. In 1897, the latter were clearly underrepresented, but were the men categorized this way in 1903 actually members of the upper class? For two of the six individuals, we do not have sufficient information to be able to decide. The other four—Pál Elek de Malomszeg, chief executive of the Hungarian Bank and Commerce Company; Zsigmond Hercz, the founder and chief executive of the Hungarian General Coal Mine Company; Lajos Egyedi, a distiller and prominent racing-stable owner; and Gyula Kelemen, managing director of the Domestic Bank—were clearly members of the upper class. Those 4 individuals constituted 2.4 percent of the 169 men who disaffiliated from the ICP in 1903. Social historian Károly Vörös calculated that from 1896 to the outbreak of World War I, Budapest's haute bourgeoisie—its economic elite and the intellectual elite (primarily lawyers) providing it with political representation—amounted to about 500 individuals.[87] If we accept the conservative estimate that Jews made up half of the Hungarian upper class in the period, then the 250 Jews of the haute bourgeoisie represented just 0.3 percent of Budapest's 1910 population of economically active Jewish men (73,058), compared to 2.4 percent of the Jewish men who disaffiliated from the ICP in 1903.[88] Even if we accept the possibly exaggerated estimate that the haut bourgeois Jewish population of Budapest amounted to 400 individuals, members of this class would still have made up a mere 0.5 percent of the economically active Jewish male population of Budapest in 1910.

Clearer evidence that middle- and upper-class individuals were overrepresented among the ICP's disaffiliates is the fact that lawyers, lawyer candidates, doctors, veterinarians, editors, journalists, and engineers made up only 4.9 percent of Budapest's 1910 population of economically active Jewish men, but 21.9 percent of the disaffiliates who announced their intentions to the ICP in 1907.[89] There is no question university students were overrepresented among converts: in the first half of 1907, Budapest's 2,646 Jewish university students constituted 3.4 percent of the city's Jewish males over the age of fifteen and 4.0 percent of its Jewish males over the age of twenty, yet they made up 14.8 percent of male disaffiliates who announced their intentions to the ICP that year.[90] The proportion of high school and university students who converted rose most dramatically in the period between 1897 and 1907, which may help explain the drop in the proportion of civil servants who converted in this period. In 1897, eight civil servants and two law students told the ICP they planned to disaffiliate while six civil servants and ten law students did so ten years later. It is possible that young Jews who aspired to public sector careers were increasingly inclined to "settle" their religious circumstances before beginning their professional lives. The number of teachers who disaffiliated from the ICP went from zero in 1897 and 1903 to seven in 1907, which may reflect a proliferation of the obstacles Jewish candidates faced in their efforts to find jobs or get promoted once they were appointed. It may also reflect dwindling resistance to such impediments.

Private sector clerks made up a significantly smaller proportion of the ICP's disaffiliates (roughly 15 percent in each of the three years in question) than they did of the capital's population of economically active Jewish men (25.4 percent in 1910). Given that private sector clerks tended to work in predominantly Jewish environments where their religious affiliation did not hinder their professional advancement, this is not particularly surprising.[91]

In contrast to individuals who could be categorized as middle class, the proportion of artisans, artisans' and merchants' assistants, shop clerks, and laborers among men who disaffiliated from the ICP shrank from 1897 to 1907. Workers in the foregoing fields constituted 14.8 percent of the ICP's disaffiliates in 1907 but 44.2 percent of Budapest's economically active Jewish men in 1910. Though their share of the converted population rose slowly in this period, merchants—the most traditionally "Jewish" occupation of those listed here—disaffiliated relatively infrequently. Merchants made up 14.8 percent of Budapest's economically active Jewish male population in 1910 but just 4.7 percent of the ICP's male disaffiliates in 1907.

The overall picture painted by this data fits with the established socioprofessional profile of the Jewish converts of turn-of-the-century Vienna, Prague, and Berlin.[92] Compared to their proportion of the overall Jewish male population, members of the upper class and the (vocational) intelligentsia, licensed professionals, and university students—the most secularized and acculturated strata of Jewish society, who in social and professional terms stood to gain the most from conversion—were overrepresented among male disaffiliates from the Jewish faith.

The majority of the 250 women listed in the ICP's disaffiliation reports did not specify an occupation; it is thus more difficult to determine their socioeconomic profile. We only know whether they were single or married when they disaffiliated, with the married category also including a few divorcées and widows. When a wife disaffiliated with her husband or witnessed her husband's disaffiliation, the husband's occupation supplies us with indirect information about her socioeconomic status.

Of the 250 women disaffiliates, 58.8 percent disaffiliated before they were married while 41.2 percent did so after they were married (including a few divorcées and widows). The percentage of married women among the ICP's female disaffiliates rose from 34.8 percent in 1897 to 45.1 percent in 1907. Over the three years in question, 44.8 percent of the ICP's female disaffiliates were either employed or women of independent means. Their proportion of the ICP's female disaffiliates declined in this period, from 54.7 percent in 1897 to 44.2 percent in 1903 and 40.2 percent in 1907. Yet even in the latter year, the percentage of disaffiliating women who were employed or had independent means was nearly double the 21.9 percent of the Jewish female population of Budapest that was economically active in 1910.

The following table lists the occupations of the ICP's female disaffiliates who had independent sources of income in 1897, 1903, and 1907. The overwhelming majority of these women (100 of 112) were unmarried; 5 were married, 4 were widows, and 3 were divorcées. Of these latter 12 individuals, 8 were women of independent means.

Table 3.5 Occupations of Female Disaffiliates from the ICP in 1897, 1903, and 1907 (Percentages)

Occupation	1897 (29 women)	1903 (42 women)	1907 (41 women)
Woman of Independent Means	20.7	26.2	29.3
Intellectual	3.5	2.4	12.2
Governess, Nursery School Teacher		4.8	4.9
Artist, Acrobat	17.2	2.4	7.3
Civil Servant	3.5	–	–
Private Sector Clerk	3.5	4.8	4.9
Civil Servant or Private Sector Clerk	–	–	2.4
University or High School Student	3.5	2.4	4.9
Merchant	–	–	–
Support Staff in Artisanal, Industrial, or Commercial Enterprises; Domestic Servant	48.3	54.8	34.1
Other	–	2.4	–
Total	100	100	100

Though economically active female disaffiliates were more likely to belong to the petty bourgeois and working classes than their male counterparts, the social status of female disaffiliates rose over time, as evidenced by the growing proportion of intellectuals and the declining percentages of industrial

184 JEWISHNESS AND BEYOND

and commercial assistants and domestic servants. As was the case with their male counterparts, female intellectuals were substantially overrepresented among the economically active women who disaffiliated from the ICP. With the exception of Mrs. Mór Fuchs (née Malvin Kohn)—who identified herself as a "writer" when she disaffiliated in 1903—all the female intellectuals listed in the ICP's disaffiliation records in this period were elementary and secondary school teachers; educators thus made up 12.2 percent of the economically active women who disaffiliated from the ICP in 1907 but only 1.2 percent of Budapest's overall population of economically active Jewish women in 1910. Female private sector clerks resembled their male counterparts inasmuch as they were underrepresented among the ICP's economically active female disaffiliates, of whom they constituted 4.9 percent, while private sector clerks made up 17.4 percent of Budapest's economically active Jewish female population. None of the ICP's economically active female disaffiliates in this period were independent merchants, even though that group made up 8.7 percent of the city's economically active Jewish women in 1910. Given that 55.6 percent of Budapest's economically active Jewish women were classified as artisans, domestic servants, or assistants in the industrial, commercial, and transportation sectors in 1910, women who worked in these fields were underrepresented among the ICP's female disaffiliates even in 1903.

The social positions of the thirty-one women who disaffiliated from the ICP in the company of—or in the same year as—their husbands in 1897, 1903, and 1907 differed sharply from those of the ICP's predominantly unmarried, economically active female disaffiliates in this period. Their husbands' occupations indicate that a significant majority of these women belonged to the middle and upper classes; their spouses included the aforementioned Pál Elek, Zsigmond Hercz, and Gyula Kelemen as well as three lawyers, two engineers, the director of a bank, the owner of a printing house, an entrepreneur, an industrialist, a teacher at the Oriental Academy in Vienna, a doctor, a veterinarian, a pharmacist, and a journalist.[93] The social status of the sixteen Jewish women whose husbands served as their witnesses (Christians for the most part, judging by their names) was a step below that of the women cited above but generally higher than that of the ICP's economically active female disaffiliates. The husbands of these sixteen women included three office workers, two pharmacists, an industrialist, a sculptor, an engineer, an architect, a veterinarian, a middle school teacher, a ministerial secretary, a baker's assistant, and a cobbler; two of the husbands' occupations were not recorded.

Disaffiliation and (mixed) marriage. I have yet to address the proportion of Jewish men who might have converted for a Christian wife or fiancée because the ICP's records do not contain any concrete information on this subject. It is a crucial issue, since one might reasonably assume that wanting to marry a Christian was nearly as common a motive for converting as socio-professional advancement. Árpád Welker's research indicates that 23.7 percent of Jews who converted to a Protestant denomination in Pest between 1800 and 1895 got married within a month of being baptized.[94] Welker's analysis did not provide any information about the chronological variation in the proportion of Jews who converted to marry Christians in this period, but one of his earlier studies demonstrates that such conversions became more common in the latter half of the nineteenth century. As I have noted, 52 (38.2 percent) of the 136 Jews who were baptized into the Kálvin Square Reformed Church in Budapest in the years 1873–75, 1884–85, and 1894–95 married a member of the congregation within a month of their conversion.[95]

Once the Hungarian parliament introduced civil marriage in 1895, Jews were no longer legally required to convert in order to marry Christians, but in practice many Jewish brides and grooms were still obliged to do so. The ICP's disaffiliation records for the period do not contain information about converts' motives. I have therefore used purely speculative methods in attempting to estimate the proportion of the ICP's female disaffiliates who left the congregation for a Christian fiancé or husband. First, I assumed that every unmarried, unemployed woman who disaffiliated from the ICP did so for a Christian fiancé. Some unmarried Jewish women probably abandoned their faith for other reasons (to get a job, for instance), but there were also surely employed unmarried women who disaffiliated in order to marry a Christian fiancé, so the two groups might cancel each other out. Second, from the pool of unemployed, dependent wives, I have omitted those whose husbands were obviously Jewish—that is, the twenty-nine women who announced their disaffiliation in the company of their husbands; women whose married names are clear evidence that their husbands were born Jewish; older widows who were wed before the introduction of civil marriage in 1895 and thus must have had Jewish husbands, and clearly could not have disaffiliated to marry a Christian since then; and finally, three women whose husbands were known to be Jewish or Jewish-born. The remaining ninety-five women (forty-nine were dependent wives and forty-six were unemployed singles) made up 24.5 percent of the ICP's disaffiliates in 1897, 38.9 percent in 1903, and 44.1 percent in 1907. Despite this rather spectacular growth, even in 1907 a majority of the ICP's female disaffiliates left the congregation for socio-professional reasons or in the company of their Jewish husbands. Given that women's subordinate positions made them more likely to convert to the Christian faith of a husband or fiancé, it is likely that an even greater majority of the ICP's male disaffiliates left the congregation for reasons other than planned marriage, primarily to further their socio-professional interests.

Magyarization of names. Since a growing proportion of converts could be categorized as middle class, it is not surprising that an increasing percentage of the ICP's disaffiliates had Magyarized surnames between 1897 and 1907. Men with Magyarized surnames made up 38.9 percent of the ICP's male disaffiliates in 1897, 53.8 percent in 1903, and 66.2 percent in 1907. For female disaffiliates, I have limited the calculations to unmarried women, as married women's surnames reflected their husbands' decisions. Women with Magyarized surnames made up 17.7 percent of the ICP's unmarried female disaffiliates in 1897, 19.3 percent in 1903, and 39.3 percent in 1907. However, the ICP's records for the four-month period from February to May of 1910 indicate that the proportions leveled off or dropped back sharply: 66.0 percent of the fifty men and only 23.8 percent of the twenty-one unmarried women who disaffiliated in this period had Magyarized surnames.

Male disaffiliates were more likely to have Magyarized surnames than unmarried female disaffiliates for three probable reasons: first, unmarried women were younger than the average man (including married men) and thus had less time to decide to Magyarize their surnames; second, unmarried women were more likely than men to belong to the petty bourgeoisie and be less inclined to Magyarize their names; and last, but not least, unmarried women intending to marry would not have needed to Magyarize their maiden names as they would no longer have used them once they adopted their husbands' surnames.

Men with Magyarized surnames made up a substantially higher proportion of the ICP's male disaffiliates than of Budapest's Neolog Jewish middle class.[96] Of the 200 members of the representative body of Pest's Neolog *Chevra Kadisha*, which consisted mostly of well-to-do merchants, industrialists, intellectuals, and landlords, the proportion with Magyarized surnames increased from 11 percent in 1899 to 18 percent in 1915.[97] Individuals with Magyarized family names made up 20.7 percent of the 241 men elected to the board of the ICP in December of 1910.[98] The proportion of Budapest's Jewish university students

PROFILES OF HUNGARIAN JEWISH CONVERTS 187

who had Magyarized surnames was even higher, reaching 39 percent in the 1900–01 academic year.[99]

Given that Hungarian Jews Magyarized their names in the hope of reducing the otherness that separated them from the country's Christian majority, it is hardly surprising that in comparison with the Jewish middle class as a whole, the proportion of individuals with Magyarized surnames was higher among Jews who took the ultimate step in attempting to eradicate this otherness and converted. The real surprise may be that so few of the ICP's disaffiliates had Magyarized their names. In 1907, 60.7 percent of the unmarried women and 33.8 percent of the men who disaffiliated from the ICP had names that would immediately have alerted their contemporaries to their Jewish origins. It is possible that some of the male converts Magyarized their surnames after converting to Christianity, and some of these unmarried women may have later adopted their Christian husbands' last names. In any case, though it was increasingly common for Jewish converts to Magyarize their names, thirty-three-year-old dentist Oszkár Kohn, twenty-eight-year-old office worker Hermina Fischel, thirty-three-year-old waiter Mór Herschkovits, eighteen-year-old bookbinder Szerén Schwarz, twenty-nine-year-old postal official Ödön Hirschler, and twenty-seven-year-old day laborer Regina Herschkovits (to mention just a few disaffiliates from 1907) illustrate that a significant number of converts do not seem to have wanted to erase their Jewish otherness.

Conversion affected every segment of Jewish society in turn-of-the-century Pest. Still, there is no question that the ICP's male disaffiliates were increasingly better represented by twenty-four-year-old mining engineer István Kovács than by twenty-five-year-old cobbler Hermann Kohn. And while twenty-three-year-old seamstress Jozefin Kohn and twenty-five-year-old teacher Irma Révész both disaffiliated, unmarried salesgirls, artisans, laborers, and domestic servants constituted a diminishing proportion of the ICP's female disaffiliates. More and more of the group was made up of intellectuals and women who wanted to convert for their (converted) Christian husbands or fiancés. If the majority of the Hungarian Jews who converted to Christianity in the first few decades of the Dualist era were of humble economic standing, conversion had certainly become more common among Budapest's middle-class Jews—and presumably among provincial Hungary's middle-class Jews—by the early years of the twentieth century. By the final years of the Dualist era, a significant proportion of the country's Jewish economic elite

188   JEWISHNESS AND BEYOND

and progressive intelligentsia, an even larger proportion of its Jewish political elite, and a majority of Hungary's Jewish cultural elite had abandoned the
Jewish faith.

How did they come to this decision? Some Hungarian Jews who converted
to Christianity between 1825 and 1914 were brought up in strictly religious settings; others grew up in families that disregarded Jewish religious traditions.
Some were active participants in Jewish religious life before they converted,
and some even served in the vanguard of the struggle for Jewish emancipation
while others exhibited no particular interest in Jewish affairs prior to converting. Some converts apparently abandoned their faith without experienc-
ing any sort of inner conflict while others suffered through lengthy spiritual
struggles before taking this step. In the next chapter, I will attempt to follow
some of the paths individual converts took in hopes of shedding light on the
various predicaments and decisions they faced.

Notes

1. Géza Eperjessy, "Városi kereskedők a reformkorban," in *A polgárosodás
útján: Tanulmányok Magyarország társadalmának átrétegződéséhez a polgári átalakulás korában*, ed. György Szabad (Budapest: Tankönyvkiadó, 1990), 57–67.

2. Katz, *Out of the Ghetto*, 25–26, 122.

3. Mordechai Breuer, "The Early Modern Period," in *German-Jewish History in
Modern Times*, vol. 1, *Tradition and Enlightenment 1600–1780*, ed. Michael A. Meyer
(New York: Columbia University Press, 1996), 123, 160, 250; Hertz, "Seductive
Conversion in Berlin, 1770–1809," 52, 61; id., *How Jews Became Germans*, 35–36, 49.

4. Marczali, "A magyarországi zsidók II. József korában," 353–63; Mózes
Richtmann, *Landau Ezekiel prágai rabbi (1713–1793) és a magyar zsidók* (Budapest:
Athenaeum, 1905), 35–36; Sándor Büchler, "Egy sábáteus vándorrabbi kitérése
Magyarországon," *Magyar-Zsidó Szemle* 24, no. 2 (1907): 127–40; Mózes Richt-
mann, "A régi Magyarország zsidósága," *Magyar-Zsidó Szemle* 29, no. 4 (1912): 311–
17; Raphael Patai, *The Jews of Hungary: History, Culture, Psychology* (Detroit, MI:
Wayne State University Press, 1996), 197–200; Géza Komoróczy, *A zsidók története
Magyarországon*, vol. 1, *A középkortól 1849-ig* (Pozsony: Kalligram, 2012), 641–42.

5. Richtmann, "A régi Magyarország zsidósága," 311, 316.

6. Vera Bácskai, *A vállalkozók előfutárai: Nagykereskedők a reformkori Pesten*
(Budapest: Magvető, 1989), 14.

7. In order of the dates of their conversions, these individuals were Mózes Ullmann, Zsigmond Adelsberg, Mór Wodianer, Bernát Ferenc Weisz, Fülöp Koppély,

PROFILES OF HUNGARIAN JEWISH CONVERTS   189

Sámuel Wodianer, Simon Biedermann, Fülöp Kunewalder, Jónás Kunewalder, and Manó Kanitz.

8. These converts were Móric Gottlieb Saphir, Viktor Móric Kornfeld, Móric Bloch, Károly Beck, Károly Hugó, Zsigmond Hirsch, Frigyes Szarvady, Gyula Lipót Klein, Hermann Klein, Fülöp Korn, Fülöp Hirschfeld, Mór Szegfi, Miksa Falk. This list does not include foreign Jewish intellectuals who lived and worked in Hungary for limited periods, such as Leopold Kompert, Adolf Neustadt, or Isidor Heller.

9. László Németh, ed., *A Zala megyei zsidóság történetének levéltári forrásai, 1716–1849* (Zalaegerszeg, Hungary: Zala Megyei Levéltár, 2002), 77.

10. *Religio és Nevelés*, no. 15 (1st Half 1844): 118; no. 2 (2nd Half 1844): 14; no. 44 (2nd Half 1844): 349; no. 36 (1st Half 1846): 296.

11. Robert Smith, "Personal Narrative of a Ten Years Mission in Hungary," *The Sunday at Home*, December 8, 1866, 772–75; Carlyle, *"Mighty in the Scriptures,"* 15–40; Kovács, *The History of the Free Church of Scotland's Mission to the Jews in Budapest*, 81–86.

12. Endelman, *Radical Assimilation in English Jewish History*, 144–72.

13. Kovács, *The History of the Free Church of Scotland's Mission to the Jews in Budapest*, 84; Welker, "Vegyes házasságok és vallásváltások a Kálvin téri gyülekezetben a 19. században," 152. According to the Reformed pastor Gyula Forgács, between 1841 and 1940, a total of 1,069 Jews converted to the Reformed faith at the Scottish Mission, including 612 in 1919–20 and 131 in 1939. That leaves 316 conversions for the other 97 years, or an annual average of just over 3. See Gyula Forgács, *A százéves skót misszió* (Budapest: Szerző kiadása, 1941), 413.

14. Endelman, "Jewish Converts in Nineteenth-Century Warsaw," 31–33, 36–38; Staudacher, *Jüdische Konvertiten in Wien 1782–1868*, vols. 1–2.

15. Katz, "The Identity of Post-Emancipatory Hungarian Jewry," 26; Silber, "Hungary before 1918," 781.

16. Nathaniel Katzburg, *Hungary and the Jews: Policy and Legislation 1920–1943* (Ramat-Gan, Israel: Bar-Ilan University Press, 1981), 18; Karády, "Zsidó identitás és asszimiláció Magyarországon," 71.

17. Along with their four daughters, Karinthy's parents were baptized at the Deák Square Lutheran Church. They had five more children after their conversion, and thus Frigyes Karinthy's 1887 birth certificate lists him as Lutheran. See Gábor Merényi-Metzger, "Karinthy Frigyes származásának anyakönyvi forrásai," *Irodalomtörténeti Közlemények* 107, no. 4–5 (2003): 535–44.

18. Marjanucz, *A szegedi zsidó családok a 19. században*, 35–37.

19. Welker, "Vegyes házasságok és vallásváltások a Kálvin téri gyülekezetben a 19. században," 155–56.

190 JEWISHNESS AND BEYOND

20. See also R., "Regényes házasság," *Pápai Lapok*, September 23, 1876, 165; "Eljegyzések, esküvők," *Pesti Napló*, January 14, 1882, [5]; "Kikeresztelkedés szerelemből," *Budapesti Hírlap*, November 3, 1883, 6; "Áttért zsidó," *Budapesti Hírlap*, February 16, 1884, 6; "Hymenhir," *Esztergom és Vidéke*, October 27, 1889, [2].

21. *Főrendiházi napló, 1881–1884*, vol. 2 (Budapest: Pesti Könyvnyomda, 1884), 38.

22. Biró Lajos vegyes feljegyzései [Lajos Biró's miscellaneous notes]. Petőfi Irodalmi Múzeum, Kézirattár, I. V. 5586/48/17.

23. See, for instance, [Ferenc Molnár], "Tarka krónika: Társadalmi körök," *Pesti Napló*, February 24, 1905, 12; id., "Tarka krónika: Új állomás," *Pesti Napló*, July 20, 1905, 12; Andor Gábor, "A Zsazsa," in *Erélyes elégia* (Budapest: Szépirodalmi, 1967), 37; Ágnes Alpár, *A fővárosi kabarék műsora 1901–1944* (Budapest: Magyar Színházi Intézet, 1979), 88.

24. Adolf Strausz, "A guvernántok," *Egyenlőség*, February 11, 1900, 6.

25. Singer, "A kitérések, I," 4.

26. Lipót Goldschmied, "A mi jövőnkről," *Hitközségi Szemle* 3, no. 4 (1912): 83.

27. István Lőrintei, *Magyarország nagybirtokosai* (Szatmár: "Szabad Sajtó" Könyvnyomda, 1893), 3–8.

28. Varga, "A hazai nagyburzsoázia történetéből," 86.

29. Károly Halmos, "Lánczy Leó: Hagyomány és nonkonformizmus egy bankvezér történetében," in Sebők, *Sokszínű kapitalizmus*, 182.

30. "A magyar izr. kézmű és közművelési egyesület," *Egyenlőség*, June 24, 1916, 13.

31. *A Pesti Chevra Kadisa választóképes tagjainak névjegyzéke* ([Budapest]: n.p., 1914).

32. Hungarian Jewish families who received Austrian baronies were not included in the calculation. This was the case with the unconverted Philip Schey and his nephew Frederick Schey in 1869, the baptized Mór Wodianer in 1863, and the unconverted Lipót Popper in 1882.

33. The individuals who were still Jewish when they were granted their baronies were Zsigmond Schosberger de Tornya (granted his title on March 12, 1890), Péter Herzog de Csete (January 2, 1904), Ödön Gutmann de Gelse and Belišće (September 16, 1904), Vilmos Gutmann de Gelse and Belišće (September 16, 1904), László Gutmann de Gelse and Belišće (September 16, 1904), Gutmann Aladár de Gelse and Belišće (September 16, 1904), Ármin Groedel de Gyulafalu and Bogdány (September 11, 1905), Bernát Groedel de Gyulafalu and Bogdány (September 11, 1905), Albert Groedel de Gyulafalu and Bogdány (September 11, 1905), László Dirsztay de Dirszta (November 30, 1905), Lajos Schosberger de Tornya (December 11, 1905), Rezső Schosberger de Tornya (December 11, 1905), Béla Dirsztay de Dirszta (May 14, 1910), Nándor Beck de Madaras (April 7, 1906), Sándor Hatvany-Deutsch de Hatvan (October 23, 1908), József Hatvany-Deutsch de Hatvan (October 23, 1908), Károly Hatvany-Deutsch de Hatvan (October 23, 1908), Béla Hatvany-Deutsch

PROFILES OF HUNGARIAN JEWISH CONVERTS

de Hatvan (October 23, 1908), Zsigmond Kornfeld (February 22, 1909), Henrik Ohrenstein de Beočin (November 24, 1910), Miksa Beck de Madaras (February 23, 1911), Adolf Kohner de Szászberek (July 2, 1912), Alfréd Kohner de Szászberek (July 2, 1912), Jenő Kohner de Szászberek (July 2, 1912), Vilmos Kohner de Szászberek (July 2, 1912), Manó Herczel de Pusztapéter (July 15, 1912), Adolf Neumann de Végvár Sr. (September 29, 1913), Adolf Neumann de Végvár Jr. (September 29, 1913), Dániel Neuman de Végvár (September 29, 1913), Adolf Ullmann de Baranyavár (April 6, 1918), Manfréd Weiss de Csepel (September 16, 1918), Tivadar Wolfner de Újpest (September 16, 1918).

The individuals who had already converted to Christianity when they received their baronial titles were Mór Wodianer de Kapriora (April 23, 1874), Albert Wodianer de Kapriora Sr. (December 1, 1886), Frigyes Harkányi de Taktaharkány (October 24, 1895), Károly Harkányi de Taktaharkány (October 24, 1895), Hermann Königswarter de Csabacsüd (March 13, 1897), Henrik Lévay de Kistelek (April 22, 1897), Lajos Dóczy de Németkeresztúr (March 13, 1900), Károly Kuffner de Diószeg (December 7, 1904), Fülöp Orosdy de Orosd (February 15, 1905), István Lévay de Kistelek (August 21, 1905), Frigyes Korányi de Tolcsva (November 21, 1908), Samu Hazai (December 12, 1912), József Szterényi de Brassó (July 7, 1918).

34. Henrik Lenkei, "A jánosi Engel-család," *Múlt és Jövő* 20, no. 2 (1930): 62–68; Kristóf Baiersdorf, "A jánosi Engel családról: Adatok és kérdőjelek, III. rész," *Pécsi Szemle* 12, no. 4 (2009): 72–87.

35. Károly Halmos, "Két építési nagyvállalkozó a századfordulón," in *Gazdaság—Politika—Kultúra: Tanulmányok Kelet-Közép-Európa történetéből*, ed. Sándor Gyimesi (Budapest: Aula, 1992), 51.

36. This information is derived from the disaffiliation records of the ICP and from civil marriage records. Vital records can be examined at the Budapest City Archives or on the website https://familysearch.org.

37. Lajos Szabolcsi, *Két emberöltő: Az Egyenlőség évtizedei (1881–1931): Emlékezések, dokumentumok* (Budapest: MTA Judaisztikai Kutatócsoport, 1993), 209.

38. "Glosszák a hétről," *Egyenlőség*, August 18, 1917, 7.

39. Duplicate of the civil marriage records of the fifth district of Budapest, November 5, 1912. Their conversion was recorded under the heading "subsequent notes/modifications."

40. Duplicate of the civil marriage records of the sixth district of Budapest, March 24, 1903. Their conversion was recorded under the heading "subsequent notes/modifications."

41. Daisy Strasserné Chorin and András D. Bán, *Az Andrássy úttól a Park Avenue-ig: Fejezetek Chorin Ferenc életéből (1879–1964)* (Budapest: Osiris, 1999), 27; Budapest—Neológ (Pesti Izraelita Hitközség) születési anyakönyvei [Budapest—Neolog birth records (of the Israelite Congregation of Pest)]. MNL OL, A3562.

192   JEWISHNESS AND BEYOND

42. Duplicate of the civil marriage records of the fifth district of Budapest, June 22, 1913. Their conversion was recorded under the heading "subsequent notes/modifications."

43. Duplicate of the civil marriage records of the fifth district of Budapest, January 5, 1899. Their conversion was recorded under the heading "subsequent notes/modifications."

44. Duplicate of the civil marriage records of the sixth district of Budapest, July 2, 1906. Her conversion was recorded under the heading "subsequent notes/modifications."

45. Duplicate of the civil marriage records of the second district of Budapest, April 10, 1904. His conversion was recorded under the heading "subsequent notes/modifications."

46. Duplicate of the civil marriage records of the fifth district of Budapest, April 14, 1897. Their conversion was recorded under the heading "subsequent notes/modifications."

47. Zeke, "Statisztikai mellékletek," 195.

48. "A Kohner-bárók kitérése," *Egyenlőség*, January 13, 1938, 5.

49. Kempelen, *Magyar zsidó családok*, 2: 84.

50. "Vidék," *Fővárosi Lapok* 18, no. 138 (1881): 805.

51. Dániel Szabó, "Kortesdalok (avagy a választás, mint a poéták paradicsoma)," in *Polgárosodás Közép-Európában: Tanulmányok Hanák Péter 70. Születésnapjára*, ed. Éva Somogyi (Budapest: MTA Történettudományi Intézet, 1991), 238, 241.

52. "Kölesden," *Az Est*, May 5, 1910, 7.

53. "Zsidóhitű országgyűlési képviselők," *Egyenlőség*, June 5, 1910, 10.

54. William McCagg's book mentions 102 (or 103) "Jewish" members of the Hungarian parliament, which number includes the children of converted parents. However, McCagg does not address the question of these representatives' denominational affiliation—that is, how many of them remained in the Jewish faith. See McCagg Jr., *Jewish Nobles and Geniuses in Modern Hungary*, 129, 185. McCagg's book and the (often mistaken) information in the *Zsidó Lexikon* (*Jewish Lexicon*) led Andrew Janos to the conclusion that "at least" three-quarters of these Hungarian Jewish representatives had converted. See Andrew C. Janos, *The Politics of Backwardness in Hungary, 1825–1945* (Princeton, NJ.: Princeton University Press, 1982), 180.

55. The six converts who served as state secretaries were Károly Csemegi (in office from 1872 to 1879), István Teleszky (1887–93), József Szterényi (1905–10), Elemér Hantos (1917–18), Lajos Beck (1917–18), and Imre Neményi (1917–19). The three converts who served as minister were Samu Hazai (minister of defense from 1910–17), Béla Földes (minister without portfolio responsible for transitional

economic affairs, 1917–18), and József Szterényi (minister of commerce, 1918). They were joined by two ministers of Jewish origin whose fathers had converted: János Teleszky (a state secretary from 1911 to 1912 and minister of finance from 1912 to 1917) and Baron János Harkányi (minister of commerce, 1913–17).

56. Kovács, *Diszkrimináció, emancipáció*, 152–55.

57. R. S. [Rezső Seltmann], "Akadémia tagjai," in Ujvári, *Zsidó Lexikon*, 17–18.

58. For discussions of progressive intellectuals' relationships to their Jewishness, see György Litván, "Szellemi progresszió a századelőn," in *A zsidókérdésről*, ed. Balázs Fűzfa and Gábor Szabó (Szombathely: Németh László Szakkollégium, 1989), 11–27; id., "Zsidók a huszadik századi magyar modernizációban és progresszív mozgalmakban," in *1100 éves együttélés: A magyar és magyarországi zsidóság a haza és a fejlődés szolgálatában*, ed. Péter Püspöki Nagy (Budapest: Magyarországi Holocaust Emlékalapítvány, 2001), 308–16; Mary Gluck, *Georg Lukács and his Generation 1900–1918* (Cambridge, MA/London: Harvard University Press, 1985); Gyurgyák, *A zsidókérdés Magyarországon*, 471–553.

59. See volumes 4–22 of the *Hungarian Statistical Yearbook* (for the years 1896–1914, published from 1897–1916).

60. We do know that more than two-thirds of the German Jews who formally withdrew from the Jewish community while remaining in the Jewish fold between 1873 and 1918 were men. Honigmann, *Die Austritte aus der Jüdischen Gemeinde Berlin 1873–1941*, 134.

61. Kitérési és prozelita jegyzőkönyvek [Records of converts and proselytes]. MZsML, TB. B/67.

62. *A magyar szent korona országainak 1900. évi népszámlálása: A népszámlálási mű VII. kötetének kiegészítő része* (Budapest: Athenaeum, 1906), 9, 85; *Magyar Statisztikai Közlemények*, new series, 56: 313, 429.

63. Viktor Karády, "A felekezetek közötti házasságok általános szociológiája a régi rendszer idején," in *Zsidóság, modernizáció, polgárosodás*, 228–31; Lowenstein, "Jewish Intermarriage and Conversion in Germany and Austria," 31.

64. Rozenblit, *The Jews of Vienna, 1867–1914*, 132.

65. Kaplan, "Tradition and Transition," 18.

66. Riff, "Assimilation and Conversion in Bohemia," 76.

67. Todd M. Endelman, "Gender and Conversion Revisited," in *Gender and Jewish History*, ed. Marion A. Kaplan and Deborah Dash Moore (Bloomington/ Indianapolis: Indiana University Press, 2011), 170–86.

68. Between 1900 and 1910, the number of Hungarian Jewish women employed outside the home increased from 69,331 to 70,018; in Budapest, this number rose from 17,671 to 21,607. *A magyar szent korona országainak 1900. évi népszámlálása*, 5, 9, 85; *Magyar Statisztikai Közlemények*, new series, 56: 313, 429.

69. These numbers are derived from the *Hungarian Statistical Yearbooks* published between 1896 and 1914.

70. For a discussion of antisemites' views, see Egy jogász és egy bölcsész, *Kereszt, zsidó, vallás*, 39.

71. Miksa Szabolcsi, "Meturgeman: Haypál Benő szózatáról," *Egyenlőség*, January 25, 1903, 6.

72. Karády, "Zsidó identitás és asszimiláció Magyarországon," 73.

73. Balogh and Gergely, *Egyházak az újkori Magyarországon 1790–1992*, 163.

74. Ibid.

75. See volumes 4–22 of the *Hungarian Statistical Yearbook* (published from 1897–1916).

76. Dezső Bánffy, *Magyar nemzetiségi politika* (Budapest: Légrády Testvérek, 1903), 167.

77. See Felix A. Theilhaber, *Der Untergang der deutschen Juden: Eine volkswirtschaftliche Studie* (München, Germany: Ernst Reinhardt, 1911), 97, 122–23; Ruppin, *The Jews of To-Day*, 188.

78. Steven M. Lowenstein, "Was Urbanization Harmful to Jewish Tradition and Identity in Germany?" in *People of the City: Jews and Urban Challenge*, ed. Ezra Mendelsohn (New York/Oxford, UK: Oxford University Press, 1999), 80–106.

79. Alajos Dolányi (Kovács), "A keresztény vallású, de zsidó származású népesség a népszámlálás szerint," *Magyar Statisztikai Szemle* 22, no. 4–5 (1944): 95–103, esp. 102–03.

80. Kitérési és prozelita jegyzőkönyvek [Records of converts and proselytes]. MZsML, TB. B/67.

81. *A Pesti Izr. Hitközség elöljáróságának jelentése az 1907-iki közigazgatási évről*, 17.

82. Given that names are not always reliable indicators of family relationships, the number of relatives who served as witnesses may have been somewhat higher. In June of 1906, twenty-two-year-old Zsófia Dénes reported her intention to disaffiliate in the company of her cousin Sándor Ferenczi, who would go on to become a renowned psychoanalyst (and remained unconverted throughout his life). Judit Mészáros, ed., *In memoriam Ferenczi Sándor* (Budapest: Jószöveg Műhely, [2000]), 31–32.

83. Of the 621 disaffiliates in the ICP's records, 12 were listed without dates of birth, thus the age ranges in this table comprise 609 individuals.

84. Riff, "Assimilation and Conversion in Bohemia," 84–85.

85. Endelman, "Conversion as a Response to Antisemitism in Modern Jewish History," 71–72.

86. Rozenblit, *The Jews of Vienna, 1867–1914*, 137.

87. Károly Vörös, "A világváros útján, 1896–1918," in *Budapest története a márciusi forradalomtól az őszirózsás forradalomig*, ed. id., 625.

88. The figure for the economically active Jewish population of Budapest comes from the *Magyar Statisztikai Közlemények*, new series, 56: 429.

89. Ibid., 429–780.

90. The age distribution is derived from data for the year 1910; see *Budapest Székesfőváros Statisztikai és Közigazgatási Évkönyve*, vol. 11, *1909–1912*, tables, 41. The numbers of university students are taken from the *Magyar Statisztikai Évkönyv*, new series, vol. 15, *1907* (Budapest: Athenaeum, 1909), 368, 370.

91. In 1910, Jews made up 56.2 percent of the private sector clerks employed in manufacturing in Budapest and 67.2 percent of the city's private-sector clerks employed in commerce and finance.

92. Ruppin, *The Jews of To-Day*, 190–91; Riff, "Assimilation and Conversion in Bohemia," 83–85; Rozenblit, *The Jews of Vienna 1867–1914*, 135–39; Ivar Oxaal and Walter R. Weitzmann, "The Jews of Pre-1914 Vienna: An Exploration of Basic Sociological Dimensions," *Leo Baeck Institute Year Book* 30 (1985): 416–17.

93. In 1905, after Zsigmond Hercz's death, his wife, Róza (née Freyenfeld), married the finance minister László Lukács (who would serve as prime minister in 1912–13). See "Házasságok és eljegyzés," *Vasárnapi Újság* 52, no. 7 (1905): 108–09.

94. And of course, others might have married Christians elsewhere or later. See Welker, "Zsidó betérések a protestáns felekezetekbe Pesten," 104–05.

95. Welker, "Vegyes házasságok és vallásváltások a Kálvin téri gyülekezetben a 19. században," 155–56.

96. Michael Silber has estimated that the proportion of Hungarian Jews with Magyar family names at the end of the Dualist era did not exceed 5 percent. Silber, "Hungary before 1918," 779.

97. Hajehudi Mardochai [Miksa Szabolcsi], "A zsinagóga, mely legyűrte a templomot," *Egyenlőség*, April 9, 1899, supplement, 3–4; Zsuzsanna Toronyi, "A zsidó asszimiláció a Pesti Chevra Kadisa elöljáróinak társadalmi pozíciói alapján," in *Otthonkeresők, otthonteremtők: Zsidó társadalomtörténeti tanulmányok*, ed. György Gábor, Piroska Hajnal, and Gábor Schweitzer ([Budapest]: Universitas/Judaica Alapítvány, 2001), 92.

98. A Pesti izr. hitközség teljes képviseletének tagjai [Complete membership list of the board of the Israelite Congregation of Pest], 1910. MZsML, PIH, I-C-1.

99. Victor Karady, "Assimilation and Schooling: National and Denominational Minorities in the Universities of Budapest around 1900," in *Hungary and European Civilization*, ed. György Ránki and Attila Pók, eds (Budapest: Akadémiai, 1989), 292.

4

Paths to Conversion—Portraits

In analyses of the causes of conversion, historical scholars will generally present a specific (often famous) individual as an exemplification, an illustration of a particular reason for converting. This method precludes the presentation of individuals whose baptisms cannot be explained unambiguously and frequently results in a one-sided and reductive portrayal of a given individual's generally complex motivations for converting. Finally, and most importantly, this method fails to accord sufficient space to the subjects of the research. In the present chapter, a portrait gallery of Jews who converted to Christianity between the Reform Era and the First World War, flesh-and-blood individuals will take center stage.

Only a fraction of the period's Hungarian Jewish converts to Christianity left behind even minimal information about the circumstances of their conversions or their possible motivation. Information of the sort is limited largely to members of the economic elite and in particular to a few members of the intelligentsia. The question is the degree to which one can use the cases of a few individuals to draw general conclusions about the unknown multitudes of Jewish men and women who abandoned Judaism. The approach is doubly speculative in cases where lack of personal testimony limits our knowledge to major events in individuals' lives, or contemporaries' opinions of their conversions, because we are then forced to rely on conjectures concerning their reasons for getting baptized. At the risk of generalization, one might draw certain conclusions from the stories of individuals who wrote down their views on the situation and future of Jewry, some of whom described their relationship with the Jewish religion and community before and/or after their conversion and, in ideal cases, also discussed the process of conversion itself. One might boldly assume that individuals who pursued similar careers before and after their conversions, or who lived in comparable environments and were baptized around the same time and at the same age, would have converted for many of the same reasons. Could examining the experiences of a wealthy Reform Era entrepreneur or a turn-of-the-century intellectual allow us to draw any reasonable conclusions about the inner motives and life paths that might have led a Reform Era peddler or a turn-of-the-century day laborer to convert?

In any case, the stories of the converts presented below may shed light on certain characteristics of conversion among Hungary's Jewish upper class and Jewish intellectuals, some of whose motives for converting were constant, while other rationales evolved over the course of the nineteenth century. What prompted entrepreneurs, bankers and their descendants, intellectuals, poets, writers, and scholars to register a formal break with their religion and their community? What might have led them to make such a decision? This chapter is an effort to answer those questions. In selecting the converts whose stories are recounted in this chapter, I used one simple criterion: the volume of relevant information I was able to gather. However, since converts rarely discussed their conversions (and even those who did sometimes limited themselves to a few sentences), one is often reduced to speculating about their motives and feelings. Sometimes even that much is impossible; we may have no clues to guide us to an explanation of a given individual's choice to convert. In some cases, that might be what makes their stories interesting. Finally, I should note that the subjects of the sketches presented below are not a representative sample, neither in terms of their socio-professional profiles nor in terms of their gender; they are almost all men.

Hungarian Jewry underwent an enormous transformation between the Reform Era and the First World War. In 1825, Hungary's roughly 185,000 Jews had no political rights and lived mostly in a culturally isolated world of tradition; by the time of the First World War, Hungary had over 900,000 Jews (911,227 according to the 1910 census) who enjoyed legal equality in every respect (on paper, at least). A majority had become largely secularized and Magyarized in language and culture. By the turn of the century, Hungary's Jewish population had developed a considerable degree of social diversity. Of course, Central Europe's traditional Jewish communities were also characterized by social and cultural stratification,[1] though it cannot be compared to the diversification of

Jewish society in the early decades of the twentieth century. As the sociocultural backgrounds and upbringings of Hungarian Jewish converts changed and became more heterogeneous over time, their motivation to convert (while generally characterized by certain constants) was also diversifying. While all periodization is essentially arbitrary, I believe the profiles of these converts justify classifying them into three chronological segments: from the beginning of the Reform Era in 1825 to the emancipation of Hungary's Jews in 1867; the 1880s; and the quarter century preceding the outbreak of the First World War. I have omitted the 1870s because so few Hungarian Jews converted to Christianity in that decade and because we do not have a sufficient volume of reliable information about any of their conversions.

Conversions before the Emancipation of 1867

In discussing Central European Ashkenazi Jews, Jacob Katz wrote that until the late eighteenth century, conversion to Christianity had to be justified theologically by acknowledging Jesus of Nazareth as the messiah, whereas "it is the mark of the new era that the Jewish convert was no longer expected to arrive at the truth of the central tenets of Christianity."[2] Thereafter, the expectations associated with conversion to Christianity became increasingly secular—justifications were based primarily on sociocultural grounds in the age of the Enlightenment and took on an increasingly political-ideological character with the rise of nationalism. The linguist and Protestant theologian **Móric Bloch/Mór Ballagi** (1815–91), who converted to Lutheranism in 1843 and later joined the Reformed Church, was the first baptized Jew whose conversion would be depicted as a sacrifice on the altar of the Hungarian nation.[3]

The most detailed description of Móric Bloch's early years—as well as this nationalistic interpretation of his conversion—can be found in an 1879 portrait written by his son, historian Aladár Ballagi. Born in the Zemplén County village of Inócz (Inovce, Slovakia), Bloch grew up in an impoverished Yiddish-speaking family. When he was six, his tenant-farmer father lost everything in a fire. The elder Bloch then earned a meager living as a *melamed* (private tutor), perpetually wandering with his eight-member family. Bloch learned the fundamentals of the Jewish faith from his father before moving on to study at the yeshiva in Nagyvárad in 1829 and in Pápa in 1831. Bloch then went to work as a tutor in Mór in 1832 and in Surány in the mid-1830s. This was where—in the words of his son Aladár, who never reconciled himself to his Jewish origins—Bloch first came into contact with "decent society." After Surány's parish priest helped familiarize him with the Greek and Latin languages and classics, Bloch enrolled at the Reformed College in Pápa. In 1837, Bloch moved to Pest to study advanced mathematics at the Institutum Geometricum, the predecessor of the Budapest University of Technology and Economics. Meanwhile, he studied the fundamentals of the Hungarian language and published his first articles in the German-language *Pesther Tageblatt* and the Hungarian-language *Hasznos Mulatságok* (*Useful Amusements*). Because the Institutum Geometricum would not issue a diploma to a Jew, Bloch moved to Paris to continue his engineering studies in 1839. It was there that Bloch received József Eötvös's request to participate in the movement to emancipate Hungary's Jews.[4]

In Paris in late February of 1840 (before the issue was debated in the Hungarian national assembly), Bloch wrote a pamphlet demanding that Hungarian Jews be granted equal rights, which immediately made him a leading proponent of—and the most prominent Jewish spokesman for—the emancipation of Hungarian Jewry. His argumentation was largely consistent with the liberal rationales of the era, endorsed by Eötvös as well.[5] According to this reasoning, the (supposed) moral degradation of Jews was a byproduct of their being banned from engaging in "useful" trades, a direct result of their oppression. Emancipation would nourish their sentimental attachment to the Hungarian homeland, which had been smothered by oppression but would naturally flourish in conditions of liberty. Both the public interest and a humane sense of justice demanded equal rights for Jews.[6] Bloch's pamphlet makes it clear that he identified as a Hungarian: "An educated Jew, born and raised in Hungary, speaking the language of his homeland? What else could he consider himself, if not Hungarian?"[7] At the same time, Bloch was also speaking out as a Jew, and as such, he pointedly criticized conversion to Christianity: "Honestly, do you not respect the Jew who is loyal and clings to his faith out of conviction, not abandoning it for some paltry advantage? And do you not despise the miserable creature who—for this year's profits (and trust me, that's mostly how it happens)—switches faiths like changing his coat and converts?"[8]

Bloch returned to Pest in 1840. In order to promote the Magyarization—and thus facilitate the emancipation—of his fellow Jews, Bloch translated the Torah into Hungarian and published it alongside the Hebrew text and a commentary.[9] On September 5, 1840, shortly after the publication of the first

Figure 4.1. Móric Bloch, c. 1860–61. Petőfi Literary Museum, F.4837.

volume, Bloch became the first Jew elected to the Hungarian Academy of Sciences. His election was partly an acknowledgment of his work, but as noted by the members of the academy who recommended his nomination, it was also a symbolic gesture "in consideration of the progress of the age."[10] That same year, Bloch translated *A zsidók* (*The Jews*), a pamphlet by the chief rabbi of Pest, Löw Schwab.[11] In 1841, he wrote his first studies of linguistics while collaborating on the first Hungarian translation of the Jewish prayer book[12] and publishing the Book of Joshua in Hungarian[13]. In 1842, he became the only Jewish member of the Kisfaludy Society, an organization dedicated to the promotion of Hungarian belles-lettres.[14]

Móric Bloch left Hungary again in early April of 1843.[15] On May 28, he converted to Lutheranism in Notzingen, a village near the city of Tübingen in Württemberg.[16] On July 4, he enrolled at the University of Tübigen to study theology.[17] After his conversion, Bloch wrote a letter—which Rabbi Lipót Löw said "could not have been angrier in tone"—calling on the members of the Jewish community of Pest to follow his example.[18] In an article published in the *Allgemeine Zeitung des Judenthums* in the autumn of 1844, Lipót Löw expressed his certainty that Bloch had been driven to convert by a desire to purchase "civil rights." Two years before, Löw noted, Bloch himself—"in the presence of one of the leading statesmen of our homeland"—had characterized Sámuel Wodianer's baptism as "abject cowardice." Löw acknowledged that had Bloch remained affiliated with his faith, his opportunities would have been limited to a teaching position in a Jewish community. However, as Löw reported, shortly after Bloch converted to Christianity, he had been hired to teach at the Lutheran high school in Szarvas.[19] And this much is true: Bloch could not have relished the prospect that, despite his scholarly reputation and fame, he might have to earn his daily bread as a melamed, just as his father had. It is clear that Bloch hoped to win laurels of another kind: by the summer of 1841, he had informed several members of the Danube Regional (Dunamelléki) District of the Reformed Church that he was interested in teaching eastern languages—even on a temporary volunteer basis—at the central Reformed high school to be established in Pest.[20]

As I have mentioned, the ideological interpretation of Bloch's conversion originated with his son. According to Aladár Ballagi, in 1841, his father launched a movement to found a rabbinical seminary with the intention of promoting the Magyarization of Hungarian rabbis. Bloch published several articles on the subject, then launched a donation campaign that Count István

Széchenyi inaugurated with a contribution of 200 forints. Bloch then turned to the "immensely wealthy" Jewish community of Pest, which—instead of the "rightfully expected thousands"—voted to donate only 140 forints. As Aladár Ballagi described his father's reaction, "His castles in the air collapsed; his most beautiful and ardent plans and wishes fell into an ice cellar, and he thought he saw a suddenly heavy, suffocating fog roll in and settle between Jewry and himself, separating them from one another forever. The day that 'Protocolls-Extract' informed him of the community's miserly resolution, he made a firm and final commitment to leave his denomination, the egoism and caste-like isolation of which made them incapable of following—and less and less inclined to follow—his grand, far-reaching plans."[21] According to Aladár Ballagi, his father abandoned the Jewish faith when he realized that his fellow Jews were unwilling to accommodate themselves to Hungarian society.

Because Móric Bloch never discussed his conversion publicly, authors who have considered his case tend to adopt the interpretations of Lipót Löw[22] or, more frequently, that of Aladár Ballagi,[23] or to use them as the foundations of their own evaluations of Bloch's possible motives for converting.[24] However, Aladár Ballagi's explanation of his father's conversion is erroneous. First, the school Móric Bloch proposed to establish in February of 1841 was a Jewish teachers' training institute, not a rabbinical seminary. And the article in which Bloch advocated the establishment of this teachers' training institute—expressing sympathy for Jewish parents reluctant to enroll their children in Christian schools—suggests his commitment to the Jewish faith was still firm. Instilling a "religious mindset" being the primary objective of Jewish education, Bloch wrote, Jewish parents' reluctance was justified, "as experience has taught them that Jewish youths who emerge from the schools of other denominations are usually irreligious, a natural consequence of which is that they are by and large morally corrupt as well."[25] Second, Széchenyi's "one-time" donation in support of the teachers' training institute amounted to 50 forints (not the 200 Ballagi claimed), and thus the Pest Jewish community's proposed contribution of 140 forints per year was by far the most generous offer Bloch received.[26] At the same time, it is clear that Bloch's primary motive for establishing the teachers' training institute was to promote the Magyarization—and thus the eventual emancipation—of his fellow Jews. Bloch was hopeful: "Finally my coreligionists are beginning to see that if they ever want to become citizens of Hungary, they will have to raise their children to be Hungarian, not German or French or English."[27] Given that the Jewish communities of the era were clearly wary of establishing modern primary schools and showed little inclination to learn Hungarian,[28] it is possible that Bloch was genuinely disappointed by his fellow Jews and that this disappointment alienated him from his community.

Finally, we cannot exclude the possibility that Bloch's conversion was motivated at least in part by religious conviction. In February and March of 1842, Bloch paid several visits to the Scottish missionary William Wingate, whose diary indicates that Bloch declared "his faith had found repose in Christ."[29] While Bloch kept his distance from the pietism of the Scottish Mission, his sympathy for liberal Protestantism may have played a role in his decision. After all, he went on to become a theologian, teaching at the Reformed theological academies in Kecskemét (1851–55) and Budapest (from 1855 until his retirement).

While it is difficult to come to an unambiguous understanding of Bloch's motives, the clearly embittered **Jónás Kunewalder** (1804–88) was certainly led to the baptismal font by feelings of despair. A native of Óbuda, Kunewalder and his younger brother Fülöp converted together to Catholicism in 1848. Major produce wholesalers, Jónás and Fülöp were spectacularly successful at integrating themselves into the social life of the city of Pest in the 1840s. They became founding members of the Industrial Association in 1840; in 1844, they joined the National Circle (an organization of liberal intellectuals and political officials founded in 1841); in 1846, they became members of the Art Association of Pest, established seven years earlier to provide support for the fine arts. Jónás Kunewalder also played a role in organizing the National Association for the Establishment of Art Galleries, founded in 1846.[30]

Built in 1838 near the National Museum in Pest, their headquarters were the scene of ornate receptions. The liberal daily *Pesti Hírlap* described a soirée the Kunewalders hosted for the Industrial Association in March of 1844 as an exemplary instance of "social union without regard to difference in rank and religion."[31] Starting in the summer of 1844, the Kunewalders' residence served as the headquarters of the National Circle, a gathering of young liberal intellectuals in Pest. Three years later, the Kunewalder residence would serve as temporary headquarters of the Opposition Circle, an organization associated with Hungary's liberal reform opposition.[32]

Beginning in the latter half of the 1840s, Jónás Kunewalder would become—in the words of Michael Silber—"the unofficial head of Hungary's Jewry." On December 26, 1845, Jónás Kunewalder and silver trader Herman

Figure 4.2. Jónás Kunewalder. Hungarian Jewish Museum and Archives, Budapest, F72.28.

Löwy were chosen as the co-presidents of the Jewish community of Pest; in 1846, Kunewalder was appointed chairman of the national committee supervising the settlement of the unpaid tolerance taxes that King Ferdinand V (Emperor Ferdinand I of Austria) had abolished on June 24, 1846.[33]

Kunewalder first spoke out as a Jew in 1844. This first statement is a striking exemplification of the themes and sentiments that would characterize public pronouncements Kunewalder would make on behalf of Hungary's Jews and in his own name: a defiant affirmation of his Jewishness paired with wounded pride, stemming from his homeland's failure to provide him with civil rights and to distinguish him from the multitudes of destitute Jews whom he himself disdained. When Kunewalder was elected to the board of the Defense Association, an organization set up to protect Hungarian industry, he declined to participate on the following grounds:

> Last year's negotiations, when [the 1843–44 session of the Hungarian Diet] deliberated over the fate of some 240,000 Hungarians who, like me, were decreed by providence to have been born Jewish, and on which occasion wicked and mean-spirited Jews served as the basis of judgement while honorable and unsullied Jews who are steadfastly devoted to their homeland—like me, thousands of whom live in our country—were completely ignored, inflicted deep wounds on my heart. . . . I consider it to be an anomaly of the highest order that, on the one hand, I should be counted among the most wicked, while on the other, I should enjoy the lofty distinction of deliberating the good of the country alongside men we regard as the pride of our homeland.[34]

Kunewalder issued his first major public political declaration as semi-official spokesman for "Hungary's Jewry" in the form of a circular letter dated September 23, 1847. As president of the Israelite community of Pest and head of the executive board of the Israelites of Hungary and Croatia, Kunewalder asked the country's county assemblies and newspapers to support the cause of Jewish emancipation at the next session of the national assembly. Kunewalder was well aware that "antipathy to us is prevalent throughout the country," and indeed, the cause of emancipation was significantly less popular in 1847 than it had been in the early 1840s.[35] Lacking a better alternative, Kunewalder recited the arguments generally adduced in support of the emancipation of Hungary's Jews, emphasizing its advantages for the country.[36]

Kunewalder's circular is distinguished by the bitterness of its tone: "To be Hungarian was our aspiration and our pride, and yet we are constantly warned

that we are not entitled to regard ourselves as such"; this "stiff punishment . . .
brands [Jews'] foreheads with the stigma of disadvantage from the time they
are born." Theoretically, Kunewalder was speaking on behalf of all the country's Jews, yet the lamentations in his circular focused on the fates of members
of his social stratum—and on his own fate in particular: "Will Hungarians of
the Mosaic faith generally aspire to elevation and moral advancement when
the masses can see that even their most noteworthy coreligionists—whose
steadfast patriotism, pure moral lifestyles, and devotion to their countrymen's
language, morals, and customs are beyond dispute—stand on the same civil
and political rung as the lowliest among us?"

This passage seems to call for partial emancipation. While ostensibly
speaking in the name of all the country's Jews, Kunewalder dissociated himself from the bulk of them in articulating his hope that the "noble-souled
Hungarian nation will no longer associate the good with the evil, the worthy
with the unworthy," and thus not drive respectable merchants and industrialists, artists and scholars, artisans and farmers "to despair over the prospect of
improving their fate."[37]

Then came the revolution. The fourth of the "Twelve Points" published on
March 15, 1848 was a demand for "civil and religious equality before the law."
On March 16, Jónás Kunewalder was elected to the Public Courage Committee formed the previous evening.[38] At its meeting on March 17, Kunewalder
said "as the Jewish community [of Pest] is dissolving itself, it will function
only temporarily."[39] That same day, Kunewalder issued another circular letter
in his capacity as the chairman of the committee supervising the settlement
of unpaid tolerance taxes. This letter suggests that his bitterness had been
transformed into euphoric confidence in the future. Selected to the delegation
entrusted with delivering the revolutionaries' twelve demands to the diet in
Pozsony, Kunewalder was certain the time for emancipation had come: "Now
that our homeland has accepted us into its bosom and made us equal with its
other inhabitants, we are simply patriots, simply Hungarians; behold! what
the word of the legislature promised more than half a century ago has now,
thank God, become reality." At that point, Jews' only concern was to take care
"as virtuous patriots [. . .] *to merge into the broader population.*"[40]

On March 18, Kunewalder's delegation took a steamer from Pest to Pozsony, where it presented the Hungarian revolutionaries' twelve-point petition
to the diet. According to a report published in the *Pesti Hírlap,* as Móric Szentkirályi read the petition aloud, representatives "responded to certain of the

points by exclaiming: it is done! and to others with: so be it!"[41] Kunewalder might have concluded the emancipation of Hungary's Jews was a fait accompli. Bitter disappointment awaited him. Under the influence of antisemitic disturbances that broke out in the city on March 18 and continued for several days, on March 21 legislators approved section 6 of Act XXIII of 1848 (*"on the royal free cities"*). Originally designed to accord voting rights to the citizens of free cities "without regard to difference of religion," section 6 ultimately granted suffrage to citizens "without regard to difference of received religion," thus excluding Jews. Revolutionary leader Lajos Kossuth declared, "It pains a person's soul to see the land of freedom expanding everywhere and only the Jewish people excluded from it. But prejudice exists, and according to the poet, even the gods struggle in vain with its blindness."[42]

Kunewalder and his delegation left Pozsony three days after their arrival. The next day, March 22, 1848, Kunewalder (now as a private citizen) published a leaflet addressed "to Hungarians of the Mosaic faith": "given the current state" of things, he said, Hungarian Jews were duty-bound to launch "the most fundamental reforms."[43] Kunewalder offered no details, but according to the *Pesti Hírlap*, his proposed reforms included moving the sabbath to Sunday, a standard element of the repertoires of the radical reform associations that proliferated in the spring and summer of 1848.[44] However, Kunewalder's colleagues in the leadership of Pest's Jewish community did not share their president's radical views, from which they explicitly distanced themselves at a March 26 meeting of the community board—the last session Kunewalder ever attended.[45] On March 31, the diet adopted Act XX of 1848 on the equality of "legally received" religious denominations, which excluded the Jewish religion. Responding to a representative's speculation about what might happen to the Jews, Kossuth reiterated an earlier assertion: "Under the present circumstances, it is precisely the friends of emancipation who should wish that nothing concerning this affair occur at this moment, because at certain times there are obstacles with which even the gods cannot contend."[46] In the words of rabbi and historian Béla Bernstein, "With this, the issue of Jewish legal equality was buried."[47] The funeral officially took place on April 3, 1848, when the Ministerial National Provisional Committee sent Kunewalder a letter informing him, as co-president of the Jewish community of Pest, that Hungary's Jews would have to be satisfied with the rights they had already been granted until the convocation of the next session of the legislature.[48] On April 6, a few days after promising physician József

208   JEWISHNESS AND BEYOND

Bergl of Kaposvár that he would continue to fight to improve the status of Hungarian Jews,[49] Jónás Kunewalder and his family were baptized at Saint Roch parish church in Pest.[50] There is no doubt Kunewalder converted to Christianity in a state of bitterness and despair, though it remains an open question whether these feelings were occasioned by his Christian compatriots—unwilling to grant him and his ilk the equal rights he believed they deserved more than did the broad mass of Jews—or by his coreligionists, who refused to support the radical religious reform he believed necessary for Jews to achieve legal equality.

Among converted members of Hungary's Reform Era Jewish economic elite (wholesalers, entrepreneurs, and bankers), Jónás Kunewalder was atypical: he was the only such individual who repeatedly and publicly expressed his perspective on the present and future of Hungary's Jews, and whose writings demonstrate that his conversion took place in the midst of considerable emotional turmoil. This does not mean other converts' decisions were without emotional friction, but the most prominent Jewish wholesalers who converted in the period (Mózes Ullmann, who became a Catholic in 1825; Mór Wodianer, who did likewise before 1834; and the latter's father, Sámuel Wodianer, who joined the Reformed Church in 1841) clearly experienced much less, if any, emotional turmoil in connection with conversion.

Along with his three brothers, Ábrahám Ullmann—father of **Mózes Ullmann** (1783–1847), founder of the Szitányi family—immigrated to Pozsony from the Bavarian city of Fürth in the late eighteenth century. Ábrahám Ullmann died a wealthy merchant in Pest in 1823—before his son Mózes's conversion.[51] The latter was granted the right to settle in Pest in 1805[52] and acquired his wealth by trading wool, grain, rawhide, and tobacco. Though his entrepreneurial activities are well documented, we know very little about Ullmann's relationship to his Jewishness. Though the Reform Era's most famous businessman became a member of the leadership council of the still officially unrecognized Jewish community of Pest in 1806, this fact reveals nothing about his commitment to the faith, given that he did not seek this post and was not elected by his coreligionists. Until 1833, when the lord-lieutenant approved the bylaws of the Jewish community of Pest, it was not the "Jews of Pest" (*Judaei Pesthienses*) who elected their representatives (*Deputirtes*) but rather city officials who chose among the Jews who had obtained rental rights to operate kosher restaurants and sell kosher wine and meat. The Jews who paid the city the largest rental fees became their community's leaders.[53]

Mózes Ullmann's relations with his fellow merchants who had already acquired the right of tolerance—that is, the other leaders of Pest's Jewish community—did not begin in a spirit of solidarity. In 1802, Mózes Ullmann and his father applied to Pest's city council for the right of tolerance and permission to maintain an open warehouse in the city. Jewish textile merchants who wanted to preserve the local market for themselves pressured the council to reject the Ullmanns' request. The textile merchants' intervention contributed to the council's decision to reject the Ullmanns' application for permanent residence in the city; it took two years of wrangling for the Royal Governor's Council to grant them a residence permit by decree.[54] In 1813, the other leaders of Pest's Jewish community chose Mózes Ullmann to serve as their "primary" leader (de facto executive), largely on the strength of his prominence in commerce.[55] However, Ullmann's relationships with his fellow merchants at the head of Pest's Jewish community were not harmonious even after he settled in the city. On November 13, 1822, a certain Izsák Rosenthal submitted a petition to Pest's city council portraying Mózes Ullmann as a quarrelsome, aggressive man who, despite the dignity of his position, had caused a public scandal by getting into a fight at the local market on St. Medard's Day (June 8) of 1814.[56] As a leader of Pest's Jewish community, Ullmann acquired numerous enemies.[57]

On March 1, 1825, at the age of forty-two, Mózes Ullmann converted to Roman Catholicism in Vienna, taking the Christian name Moritz Johann or Mór János.[58] He and his wife had eleven children; six sons and three daughters reached adulthood. His wife, Frumet (or Szidónia, or Veronika) Hirschl, whom he divorced in 1832, remained Jewish, as did his three daughters. His six sons joined him in converting to Catholicism at the Lipótváros Parish Church eight months after their father, between November 12–15.[59] In a 1921 issue of *Egyenlőség*, the teacher and historian Bernát Mandl attributed Ullmann's conversion to the conflicts within Pest's Jewish community: "At that time, two powerful factions stood in opposition to one another and quarreled with one another for years. . . . The central figures around whom these two factions crystallized were Mózes Ullmann and Izsák Rosenthal (the grandson of the famous Naftali Rosenthal, the childhood friend of Mózes Mendelssohn). The fierce hatred and mutual recrimination between the Montague and Capulet families could not have been greater than it was between the Rosenthal and Ullmann clans. Insinuations, reproach, and accusations went flying back and forth."[60] According to Mandl, when the former notary of the

Jewish community of Pest, Simon Feuchtmann, also turned against Ullmann, the headstrong businessman abandoned the Jewish faith.[61] Zsigmond Groszmann expressed a similar opinion, concluding that Ullmann—a difficult man on bad terms with his fellow Jewish leaders—was prompted to convert when he lost the confidence of his coreligionists.[62] This much is clear: Ullmann resigned from his leadership position within Pest's Jewish community in 1823, two years before he converted to Christianity.[63] On the subject of his Jewish identity, members of Pest's Jewish community submitted a petition to the city council in 1817, criticizing Ullmann's autocratic leadership and claiming that "he belongs to our religion only insofar as he bears the entirely unjustifiable designation 'Jewish.'"[64] We do not know the community members' reasons for judging him in such a way. One might reasonably assume that Ullmann had distanced himself from the Jewish religion and its values years before he converted. Otherwise, it is unlikely that he would have taken Károly Kohlmann (who converted to Roman Catholicism in 1816) into his personal service in 1822. According to Groszmann, Kohlmann was an employee at one of Ullmann's commercial enterprises while according to Béla Kempelen, he served as Ullmann's accountant and tutored his children.[65]

An interesting aspect of Groszmann and Mandl's explanations of Mózes Ullmann's conversion is that they deviate from the usual interpretations of observers like Rabbi Lipót Löw and the journalists of the Jewish press in the 1910s, who attributed such conversions to opportunism. In my opinion, however, William McCagg and Vera Bácskai have offered a more convincing explanation, based on Ullmann's commercial ambitions. Ullmann's conversion made it possible for him and his six sons to acquire a noble title on December 2, 1825. In Hungary's feudal society such a title carried with it significant economic advantages including the right to own property and a blanket exemption from taxation. According to Vera Bácskai, "for Jewish wholesalers . . . ennoblement made it possible for their entrepreneurial activities to develop to their fullest."[66] Ullmann may also have been motivated by the prospect of integration into the traditional elite. In 1832, not long after divorcing his unconverted Jewish wife, Ullmann remarried, this time to a Hungarian woman of noble birth, Borbála Szentiványi, who blessed him with two more daughters.[67] Even more revealingly, though Ullmann founded the Pest Hungarian Commercial Bank (Hungary's first modern bank) in 1841 and remained an active businessman throughout his life, he wanted his sons' futures to be different. In his will, Ullmann forbade them from engaging in any further

Figure 4.3. Mózes Ullmann, 1840s. Painted by Miklós Barabás. Courtesy of Kieselbach Gallery and Auction House

business activities and left five hundred thousand forints with which to purchase an entailed estate to be held in an inalienable family trust, its income destined to provide five young nobles of modest means with an annual sixty forints each to finance their studies.[68]

Among Jewish wholesalers of the Reform Era, Mózes Ullmann's only rivals in wealth and renown were **Sámuel Wodianer** (1785–1850) and his son **Mór** (1810–85), who were granted their noble title on July 4, 1844. The Wodianers converted chiefly to further their commercial ambitions. Sámuel Wodianer's grandfather emigrated from Bohemia to Bács County. In 1789, Wodianer's father moved to Szeged, where he earned his living as a produce merchant. Sámuel began his career at his father's firm and married into a wealthy family of wholesalers in Pest. He served as the president of the Jewish community of Szeged in 1816–17 and 1820–21. Like the Ullmanns, Sámuel earned his fortune transporting government-owned grain and, above all, by purchasing tobacco on government contracts. His operations had outgrown the city of Szeged by the late 1820s, so in 1828 he petitioned Pest's city council for a residency permit, which he received that same year. In 1834, Sámuel was granted the right to engage in wholesale trade. But it seems Pest was too small for him, too; that same year, he asked the city of Vienna for a residency permit and a wholesaler's license. His applications were rejected.[69]

Sámuel Wodianer had become a major player in the Hungarian wool trade by the 1830s, automatically assuming a leading role in Pest's Jewish community and serving as a member of its board starting in 1830. However, he seems to have put his own interests above those of the Jewish community. In 1833, when the community finally approved a new set of bylaws that put an end to the decidedly arbitrary rule of its wealthiest merchants by introducing a multilevel system of representation, Wodianer and six associates lodged a protest with the city council. Despite his opposition to the new system, Wodianer's fellow congregants elected him to serve as a representative (*Wahlmann*) in 1833 and as one of five board members in an 1836 by-election, though he was not among the board members chosen in the regular election held later that year.[70] It is not clear why Wodianer stopped participating. Probably because of the prominent role he played in the country's economy, the members of the national Jewish assembly held in Pest in November of 1839 elected Wodianer to the twelve-member delegation that would submit a petition to the Hungarian national assembly in 1840 calling for the emancipation of Hungarian Jewry.[71]

By that time, Wodianer had personal experience of the limits his religious affiliation imposed on his prospects for social integration. In 1837, Wodianer became the first unconverted Jew to apply for membership at the National Casino.[72] He was certainly aware that the National Casino had rejected Mózes Ullmann's application in 1832, seven years after Ullmann converted to Catholicism. That Wodianer applied anyway is a testament to his self-confidence; his having done so as an unconverted Jew might be taken as a sign of a kind of Jewish self-esteem. Perhaps he believed that his being one of the richest merchants in Hungary entitled him to membership at the National Casino. Along with his commercial ambitions, the casino's rejection presumably played a role in his decision to convert to the Calvinist faith in February of 1841.[73] Later that same year, Wodianer was admitted to the National Casino, becoming its first member of Jewish origin. Four years later, Wodianer was also admitted to the very exclusive Hungarian Jockey Club, founded in 1827. He and his son Albert were the organization's first Jewish-born members.[74]

Sámuel Wodianer clearly subordinated traditional Jewish values to his business interests even while he was still playing a leading role in Pest's Jewish community. After his son Mór converted to Christianity, Samuel continued to engage in joint business activities with him.[75] Mór Wodianer (who moved his business headquarters to Vienna in 1840) achieved even greater professional success than his father, but we have almost no information about his connection to the Jewish community or his own Jewishness. We know only that he and four other members of his family joined the *Chevra Kadisha* of Pest in 1830.[76] We have no evidence that Mór Wodianer played any other role in Jewish public life, and he may not have, given that he converted to Christianity as a young man, probably before he turned twenty-four. The precise date of Mór Wodianer's conversion to Catholicism is not known. William McCagg concluded that it took place in 1830, although this is rather unlikely considering that he joined the Pest Chevra Kadisha in the same year. Vera Bácskai surmised that he converted before 1834.[77] Neither McCagg nor Bácskai cited a source for their dates. Like Mór Ullmann, Mór Wodianer—who was admitted to the National Casino and the Jockey Club in 1852 and was granted the title of baron in Austria in 1863 and in Hungary in 1874—remained a businessman throughout his life.[78] And again like Ullmann, Wodianer used a significant portion of his wealth to establish an entailed estate, a long-term strategy reflecting his desire to integrate his descendants into Hungary's traditional elite. As Vera Bácskai put it, "However talented and profit-oriented Mór Wodianer proved to be over the course of his entrepreneurial life, he used his wealth and success in the service of his children's social advancement. His 1853 will stipulated that his company was to be liquidated after his death. He advised his only son and sole heir Albert (born in 1834) to go into agriculture instead."[79] One might also add that two of Wodianer's three daughters married counts, with the third wedding a "mere" knight.[80]

Among the Jewish intellectuals who converted to Christianity in the three decades following the suppression of the Hungarian Revolution of 1848–49,

Figure 4.4. Mór Wodianer. In *Die Bombe*, February 21, 1875. Wien Museum, W 7207. https://sammlung.wienmuseum.at/en/object/552905-baron-moriz-wodianer.

only the world-famous Orientalist **Ármin Vámbéry** (1832–1913) published a written account of the factors that led him to his decision to convert, in his case, to Calvinism in 1864. In the autobiography he wrote near the end of his life (published in English in 1904 and Hungarian in 1905), Vámbéry—born Hermann Wamberger in the village of Szentgyörgy (Svätý Jur, Slovakia) near Pozsony—said his mother put him on the path toward the non-Jewish world.[81] Ármin's father earned a living as a peddler for a time before dedicating himself almost exclusively to the study of the Talmud. He died in the devastating cholera epidemic of 1832, the year Ármin was born. Widowed at twenty-two, Vámbéry's mother was illiterate but clever and energetic. She soon opened a tavern and by 1836 had married a merchant from Dunaszerdahely (Dunajská Streda, Slovakia). The family then moved to Dunaszerdahely, which had a significant Jewish population, and earned a living selling medicinal leeches. The setting of Vámbéry's childhood was the traditional Jewish world of the *Oberland*, which he called a relic of the "pure and unadulterated Middle Ages." Extremely devout and strictly observant, Vámbéry attended cheder until he was eight, at which point his mother—convinced that "knowledge of the Torah and the Talmud is useful enough as a key to the gates of paradise, but is not really fit for getting by in this world,"—decided to guide her son toward a "secular career" by transferring him to the local Protestant elementary school. In his autobiography, Vámbéry posited a direct causal relationship between his growing detachment from religion and this contact with Christians and secular scholarship:

> As long as I went to Jewish school and believed that any kind of association with the Christian world was damning, no shadow of a doubt could cast itself across my soul. . . . Contact with my Christian schoolmates made my childhood mindset freer and less prejudiced, because we played together and I made friends with them, though I never visited their houses and did not dare touch their food. . . . Nevertheless, the ice had broken. Though I did not dare cross the boundary my upbringing had put between me and the non-Jewish world, I had already begun casting timorous glances at it.

Though he was no longer fully convinced of his faith, when Vámbéry turned thirteen, he celebrated his bar mitzvah with an *aliyah* to the *bimah* for a reading and discussion of his weekly Torah portion. "The entire ritual left me completely cold. My main concerns were making my mother happy and earning the admiration of my listeners; the religious significance of the occasion did not really interest me because by then, my youthful impression of the Orthodox Jewish faith had been obscured by the German books that had made their way into my hands. I was not yet a skeptic, but the violation of ritual commandments no longer filled me with anguish."[82]

After his bar mitzvah, Vámbéry enrolled at the Piarist high school in Szentgyörgy, where he was miserable and hungry and found that the majority of his teachers were antisemites, thus "the Jewish boy of that time could already by his early youth have acquired the most dismal ideas about the kind of future that might await him." Vámbéry studied and read even more, and by the time he was fourteen, as a consequence of his expanding horizons and the failure of most of his teachers to act in accordance with the commandments of Christian love, Vámbéry's alienation from Jewish religious observance had deepened into a general skepticism of all religion. "Complete irreligiousness would not yet have been possible for me, nor could I yet have joined some other denomination of my choice, but many of the rungs on the ladder by which I might have made it to heaven had already been broken or fallen out."[83]

In 1846, Vámbéry left Szentgyörgy to study at the Benedictine gymnasium in Pozsony, where he would complete a sixth and final year at the city's Lutheran gymnasium. The outbreak of the revolution in March of 1848 filled him with enthusiasm. After the Austrian and Russian armies put an end to Hungary's war of independence in 1849, Vámbéry left Pozsony and spent several years wandering the country as a private tutor. During this time, he added to the French and Italian he had learned in high school by teaching himself Latin and a dozen other languages, including Turkish, Arabic, and Persian. With the support József Eötvös, Vámbéry set out on his first trip to the East in 1857. His first publication, a German-Turkish pocket dictionary, appeared in Constantinople the following year; according to Vámbéry, it was the first German-language book ever printed there. In his autobiography, he asked, "Is it not a peculiar coincidence that this [book] was also written by a Hungarian? By that time, I was a Hungarian in name as well—because I did not want a foreign name to appear on its title page, I chose to call myself *Vámbéry*."[84] Though he had been elected a corresponding member of the Hungarian Academy of Sciences, Vámbéry found bitter disappointment upon his return to Hungary:

> In 1862 [actually 1861], when I got back from Constantinople on the
> Danube steamer and first set foot on the soil of the homeland at Mohács, I
> fell to my knees and—crying in genuine rapture—kissed a clump of earth. . . .

But I was soon compelled to the realization that many, indeed, most people do not consider my Hungarian patriotism sincere and in fact disparage and mock it because, as they have said, a Jew cannot be a Hungarian, only a Jew. I countered that in matters of religion, like most educated people, I was actually an agnostic and had thus long since left the Jewish fold. Later, I alluded to the mortal dangers I had faced in the interest of researching Hungary's ancient history, which had undoubtedly put my patriotism to the test in a way that few people in the country have experienced. And I brought up many other reasons, but to no avail.[85]

Having arrived home in the spring of 1861, Vámbéry set out again just a few months later. On this second journey to the East, he became entangled in a religious dispute with a high-ranking Shiite cleric, whereupon Vámbéry declared himself a "sworn enemy" of all positive religion.[86] In May of 1864, he returned to Pest with the same ecstatic joy as in 1861 and experienced the same bitter disappointment: "I will not even try to describe the impression that seeing my dear homeland again engendered in my soul.... More painful to my soul was the sad moment of my entirely unnoticed arrival and the insulting indifference of my compatriots. No one came to visit me; no one took note of me apart from my only loyal supporter, Baron József Eötvös."[87] As a result of Eötvös's intervention, the Hungarian Academy of Sciences agreed to finance Vámbéry's planned trip to London, though the academy's president, Count Emil Dessewffy, would not agree to the loan unless Vámbéry would leave behind the valuable manuscripts he had collected in the East as collateral. "For me, this episode was deeply wounding and insulting.... I ask you now, dear reader: in these circumstances, how could I not have arrived at the thought that all this humiliation and suspicion, all this dreadful misjudgment and the deliberate disregard for my painstaking labor should be attributed exclusively to my obscure origins and the sinister omen of my Jewish ancestors' star."[88]

In late 1864, upon his return from London, Vámbéry was baptized in Pest. The final chapter of Vámbéry's book features an exposition of his thoughts on religion and a theoretical justification for his conversion (more precisely, conversions). In Vámbéry's opinion, religion in the modern world was hypocrisy; a modern man was not—and could not be—religious. Religion did not elevate humanity in the least but rather raised irrational barriers between people. As an obstacle to the peaceful coexistence and enlightenment of humanity, it was to be eliminated. This task would have to wait for the twentieth century. In

Figure 4.5. Ármin Vámbéry, 1865. Petőfi Literary Museum, F.7736.

Vámbéry's own lifetime, his "confession of faith" functioned as an apologia for opportunistic conversion:

> When the circumstances have required it to be so, I have, as a matter of form—first, out of respect for the laws of the land, and second, as a courtesy to the society in whose circle I belonged—always adapted to the predominant religion of the country in question. . . . In matters of subordinate significance, such as religion, I have always adhered strictly to the principle *Si fueris Romae, Romano vivito more,* and if perchance the religious moralists were to reproach me for changing my religion with such ease, my response to them would sound like this: "The reason for switching religions lies primarily in an absence of religion, and he who has nothing cannot exchange anything." This is the case with most denominational changes. There is nothing in the world more abominable than the holy indignation with which hypocrisy—now conventional throughout Europe—condemns and stigmatizes conversion without conviction.[89]

This pragmatic, unemotional view of conversion contradicts the previously cited passages of his autobiography that suggest he was driven to convert by the painful experience of exclusion and by a desire to be recognized as a Hungarian scholar. This account also fictionalizes the circumstances of his baptism. On July 21, 1865, Vámbéry was hired as a lecturer by the department of eastern languages at the Royal University of Pest.[90] Since Hungarian Jews had not yet been emancipated, this position could be filled only by a Christian. According to Vámbéry's professed principle ("when in Rome, do as the Romans do"), he should have converted to Catholicism; his potential employer was a historically Catholic university staffed, with few exceptions, by Catholic instructors. On December 30, 1864, Vámbéry instead converted to Protestantism, which his contemporaries considered "inherently liberal and national" in spirit,[91] and specifically to the Reformed faith, regarded as the most Hungarian denomination.[92] Vámbéry's autobiography does not discuss the causes and circumstances of his baptism nor even its date. His narration of this episode at the Royal University features only a cursory reference to his conversion, which he mentions as a fait accompli: "The first complaints came from the Catholic Church because I'd become a Protestant, not a Catholic. As if an uncompromising free-thinker like me would have concerned himself with sectarianism of any kind."[93] But if his religious affiliation really did not matter to him, why not choose Catholicism?

Vámbéry's autobiography, *The Story of My Struggles*, is the only work published under his own name during his lifetime in which he articulated his opinions on the subject of conversion. His first memoir (published in English in 1884 and never translated into Hungarian) does not even mention his Jewish origins.[94] Four months after Vámbéry's death in September of 1913, the bourgeois radical *Huszadik Század* published a text it claimed he had written in German in the early 1880s. The narrator of this meditation, patterned after Montesquieu's *Persian Letters*, is a Tatar describing his travels through Europe for his compatriots back East. In the opening subchapter, entitled *A zsidóság (Jewry)*, the narrator stresses that his opinions concerning the "Jewish question that has become important in Eastern Europe" are perfectly impartial, since he is neither Jewish nor Christian, "neither Semite nor Aryan," and thus is able to examine this issue with "complete objectivity."[95] Like others who wrote in defense of Jews in the period, Vámbéry attributed the antisemitism of Christian society to the "envy and jealousy" aroused by Jews' economic success. Vámbéry's solution to antisemitism, however, diverged from conventional liberal perspectives. The "remedy for the problem" was for Jews who were "neither internally nor in their outward appearance" attached to the faith of their forebears to cross over from "Jewish irreligiousness to Christian irreligiousness." The masses of religious Jews, said Vámbéry, should remain Jewish. "However, unbelieving Jews, as a minority, would do better to associate with unbelieving Christians, for if both could fit their pathetic nothings into a shared satchel, I see no reason why they would start a fight and wrestle each other over such a nothingness."[96]

In 1882, around the time Vámbéry wrote his German-language Tatar travelogue, an anonymous "liberal"—who, as previously noted, was identified by the weekly *Somogy* as a law student from Kaposvár named Gyula Fekete—published a pamphlet in Budapest. Unaware that *Somogy* had attributed its authorship to Fekete, the literary historian Aladár Komlós assumed Vámbéry had written it, as the latter was the only person "among Hungary's leading Jews at that time" whose thinking resembled the ideas in the pamphlet.[97] One thing is certain: Fekete never published anything under his own name. And the reasoning in this pamphlet certainly suggests that Vámbéry was its author. According to this "liberal," the advance of science inevitably estranges educated people from organized religion. If they remain affiliated with the religion into which they were born, irreligious Jews are just as hypocritical as those who declare themselves believers in another faith. The act of conversion means nothing to an irreligious Jew; he who has no religion cannot betray his faith—"only the name changes." Under ideal circumstances (if people would be judged "without regard to their religion"), nominal affiliation would not matter. Yet "prejudice exists and must be taken into account." "Uneducated" (i.e., religious) Jews should adhere to their faith, because in their case conversion would be a lie; however, members of the "Jewish middle class" should convert, preferably to the Reformed faith, which "does not promise outer splendor or rank." Choosing it "is a sign that the motive that spurred the will to act was noble." Only as members of the Reformed Church could educated Jews fight effectively against the prejudices afflicting the masses of religious Jews while also struggling for the creation of a world "in which there is no religion no sectarian prejudice." The conversion of the Jewish middle class was ultimately "in the political interest of Hungarian society" because "its members would become a homogenous element of society," and thus "the vital forces that would have been lost in friction . . . will be saved for the common good."[98] Such were the altruistic grounds for conversion. But what did the Jewish middle class have to gain from it? Recognition as Hungarians—which, as Vámbéry noted, they could *force into being*, if not by any other means then by converting: "We will be Hungarians, and all the more gladly if you wish it to be so; if you do not, we will be Hungarians against your will; we have this right by birth and in our hearts; we have the right to be of equal rank with you by virtue of our education. We have discarded that ancient nature that follows a religion and forsakes the homeland; we want a homeland, and honor."[99]

Vámbéry's writings present conversion as a logical, practical, coldly rational step as well as a means of putting an end to the painful exclusion associated with Jewish existence. This duality suggests that Vámbéry, consciously or not, wanted to use the rational argumentation of the modern era to cloak his desire to escape the stigma of Jewishness and find acceptance as a Hungarian. This does not mean that he ignored all pragmatic considerations in converting to Christianity. In any case, it does seem clear that the author of the 1882 pamphlet was Ármin Vámbéry, who was thus the first Hungarian Jewish convert to publish a call for his fellow Jews to abandon their religion for purely *secular* reasons.

Conversions in the 1880s

The decision to present this decade as a distinct era is justified by the wave of antisemitism that swept over Hungary in the early 1880s. On April 8, 1875, modern political antisemitism made its appearance in the Hungarian House of Representatives in the form of an interpellation Győző Istóczy addressed to the prime minister, concerning the allegedly "overwhelming" immigration of Galician Jews into Hungary.[100] It was some time before increasingly frequent bouts of antisemitic incitement like Istóczy's began to trouble the Hungarian public or even most Jews. As late as the autumn of 1880, the *Pesti Hírlap* declared that, with the exception of Istóczy, no one in the country was disturbing the "positive understanding" between Jewish and Christian Hungarians.[101] Two years later, following the explosion of the Tiszaeszlár blood libel affair, the daily could no longer make this claim. After taking a position in support of the Jews who were brought to trial, the *Pesti Hírlap* lost almost a quarter of its subscribers.[102]

The Tiszaeszlár crisis gave the Jewish public sphere new life. The two most authoritative Neolog Jewish publications of the following decades were launched around that time. The first issue of the weekly *Egyenlőség* hit newsstands on November 5, 1882 while the journal *Magyar-Zsidó Szemle* appeared in early 1884. The intellectuals grouped around the two periodicals were unanimous in proclaiming that the country's Jewish citizens were as Hungarian as anyone else, certainly by law and increasingly in sentiment. For Neolog intellectuals, *Jew* and *Hungarian* were not and could not be mutually exclusive terms. They presented the transformation of Jews—defined by religion and cultural heritage—into Hungarians as a natural and unproblematic process. Obviously, not all Jewish intellectuals shared their understanding of the place and future of Hungary's Jews.

In conversion, linguist Zsigmond Simonyi, lawyer and economist Jakab Pólya, and historian Dávid Angyal saw or sought a response to the antisemitism of 1880s Hungary and to what felt to them like an antagonistic relationship between "Jews" and "Hungarians." Of these three men, one started his education at a cheder, and the others received thorough religious instruction at Jewish public schools in their hometowns, though none had been *yeshiva bochurim*. Only one had participated (briefly) in Jewish religious life before converting. However, they all discussed their conversions (or conversion in general), though not always publicly.

In a late 1884 issue of *Magyar-Zsidó Szemle*, József Bánóczi published an account of the conversion of "a young scholar" whose example had been followed by four Jewish student teachers in the months since. "One of them is traveling on a state scholarship, they say, and the other three

Figure 4.6. Zsigmond Simonyi, 1874. Hungarian Jewish Museum and Archives, Budapest, F66.309.

have jobs already." Though Bánóczi described the young scholar's baptism as an "embarrassing" surprise to his fellow Jews, who had until then been proud of him, the *Szemle*'s coeditor did not identify the convert, as he was Bánóczi's childhood friend **Zsigmond Simonyi** (1853–1919).[103] At the time of Simonyi's death, the *Magyar Nyelvőr* (*Guardian of the Hungarian Language*) published Bánóczi's warm recollections of the youth of the illustrious scholar of modern Hungarian linguistics. Simonyi was born in Veszprém, where his parents ran a small flour store. He attended the local Jewish elementary school, where Veszprém's Chief Rabbi Ábrahám Hochmuth took note of his keen intellect. After completing a degree at the University of Budapest, he studied in Leipzig, Berlin, and Paris before habilitating as an assistant professor at his alma mater in 1877. Since the position was unpaid, Simonyi took a job as an assistant instructor at the Rabbinical Seminary, where he was unhappy teaching Latin to students in lower-level, secondary classes. Bánóczi's piece makes no mention of the conversion of Simonyi, who in 1874 had joined his brothers and their father, Simon Steiner, in Magyarizing their family name.[104]

Simonyi was hired as a teaching assistant by the newly established department of Hungarian linguistics at the University of Budapest in 1878. He was elected to the Hungarian Academy of Sciences as a corresponding member in 1879, but his career soon stalled because education minister Ágoston Trefort was unwilling to appoint him to a full-time position at the university.[105] In 1882, *Szombati Újság* identified Zsigmond Simonyi and Ignác Goldziher as two of the prominent Hungarian Jewish scholars whose religion had prevented them from advancing beyond the rank of assistant professor—or, in Simonyi's case, teaching assistant.[106] Goldziher and Simonyi's letter to the editor appeared in the weekly's next issue: "We do not feel that the arms of our faith should embrace our cause, and might with even greater justification protest the public discussion of our cases, as we have never asked anyone to do so."[107] Two years later, *Egyenlőség* published several references to the thirty-one-year-old Simonyi's conversion, first on July 6, 1884: "Teacher Zsigmond Simonyi recently followed the advice publicized by Mr. Trefort and converted to the Roman Catholic faith so that he might finally be appointed as a university professor."[108] The day before, a Pest daily noted that "Zsigmond Simonyi and his wife recently converted from the Israelite to the Roman Catholic faith; a large gathering observed the ceremony."[109]

That Zsigmond Simonyi was not motivated to convert by religious conviction or by long-term integrationist considerations is suggested by the fact that he did not baptize his one-year-old son.[110] We have no record of the personal deliberations that led Simonyi to convert, but we do know how he explained and justified his decision to Lajos Haynald, the Archbishop of Kalocsa. On May 8 of 1884, Simonyi sent Cardinal Haynald a letter asking for his support in a "matter of paramount importance." Simonyi began by summarizing his scholarly achievements before turning to his pedagogical career at the university, specifically its stagnation at the rank of teaching assistant:

Having obtained definitive information from the responsible parties, I know that the religion to which I belong is the reason I have been sidelined: the reason is that I was born a Jew. Your Eminence! The members of my religion who have, like me, attempted to scale the heights of European scholarly culture are only nominally Jews. In fact, we are so steeped in the spirit of Christian civilization that generally only a small step, only a certain false modesty that keeps us from converting, separates us from the faithful of the Holy Church of Christ. After mature reflection, I have come to the conclusion that wherever the failure to take this step clips the wings of the most noble and altruistic ambitions, it is a human and patriotic duty to overcome this false modesty and stand where we belong as a result of the direction of our spiritual lives. I made up my mind to take the step of conversion and brought myself into the bosom of the Roman Catholic Mother Church. I would thus ask Your Eminence to be so kind as to support me in the effectuation of this decision and—the next time you pay a visit to the capital city—to consent to appoint a day and hour at which I might present my request in person.[111]

Cardinal Haynald received the illustrious scholar on May 14, 1884. The most striking characteristic of Simonyi's letter is its complete omission of the religious aspects of converting to Christianity—theoretically, his chief motive for doing so. According to Simonyi's reasoning, he decided to convert not because he was "steeped" in the "spirit of Christian civilization" but rather with the admittedly pragmatic objective—wrapped in the cloak of "patriotic duty"—of preventing his religious affiliation from "clipping the wings" of his scholarly aspirations. Of course, Simonyi did not need the archbishop's support to achieve the desired result; displaying a baptismal certificate would have been enough to get him an appointment at the university. Simonyi presumably wanted to be absolutely sure. On February 21, 1885, the University of Budapest hired Simonyi as an assistant professor, and by July 4, 1889 he was a full professor there.[112]

In contrast to Simonyi, the distinguished economist **Jakab Pólya** (1844–97) converted to Catholicism with his entire family in 1886. Two years after Pólya's death, Gyula Vargha, deputy director of the Central Statistical Office, delivered a memorial address to the Hungarian Academy of Sciences, to which Pólya had been elected as a corresponding member in 1894. He thanked Pólya's son, doctor Jenő Pólya, for his written account of his father's life and recited several passages from the diary of the deceased.[113] The diary, which Jenő

Figure 4.7. Jakab Pólya. Library and Information Centre of the Hungarian Academy of Sciences, Department of Manuscripts and Rare Books, Ms 315/108.

Pólya presumably made available to Vargha, has been lost. The confessional character of the passage dealing with conversion suggests that the liberal Vargha was summarizing the relevant portions of the diary. But Vargha did not state he was quoting directly from the diary, and thus we face an insoluble conundrum: we cannot know how much of the justification for conversion reflected Pólya's own opinions and how much was shaped by the attitudes of his son Jenő, baptized at the age of nine, or of Pólya's eulogist Gyula Vargha.

Born on the Great Hungarian Plain in the village of Békésszentandrás, Jakab Pollák Magyarized his and his children's surname to Pólya in 1882. His father, Mózes Pollák, was a poor grocer; his mother, Johanna Diamant, was the daughter of an equally poor innkeeper from Nagykőrös. The eldest of eight children, Jakab's parents enrolled him at the local cheder at the age of five; he moved on to the Lutheran gymnasium in nearby Szarvas at the age of ten and spent two years there before transferring to the Reformed high school in Nagykőrös, where he lived with his grandparents. After graduating at the age of nineteen, he complied with his father's wishes and enrolled at the medical school in Pest but transferred to the law school at the end of his first year. With his parents unable to support him financially, Jakab was forced to eke out a meager living as a private tutor. According to Vargha's version of Jenő Pólya's account of his father's life, one Sukkot, "when every Jewish household was baking and cooking and cheerful, [Jakab] strolled the bank of the Danube all day long, hungry and thirsty, with nothing but a day-old roll."[114] After completing his studies at the university, Pólya joined a law office, taking over its management in 1871. In 1873, he married Johanna Deutsch of Lugos (Lugoj, Romania). In the Panic of 1873, he lost both his savings and his wife's dowry, and in 1883, with his law office generating less and less revenue, he gave it up and took a position at the Trieste General Insurance Company, where he would work until his death. In addition to his office work, Pólya also began to write and publish. Before presenting Pólya's scholarly work, Vargha read out a lengthy set of passages from his 1882 diary in which the young lawyer wondered whether his writing would allow him to serve the cause of his homeland and nation.[115] Vargha then turned to the story of Pólya's baptism:

> An even more interesting episode in his spiritual life: his conversion from the Jewish faith. He, a man of strong conviction, was not led here by self-interest or momentary enthusiasm, but by serious deliberation and a resolve based on solid foundations.

Conversion did not promise him title, rank, or material benefit; on the contrary. It exposed his family, whom he loved to the point of idolatry, to a future of uncertainty. It was precisely his family's future that kept him from taking this step for so long. He thought about the fate of his daughters. If he were to remain among his coreligionists in the faith of his forefathers, surely his upstanding daughters, who had been blessed with so many favorable qualities, would meet with good fortune. If he were to convert, though, might he forfeit this good fortune? He ruminated on it for a long time, but finally fought the good fight and in 1885 [actually 1886[116]], along with his wife and children, he made his way into the bosom of the Roman Catholic mother church.

It was not religious conviction, but rather national sentiment that led him to this important step. Among his estimable traits was a profound piety, but this was not the same as sectarianism. He knew, he felt, that the essence [of religion], its truly valuable content—the most precious thing humanity possesses—is the concept of the One God, omnipotent and eternal, which treasure is shared by every Christian denomination, just as it is by the Jewish faith. . . .

We know—and Pólya knew this very well—that religion has essentially nothing to do with nationality; a believer in any creed can be a good Hungarian. Despite his Jewish faith, he felt himself to be as Hungarian in language and sentiment as any member of the denomination known as the Hungarian faith. However, despite the great progress Jews have made in their Magyarization, he was broken-hearted to see how difficult it is to achieve complete fusion. It pained him to see social discord—the rigid, dismissive behavior of Christian society on the one hand and the closed-off, separatist spirit of the Jews, which seems to draw even greater strength from material progress and worldly successes. He felt its harmful effects on the development of national unity and saw no other proper solution than for Jews to convert and enter into the bosom of a Christian church. He did not consider this to be an unachievable utopia, or even a difficult step. The two religions share the same foundation; moreover, Jewish youths, having grown up in mostly Christian schools, are thus party to Christian moral concepts and worldviews. So why, asked the Hungarian patriot in his soul, should we preserve the barriers of division when there is no genuine, serious obstacle to complete amalgamation?[117]

This lengthy assertion that Pólya converted out of inner conviction, free of any self-interest, is a revealing indicator of the extent to which the Hungarian public of the era saw Jews' conversions as driven primarily by opportunism. The most fragile aspect of Vargha's argument is his attempt to reconcile a justification of conversion with a liberal's differentiation of religious identity and Hungarianness. Logically, this reconciliation inevitably ran aground. If "a believer in any creed" could be "a good Hungarian," then how much did conversion actually advance the cause of integration? If Hungarianness was not defined by denominational identity, then conversion could not have a "national" justification.

There is no trace of such self-contradiction in the autobiography of eminent historian **Dávid Angyal** (1857–1943), who characterized Christianity as a superficial but self-evident attribute of Hungarianness. Angyal converted the year before Pólya, and like him, to the Roman Catholic faith, though as noted in chapter 2, Angyal considered the Reformed Church first. A conversation with his mentor Pál Gyulai ultimately led him to choose Catholicism, suggesting his primary consideration was to join the majority faith. Angyal began writing his autobiography in July of 1943, at the age of eighty-five—fifty-eight years after his conversion and five months before his death. Though the title of full professor exempted Angyal from Act IV of 1939 (the so-called Second Jewish Law), the perilousness of the period inevitably left its mark on his writing. As he wrote in the second paragraph of his autobiography, "I was born in Nagykunszentmárton on November 30, 1857. However, I am unfamiliar with this upstanding community, because I was two years old when my parents moved to Szentes, the current seat of Csongrád County. My parents were Jews. I have been made to feel the curse of Jewish origins many times, up to this very day. Börne was right to say that Judaism (*Judenthum*) is not a religion, but a misfortune."[118]

A misfortune, one might add, that by 1943 had befallen converted Jews (and/or their descendants) just as much as it befell Jews who remained in the fold. However, Angyal continued to assert that the solution was the integration of the "Jewish minority" into the majority society of the given nation and that conversion was a necessary, natural condition of such integration. The reason the "Jewish question" had not been resolved was that "the large majority of Jews have not wanted to acknowledge the wise humanism of this suggestion"—that is, they had not converted.[119]

Angyal dedicated a paragraph of his autobiography to his motivation for converting and the circumstances of his doing so, yet he said little about the path that led him to take this step. After his digression on the subject of the "Jewish question," Angyal set about telling the story of his life, first clarifying his relationship with the Hungarian nation and his own Hungarianness:

Figure 4.8. Dávid Angyal. In *Vasárnapi Újság* 42, no. 36 (1895): 585.

"Returning to the narrative: I spent my childhood in Szentes. Everyone there spoke Hungarian, so I naturally spoke to my parents in my mother tongue, too. I believed the Jewish [faith] to be a denomination, like the Catholic or the Reformed. And though I heard the word 'Jordan' cast in my direction once or twice, it did not wound my Hungarian pride. I had no need of assimilation; I spoke only Hungarian, and along with my playmates, whether Jewish or not, I rhapsodized over everything Hungarian."[120] Angyal had expressed this thought a few years earlier, in a 1939 letter to historian Gyula Szekfű: "In any case, I am not assimilated. I never felt the process of transformation in my soul. Hungarian is my mother tongue and I have been passionate ... about Hungarian writers since my childhood. To me, Jewishness was always just a denomination."[121]

Perhaps to avoid disturbing this image, Angyal did not mention the "German-Jewish" sounding name of his grain wholesaler father, Márton Engel, nor that he had Magyarized his name in 1880.[122] Perhaps his maternal grandparents made a greater impression on him than his own parents did, as he barely mentioned the latter. The three generations lived together, and the grandparents were religious Jews who spoke Yiddish to each other and to Angyal's parents. Angyal understood Yiddish, though he claimed he could not speak it. Angyal's grandfather, who spent his time reading "mostly Hebrew or German" books, introduced his grandson to the Hebrew language. When Angyal began attending Jewish elementary school at the age of five, he was already able to read Hebrew, though he did not yet understand the language. His grandmother, whom he never saw at rest, "either worked or prayed, just like my mother."[123] This is the only reference in Angyal's autobiography to his parents'—or at least his mother's—religiosity. In 1867, at the age of ten, Angyal enrolled at the Reformed gymnasium in Szentes, and like Ármin Vámbéry, he later attributed his drifting away from the Jewish faith to his contact with Christian members of his generation: "My grandmother made sure that I was precise in satisfying my obligations to my religion.... My religious zealotry initially filled me with joy, but with the passage of time my zeal began to wane. Probably because Jewish boys were a tiny minority at my gymnasium, I made friends with lots of my Christian classmates. I was dazzled and moved when, courtesy of one of our servants, I was able to listen to an entire midnight mass on Christmas at the Catholic church. On several occasions, my school and I went to the neighboring Calvinist church."[124]

A few pages later, Angyal mentions that after he and his family moved to Szeged in 1871, the religious instruction for Jewish students at the local Piarist gymnasium was provided by Lipót Löw, "the rabbi of Hungarian sensibilities known from the time of the war of independence," who delivered engrossing lectures on the history of the "Jewish Church."[125] Except for these remarks, Angyal said nothing about the process by which he drifted away from the Jewish faith and toward his—decidedly ecumenical—form of Christianity. Angyal had slightly more to say about the difficult fate of the young Jewish intellectual. While still a student at the University of Budapest, Angyal began publishing in newspapers and periodicals like the prestigious *Budapesti Szemle*, where he found a steadfast supporter in editor Pál Gyulai. Once he graduated from university, it became clear these credentials would not be enough to get Angyal a teaching position at a high school. There was always tutoring. Angyal was hired by the wealthy Kohner family, then in 1883—when the Tiszaeszlár blood libel trial had not helped create a "favorable atmosphere... for the appointment of Jewish teachers"—he took a job with the equally affluent Brüll family. Angyal tutored Henrik Brüll's son Alfréd until February of 1885, when Pál Gyulai found him a temporary position as a clerk at the University Library in Budapest.[126]

Having by then come to the decision to convert, Angyal described his feelings as follows:

> When I entered the civil service in early 1885, I decided I could not put off conversion to the Christian faith any longer. The question of financial advantage argued against this decision. As a tutor, my pay was 100 forints a month and full board, not to mention smaller gifts and trips. Nor was that all. Had I committed to leading my student through the eight grades of gymnasium, my guaranteed severance pay would have been 10,000 forints. And after these eight years, I could have hoped for the support of powerful financiers in finding adequately paid employment. Compared to these reliable material considerations, 50 forints a month and uncertain professional advancement were not sufficiently weighty motivation. Also, as a result of these financial circumstances, I had to struggle with the indignation of parents and relatives, as well as the feeling that I had been ungrateful to those who had always supported me as a poor student in the name of the community of faith. These considerations discouraged me and raised doubts, but the desire to belong externally to something that my feelings bound me to vanquished all doubt.[127]

To what did his "feelings bind him?" Since Angyal never said a word about religious conviction, it was clearly not Christianity but rather the Hungarian nation, which was understood to be coterminous with Christianity.

So far, this seems to be the self-justification of old age. The account is contradicted somewhat by an article published in *Egyenlőség* the year after Angyal's conversion; a young author reported that he knew of converted Jews—including Angyal and the aforementioned linguist Zsigmond Simonyi—"who declare *palam* and *publice* [openly and publicly] that they were baptized out of simple self-interest, to achieve a certain objective or obtain a certain position."[128] That Angyal was guided by practical considerations is suggested by the fact that in the summer of 1896, eleven years after joining the Catholic Church, he married a Jewish woman named Alice Mandl, and not only did he not insist that his bride belong to that which he claimed he was bound by his feelings, he did not even negotiate a prior agreement about the faith in which their children were to be raised. Thus, when the Angyals' daughter Paula was born on August 28, 1898, she was registered as an "Israelite" in accordance with her mother's religion.[129]

Conversions in the Final Decades of the Dualist Era

By the end of the 1880s, Hungarian political antisemitism had disappeared almost completely. The National Antisemitic Party, which had won seventeen seats in the House of Representatives in 1884 and eleven seats in 1887, was not among the contestants in the 1892 general election.[130] The optimism of *Egyenlőség*'s contributors peaked around the time Judaism was granted "received status" (1895) and Hungary celebrated its millennium (1896). It would gradually turn to pessimism over the course of the following twenty years. The Neolog weekly's outlook darkened, increasingly disillusioned with the traditional political elite and disheartened by the lack of hope that Jews would ever achieve social acceptance. From the perspective of conversion, these two decades can be regarded as a single era. Most Jews who converted in this period had grown up in acculturated and secularized families. Some Jewish intellectuals who converted were born into families of artisans and retailers, but by this time many were the children of intellectuals while a few were scions of the upper class.

Let us begin this series of fin-de-siècle portraits with social scientist, library director, and anarcho-syndicalist revolutionary **Ervin Szabó** (1877–1918), who grew up in an impoverished bourgeois family, and philosopher György Lukács, whose family was very well to do. Despite different social backgrounds, they were united by their absolute rejection of the Hungarian political and social order. They also shared a classically pragmatic set of reasons for conversion. Born Sámuel Ármin Schlesinger in the largely Slovak Árva County village of Szlanica (now Slanica, Slovakia), home to roughly forty Jewish families, Szabó Magyarized his surname in 1892 and adopted the given name Ervin when he joined the Reformed Church in 1895, shortly

234   JEWISHNESS AND BEYOND

before his eighteenth birthday. His grandfather, Sámuel Hirsch, a native of Moravia or Silesia, left Szabó's father, Gyula Schlesinger, a profitable blue-dye factory that allegedly employed 150 workers at its peak. The educated Gyula Schlesinger was committed to Judaism, as evidenced by his paying for the construction of Szlanica's synagogue. Szabó's mother, Lujza Pollacsek, grew up in the village of Dluha (Dlhá nad Oravou), near Szlanica. According to György Litván's biography of Ervin Szabó, the Pollacseks "likely outranked the Schlesingers in terms of affluence and embourgeoisement." Szabó was the sixth of Gyula Schlesinger and Lujza Pollacsek's seven children. His father committed suicide not long after the birth of the seventh child, "allegedly because the developing manufacturing industry ruined his small factory and forced it into bankruptcy." After the elder Schlesinger's death, his family moved to Ungvár, where Szabó's mother sought the support of her still prosperous relatives, who gave her a place to stay. With help from her parents, her own labors, and a great deal of sacrifice and self-denial, Szabó's widowed mother managed to maintain an almost bourgeois lifestyle and provide for her children's education.[131]

The bookshelves of the Schlesinger family home were lined with the complete novels of Charles Dickens, the philosophical writings of Friedrich Schiller, and the published speeches of Ferdinand Lassalle. As Szabó recalled, "When my classmates were still struggling with school authors, I was already familiar with the best of world literature."[132] Having lost her presumably more devout husband, Szabó's widowed mother and her family behaved in accordance with bourgeois expectations for religious behavior. As Litván put it, "Even the older generation had already completely discarded Jewish orthodoxy. Their correspondence shows no trace of religious life, though it does reveal that they celebrated Christmas and Easter. The younger generation was obviously even more affected by the spirit of the Enlightenment, desires for education and advancement, and aspirations to national assimilation." The latter ambition is illustrated by the fact that Adolf, Ottó, Alfréd, and Sámuel Schlesinger all Magyarized their surname to Szabó as minors in 1892.[133]

Litván attributed Ervin Szabó's conversion to his aspiration to "assimilate." At the age of ten, Szabó was enrolled at the Catholic gymnasium in Ungvár. He was a diligent, ambitious, and outstanding student—the pride of the school. Letters Szabó wrote to his mother (living in Budapest at the time) indicate he was hard at work preparing for his graduation exam in the spring of 1895.

Figure 4.9. Ervin Szabó, 1910s. Petőfi Literary Museum, F.2205.

In a letter dated March 22, reporting on his everyday affairs, Szabó informed his mother, almost as an aside, "I want to convert after the Easter break, but before the year-end exam, and I have chosen principal [László] Hódoly as my godfather. What do you say to the former and the latter?"[134] We have no record of his mother's response, though she herself converted sixteen years later. Szabó was baptized in April; his school report for the 1894–95 academic year already listed him as "of the Helvetic confession." According to Litván, "he had clearly come to this decision long before; it was among his conscious steps on the path to assimilation. Religious conviction did not bind him to his old denomination, nor attract him to the new one; he probably chose the

236   JEWISHNESS AND BEYOND

Reformed faith precisely because of its relative liberalism. The timing [of his conversion] may have been a function of his graduation exam."[135]

There can hardly be any doubt Szabó consciously scheduled his conversion for the month before this exam. He had to have known that it would be advantageous to his career to have his graduation records identify him as a Christian. His indifference to religion was indisputable as well. As regards "assimilation," György Litván emphasized in several of his writings that turn-of-the-century Jewish progressive intellectuals "had no Jewish consciousness; on the contrary, they were passionate assimilationists."[136] A "good half" of Hungary's bourgeois-radical leaders were of Jewish origin, and as Litván wrote elsewhere, "they were convinced assimilationists who wanted to address the national intelligentsia not as Jews, but as Hungarian intellectuals, or more precisely, as intellectuals who had become Christian Hungarians."[137] Litván never discussed how being a "passionate," "convinced assimilationist" led one to become a "Christian Hungarian." Ervin Szabó hardly thought conversion was a necessary condition of becoming Hungarian or of showing respect for Hungary's Christian cultural tradition. What is certain is that there is no evidence he ever possessed any "Jewish consciousness." Lacking any meaningful experience—religious, cultural, or communal—of his Jewish heritage, Szabó's awareness of his religious status was limited to the wearying knowledge that it constituted a disadvantage. From this perspective, liberating himself from his ties to the Jewish faith was a logical, self-evident step.

Unlike Szabó, the philosopher **György Lukács** (1885–1971) was born to wealth, into what he called a "capitalist, 'Lipótváros' family."[138] Lukács's paternal grandfather, a quilter from Szeged named Jakab Löwinger, was a religious Jew and a Hungarian patriot who left his family to join the army during the 1848 revolution. Jakab Löwinger was unable to pay for his youngest son József's education beyond the age of thirteen, at which point the young man was forced to abandon the *Realschule* and find work. In 1873, at the age of eighteen, József Löwinger (he would Magyarize his surname to Lukács in 1890) found a job as correspondence supervisor at a Budapest bank. In a 1971 interview conducted in London, György Lukács' younger sister Mária described their father's rise as follows:

> In the evening, after [finishing his work at] the bank, he did bookkeeping for private firms to earn extra money, which money he used to continue his

studies. Languages. So he really educated himself. When he was 18 years old, he read a job listing: a large Budapest bank was looking for a correspondence supervisor. Because he spent whole nights studying, he could write in various languages and got the position. . . . By the time he was 24 years old, he was already the director of a branch of the English-Austrian Bank. And he never forgot what it meant to be poor. That feeling made him help [my brother] Gyuri and every young person with whom he came into contact.[139]

József Lukács provided financial support to many young intellectuals and artists around the turn of the century and hosted figures like Max Weber and Thomas Mann at his home. He exhibited a combination of cultural openness and political conservativism. Like many members of the Jewish upper class of his era, Lukács supported the modernist literary journal *Nyugat* (*West*) in cultural affairs and the liberal conservative prime minister István Tisza in politics. According to literary historian Albert Gyergyai, who spent six years as a tutor at the Lukács home beginning in 1920, József Lukács admired Tisza "for his faith, his determination, and his integrity."[140]

In 1883, József Lukács married Adél Wertheimer, who had grown up in a wealthy family in Pest and Vienna, where the couple met. According to Mária Lukács, her mother had little more than a superficial education, but she spoke several languages and played the piano beautifully. Adél spoke Hungarian well, but the Lukács family spoke German at home.[141] The couple had four children, the youngest of whom—Pál—died of diphtheria at the age of three. On May 1, 1899, József, Adél, and their three surviving children (János, György, and Mária) were ennobled and granted the *praedicatum* "szegedi." József Lukács built a successful career as managing director of Hitelbank (Credit Bank) and later as chief executive of the English-Austrian Bank.[142] Even so, his social ascent plateaued. In the words of Albert Gyergyai, "he was not of the new nobility's first rank, the world of the Hatvanys, Kornfelds, Kohners, Herzogs, and Ullmanns; though he surpassed them all intellectually, they were significantly wealthier and more politically influential than he."[143]

In any case, József Lukács made enough money to complicate his relationships with his poorer kin. As Albert Gyergyai recalled, "He was not ashamed of his humble origins, nor of his ambition to rise as high as possible. He was constantly helping poor relatives, though he kept them away from the house."[144] When Szeged was devastated by the great flood of 1879, József Lukács brought his parents to Budapest, but they lived on their own, not even visiting their son at his home.[145] Instead, the Lukács family visited them, regularly hosting their Passover seders at the elderly couple's house. As Mária Lukács recalled, they did so "because the old man really liked it. One time he asked my father to bring a Christian colleague because he wanted to talk to a Christian person at his house for once. My father brought one of his colleagues, who really enjoyed himself there."[146] That was about the extent of the Lukács children's religious experiences in the home. József Lukács was a member of Pest's Neolog Chevra Kadisha, a representative on the council of the Israelite Congregation of Pest, and a member of the Hungarian Israelite Cultural Association; his sons' tutors included two sons of rabbi Márk Handler of Tata.[147] Nevertheless, Mária Lukács said their religious life at home "was nothing." By way of explanation, she added, "My father was a great assimilationist. He said that the one thing intelligent Jews must keep in mind is that they belong to a homeland, not to a religion."[148]

For György Bernát Lukács (born György Löwinger and known at the synagogue by his Hebrew name, Berl), Jewishness was reduced to another of the empty formalities of haut bourgeois life in Pest. In an autobiographical sketch taken down in the final months of his life, he wrote:

> From a pure Jewish family. Precisely for this reason: the ideologies of Jewry [had] no influence on my intellectual development.... [Jewishness] affected my childhood life episodically, as protocol: social participation in acquaintances' weddings, funerals, etc.: participation in rituals. As they put no emphasis even on the acquisition of the Hebrew language, these [rituals] were utterly meaningless to children, purely "protocolaire" (hat in the church; it never crossed my mind that the texts spoken or sung there could have any meaning). In this way, religion arranges itself into a normal social life: how one was to greet the (unknown) guest respectfully, how one was to respond politely (and with apparent interest) to his questions and statements, which from a child's perspective, were almost entirely meaningless: it made no difference. How this system of formal-meaningless obligations to react is built around the child's normal life: already characteristic of the first years of childhood. Spontaneous rebellion.[149]

The rebellion was directed at Lipótváros and broadened out to a rejection of "the whole of official Hungary."[150] When György Lukács was fifteen, his father introduced him to the Benedek family, and the things that attracted him to Elek Benedek were those he thought he could not find in his own milieu. As

Figure 4.10. György Lukács, Anna Hamvassy, and Béla Balázs, c. 1915–16. Petőfi Literary Museum, F.11063.

Lukács said in a conversation with Erzsébet Vezér and István Eörsi, "I never had anything to do with Elek Benedek as a writer, not even then. But unlike the milieu in which I lived, where success achieved by means of compromise or worse was essentially the only standard of human value, Elek Benedek always stood up for his convictions in his own puritan way."[151] In that same conversation, Lukács commented on the portrayal of his family's Jewishness in his autobiographical sketch: "Only as part of our domestic protocol did religion actually interest us, insofar as it played a role in the arrangement of weddings and other ceremonies.... The Jewish religion itself was a subject of utter indifference among us."[152] Neither Lukács's intellectual development nor his reading interests were oriented toward religion. According to the diary of Marcell Benedek, Elek Benedek's son and a teenage friend of Lukács, the would-be philosopher had moved beyond all religion by the age of fifteen: "He does not generally speak about religion; he'll occasionally make an ironic observation about his own faith, but I've never heard him talk about

Christianity. However, the way he deals with philosophical and metaphysical questions makes clear as day that he regards the question of religion as having been settled long ago."[153]

Asking about the years Lukács spent at the Lutheran gymnasium on Deák Square in Budapest, Erzsébet Vezér and István Eörsi raised the issue of his relationship with his own Jewishness:

Questioner: Did the problem of Jewishness not influence your development in secondary school?

Lukács: No. Neither pro nor contra.

Questioner: And it did not affect you even in the sense that—involuntarily, or independently of your own consciousness—it caused you problems, and...?

Lukács: At the Lutheran gymnasium, Lipótváros was the aristocracy. I was not treated like a Jew there, but like a Lipótváros lad, who counted as an aristocrat at that school. Thus questions of Jewishness didn't arise. I've always known myself to be Jewish, but it never had any substantial effect on my development... I didn't feel like a Jew. I understood my Jewishness to be a fact of birth and that was the end of the matter.[154]

Lukács never spoke publicly about his conversion to Christianity, nor—with the exception of the foregoing citations—did he ever write about his relationship with his Jewishness. The proximate cause of his conversion was a banality. After earning a law degree in Budapest and a doctorate in political science from the Franz Joseph University in Kolozsvár, Lukács attended the University of Berlin from November 5, 1906 to March 7, 1907. He finished the academic year at the University of Budapest, where he received a doctoral degree from the faculty of humanities in 1909.[155] Shortly after his return from Berlin, Lukács decided he should find a job in Pest. His family began putting out feelers; it was suggested Lukács might find work at the House of Representatives.[156] Eventually, in September of 1907, Lukács was hired as an assistant clerk at the Ministry of Commerce.[157] On August 19 and September 2, 1907 (that is, immediately preceding his appointment), Lukács announced his intention to disaffiliate at the rabbinical office of the Israelite Congregation of Pest, then converted at the Fasori Lutheran Church in Buda on September 3.[158] Lukács's decision was almost certainly a function of his job at the ministry. He never mentioned his conversion in any of his correspondence, neither at the time nor later. There is nothing to suggest that it was of any significance to him at all.[159]

Iván Moscovitz (1875–1916), who died as a hussar captain on a Transylvanian battlefield in the First World War, was likely driven to convert by combination of practical considerations (such as winning election to the National Assembly and finalizing his integration into Hungary's traditional elite) and deeper psychological impulses. His grandfather Mór Moscovitz and his father, Géza, have already come up several times in the course of this book. In the Reform Era, Mór Moscovitz was the family doctor of future prime minister Gyula Andrássy and became the first Jewish member of the National Casino in 1848. In 1867, during Gyula Andrássy's tenure as prime minister (but before the emancipation of Hungary's Jews!), Moscovitz was ennobled and granted the praedicatum "zempléni." In 1872, this son of a poor innkeeper purchased 4,000 *hold* (2,280 hectares) of land, along with a single-story Baroque-ified mansion, in the Zemplén County village of Alsókörtvélyes (now Nižný Hrušov, Slovakia).[160] As the *Pesti Hírlap* said at the time of Moscovitz's death in 1880, "As a result of his erudition and his witty, refined manner, he was always received with joy in the capital's most distinguished salons."[161]

Géza Moscovitz, Mór Moscovitz and Amália Boscovitz/Boskovitz's only child, was sixteen when he was ennobled alongside his father. After earning a doctorate in law at the University of Vienna, he stayed in the city to do secretarial work for Gyula Andrássy, by then foreign minister of the Austro-Hungarian Monarchy. Moscovitz resigned after a short time, allegedly having taken offense at being told to go fetch the foreign minister's carriage. He returned to his family's estate and in 1874 married Hermina Deutsch, daughter of József Deutsch and younger sister of the future baron Sándor Hatvany-Deutsch. Moscovitz was a free-spending hunter, the last of the National Casino's members of the Jewish faith, and a good neighbor to the local landowners, who welcomed him into their social circles.[162] The remarkable degree of acceptance he found within the traditional elite was not merely the result of his close association with the Andrássys. Géza Moscovitz was the type of man who simply knocked people off their feet. Gyula Andrássy Jr., the last foreign minister of the Austro-Hungarian Monarchy, called him a "magnanimous, witty, endearing personality"[163] while his brother-in-law Oszkár Jászi, whom he met in the early 1890s at his family's home in Budapest, remembered him as "a lovable *causeur* . . . a witty, brilliant, generous lord of the manor."[164] In its obituary, *Egyenlőség* noted that Moscovitz "was known as a very amiable, witty, and always clever gentleman—which is obviously why they forgave him for his Jewishness."[165]

In her fictionalized autobiography *Kezdetben volt a kert* (*In the Beginning Was the Garden*), Moscovitz's daughter Anna Lesznai wrote that her

Figure 4.11. Hermina Hatvany-Deutsch and Géza Moscovitz, 1902. Petőfi Literary Museum, F.15135.

grandfather raised his son to be a Hungarian gentleman above all, purchasing him an estate so that "he might be a gentleman just like the rest of them—those happy Christians who were born into the framework of a ready destiny." This upbringing succeeded perfectly. "István Berkovics," the young Géza's stand-in, "knew that his father was Jewish—but today, in the age of Enlightenment, everyone sees clearly that nothing is determined by religion. Just let the person be an honorable, learned, generous gentleman." As a mature man, Berkovics laughs when his wife tells him that Körtvélyes' parish priest hopes to baptize the family one day: "The priest is an upright man, but a bit narrow-minded! Convert to Catholicism? These days, the enlightened Hungarian does not belong to any religious sect. Let the barons of finance, the social climbers, the Jews become Catholics. . . . István Berkovics is not a Jew or a Catholic, but rather a Hungarian gentleman, period!"[166]

Géza Moscovitz's son Iván did not inherit his father's rock-solid sense of self. In 1891, he began studying law at the University of Budapest, earning a doctorate in 1897. He then took a series of public service positions beginning with clerk at the royal court in Budapest. In 1901, Iván Moscovitz launched an unsuccessful bid to represent the city of Ungvár at the National Assembly.[167] In the fall of that same year, Moscovitz was engaged to Erzsébet Brüll (also known as Lili or Lily), daughter of Ignác Brüll, vice president of the Bar Association of Budapest. After a civil ceremony, Moscovitz and Brüll celebrated their marriage at the Dohány Street Synagogue in Budapest in July of 1902. According to a report in *Egyenlőség*, their service at the synagogue took place in the presence of "a large and brilliant gathering, [including] numerous luminaries of political and social life."[168] Moscovitz's choice of spouse suggests he envisioned a social future that would unfold at least partly within Jewish upper-class circles.

The "subsequent notes/corrections" section of their civil marriage certificate indicates that Moscovitz (who spelled his name *Moskovitz* from 1904 onward)[169] converted to the Unitarian faith in 1905. His political ambitions may have been the immediate motive for his conversion. Though his newfound faith may not have been the deciding factor, he did win the 1906 election to represent the village of Dobra in Hunyad County, Transylvania. Following the collapse of Sándor Wekerle's coalition government, Moskovitz ran again in 1910, but after losing that election, he went to work as a lawyer in Budapest. Unhappy in their childless marriage, Moscovitz and his wife divorced in February of the same year. By July 6, the beautiful Lily Brüll had already remarried, converting to Catholicism for Baron Lipót Bornemisza de Nagykászon. On October 24, at Saint Stephen's Basilica in Budapest, Moskovitz—now a Catholic himself—married the Greek Catholic Róza Nyegre de Uglya, whom he had probably met through her father, Moscovitz's parliamentary colleague László Nyegre.[170]

Back in Körtvélyes, Moscovitz's companions were members of the county's land-owning nobility, but at the university and at his home in Pest he socialized with anarcho-syndicalists and radicals like Ervin Szabó and Oszkár Jászi. Described by Hilda Bauer—the younger sister of film critic and poet Béla Balázs— as "very Jewish" in appearance, by Endre Ady as "too upright," by Erzsébet Vezér as endowed "with excessive sensitivity and an excessive sense of duty," and by Jászi as "a conservative seeker of truth steeped in humanism," Moscovitz began his career as a lawyer in the service of the state, but he also wrote for periodicals like *Huszadik Század* and *Nyugat*.[171] He moved along the boundaries of many worlds but without his father's good cheer. Anna Lesznai

Figure 4.12. Iván Moscovitz. http://www.geni.com

attributed her older brother's emotional uncertainty to his unique social situation; more precisely, her account of her "older brother" in her novelized autobiography uses excerpts from his imaginary diary to make this point. As Iván Moscovitz, alias János Berkovics, wrote in 1899, "It's odd that I apparently live in the same world as these gentry—yet some kind of estrangement separates me from them. I feel this barrier more acutely than they do." Berkovics believes his acceptance is superficial; even if his noble friends embrace him, they see him as different, as a Jew. In a 1901 diary entry, Moscovitz's alter ego describes his situation as unbearable: "We're an abnormal sort, the Berkovicses. I myself was certainly not made for happiness. I have too much gnawing duality inside me—for instance, my unfortunate half-Jewish, half-gentry condition. János Berkovics de Rozgony. I don't trust this amalgam. My father can take it, but even today it's difficult to emulate him, and tomorrow it will be impossible."[172] We cannot know how much these words reflected the feelings of Anna Lesznai and how accurately they portrayed her actual brother Iván. One could assume that he converted partly in search of a balm for his identity crisis and relief from the feeling of "nagging duality." He never found it. The eulogies published at the time of Moscovitz's funeral in Pest in February of 1917, including one by Gyula Andrássy Jr., all emphasized his boundless politeness, conscientiousness, love of justice, and idealism. They also agreed that Moscovitz was not merely courageous on the battlefield but "downright defiant" in confronting the enemy, willing to face "a hail of bullets," yet he was extremely sensitive, a brooding "wounded soul" who took offense easily, often for no apparent reason.[173]

In addition to career advancement, marriage was the other "tangible" goal of conversion. **Lajos Dóczi** (or Dóczy, 1845–1919), who worked as a press official under Austro-Hungarian foreign minister Gyula Andrássy Sr. starting in 1871, and as head of the joint foreign ministry's press office from 1895 until his retirement, converted at the age of forty-eight in order to marry his second wife. Dóczi was thus a generation older than most of the Jews who converted in the final decades of the Dualist era. Born Baruch Dux in Sopron, Dóczi Magyarized his name in 1872 before being ennobled in 1878 and elevated to the rank of baron in 1900. His father, leather merchant Móric Dux, moved his family from Sopron back to his hometown of Németkeresztúr (Deutschkreutz, Austria) as a result of the antisemitic disturbances that broke out in 1848. According to a portrait of Lajos Dóczi published in *Egyenlőség* in 1890, his mother, Róza Rosenberg, "was a woman of rare erudition, considering the era and the conditions then"—meaning she had received some secular education.[174] Dóczi's family had thus started down the path of acculturation, though their milieu was still traditional. In the 1840s, the Jewish residents of Németkeresztúr—where a yeshiva opened in 1860 and the community sided with the Orthodox camp in the schism of 1868–69—spoke Yiddish while the village's Christians spoke a local dialect of German. As Dóczi remembered it, "nobody knew Hungarian."[175] The Yiddish-speaking Baruch Dux thus started primary school in Németkeresztúr before going to live with his mother's relatives in Nagykanizsa, where he finished his elementary education at the local Jewish school. He then returned to Németkeresztúr, where—according to *Egyenlőség*—"the community's gray-haired teacher introduced him to Talmudic scholarship at his father's home."[176]

However, the young Dóczi's parents did not want him to become a *yeshiva bochur* but rather a merchant. When he failed to make it as a shop assistant, his father took him to Sopron to enroll him in high school in 1857.

After graduating from the gymnasium, Dóczi began studying law at the University of Vienna in 1865. Two years later, at an assembly the Equality Circle had organized in support of the emancipation of Hungary's Jews, he spoke up as the Pest correspondent for the Viennese newspaper *Neue Freie Presse*. As Equality Circle official Pál Tenczer recalled in the pages of *Egyenlőség* in 1892, Dóczi made a mess of it, his sparkling intellect fettered by his miserable oratorical skills.[177] Tenczer told the story again six years later, now set at a meeting of the Israelite Hungarian Association rather than the Equality Circle, but the punchline was the same: the twenty-two-year-old journalist had "fumbled his speech and left the podium in shame."[178] In any case, the anecdote suggests that the young man was committed to the Jewish community.

Conversion might have accelerated Dóczi's career along its upward trajectory, but he refused to do so. As a Jew working at the Ballhausplatz in Vienna, he considered his career an edifying example for his coreligionists. In 1878, foreign minister Andrássy informed Dóczi that he could not arrange for him to receive the Order of Saint Stephen unless he converted. Dóczi recounted Andrássy's offer and his response to it in a letter to Manó Kónyi dated December 30, 1878:

> I replied that I would nonetheless remain a Jew, and only as a Jew would I consider it worthwhile to obtain such recognition, because, I say, we must maintain Jews' belief that if they are honorable patriots, nothing is out of their reach.... I then told him that my career is very good and useful, one might say an important example, and for this reason, my religion, which I

PATHS TO CONVERSION—PORTRAITS

might discard for a young girl, shall never be discarded for the sake of my career, and it is really a shame if His Majesty prefers converted Jews to the unconverted. Andrássy responded by saying I was completely correct.[179]

In addition to serving at the joint foreign ministry, Dóczi also tried his hand at literature. His play *Vegyes párok* (*Mixed Couples*), first staged at the National Theater in Budapest in 1889, was well received. In her review, Ilona Fürst wrote, "This is perhaps the first instance in which a Jew has brought the Jewish question to the stage, though—in a very interesting and distinctive fashion—the word *Jew* is never uttered in the piece."[180] Dóczi was, of course, aware of the fact. The director of the National Theater had told him that the delicate subject "harms no one, but makes everyone uncomfortable,"[181] so he avoided the word in order to refine his theme into something presentable. In *Mixed Couples*, the noble-minded Malvin Rózsay falls in love and converts in order to marry a ministerial secretary who has lost his land. Malvin's entire family converts along with her. The young woman has to insist on her love in order to convince her father—a nouveau riche named Náthán (Rosenberg) Rózsay—to agree to the wedding, but once his daughter marries into the old noble family, he does everything he can to insinuate himself into the traditional elite. However, conversion alone is not enough to achieve this goal. As Malvin bitterly tells her new husband, regarding his noble friends, "Their esteem has to be begged for or bought." Malvin's father chooses the latter, paying off his new relatives' debts while donating substantial sums of money to Christian charitable organizations and supporting the restoration of Catholic churches. As a result, he tells his children with satisfaction, "the lord-lieutenant and the landowners come to our house, hunt with you, and pal around with me."[182]

Leaving their religion and community behind does not do these characters any spiritual harm. Dóczi is sympathetic and succinct in presenting the young heroine's reason for converting: "Wherever the boundless faith of primeval love converses from two pairs of eyes, everything else shrinks to nothingness."[183] Dóczi is much more interested in the experience of Jewishness as a social stigma and the emotional factors that encouraged attempts to escape it, as he articulated through Malvin's older brother, hussar lieutenant Zoltán Rózsay:

> There was a time when I wanted to cloak myself in pure self-esteem; I decided to be contemptuous of those who look down on me for no reason, to despise them for their intolerance, their injustice, their stupid cruelty; to

248 JEWISHNESS AND BEYOND

stick to my own kind, to seek consolation for the contempt of those who don't want to know me in the affection and respect of those who do. But I struggled in vain! There were many who disdained me, and of my kind there were few. . . . Why should I have to peek with my heart pounding to see if someone's in the mood to treat me like a human being? Why should I have to extend my hand in fear, at the risk of being ignored and pulling it back like a thief caught in the act? Why should I have to rejoice if a gentleman dignifies me with a nod of the head? I'm tired of this feeling that degrades me in my own mind. I'd rather renounce my own self-esteem than the respect of others.[184]

Egyenlőség's critic understood Lieutenant Rózsay's monologue as an apologia for conversion.[185] However, Dóczi's play was neither a glorification nor a condemnation of conversion; it was a proclamation of the supremacy of love and a denunciation of the prejudices of noble society.

In the 1880s, Lajos Dóczi visited Turin to thank the exiled Lajos Kossuth for having come to the defense of Hungary's Jews at the time of the Tiszaeszlár blood libel trial. In December of 1892, Dóczi wrote a eulogy praising the banker Mór Wahrmann for having remained loyal to his faith.[186] But then in 1893, Dóczi converted to Catholicism in order to marry eighteen-year-old Paula Dassl-Rosenberg, who was also of Jewish origin but had been baptized at birth. Earlier that year in Vienna, the forty-seven-year-old Dóczi had written an undated letter informing Manó Kónyi of his intention to get married: "Disown me, curse me, but I can no longer conceal the fact that I have a kind, beautiful, good—but youthful—fiancée." Dóczi was still uncertain about conversion: "Advise me: should I be baptized or should she become a Jew? If the latter were to happen *here*, would my marriage be *valid back home?*"[187] We do not know how Kónyi responded, but Dóczi obviously came to the realization that marriage to a woman who had converted to Judaism would be invalid in Hungary. If he wanted his marriage to Paula to be considered legal in Hungary, he had no choice. On April 21, 1893, he wrote to Kónyi: "Pray for me tomorrow around noon—if nothing else, say Kaddish for me, because that's when they baptize me, or convert me, or christen me. It really bothers Paula that she's let it come to this, but to no avail; when a young girl like her marries a man of my sort, he can't accept her making this kind of sacrifice, too. *Die Rechnung ist ohnehin zu ungleich* [The tally's too uneven as it is]."[188] Dóczi's consciously self-deprecating tone may have been a defense mechanism, but his justification for conversion was utterly pragmatic. It may not have been

Figure 4.13. Lajos Dóczi. In *Vasárnapi Újság* 44, no. 13 (1897): 196.

among his motives for converting, but it is worth noting that Dóczi and his first wife, Helene Mayer of Vienna, had a son named Péter who was baptized before his father, perhaps at the time of his birth in 1881.[189] Though Dóczi would speak freely about his Jewish origins after he converted, he seems to have decided not to pass his Jewishness on to his son even before he himself was baptized.

Unlike Dóczi, writer, painter, and designer **Anna Lesznai** (1885–1966), the younger sister of Iván Moscovitz, believed in Jesus in her own peculiar and intimate manner. Yet to her, this faith was completely separate from the issue of religious affiliation.[190] In 1917, when her second husband, Oszkár Jászi, initiated a survey on the "Jewish question" in *Huszadik Század*, Lesznai was among those who sent the monthly a response. While most of the other participants examined the political, economic, and social dimensions of the issue, Lesznai wrote exclusively about its psychological aspects. The former Amália Moscovitz was the only converted Jew who responded by submitting an emphatically personal account in the style of a confession:

> The Jewish question persists even when a person of Jewish origin sits alone in a room behind closed doors. It is not merely part of the relationship between the individual and the public; its fateful seriousness derives from the fact that a Jew is a Jew even to [herself]. Thus what are—and what are the origins of—the characteristics that differentiate the non-Jew from the cultivated Jew who has emerged from the ghetto?
>
> In seeking a response to this question, I have to reach back to semi-conscious childhood memories, insofar as I—a woman not confronted with any external competition or social struggle—have become familiar with the problem only as it has been reflected in my own life. As a result of the happenstance of my upbringing, I lived among Christians and Jews—my memories, my feelings, my friends were recruited from both circles—and at the very beginning of things, the broad-crowned trees of a village manor swayed above me.
>
> At eight, in the pipe smoke of respectable rural "gentlemen" who hunted and talked politics, I was "the most Hungarian little rich kid," growing up in an atmosphere of patriotism and—insofar as it was possible to absorb such things unconsciously—"the sentiments of the lordly class." Other elements in my spiritual inventory included the Pest home of my religious Jewish grandparents, their more narrowly strict customs, the white-bearded old man who observed Yom Kippur. My consciousness accommodated both the Yom Kippur and Good Friday fasts. I prayed at the sound of the Catholic church's bell.

I knew of the existence of sidelocked rural grocer-innkeepers who were "Jews," but like the Slovak peasants [there], these "professional Jews" who sold ribbon were not the same kind of people we were. I must have expressed something like this to my mother once (I think I asked what sort of military deeds my ancestors had done to deserve their nobility); my mother began to laugh out loud, and this derisive laughter, along with the commentary she added, made clear to me for the first time that I was not "a true, purely Hungarian child of the upper class" and that Jewishness represented a kind of separate reality, something inferior, not necessarily to be concealed, but to be avoided in society. This was the beginning of the Jewish question for me. I wanted to know *where I belonged*: to the kind company that had coddled me from the cradle; to my strict grandparents who had condemned and misunderstood us and whose atmosphere was alien to me; or perhaps to the ribbon-selling Jews down there in the village. I learned that my paternal great grandfather was an innkeeper, so I slipped down to the little store next to the inn and observed the lady grocer at the counter for a long while, her busy hands, her drawling singsong. I invited her children out to play, but we could hardly understand each other; they spoke German, they were filthy, and they said "it wasn't allowed to eat from the same food as me." This impatient, painful quest accompanied me throughout my development. I sometimes took pleasure in believing myself to be "at home" among Jews or Christians with whom I felt a particular sense of community as a result of my memories and inclinations. Even so, I never found in any milieu a synthesis of memory, culture, and temperament into which I fit perfectly. *Jews have friends, but no social circle.* A thousand hurtful words flew at me, a thousand arrogant witticisms, Jewish and Christian, each of which wounded me in some way. And that which in my life has remained a faint, lyrical, voiceless feeling of absence, without tragedy, has more or less decisively stamped the fate of the Jewish intelligentsia. *To be a Jew signifies a distinctive, pathologically agitated nervous state.*[191]

By the time Anna Lesznai wrote these lines, she had already converted to the Reformed faith; in a diary entry written six years later, she described that period of her life with the following remark about the Slovak peasants of Körtvélyes (Hrušov): "With my faith that recognized no denomination, and yet as a Jew who had been baptized a Calvinist, I could pray with them wholeheartedly, zealously, in tears."[192] However, Lesznai did not mention her conversion in her response to the survey. In the latter part of her piece in *Huszadik Század*, she stopped writing about herself and instead offered a detailed analysis of the factors that contributed to the neurosis associated with

Figure 4.14. Anna Lesznai, 1920s. Petőfi Literary Museum, F.2009.149.1.

"cultivated Jews" and their "belonging nowhere." A 1932 diary entry indicates that one of the objectives of the autobiographical novel she was planning to write was to present the way in which "a young girl raised to be 'gentry'" becomes conscious of "being a Jew and an outsider,"[193] but in the book itself (which she completed after emigrating to the United States), Lesznai attributed this realization to her narrator's older brother. The novel does not refer to her own conversion, nor do the known portions of the diaries she kept between 1912 and 1945.[194]

Lesznai was still a member of the Jewish community when, at the age of seventeen, she married Károly Garay, whom she divorced within a year.[195] In her autobiographical novel, she depicted Garay as boorish, calculating, and two-faced. She gave his stand-in the name Jenő Weiszberg, effectively re-Judaizing Garay even though he had already converted to Catholicism in 1902, when he and his still-Jewish bride tried unsuccessfully to convince the chief rabbi of Arad, Sándor Rosenberg, to bless their civil marriage.[196] Thus, it would seem that Lesznai still maintained some sort of commitment to the Jewish community at the time of her marriage, though she may have asked for the rabbi's blessing merely out of concern for her parents. The precise date of her conversion is unknown, though she was already a member of the Reformed Church by the time of her civil marriage to her second husband, Oszkár Jászi. She presumably converted at his request, shortly before they were wed on June 19, 1913.[197]

Lesznai never spoke about her conversion, which we could interpret as a form of self-censorship. Perhaps she could not reconcile her self-image as an independent, sensitive, and sincere artist with the pragmatic decision to convert to please her future husband. It is also possible that Lesznai never discussed her conversion because she considered the issue insignificant. Perhaps the formal change of religious affiliation did not signify a caesura in her spiritual growth or in her relation to her Jewishness and thus had no symbolic significance for her. As her response to the *Huszadik Század* survey demonstrates, she was primarily interested in the "cultivated Jews" of her own milieu and in their state of mind. She believed that being a modern Jewish intellectual necessarily induced a pathological nervous condition. Yet the legal act of switching religions could not serve as a means of escaping this condition, the primarily inward sensation of "belonging nowhere." It is no coincidence that at the end of her response to the survey, among her recommendations for "resolving" the "Jewish question," Lesznai did not mention conversion.

254 JEWISHNESS AND BEYOND

Despite her confused attraction to Jesus, there is no sign Anna Lesznai was particularly affected by the Christian religion as an adolescent. An example of conversion stemming from genuine religious conviction was **Sándor Hevesi** (1873–1939), director, theater manager, translator, and critic.

On September 20 and October 11, 1900, at the age of twenty-seven, Sándor Hevesi informed the rabbinical office of the Israelite Congregation of Pest of his intention to disaffiliate and convert to Catholicism.[198] His testimonial on the subject was published in the Catholic periodical *Vigilia* in 1948. The precise date on which Hevesi produced the text is unknown, though *Vigilia's* editor noted that one of Hevesi's friends had asked him to write an account of his journey to Catholicism in 1930.[199] Hevesi, who had Magyarized his name in 1893, was born in Nagykanizsa. His father, Mór Hoffmann, began his career teaching at a Jewish elementary school, then transferred to a middle school in Nagykanizsa, where he taught Hungarian literature and German language until his retirement. An active participant in the cultural life of Nagykanizsa, Mór Hoffmann wrote an early Jewish-themed volume of poetry, a novel, nineteen textbooks, and several pedagogical studies; he also edited a handful of periodicals for young people. Hevesi's village-born mother, the cheerful Wilhelmina (Anna) Wesel, strove to bring herself up to her husband's level of culture. She read extensively and created a peaceful home for her family.[200]

Hevesi completed his primary education at the Jewish elementary school in Nagykanizsa. According to his testimonial, "My religious education at school was built around the Old Testament, in which I was very well versed." He initially encountered the Catholic faith as a student at the Piarist gymnasium in Nagykanizsa: "My first sensation of the Catholic religion was a vague, peculiar mysticism. The children went to mass in the morning and I envied them. I would have loved to assist the priest; I found the liturgy very interesting. I felt like the adults were cheating me, shortchanging me by preventing me from participating in something I would have liked." The synagogue, on the other hand, did not inspire him: "I have only this memory, from when I was a little boy: a cantor with a beautiful voice was singing (and I was happy to listen because I had liked music from a very early age), but he sang as if he were condescending to the Lord God, and then the rabbi and the cantor carried the Torah around. Everything else in me has faded away, perhaps because this impression had no effect on my soul."[201]

PATHS TO CONVERSION—PORTRAITS

The piety of his parents' household left more of a mark; according to Hevesi's testimonial, his family was the source of the faith that eventually took shape as Catholicism:

> In my family, belief in God and prayers were separate from Jewish rites; as soon as I could speak, my first prayer was the same one that many thousands of children besides me prayed in every European language. It was written by the German poetess Luise Hensel, who grew up in a Protestant preacher's family and later returned to the Church. . . . There was no ceremony in my parents' house on holidays; they did not follow the dietary laws. In this age of surging liberalism, they raised children with strong national—but not particularly religious—sentiments. Inwardly, both of my parents were believers in God, and thus I was not driven to the Catholic faith by the frigid air of atheism, but rather by a belief that I had absorbed in childhood, and which later sought form. I desired a religion that would serve as a framework for my actual life, as content for my inner world.[202]

Hevesi had nothing more to say about his early impulses and thus did not explain why Judaism had failed to serve as the religion his soul "desired." His testimonial did not recount what it had been like for him to grow up as a Jew, nor did it mention any aspect of his parents' Jewishness beyond the religious. Hevesi's father, Mór Hoffmann, was an active participant in Jewish public life from the late 1860s to the 1880s. He wrote articles for *Izraelita Magyar Néptanító* (*Hungarian Israelite Schoolteacher*), *Izraelita Közlöny* (*Israelite Gazette*), and *Szombati Újság* (*Saturday News*). He also published several pamphlets, some of which advocated a more complete Magyarization of his fellow Jews, while others offered defenses against attacks they had suffered.[203] Another of Hoffmann's interests was the rearing of Jewish children; he wrote regularly for *Magyar-Zsidó Ifjúság Lapja* (*Journal of Hungarian-Jewish Youth*; 1885–87). In his articles, Hoffmann tried to inspire his young readers with the religious zeal that "constitutes the foundation of pure morality."[204] In most of his writings, Hoffmann attempted to arm young Jews against the spiritual effects of antisemitism, and like many Neolog intellectuals, he believed the most effective means of equipping them was to present Jewish history as a tale of suffering.[205] It is hard to imagine that Mór Hoffmann did not strive to make "a good Jew" of his own son. Yet Hevesi's testimonial says nothing about his father's efforts to raise him as Jew, possibly because these efforts were not particularly effective, or perhaps

Figure 4.15. Sándor Hevesi. https://hu.wikipedia.org/wiki/Hevesi
_Sándor

because his assignment was to write the story of his path to the Catholic faith, rather than his abandonment of Judaism.

For Hevesi, Christianity was not merely a religion but a civilization—the European civilization that had grown up out of the soil of "Christlike thought." However, his description of the journey that culminated in his conversion to Christianity is primarily a spiritual phylogenesis. A decade before his conversion, "the figure of Jesus Christ" had already "moved" into him, though he knew he could not become a Christian "without the supernatural, mystical force known to theologians by the name of *grace*." After several years of struggle, the moment finally arrived: "It was summer. I had gone off to Venice. The Gospels were in my pocket, my thoughts constantly engaged with them. One morning in a little abandoned church, before its little altar, these years-long conflicts broke forth and I fell to my knees in tears. I was comforted; Christ spoke clearly to me through it all, and His Church showed my thoughts their exact subsequent path, which I now knew would be straight as an arrow and lead to the Catholic faith. My religious doubts had come to an end. I no longer wanted to be smarter."[206]

Even so, Hevesi continued to wait because "I knew that I still had much work to do, that I had to be completely worthy of reaching the place where I yearned to be—though I already had my arguments for all sorts of things." He finally converted at the dawn of the twentieth century: "I sealed my profound conviction in 1900 by having myself recorded as a member of the Church."[207]

Unlike Hevesi's, the conversion of the film critic, screenwriter, and poet **Béla Balázs** (1884–1949) had nothing to do with religious conviction. Balázs set about justifying his conversion in two separate diary entries: his first attempt, written three months after he became a Catholic in March of 1913, was essentially incomprehensible; the second explanation of his convictions (written four years later, in 1917) was grounded in a philosophy of history. Other passages of Balázs' diary and autobiography suggest that he omitted a more personal motive for converting—namely, a desire to find acceptance, spiritual community, and a sense of his own identity as part of the majority society.

Born in Szeged, Herbert Bauer—the eldest child of Simon Bauer and Prussian-born Eugénia (Jenny) Levy—legally adopted the nom de plume Béla Balázs at the age of twenty-nine, shortly after converting. Balázs's sister Hilda Bauer was among the loves of György Lukács' youth, while his brother, biologist Ervin Bauer, was the second husband of writer Margit Kaffka. Their father, Simon Bauer, was born in Pest and attended the University of Vienna to study pedagogy and philosophy. Upon returning to Hungary, he passed his teacher's examination and earned a doctoral degree. In 1875, he took a teaching position at the state *Realschule* in Szeged. He translated Leibniz and wrote introductions to the works of Goethe, Schiller, and Molière. After fifteen years of teaching in Szeged, when his son Herbert was six, Bauer was

258 JEWISHNESS AND BEYOND

transferred to Lőcse. The year after Simon Bauer's death in 1897, in compliance with his dying wish that his children would grow up in a purely Hungarian environment, the family moved back to Szeged, where Balázs's mother found a teaching position at the girls' secondary school.[208]

In his 1946 autobiography, Balázs recalled the relationship he and his father had with Judaism and Jewishness during their time in Lőcse. Balázs attended the local German Lutheran school: "This was *my* school. These people were *us*"; the students at the nearby Catholic school "were *them*. Those over there." The Lutheran school was attended primarily by the children of German burghers and "liberal" Hungarian civil servants from Lőcse and the rest of Szepes County. The Catholic school was for the offspring of Slovak peasants, "bigoted Catholic" civil servants, and the gentry:

> Thus with my whole heart and a passionate partiality, I felt I belonged to the fellowship of Lutherans. And so I went to the Lutheran church every Sunday. However, given that I had no place in the pews beside my parents like the other children did, I went up into the choir and with great zeal helped pump the huge beam of the organ's bellows. If I was not allowed to sing down there with the others, I thought, then I'd do my part like this. I did not lack for zeal.
>
> But my ardent zeal and solidarity were in vain; I still did not fully belong to the others. My father, who otherwise never went to church and never prayed, brought me to a sort of mysterious ceremony once a year. He took me by the hand and led me to a small house by the Polish Gate, then to the end of a courtyard that opened onto an utterly ordinary room which nevertheless had pews like a church. It was all men there, no one I recognized, no one with whom my parents socialized. With white shawls on their shoulders, they pounded their chests and wailed. The only frightening thing for me was that my father had also dressed himself in one of these white shawls, bordered with black stripes, as if he had joined and lined up alongside some mysterious foreign alliance. He did not pound his chest, and mumbled the prayers so mechanically, it felt like he was reciting some ambivalent data at the office. And yet it was precisely that which gave me the impression of some enigmatic, higher constraint. Because it seemed like my father was being *forced* to submit to this ritual, reluctantly, against his will. . . .
>
> Otherwise, for the rest of the year, I had no reason to notice that we were Jews. There was no Jewish religious instruction at the Lutheran school and my father, a committedly non-denominational Freemason, did not invest it with any significance. The first inkling of my isolation and loneliness cast its painful shadow across me when they told me I could go home during religious

PATHS TO CONVERSION—PORTRAITS

instruction. I simply could not comprehend how I was to leave school totally alone in the morning. Why?—everybody then asked me in amazement. Why isn't Herbert Bauer there with the others at school? And I, equally amazed and with an anxious heart, answered without understanding: because I'm a Jew. . . . I loitered in the hall in front of that classroom, waiting for Bible class to end with a sad desire in my heart.

Then one day I made up my mind and asked the pastor to allow me to attend his class. I promised to behave myself and I was very much satisfied that he allowed it. But I remained isolated and lonely because I was never called on and never asked anything. I knew the Bible stories and the Psalms better than the others did, but the reverend pastor always left my row as if he hadn't even seen me. I was still excluded.

The fact that I was excluded from one community without belonging to another—that I, even in my early childhood, stood outside any denomination or community, a solitary individual, isolated—has determined my conduct and my destiny throughout my life.[209]

At that time, Balázs was only sentimentally divorced from the Jewish community; when he returned to Szeged at fourteen, he was enrolled in the required Jewish religion classes. However, as his diary articulates, this compulsory instruction had no emotional effect on him. An entry dated January 8, 1899 reads:

Unfortunately, I studied precisely the [part] that was left out of religion class, not the lesson itself, but luckily I didn't have to answer. After religion, I went ice-skating.

January 15, 1899: I woke up early this morning and studied a little more religion in bed, but then I just put out the lamp and slept some more, so I was almost late for religion class.

January 21, 1899: I don't intend to go to religious instruction tomorrow because I want to do a drawing. I don't think it will do much harm to miss this religion lesson. I don't want to be a rabbi anyway.[210]

As a teenager, Balázs seems to have been entirely indifferent to his Jewishness. His diaries for the years 1899 and 1900, in which he dissected the great questions of life with an adolescent's élan, do not contain a single line on the subject.

After graduating from the *Realschule* in Szeged, Balázs began studying Hungarian and German at the University of Budapest in the fall of 1902. In 1904, he joined the Thália Society, a theatrical company modeled on the Freie

260   JEWISHNESS AND BEYOND

Bühne and the Théatre-Libre. He and György Lukács became friends in the same year. Balázs earned a diploma in Hungarian and German in 1906 and a doctoral degree in 1909. Meanwhile, he worked as a substitute teacher at several schools in Budapest and wrote poems and prose for publications like the 1908 literary anthology *Holnap* (*Tomorrow*) and *Nyugat*. His drama *Doctor Margit Szélpál* was staged at the National Theater in 1909, and his first volume of poetry was published the following year. Balázs identified himself as a teacher when he registered his disaffiliation with the rabbinical office of the Israelite Congregation of Buda in 1913, although soon afterward he was hired by the Pedagogical Library of Budapest.[211]

Balázs ends the autobiography he wrote in his dotage with an account of a mystical-erotic experience that took place the summer after he graduated from high school. After a failed attempt to establish an intimate relationship with "the Hungarian people" as the assistant superintendent of the Pálffys' estate in Szilágypuszta, Balázs found release in the arms of a servant girl in a freshly mown field. "I could hardly see Marika's face. It was like I'd dug myself into the earth, which wanted to push me away, but called me back and embraced me."[212] Though this incident played a significant role in Balázs's autobiography, his diary—which he resumed writing in November of 1903 after a three-year hiatus—does not mention it. He frequently touched on his relationships with Jews, Judaism, and his own Jewishness, though always in a cursory manner. On November 24, 1905, "after a long pause," he went to a synagogue for a Friday evening service where the rabbi's sermon "made something clear" to him: "I know why the Jewish religion and Jewish spirituality have been antipathetic to me from the start. They are conceptualizing, but totally metaphysical and antithetical to art." A brief, somewhat murky comment dated January 1909 suggests he felt a sort of opposition between his Jewishness and his ability to find spiritual equilibrium or his own inner path.[213] In a letter to György Lukács on June 25, 1910, Balázs expressed his desire to find a full-time teaching position at one of the state secondary schools in Budapest, casually adding, "Too bad I'm Jewish, or that I didn't convert long ago, because now—out of a possibly unjustifiable but insuperable 'defiance, self-respect, or sense of shame,' or whatever—I'd be totally incapable of doing so."[214]

Not much later, on October 6, 1910, Balázs informed Lukács that he had found a position, "an outstanding job," at a gymnasium operated by the city of Budapest rather than the state.[215] As for the dilemmas of his art and artistic career, they would not have been resolved by conversion. On

Figure 4.16. Béla Balázs, c. 1915. Petőfi Literary Museum, F.6982.

November 26, 1911, the editors of *Nyugat* organized a matinée in honor of novelist Zsigmond Móricz. All the readers at this event were Christian writers, which some interpreted as evidence of a sort of anti-Jewish conspiracy within Hungary's modern literary camp. The poet Endre Ady protested vehemently,[216] but Balázs's diary entry for December 12, 1911 suggests Ady had not convinced him:

> I've known for some time that they hate the Semitic literature that hangs around the neck of Pest, for which reason they're hostile to—and suspicious of—every writer who's a Jew. They want to form an alliance and seize a controlling influence for themselves.... They're right ... within 10 years, antisemitism will be a force in Hungarian literature and Jewish journalists will no longer be as important as they are today. They're right. They proclaim the cult of race in art, in literature—this is their means of eliminating those who aren't "full-blooded Hungarians." And again, they're right. But what's to become of me? I hate contemporary Jewish literature more than they do—yet I don't belong to them, either. They don't accept me. My name is German, my tribe is Jewish, my writing will never reflect the particular character of the Hungarian race. I can't make a cult of something I lack. What's to become of me? Will I be excluded, isolated, and rootless, without any neighbors, any followers, any resonance, no matter what? That would appear to be the end of this. I won't be needed, neither here nor there.[217]

For Balázs, Jewishness was clearly nothing but exclusion and belonging nowhere—a substantial obstacle to his self-expression as a Hungarian writer.

On March 6, 1913, alongside economic historian Károly Polányi, Balázs reported his disaffiliation to the rabbinical office of the Israelite Congregation of Buda for the second time. Though both men declared an intention to remain unaffiliated, Balázs was baptized at the Roman Catholic parish church of Buda a couple of weeks later. On March 29, 1913, he married the equally converted Edit Hajós.[218] In a letter dated February 19, 1913, shortly after he first announced his disaffiliation, Balázs notified György Lukács of his conversion, letting the news drop parenthetically among some other rather minor matters: "Besides that, I have succeeded in getting off Moses' lap."[219] After another year-long pause, Balázs returned to his diary in July of 1913 and recalled his conversion as follows:

> I converted, Magyarized my name, and got married. I thus changed all the accidental properties of my existence. I shed and exposed a new skin. Now I'm a Roman Catholic, and known officially as Béla Balázs, too. Of course,

all this entailed an enormous amount of effort. That and getting ourselves established at the villa took up the whole spring.

Among the most serious of these [events] was perhaps my conversion. It was the result of conviction. If one must belong to a religion, this one is the most sympathetic to me. On the other hand, I don't feel like I have anything to do with Jews—although, as I've recently noticed, this applies only to Jewish men. I'm much more attracted by Jewish *women*; perhaps only they truly attract me. There's still something there that I haven't figured out. Aryan-Jewish cross-breeding suits me best. I suspect that I myself am a hybrid of this sort . . . because there's a lot of Jew in me. One day soon I'll systematically analyze this. Only my final *intentions* are Aryan.[220]

This entry is something of a muddle. It does not indicate which of Balázs's intentions were "Aryan," nor what that might have meant. Neither does it make clear what sort of "conviction" had prompted him to convert. Was it his conviction that the Catholic faith was "most sympathetic?" Or that he had nothing in common with Jews, despite his attraction to Jewish women and his having "a lot of Jew" in him? Perhaps Balázs himself was dissatisfied with this explanation; perhaps even his friends did not truly understand his reasoning. In any case, Balázs returned to this subject four years later, in May of 1917:

They asked me why I converted. "Out of conviction." Do I believe in the modern Catholic creed and church? "No."—?—

I believe, and I consider myself deeply religious, but I do not recognize any of the presently "available" denominations as my home. However, I do not believe it is possible to invent a religion, or that I could fashion some sort of private faith for myself. I hate "religions" that are tailored to the personal comfort of modern, individualistic aesthetic philosophy.

I did not wish to be without a denomination, so I joined the most *up-to-date* denomination in historical-philosophical terms. Because even if I'm not at home in a particular tent, one cannot go without shelter. Religions *happen*, just as the world and God happen. A train is passing before me; the car that's right *here* in front of me, right now, is not mine, but I have to jump on or get left behind. Jewishness has already been uncoupled from the train. Catholicism is not my home, but here it is, moving along in front of me, the living religion. I have to step in under its roof. And there I can continue seeking and waiting.[221]

This explanation is more coherent, though it was not particularly original to justify conversion by citing the obsolescence of Judaism. The essential

264   JEWISHNESS AND BEYOND

element here, as reflected in both the text and especially its context (the other diary entries Balázs wrote in the period), is the final reference to "seeking": Béla Balázs was a seeker who did not find what he was looking for in the Catholic Church (nor did he really look for it there). After the outbreak of the First World War, the young writer was seized by a burning desire to experience an inner sense of community with his "society, race, country" and thus to be able, like Ady, to speak "in the name of the Hungarians." At the same time, Balázs was increasingly sensitive to the notion that he would never have a chance to do so unless he clarified his relationship with the Hungarian "people" and with his own "Hungarianness."[222] His conversion was a way station along that path.

Strictly observed, the periodization of the present volume (ending with the outbreak of the First World War) would sever the ends of several tales that continued on past the war. One concerns writer, critic, literary historian, and patron of the arts **Lajos Hatvany** (1880–1961), who did not convert until 1919 but would otherwise serve as a fitting epilogue to this series of portraits of Jewish intellectuals who converted to Christianity. The year before Lajos Deutsch was born, his family was ennobled and granted the praedicatum "hatvani," which young Lajos bore from birth. In 1897, his father and uncles formally changed their name to Hatvany-Deutsch. Having been granted the title of baron alongside their father in 1908, Lajos Hatvany-Deutsch and his brother Ferenc shortened their surname to Hatvany in March of 1917. A line of commodities traders who had come to dominate Hungary's sugar and milling industries, the Deutsch dynasty was then in its fifth generation. Lajos Hatvany was not the only member of that generation who declined to pursue his forefathers' occupation and instead chose to focus on scholarship or the arts. Among them were Sándor Hatvany-Deutsch's younger son Ferenc (painter and art collector) and József Hatvany-Deutsch's children Lili Hatvany (writer) and Bertalan Hatvany (Orientalist). Lajos, Ferenc, and Lili converted to Christianity while Bertalan turned to Zionism—which, in its own way, was at least as alien to his parents' worldview as the baptisms of his sister and cousins.

The family's dominant personality, Sándor Hatvany-Deutsch (Lajos Hatvany's father), ran an assortment of industrial and financial enterprises while acting as vice president of the National Association of Industrialists. Unlike his cousin József, Sándor Hatvany-Deutsch was not an active participant in the public life of the Jewish community, though he did serve as an honorary officer of several Jewish organizations. He donated significant sums to Jewish organizations and provided generous support for Russian and Romanian Jews who fled through Hungary to escape pogroms in their home countries. On the occasion of Sándor Hatvany-Deutsch's death, *Egyenlőség* wrote, "A multitude of tasks kept him from playing an active role [in Jewish communal life], but he displayed his Jewish heart and Jewish sensibilities in embracing the cause of—and generously supporting—the forsaken."[223] The notion of his *Jewish heart* is undercut somewhat by the fact that a few months before his death in 1913, Sándor Hatvany-Deutsch—whose first wife died in 1901—married a converted Jewish widow, Ottilia (Tilly) Amberg, a union the Jewish press discreetly ignored.[224]

Our only information about the manner in which Hatvany-Deutsch and his wife, Emma, raised their children comes from a 1928 recollection penned by teacher and pedagogical specialist János Waldapfel, who became the ten-year-old Lajos Hatvany's private tutor in the autumn of 1890 (he resigned on March 31, 1891). Waldapfel's account suggests that Emma Deutsch was rather tightfisted and that "Laci"—as the darling of the family was known—was extremely spoiled by his grandmothers. Laci's father apparently "considered him a genius," though Waldapfel thought Laci's younger brother Ferenc was more talented.[225] In any case, neither Waldapfel nor anyone else ever discussed the Hatvany-Deutsches' relationships to their Jewishness or whether they attributed any significance to it in raising their children.

Lajos Hatvany's acclaimed family saga *Urak és emberek* (*Men and Gentlemen*), which depicts the rise of the Bondy family over the course of several generations, provides no grounds for speculation on the subject. Hatvany wrote the first volume after emigrating in 1919, publishing it upon his return to Hungary in early 1927. (The day after his homecoming, he was charged with "defamation of the nation" and eventually sentenced to a year and a half in prison.[226]) *Egyenlőség* characterized the first volume of the cycle, *Zsiga a családban* (*Zsiga in the Family*, published in English as *Bondy Jr.*), as a work of antisemitism, which surprised and discouraged Hatvany. He nevertheless continued to work on the series, though it is not clear when (or whether) he completed it. Literary historian György Belia found the (possibly) unfinished, partially typewritten manuscripts of two other volumes, publishing them along with *Zsiga in the Family*, after Hatvany's death.[227] Hatvany's contemporaries assumed the series was a portrait of his own family, but he himself emphatically rejected any such comparisons in March of 1927, when he responded to *Egyenlőség*'s accusations of antisemitism: "My great grandfather,

Figure 4.17. Lajos Hatvany, c. 1905. Petőfi Literary Museum, F.14840.

Ignác Deutsch, my grandfathers Bernát and József, my father Sándor Hatvani Deutsch, and my uncle József Hatvani Deutsch *were merchants and industrialists of a spirit entirely different from that of the heroes of my novel.* It is thus senseless to say that I wrote my novel about my family."[228] I should also note that this reading of the work as a depiction of Hatvany's father's generation is made yet more absurd by the fact that the protagonist of the post-1927 volumes, bank director Zsigmond Bondy, marries into a family of Hungarian counts as a defiantly bourgeois, unconverted Jew, making him a historical impossibility, a character who could never have existed.

Having earned a doctoral degree in Budapest in 1905, Lajos Hatvany provided financial support for the highly influential literary journal *Nyugat* from the time of its first appearance in 1908. After a disagreement with the journal's editors, he parted ways with them in 1911 and subsequently moved to Berlin, where he lived for several years. Up until 1917, Hatvany never made any public statements about his Jewish identity or the "Jewish question." He does not seem to have been particularly interested in the subject, although he did make a few offhand remarks about his Jewishness in his letters, such as the one he wrote to poet Endre Ady from Saint-Germain-en-Laye on July 10, 1914. In response to Ady's request for advice on marrying Berta Boncza (known by her pen name, Csinszka), Hatvany discussed his multiple identities with cheerful irony, or at least affected an ironic attitude in this exchange with his friend:

> Concerning your beloved. With my level Deutsch head: the givens are a poet who is neither healthy nor young and a little girl, a little 20-year-old hysteric. Because that's what she is, isn't she . . . trouble, trouble, trouble . . . in every way, trouble. That's what the Deutsch says. The *Hatvany*, on the other hand, with the *y* on his name [signifying nobility], almost gentry, almost a carouser, almost a Hungarian, who has always battled the cautious Jew in me, recommends that you get on with it: life is worth as much as the experiences in it. Are you any wiser?[229]

Among the respondents to the aforementioned 1917 survey on the "Jewish question," Hatvany was the only Jew who urged his coreligionists to settle the issue definitively by choosing the path of self-liquidation through intermarriage. His brief response to the *Huszadik Század* survey reads as follows:

> Those who've suffered half their lives for their race and their religion, even if they've hardly cultivated a sense of racial belonging and have long since outgrown religious superstition, can no longer really help themselves. They

268   JEWISHNESS AND BEYOND

must bear the cross, which in this case is the *cross of Jewishness*. Yet it's the duty of every enlightened Jewish father to raise Christian children. "If one goes to the ball, one dons tails," [Maximilian] Harden said to justify his own apostasy. One cannot leave the ghetto in a kaftan, neither a physical nor a spiritual kaftan. You must dress your children in tailcoats, my Jews, definitely tails, so that closed doors will open before them and they will be able to take part, *unimpeded*, in all the work of mankind. Because the quantity of energy you spend overcoming obstacles to Jewishness could be used more efficiently and fruitfully if you commit it directly to the work of life rather than the surmounting of pointless, yet still insurmountable prejudices. . . .

You can't fight primeval stupidity or innate, bestial, instinctive passions. You're crazy if you stand in their way; you're wise to sidestep them. It's here— the time has arrived for Jewry to draw its own conclusions from the great and eternal lessons of the world war, according to which antisemitism cannot be fought with clever or logical arguments, but only with the Semites' assimilation into the Aryan race. As many mixed marriages as possible! Let this be the slogan that leads to what I consider the only sure solution to the Jewish question. Let Jewish racial character, which cannot be defended against humanity's antipathy (the more irrational, the more invincible) fade into [our] Christian descendants as much as possible. This is the goal, the one sensible, blessed goal for the new Jewish generations.

Et salvavi animam meam, I wrote on the Feast of Corpus Christi, though in the spirit and the interest of humanity.[230]

Hatvany's argument seems unassailable: when there are no longer any Jews, neither will there be any Jewish question. Otherwise, it is difficult to make sense of the piece. Why did Jews have to disappear? As an inevitable condition of their integration into the majority society, or because it was the only way Jews could overcome ineradicable antisemitic prejudices? Furthermore, what exactly was Hatvany advocating? That fathers who were fated to continue to bear the stigma of Jewishness should baptize their children? As Hatvany must have known, this was not legally possible. Children under the age of seven could not convert unless their parents did, while those between seven and eighteen could not convert at all (excepting married women). What remains is the proposal at the end of the piece, according to which members of the younger generation of Jews should marry Christian partners to dilute the "racial character" of the children they would bear.

The closing Latin citation (from the confessional oath *Dixi et salvavi animam meam*, "I have spoken and saved my soul") and the reference to a Catholic feast day suggest that Lajos Hatvany had already converted. *Egyenlőség* reached the same conclusion in a reaction to the *Huszadik Század* survey.[231] In an article published in early 1918, the Zionist journal *Zsidó Szemle* reported that when Hatvany announced his disaffiliation to the Israelite Congregation of Pest "on that famous feast day of Corpus Christi," he had given the rabbi a large sum of money to promote "Israelite literary objectives."[232] Hatvany was, in fact, still legally of the Jewish faith when he wrote the piece. According to the "notes" section of his Jewish birth certificate, Hatvany was baptized at the Catholic Inner City Parish Church of Budapest on May 30, 1919, during the time of the short-lived Hungarian Soviet Republic.[233]

Hatvany's response to the *Huszadik Század* survey does little to clarify his motives for converting. He had already entered into a "mixed" marriage of his own in 1915 with Lutheran Christa Winsloe. Though they never had children and would divorce in 1924, he and his wife had agreed that their offspring would be raised in the Lutheran Church like their mother.[234] The logic of Hatvany's piece suggests that conversion would do nothing to alter his Jewishness, thus it is not a coincidence that he avoided words like *conversion* and *baptism* in his response to the survey. In his view, the "Jewish question" could be resolved only over multiple generations, by gradually diluting Jews' "racial character" through mixed marriages.

Having begun his writing career under the tutelage of conservative literary historian Pál Gyulai, Hatvany supported the Aster Revolution that broke out in Hungary in late October of 1918. He served as a member of the Hungarian National Council, which functioned as the legislative body of the independent Hungarian People's Republic proclaimed the following month. Hatvany emigrated to Austria in 1919, during the summer of the Hungarian Soviet Republic. Starting in 1921, the Vienna-based Hungarian-language periodicals *Jövő* (*Future*) and *Ember* (*Man*) would publish his vehement denunciations of white terror and the inchoate regime of Miklós Horthy. On February 1, 1928, at the first hearing of Hatvany's trial on charges of "defaming the nation," chief justice of the criminal court Géza Töreky spoke for the regime in declaring, "You might be a citizen of this country, but you cannot be a son of this fatherland."[235] By then, Hatvany could hardly have been surprised by his guilty verdict. As he wrote in the May 1927 edition of the Kolozsvár-based journal *Korunk* (*Our Age*), "Woe unto us, a hundred times woe, who can only argue that we grew up on Hungarian soil, breathed Hungarian air and spoke Hungarian, gave our bodies and souls, our blood, our marrow, and our sweat to the Hungarian nation, and yet if our Hungarianness is subjected to insult or injury, we cannot open our mouths to complain because the wits of the regime immediately taunt us: *Jew! Jew!*"[236]

Hatvany expressed himself even more pithily at an appeal hearing on May 9, 1928: "I have heard these charges for 10 years: a person of Jewish origin cannot truly be Hungarian, there is no assimilation, there is no genuine integration into the Hungarian race."[237] Hatvany presented himself as evidence that disproved these charges: "I stand here now as a warning sign, my entire nervous system a trembling manifestation of protest against this false doctrine."[238]

These statements highlight the peculiarity of Hatvany's response to the 1917 survey. Though *Huszadik Század*'s query specifically addressed the "Jewish question" in Hungary, Hatvany responded only in general terms, citing German convert Maximilian Harden, comparing and contrasting kaftans and tailcoats, Jews and Christians, the "Semite" and "Aryan" races; however, "Hungarians" and "the Hungarian nation" do not appear. Even so, and even though Hatvany would not convert for another two years, his Hungarianness was the subject of this piece. The statements he made during his trial and the writing he produced in that period indicate that he was deeply affected by the accusation of un-Hungarianness, which denied him the possibility of identifying, fully and spiritually, with the Hungarian nation—even if the charges were brought by a regime that he despised. His response to a 1924 interview question—"I have only Hungarian things to say"—says it all.[239] His conversion to Catholicism in late May of 1919 could, of course, be interpreted as a simple act of escape. However, given the pain it caused Hatvany to have the Horthy regime question his belonging to the Hungarian nation, I believe the deeper motivation for his conversion (as well as that of his more ideologically conservative intellectual predecessors) lay in his desire to be accepted as a Hungarian. He hoped that becoming a Christian would somehow fend off the accusation that "a person of Jewish origin cannot truly be Hungarian" and earn him recognition as that which he felt himself to be—a Hungarian writer. That Hatvany—who converted when racialized antisemitism was flaring up in Hungary and resisted the Horthy regime after his baptism—never had a chance to gain such recognition is, as they say, another story.

In the final decades of the Dual Monarchy, the primary motivation for conversions of upper-class Hungarian Jews of more conformist worldviews was a desire to integrate themselves into the traditional elite. I will bring this next section of short portraits to a close with the story of Mór Wahrmann and his children. The case of the Wahrmann family in particular raises questions about the reasons why the Jewish fathers of the era—apparently committed to Judaism and the Jewish community—were unable to pass that sense of commitment on to their children. The elder Wahrmann's case may provide us with some answers.

Hermann Königswarter (1864–1915) converted to Catholicism in 1895 at the age of thirty-one, as the scion of a prominent family of bankers and entrepreneurs that played a significant role in Viennese Jewish public life. Hermann's grandfather, Jonas von Königswarter, a loyal observer of traditional religious laws, was elevated to the Austrian nobility in 1860. His son, Moritz von Königswarter, who was granted an Austrian baronial title in 1870, was known for his considerable economic accomplishments, his philanthropy, his art collections, and his piety, which was increasingly anachronistic in upper-class Jewish circles. He maintained a strictly kosher household throughout his life.[240] His marriage to Charlotte von Wertheimstein produced four children, including Hermann, who abandoned not only the piety of his parents' home but also his forebears' economic activities, instead becoming a well-known figure among the gilded youth of Budapest.[241] Hermann Königswarter met his future bride, Melánia Blaskovich (of the distinguished Blaskovich de Ebeczk family) as a young hussar captain stationed in Nagyvárad. When they were wed in the spring of 1887, it was not the groom who converted. As a condition of his blessing, Moritz von Königswarter insisted that his son's Christian fiancée convert to Judaism, which she did in Vienna.[242] In 1888, Hermann Königswarter purchased 350,000 forints' worth of land near the Bihar County town of Kisszántó (Sântăul Mic, Romania),[243] where he lived at the time of his father's death in 1893. Toward the end of his life, Moritz Königswarter feared that Hermann would abandon the Jewish faith once he was gone and stipulated in his will that if Hermann converted, he would have to donate one million forints (two million crowns) of his inheritance to several (mostly Jewish) charitable organizations. Hermann did just that following his Catholic baptism. News of his conversion appeared in the press in late 1894, though Hermann, his wife, and their young son, János, actually converted in early 1895. Given that his father had left him assets totaling thirty-four million crowns, a penalty amounting to two million was not a significant burden to him.[244] Hermann's baptismal ceremony was conducted in Nagyvárad by the city's bishop, Cardinal Lőrinc Schlauch, who was rewarded for his troubles with a brooch valued at one hundred thousand crowns.[245] In 1896, the year after he converted, Hermann Königswarter and his wife were admitted to the Park Klub; in 1897, Königswarter was granted the title of baron; in 1898, he became a member of the National Casino.[246] Unlike his father and his grandfather, Hermann Königswarter had no economic achievements to show for himself; he may have hoped converting would help him acquire a Hungarian barony.

Henrik Lévay (1826–1901) seems even more clearly to have converted to Catholicism in order to acquire the title of baron. Born in the Bács County village of Jankovác in southern Hungary, Lévay grew up in a poor family that raised him with what *Egyenlőség* called "a pure-blooded Hungarian mindset."[247] He was working for a merchant in Szeged when the Hungarian Revolution broke out in 1848; Lévay fought and attained the rank of lieutenant in the subsequent war of independence. In 1857, he was among the founders of the First Hungarian General Insurance Company, serving as chief executive from 1883. Lévay provided regular and generous financial support to cultural and philanthropic organizations: in 1878, he established a ten thousand forint fund at the Hungarian Academy of Sciences for the recognition of studies of economics; to commemorate the twenty-fifth anniversary of the founding of his insurance company, he created another ten thousand forint fund to finance a national foundation for the deaf. He was also a founding member of a benevolent society for Hungarian writers and a pension fund for Hungarian journalists.[248] Though Lévay contributed less to Hungarian Jewish religious charities, he was elected to the representative body of the Israelite Congregation of Pest in 1886. In 1892, he became a member of the executive committee of the Neolog movement fighting for the legal "reception" of the Jewish religion.[249] Lévay contributed to the 1893 founding of the *Israelitisch-Theologische Lehranstalt*, the Viennese theological seminary for rabbis and teachers.[250]

One of the first Jews to be ennobled in Hungary, Lévay was granted the praedicatum "kisteleki" on August 25, 1868. An 1885 reform authorized the king of Hungary to appoint fifty members to the House of Lords on the recommendation of the council of ministers, and in December of 1886, King Franz Joseph made Lévay the third Jew (after landowner Károly Sváb and ophthalmologist Ignác Hirschler) to be rewarded for his merit with a lifetime appointment to the upper chamber of the Hungarian National Assembly.[251] When he converted to Christianity in the summer of 1896, Lévay was seventy years old and lived in a childless marriage, so his decision could not have been influenced by family or career considerations. Nor did he need to seek the acceptance of the country's Christian elite, as he had become the fourth Jew admitted to the National Casino in 1862 and the first (along with the journalist Mór Ludassy) to become a member of the Hungarian Jockey Club in 1865.[252]

In April of 1896, Lévay donated thirty-five thousand crowns to six orphanages in Budapest, including five thousand crowns each to the boys' orphanage of the Israelite Congregation of Pest and the girls' orphanage of the Israelite Women's Association of Pest. Two months later, on June 16 and again on July 10, Lévay and his wife reported to the rabbinical office of the ICP to announce their disaffiliation.[253] On July 5, the *Pesti Hírlap* reported that Lévay would soon convert to Catholicism and added, "According to the news flying around the capital, Lévay—who has no children, by the way—will soon obtain the rank of baron in recognition of his long and meritorious service to the public."[254] *Egyenlőség* did not wait for his actual conversion either but published a piece feigning incomprehension of the reasoning behind the conversion of a chief executive who had achieved everything: "Or might there perhaps be something that Henrik Lévay is still awaiting, and which he can obtain by switching religions?"[255] On July 14, 1896, Lévay, his wife, and his nephew's newborn son were baptized at a chapel he had renovated on his estate. The ceremony was conducted by the bishop of Győr, János Zalka; attendees included friends, relatives, and a correspondent from the newspaper *Alkotmány*.[256]

Lévay's conversion was among the few discussed in the Hungarian national press of the period.[257] The event may have attracted attention as a result of Lévay's prominence and advanced age, but as the presence of the correspondent from *Alkotmány* demonstrates, Lévay himself took care to ensure his conversion would be discussed in the press. Nine months later, on April 22, 1897, Lévay and his wife were elevated to the rank of baron and baroness. There is no hard evidence of a link between their conversion and the granting of their titles, but there very likely was one. Only five other Jewish-born individuals had been granted Hungarian baronies at the time: Mór Wodianer in 1874; his younger brother Albert Wodianer Sr. in 1886; Zsigmond Schosberger in 1890; and the brothers Ferenc and Károly Harkányi in 1895. Given that four of these five Jewish-born Hungarian barons—all except Schosberger—converted to Catholicism before they were granted their titles, Lévay's decision to do the same may have been entirely pragmatic.

Hermann Königswarter's father died in 1893, shortly after Mór Wahrmann's death at the age of sixty on November 26, 1892. Though there are obviously

Figure 4.18. Henrik Lévay. In Samu Borovszky, *Magyarország vármegyéi és városai. Győr vármegye* (Budapest: Országos Monografia Társaság, 1908), 190.

limits to parental influence, the conversion of all three of Wahrmann's children to Christianity raises the question: why was he unable to instill in them a dedication to his faith and community?

On the occasion of Wahrmann's passing, *Egyenlőség*'s Miksa Szabolcsi wrote, "I fear that what he was to us, to his denomination—what Hungarian Jewry has lost in him—shall not be truly understood until later. A void, an unfillable void has been struck in our ranks."[258] Ferenc Mezey, the co-editor of the scholarly journal *Magyar-Zsidó Szemle*, agreed with Szabolcsi completely; in lamenting the death of "the greatest Hungarian Jew," Mezey asserted that the community had "suffered an irreparable loss."[259] Szabolcsi proudly remembered Wahrmann as a financial authority of national renown and the first Jewish representative elected to Hungary's National Assembly, but he eulogized Wahrmann primarily as the president of the Israelite Congregation of Pest, as a *good Jew* whose personal example served to encourage his coreligionists: "Who could replace him for us? Who could, like him, win a large circle [of his people] back to religious life with his own example? Who could arouse new, fresh interest in our affairs where it is dying out or disappeared long ago? Who could, like him, fill synagogues with his own example? Who could, like him, revive Jewish communal life and Jewish consciousness with his own example?"[260]

Egyenlőség's eulogy failed to mention Wahrmann's children, presumably because it was common knowledge that they had completely ignored their father's supposedly inspiring example. After marrying Wahrmann in 1861, Lujza Gold bore him a girl, **Renée Wahrmann** (1862–1926), and two boys, **Ernő Wahrmann** (1863–1906) and **Richard Wahrmann** (1865–1912). Lujza died giving birth to Richard, and Mór Wahrmann never remarried; his children were raised by governesses and private tutors. Ernő and Richard, both lieutenants in the hussar reserves, did not follow in their father's professional footsteps, shining instead at the card table and the racetrack. Ernő was fond of ethereal English ladies; Richard was attracted to music-hall singers.[261] Ernő Wahrmann went to the University of Halle-Wittenberg to study agriculture in 1887,[262] then spent a couple of years in London as an analyst for the Hungarian Ministry of Commerce in the early 1900s. Most of the Budapest dailies attributed Wahrmann's resignation from the ministry to health problems; an article published in the *Pesti Hírlap* on the occasion of his younger brother's death suggested that Ernő had quit after a "quarrel with the ambassador, who did not wish to introduce him to the English court."[263] Richard Wahrmann never worked; he was a passionate hunter of game in distant, exotic lands. He was in Bombay when his father died and was unable to join his brother Ernő at the funeral.[264] Neither brother attended the memorial service organized at the synagogue of the Rabbinical Seminary of Budapest on December 12, and by the time of the ceremony to mark the thirtieth day of mourning at Dohány Street Synagogue, Ernő had traveled on to Italy. Richard had arrived home from India the day before, but he was not willing to be seated on the dais reserved for the family. *Egyenlőség*'s correspondent "overheard [Richard] explaining his reluctance: 'I believe I will be acting in accordance with my departed father's intentions if I do not go up to the designated location.'"[265] *Egyenlőség* clarified the context of this rather enigmatic statement a few months later, reporting that Richard Wahrmann had abandoned the Jewish faith and converted to Protestantism in India while his father was still alive, then converted again to Catholicism at the Franciscan church of Nyitra (Nitra, Slovakia) in May of 1893; Ernő had been baptized Catholic in Brussels months earlier, during the week of Easter.[266]

At her father's house, Renée Wahrmann maintained a large domestic staff and entertained illustrious guests like Archbishop (and later Cardinal) Lajos Haynald of Kalocsa. According to an anecdote, Haynald once asked Renée when he was going to officiate her wedding and she replied, "When your Eminence becomes a rabbi!"[267] In 1883, Renée married the distiller Izidor Krausz de Megyer, who had been ennobled with his father the year before.[268] Their daughter, Amália Lujza, was born in 1895. In April of 1897, Renée Wahrmann reported to the rabbinical office of the Israelite Congregation of Pest to register her intention to convert, but Chief Rabbi Sámuel Kohn managed to dissuade her.[269] Eight months later, in late December, she made a deliberate spectacle of announcing her disaffiliation in accordance with the established procedure, reporting to the rabbinical office of the ICP in the company of two witnesses, parliamentary representative (and chair of the finance committee) Sándor Hegedüs and sitting prime minister Dezső Bánffy. After divorcing Izidor Krausz, Renée had herself and her daughter baptized as members of the Reformed Church in January of 1898 at a ceremony conducted by Bishop Károly Szász in the palace she had inherited from her father, at 23 Andrássy Avenue in Budapest.[270] Shortly before disaffiliating, Renée Wahrmann ordered an elaborate Torah ornament from a Budapest goldsmith, and not long after her conversion she donated two thousand crowns to the Israelite Women's Association of Pest.[271] These gestures do nothing to alter the fact that within five years of Mór Wahrmann's death, all three of his children had abandoned their father's faith.

After converting, Ernő and Richard Wahrmann spent most of their time abroad; the former preferred Monte Carlo and Nice while the latter circulated in Vienna, London, Monte Carlo, and Paris. The brothers lived in luxury, losing enormous sums of money betting on cards and racehorses, and squandered their inheritance within a couple of years. Their sister then provided them with a monthly allowance that they found insufficient; Ernő dueled ever more maniacally while Richard gambled with ever greater passion. At the age of forty-three, Ernő Wahrmann poisoned himself with gas in Paris. His friends paid for a funeral at Montparnasse Cemetery. In 1911, out of respect for the late Mór Wahrmann, King Franz Joseph paid off Richard's debts on the condition that he emigrate to America. Richard did but soon returned to Europe, ultimately settling in Paris as his older brother had. On the night of September 25, 1912, Richard shot himself in the head; he was interred in the cemetery of Bagneux, just south of Paris, at his sister's expense.[272]

Three days after her baptism in 1898, Renée Wahrmann married Endre Beretvás, an imperial and royal chamberlain twenty-one years her senior. The couple had no children, but their marriage was a happy one; the hunting excursions they organized on Renée's estates were discussed nationwide. Beretvás died of heart failure in 1902; two years later, Renée married another imperial and royal chamberlain, Béla Fáy. By then, Renée had withdrawn to the countryside and avoided social engagements. After divorcing Fáy in 1907, Renée lived alone with her adolescent daughter under her second husband's surname. Her financial situation deteriorated in the wake of the First World War; she developed an addiction to morphine and died in a hotel room in Pest at the age of sixty-four. Her daughter, Amália Lujza Krausz de Megyer, Mór Wahrmann's last surviving direct descendent, died only four years later at the age of thirty-five. Dependent on morphine and other medications, Amália Lujza spent most of her final years in sanatoria; she overdosed on tranquilizers in the summer of 1930 and died of thrombosis on July 22.[273]

Mór Wahrmann spoke fondly of his children in his 1882 will, which divided his estate among them in three equal shares.[274] But relations between the elder Wahrmann and his worldly sons deteriorated as Ernő and Richard bombarded their father with repeated requests for money. Mór Wahrmann was increasingly reluctant to dip into his own pocket on his sons' behalf.[275] According to the otherwise unknown terms of the 1888 revision of Mór Wahrmann's will,

Renée was to receive two-thirds of his estate, with Ernő and Richard sharing the remaining third.[276] Thus, while he appears to have repudiated his sons in the final years of his life, Wahrmann was known to adore his daughter, who had remained loyal to her father's faith and milieu in her first marriage.[277] Renée's younger brothers' conversions made her the last hope of the Jewish community, so her baptism was a particularly bitter pill for the Jewish press to swallow. On the occasion of Renée's conversion in January of 1898, *Egyenlőség's* Miksa Szabolcsi wrote, "Mór Wahrmann's daughter had an obligation to her father's memory, to her father's religion.... Yet behold, like his outcast sons, his only daughter, whom he worshiped from the grave, has shamed him, too."[278]

How could this have happened? Szabolcsi's piece was an attempt to answer that very question. He seems to have withheld publication of his article until the last of Wahrmann's children had converted, presumably because his explanation involved criticism of Mór Wahrmann and thus the partial demolition of an idol:

> Mór Wahrmann's children spent their tender youth in an era when a portion of Jewry, in its ecstasy, believed it could do nothing better or more beautiful than to squeeze their now-emancipated religion into the narrowest possible space at home. Of course, this logic is upside-down, but that is still how it happened. To teach their children as little as possible about what's Jewish, to socialize them exclusively among Christians if possible, to have them educated exclusively by Christian governesses and teachers; that is, to avoid everything Jewish, everything that reminds us of the past: this was the shibboleth. Then in the early eighties, when they began reminding us of our Jewishness from without, the education of the generation that included Mór Wahrmann's children—who also grew up without the supervision of a mother—was essentially complete. Their parents would have summoned back the banished spirit that had kept them warm in hard times, but that rising generation was no longer familiar with it, and thus only a lamentable few could lead it back to the hearths of their homes again. The Wahrmann children were never acquainted with this spirit. Their father later turned toward his fellow Jews with ever greater dedication, but his children did not understand it; for them, the spirit of Israel remained a foreign spirit.[279]

Other than Szabolcsi's piece, we have very few sources of information about the Wahrmanns' experiences of childhood and adolescence, and the sources we do have are unverifiable. The anonymous author of an 1886 portrait of "Budapest society" dedicated a single sentence to Mór Wahrmann's child-rearing principles: "[he] raised his children very well; let us take into consideration both European culture and genuine Hungarian patriotism in the raising of [our] children—this was his motto."[280] A few contemporaries, notably writers Tamás Kóbor, Sándor Bródy, and Dénes Pázmándy, discussed the Wahrmann children's upbringing in print, but only after their deaths. The foregoing authors approached the subject from the perspective of bourgeois rather than Jewish identity—not as the converted children of a Jewish father but rather as prodigal sons of a hard-working man. They nevertheless joined Szabolcsi in tracing the Wahrmann boys' troubles back to the upbringing they had received from their father. An experienced journalist, Tamás Kóbor led with a vicious uppercut: "Ernő Wahrmann was killed by his father. His uncomplicated, wise, sensible, all-seeing father. For no matter how uncomplicated and sensible he might have been, he raised his children in the lap of luxury and all its forms. Before his father's eyes, the child grew up into a dissolute lordling who squandered money, his father's money, and never learned to work with his father's knowledge."[281]

Sándor Bródy expressed similar sentiments when Richard Wahrmann killed himself six years later, writing that Mór Wahrmann had

> raised [Richard] to be a count, his older brother to be a duke, and their sister to be a duchess. He enjoyed that he remained an abject merchant, now that he had young sons as accustomed to horseback as to walking on their own. The two little high-schoolers moved like hussar captains: beneath their feet, the earth trembled like an unworthy element. If they were guests, they ate from genuine Sèvres. They were always one's most distinguished guests, and [Richard] . . . was expected to pursue a diplomatic career. He'll win a derby and marry a Czech countess. Then he became a hussar. His round-headed, big-brained, big-bellied father beamed with happiness at having such a slender, elegant, heroic and gentlemanly son. Thus it was actually he who . . . launched [his son's] career as a socialite, which has now come to a sudden end.[282]

Neither Kóbor nor Bródy were acquaintances of the Wahrmanns, but the parliamentary representative Dénes Pázmándy, a close friend of the family, agreed with their conclusion that Mór Wahrmann had sent his sons down the path that ended in tragedy. As Pázmándy recalled in 1934, "Móric was terribly lavish in providing them with money. He was giving them 300 forints a month in pocket money when they were still in high school. This abundance went to the boys' heads. All their friends were magnates."[283]

While these journalistic sources have to be handled with skepticism, we do know with certainty that Mór Wahrmann covered the considerable expenses his sons incurred during the year they served as volunteers with the hussars, just as he had financed his children's other aristocratic passions. There is no reliable information about the quality of the presumably limited amount of time Mór Wahrmann spent with his children when they were young, but we have not found even anecdotal evidence that he instilled in them any respect for the bourgeois ethos or Jewish traditions.

According to Miksa Szabolcsi, when the rising antisemitism of the early 1880s made parents conscious of their Jewishness, they had tried to bring back "the banished spirit that had kept them warm in hard times," but this effort made no impression on their adult children. The period represented a dramatic turning point in Mór Wahrmann's life; he "turned toward his fellow Jews with ever greater dedication." We do not know if this dedication ever manifested itself in the education Wahrmann provided his adolescent sons, but the man himself clearly turned to his fellow Jews.

Mór Wahrmann was elected to the House of Representatives in 1869 and remained a member of parliament until his death in 1892, though he spoke less and less frequently after 1882.[284] After being offered the presidency of the Israelite Congregation of Pest in 1880 and refusing it, Wahrmann was unanimously elected to the post three years later, in November of 1883. The congregation's everyday operations assumed an ever greater share of his attention over the last nine years of his life.[285] Wahrmann took his position at the ICP very seriously, personally examining all its documents and attending every session of its leadership council. Nothing was decided there without his knowledge and approval.[286] The obituary his family published listed the presidency of the ICP before his political accomplishments, a reflection of a profound change in Wahrmann's priorities.[287]

Wahrmann's ideas about the future and obligations of Hungary's Jews underwent a dramatic transformation. Twice in the course of his twenty-three-year career in the House of Representatives, Wahrmann spoke out about the path he believed Hungarian Jews should follow. On February 17, 1870, he fumbled his attempt to convince the House to prevent the schism that resulted in establishment of separate Orthodox and Neolog Jewish organizations. Wahrmann attempted to present himself as a spokesman for enlightened Jews who wanted closer relationships with Hungarian society, but his colleagues in the legislature heard a certain religious intolerance

Figure 4.19. Mór Wahrmann, 1880s. Hungarian National Museum, 187–1934.

282   JEWISHNESS AND BEYOND

in his remarks. He underestimated their commitment to the fundamental principles of liberalism, and in the name of religious freedom, a majority of the house—led by Ferenc Deák and Mór Jókai—sided with the Orthodox schismatics.[288]

Over a decade later, on June 9, 1882, Wahrmann delivered his only other parliamentary statement on the condition of his fellow Hungarian Jews and the future he desired for them. The timing was not a coincidence; seventeen days earlier, the Tiszeszlár blood libel affair had exploded into Hungarian political life with a speech by representative Géza Ónody of the Independence Party. Immediately preceding Wahrmann's address to the House, Győző Istóczy spouted another of his antisemitic diatribes.[289] The subject of debate in the House that day was the possibility of obstructing an influx of Jews who were allegedly inundating Hungary as they fled from pogroms in Russia. Wahrmann declared that the ultimate objectives were to ensure the triumph of the "Hungarian element" and to transform the "Hungarian state into a perfect Hungarian state." Anything that might slow these processes— like mass immigration—had to be avoided. Yet Wahrmann spoke out not only as a member of the Liberal Party but also explicitly as a Jew. He briefly summarized his personal views: "I do not consider mass immigration to be in the interest of Hungarian Jews. The legislature was explicit in declaring political emancipation and thereby satisfied its obligation to humanity. But social emancipation cannot be decreed. Social emancipation depends entirely on the perfect absorption of Jews into the Hungarian nation."[290] It is unclear what Wahrmann meant by "perfect absorption." The rest of his speech suggests that he simply wanted Jews to speak Hungarian and participate in Hungarian national culture. In any case, it is clear that in 1882, Mór Wahrmann the politician believed that the primary task facing Hungary's Jews was to incorporate themselves into the Hungarian nation.

It was the last time Wahrmann used his parliamentary platform to advise his coreligionists to adopt a particular course of action. As president of the Israelite Congregation of Pest, however, he made increasingly frequent recommendations in the final years of his life. The focus of the statements he issued as his congregation's leader shifted from the Magyarization of Hungary's Jews to the preservation of their religious and cultural heritage and the cultivation of their collective identity. At the dedication of the ICP's new hospital in 1889, he expressed regret and grief that modern life had "upstaged immersion into the Holy Scriptures and other religious documents" and that young Jews

PATHS TO CONVERSION—PORTRAITS

"barely [knew] the glorious story of their forefathers, barely [knew] the book of books which is Jewry's holiest legacy."[291] In December of 1891, less than a year before his death, Wahrmann spoke at the closing ceremony of a session of the membership committee of the Neolog Chevra Kadisha of Pest. Joining the Chevra Kadisha, he declared,

> chips the gloss of fashion off the Jewish heart. Many, many Jews have made a genuine discovery at this time, discovering themselves, the Jewish heart that beats with warmth for the faith of their fathers. Fashion, imitation, and self-indulgence suddenly appear before him in all their emptiness and vulgarity; he feels that the things he pursued are no longer of his world and that he has become estranged from the place where he belongs. Then he comes to us and renews his covenant with his Jewish being, with Jewish charity and love, with Jewish loyalty and faith, with devotion, with a Jewish spirit and understanding.[292]

Wahrmann may have been thinking of affluent young Jews who sought the favor of the traditional elite, like his own sons. However, considering that the opposition he set up was not one between the gilded Jewish youth and the world of Christian magnates, but rather between the Jewish and non-Jewish communities pure and simple, his speech came close to advocating Jewish dissimilation.

His problem, of course, was with those Jews who, like his own sons, never returned to the Jewish fold. In reporting the conversions of Ernő and Richard Wahrmann in the April 14, 1893 edition of *Egyenlőség*, Miksa Szabolcsi asked,

> Have you seen, dear reader, the special religious service we've recently introduced for the youth? Shortly before his death last year, the distinguished president of the Israelite Congregation of Pest attended such a service, and as he was filing out of the temple, he raised a bitter voice to a friend standing nearby: "Perhaps I will succeed at putting right in others' children that which I got wrong with my own sons. God knows what faulty principles we practiced in raising our children; we raised them without religion. I know that my sons will deny their faith before I've spent half a year in my grave.[293]

In blaming the Wahrmann children's conversions on their father's parenting, Miksa Szabolcsi considered only half of the question, limiting his discussion to the things young Jews had *not* been taught by Mór Wahrmann and his generation. But *why* did it make Wahrmann so proud to have elegant hussars

284 JEWISHNESS AND BEYOND

for sons? Tamás Kóbor may have answered the question in his piece on Ernő Wahrmann's suicide:

> I know more than one old Wahrmann. And every time I scratch at an old-fashioned man of labor and simple habits, I uncover the snobbery that eats away at him, goads him, makes him dissatisfied and misanthropic. Yet common sense makes him conscious of the petty nature of his mistake, and he sees that he cannot acknowledge it without losing esteem. Such people do not change their lifestyles; they . . . sit at the office from morning to night, work more than the interns, and never ask for any accolades. . . . But then here come [his] children! Things he was never given, he can get for them. And things he has been forbidden, he can acquire through his children. . . . Mór Wahrmann cannot maintain a stable; they would crack a thousand jokes about it and he would cease to be a patriarch. But Richard or Ernő, using his money—why not? And so, without knowing it himself, he raises his children to be more distinguished, transmitting his weaknesses to them and living them out through their personalities. Thus and only thus does the apple fall so far from the tree.[294]

While it is impossible to confirm or refute Kóbor's claims about Mór Wahrmann's unconscious desires, this much is certain: although Wahrmann—like other wealthy Jews of the period—could easily have acquired a noble title, perhaps even the rank of baron, he died a simple commoner. How then can one explain that Wahrmann's adult children, particularly his sons, chose paths that diverged so radically from their father's? I might venture to hypothesize that the factors behind the Wahrmann children's conversions included their father's more or less unconscious failure to raise them as Jews in the feverishly patriotic atmosphere of the age of emancipation, as well as his more or less unconscious decision to teach them a sense of belonging to Hungary's traditional elite, full integration into which could not be achieved without abandoning Judaism. Mór Wahrmann clearly never wanted the latter. In time, perhaps partly as a result of his own children's example, he came to his senses and reconsidered, though too late as far as his children were concerned. And so it was that by the time of his death, Wahrmann had become both a paragon of Jewishness and the father of three children who had betrayed, or would soon betray, his faith.

In Miksa Szabolcsi's telling, Wahrmann's children abandoned the Jewish faith because their father had raised them without any feeling for the "spirit of Israel." Again, this is only half the story. The Wahrmann children were assuredly driven to convert by their ambition to find complete acceptance in aristocratic society. Renée and her younger brothers had begun to move in such circles as adolescents. Had she remained a Jew, Renée would not have been able to marry an imperial and royal chamberlain, nor would she have been admitted to the Park Klub—which accepted her within a year of her joining the Reformed Church in 1898.[295] Had he not converted, Ernő could hardly have hoped to spend time in the company of "a young Metternich duke" in Nice,[296] nor would Richard have been admitted to the Jockey Club in Vienna or (like his sister) the Park Klub in Budapest.

By the 1900s, the pious family members of Reform-Era converts—like Frumet Hirschl, who divorced her husband rather than renounce her faith, or Móric Bloch's itinerant *melamed* father—had been largely supplanted by Magyarized and secularized Jewish families. Despite the changing circumstances of the era, most of the conversions that took place between 1825 and 1914 were driven by pragmatic considerations and a desire to overcome disadvantages associated with Jewish status. In feudal Hungary, Mózes Ullmann had been obliged to convert to acquire the noble title that would allow him to hurdle any legal obstacles to his economic ascent. Three years before the 1867 emancipation of Hungary's Jews, Ármin Vámbéry had to convert in order to teach at the university. After the emancipation, in the Dualist era, abandoning the Jewish faith in theory no longer conferred any professional advantages, and while that may have been the case in economic life, there were many other spheres in which conversion could advance one's career. Ervin Szabó's decision to have himself baptized just before his high school graduation exam was driven by a pragmatic acknowledgment of that fact. A similar continuity characterizes the conversions of individuals who hoped to integrate themselves into the country's traditional elite. While the 1895 introduction of civil marriage made mixed marriages possible in Hungary, Lily Brüll would not have been able to marry Baron Lipót Bornemisza de Nagykászon as a Jew, just as Mózes Ullmann was unable to marry Borbála Szentiványi as a Jew in 1832.

The 1880s represented a caesura in terms of ideological justifications for conversion. In an anonymous pamphlet he wrote in that period, Ármin Vámbéry articulated a purely secular rationale for conversion. Jakab Pólya gave voice to the notion that national unity, the fusion of the Jewish and Christian members of the Hungarian nation, could be achieved only by means of the collective conversion of the country's Jews.

286 JEWISHNESS AND BEYOND

The most significant changes associated with the transformation of converts' familial and social environments manifested themselves in the emotional burdens of conversion. Dávid Angyal still struggled to justify his decision to forsake his religion, his parents and relatives, and the milieu that had supported his studies "in the name of the community of faith." György Lukács had no community of this sort to abandon and thus no one to whom he needed to justify himself. In disavowing the Jewish faith, Móric Bloch and Jónás Kunewalder forsook their communities as well while Béla Balázs, who was always estranged from the Jewish community, converted in an attempt to find a community of his own.

Notes

1. Jacob Katz, *Tradition and Crisis: Jewish Society at the End of the Middle Ages*, trans. Bernard Dov Cooperman (Syracuse, NY: Syracuse University Press, 2000), 170–79.

2. Katz, *Out of the Ghetto*, 106.

3. Móric Bloch and his brother Károly changed their name to Ballagi in May of 1848. *Jelenkor*, June 11, 1848, 283.

4. Aladár Ballagi, "Ballagi Mór," in *Protestáns Új Képes Naptár 1879. Évre*, ed. Sándor Dúzs (Budapest: Franklin-Társulat, 1879), 17–19.

5. Bloch's pamphlet (which he finished on Feb. 27, 1840) anticipated the pro-emancipation speech that Eötvös delivered to the Hungarian House of Lords on March 31 (and published in expanded form in February of 1841).

6. Bloch, *A zsidókról*, 39–55.

7. Ibid., 47.

8. Ibid., 52.

9. [Móricz Bloch], *Mózes öt könyve*, vols. 1–5, trans. and notes Móricz Bloch (Buda: Magyar Kir. Egyetem, 1840–41).

10. Gyula Viszota, "Tagajánlások az akadémiában: A megalakulástól 1847-ig," *Akadémiai Értesítő* 17, no. 11 (1906): 618.

11. Schwab, *A zsidók*.

12. *Jiszrael könyörgései egész évre*, trans. Móricz Rosenthal, ed. Móricz Bloch (Pozsony, Hungary: Korn Fülöp, 1841).

13. *Első jósok*, trans. and notes Móritz Bloch (Buda: Magyar Kir. Egyetem, 1841).

14. "Kisfaludy-társaság," *Pesti Hírlap*, February 24, 1842, 128.

15. "Budapesti napló," *Jelenkor*, April 9, 1843, 138.

16. Ballagi, "Ballagi Mór," 20. Eight years later, in 1851, Ballagi joined the Reformed Church. Kovács, *Diszkrimináció, emancipáció,* 32.

17. László Szögi, *Magyarországi diákok németországi egyetemeken és főiskolákon 1789–1919* (Budapest: Eötvös Loránd Tudományegyetem Levéltára, 2001), 479; István Gémes, *Hungari et Transylvani: Kárpát-medencei egyetemjárók Tübingenben (1523–1918)* (Budapest: Luther, 2003), 54, 103.

18. Löw, "Sendschreiben an Herrn Dr. Jos. Szekács," 682.

19. Ibid., 682–83, 689–90. According to Löw, he heard about Bloch's outburst directly from the statesman in question; Löw's son Immánuel, who edited his father's collected works, identified this statesman as Ferenc Deák; see Löw, *Gesammelte Schriften,* 4: 336. In June of 1844, the gymnasium hired Bloch to teach Hebrew, Greek, French, mathematics, and Hungarian literature. Pál Balassa, "Békési ev. egyh. megyei közgyűlés," *Protestáns Egyházi és Iskolai Lap* 3, no. 28 (1844): 665–68; "Vegyes Közlemények," *Pesti Hírlap,* July 28, 1844, 518.

20. "Megyei dolgok," *Pesti Hírlap,* July 17, 1841, 480.

21. Ballagi, "Ballagi Mór," 20.

22. Komlós, *A magyar zsidóság irodalmi tevékenysége a XIX. században,* 51.

23. Béla Kenessey, "Dr. Ballagi Mór," *Protestáns Egyházi és Iskolai Lap* 34, no. 36 (1891): 1145–62; Sándor Imre, *Emlékbeszéd Ballagi Mór M. T. Akad. r. tagról* (Budapest: Akadémiai, 1893), 169–70; Andrea Waktor, "A XIX. századi családmodell működése és változásai a Ballagi család levelezésének tükrében," *Sic Itur ad Astra* 9, no. 1–2 (1995): 44–45.

24. Kinga Frojimovics, Géza Komoróczy, Viktória Pusztai, and Strbik Andrea, *A zsidó Budapest: Emlékek, szertartások, történelem,* vol. 1 (Budapest: Városháza/ MTA Judaisztikai Kutatócsoport, 1995), 126, 129; Ábrahám Kovács, "Ballagi Mór és a Skót Misszió: megtérés, áttérés vagy kitérés? Egy liberális protestáns zsidó életútjának kezdete," *Confessio* 31, no. 3 (2007): 119–20.

25. Móricz Bloch, "Felszólítás egy magyar-zsidó tanítókat képző intézet ügyében," *Pesti Hírlap,* February 6, 1841, 86–87.

26. Móricz Bloch, "A Pesten állítandó magyar-zsidó tanítókat képző intézet ügyében," *Pesti Hírlap,* June 30, 1841, 434.

27. Bloch, "Felszólítás egy magyar-zsidó tanítókat képző intézet ügyében," 87.

28. In 1846, after several years of intense efforts at reform, Lipót Löw counted only twenty-nine communities with modern primary schools. Silber, "The Historical Experience of German Jewry and Its Impact on Haskalah and Reform in Hungary," 132.

29. Kovács, "Ballagi Mór és a Skót Misszió," 116.

30. Károly Vörös, *Budapest legnagyobb adófizetői 1873–1917* (Budapest: Akadémiai, 1979), 62; Árpád Tóth, *Önszervező polgárok: A pesti egyesületek társadalomtörténete a*

reformkorban (Budapest: L'Harmattan, 2005), 190, 205, 252; Sándor Takáts, "A Kör és a Gyülde," in *Hangok a múltból* (Budapest: Athenaeum, [1930]), 258; *A Pesti Műegyesület részvényeseinek névsora 1846* (Pest: Landerer és Heckenast, [1846]), 9. Országos Széchényi Könyvtár (hereafter, OSZK), Plakát- és Kisnyomtatványtár (hereafter, PK), Kny. 1846. 8°/22.

31. "Fővárosi újdonságok," *Pesti Hírlap*, March 31, 1844, 222.

32. Takáts, "A Kör és a Gyülde," 258; Béla Dezsényi, "A Nemzeti Kör a negyvenes évek irodalmi és hírlapi mozgalmaiban," *Irodalomtörténeti Közlemények* 57, no. 1–4 (1953): 172–73; István Barta, ed., *Kossuth Lajos 1848/49-ben*, vol. 1, *Kossuth Lajos az utolsó rendi országgyűlésen 1847/48* (Budapest: Akadémiai, 1951), 122; Az Ellenzéki Kör pénztári könyve [Treasurer's Ledgers of the Opposition Circle], 1847–1849. OSZK Kézirattár (hereafter, Kt.), Fol. Hung. 980.

33. Silber, "The Entrance of Jews into Hungarian Society in *Vormärz*," 322; Groszmann, "A pesti zsidó gyülekezet alkotmányának története," 148; *Első magyar zsidó naptár és évkönyv 1848-ik szökőévre* (Pest: Landerer és Heckenast, 1848), 37–38.

34. Joseph Bergl, *Geschichte der ungarischen Juden* (Leipzig: Wilhelm Friedrich, 1879), 96–97.

35. Károly Kecskeméti, *Magyar liberalizmus 1790–1848* ([Budapest]: Argumentum/Bibó István Szellemi Műhely, 2008), 181–83.

36. Zeller, *A magyar egyházpolitika 1847–1894*, 1: 4–7.

37. Ibid.

38. Bernstein, *A negyvennyolcas magyar szabadságharc és a zsidók*, 28; György Spira, *A pestiek Petőfi és Haynau között* (Budapest: Enciklopédia, 1998), 34.

39. Ákos Birányi, *Pesti forradalom (Martius 15–18.): Hiteles adatok nyomán* (Pest: Trattner Károly, 1848), 47.

40. Zsoldos, *1848–1849 a magyar zsidóság életében*, 63–64.

41. Birányi, *Pesti forradalom*, 54; György Gracza, *Az 1848–49-iki magyar szabadságharcz története*, vol. 1 (Budapest: Lampel Róbert, [1895]), 186; "Országgyűlés," *Pesti Hírlap*, March 23, 1848, 247.

42. "Pozsony, márt. 21-én," *Pesti Hírlap*, March 24, 1848, 251. For discussions of the antisemitic riots of the spring of 1848, see György Haraszti, "Az 1848. évi magyarországi zsidóösszeírás háttere és mozgatórugói," in *Két világ határán* (Budapest: Múlt és Jövő, 1999), 190–94; Kádár and Vági, "Hosszú évszázad," 79–83.

43. Jónás Kunewalder, *Moses vallású magyarokhoz: Tisztelt testvérek! An die Ungarn mosaischer Confession: Geehrte Brüder!* ([Esztergom]: Beimel, n.d.). OSZK PK. Kny. 1848.2°/49; Zsoldos, *1848–1849 a magyar zsidóság életében*, 75–77.

44. "Pest, április 7-én," *Pesti Hírlap*, April 8, 1848, 309. For more on radical reform societies, see Silber, "The Social Composition of the Pest Radical Reform Society," 99–128; Michael A. Meyer, *Response to Modernity: A History of the Reform Movement in Judaism* (Detroit, MI: Wayne State University Press, 1995), 161–63.

45. Groszmann, "A pesti zsidó gyülekezet alkotmányának története," 149–50.

46. "Országgyűlés," *Pesti Hírlap*, April 7, 1848, 305.

47. Bernstein, *A negyvennyolcas magyar szabadságharc és a zsidók*, 33.

48. Büchler, *A zsidók története Budapesten*, 450.

49. Bergl, *Geschichte der ungarischen Juden*, 97.

50. "Kunewalder," *Reform*, April 9, 1848, 15; "Pesth-Ofner Neuigkeitsbote," *Der Ungar*, April 9, 1848, 679; Jakab István miniszteri tanácsos naplója 1848–1849-ből [Diary of the ministerial counselor Jakab István, 1848–1849]. OSZK Kt. Quart. Hung. 1315, 6. For a discussion of Jewish reactions to Kunewalder's conversion, see Einhorn, *Die Revolution und die Juden in Ungarn*, 81–82.

51. For more on the Ullmann family, see Bácskai, *A vállalkozók előfutárai*, 141–53; Silber, "Ullmann Family"; McCagg Jr., *Jewish Nobles and Geniuses in Modern Hungary*, 59–61.

52. Before Law XXIX of 1840 finally allowed Jews to settle in Hungarian cities (with the exception of the kingdom's mining towns), Jews were allowed to stay in Pest either as "tolerated" residents who payed a special toleration tax or as *kommoráns* ("commorant") Jews, in which case they had a temporary residence permit.

53. Groszmann, "A pesti zsidó gyülekezet alkotmányának története," 127–28.

54. Bácskai, *A vállalkozók előfutárai*, 141–42.

55. Groszmann, "A pesti zsidó gyülekezet alkotmányának története," 129.

56. Ibid., 137; Zsigmond Groszmann, "Az Ullmann-botrány," *Egyenlőség*, September 7, 1935, 12.

57. Bernát Mandl, "Két tragikus zsidó asszony," *Egyenlőség*, April 9, 1921, 11.

58. Staudacher, *Jüdische Konvertiten in Wien 1782–1868*, 2: 506.

59. Löw, *Der jüdische Kongress in Ungarn*, 108; Mandl, "Két tragikus zsidó asszony," 10–11; Bácskai, *A vállalkozók előfutárai*, 145–46; Silber, "Ullmann Family"; Szentistvánvárosi (Lipótvárosi) r. kath. plébánia, kereszteltek anyakönyve [Baptismal records of the Roman Catholic parish of Szentistvánváros (Lipótváros)]. MNL OL, A60. At least two of Mózes Ullmann's daughters later converted to Catholicism. Franciska Ullmann (who would later marry Mór Wodianer) was baptized in Pest in 1829 at the age of fifteen. Antónia Ullmann, who married her father's younger brother Gábriel Ullmann (a faithful Jew till the day he died), converted in Vienna in 1852. See Erzsébet Mislovics, "A magyarországi zsidóság áttérési gyakorlata Buda, Óbuda, Pest településeken és Bécsben 1746 és 1850 között," *Aetas* 30, no. 1 (2015): 52; Staudacher, *Jüdische Konvertiten in Wien 1782–1868*, 2: 505.

60. Mandl, "Két tragikus zsidó asszony."

61. Ibid. According to Zsigmond Groszmann, Mózes Ullmann's chief antagonist was not Izsák Rosenthal but rather Rosenthal's father Salamon. Groszmann, "A pesti zsidó gyülekezet alkotmányának története," 137.

62. Groszmann, "A pesti zsidóság vezetői," 52.

290   JEWISHNESS AND BEYOND

63. Ibid.

64. Groszmann, "Az Ullmann-botrány," 12.

65. Groszmann, "A pesti zsidó gyülekezet alkotmányának története," 137; Kempelen, *Magyar zsidó családok*, 2: 37. In providing the dates of Kohlmann's employment, Bernát Mandl says only that "he was employed in Mózes Ullmann's home." Bernát Mandl, "A pesti izr. hitközségi fiúiskola monográfiája," in *A magyar-zsidó felekezet elemi és polgári iskoláinak monográfiája*, vol. 1, ed. Jónás Barna and Fülöp Csukási (Budapest: Corvina, 1896), 15.

66. Bácskai, *A vállalkozók előfutárai*, 140; McCagg Jr., *Jewish Nobles and Geniuses in Modern Hungary*, 60; id., "Jewish Conversion in Hungary in Modern Times," 149.

67. Vörös, "Pest-Budától Budapestig 1849–1873," 225; Silber, "Ullmann Family"; Bácskai, *A vállalkozók előfutárai*, 148.

68. Bácskai, *A vállalkozók előfutárai*, 150–51.

69. For discussions of the Wodianer family, see Löw and Kulinyi, *A szegedi zsidók 1785-től 1885-ig*, 98–99; Bácskai, *A vállalkozók előfutárai*, 153–59; Michael K. Silber, "Wodianer Family," in Hundert, *The YIVO Encyclopedia of Jews in Eastern Europe*, http://www.yivoencyclopedia.org/article.aspx/Wodianer_Family; McCagg Jr., *Jewish Nobles and Geniuses in Modern Hungary*, 55–56; Kempelen, *Magyar zsidó családok*, 1: 42–46.

70. Groszmann, "A pesti zsidó gyülekezet alkotmányának története," 144–46.

71. Bernstein, *A negyvennyolcas magyar szabadságharc és a zsidók*, 12, 197. This organization would soon become the executive board of the Israelites of Hungary and Croatia.

72. Széchenyi, *Naplói*, vol. 5, *(1836–1843)*, 122.

73. According to Vera Bácskai, Sámuel Wodianer converted in 1839. However, *Jelenkor* and the *Pesti Hírlap* published reports of Wodianer's conversion in 1841, and I consider the latter accounts to be authoritative. See "Budapesti napló," *Jelenkor*, February 27, 1841, 65; "Fővárosi újdonságok," *Pesti Hírlap*, March 3, 1841, 140.

74. *A nemzeti kaszinó évkönyve 1841*, 54; *1845-dik évi jelentés a pesti lovaregylet munkálódásairól* (n.p.: n.p., n.d.), 5. Albert Wodianer Sr. converted to Catholicism in 1843, two years after his father. Mislovics, "A magyarországi zsidóság áttérési gyakorlata," 50.

75. Bácskai, *A vállalkozók előfutárai*, 160.

76. Chevra-tagok névjegyzéke [List of Chevra members], 1804–1882. MZsML.

77. McCagg Jr., "Jewish Conversion in Hungary in Modern Times," 162; Bácskai, *A vállalkozók előfutárai*, 160.

78. *A nemzeti kaszinó évkönyve 1852*, 26; *1852dik évi jelentés a pesti lovaregylet' munkálódásairól* (n.p.: n.p., n.d.), 6.

PATHS TO CONVERSION—PORTRAITS

79. Bácskai, *A vállalkozók előfutárai*, 163.

80. OSZK, obituaries, FM8/35797/569: Baron Mór Wodianer de Kapriora.

81. Arminius Vambéry, *The Story of My Struggles*, vols. 1–2 (London: T. Fisher Unwin, 1904); Ármin Vámbéry, *Küzdelmeim* (Budapest: Franklin-Társulat, 1905). The following citations are taken from the considerably expanded Hungarian edition.

82. Vámbéry, *Küzdelmeim*, 19–20, 22–23, 34.

83. Ibid., 44, 46.

84. Ibid., 154. The dictionary in question is Hermann Vambéry, *Deutsch-Türkisches Taschen-Woerterbuch* (Constantinopel: Gebrüder Koehler, 1858).

85. Vámbéry, *Küzdelmeim*, 494. While he was abroad (on October 9, 1860), Vámbéry was elected to the Hungarian Academy of Sciences as a corresponding member; he delivered his inaugural lecture (*On Turkish Historical Literature*) soon after his return (on April 29 and May 6, 1861).

86. Ibid., 186.

87. Ibid., 239–40.

88. Ibid., 245–46.

89. Ibid., 487–89.

90. Kovács, *Diszkrimináció, emancipáció*, 140–41.

91. Mihály Bucsay, *A protestantizmus története Magyarországon 1521–1945* (Budapest: Gondolat, 1985), 211.

92. László Kósa, "Felekezeti és nemzeti azonosságtudat kapcsolódása: A magyar protestáns példa," in *Bennünk élő múltjaink: Történelmi tudat—Kulturális emlékezet*, ed. Richárd Papp and László Szarka (Zenta: Vajdasági Magyar Művelődési Intézet, 2008), 391–400; Kálvin téri református gyülekezet, keresztelési anyakönyvek [Baptismal records of the Reformed congregation of Kálvin Square]. MNL OL, A620.

93. Vámbéry, *Küzdelmeim*, 279.

94. Arminius Vambéry, *His Life and Adventures Written by Himself* (London: T. Fisher Unwin, 1884).

95. Ármin Vámbéry, "Egy tatár emlékirataiból," *Huszadik Század* 15, no. 1 (1914): 5.

96. Ibid., 8.

97. Komlós, *A magyar zsidóság irodalmi tevékenysége a XIX. században*, 292.

98. Egy szabadelvű, *A zsidókérdés Magyarországon*, 12, 14–18, 20, 26, 28.

99. Ibid., 18–19.

100. Istóczy, *Országgyűlési beszédei, indítványai és törvényjavaslatai, 1872–1896*, 1–14.

101. "A magyar zsidókhoz," *Pesti Hírlap*, November 23, 1880, 1.

102. "A szerkesztőség története," in *Pesti Hírlap naptára az 1919. közönséges évre*, ed. József Schmittely (Budapest: Légrády Testvérek, n.d.), 82.

103. Bánóczi, "A zsidó tanárok," 511.

104. József Bánóczi, "Emlékeimből," *Magyar Nyelvőr* 48, no. 10 (1919): 187, 192.

105. Kovács, *Diszkrimináció, emancipáció*, 133.

106. "A köztisztviselők minősítése," *Szombati Újság*, February 11, 1882, 49.

107. "Levelezések," *Szombati Újság*, February 18, 1882, 63.

108. "Trefort úr mint hittérítő," 7.

109. "Rövid hírek," *Fővárosi Lapok* 21, no. 157 (1884): 1020.

110. Károly Simonyi, who would become an engineer, was still Jewish when he married the likewise-Jewish Rézsi Landeszman in 1914. Duplicate of the civil marriage records of the ninth district of Budapest, March 20, 1914.

111. Kálmán Timár, "Simonyi Zsigmond levele Haynald érsekhez," *Irodalomtörténeti Közlemények* 41, no. 3 (1931): 332–33.

112. Kovács, *Diszkrimináció, emancipáció*, 133.

113. Gyula Vargha, "Pólya Jakab emlékezete," *Akadémiai Értesítő* 10, no. 1 (1899): 5–16.

114. Ibid., 6–10.

115. Ibid., 8–10.

116. Jakab Pólya, his wife, and their three children converted to Catholicism in July of 1886. "Áttérés a katolikus vallásra," *Budapesti Hírlap*, July 26, 1886, 6. Born a year later, the couple's fourth child, the famous mathematician György Pólya, was thus baptized Catholic at birth.

117. Vargha, "Pólya Jakab emlékezete," 10–11.

118. Angyal, *Emlékezések*, 31. For a discussion of the circumstances in which Angyal composed his autobiography, see Gábor Schweitzer, "Reflexiók a 'zsidókérdés'-ről: Két magyar történész memoárjai: Angyal Dávid és Marczali Henrik," *Budapesti Negyed* 16, no. 1 (2008): 175.

119. Angyal, *Emlékezések*, 33–34.

120. Ibid., 34.

121. Cited in Schweitzer, "Reflexiók a 'zsidókérdés'-ről," 177.

122. [Zoltán Szentiványi], *Századunk névváltoztatásai 1800–1893* (Budapest: Hornyánszky Viktor, 1895), 27.

123. Angyal, *Emlékezések*, 34–35.

124. Ibid., 40.

125. Ibid., 45–46.

126. Ibid., 68–69, 78, 80.

127. Ibid., 84.

128. Dezső Lévay, "Néhány szó az ösztöndíjegyletről," *Egyenlőség*, December 19, 1886, 6.

129. Alice Mandl finally converted to her husband's faith on March 14, 1905; Paula was five months shy of her seventh birthday and thus became a Catholic automatically. Duplicate of the civil marriage records of the sixth district of Budapest, August 6, 1896; Duplicate of the civilb irth records of the sixth district of Budapest, annotation dated September 3, 1898. Alice Mandl's conversion was recorded under the heading "subsequent notes/modifications.

130. Kubinszky, *A politikai antiszemitizmus Magyarországon 1875–1890*, 212, 222–23; Paksy, *Istóczy Győző és a magyar antiszemita mozgalom*, 203, 253.

131. György Litván, *Szabó Ervin, a szocializmus moralistája* (Budapest: Századvég, 1993), 17–22; Árpád Juhász, "Szabó Ervin szülőháza a szlanicai keresztúton," *Magyar Nap*, May 23, 1937, 4.

132. Béla Kőhalmi, *Könyvek könyve* (Budapest: Lantos, [1918]), 206–07.

133. Litván, *Szabó Ervin*, 22.

134. Ibid., 24. For the full text of this letter, see Ervin Szabó, *Levelezése*, vol. 1, *1893–1904*, ed. György Litván and László Szűcs (Budapest: Kossuth, 1977), 22–26.

135. Litván, *Szabó Ervin*, 21–24.

136. Litván, "Szellemi progresszió a századelőn," 23.

137. Litván, "Zsidók a huszadik századi magyar modernizációban és progresszív mozgalmakban," 313.

138. György Lukács, "Előszó," in *Magyar irodalom—magyar kultúra: Válogatott tanulmányok* (Budapest: Gondolat, 1970), 5. The Lukács family did not actually live in Lipótváros. Having grown up on Andrássy Avenue, then Nagy János (now Benczúr) Street, Lukács followed the custom of the day in using "Lipótváros" as a designation of social class.

139. Vezér, "A mindennapi élet története," 27; [Szentiványi], *Századunk névváltoztatásai*, 152.

140. László Péter, "Lukács György apja," in *A szerette város: Írások Szegedről* (Budapest: Szépirodalmi, 1986), 429; Albert Gyergyai, "Egy barátságos ház története," in *Magyar zenetörténeti tanulmányok Kodály Zoltán emlékére*, ed. Ferenc Bónis (Budapest: Zeneműkiadó, 1977), 415.

141. Júlia Bendl, *Lukács György élete a századfordulótól 1918-ig* (Budapest: Scientia Humana, 1994), 11–12; Vezér, "A mindennapi élet története," 25, 27.

142. Vörös, *Budapest legnagyobb adófizetői 1873–1917*, 136, 148.

143. Gyergyai, "Egy barátságos ház története," 415.

144. Ibid.

145. Mici Popperné Lukács, "Emlékeim Bartókról, Lukács Györgyről és a régi Budapestről," in Bónis, *Magyar zenetörténeti tanulmányok Kodály Zoltán emlékére*, 384.

146. Vezér, "A mindennapi élet története," 27.

294 JEWISHNESS AND BEYOND

147. *A Pesti Chevra Kadisa választóképes tagjainak névjegyzéke*, 26; *A Pesti Izr. Hitközség elöljáróságának jelentése az 1914. közigazgatási évről* (Budapest: n.p., 1915), 32; Ernő Weiller, "Jelentés," in *Cultur-Almanach*, vol. 2, *1911–12*, ed. Simon Hevesi (Budapest: OMIKE, 1912), 117; Vezér, "A mindennapi élet története," 26.

148. Vezér, "A mindennapi élet története," 27.

149. Károly Kókai, "A fiatal Lukács György és a zsidóság," *Szombat* 12, no. 2 (2000): 21; György Lukács, "Megélt gondolkodás" (1971), in *Curriculum vitae* (Budapest: Magvető, 1982), 11.

150. Lukács, "Előszó," 6.

151. Lukács, *Megélt gondolkodás: Életrajz magnószalagon*, 97.

152. Ibid., 88–89.

153. Benedek, *Naplómat olvasom*, 77.

154. Lukács, *Megélt gondolkodás: Életrajz magnószalagon*, 95.

155. Szögi, *Magyarországi diákok németországi egyetemeken és főiskolákon 1789–1919*, 154.

156. Bendl, *Lukács György élete a századfordulótól 1918-ig*, 75–76.

157. "Hivatalos rész," *Budapesti Közlöny*, September 22, 1907, 1; György Lukács, *Levelezése (1902–1917)*, ed. Éva Fekete and Éva Karádi (Budapest: Magvető, 1981), 716–17.

158. Kitérési és prozelita jegyzőkönyvek [Records of converts and proselytes]. MZsML, TB. B/67.; Bendl, *Lukács György élete a századfordulótól 1918-ig*, 76.

159. Bendl, *Lukács György élete a századfordulótól 1918-ig*, 76–77. Lukács lasted just a few months at the ministry. His father saw that this type of work was not for him and offered his son an allowance for an unlimited period.

160. Tamás Repiszky, "Emlékkép-foszlányok: Adalékok Lesznai Anna családtörténetéhez," *Enigma* 14, no. 52 (2007): 18–21; Judit Majoros, "Egy elfeledett irodalmi emlékhely Zemplénben: Az alsókörtvélyesi kúria," *Enigma* 14, no. 51 (2007): 25–41.

161. "Dr. Moskovicz Mór," *Pesti Hírlap*, July 6, 1880, 5.

162. Lesznai, *Kezdetben volt a kert*, 1: 116–17; Vezér, *Lesznai Anna élete*, 11–12; Repiszky, "Emlékkép-foszlányok," 21–25.

163. Gyula Andrássy, "Moskovitz Iván emlékére," *Pesti Napló*, February 15, 1917, 1.

164. Oszkár Jászi, "Emlékeimből: Szülőföldemen" (1953–1955), in *Publicisztikája: Válogatás*, ed. György Litván and János F. Varga (Budapest: Magvető, 1982), 557–58.

165. "Zempléni Moskovitz Geyza," *Egyenlőség*, April 13, 1913, 11.

166. Lesznai, *Kezdetben volt a kert*, 1: 95, 97, 105, 138.

167. "Kinevezések és áthelyezések," *Igazságügyi Közlöny* 6, no. 9 (1897): 438; *A magyar országgyűlés: A főrendiház és képviselőház tagjainak életrajzi adatai* (Budapest: Magyar Tudósító, 1906), 293.

168. "Hymen," *Egyenlőség*, October 27, 1901, 11; "Házasság," *Egyenlőség*, July 13, 1902, 10.

169. Members of the family have spelled their name in various ways: Moscovitz, Moskovitz, Moskovicz.

170. Vezér, *Lesznai Anna élete*, 58; Duplicate of the civil marriage records of the fifth district of Budapest, July 6, 1910; duplicate of the civil marriage records of the ninth district of Budapest, October 22, 1910; Repiszky, "Emlékkép-foszlányok," 28.

171. Bauer, *Emlékeim*, 44–45; Hatvany, *Levelei*, 131; Vezér, *Lesznai Anna élete*, 27, 58; Jászi, "Emlékeimből: Szülőföldemen," 558.

172. Lesznai, *Kezdetben volt a kert*, 1: 308, 355.

173. "Moskovitz Iván," *Magyar Hírlap*, February 15, 1917, 3–4; Andrássy, "Moskovitz Iván emlékére," 1–2; Henrik Gonda, "Moskovitz Iván halálára," *Magyar Hírlap*, February 27, 1917, 5.

174. Sándor Feleki, "Zsidó magyar írók és tudósok, III, Dóczi Lajos," *Egyenlőség*, October 17, 1890, 10; [Szentiványi], *Századunk névváltoztatásai*, 61. Studies of Dóczi's life include Ilona Fürst, *Dóczi Lajos mint német író: Egy zsidó írói nemzedék típusa* (Budapest: Pfeifer Ferdinánd, 1932); József György, *Dóczi Lajos* (Budapest: Pécsi Egyetemi Könyvkiadó, 1932); Éva Somogyi, "Egy magyar hivatalnok a bécsi külügyminisztérium szolgálatában: Báró Dóczy Lajos," in *Hagyomány és átalakulás: Állam és bürokrácia a dualista Habsburg Monarchiában* (Budapest: L'Harmattan, 2006), 120–36. Dóczi would be ennobled as "Baron Dóczy," but he always he signed his literary work as "Dóczi." Szabolcs Boronkai, "Német–magyar kétnyelvűség: Ludwig Dux—Báró Dóczi Lajos (1845–1919)," *Irodalomtörténeti Közlemények* 105, no. 1–2 (2001): 73.

175. Lajos Dóczi, "Hogy tanultam magyarul," in *Magyar szellemi élet: Elbeszélések és rajzok a magyar írók és művészek életéből*, ed. Mihály Igmándi (Budapest: Hornyánszky Viktor, 1892), 8.

176. Feleki, "Zsidó magyar írók és tudósok, III, Dóczi Lajos," 10.

177. Pál Tenczer, "Reminiszcenciák," *Egyenlőség*, December 23, 1892, 3.

178. Tenczer, "Sváb rabbi jóslata Falk Miksáról," 3.

179. Ilona Fürst, "Dóczi Lajos báró zsidósága eddig ismeretlen leveleiben," *Múlt és Jövő* 24, no. 4 (1934): 118.

180. Fürst, *Dóczi Lajos mint német író*, 45.

181. Dóczi quoted the director of the National Theater, Ede Paulay, in a letter to Kónyi dated September 28, 1888. See Fürst, "Dóczi Lajos báró zsidósága eddig ismeretlen leveleiben," 118.

182. Lajos Dóczi, *Vegyes párok* (Budapest: Ráth Mór, 1889), 145, 174.

183. Ibid., 266.

184. Ibid., 92–95.

185. Dixi, "Vegyes párok," *Egyenlőség*, May 12, 1889, 1–3.

186. "Szerkesztői üzenetek: H. P. úrnak B–t," *Egyenlőség*, December 30, 1888, 14; Fürst, *Dóczi Lajos mint német író*, 61–62.

187. Lajos Dóczi to Manó Kónyi. Undated letter [1893]. Kónyi–Lónyay Papers, Library of the School of Slavonic and East European Studies [SSEES], University College of London. I would like to thank Éva Somogyi and András Cieger for providing me with photocopies of several of Dóczi's letters.

188. Lajos Dóczi to Manó Kónyi, April 21, 1893. Kónyi–Lónyay Papers, Library of the School of Slavonic and East European Studies [SSEES], University College of London. Dóczi and his fiancée were married three weeks later. "Dóczy Lajos," *Pesti Hírlap*, May 14, 1893, 7.

189. Bernát Singer, "A kitérések, VIII," *Egyenlőség*, January 1, 1905, supplement, 1.

190. For discussions of Lesznai's religious beliefs, see Vezér, *Lesznai Anna élete*, 71; Petra Török, "'Gránit a siratófalban, ütem magyar ajkú dalban,'" *Múlt és Jövő*, new series, 12, no. 1 (2001): 60–61.

191. *A zsidókérdés Magyarországon: A Huszadik Század körkérdése*, 104–05.

192. *Sorsával tetováltan önmaga: Válogatás Lesznai Anna naplójegyzeteiből*, sel. Petra Török (Budapest: Petőfi Irodalmi Múzeum/Hatvany Lajos Múzeum, 2010), 326–27; Török, "'Gránit a siratófalban, ütem magyar ajkú dalban,'" 73.

193. *Sorsával tetováltan önmaga*, 422.

194. In her selection of writings taken from the twenty notebooks of Lesznai's diary (housed at the Petőfi Literary Museum), Petra Török published all but a few of Lesznai's observations on the subject of Jewishness; the minor passages she omitted do not discuss Lesznai's conversion either. I would like to thank Petra Török for facilitating my examination of these passages.

195. "Házasság," *Budapesti Hírlap*, February 4, 1902, 7.

196. Lesznai, *Kezdetben volt a kert*, 1: 566, 578, 682; "Az aradi rabbi pálfordulása," *Aradi Közlöny*, January 15, 1902, 6–7; "A főrabbi áldása és az aradi zsidó hitközség," *Aradi Híradó*, January 20, 1902, 1.

197. Duplicate of the civil marriage records of the second district of Budapest, June 19, 1913; György Litván, *A Twentieth-Century Prophet: Oscar Jászi 1875–1957* (Budapest/New York: Central European University Press, 2006), 88; Repiszky, "Emlékkép-foszlányok," 30–31.

198. Kitérési és prozelita jegyzőkönyvek [Records of converts and proselytes]. MZsML, TB. B/67.

199. Sándor Hevesi, "Egy magyar író konverziójának története" (1930s), *Vigilia* 13, no. 4 (1948): 203–10.

200. [Szentiványi], *Századunk névváltoztatásai*, 103; József Németh, "Hoffmann Mór," in *Zalai Múzeum 12*, ed. László Horváth (Zalaegerszeg, Hungary:

Zala Megyei Múzeumok Igazgatósága, 2003), 255–66; Anna László, *Hevesi Sándor* (Budapest: Gondolat, 1960), 5–6.

201. Hevesi, "Egy magyar író konverziójának története," 204.

202. Ibid.

203. Mór Hoffmann, *A nemzetiség és a nemzeti nyelv* (Nagykanizsa: Fischel Fülöp, 1877); id., *Zsidóinkról! Igaza van-e Csernátony Lajos úrnak vagy nincs?* (Nagykanizsa: Fischel Fülöp, 1874); id., *A sémiták és antisemiták* (Budapest: Franklin, 1883).

204. M. H. [Mór Hoffmann], "Chanukka," *A Magyar-Zsidó Ifjúság Lapja* 1, no. 24 (1886): 371.

205. See, for instance, Mór Hoffmann, "Egy zsidó gyermek pályája," *A Magyar-Zsidó Ifjúság Lapja* 1, no. 2 (1886): 22; id., "Magyar-zsidó (Vers)," *A Magyar-Zsidó Ifjúság Lapja* 1, no. 3 (1886): 36.

206. Hevesi, "Egy magyar író konverziójának története," 207.

207. Ibid., 209–10.

208. For more biographical data, see Magda K. Nagy, *Balázs Béla világa* (Budapest: Kossuth, 1973); Béla Balázs, *Álmodó ifjúság* (1946) (Budapest: Magvető/Szépirodalmi, 1976).

209. Balázs, *Álmodó ifjúság*, 82–86.

210. Balázs Béla naplója [The Diary of Béla Balázs]. MZsML, XIX: Hagyaték.

211. "Hitehagyottak," *A Budai Izraelita Hitközség Értesítője* 4, no. 3 (1913): 32.

212. Balázs, *Álmodó ifjúság*, 423, 442.

213. Béla Balázs, *Napló 1903–1914* (Budapest: Magvető, 1982), 281–82, 483.

214. Béla Balázs, *Levelei Lukács Györgyhöz: Egy szövetség dokumentumai*, ed. Júlia Lenkei ([Budapest]: MTA Filozófiai Intézet/Lukács Archívum, 1982), 21.

215. Ibid., 31.

216. Endre Ady, "Ünneprontás: A Nyugat matinéja körül" (*Világ*, 30 November, 1911), in *Összes prózai művei*, 10: 163.

217. Balázs, *Napló 1903–1914*, 540–41.

218. "Hitehagyottak," *A Budai Izraelita Hitközség Értesítője* 4, no. 3 (1913): 32; "Balázs Béla vallása," *Délmagyarország*, March 27, 1913, 7. According to Kempelen, Béla Balázs was baptized on March 22; Kempelen, *Magyar zsidó családok*, 3: 62. Polányi did not remain *konfessionslos* either; he converted to the Reformed faith, though we do not know when—perhaps years later. Ilona Duczynska Polanyi, "'I first met Karl Polanyi in 1920 . . . ,'" in *Karl Polanyi in Vienna: The Contemporary Significance of the Great Transformation*, ed. Kenneth McRobbie and Kari Polanyi Levitt (Montréal: Black Rose Books, 2006), 304.

219. Balázs, *Levelei Lukács Györgyhöz*, 107.

220. Balázs, *Napló 1903–1914*, 601–02.

221. Béla Balázs, *Napló 1914–1922* (Budapest: Magvető, 1982), 246–47.

298   JEWISHNESS AND BEYOND

222. Ibid., 9, 44.

223. "Hatvany-Deutsch Sándor báró," *Egyenlőség*, February 23, 1913, 6–7. For more on the Hatvany-Deutsch family, see György Kövér, "'Deutsch Ig. és fia,'" in *A Hatvanyak emlékezete*, ed. László Horváth (Hatvan, Hungary: Hatvany Lajos Múzeum, 2003), 13–21; Károly Halmos, "A Hatvany-Deutsch dinasztia," in Sebők, *Sokszínű kapitalizmus*, 84–97.

224. Holitscher Szigfrid közjegyző iratai: 1912, Hatvany-Deutsch Sándor báró házassági szerződése [Szigfrid Holitscher's notarial documents: Baron Sándor Hatvany-Deutsch's marriage contract, 1912]. Budapest Főváros Levéltára (hereafter, BFL), VII.187.—1912—1940.

225. Waldapfel János: Hatvany Lajosról [János Waldapfel: concerning Lajos Hatvany], 3. f. Magyar Tudományos Akadémia Könyvtár és Információs Központ, Kézirattár (hereafter, MTA KIK Kt.) Ms 5371/116.

226. Lajos Hatvany, *Zsiga a családban* (Budapest: Genius, [1927]). This book was translated into German and later into English; see Ludwig Hatvany, *Bondy Jr.: Ein Roman* (München, Germany: Drei Masken, 1929); id., *Bondy Jr.*, trans. Hannah Waller (London: Hutchinson, 1931). After nine months in prison, Lajos Hatvany was paroled as a result of a stomach ailment. For a summary of his trial, see Péter Sz. Nagy, *Hatvany Lajos* (Budapest: Balassi, 1993), 83–89.

227. György Belia, "Utószó," in Lajos Hatvany, *Urak és emberek* (Budapest: Szépirodalmi, 1980), 727–29; Nagy, *Hatvany Lajos*, 65–71.

228. "Hatvany Lajos levele," *Egyenlőség*, March 19, 1927, 3.

229. Hatvany, *Levelei*, 120.

230. *A zsidókérdés Magyarországon: A Huszadik Század körkérdése*, 92–93.

231. Lajos Szabolcsi, "Hitvita a Huszadik Században, II," *Egyenlőség*, August 11, 1917, 4.

232. Ármin Schönfeld, "Zsidó sajtó s közéleti morál," *Zsidó Szemle*, January 11, 1918, 2.

233. Budapest—Neológ (Pesti Izraelita Hitközség) születési anyakönyvei [Budapest—Neolog birth records (of the Israelite Congregation of Pest)]. MNL OL, A3562.

234. Duplicate of the civil marriage records of the fifth district of Budapest, December 4, 1915; note recorded under the heading "Marital declarations/Miscellaneous notes prior to signing."

235. "Hatvany Lajos jószándékával védekezik a bíróság előtt," *Magyarország*, February 2, 1928, 4.

236. Lajos Hatvany, "Egy zsidó-magyar monológja," *Korunk* 2, no. 5 (1927): 330.

237. "A Tábla ítélt a Hatvany-perben," *Pesti Napló*, May 9, 1928, 4.

238. Ibid.

PATHS TO CONVERSION—PORTRAITS

239. Lajos Hatvany, "Magyar írók száműzetésben" (1924), in *Utak, sorsok, emberek* (Budapest: Szépirodalmi, 1973), 445.

240. (H-r.), "Königswarter Móricz báró," *Egyenlőség*, November 17, 1893, 4–5; Kempelen, *Magyar zsidó családok*, 2: 18; Wistrich, *The Jews of Vienna in the Age of Franz Joseph*, 122, 166; William O. McCagg, "Austria's Jewish Nobles, 1740–1918," *Leo Baeck Institute Year Book* 34 (1989): 178.

241. István Bródy, *Régi pesti dáridók: Egy letűnt világ regénye* (Budapest: Szerző kiadása, 1940), 61–62.

242. "Érdekes hymen-hír," *Budapesti Hírlap*, January 23, 1887, 6; "Zsidóvá lett keresztény lány," *Budapesti Hírlap*, May 27, 1887, 6.

243. "Königswarter Hermann br.," *Egyenlőség*, June 24, 1888, 9; Kempelen, *Magyar zsidó családok*, 2:18.

244. "Báró Königswarter kikeresztelkedése," *Pesti Napló*, November 12, 1894, 5; "Báró Königswarter milliója," *Pesti Napló*, December 27, 1894, 3; "Báró Königswarter alapítványai," *Pesti Napló*, February 13, 1895, 6; "Báró Königswarter vagyoni bukása," *Pesti Napló*, February 9, 1906, 9.

245. "Báró Königswarter ajándéka," *Fővárosi Lapok* 32, no. 46 (1895): 518.

246. *A Park Club Évkönyve 1912* (Budapest: Hornyánszky Viktor, 1913); *A nemzeti kaszinó évkönyve 1898*, 35.

247. "Lévay Henrik," *Egyenlőség*, December 26, 1886, 7.

248. Albert Sturm, ed., *Új országgyűlési almanach 1887–1892: Rövid életrajzi adatok a főrendiház és a képviselőház tagjairól* (Budapest: Ifjabb Nagel Ottó, 1888), 143; "Zsidó hazafisága," *Szombati Újság*, March 24, 1883, 89–90.

249. "Választás," *Egyenlőség*, October 24, 1886, 6; "Többek kérdésére," *Egyenlőség*, February 10, 1889, 15; "A receptió vezérbizottsága," *Egyenlőség*, January 8, 1892, 9.

250. Lajos Venetianer, "Rabbiképzők," *Magyar-Zsidó Szemle* 34, no. 2–4 (1917): 165.

251. Venetianer, *A magyar zsidóság története*, 363; Veronika Tóth-Barbalics, "A 'korona védpajzsa' vagy 'észarisztokrácia'? A magyar főrendiház élethossziglan kinevezett tagjai," *Századok* 145, no. 3 (2011): 739, 745.

252. *A nemzeti kaszinó évkönyve 1862*, 41; *1865. évi jelentés a pesti lovaregylet munkálódásairól* (Pest: Emich Gusztáv, 1865), 8.

253. "Lévay Henrik adománya," *Budapesti Hírlap*, April 19, 1896, 7; Kitérési és prozelita jegyzőkönyvek [Records of converts and proselytes]. MZsML, TB. B/67.

254. "Főrendi kikeresztelkedés," *Pesti Hírlap*, July 5, 1896, 11.

255. Béla Pápai, "A kitérés útja," *Egyenlőség*, July 10, 1896, supplement, 5.

256. "Lévay Henrik megtérése," *Alkotmány*, July 15, 1896, 4.

257. "Lévay Henrik megkeresztelése," *Budapesti Hírlap*, July 15, 1896, 6; "Keresztény hitre térés," *Pesti Hírlap*, July 15, 1896, 8; "Lévay Henrik kikeresztelkedése," *Pesti Napló*, July 15, 1896, 3; "Lévay Henrik megtérése," *Alkotmány*, July 14, 1896, 10.

300 JEWISHNESS AND BEYOND

258. M. Sz. [Miksa Szabolcsi], "A mi nagy veszteségünk," *Egyenlőség*, December 2, 1892, 1.

259. Ferencz Mezey, "Wahrmann Mór (1832–1892)," *Magyar-Zsidó Szemle* 9, no. 12 (1892): 687, 691.

260. Sz. [Szabolcsi], "A mi nagy veszteségünk," 2.

261. Dénes Pázmándy, "A Wahrmann-család tragédiája," *Szombat*, February 3, 1934, 6–7, and February 17, 1934, 7–8; *Kais. Königl. Militär-Schematismus für 1885* (Wien: K. K. Hof- und Staatsdruckerei, 1884), 548, 586; *Kais. Königl. Militär-Schematismus für 1888* (Wien: K. K. Hof- und Staatsdruckerei, 1887), 547, 593; "Wahrmann Richárd tragédiája," *Pesti Napló*, September 28, 1912, 6; Andor Kellér, *Mayer Wolf fia (Wahrmann Mór életregénye)* ([Budapest]: Hungária, [1941]), 39.

262. Szögi, *Magyarországi diákok németországi egyetemeken és főiskolákon 1789–1919*, 277.

263. "Hivatalos rész," *Budapesti Közlöny*, January 1, 1901, 1; Nepos, "Wahrmannék: Két öngyilkosság kulisszatitkai," *Pesti Hírlap*, September 28, 1912, 10.

264. Samu Haber, "Wahrmann Mórról," *Egyenlőség*, December 2, 1892, 4.

265. "Az orsz. rabbiképző intézet," *Egyenlőség*, December 9, 1892, 9; "Wahrmann emlékezete," *Egyenlőség*, December 16, 1892, 8; "A hitközség gyászünnepe," *Egyenlőség*, December 30, 1892, 4–5.

266. Miksa Szabolcsi, "Az új nemzedékért," *Egyenlőség*, April 14, 1893, 4; "Amit Wahrmann Mór sem sejtett," *Egyenlőség*, May 19, 1893, 11; "Kikeresztelkedés," *Pesti Hírlap*, May 18, 1893, 11.

267. Pázmándy, "A Wahrmann-család tragédiája," February 3, 6.

268. "Wahrmann Renée hozománya," *Országos Hírlap*, December 2, 1897, 9.

269. [Miksa Szabolcsi], "Egy áttérés alkalmából," *Egyenlőség*, January 9, 1898, 2.

270. Kitérési és prozelita jegyzőkönyvek [Records of converts and proselytes]. MZsML, TB. B/67.; "Wahrmann René kitérése," *Budapesti Hírlap*, January 4, 1898, 8; "A miniszterelnök Kohn rabbinál," *Alkotmány*, January 4, 1898, 7; "Wahrmann René keresztelése," *Országos Hírlap*, January 22, 1898, 6.

271. "Megtörtént," *A Jövő*, January 28, 1898, 4.

272. Miklós Konrád, "Wahrmann Mór és gyermekei: Adalék a dualizmus kori zsidó nagypolgárság történetéhez," *Történelmi Szemle* 54, no. 3 (2012): 445–50.

273. Ibid.

274. György Kövér, "'Wahrmann és fia,'" in *Honszeretet és felekezeti hűség: Wahrmann Mór, 1831–1892*, ed. Tibor Frank (Budapest: Argumentum, 2006), 87.

275. "Wahrmann Rikárd—öngyilkos," *Budapesti Hírlap*, September 28, 1912, 8.

276. "Wahrmann végrendelete," *Egyenlőség*, December 2, 1892, 19; Kövér, "'Wahrmann és fia,'" 86.

277. Pál Tenczer, "Reminiscentiák," *Egyenlőség*, December 2, 1892, 8; Ármin Neumann, "Emlékbeszéd Wahrmann Mórról," *Magyar Géniusz*, December 25, 1892, 433.

278. [Szabolcsi], "Egy áttérés alkalmából," 3.

279. Ibid., 2–3.

280. *A budapesti társaság*, 452–53.

281. Tamás Kóbor, "Wahrmann Ernő," *A Hét* 17, no. 22 (1906): 369.

282. Sándor Bródy, "Oroszlánszívű Richárd utolsó órája," in *Elmélkedések* (Budapest: Lampel R., [1914]), 7–8.

283. Pázmándy, "A Wahrmann-család tragédiája," February 3, 6.

284. Tibor Frank, "Magyar és zsidó: A Wahrmann-életrajz kérdései," in *Honszeretet és felekezeti hűség*, ed. id., 29. For discussions of Wahrmann's political career, see Károly Vörös, "Wahrmann Mór: egy zsidó politikus a dualizmus korában," in Frank, *Honszeretet és felekezeti hűség*, 71–78; Árpád Welker, "Wahrmann a magyar országgyűlésben," in Frank, *Honszeretet és felekezeti hűség*, 111–70.

285. [Mór] Bogdányi, "A pesti. izr. hitközség elnöke," *Egyenlőség*, November 25, 1883, 2.

286. Veritás, "Wahrmann Mór és elöljáró társai," *Egyenlőség*, October 27, 1889, 1–2; Miksa Szabolcsi, "Wahrmann Mór," *Egyenlőség*, October 30, 1891, 3; Szabolcsi, *Két emberöltő*, 41, 57–58.

287. OSZK, obituaries, FM8/35797/561: Mór Wahrmann.

288. *Képviselőházi napló, 1869–1872*, vol. 5 (Pest: Légrády Testvérek, 1870), 408–11.

289. Kubinszky, *A politikai antiszemitizmus Magyarországon 1875–1890*, 92, 136–40; *Képviselőházi napló, 1881–1884*, vol. 6 (Budapest: Pesti Könyvnyomda, 1882), 263–67.

290. *Képviselőházi napló, 1881–1884*, 6: 263–64.

291. "Wahrmann Mór beszéde," *Egyenlőség*, November 24, 1889, 2.

292. "Wahrmann Mór beszéde," *Egyenlőség*, December 18, 1891, 2.

293. Szabolcsi, "Az új nemzedékért," 3–4.

294. Kóbor, "Wahrmann Ernő," 370.

295. *A Park Club Évkönyve 1912*.

296. József Láng, "Jókai Mórné Nagy Bella emlékirata," *Irodalomtörténeti Közlemények* 79, no. 3 (1975): 371; Pázmándy, "A Wahrmann-család tragédiája," February 3, 7.

5

After Conversion

Before 1895, Hungarian Jews who wanted to begin living their lives as Christians needed only to present themselves to a Christian clergyman, receive some theological instruction, and testify to their Christian faith. The ecclesiastical laws of 1895 required prospective converts to report to their congregation's rabbinical office to announce their intention to convert. Rabbis occasionally attempted to dissuade potential converts, treating them to heartfelt commemorations of ancestors who had died as martyrs for their faith or warning them that conversion meant defecting "to the enemy camp," as Sámuel Kohn told the violist and music historian Antal Molnár in 1908, when he converted at the age of eighteen.[1] Some tried to keep their conversions secret; others trumpeted the news. In one respect, however, every convert was the same: baptism was not the end of the story. In most cases, uncertainties would linger—would they achieve the objectives for which they had abandoned their religion? In every case, converts had to ask themselves how they would handle their Jewish past. And finally, what of the reactions of their still-Jewish family members, friends, acquaintances, and colleagues—how would they relate to former coreligionists who had formally and symbolically disavowed their faith and their community? The final chapter of this book is an attempt to find answers to these questions.

The Results of Conversion

In a journal entry composed four months after his baptism, Béla Balázs wrote, "My conversion has not been of any use. Just a disadvantage. The Jews got angry; in the eyes of the 'Christians,' I remain just a Jew."[2] Sándor Márai's memoirs feature a similar formulation of the "Christian" perception of Jews: "At that time, 'Aryan' theory had yet to flash through the minds even of those who now swear by it, yet [Hungarians] naturally considered converted Jews to be their racial brethren about as much as an American citizen would consider a black sprinkled with holy water to be a white man."[3]

At the turn of the century, Nazi-style "Aryan" theory was indeed still a long way off, but the essentializing perception that Jewishness overrode conversion was no longer a novelty. This perception was reinforced by pseudoscientific theories of race, but the notion that Jews could not divest themselves of their "Jewishness" took root long before the proliferation of the racial terminology that became a normative cultural paradigm by the late nineteenth century.[4] In Hungary, as far back as the Reform Era, it was widely believed that conversion had no effect on the character of a Jew. In 1839, lawyer and journalist Soma Varga published an article describing Jewish converts as "wolves in sheep's clothing" whose "distinctive characteristics make them immediately recognizable."[5] In a letter written on January 5, 1848 to Pál Nyáry, deputy lord-lieutenant of Pest County, actor Gábor Egressy noted in connection with the playwright and recent Lutheran convert Károly Hugó, "*In the end, a Jew's just a Jew!* Of this, I've been convinced. This race cannot deny itself, ever, in any way. The taste, smell, and color of the traits of this race can be seen and sensed in all the manifestations of its spirit."[6]

The pervasiveness of such beliefs is demonstrated by the simultaneous emergence of the notion that conversion was predestined to failure. In a drama first staged in 1847, one of the characters declared, "My father was baptized as a child, but the waters of baptism did not wash away the name *Jew*."[7] By the beginning of the Dualist era, the idea was being articulated from the Jewish side as well. As Adolf Ágai (more precisely, his satirical cartoon character Iczig Spitzig) put it succinctly in 1870, "My dear friends, if you turn Christian, the world'll still say you're converted Israelites."[8] In an 1875 pamphlet, teacher Jakab Reif took it as a given that the enemies of the Jews would be able to "detect" converts' origins for another "hundred generations."[9] In his 1862 book *Rome and Jerusalem*, the German socialist and proto-Zionist Moses Hess noted that the waters of baptism do not protect Jews from the hatred of Germans because "Jewish noses cannot be reformed."[10] Around the turn of the century in Pest, this notion circulated in the form of a joke: "Convert? What for? Listen—people forget, God forgives.... —But the nose remains!"[11]

304   JEWISHNESS AND BEYOND

It should be noted that Christians were not alone in such beliefs. In Ernő Szép's book about turn-of-the-century Pest, it is precisely this essentialized image of an unalterable Jewishness that leads Szép's alter ego to reject the idea of conversion: "I might have daydreamed about it, but I have never seriously thought of converting. Take Mr. Gergely; he transferred himself to Christianity, but when he opens his mouth, you can hear in his voice that he was a Jew. He couldn't rewrite his voice. It's a Jewish voice."[12] Hugó Veigelsberg (known by his pen name, Ignotus), future cofounder and editor in chief of the journal *Nyugat,* was of a similar mindset, as indicated by an 1895 letter to Béla Tóth, wherein he did not distinguish between the "Jews" Bernát Munkácsi (unconverted) and Zsigmond Simonyi (by then Catholic for eleven years).[13] In 1925, József Bánóczi wrote that Simonyi's conversion had been "of no use at all," insofar as "all of us, Jewish and Christian academics, continued to consider him to be Jewish."[14] By the end of the nineteenth century, this essentialist conception of Jewishness, which was not new to the traditional Ashkenazi world,[15] was as deeply rooted among acculturated Jews as it was among the Christians whose culture they shared. Once again, the notion took the form of a "Jewish" joke:

> Quiet conversation in front of the stock exchange.
> A gentleman: Did you hear? My boss . . .
> Another: What did he do?
> The gentleman: He converted.
> (Long pause)
> The gentleman: And his wife, and his two kids converted, too. All of them converted, the whole family.
> (Long pause)
> The other: That's a real Jewish tempo.[16]

While there is no doubt that both Christians and Jews *kept track* of converted Jews' origins, two clarifications are essential: first, this was an era in which people kept track of *everyone's* origins; second, and above all, when Christians took into account—or went so far as to mention—a convert's origins, they did not necessarily do so with hurtful or malicious intent. In an 1861 pamphlet advocating emancipation, the lawyer Lajos Gáspár identified a number of "Israelites" who had made significant contributions to Hungarian literature and journalism, without distinguishing between unconverted Jews and converts.[17] In an 1883 debate in the House of Representatives, Mór Jókai was praising the Jews who had taken part in the 1848–49 Hungarian Revolution and War of Independence when an antisemitic representative interrupted him to demand the name of a single Jewish war hero. Jókai mentioned Károly Ballagi, younger brother of Mór (Bloch) Ballagi, who was wounded during the 1849 siege of the Buda Castle. By that time Károly Ballagi had been a member of the Reformed Church for five years,[18] as Jókai must have known.

What might qualify a conversion as "successful"? Obviously, a convert's believing it to be so. If any Hungarian Jews converted during the period in question in hopes of concealing their Jewish origins once and for all, they were bound to fail. Given the foregoing, however, few Jews could have entertained any such inane fantasy. As far as I can tell, an overwhelming majority of Jews' conversions worked out in accordance with their calculations. For those who converted in order to free themselves from the legal restrictions imposed on Jews before their emancipation, baptism achieved their objectives automatically. Likewise, for anyone who converted in order to marry a Christian, switching religions necessarily produced the desired result. After 1867, conversion also proved useful in a majority of cases where Jews abandoned their faith in the interest of professional advancement or obtaining a particular position.

Of course, conversion was not a guarantee of success and sometimes bore no fruit. According to a pamphlet he published in 1862, Moravia-born János Koricsáner moved to Hungary in 1832 at the age of sixteen, worked as a Jewish elementary school teacher for many years, then converted to Catholicism in 1846.[19] Koricsáner printed his pamphlet as an expression of frustration at his inability to find a permanent position despite his many years of Christianity: "They despise a Jew even if he's baptized and lives according to Christ's commandment. Alas! It's happened to me. I've been a Christian for 15 years; 15 times I've applied to teach at schools in various communities, and . . . I still don't have a position. In several locations, officials told me to my face, 'We don't need anyone who was Jewish. You've got Jewish facial features.'"[20] Koricsáner described his calvary in great detail, including lengthy accounts of the setbacks he suffered in towns and villages located mostly on the Great Hungarian Plain and in the region between the Danube and Tisza rivers. In his pamphlet, Koricsáner also recounted the case of his fellow convert Ferdinand Kohn, whom he had gotten to know in Kalocsa in the early 1850s: "He complained to me with bitter indignation that despite his having graduated from secondary schools in his youth, they did not want to employ him as a teacher;

306   JEWISHNESS AND BEYOND

that with great difficulty, at the age of forty, he had been given a teaching position in a most wretched backwater; that they still, even now (thirty-five years
after his baptism) call him a Jew; that the other children still call his children
Jewish kids."[21] We have to no reason to doubt Koricsáner's account; his pamphlet is a unique source of information on Hungarian popular antisemitism in
the period from the late 1840s to the early 1860s. However, precisely because
we have no comparable sources to corroborate Koricsáner's pamphlet, we
cannot be sure of the extent to which his (and Ferdinand Kohn's) experiences
were similar to those of other Hungarian converts trying to find teaching
positions during this period.

Ármin Vámbéry's conversion, which also took place in the 1860s, did
not lead immediately to an appointment either. After joining the Reformed
Church on December 30, 1864, Vámbéry wrote to his friend Áron Szilády
from London on March 19 of the following year, telling the Reformed pastor,
Orientalist, and linguist, "The Hungarian gentlemen of Vienna, several leading German officials, and Count [Rudolf] Apponyi, the ambassador here, supported [my] cause—the emperor made a personal promise." All for naught,
however: "despite the unanimous approval of the teaching staff, the university's precious senate was largely opposed to my appointment and returned
His Apostolic Majesty's proposal with a negative response."[22] The Catholic
paper *Religio* voiced opposition to Vámbéry's appointment as well, asking in
its March 18, 1865 issue, "Is Vámbéry a Jew, a Christian, a Turk, or a fetishist?"
Of course, it was no secret that Vámbéry had converted; the problem was
his choosing Calvinism over Catholicism.[23] Vámbéry was finally hired as a
lecturer in eastern languages on July 21, 1865.

Legal scholar Bódog Somló, who converted to Catholicism at the age of
eighteen in 1891, endured an even longer struggle.[24] Somló earned a law degree from the Royal Hungarian Franz Joseph University in Kolozsvár in 1895
and a doctorate in political science in 1896. He wrote to his parents from
Leipzig on November 26, 1896 to inform them that he had not been hired to
teach at the law school in Máramarossziget (Sighetu Marmaţiei, Romania)
because it was affiliated with the Reformed Church and did not hire Catholics.[25] After studying abroad, Somló returned in 1898 and redoubled his efforts to find a teaching position. He failed again and was forced to work as a
clerk in the central administration of the Hungarian state railway company.[26]
But Somló did not give up. His efforts were supported by the eminent legal
philosopher Gyula Pikler, himself a Jewish convert. Pikler met with Gyula

Figure 5.1. Bódog Somló. In Felix Somló, *Gedanken zu einer ersten Philosophie* (Berlin/Leipzig: Walter de Gruyter, 1926)

Wlassics, Hungary's minister of religion and public education, to discuss the young convert's appointment to a teaching position at the Royal Law School of Pozsony.[27] On October 17, Somló was interviewed by Wlassics, then went to Pozsony to discuss his application.[28] Despite these efforts, Somló was not hired by the law school in Pozsony. In 1899, he became a teaching assistant at the law school of his university in Kolozsvár. The position was unpaid, and he was forced to continue earning his daily bread as an employee of the state railway company. Somló was finally hired as an associate professor at the law school in Nagyvárad in 1903; a year later, he was summoned back to the university in Kolozsvár, where he was appointed to an associate professorship in August of 1905 and a full professorship in 1909.[29]

Even if the process did not go smoothly, Somló ultimately got what he wanted. Zsigmond Simonyi earned an appointment in similar fashion, just as György Lukács managed to get a job as an assistant clerk at the Ministry of Commerce. In addition to the examples above, all available evidence indicates that Hungarian Jews who converted to advance their careers or obtain a specific position generally achieved their objectives. For decades, Neolog Jewish pamphleteers and the Jewish press reiterated that Jews who converted would "continue to bear the title of 'Jew'"[30] and that in the eyes of Christians, "their descendants would still be counted as Jewish."[31] As editor in chief József Patai of the cultural Zionist *Múlt és Jövő* (*Past and Future*) put it in 1914, "not even 100 fonts of baptismal water could wash the Jewishness off a Jew." And yet Patai had no doubt that "it could be significantly easier to advance" with a baptismal certificate.[32] In the words of Illés Adler, Óbuda's chief rabbi, "If a Jewish person commits to a change of faith, at that point, whether he believes in his new religion or not, a career opens up before him as if by magic; the wages of this career fall into his lap; roasted birds fly into his mouth."[33]

The tracking of converts' origins did not necessarily entail any unpleasantness for them, though it sometimes was a source of difficulties in their professional and public lives. Professional issues of the sort are illustrated by the complaints of journalist Mór Szegfi, an active participant in Hungarian Jewish public life before and during the 1848 revolution, who converted for unknown reasons in the mid-1850s.[34] In 1861, Szegfi married Emília Kánya, a Lutheran who was Hungary's first female newspaper editor. In 1876, he took a teaching job at the *Realschule* in Lőcse. In 1881, he moved on to the *Realschule* in Kassa,[35] whence he sent a letter, dated December 30, 1882, asking his old friend and patron, royal education commissioner Károly Szász, for assistance: "Alas, my arrival here has coincided with the first wrigglings of antisemitism in our homeland and—you are certainly better acquainted than I with the cultural level of our teachers. Half my colleagues here are openly antisemitic, while the others, with few exceptions, are more underhanded about it. . . . I made my break with Jewry long ago, but I still cannot watch calmly when a fundamentally sublime religion and a community boasting a multitude of illustrious souls is being presented like a loathsome wound to mankind." Not believing that he could change anything by speaking up, the reserved Szegfi generally ignored his colleagues' antisemitic comments. Even so, he was not always able to avoid conflict. One of his colleagues, Szegfi wrote,

AFTER CONVERSION

> ... picked me out as the target for his racial hatred straightaway. That the Jews would now like to be the apostles of the Hungarian language; that they mischievously change names and religions, etc., etc.— I pretended not to hear it, because I am afraid of uncultured persons. One day, however, on the subject of the Jews again, he reduced himself to saying: "If it were up to me, however many Jews there are in the world, I'd hang them all!" And because the principal was there in the teachers' lounge, I mustered the courage to say this much: "Dear colleague, please refrain from reviling the Jews like that, in my presence at least! Because my parents were Jews, too, and they were honorable people all the same!" That was all I had to do!

Szegfi's colleague subjected him to a torrent of profanity and became an implacable foe, using slander of every kind in an attempt to discredit him with his superiors.[36]

Public figures who converted (and their descendants) were maliciously reminded of their Jewish origins, and not only by avowed antisemites. In 1886, Independence Party politician and journalist Lajos Hentaller published a book of biographical sketches in which he mocked the nobiliary suffix on the surname of István Teleszky, a parliamentary representative of the Liberal Party and future state secretary at the Ministry of Justice: "He can put two Ys on the end of his name; he still cannot deny that they used to call him *Jajteles*."[37] Considering that Teleszky was three years old in 1839 when his father, surgeon János Jeiteles, Magyarized his name (and presumably converted), this remark shows how long it could take for one's origins to be forgotten.[38] Members of the bourgeois-radical camp were also inclined to make mention of their political opponents' Jewish origins. In 1914, *Világ* surpassed even Lajos Hentaller in noting that finance minister János Teleszky's father, István, "was still a Jajtelesz in his childhood."[39]

Converts' (and their descendants') political opponents occasionally tried to use their origins against them in their election campaigns. The 1886 *Almanac of the National Assembly* let it slip that Ödön Gajári had been elected to represent Dunapataj in 1884 "despite antisemitic provocations" there, even though Gajári—the scion of a noble family on his mother's side—had been born seven years after his father's conversion to Catholicism.[40] In 1887, when Károly Légrády (founding editor and owner of the *Pesti Hírlap*, who had joined the Lutheran Church twenty-seven years earlier) ran to represent the Békés County district of Gyoma, his political adversaries from the Independence Party attempted to disparage him by singing a campaign song emphasizing his "Jewish-sounding" birth name; Légrády lost the election.[41] Ödön Gajári's half brother Géza Gajáry had better luck in 1901. Born to another noblewoman eighteen years after his father's conversion to Catholicism, Gajáry was reelected as the Liberal Party's representative of the city of Vác in 1901 despite a campaign song his opponents in the Catholic People's Party sang to remind voters of his Jewish origins: "Gajáry's forefather was a Jew / So he can't be a Hungarian, either. / Gajáry, my dear, / You're going to fail, I'm telling you."[42] When historian and Liberal Party candidate Géza Ballagi (son of the aforementioned Mór Ballagi) ran to represent the Zemplén County district of Olaszliszka in the national election of 1901, it meant nothing that he had been born eight years after his father's conversion, nor that his mother, Ida Lehoczky, was the descendant of an old noble family; his political rivals played the Jewish card against him with another campaign song: "We just don't listen to them / Because their jabber's phony. / We don't need the Bloch boy, / Hammersberg will be our man." Ballagi won the election, though he would lose his seat to Gyula Andrássy Jr. four years later. Among the songs of the 1905 campaign, one went, "Jew, Jew, ragged Jew, / Have you any rouge? / Géza's face is pallid, / He needs some rouge on it. / Long live Andrássy!"[43] All these antisemitic attacks were directed at Liberal Party candidates because most politicians of the Jewish faith (or of Jewish origin) ran as Liberals. Moreover, the sense of political correctness on the Liberals' end of the ideological spectrum (formerly associated with the Deák Party and later with the National Labor Party) made them much less likely to draw attention to a rival's Jewish origins. Tactics of this sort were, however, permitted within the party. In the 1901 election, Géza Ballagi and his opponent Miklós Hammersberg both ran as Liberals.

Attacks like the foregoing did not meaningfully diminish the overall success politicians and public figures found in converting; at worst, they may have cast a shadow. On the one hand, such attacks could hardly have been surprising to their targets. And as the outcomes of the parliamentary elections demonstrate, the attacks did not necessarily prevent converts or their descendants from winning elections, nor is there any proof that they played a decisive role in particular candidates' losses. Certain converts attributed the failures of their political careers to antisemitism, but there is no guarantee it actually happened that way. Speaking to an 1886 gathering of the Hungarian Association of Lawyers, the organization's founder, Károly Csemegi, implied that his Jewish origins had prevented him from realizing his dreams.[44] Csemegi,

Figure 5.2. Mór Szegfi. National Széchényi Library, The Manuscripts Archive, 935/2.

312 JEWISHNESS AND BEYOND

whose parents had him baptized as a young child, was renowned for writing the first Hungarian-language criminal code. Having been appointed state secretary at the justice ministry in 1872, he was known to aspire to the office of justice minister.[45] However, his Jewish origins were not responsible for derailing his political career. When prime minister Kálmán Tisza—who could hardly be characterized as an antisemite—pressured Csemegi into resigning from his post in 1879, he did so because he thought the state secretary's efforts to detach the justice system from the state administration would diminish the government's authority.[46]

Conversion generally helped converts and their children achieve their political objectives, regardless of the possible attacks they may have endured as a result of their origins. As a person of Jewish faith, Mór Ullmann's son László could not have served as a member of the country's first representative parliament, elected in 1848. Nor could Mór Ballagi, Bernát Ullmann (another of Mór Ullmann's sons), or Lajos Máday (who converted at an unknown date) have been elected to serve as representatives in 1861; nor could Máday, Bernát Ullmann, or Albert Wodianer Jr. (the Catholic-born son of Mór Wodianer) have been seated at the National Assembly in 1865.[47] The emancipation law permitted Jews to run for the national assembly, yet while the parliamentary cycle from 1869 to 1872 featured three Jewish representatives (Mór Wahrmann, Ede Horn, and Ferenc Chorin), eight of their colleagues had either converted or were of Jewish origin. In 1872, two Jewish representatives, Wahrmann and Horn, were reelected to the assembly while the number of converts and converts' descendants in the legislature rose from eight to ten. With the election of István Teleszky in 1874, the number reached 11.[48]

While political opponents occasionally succeeded in using converts' Jewish origins against them, Miksa Falk managed as a Catholic to achieve a level of influence within the Hungarian political establishment that would have been beyond his reach as a Jew, regardless of his manifest talent. Perhaps the most influential Hungarian political journalist in the latter half of the nineteenth century, Falk converted in 1851 at the age of twenty-three.[49] He was a confidant of figures like István Széchenyi, Ferenc Deák, and Kálmán Tisza; "the highest dignitaries of the court" would make a show of walking arm in arm with him.[50] He edited the influential Pester Lloyd from 1867 to 1906, was admitted to the National Casino in 1873, and later joined the Countrywide Casino and the Park Klub. Falk was elected to the House of Representatives for eleven consecutive terms, serving from 1870 until 1905. When he died in

Figure 5.3. Károly Csemegi. In *Vasárnapi Újság* 46, no. 13 (1899): 197.

1908, the conservative *Budapesti Hírlap* eulogized him as "a towering marble pillar" among the political proponents of the Austro-Hungarian Compromise and a mainstay of the Hungarian political elite.[51]

Moreover, not all converts were attacked for their Jewish origins. There were many conflict-averse public figures who were able to integrate quietly into Christian society. The best example in political life was Bernát Ullmann (who changed his surname to Szitányi in 1867). Born in 1816 to Mózes Ullmann and Frumet Hirschl, the young Bernát converted to Catholicism alongside his

Figure 5.4. Miksa Falk, c. 1890. Hungarian National Museum, 1973/1957 fk.

father in 1825 and received his title as a result of his father's ennoblement that same year. He passed the bar exam in 1837 and became deputy lord-lieutenant in 1849. When Hungary's war of independence was put down, Ullmann fled to Turkey and eventually moved to Paris. Granted amnesty, he returned to Hungary and reclaimed his confiscated properties. Admitted to the National Casino in 1847, he became a member of the Hungarian Jockey Club in 1853.

He served as a representative in the National Assembly for almost three decades, from 1861 until his death in 1889, first as a member of the Deák Party, then as a Liberal.[52] The 1884 *Liberal Party Calendar* reported that the "well-liked" Szitányi maintained several "tender customs"; when he was pleased by a parliamentary speech, he rewarded his fellow representative with a piece of candy—two if the speaker was the prime minister.[53] He does not seem to have done much else. As Károly Eötvös put it in a eulogy, "He was what they call a 'good guy.' In the club, at home, at the office, at presidential and departmental luncheons, at a royal speech or a court soirée—he was always present. He never missed anything, but he never undertook anything either. . . . He was a familiar figure in parliament. Everybody knew him, everybody will forget him, and everybody will remember him fondly when they remember him."[54]

Similar examples in Hungarian cultural life include the Wohl sisters, Janka and Stefánia. Their father, surgeon Antal Wohl, adopted the baptismal name János Sándor in converting to Lutheranism in 1843, a month before Janka's birth. Her sister Stefánia was born on March 24, 1846 and baptized on April 18. It is not clear precisely when their mother, Johanna Löwy, converted.[55] The girls' parents entertained illustrious guests; according to Emília Kánya's memoirs, Protestant—and especially Lutheran—intellectuals of Pest were happy to socialize with an "educated, extraordinary woman" like Johanna Löwy.[56] Learned Protestants were not their only visitors; the guestbook Janka Wohl began keeping in 1858 features inscriptions by figures like Countess Teréz Brunswick, Countess Blanka Teleki, Franz Liszt, János Arany, and József Eötvös.[57] The Wohl sisters made their living as journalists, editors, and translators, never mentioning their Jewish origins. Their reputation was based above all on their hosting a literary salon with a "Western European flavor."[58] The Wohl sisters adopted and transmitted the values of genteel Christian society, and as their obituaries noted, they were fully accepted even in "the most distinguished circles."[59]

This brings us to the issue of social acceptance. How successful were those Jews who abandoned their faith partly or primarily in hopes of being fully accepted into Hungarian Christian society? With the notable exception of the aforementioned János Koricsáner, the data with which to answer this question is limited almost exclusively to the upper class. Koricsáner left a record of the extraordinarily withering experiences he endured in the early 1850s as a schoolteacher in Kalocsa, where all his efforts to establish social relationships were immediately and rudely rejected.[60] Koricsáner's precise descriptions of

Figure 5.5. Janka Wohl, c. 1892. National Széchényi Library, The Manuscripts Archive, Analekta 6786.

the various settings, incidents, and exchanges give the impression that these accounts were drawn from his own diary. In any case, he was indisputably justified in feeling bitter. However, I should again point out that the unique nature of this source makes it impossible to draw general conclusions from it. Just as Géza Moscovitz's social successes were at least partly the result of his alluring personality, it is possible that Koricsáner was simply an unpleasant person.

Figure 5.6. Stefánia Wohl, c. 1888. National Széchényi Library, The Manuscripts Archive, Fond 62/36.

Concerning the upper class, most contemporaneous observers put the emphasis on converts' failures to integrate, or at least on the limits of their acceptance. In a folk play Sándor Lukácsy set at the time of the 1848 revolution and staged in 1875, when a Jewish banker ponders whether he should have his daughter baptized and marry her to a baron who owes him money, his daughter tries to dissuade him: "You should reconsider. You'll remain but Steinberger, the Jewish banker, and the upper echelons will hardly notice anything about me but my diamonds."[61] In a story Zoltán Thury published in the *Pesti Napló* in 1904, the rich elderly Jew cites his daughter's future happiness in rejecting an indebted hussar lieutenant's request for her hand: "If she remains in her father's faith and marries some decent merchant, she'll become a celebrated woman. Over there, however, in that other society, she'll often be made to feel that she's just my daughter."[62] In his well-received 1914 drama *Liza Tímár*, Sándor Bródy voiced the same idea Lukácsy had expressed forty years earlier. The wife of Bródy's converted and ennobled merchant bursts out, "No one comes to see us except for money. We can't go anywhere unless we pay our way in."[63]

According to the general belief, wealthy Jewish converts were fated to float in a kind of intermediate social position. In 1884, an anonymous Jewish woman wrote a letter to *Fővárosi Lapok* on the subject of "wealthy Jewish girls" who converted in order to marry into prominent noble families: "What has our experience been? That the waters of baptism, which initiate one into another faith, do not wash away preconceptions and prejudices. These girls have broken away from the circle in which they were raised without having gotten in where they wanted. And now they are floating 'zwischen Himmel und Erde,' that is, between heaven and earth."[64] Two decades later, Count Miklós Zay, who had an insider's knowledge of Hungary's social elite, expressed a similar opinion using similar imagery: "Discounting the exceptional cases in which men who converted and obtained noble rank were able to find a place in Hungarian society as a result of their individual ability, the situations of most baptized Jews cannot be characterized as rosy. In reality, they belong neither to the Christian nor to the Jewish element, but like Mohamed's coffin, float between two magnets."[65]

In my estimation, however, most members of the Hungarian Jewish economic elite achieved their objectives in converting. One obvious indicator of success was admittance to the National Casino, the Countrywide Casino, or the Park Klub. Naturally, conversion did not guarantee access to these clubs.

The National Casino rejected the membership application of the converted Mór Ullmann in 1832 but accepted the unconverted Mór Moscovitz in 1848. Yet while the National Casino was mostly—the Countrywide Casino and Park Klub entirely—closed to Jews, all three clubs' doors were open to converts and particularly to their descendants. By 1918, the National Casino had accepted ten Jews and thirty-five converts or descendants of Jews; in 1913, the Countrywide Casino had around thirty-six members who were converts or sons of converts; in the early 1900s, the Park Klub had at least twenty such members.

Conversion also proved to be a successful strategy for marrying into the traditional elite. Unlike their counterparts in Germany, wealthy Hungarian Jewish men who converted were almost always able to find wives from old noble or aristocratic families, and the fathers of female Hungarian converts could almost always find them noble husbands.[66] When Baron Mór Wodianer died in 1885, his son Albert was still a bachelor (and would remain so), but his daughters had already married. According to the family's obituary, Anna was married to Count Lipót Ferri, Gabriella was married to Count Vince Nemes, and Borbála was the widow of Sir Géza Wachtler.[67] Károly Harkányi was baptized as a child, ennobled in 1867 along with his father, wholesaler and landowner Fülöp (Koppély) Harkányi, and elevated to the rank of baron in 1895. He married Emília Vörös de Monostor in 1861; all three of their children married members of the traditional elite. In 1900, András (or Andor) Harkányi wed Mária Iphigénia Csáky, daughter of Count Albin Csáky (former minister of religion and public education, president of the House of Lords at the time of the wedding). After divorcing Gyula Miklós, lord-lieutenant of Borsod County, Mária Harkányi married Count János Cziráky in 1903; in 1908, Béla Harkányi married Blanka Hieronymi (whose father, Károly Hieronymi, had compensated for his common origins by serving stints as minister of the interior and minister of commerce).[68] In 1844, a year after the death of Viennese Jewish banker Michael Lazar Biedermann (who also operated as a licensed wholesaler in Pest), his converted son Simon Biedermann married noblewoman Amália Gratze.[69] Granted an Austrian knighthood and the praedicatum "turonyi" in 1860, Simon Biedermann and his wife had five children. Their son Ottó married Margit Tüköry de Algyest, and their daughter Leontine married Guillaume Morin de Banneville, son of Gaston Morin, Marquis of Banneville, who served as France's ambassador to Switzerland, Austria, and the Vatican, then as its foreign minister. Two of the Biedermanns' sons married converted daughters of upper-class Jewish

320   JEWISHNESS AND BEYOND

families, but considering the significant financial advantages of such unions, it is highly unlikely that they did so "faute de mieux."[70]

Over the course of an integration process that spanned several generations, upper-class converts did occasionally suffer lesser indignities, and while the rejections and insults they endured may seem frivolous, they could still be painful. Distiller Dániel Néuman de Végvár of Arad was still Jewish when he was elevated to the rank of baron in 1913; his only daughter, Margit Neuman, converted to Catholicism before marrying Baron Tibor Dániel in 1906.[71] When Margit applied for a membership at the Park Klub as Mrs. Tibor Dániel in 1910, some of the organization's younger aristocratic members objected to her Jewish origins. Though the women's committee ultimately approved her application, the affair was so mortifying, Mrs. Dániel collapsed into bed and refused to leave her room for days.[72] In a book published in 1972, Pál Ignotus narrated the case of an acquaintance of his, a former National Assembly representative who converted and married a woman from an impoverished "gentry" family: "After their wedding, she was still invited to the country balls, but they received tactful warnings that he had better plead public duties on such occasions."[73] Count Albert Nemes, a high-ranking official at the Imperial and Royal Foreign Ministry in Vienna in the early 1910s, had a colleague remark that his appearance betrayed his origins—suggesting that the count, son of Count Vince Nemes and Christian-born Gabriella Wodianer, was visibly the grandson of once-Jewish Mór Wodianer, who had converted to Catholicism three-quarters of a century before.[74]

It bears repeating, however, that unless the targets of these insults had completely lost touch with reality, incidents like these could not have come as a surprise. More importantly, conversion generally led directly to the desired result—membership to a casino, a baronial title, and marriage to a member of a noble or aristocratic family. Furthermore, while the passing of several generations might not have been enough for a family's Jewish origins to fade into oblivion, there were cases in which converts themselves seem to have achieved complete social acceptance. Albert Wodianer Sr. converted to Catholicism in 1843, at the age of twenty-five, was ennobled alongside his older brother Mór and their father, Sámuel, in 1844 and admitted to the National Casino in 1845.[75] In 1853, Albert Wodianer Sr. married a woman of noble descent, Zsófia Atzél de Borosjenő.[76] Though his financial achievements did not match those of his brother, he did donate significant sums to various church-run ventures—presumably the reason he was awarded one of the highest papal distinctions, the Cross of the Order of St. Gregory the Great, in 1870.[77] In 1886, one year after the reform of the House of Lords, when Hungarian prime minister Kálmán Tisza asked the king to grant Albert Wodianer Sr. a baronial title and—as a special royal favor—a hereditary appointment to the House of Lords, which could now be effected independent of his aristocratic rank, the prime minister stressed that Wodianer enjoyed "universal respect in aristocratic circles."[78]

Frigyes Koppély also seems to have been fully accepted by the traditional elite. Having converted to Catholicism in 1842 at the age of seventeen (about two years after his wholesaler father, Fülöp Koppély, had converted), he was admitted to the National Casino in 1850. He married Baroness Zsuzsanna Podmaniczky in 1858 after bravely resisting her Lutheran family's efforts to convert him from Catholicism.[79] Frigyes was ennobled alongside his father in 1867; the family changed their surname to Harkányi the same year. Now known as Frigyes Harkányi, he won a by-election to the National Assembly in 1870[80] and would retain his seat there until 1895, at which point he and his brother Károly Harkányi were elevated to the rank of baron. Having also received a hereditary appointment to the House of Lords, Frigyes resigned from the House of Representatives. According to the anonymous author of the 1886 book *A budapesti társaság* (*Budapest Society*), the head of the Harkányi family was "a gentleman of European culture, who by virtue of his family connections was at home among livers of the highlife even before the rebirth of our constitutional existence [i.e., the compromise of 1867]. He and his brother, national representative Károly Harkányi, maintain a large house where members of the aristocracy and gentry are happy to be entertained."[81] Frigyes Harkányi was admitted to the Countrywide Casino in 1890 and joined the Park Klub in 1893, just as the latter association was getting off the ground. In 1900, Harkányi assumed a seat on the men's admissions committee at the club.[82]

One might contend that the elder Albert Wodianer and Frigyes Harkányi converted in the Reform Era, and thus their Jewish pasts, if not completely forgotten by the 1880s, would have counted as old news. The same could not be said of Hermann Königswarter and Henrik Lévay, who converted to Catholicism in 1895 and 1896, respectively. Nevertheless, *Szalon Újság*, the paper of record for Hungarian aristocratic society, treated both men to favorable coverage. In 1900, in a discussion of the 100,000-crown divorce settlement Königswarter offered his estranged wife, Melánia Blaskovich, *Szalon Újság* said he was "a gentleman in the most profound sense." The paper curtly

JEWISHNESS AND BEYOND

brushed aside the "more or less" baseless rumors concerning the "English girl," appreciatively noting that Königswarter had settled the debts of several young scions of noble families of Bihar County.[83] *Szalon Újság* also published several articles about Henrik Lévay, one describing the chapel he had had built on his estate in Táplány and consecrated by the county bishop. A lengthier piece, illustrated with numerous photos, introduced readers to his mansion, which had been "furnished with princely pomp and comfort."[84]

Finally, it should also be noted that in general, official statistics clearly indicate that the overwhelming majority of the Hungarian Jews who converted in the roughly two decades leading up to the outbreak of World War I experienced the process as a net positive. If conversion had entailed more disadvantages than advantages, larger numbers of converts would have returned to the Jewish fold, as doing so was legalized in 1896. Starting in 1897, the Hungarian statistical yearbook's annual data would feature numbers for conversions to Judaism, including those of "returnees." Between 1897 and 1914, of the 8,232 Hungarian Jews who converted to a Christian denomination, only 496 returned to the Jewish faith. The precision of this comparison is diminished by the fact that some of these returnees had converted to Christianity before 1897, though the number of Jews who converted in this period and returned to the Jewish faith after 1914 may compensate for the distortion. In any case, the 496 returnees amounted to 6.0 percent of the 8,232 Hungarian Jews who converted to Christianity in the period, a proportion that speaks for itself.

In addition to converts who hoped in vain that their Jewishness would fade into oblivion and those for whom baptism was merely an unsuccessful attempt at self-discovery, there were two other classes of "Jews" whose conversions eventually proved fruitless. Individuals who (in György Litván's words) "wanted to address the national intelligentsia not as Jews, but as Hungarian—or more precisely, Christian Hungarian—intellectuals"[85] but used their voices to articulate radical critiques of Hungary's political and social structures would ultimately experience conversion as futility—certainly at some point after 1919, if not sooner. Conversion would also prove pointless for those who, to put it bluntly, did not die soon enough. The economist and statistician Béla Földes converted to Catholicism in 1879; he was hired as an associate professor of law at the University of Budapest in 1882 and promoted to a full professorship there in 1889; he served as dean of the law school in 1896–97 and 1912–13 and was chosen as the university's rector in 1917–18. Földes was elected to the Hungarian Academy of Sciences as a corresponding member in

Figure 5.7. Béla Földes. In *Vasárnapi Újság* 64, no. 35 (1917): 559.

1893 and a regular member in 1901; he served in the House of Representatives from 1905 to 1917. From August 18, 1917 to May 8, 1918, he served as minister without portfolio responsible for transitional economic affairs. And on January 18, 1945, the day Budapest's Jewish ghetto was liberated, Béla Földes died there of starvation at the age of ninety-seven.[86]

New Christians and Their Jewish Pasts

Some Jews converted after long periods of inner struggle; others did so without any misgivings at all. In converting, some Jews were abandoning a faith to which they had felt bound and a community with which they had identified. Others left nothing behind, because they had nothing to leave. However, insofar as the society in which they lived still took note of their origins and would continue to classify them as Jews on some level, conversion was not the end of the story. Whether they liked it or not, converts could not erase their Jewish pasts. The following is a discussion of the ways in which converts related to and dealt with such personal history.

In a feuilleton published in *Pesti Napló* in 1910, journalist Sámuel Radó offered an imaginary acquaintance some advice on conversion. If Radó's interlocutor wanted his origins to be forgotten, his first task was to cut off all contact with his former coreligionists. If his professional obligations did not permit him to do so, he should at least extract his family from the old milieu: "In general, it would be best if Jews were not to cross the threshold of your home." Radó recommended an immediate change in the education of the convert's children; raising them "in a resolutely clerical spirit" would ensure the disappearance of their "racial character." Likewise, he was not to shy away from "a little clericalism" in his political convictions. Radó also addressed the sensitive subject of the convert's behavior in Christian company: "Many a neophyte wishes to improve his position with a howling antisemitism, which I would ask you to avoid.... If, for example, a blood libel is mentioned in your company, be wary of excitement and invective. It is enough to say, in a regretful and melancholy voice, 'The fanaticism of provincial Jews is unbelievable!' This is a splendid formula."[87]

By the 1900s, the cliché of the antisemitic convert was widespread among Hungarians of all denominational backgrounds. It appears as far back as an 1866 short story by the poet and journalist Bertalan Ormody, in which a "wretched apostate" delivers a passionately antisemitic speech to the rabble who plundered the Jews of Pest at the time of the 1848 revolution.[88] By the 1890s, there was an increasingly widespread belief that converts mouthed antisemitic tropes in hopes of obscuring their own Jewish origins. In 1894, Iván Szigetvári wrote that everyone reviled Jews, "even he who used to be Jewish, because he thereby hopes to conceal this congenital 'defect.'"[89] In 1901, Andor Kozma treated the convert who turns against his former coreligionists as a stereotype: "As everyone surely knows, among the Jews who turn to Christianity, there are many whose antisemitism is distinguished by the overzealousness of the renegade."[90] By World War I, the cliché of the antisemitic Jewish convert had also appeared in the humorous writings of Ferenc Molnár, Zoltán Ambrus, and Pál Farkas.[91]

More nuanced depictions were rare. One exception is Róbert Tábori's 1899 novel *Megfagyott pezsgő* (*Frozen Champagne*), in which entrepreneur and banker János Lóránd converts at nineteen, becomes a zealous Catholic, flirts with antisemitism, and is enraged when a Jewish painter proposes to marry his daughter. Because Lóránd's heart is fundamentally good, he gives the union his blessing; then he begins removing images of Christian martyrs from the walls of his villa, replacing them with paintings "in which one recognizes a certain Old Testament orientation." In plainer language, "Mr. János backslid a bit."[92]

Sándor Bródy's 1914 play *Liza Tímár* is the only work of Hungarian fiction produced in the period that does not attribute negative characteristics or attitudes, including antisemitism, to the figure of the wealthy convert. When we meet Liza Tímár's father, a wheat merchant who has amassed a fortune and been ennobled, he and his family have already converted, though he confesses to his daughter that he struggled with the decision: "I did it for your sake, against my own inclination." While Mr. Tímár abandons his faith, he remains a merchant—defiantly so. He likes to remind his family that he went to yeshiva as a young man; he ridicules his wife's piety and is contemptuous of her longing to find acceptance in aristocratic society. He looks down on the impoverished aristocrats competing for his daughter's hand, instead hoping to find her a "self-made man" like himself, preferably a Jew.[93]

Of course, Jewish newspapers were not nearly as positive in their descriptions of the "renegades." The cowardly Jew who abandoned his ancestors' faith and his besieged community to have himself baptized out of self-interest denied his own being and doomed himself to spiritual ruin. As Miksa Szabolcsi, the editor in chief of *Egyenlőség*, put it in his 1901 psychological profile of the convert,

> He knows that Christians consider him a Jew even if he is depraved enough to prove his Christianity by playing the antisemite. He knows that Jews and Christians both watch what they say around him, whether they are talking about Jews or about Christians, and they do not believe him, whether he is talking about Jews or about Christians. What he actually is, he himself does not really know. . . . This agonizing state of mind makes the unfortunate misfit into a suspicious, dissatisfied, envious, and inexpressibly unhappy individual who enjoys himself in the company of only one kind of person: other converted Jews. . . . His entire life is wandering, adaptation, spiritual turbulence, and above all, a perpetual denial of the self.[94]

The writers at *Egyenlőség* were even more emphatic than their contemporaries in asserting that converts—driven by a sick, hopeless desire to conceal their origins—would inevitably turn against their former coreligionists. According to an editorial Szabolcsi wrote in 1904, "The rule is thus that the converted Jew sides with the enemies of the Jews. . . . If the convert does not immediately become an antisemite, he will later on; and if, by chance, he never does, his children and grandchildren certainly will, as countless cases demonstrate."[95] Over the years, this view would harden into dogma. In the words of a pseudonymous author of a 1911 piece in *Egyenlőség*, "We have sufficient proof of it—every renegade not only breaks with his brethren, but betrays them the first chance he gets; his children, meanwhile, are openly antisemitic so as to conceal their origins."[96]

Another common feature of the stereotypes promulgated by the Hungarian public and the Jewish press was that the convert who becomes an antisemite was almost always a member of the wealthier strata of Jewry. As Miksa Szabolcsi noted in his 1901 portrait of the conflicted convert, "Of course, our subject here is not the poor lad who converts to get a winter coat from his godfather,"[97] and indeed, Szabolcsi consistently avoided discussing how poor converts related to their Jewish pasts and their former coreligionists.

Nor would it be possible for us to assemble a representative sample. And while it may be rash to speculate on the subject of individuals about whom we know nothing, I would venture to suggest that the majority of Hungarian Jews who converted—who left no written records of their lives and were not written about by others—simply tried to keep a low profile. They did not become antisemites or defenders of Jewry; they tried to blend into Hungary's Christian society, which required them to keep their Jewish origins under a bushel, insofar as it was possible.[98] In addition to the mass of anonymous individuals, there are only a relatively small number of converts about whom we have sufficient sources to assess how they dealt with their Jewish past. Many of these sources are unverifiable anecdotes, accounts of isolated incidents, or comments converts made (or overheard), but they run counter to the public opinion of the day and suggest that converts who attempted to conceal their origins, became zealous apostles of their new faith among their former coreligionists, and were contemptuous or belligerent in their dealings with Jews were far less common than converts who acknowledged their origins, provided financial or professional support to their former coreligionists, defended them in public, and spoke of Jews and the Jewish faith in positive terms. Of the roughly fifty converts who serve as the basis for this assertion, I will present five in greater detail below. Three of the five figures were included in the chapter on pathways to conversion. Here I will follow their stories up to 1919, at the latest.

The first was a child when his parents had him baptized and thus did not convert of his own free will. I have nevertheless included him because his origins influenced his outlook. We do not know of any Hungarian Jewish converts who dedicated their lives to denouncing their former coreligionists, like the Russian Jew Iakov (Jacob) Brafman, whose 1869 *Book of Kahal* was one of the most influential works of antisemitism ever published in Russia, or the Viennese Jew Arthur Trebitsch, who converted in 1909 and became an early adherent of Nazism.[99] Their antisemitic outbursts were far more extreme than any of **Oszkár Jászi**'s (1875–1957) intimations of antipathy to Jews and Judaism, but it is clear that the leader of Hungary's bourgeois-radical camp was never able to come to terms with his Jewish origins.[100]

On June 25, 1881, physician Ferenc Jakubovits of Nagykároly (now Carei, Romania) submitted a request that he and his three minor children be allowed to Magyarize their surname to Jászi.[101] Soon thereafter, the forty-three-year-old Ferenc Jászi (along with his son Viktor, from his first marriage), his second wife, Róza Liebermann, and their children, Oszkár and Alice, all joined the Reformed Church. Oszkár Jászi's correspondence suggests that in the mid-1930s, he could still remember the date of his conversion (the summer of 1881, when he was six),[102] though his recollection of the actual ceremony was murkier. He described it in the memoir he wrote from 1953 to 1955: "I just faintly recall that a strange man came into my mother's parlor; it was György Asztalos, the eloquent Reformed pastor. He addressed a few words to us that I did not understand and repeated our names. I could feel the solemnity of the ceremony in my parents' comportment, but I did not know what was happening."[103] Jászi's parents never enlightened their children either: "they did not explain to us the meaning or significance of switching religions; in fact, they sometimes avoided the subject when it was raised in our presence." Their conversion was thus "enveloped in a shadow of secrecy, the feeling of a sort of taboo about which one should not speak."[104]

His father's motives for converting "never served as a subject of discussion among us," so Jászi could only guess at the reasons "a humanitarian, *libre penseur*" might have had for doing so:

Knowing his intellectual disposition, I have to assume two motives. The first might have been that liberal Calvinism suited him much better than the dogmatism of Jewish Orthodoxy. And second, having seen the obstacles Jews face in life, he would not have hesitated to discard a religion in which he no longer believed, thereby smoothing the paths that his children would follow in their future lives. . . . A prior factor in my father's decision may have been my mother's profound sentimentality, insofar as humanist free-thinking could not satisfy her. I recall her frequent invocations of God. . . . Nor can there be any doubt that their decision was strongly motivated by the desire to keep the growing specter of antisemitism out of their children's lives.[105]

The background and circumstances of the Jászi family's conversion help clarify the relative significance of the various motives. Jászi alluded to his family's background in discussing the conversion ceremony he had failed to understand: "I did not even know we were Jewish. Religion played no role in our lives. In accordance with my parents'—my father's—Enlightenment principles, it was only our moral education that they considered important, in a totally undogmatic spirit. Nor was I aware of any religious differences in our social life. My parents were generally respected; most of our close friends were Christians; in fact, we were in regular contact with a few gentry families as well."[106] Jászi's parents intentionally raised their children as non-Jews, and once they had formally converted, they attempted to remove the official evidence of their Jewish past: among the belongings Jászi left behind when he died was a birth certificate issued in 1895 (two decades after the fact), according to which he had been baptized into the Reformed Church at birth.[107] Jászi family researcher Tamás Repiszky believes that the forged baptismal certificate that served as the basis for the birth certificate's erroneous data was produced at the time of their conversion by the Reformed pastor who baptized them.[108] The Jászi children's upbringing, their backdated baptismal certificates, and the family's silence on the subject of conversion all suggest that Oszkár's father, Ferenc, was motivated primarily by a desire to spare his children the trials associated with Jewish origins, which he himself had clearly experienced as a senseless burden and a stigma, despite his social standing.

In his memoirs, Oszkár Jászi characterized his parents' failure to explain the "meaning or significance" of conversion as a "serious error of parenting," since they left their children "almost totally unprepared for the situation" that would arise "a year or two later, when the Christian-Jewish question and antagonism also began to unfold in the society of our small town."[109] The somewhat murky formulation suggests that Jászi may have been forced to confront his Jewish origins for the first time in 1882–83, during the antisemitic furor surrounding the Tiszaeszlár blood libel. While Jászi does not provide any account of this confrontation, it could hardly have been a joyful experience. For Jászi, Jewishness was always negative—an embarrassing taboo that later made him the target of antisemitism, which, even in the best of circumstances, hung like a sword of Damocles over his head. Oszkár Jászi had no Jewish identity, only a "Jewish question."

After finishing high school in 1892 at the age of seventeen, Jászi studied law at the University of Budapest, and though "the shadow of antisemitism haunted the university courtyard," he characterized it as a "political rather than social phenomenon." During his time at university, which coincided with the Hungarian political elite's last great wave of liberal reforms, "it rarely happened that I took note of antisemitism as a dividing element within the student movement." On the contrary, "I saw that talented and independent-minded Christian and Jewish young people could collaborate in friendship and harmony, which would be a decisive influence on the entire remainder of my life."[110]

Jászi earned a doctoral degree in 1896 at the age of twenty-one. He and his friends would then launch the journal *Huszadik Század* in 1900 before founding the Sociological Society and the Martinovics Masonic Lodge; they would establish the daily *Világ* in 1910 and the National Bourgeois Radical Party in 1914. But the high hopes of Jászi's university years—that his public aspirations and political ambitions would not be limited by his Jewish origins—would soon be dashed. Writing from Oberlin, Ohio, on March 1, 1936, Jászi told his relative Pál Liebermann, "It often occurs to me: if I'd been born a petty noble or even the offspring of peasants, the impact of my work would have been a thousand times greater."[111] Jászi probably already came to this realization in the second half of the 1900s, especially since other members of the progressive Jewish intelligentsia had already given voice to this notion. As Ignotus wrote in 1895, "If a Jew proclaims the truth, everyone for whom this truth is painful becomes an antisemite. If István Széchenyi had been a Jew, they would have attributed the abolition of feudalism and the liberation of the serfs to purely Jewish interests."[112]

The leader of what György Litván called "the progressives locked in quarantine," Jászi learned that his baptismal certificate would do nothing to protect him from his political opponents' attempts to stigmatize him as a Jew. The efforts to smear him only intensified the aversion to Jews he had expressed in his earlier writings—as did the fact that his movement was decried as anti-Hungarian with increasing vehemence after 1905.[113] In a letter to Ervin Szabó dated November 2, 1904, Jászi declared that "the biggest problem with Hungarian soc[ialism] is that spirit of Judaism, that ghetto-hatred, which weighs heavily upon it."[114] The next year, when courses in morality replaced religious instruction in French schools, Jászi published a piece in *Huszadik Század* describing the commandments of the Old Testament as "horrific" and its atmosphere as "brutal," and expressing his joy that French children would no longer be plagued by "the ghastly curses of the Old Testament Jehovah." Jászi was significantly more forgiving in his treatment of the Gospels, the morality of which he considered "sublime, though impracticable."[115] In response to his political enemies' efforts to tarnish the bourgeois-radical camp's democratic aspirations as Jewish policies, Jászi defended himself in a piece that appeared in *Világ* in 1911, saying radicals could not be animated by a Jewish spirit, insofar as it was "a ghetto outlook from the Middle Ages," when Jews had "developed a distinctive racial character with two fundamental characteristics. One is a mentality of religious fanaticism in spiritual life, the other is usurious activity in economic life."[116]

According to Jászi, Orthodox Jews were characterized by "the zealous, fanatical racial atmosphere and usurious spirit of the ghetto."[117] As for the Jewish petty bourgeoisie, its "soul" was also "stuck in the ghetto."[118] Jászi once described the entire Jewish bourgeoisie as "descendants of wearers of the yellow badge" who "still instinctively tremble as they stand before the sinecured descendants of the warlike nobility."[119] An "inner yellow badge" had also made "rich Jews"—the most frequent targets of Jászi's attacks—"the obedient usurers of Junker class rule."[120]

In the spring of 1912, Jászi was obliged to defend these views. He published a piece in *Huszadik Század* after Hungarian authorities brutally dispersed a demonstration held in Budapest on May 23, 1912, where protestors demanded universal suffrage and the resignation of Speaker of the House István Tisza. Jászi fulminated against "Jewish usury," which in his view had never been so powerful, and denounced the "Junker-Jewish coalition," identifying it with figures like Tisza and Pál Elek (converted nine years earlier).[121] The piece was controversial even within Jászi's own camp. An anonymous contributor to *Világ*—in reality, the paper's editor—rebuked Jászi for using "the modifier 'Jewish' as a qualifying attribute" and for identifying Pál Elek—who had

Figure 5.8. Oszkár Jászi, Alice Jászi, Anna Lesznai, and Ervin Szabó, 1910s. Petőfi Literary Museum, F.4300.

been baptized and could no longer be classified a Jew—as a representative of "Jewish ruination of the people."[122] In responding, Jászi reaffirmed his views: "It is precisely for this reason that these gentlemen are to be called Jews [*lezsidózni*] at every turn, because in the interest of promoting their brand-new Christianity and nobility and in order to obscure their origins, they have allied themselves with the most wicked enemies of the people, and thus with the greatest enemies of hardworking, honorable Jews as well." In repudiating the allegations of antisemitism, Jászi offered a personal confession: "I assumed I was speaking to cultivated people, who are well aware—by virtue of my origins and my entire career in public life—that no one could presume I meant to attack the race of Jesus, Spinoza, Heine, Marx, and Lassalle in general, as well as the many noble fighters for the rights of the Hungarian people, my beloved brothers-in-arms, rather than *Feudaljud* types, and them alone, these tools who will do anything in the service of Junker-violence and the fleecing of the people."[123] His reply did not convince the editor of *Világ*, who composed a rebuttal that did not—and could not—soften Jászi's vociferousness,[124] since it did not address the driving force behind Jászi's passions—namely, his conviction that the support of the Jewish (haute) bourgeoisie enabled István Tisza to remain in power and perpetuate a regime that not only impeded Hungary's transformation into a democracy but also made it impossible for Jászi himself to fulfill his political ambitions free from the stigma of his Jewish origins.

By organizing *Huszadik Század*'s aforementioned 1917 survey on the "Jewish question," Jászi helped legitimize the notion that there was a problem with Hungary's Jews. Kati Vörös has convincingly demonstrated that the journal's elevation of the "Jewish question" to the level of social-scientific discourse had a liberating and emboldening effect on Hungarian antisemites, helping them invest their rhetoric with the appearance of objectivity and scholarship. Rather than deflating the antisemites, the *Huszadik Század* survey actually put wind in their sails.[125] In his own response to the survey, Jászi did not, of course, advocate any sort of anti-Jewish policies. First, he spent half a page listing the traits that an "overwhelming majority" of Jews had developed in the course of "a thousand years of ghetto-isolation." From the perspective "of the dominant Christian culture," these characteristics were "foreign, unpleasant, or repugnant." He then described his solution to the "Jewish question" in unambiguous terms: "There is no need for special laws or social institutions. Christian society should give every citizen as complete a democracy as possible, as honorable a legal system as possible, and the fairest possible opportunities for success. With ever-improving education, ever more disciplined manners, and a deepening experience and love of our common national and international culture, Jews . . . should no longer be a separate body, a vestige of the old ghetto, but rather a conscious and unconscious participant in that same national and international circulatory system."[126]

It is clear from Jászi's prior work that these prescriptions amounted to the self-liquidation of Hungary's Jews. According to his 1912 book *The Development of Nation-States and the Nationality Question*, "Assimilation occurs only within a certain cultural community. This cultural community finds its most articulate expression in common religion." From this, it necessarily followed that "the assimilation of the Jews cannot take place except where the Jewish religion has disintegrated once and for all, either formally, as a result of the fact of conversion, or emotionally, as a result of the rejection of ancestral traditions."[127]

AFTER CONVERSION   333

According to János Gyurgyák, writers who discussed the "Jewish question" for bourgeois-radical papers "essentially followed Jászi's line, which they tended only to modify, rather than saying anything radically new."[128] Numerous pieces affirm this assessment, though I would add an important clarification. Contributors to bourgeois-radical dailies often spoke well of the Jewish bourgeoisie, certain individual upper-class Jews, and even Orthodox Jews, whose culture merited attention despite its backwardness; they sometimes wrote empathetically about their Jewish subjects, whether they lived in Pest, Máramarossziget, or elsewhere in Eastern Europe. Jászi's writings show no sign of any such empathy.[129]

Other converts occasionally demonstrated an unambiguous empathy for or connection to their former coreligionists and their faith. Mór Ullmann was said to have visited his Jewish ex-wife every Friday evening to watch her light candles for Shabbat.[130] Not long before his death in 1850, Sámuel Wodianer donated a parcel of land to the Jewish community of Gyoma to serve as the site of its new synagogue.[131] Károly Kohlmann, the first teacher hired by the elementary school the Jewish community of Pest opened in September of 1814, converted to Catholicism in 1816, but when the Dohány Street Synagogue in Budapest was consecrated in 1859, Kohlmann sent the community board of the Israelite Congregation of Pest a Hebrew-language hymn he had composed for the occasion.[132] In 1868, a year after the emancipation of Hungary's Jews, Mór Ballagi's younger brother Károly—who had joined the Reformed Church in 1843—wrote a textbook for Jewish elementary schools. The first sentence of the preface expresses his gratitude to God that "we are able, at long last, to declare that we are all the children of one and the same homeland."[133] Over the thirty-nine years he spent editing *Pester Lloyd*, Miksa Falk was always a defender of Jews. His account of his youth makes no mention of his Jewish past, but Falk willingly acknowledged his origins in the company of his former coreligionists.[134] Frigyes Harkányi, elected to several consecutive parliamentary terms as representative of the Krassó-Szörény County town of Facset (Făget, Romania), provided the local Jewish community with financial support including a contribution to the construction of a new synagogue, consecrated in 1897.[135] Linguist Zsigmond Simonyi was a consistent source of support for early stage Jewish scholars, because—as he told the Catholic provost Emil Concilia in 1908—"in scholarship, I do not take note of religion or race."[136] On the occasion of his death in 1919, *Egyenlőség* asserted that Simonyi had become "a discoverer and patron of

334   JEWISHNESS AND BEYOND

poor Jewish philologists" because "in his soul" he had never truly abandoned his fellow Jews.[137]

Illustrative examples of converts who publicly expressed solidarity with—or clearly maintained their ties to—their former coreligionists include the following four, all born in the first half of the nineteenth century. The oldest, Mór Ballagi, was born in 1815; the youngest, Lajos Dóczi, in 1845. We know that Ballagi and Ármin Vámbéry (b. 1832) grew up in unacculturated families while Ignác Helfy (b. 1830) likely did so as well. Dóczi's family had already started down the path to acculturation. Nevertheless, like Ballagi, Vámbéry, and Helfy, he grew up speaking Yiddish in a fundamentally traditional Jewish environment.

The relationship between Móricz Bloch (who converted to Protestantism in 1843 and Magyarized his name to **Mór Ballagi** in 1848) and his former coreligionists was initially fraught. Seventy years after Ballagi sent his letter to the Jewish community of Pest urging its members to convert en masse, the noted educator Mór Kármán wrote, "Lest I label it too harshly, let us say this move created a scandal."[138] However, this letter was the last time Ballagi would express himself publicly in this way, and some of his later gestures suggest a very different attitude. The *First Hungarian Jewish Calendar*, published in early 1848, features an entry by Márton Diósy outlining the history of the *Magyarító Egylet* (the Magyarization Society, founded in 1844 to encourage Jews to learn Hungarian) and thanking everyone who had donated money, books, or furniture to the association, including Ballagi (still listed here as Móric Bloch).[139] Ballagi was a consistent supporter of young Jewish scholars. His recommendation helped Ármin Vámbéry land an interview with József Eötvös, whose financial support would enable the young Orientalist to set off for Constantinople in 1857, his first trip to the East.[140] Ignác Goldziher was still in high school when he got to know Ballagi; among the introductory recollections Goldziher recorded in a diary he began keeping in 1890, he wrote that Ballagi had allowed him to use his library and was always ready to help him, just as "he supported every Jewish talent to the best of his ability."[141] Like Vámbéry, Goldziher had Ballagi to thank for his introduction to Eötvös, who began his second stint as minister of religion and public education in 1867. The minister's involvement helped Goldziher become the first Jewish winner of a Hungarian state scholarship, enabling him to study abroad for two years starting in 1868. As editor of *Protestáns Tudományos Szemle* (*Protestant Scholarly Review*), Ballagi published Goldziher's work. In 1872, Ballagi sponsored

AFTER CONVERSION   335

Goldziher's application to the Reformed Theological Academy of Budapest, where he would teach Hebrew language and literature for a few months.[142]

Ballagi was elected to the National Assembly in 1861, and though he never used his seat in parliament to speak out on Jewish affairs, he did use the pages of a periodical he edited, *Protestáns Egyházi és Iskolai Lap* (*Protestant Ecclesiastical and Scholastic Journal*), to applaud the 1867 legislative proposal to emancipate Hungary's Jews.[143] Ballagi also expressed willingness to voice his opposition to antisemitism in public, though his article on the subject was never published. In the fall of 1882, a few months after the explosion of the Tiszeszlár blood libel affair, Miksa Szabolcsi asked Ballagi to speak out on the issue. Ballagi promised to write a piece for *Vasárnapi Újság* (*Sunday News*). According to Szabolcsi, Ballagi told him, "My young brother, tell the Jews that I am very happy to have the opportunity to defend my brethren's truth."[144] Ballagi wrote an article that he showed to Sámuel Kohn and his housemate Ignác Goldziher; not only was the piece a demonstration of the absurdity of the blood libel, it was also a fierce attack on the individuals who had lodged the accusation. In the end, however, *Vasárnapi Újság* did not publish Mór Ballagi's discussion of the Tiszaeszlár affair but an article written by his son, historian Aladár Ballagi, on the 1529 blood libel of Bazin (Pezinok, Slovakia).[145] It later came to light that Aladár Ballagi had pressed his father not to publish the piece.[146]

Since the source of this story are articles that appeared in *Egyenlőség* years after the event, we can't be sure that it really happened that way. However, it is beyond dispute that Mór Ballagi published a study in *Protestáns Egyházi és Iskolai Lapok* in 1864 (and in book form a year later) in which he expressed an effusive admiration for the Jewish nation of old, even if he—as a Protestant theologian, quite naturally—presented Jesus Christ as the culmination of the spirit of its prophets.[147]

Unlike Mór Ballagi, whose active participation in political life was brief, **Ignác Helfy**—born Nátán Helfer in 1830 and a yeshiva student before converting to Catholicism in 1855—was a natural politician.[148] Helfy won a by-election to the House of Representatives in October of 1870 and would keep his seat until his death in 1897. Though Helfy spoke out on behalf of the Independence Party on countless occasions, he rarely publicized his thoughts on his former coreligionists. Still, he did so more often than any other Hungarian Jewish convert. In an 1874 parliamentary debate concerning the establishment of the Rabbinical Seminary of Budapest, Helfy was critical of Jews: "If they

Figure 5.9. Ignác Helfy, c. 1865. Petőfi Literary Museum, F.7665.

are interested in someone's identity, Jews themselves will commonly ask what sort of person he is: Jewish or Hungarian?" This led Helfy to the conclusion that "many Hungarian Jews do not consider themselves to be Hungarians." Characteristically, the evidence he cited was what he perceived as a lack of linguistic Magyarization among the country's Jews. In elaborating the idea that belonging to the Hungarian nation was a function of one's command of the Hungarian language, Helfy proffered a curious observation: "If one walks down the street in front of a Jewish person's shop, one sees a sign with Jewish letters. One would think he is a Hebrew person, and is thus attached to the Hebrew language. And what does one see if one knows Hebrew? What is written there in Hebrew letters is *Nürnberger Waarenhandlung*." Having inadvertently disclosed his knowledge of Hebrew, Helfy proceeded to advocate an unorthodox variant of linguistic Magyarization: "Fine, let them use Hebrew letters, but use them to write it in Hungarian: *Norinbergi Áruraktár* [Nuremberger Warehouse]." Helfy went on to voice his support for the rabbinical seminary on the grounds that "its aim, in essence, is to provide Jews with an education in the Hungarian language."[149]

During the parliamentary debate over Jewish-Christian civil marriage in November of 1883, Helfy reserved his criticism for his fellow representatives. Beyond simply arguing in favor of the proposed bill, Helfy insisted on its necessity as a symbolic gesture to compensate for the national assembly's history of flawed responses to antisemitism: "For we cannot deny that the behavior exhibited by the individual parties and the legislature itself throughout the life of the antisemitic movement has misled the people of the homeland, and foreigners as well. Indeed, the people themselves have often believed that this is not the work of a faction, not the activity of a few fanatics, but rather that the most serious people, even legislators themselves, actually approve of these things and that only a few are courageous enough to say so, while the others lack this courage."[150]

As Helfy saw it, the legislature's "only correct response to the antisemitic movement" was to approve the proposed civil-marriage law.[151] However, after the House of Lords rejected the bill for the second time on January 11, 1884, the House of Representatives spent five days in heated debate before voting in favor of prime minister Kálmán Tisza's motion not to submit a third proposal to the upper chamber. When most of his fellow legislators digressed from the session's agenda in order to address "the Jewish question," Helfy felt it was his duty to express his own opinion. In addressing the lower chamber on February 4, 1884, Helfy established his perspective by citing the opening line of a letter Lajos Kossuth had written to him on October 11, 1882: "The Jewish question, he said: it is a shame and a scandal that such a thing could still exist in Hungary. And in fact, this parenthesis contains the only correct conclusion that could be articulated on the subject."[152] But given that the Jewish question did still exist in Hungary, Helfy believed it had to be confronted and resolved: "There exists in our country a denomination, let's say a race, a large part of which has yet to be absorbed into the body of the nation;

thus we must strive to find methods by which we can absorb this part into the body of the nation so that it blends in seamlessly. In my opinion, this is how the issue stands." Helfy emphasized "assimilation requires the concordant will of two factors: the assimilating party and the party to be assimilated," and the only objectionable behavior he had seen was exhibited by the former in its dealings with the latter. Helfy reiterated his belief that Hungarian Jews' primary duty was linguistic Magyarization, though he went on to opine that they were doing enough to fulfill this obligation; in fact, "among all the foreign-speaking [Hungarian] citizens, it is precisely the Jews who are most likely to Magyarize." In Helfy's view, however, Hungarian Christian society had neglected its obligation to accept its Jews. The solution to the Jewish question—that is, the success of "assimilation"—thus depended not on the Jews but on Christian society: "If we genuinely desire assimilation, we should approach them with love and demonstrate that we can honor and respect the honorable, educated Jew in the same manner as the honorable, educated Christian, and in doing so, we will attract those who have been left behind; [when] they see that their educated coreligionists are welcome in good company, even though they maintain their faith, they will extricate themselves from their narrow sectarianism."[153]

Helfy never acknowledged his Jewish origins in a public forum. Though he had gone to yeshiva till he was fourteen, Helfy spent his entire public career as a pro-independence (Christian) Hungarian politician—and nothing more. His private life was a different matter. As Miksa Szabolcsi put it on the occasion of Helfy's death:

> He honored his origins and honored Jewish scholarship in particular. He
> once told the author of these lines that he had long since absorbed Platonic
> and Aristotelian philosophy from Maimonides and legal principles from the
> Talmud by the time he began to study in Hungarian and German. . . . The
> magnitude of the reverence he felt for his former religion is demonstrated
> in particular by the fact that—as many of us are aware—when his father,
> an exceedingly religious Jew, died, Helfy—who at that time was already
> a representative of the Hungarian National Assembly—mourned him in
> accordance with the Jewish rite. He observed the seven days of mourning,
> and in the morning and in the evening, perhaps after the Lord's Prayer, he
> said the Hebrew *Kaddish* prayer in memory of his father.[154]

Lajos Dóczi, who converted to Catholicism in April of 1893 to marry eighteen-year-old Paula Dassl-Rosenberg, never spoke about his conversion in public, but unlike Helfy, he did discuss his Jewish origins, particularly the Jewish milieu of his childhood, with affection, warmth, and nostalgia.

Dóczi's experience of conversion was not as straightforward as one might expect given the letter he wrote in April 1893 informing Manó Kónyi of his intention to get baptized. In a letter written seven months after his baptism, Dóczi asked Manó Kónyi to convey his greetings to Countess Katinka Andrássy: "Notify the gracious Lady that I kiss her hand," he said, adding, "If I had not angered the old God and did not have a tense relationship with the new one, I would pray for her."[155] In addition to his pangs of conscience, Dóczi was also distressed because some people believed he had abandoned his faith in the hope of obtaining "vulgar" benefits. Suspicions of this sort seem to have been on display in a letter Dóczi received from an unnamed correspondent, mentioned to Kónyi in a missive dated August 29, 1893: "The letter bothers me precisely because it comes from a literate person. I cannot speak publicly about myself and the motives for my conversion. But if any fair-minded person entertains doubts about my character for this reason, I would consider it worthwhile to tell him what weighs on my soul."[156] Dóczi never seems to have done so. After he retired and moved from Vienna back to Pest in 1902, the humor magazine *Kakas Márton* (*Martin Rooster*) published an article speculating about his future plans. It identified Dóczi as the ideal candidate to succeed Miksa Falk as president of the Lipótváros Casino (which he did) because he, like Falk, satisfied the complicated requirements for the post: "We need a Jew, we don't need a Jew, and yet we still need a Jew—perhaps we could agree on 50%?" *Kakas Márton* then enumerated Dóczi's "virtues," among them that he had "abandoned his old faith with results."[157] A few days later, Dóczi composed a letter to the magazine's editor (which he ultimately did not send):

> I am certainly not going to polemicize in public against something that was put before your readers in the guise of a joke. But I will not hesitate to ask you personally, why do you print such ugly things about me? Do you believe that I abandoned my old faith for some sort of "result?" Do you not know that I did it when I married a Catholic girl, and did so only because the law at that time did not make it possible for me to enter into a valid mixed marriage, and that I would have had to become an Austrian citizen for my woman to be regarded as my lawful wife here at home?[158]

Though Dóczi was preoccupied with social perceptions of his conversion, his baptism had no effect on his journalistic career. From 1881 to 1915, he was a regular contributor to the *Neues Pester Journal* (a German-language daily founded by Zsigmond Bródy in 1872), whose readership was composed largely of members of the Jewish petty bourgeoisie.[159] Dóczi wrote a number of pieces on Jewish themes, primarily childhood memories that his conversion had done nothing to alter. In fact, in a letter to Kónyi dated February 23, 1895, Dóczi complained that Bródy had not given him enough space for a feuilleton about his native village: "The Deutsch-Kreutz [Németkeresztúr] feuilleton could have been good if, as I intended, I had described life there truthfully, particularly the Sabbath, the wintertime revelries, the atmosphere of *Chalemoid* [the intermediate days of Passover], the milieu. But as a result of Zsigmond's stunted perspective, I must always suppress the better part of what I could write."[160] Nevertheless, Dóczi's feuilleton conveyed the "milieu" well enough that even *Egyenlőség* would publish a Hungarian translation of the piece—and maintain a tactful silence about the fact that its author was a "renegade." Dóczi had been prompted to write this account of his native village by Károly (Karl) Goldmark's visit to Pest; the famous composer had moved to Németkeresztúr in 1834 and spent a decade of his childhood there. "Allow me to link the glory and memory of our little village to your name before the cheerful world of ghetto life disappears from it forever," Dóczi wrote, expressing his regret that the old Jewish communities, "with their faith and their foibles, their obsolescence and their originality, their poverty and their poetry," were vanishing into the past. "With them, an idiosyncratic world is foundering, a peculiar way of thinking and feeling, inimitable good humor and melancholy, a world that cannot be expressed except in its own language.... Tell me, do you not long to escape your worldly glory (from which, of course, you have gladly hidden yourself in Gmunden) and return to this little Jewish nest?" Dóczi went on to describe his master-baker grandfather, the attire of the local Jews, the cheder, the early days of Goldmark's career. The successes for which Goldmark was being celebrated in Pest reminded Dóczi of "our dear mother, the Jewish village." He concluded by noting, "If the people of Németkeresztúr read these lines, the young will ask the old, and the old the even older, till they find a trembling graybeard who knew your father. All will be terribly proud of Károly Goldmark, though none will fail to add: He's great, a truly great man. But does he still eat kosher?"[161]

Dóczi also expressed sympathy for persecuted Jews. In 1912, the *Neues Pester Journal* published a four-act drama in thirty installments whose protagonist—a student from Sopron who becomes a journalist and the confidant of a powerful minister—was clearly a fictionalized version of Dóczi himself. Despite his excellent job and the authority he enjoyed, the author's alter ego says, "I now see that they injure me when they beat a usurer, and I feel myself being tortured alongside the distillers of Kiev."[162] Dóczi effectively re-Judaized himself in this play: though his protagonist was not a religious Jew, he could not imagine abandoning his people as long as it could occur to a Christian "*einen Juden gering zu achten*" [to look down on a Jew].[163]

In her 1932 monograph on Dóczi's career, Ilona Fürst concluded by noting that the writer's 1919 death had "caught him with a Hebrew Bible in his hand."[164] In a piece published in *Múlt és Jövő* two years later, Fürst went considerably further: "According to family tradition, toward the end of his life, the increasingly sickly baron wanted to convert back to the Jewish faith, and reportedly breathed his last with a Hebrew Bible in his hand."[165] Dóczi may have considered converting back to Judaism, but he never did. It is nonetheless clear, as his old friend Ignác Peiser recalled a few months after his death, that Dóczi "never disavowed his Jewishness."[166]

Although **Ármin Vámbéry** was thirteen years older than Dóczi (and his conversion preceded Dóczi's by almost thirty years), I have saved his story for last because none of the converts who came of age in the period under discussion demonstrated such a profound attachment to his origins and former coreligionists. After joining the Reformed Church in late 1864, Vámbéry signed a series of letters in 1865 and 1866 with a monogram consisting of a crescent moon encompassing a Star of David above the initials *V.* and *A.*, woven into a coat of arms.[167] In 1868, he and Mór Ballagi brought the young scholar Ignác Goldziher to the attention of education minister József Eötvös. According to *Izraelita Közlöny* (*Israelite Gazette*), Vámbéry's enthusiastic support was an instrumental factor in the state scholarship Goldziher subsequently received.[168] None of that compares to Vámbéry's becoming a staunch supporter and effective advocate of the Zionist movement in the late 1890s. How might that have happened? As we have seen, in the early 1880s, Vámbéry demanded that Christians fully accept the Jews who "associate with them"— that is, converts.[169] But in his 1905 memoirs, Vámbéry expressed incomprehension and disapproval in discussing the integrationist urges of (denominationally indeterminate) "Jews": "One is simply astonished that European Jews, who are called foreigners everywhere, want to force their way into the ties of these nations, when they should simply say: 'If you don't need me, fine. I'll be just a Jew, and I won't care if you curse me as a cosmopolitan; do as you please.'"[170] We do not know what sorts of inner factors may have changed Vámbéry's views, but the fact remains that Theodor Herzl had Vámbéry to thank for his meeting with the Ottoman sultan. Vámbéry's longtime friend Max Nordau (like Herzl, a native of Pest) provided the Zionist leader with a letter of introduction to Vámbéry in 1898. A letter Vámbéry wrote to Herzl on September 21 of that year demonstrates the two were in contact then,[171] but their first meeting did not take place until June 17, 1900, in the Tyrolean town of Mühlbach. During the meeting, the father of modern political Zionism asked the famed Orientalist to help him arrange an audience with the sultan. According to Herzl's diary, Vámbéry began their conversation by saying, "I don't want any money; I am a rich man. I can't eat gold beefsteaks. I've got a quarter of a million, and I can't spend half the interest I get. If I help you, it's for the sake of the cause."[172] Having ended their meeting without being certain whether Vámbéry intended to intervene on his behalf, Herzl wrote Vámbéry another letter later that same day: "*Kedves Vámbéry bácsi* [Dear Uncle Vámbéry]: The Hungarian word is good: *zsidóember* [a Jewish man]. You are one, so am I. That is why we understood each other so quickly and fully—perhaps even more on a human plane than on a Jewish one, although the Jewish element is strong enough in both of us. Help me—no us! . . . Crown your pyramid with the chapter: How I Helped Prepare the Homecoming of My People the Jews."[173]

Vámbéry complied with Herzl's request. From that point on, he wrote to Herzl regularly, most often counseling patience and caution as he succinctly recounted the diplomatic steps that eventually resulted in Herzl's being received by Abdul-Hamid II on May 18, 1901.[174] According to Nordau, Vámbéry considered the plan to establish a Jewish state in the Holy Land unrealistic from the start. In Budapest, before Herzl's audience with the sultan, Vámbéry warned him, "You mustn't talk to him about Zionism. That is a phantasmagoria. Jerusalem is as holy to these people as Mecca. . . . I want the continued existence of Zionism—and that is why I have procured the audience for you, because otherwise you wouldn't have been able to face your Congress. You must gain time and keep Zionism alive somehow."[175]

Though Vámbéry called Herzl's plan a phantasmagoria, he publicly expressed his support for Zionism. Contacted by Gyula Gábel, editor of the bilingual German Hungarian Zionist weekly *Ungarische Wochenschrift*, Vámbéry responded on May 27, 1902 with a letter he clearly intended for publication:

AFTER CONVERSION

343

> Zionism has set a noble, philanthropic goal for itself in its desire to help persecuted and oppressed Jewish people who have been stripped of all their rights. . . . This praiseworthy, global movement, which you yourselves represent . . . is worthy of every good person's most energetic support. Zionism—and this is my unassailable conviction—not only does not oppose patriotism and the national sentiments of the Hungarian people, it is precisely Hungarian chivalry that makes it the peremptory duty of every Hungarian Jew to support something which, while it does impose obligations on Hungarian Jews, does not promise any direct benefit either, if only because Hungary is among the countries in which citizens of the Jewish faith, relatively speaking, enjoy the greatest degree of liberty. This, my dear sir, is my understanding of the blessed nature of Zionism.[176]

Vámbéry may have embraced this "philanthropic" variant of Zionism (which was representative of the early Hungarian Zionist movement) in order to parry accusations of lack of patriotism. But his letter to Gábel is more likely a reflection of genuine conviction and his sense of pragmatism. Evidence of the latter is demonstrated by Vámbéry's decision in 1906 to join the Jewish Territorialist Organization (ITO) founded by Israel Zangwill the previous year with the intention of establishing an autonomous territory for persecuted Jews somewhere outside the Holy Land, preferably in one of the colonies of the British Empire. Of the letters of support for his plan Zangwill published in the influential *Fortnightly Review* in the summer of 1906, Vámbéry's was the longest and most detailed.[177] *Egyenlőség*, which also supported the ITO, was grateful for the opportunity to report that Vámbéry agreed the "Jewish question" could not be resolved on the basis of "nationhood or nationality," tactfully neglecting to recall that Vámbéry was a convert.[178]

Six years later, *Hitközségi Szemle* published a lengthy excerpt from the eighty-year-old Vámbéry's interview with *The Jewish Chronicle* of London:

> I am not a Jew in the ordinary sense; many call me a Christian, but I am not, nor have I ever been. I was born a Jew and wish to remain so. Whenever I have been asked, I have always proudly declared that I am Jewish, though not in the religious sense of that word. My father, grandfather, and great grandfather were all rabbis, and I am loyal to my people as a result of my early experiences as well . . . I am not a Jew by faith, but rather a national Jew, and I do not despair of my race at all. Jewry will not die out, because what it means is to be proud of the race, to be proud of the great men of the past.[179]

344 JEWISHNESS AND BEYOND

Gyula Weiszburg, editor of *Hitközségi Szemle* and general secretary of the Israelite Congregation of Pest, may not have approved of Vámbéry's self-identification as a *national* Jew, but he shared Vámbéry's understanding of the *racial* qualities of Jewry and thus printed this passage without commentary.[180] In doing so, he failed to draw his readers' attention to a real piece of news: Vámbéry's public repudiation of his Christianity. In private conversations, Vámbéry spoke in greater detail about this final twist in his process of self-definition, at least according to a letter submitted to *Egyenlőség* after the Orientalist died on September 15, 1913. The letter's author, Mór Halász of Nyíregyháza, had met Vámbéry in the Bars County town of Vihnye (Vyhne, Slovakia) in the summer of 1912 and claimed that in the course of their conversations there, Vámbéry insisted he had never converted:

> When I arrived back in my homeland, and instead of deserved recognition, they wanted me to convert as a condition of my appointment as a university professor, a certain melancholy seized me and I began to feel pity for my country. I did not comply with this condition. *I did not have myself baptized.* I presented myself for an audience with His Majesty. . . . A couple of weeks later, he appointed me to the faculty of the University of Budapest, but before the government would carry out His Majesty's orders, I was asked to *record in the faculty registry that I am a Christian. I never had myself baptized. Baptismal water never touched me. I only registered myself as a Christian.*[181]

In 1935, at the age of sixty-three, Vámbéry's son Rusztem recounted a similar story in an interview with *Múlt és Jövő*. According to Rusztem, his father—accompanied by József Eötvös—had gone to the governor's office to apply for a passport in 1857 (before his first trip to the East), and when he was asked to declare his religious affiliation, he lodged a protest against religious distinctions of any kind. "Whereupon Eötvös replied, 'That means you're a Protestant,' and this is how a Christian denomination was recorded in my father's passport in place of the Jewish faith."[182] Whether Rusztem Vámbéry told the story because he had always heard it that way or because he did not want to contradict the legend his father manufactured in the final years of his life, it does nothing essential to alter the image the elderly Orientalist wished to project: while some converts did everything in their power to conceal their Jewish roots, the "convert" Ármin Vámbéry did not disavow his Jewishness but rather his conversion.

Jews and Converted Jews

Since there are two sides to every coin, there is another possible reading of the relationships converts maintained with their former coreligionists. If we are to believe the legend that circulated in Pest, Mór Ullmann's unconverted first wife did not object in the 1830s when her now-Catholic ex-husband visited her on Friday evenings. Mór Ballagi's conversion did not dissuade Ignác Goldziher from making contact with him. In December of 1867, Miksa Falk became editor in chief of *Pester Lloyd* on the recommendation of his childhood friend Mór Wahrmann and the equally Jewish lawyer and publicist Mór Mezei.[183] The following year, Károly Ballagi published a textbook for Jewish elementary schools because "many Isr[aelite] teachers" had asked him to do so.[184] Mór Ballagi's apostasy did not discourage Miksa Szabolcsi from asking for his help in repudiating the Tiszaeszlár blood libel in 1882, nor did it stop the chief rabbi of Pest from receiving Ballagi at his home. Szabolcsi and Ignác Helfy discussed the latter's experiences at yeshiva, and in 1891 a delegation from the National Israelite Teachers' Association made a pilgrimage to pay tribute to Miksa Falk. Lajos Dóczi's conversion did nothing to change his friendship with the unconverted Manó Kónyi, nor did it prevent the members of the Lipótváros Casino, a bastion of Hungary's Jewish upper class, from electing Dóczi as their president in 1902—which was no surprise, since his presidential predecessor was another convert, Miksa Falk.[185]

Regular, informal social interactions between Jews and converted Jews was a new phenomenon in the history of Ashkenazi Jewry. Before modern-era secularization, acculturation, and emancipation of the Jews, those who turned to the Christian faith were also obliged to switch communities (though this does not mean they were seamlessly integrated into their new milieux). Converts' new religious standing, legal status, and social environments often entailed new occupations as well, not only for those who had earned their daily bread as employees of Jewish communities; converted merchants could find themselves in the same predicament when their Jewish trading partners refused to do further business with them.[186] By the turn of the twentieth century, a Jewish university student who converted remained a university student; a Jewish doctor remained a doctor; a Jewish schoolmistress continued to teach. Even the Jewish clerk whose conversion earned him a position in the civil service would not be entering an entirely different world. Some newly converted Jews frequented new clubs or cafés in their attempts to socialize with Christians, but at the university, at lawyers' and doctors' offices, in their various professional, charitable, and cultural associations, and even in their new workplaces, they would inevitably continue to associate with their former coreligionists. At the dawn of the twentieth century, Hungarian Jewish converts changed their religious affiliation but did not move from one world to another. They continued to live in the same Hungarian society as their former coreligionists, whose relationships with converts differed markedly from those of their forebears.

Though Jewish religious law (*halakha*) holds that a Jew remains a Jew even after conversion,[187] traditionally Jewish family members would not mourn converts when they died and sometimes went as far as sitting shiva to mourn their "passing" at the time of their conversion. According to Jewish tradition, the despicable *meshumad* was an even greater danger to the Jewish people than a Christian, to be shunned and cut off by his family members and other former coreligionists, even if it could take time to sever all ties between a convert and his Jewish spouse or business partners.[188] Jewish attitudes toward converts were transformed by the Enlightenment, by rationalist reinterpretations of the Jewish and Christian religions, by the disintegration of the traditional system of Jewish values, by the secularization and acculturation of European Jews, and by the diminution of the social, cultural, and mental distances between Jews and Christians. It became tricky to advocate religious tolerance while simultaneously condemning someone for praising God in another house of worship. Voicing a desire for closer relations with the Christian majority could hardly be reconciled with the shunning of Jews who converted to the majority faith. Whether they no longer attributed significance to conversion or simply could not avoid further contact, Jews were less and less likely to avoid their former coreligionists.

This new approach to converts manifested itself in Germany and Vienna by the end of the eighteenth century.[189] In Hungary, where the disintegration of traditional Jewish society began decades later, this change in outlook was not perceptible until the Reform Era. Most Hungarian Jews continued to live in the world of tradition, so the old hostility toward converts could not simply disappear. Gyula Lipót Klein (who converted to Catholicism in Vienna in 1826 at the age of twenty-two and later published plays and literary history in German) returned to his hometown of Miskolc in 1830, and when his devout mother found out that her son had forsaken his faith, she collapsed onto her bed in shock and died of grief.[190] In 1844, the Catholic periodical

Religio és Nevelés published a Somogy County parish priest's detailed account of the conversion of an eighteen-year-old domestic servant named Francziska Klein. The priest may have exaggerated the hardships she faced, but he claimed that when she informed her family of her intention to convert, she was forced to flee her home. As she was receiving her religious instruction, family members visited her on several occasions to try to talk her out of getting baptized and repeatedly offered her money in hopes of dissuading her.[191] In 1846, Lajos Arányi, the father of Hungarian anatomic pathology, reported similar impulses among Hungary's wealthy and "reformed" Jews, claiming that if a member of these circles wanted to convert, "the enlightened rich" would collect a few thousand forints to "bribe them and return them to the fold."[192]

Yet by the Reform Era, the first signs of change had clearly begun to appear in associational life, friendships, and families. In the 1840s, the Commercial Casino of Pest, the Art Association of Pest, and the Musicians' Association of Pest and Buda all had both Jewish and converted Jewish members.[193] The former could hardly have avoided interaction with the latter, even if they had wanted to. Moritz Gottlieb Saphir—who was born in Lovasberény, moved abroad in 1822, and achieved fame throughout Central Europe writing satire in German—was not abandoned by his friends among the Jewish intellectuals of Pest when he converted in 1832. In 1845, Fülöp Weil—known for his humorous German verse—marked the occasion of Saphir's fiftieth birthday by saluting him with a poem written in what Sára Friedländer called an "effusive tone."[194] Concerning familial relationships, Mór Ullmann's wife and siblings did not sever their personal ties with him when he converted to Catholicism in 1825. Putting an end to their everyday interactions would have been particularly difficult given that Ullmann and his converted sons continued to occupy the same house as his unconverted wife and daughters, though the two groups did live on separate floors.[195]

There is less information concerning Jewish behavior toward converts during the neoabsolutist period (1850–67), but the available evidence suggests that the trends of the Reform Era continued. The Catholic periodical *Religio* (formerly known as *Religio és Nevelés*) continued to publish detailed reports about Jews willing to use all available means to deter their coreligionists from converting.[196] Meanwhile, converted and unconverted Jewish members of Hungary's emergent modern bourgeoisie frequently worked alongside one another at a growing number of organizations in the city of Pest. Among them were the Lloyd Society of Pest, founded in 1853; the editorial committee that oversaw the publication of the society's paper, *Pester Lloyd*, beginning in 1854; the Pannónia insurance company, established in 1861; and various philanthropic organizations active in the city.[197]

With a few exceptions, contemporaneous observers did not discuss Jews' relationships with apostates. This sort of discourse was rare until the turn of the twentieth century, and even then, more detailed accounts were limited almost exclusively to the Neolog intelligentsia. I have found only two instances of Christian observers making reference to the issue. In 1893, in response to a letter from a converted, presumably middle-class Jew, Géza Kenedi—Catholic editor of the *Pesti Hírlap*—asserted that one of the "undeniable" difficulties of conversion was that "Israelite society, particularly its more zealous stratum, turns its back on the family in question."[198] Writer Ferenc Herczeg made precisely the opposite point in a 1900 feuilleton he published in his family weekly *Új Idők*. A recurring character, a provincial landowner of noble descent named Mrs. Horkay, describes the first ball hosted by the recently ennobled Kaplers. Though the ball was attended by "flirtatious, spirited ladies and boisterous gentry-girls," Mrs. Horkay would not be fooled: "Other than myself, the Christians who were there were Jews."[199] In Herczeg's feuilleton, it was taken for granted that converted and unconverted Jews would socialize together in these lofty circles.

While Herczeg made light of the phenomenon, *Egyenlőség*'s contributors were incensed and embittered by it, characterizing it as yet another of the many signs that traditional Jewish values had disintegrated and that modern Jews lacked self-respect. This begs the question: how could *Egyenlőség* have shown such obvious goodwill toward certain converts? Miksa Szabolcsi's answer was simple: men like Miksa Falk, Ármin Vámbéry, and Lajos Dóczy were just the exceptions that proved the rule.[200] There were certainly foreign figures such as Heinrich Heine, Benjamin Disraeli, and the Russian Orientalist Daniel Chwolson who were "defenders of the Jews," but they too were exceptions, for "most converts are unprincipled."[201]

This stereotypical image of the convert was rooted in the conviction that conversion itself was essentially deceitful and motivated by base concerns. In 1902, Rabbi Meyer Kayserling of Pest declared, "No Jewish man or woman has ever professed the Christian faith out of conviction."[202] Miksa Szabolcsi thought it absurd to assume that one could. "Here is how things stand: no pious Jew has ever converted; only a disbelieving Jew could be baptized. So

AFTER CONVERSION 349

who will believe the convert who says he did not believe in the One God, but now believes in three?"[203] And needless to say, since Neolog intellectuals firmly believed that worshipping God in a Jewish temple was perfectly compatible with belonging to the Hungarian nation, they did not consider the desire to merge with the nation a legitimate justification for conversion.[204] The conclusion was self-evident. In the words of Rabbi Simon Hevesi of Pest, "He who strays from the faith of Israel does so either under pressure from his environment, in which case he bears witness to his own spiritual weakness; or in order to liberate himself from the ill will that accompanies the practice of Judaism and manifests itself in the social sphere, in which case he is a quaking, timorous deserter; or, as in most instances, with the objective of obtaining material advantages, in which case he is a wretched, whorish profiteer who traffics in souls and convictions."[205]

While conversion was considered a *betrayal* in religious terms, it constituted *treason* to the Jewish community—the transgression of a moral duty to maintain one's loyalty to a once persecuted, now besieged community. In adopting the Christian faith, the renegade crossed over "from the persecuted minority to the belligerent majority," relinquishing a "long-suffering, eternally beleaguered flag."[206] From his pulpit, Chief Rabbi Ármin Perls of Pécs fulminated against the Jew "who flouts his faith like a huckster, denies his blood, forsakes his forefathers, deserts and betrays his people."[207] Some observers were more forgiving of individuals who felt compelled to convert in order to earn a living.[208] But most Neolog intellectuals—and, it should come as no surprise, rabbis—considered apostasy an unforgiveable sin even in cases of financial hardship. As Chief Rabbi Bernát Singer of Szabadka asked in 1904, "Are the crimes customarily committed by evil-doers—theft, fraud, and robbery—not committed in the name of subsistence? It is impossible to change this fact. There is only one morality."[209]

The condemnation of converts and conversion was to determine faithful Jews' behavior and attitudes. Up to the middle of the first decade of the twentieth century, Hungary's Neolog press would urge Jews to sever all social relations with converts, as they represented a threat to all Jews. "In a family where one *meshumad* arises, another *meshumad* shall spring forth," Miksa Szabolcsi wrote in 1903. "Wherever the *meshumad* is admitted, he spreads *shmad*, which means annihilation, i.e., the spirit of annihilating the Jews."[210] A year earlier, Chief Rabbi Arnold Kiss of Buda warned his fellow Jews that a permanent shunning was the only appropriate response to the

350 JEWISHNESS AND BEYOND

convert, who had "breathlessly jumped a ship he believed to be sinking, like a miserable rat," and had sacrificed his past and his honor "like a dog for a bone."[211] As with Szabolcsi, the chief rabbi's unusually coarse tone was rooted in the belief that his fellow Jews had become too tolerant, forgetting the only acceptable response to *meshumadim*: "Apostasy is no longer a sin among us. Those gentlemen . . . who have trampled on our Holy Scriptures, who have branded as lies the things for which our forefathers were burnt at the stake, who have flung filth on our centuries-old banner—settle in at our tables with their affable faces . . . and make us believe that nothing happened—it's just a meaningless formality, a trifle, minutiae not worth mentioning. And we continue to shake their hands as if, indeed, nothing had happened at all."[212]

Complaints like these first appeared in the Jewish press just after the turn of the twentieth century and would soon become a regular feature of Neolog public discourse. They were clearly a function of alarm over the growing number of conversions observed since Hungarian officials began publishing such statistics in 1896. Unsurprisingly, members of the Jewish upper class were the most frequent targets of such charges. In the summer of 1908, a group of four painters—Ede Kallós, Lajos Márk, Gyula Kann, and Károly Reinhard—reported to the rabbinical office of the Israelite Congregation of Pest to announce their intention to disaffiliate. According to *Egyenlőség*, the artists justified conversion by saying they hoped it would help them find Christian patrons more easily. The Neolog weekly speculated that the painters' decisions were made easier by the knowledge that they would not thereby risk the support of their Jewish buyers: "Is it their experience that well-to-do, Jewish patrons of the arts turn away in anger and contempt from artists who make a business of their religion? They could not have experienced it thus. They are more likely to have seen the opposite. Converts are fawned over. Who on earth knows why. Perhaps they want to make a spectacle of their impartiality."[213]

Charging others with the sin of kindliness to converts was not limited to "Lipótváros." In 1904, *Egyenlőség* indignantly reported that a provincial landowner's wife had laughed while telling her friends "she had never enjoyed as much respect among Jews as she had since disavowing her Jewishness. If she appears at a synagogue for a friend's wedding, their respect is so great, they hardly know where to put her."[214] The Neolog press sometimes printed blanket condemnations of the Jews of the Hungarian capital, noting with horror that many of the witnesses who reported to rabbinical offices alongside converts-to-be were themselves Jews; "day after day," fathers accompanied their soon-to-be baptized sons through the rabbi's gate and seemed to do so with idyllic calm.[215]

Partly because *Egyenlőség*'s contributors recognized the impossibility of severing all contact in a modern (urban) setting, and partly because they wanted to avoid accusations of religious fanaticism, by the end of the first decade of the twentieth century the calls for general ostracism softened to pleas that the congregation's leadership positions be off-limits to anyone who, "in his family, not only tolerated, but facilitated defection from the Jewish faith."[216]

In reality, benevolently neutral treatment of converts among Jews was not as widespread as Neolog intellectuals claimed. In the jokebooks, short stories, plays, and novels they produced around the turn of the century, Jewish authors tended to portray converts as negative figures who had had themselves baptized out of naked opportunism, then attempted to conceal their Jewish origins. I have taken several opportunities to mention Ferenc Molnár's first novel, *The Hungry City*, about the rise and fall of Pál Orsovai, who converts at the age of twenty-three; I should note here that Orsovai is an unambiguously unsympathetic protagonist—calculating, vain, and mendacious, a pompous and self-aggrandizing arriviste.

According to a letter a young Jew submitted to the editor of the *Pesti Hírlap* in 1895, his fellow Jews were unanimous in thinking that conversion signified a lack of character. The author took up his pen in the name of "modern Israelite youth" to express his indignation that Neolog rabbis would refuse to bless mixed civil unions at their synagogues. "For us, rabbis are nothing and nobody," exclaimed the young man. The Jewish religion "in all its forms" had to be sacrificed on the altar of "Hungarian national progress," especially considering the "implacable law of nature" that "the larger mass swallows, dissolves, absorbs into itself, and assimilates the smaller." And yet he rejected the idea of converting precisely because his fellow Jews "today consider it to be a question of character."[217]

Despite running counter to the views of the Neolog press, this generalization is often supported by the available sources. My research indicates that the broad masses of Neolog Jews were consistently hostile in their dealings with converts. I do not mean to suggest that Neolog journalists' complaints about the dramatic erosion of traditional Jewish values were completely unfounded. In the final decades of the Dual Monarchy, Jews who supported the conversion

352   JEWISHNESS AND BEYOND

of their children and even converts themselves were occasionally allowed to retain the positions they occupied within the Jewish community. However, minor officials and scholarship recipients did sometimes suffer reprisals. In 1908, *Népszava* reported the case of religious instructor Emil Koralek of Budapest, one of whose daughters married a Christian and then converted to her husband's religion. The ICP responded by dismissing Koralek and refusing to rehire him even after his daughter was widowed and converted back to Judaism.[218] According to a diary entry Béla Balázs recorded in 1913, his conversion had cost his younger brother Ervin Bauer his "Jewish scholarship."[219] The situation could be different for occupants of higher offices. An extreme case involved the leaders of the Jewish community of Tápiószele, who allowed their rabbi, Ignác Lichtenstein, to maintain his position for years even as he was publishing pamphlets urging his fellow Jews to convert. Only after Lichtenstein was repeatedly attacked in the pages of *Egyenlőség* was he finally forced to resign in 1892. The congregational leadership's patience with him might have had something to do with his wealth, which allowed him to serve without pay, or to his having several relatives on the congregation's board.[220] In Budapest, wholesaler and landowner Henrik Schosberger de Tornya remained a member of the representative body of the Chevra Kadisha even after his daughters, Ottilia and Ilona, were baptized (in 1882 and 1883, respectively) in order to marry Christian aristocrats; Schosberger's wife also retained her position with the Israelite Women's Association of Pest.[221] When Rose Ormody converted to Catholicism in 1897, her father, Vilmos was also able to retain his leadership positions at several Jewish institutions.[222] Between 1899 and 1914, Ferenc Chorin Sr.—who served eight terms in the House of Representatives and was granted a lifetime appointment to the House of Lords in 1902—had three daughters convert in order to marry Christians. Chorin himself would convert not long before his death in 1925. Yet in 1913, he was still a member of the governing body of the Jewish community of Pest and served on the board of directors of the National Hungarian Israelite Public Fund until 1916.[223] This phenomenon was not confined to the Hungarian capital. In 1903, *Egyenlőség* upbraided a Jewish women's association in the countryside for its failure to shun a member who had "held her daughter and grandchildren under the waters of baptism."[224] In 1911, *Egyenlőség* pilloried the Jewish congregation of Fiume (Rijeka, Croatia) and its president, the wealthy lawyer Henrik Sachs, for their scandalous behavior. In the interest of an advantageous match, Sachs had given his blessing to his daughter's conversion and resigned from his post,

AFTER CONVERSION

whereupon the community's voting members unanimously reelected him—and Sachs accepted the honor.[225]

The recollections of Miklós Práger (born in Kiskunhalas, Pest County, in 1904) speak volumes about the attitudes of Orthodox Jews and their hostility to converts, particularly because the lukewarm Orthodox Judaism of the Great Plain was light years away from the ultra-Orthodoxy of northeastern Hungary. Práger recalled that during an elementary school recess one day, he and his classmates saw the son of the local beer wholesaler walking down the street to the *dayan*'s office to reaffirm his intention to disaffiliate, and all the children fled back to their classroom in horror.[226] This sort of revulsion was not limited to Orthodox Jews. In September of 1904, *Egyenlőség* reported that missionaries preaching the Christian gospel had appeared at the outdoor High Holiday services the Neolog congregation of Pest hosted every year at City Park. The indignant faithful, mostly poor Jews, thoroughly thrashed one of the missionaries, who "very much bore the traces of his former denominational affiliation."[227] However, this incident is less representative of the era than a speech Vilmos Vázsonyi delivered to the Central Democratic Circle in Budapest on April 27, 1912. Before a gathering of his own people, mostly petty bourgeois Jews of Terézváros who had elected him to four consecutive terms in the House of Representatives starting in 1901, the founder of the Bourgeois Democratic Party devoted his speech to denigrating his bourgeois-radical rivals as cloistered scholars and inexperienced extremists. Among the shots Vázsonyi took at "these ritual *Jünglinge* who haven't reached the age of thirteen" was the observation that "these cunning kids . . . are also cunning insofar as they've switched faiths for pennies, and baptism starts them down the path to becoming freethinkers."[228] Vázsonyi knew his voters well and was clearly convinced that statements of this sort would arouse or intensify ill will toward his rivals in the democratic camp.

István Kulcsár and his high school classmates were no fans of converts either. Most of Kulcsár's classmates were children of the "suburban bourgeoisie" of craftsmen and tradespeople. His Jewish classmates—like Kulcsár himself—received very little religious education at home and generally laughed their way through religion classes and mandatory religious services. The First World War had broken out by the time Kulcsár and his classmates enrolled in high school; were they already the sons of Vázsonyi's early supporters? Either way, it is clear that they were not indifferent to the subject of conversion. Kulcsár recalled "that Christians of Jewish origin were the subject of jokes among

354   JEWISHNESS AND BEYOND

the Jews. They investigated their parents' pasts with great diligence and on a given occasion even brought it up in front of them. Once, the day after Yom Kippur, one of the Jewish boys—my only Jewish friend, the most impudent kid in the class—asked our converted homeroom teacher how his fast had been. We felt a kind of malicious satisfaction with the converts: 'What are you bragging about? You are exactly like I am.'"[229]

In light of the foregoing, it should come as no surprise that the act of conversion (or the fact of being a convert) occasionally elicited hostile reactions from Jews in public, organizational, and professional life. According to the 1886 *Almanac of the National Assembly*, Miksa Falk ran to represent Terézváros in 1875 but "withdrew his candidacy because a portion of the voters made an issue of the religious question." Falk was ultimately elected to represent the legislative district of Keszthely.[230] The raconteur Pál Tenczer, whose political reminiscences supplied Jewish publications with anecdotes for decades, was franker in his assessment of Falk's reasons for withdrawing from the race in Terézváros. Before the parliamentary election of 1878, when prime minister Kálmán Tisza asked Tenczer whether the Liberal Party should nominate Frigyes Harkányi to represent Terézváros, he replied, "[Harkányi] is truly an upstanding man . . . though the Falk election three years ago showed that they will gladly vote for a Christian in Terézváros, and they will elect a Jewish candidate, too, but they do not like to vote for both in one person. Presently a Christian, in the past a Jew."[231] Like Falk, Ernő Schwimmer, who ran to represent Lipótváros in the municipal elections of 1885, had his candidacy sunk by his conversion. Along with his wife and three children, the groundbreaking dermatologist converted to Catholicism on April 10, 1883.[232] Reporting on the 1885 municipal elections, the *Pesti Hírlap* noted that voters had rejected Schwimmer "because he had sprinkled himself with the waters of baptism."[233]

In the age of the Dual Monarchy, Hungarian Jews and their former coreligionists continued to live together as citizens of the same communities, inevitably making regular contact with one another in "institutional" social settings, professional associations, cultural and philanthropic organizations, and various social clubs. By my count, from the founding of the Lipótváros Casino in 1883 to 1907, just under a third of the organization's Jewish-born elected officials were converts.[234] The latter sometimes experienced unpleasant surprises. At the 1914 general assembly of the Budapest Bar Association, the New Lawyers' Party was elected over three slates of rivals, but Zionist members of the party ignored the principle of party solidarity and, on the first day of the voting, circulated a pamphlet featuring the following request: "Our colleague J. D. has converted. We ask our Israelite colleagues to delete his name from the list of candidates for the executive committee and to choose a Christian candidate in his stead." The move produced a minor scandal; "J. D." lodged a complaint with the New Lawyers' leadership, asking why other members of his own movement were campaigning against him. To no avail—sufficient numbers of Jewish and Christian lawyers struck the convert's name from their ballots. József Keresztessy, the candidate who won this seat on the bar association's executive committee, expressed his gratitude by donating the cost of planting an olive tree in the Jewish National Fund's olive grove in Palestine.[235]

Jews sometimes turned their backs on former coreligionists in professional life as well. In 1909, *Egyenlőség* reported with some satisfaction the misfortune of a converted Budapest lawyer. His coreligionists in the capital did not ostracize him when he was baptized "nor—most importantly—was there any change in his clientele." When the convert's father, a provincial lawyer, passed away, leaving his son a law practice, the convert moved out to the country, where he discovered that "in some places, rural Jews don't think the way they do in the capital." His father's Jewish clients shunned him until he finally converted back to Judaism.[236]

While the converted lawyer came to grief in provincial Hungary, *Egyenlőség* asserted that in Budapest, "his relatives had not disowned him and his friends had not turned their backs on him."[237] This brings us to the conclusion of this section. Though Jews persisted in condemning converts, making them targets of resentment, hostility, and even unpleasant public outbursts, this was only one side of the coin. According to the laments of the Neolog press, conversion had no negative consequences in private life. Converts were not cut off by their devoted friends and relatives; friends continued to help friends convert, as fathers did their children.

In terms of social relations, some proportion of Hungary's acculturated and secularized Jews had become largely or utterly indifferent to the conversions of their friends and acquaintances. Such indifference was prevalent in the haute bourgeoisie and the art world, and among progressive intellectuals affiliated with *Huszadik Század* and *Nyugat*. In the case of the latter, all accounts agree: from the New York Café to the salons of Géza Moscovitz and the Polányi family, Christians, new Christians, and Jews who were still loyal to the faith formed a circle of friends and acquaintances in which religious affiliation (or a change thereof) did not affect their relationships in any way.[238] Given the prevailing opinion that upper-class Jews were largely indifferent to their Jewishness, one might be even surprised by *Egyenlőség's* indignation in reporting that banker Pál Elek's post-conversion soirée had been attended by all his Jewish friends, or that the cream of Lipótváros society had paraded itself through Saint Stephen's Basilica in Budapest to celebrate the nuptials of the newly Christian daughter of local businessman Lázár Reinmann.[239] In his 1937 memoir, the unconverted bank executive Simon Krausz recorded a long list of businessmen, politicians, writers, stage directors, actors, painters, and musicians who gathered at his home in Budapest in the years leading up to the Great War; Krausz's regular guests included Christians, Jews, and converts representing both the haute bourgeoisie and the art world.[240]

Considering the value system at work in premodern Jewish society, the fact that so many Jews no longer cut their ties with acquaintances who converted, or even befriended converts, was in itself an enormous change. The question is what general conclusions might be drawn about Neolog Jewish identity in the Dualist era, beyond the evidence that a large majority defined their "Jewishness" in ways that differed from those of their parents and grandparents.

Maintaining a relationship with a convert is not the same as approving of conversion. Nevertheless, we have no way of gauging how many Hungarian Jews maintained friendships with converts even though they condemned, resented or mocked their baptism for years afterward. Furthermore, just as converts exhibited a range of attitudes toward their old faith and their former coreligionists, unconverted Jews also distinguished between "good" and "bad" converts.[241] Jews presumably severed all their ties with antisemitic converts, but even Jews active in Neolog community life sometimes maintained relationships with "good" converts. Miksa Falk would remain one of Mór Wahrmann's closest friends throughout his life.[242] In their letters, Adolf Ágai, József Kiss, Mór Mezei, and several regular contributors to *Egyenlőség* addressed Falk in tones of profound respect and genuine friendship.[243] In 1895, Zsigmond Simonyi served as a witness to the civil marriage ceremony of Rabbi Kornél Heves of Szolnok.[244] Simonyi, Bernát Alexander, and their families spent many summer vacations together.[245] And though Henrik Marczali once slapped his young daughter for asking him why they did not convert to Catholicism, he counted Simonyi and Ármin Vámbéry among his closest friends.[246]

Given the enduring nature of such friendships, it is less than surprising that even *Egyenlőség* essentially reclaimed "good" converts as Jews when they died. *Egyenlőség* was in fact happy to note exceptions that proved its "rule" about converts inevitably becoming antisemites. On the occasion of Ignác Helfy's death, *Egyenlőség* asserted that his respect for the faith of his forefathers and his public advocacy for his former coreligionists merited commemoration "by Jews as such."[247] When Miksa Falk—the embodiment of steadfast liberalism—died, *Egyenlőség* said Hungarian Jews should mourn him twice—once as patriots and "again as people of Jewish faith. . . . Indeed, in the age of liberalism's decline, we have been repeatedly embittered by the passing away of *our good people*."[248] Ármin Vámbéry was the first departed convert whom *Egyenlőség* would explicitly re-Judaize in racialist terms: "We do not wish to reclaim him as a denomination. But racially, we can establish that he was one of ours."[249] Another of the weekly's anonymous obituaries bid farewell to linguist Zsigmond Simonyi's "orphaned Jewish soul."[250]

Finally, there remains the most intimate sphere, the family. Jews' reactions to their relatives' conversions (or contemplation of conversion) exhibited an extraordinary degree of variability, ranging from loving support to disinheritance and tragedy. To begin with the obvious, there was generally little to no change in the relationships between upper-class Jews and children (generally daughters) they permitted or encouraged to convert. Ottilia Schosberger's Jewish family members expressed symbolic approval of her conversion to Catholicism by attending her wedding to Baron Pál Bornemisza in 1882, with her male relatives dressed in traditional-style Hungarian dress uniforms.[251] Nor is there any indication in József Lukács's letters to his son György that the latter's conversion did anything to change the respect and caring affection his father felt for him.[252]

In 1907, József Bánóczi's daughter Margit married a converted Jew, legal scholar Bódog Somló. We do not know how the Bánóczis reacted to their daughter's intentions, but the letters Somló wrote to his in-laws suggest their relationship was harmonious and intimate. Somló would maintain the relationship even after he and Margit were divorced in 1912.[253] If it is surprising that Bánóczi—who played a central role in Neolog community life for several decades—maintained a close relationship with his daughter's converted ex-husband, Tamás Kóbor's behavior may seem even more perplexing. Though the renowned journalist wrote features for *Egyenlőség* around the turn of the century and defiantly embraced his Jewishness throughout his life, he encouraged his daughter Noémi to marry composer and music historian Antal Molnár, a recent convert to Calvinism. Molnár proposed to Noémi in 1915, but after a lengthy period of inner struggle, he broke off their engagement three years later. According to a letter from Molnár to his mother on July 29, 1918, he had been direct with Tamás Kóbor early in his engagement to Noémi, telling his prospective father-in-law that "the issue of wealth was also an important consideration" in their engagement. Kóbor responded that Molnár "should just make his daughter happy and leave the rest to him."[254]

Such cases were not limited to the Jewish upper class or intelligentsia; members of the petty bourgeoisie sometimes demonstrated a certain tolerance in their dealings with converted relatives as well. Born in the Bács-Bodrog County village of Mélykút in 1877, *Nyugat*'s cofounder Miksa Fenyő was ten when he moved to Budapest to live with his paternal uncle, who ran a clothing store and lived in a two-room apartment with his family of nine. They kept a kosher kitchen, a sign of their enduring commitment to traditional religious values. Yet young Miksa was allowed to have regular lunches with his mother's brother, who had fallen in love with a Christian music hall singer and converted in order to marry her.[255]

In Ervin Szabó's similarly middle-class but completely secularized family, his conversion to Calvinism at the age of eighteen in 1895 did not engender any hostility. According to György Litván's biography, Szabó's "family presumably approved of the step; in 1911, his mother would convert to Lutheranism as well."[256] István Kulcsár's decision to join the Reformed Church in 1920 falls just outside the chronological framework of this investigation but is nonetheless worth mentioning. According to Kulcsár's memoirs, he had been encouraged to convert by his mother's relatives, among whom "conversion had been routine for generations, and thus there were no obstacles to it." Kulcsár's father had no objection to his son's baptism either.[257]

In enumerating examples of more adversarial familial reactions to conversion, I will again begin with a case involving members of the upper class. In accordance with the terms of a will dated June 29, 1893, Mór Wahrmann's older brother Sándor Wahrmann (a philanthropist who died a bachelor in 1899) left 805,000 crowns to various Jewish causes and divided the remainder of his estate equally among three of his siblings. The sibling left out of his will was his sister Amália (also known as Mrs. Bernát Pollák). She had only

AFTER CONVERSION 359

one child who did not convert; Sándor Wahrmann left this nephew 200,000 crowns. All three children of Mór Wahrmann (who had died two months earlier) were omitted from Sándor Wahrmann's will, though only Mór's sons, Ernő and Richard, had converted by that time.[258] Mór Wahrmann's descendants seemed to be plagued with bad luck; when his daughter Renée and her three-year-old daughter converted in 1898, Lajos Krausz, the childless brother of Renée's ex-husband Izidor Krausz, disinherited her.[259] And finally, *Egyenlőség* reported in 1910 that Károly Hatvany-Deutsch's family had attempted to discourage him from converting, then severed their ties with him when he, his wife, and his children were baptized into the Catholic Church.[260]

Let us take leave of turn-of-the-century Lipótváros and return to the pettybourgeois milieu of Terézváros in the early 1870s, where Tamás Kóbor grew up as one of seven siblings. Kóbor's father, a strictly observant tinsmith, found his eighteen-year-old daughter Anna a job a few streets away, working as a domestic servant at the home of his wife's sickly, elderly brother. This form of servitude was very hard on the young lady, who begged her parents—in vain—to let her come home. Then one day she fled from her uncle's house; a few weeks later, her family learned that she had converted and become a nun. Kóbor's parents lit a memorial candle and sat on low stools to weep and pray, mourning their daughter as if she were dead. According to Kóbor, "The mourning lasted for eight days. Then my father got off his stool and resumed his old life, grayer, more dejected, more embittered. We were forbidden from mentioning Anna's name again, and no one ever did."[261]

There is no evidence that petty bourgeois families subjected their converted relatives to similar treatment in the early aughts. This does not mean ostracism did not exist among them, given that conversion (and even the act of considering conversion) could lead to serious conflict, disinheritance, or tragedy even in bourgeois families. According to Géza Hegedüs's memoirs, when he was born in 1912, his father, Andor, told Geza's mother he very much wanted their family to convert, but his devout relatives would make it impossible. Andor Hegedüs knew what he was talking about. His father, a cobbler and shoe salesman who joined the Orthodox congregation of Nagyvárad after the Neolog-Orthodox schism, had six sons, most of whom distanced themselves from their father's piety. Nevertheless, when their father died in 1908, the family "'sat *shiva*' in accordance with ancient religious law." After observing the traditional weeklong ritual of mourning, Andor's brother Miksa went

Figure 5.10. Tamás Kóbor, c. 1920. Petőfi Literary Museum, F.13040.

back to Szombathely (where he ran a profitable toy shop) and wrote his mother a letter informing her that he had fallen in love with a Catholic girl and was going to convert in order to marry her. In his capacity as the new head of the family, Andor's eldest brother, Arnold (a bank clerk), wrote the response to Miksa's announcement: "Its essence was that the family would rather hear their faithless son was dead than an apostate." If he converted, "they would sit *shiva* for him just as they would for the deceased, and if they saw him alive, they would spit at him." Upon receiving Arnold's letter, Miksa shot himself in the head—though not before drawing up a will in which he left the pistol to Arnold, who then turned the weapon on himself, but unlike his younger brother, he survived his attempt at suicide.[262]

The family of Ignác Hoffmann (born in Szombathely in 1855) abandoned the traditional pieties long before the Hegedüs family, as evidenced by a painting of Hoffmann's beardless paternal grandfather. Hoffmann's father opened a general store in 1847, joined the Hungarian national guard during the 1848 revolution, and later expanded his business to include a vinegar factory, which Ignác and his brother Henrik took over in the 1890s. Ignác Hoffmann was among the leaders of the Neolog congregation of Szombathely, serving as a board member of the local Chevra Kadisha for thirty years. He generally went to synagogue on Fridays and never missed High Holiday services. He fasted in the temple on Yom Kippur, though he did take time between prayers to read business correspondence that was brought to him. In the 1910s, Hoffmann's Frankfurt-born sister-in-law tried to persuade his younger brother Lajos, a military physician, to convert. According to the memoirs of Ignác Hoffmann's son János,

> Uncle Lajos was not pleased to hear it, because his coreligionists' respect was very important to him. . . . But Aunt Mally had set her heart on conversion—if I remember correctly, right before the birth of her first child. And that's when an unforgettable and shocking incident took place—my father, who idolized his younger brother and respected his sister-in-law, ordered Aunt Mally out of the house and declared that if Lajos converted, he would no longer have any contact with him. I have no way of knowing whether my father's dramatic display—or something else—had an effect on them, but Lajos Hoffmann's family would remain Jewish.[263]

As we work our way down from tragedy to more moderate instances of discord, I should mention the case of the leaseholder József Goldschmied of Dombóvár. József's father, Lipót Goldschmied, who was well versed in Jewish scholarship, had two other sons—Izrael, who became a rabbi, and Ede, who served as the president of Dombóvár's Status Quo congregation just after the turn of the century. József was also an active member of the local community and its Chevra Kadisha. In 1917, the Zionist *Zsidó Szemle* wrote that Dombóvár, "from the perspective of Jewry, [was] one of the most neglected congregations in the country."[264] That may have been the case, but József Goldschmied's will stipulated his grandson would be disinherited if he were to repudiate his faith (or change his surname!).[265]

362   JEWISHNESS AND BEYOND

Could it be coincidence that I have found only one case in which a Hungarian Jewish intellectual expressed any hostility to a converted family member? On the occasion of Sándor Bródy's death in 1924, *Múlt és Jövő* published a piece by Irén Sas featuring lengthy excerpts of a conversation she had with the prominent writer in 1920. Sas recalled that the elemental force of the antisemitism that swept over Hungary following the revolutions of 1918–19 had affected Bródy, who was subsequently "very much inclined back toward Jewry." Bródy told Sas the story of the only convert in his family, a niece who was baptized at some point prior to the war. According to this account, the young woman had visited Bródy after her conversion, tearfully begging him for forgiveness: "She grabbed at my hand, wanting to kiss it, but I did not allow it. I showed her the door, and I didn't say a word to her, though my heart was nearly broken, I loved that girl so much."[266]

How many more stories might we be able to tell if we could peek into the Hungarian Jewish homes of the early twentieth century? How much would it change our overall impression? It is impossible to know, and thus we must stress the diversity of the accounts recorded in the available sources. Over time, fewer and fewer of Hungary's secularizing and acculturating Jews would consider conversion—whether of a coreligionist, colleague, acquaintance, or family member—to be a mortal sin. Most Hungarian Jews probably continued to condemn conversion, but many no longer accorded it particular significance. Some Jews disowned—or at least disinherited—their newly Christian family members while others accepted conversion grudgingly, ambivalently, or even sympathetically; still others were explicitly supportive. Clearly, to assume that Neolog Jewish identity was homogeneous in the Dualist era is to ignore the fact that by the dawn of the twentieth century, the Neolog Jewish community had lost its internal cultural cohesion.

Notes

1. *Boëthius boldog fiatalsága: Demény János válogatása Molnár Antal leveleiből és írásaiból* (Budapest: Magvető, 1989), 326–27.

2. Balázs, *Napló 1903–1914*, 602.

3. Márai, *Egy polgár vallomásai (1934–1935/1940)*, 227.

4. For circumstances in Spain in the fifteenth to seventeenth centuries, see Yosef Hayim Yerushalmi, *Assimilation and Racial Anti-Semitism: The Iberian and the German Models (The Leo Baeck Memorial Lecture 26)* (New York: Leo Baeck Institute, 1982). For Germany in the sixteenth to eighteenth centuries, see Carlebach, *Divided*

AFTER CONVERSION 363

Souls, 1, 35–37. For Germany in the late eighteenth and early nineteenth centuries, see Endelman, "Conversion as a Response to Antisemitism in Modern Jewish History," 76–77; Ritchie Robertson, *The 'Jewish Question' in German Literature 1749–1939: Emancipation and Its Discontents* (Oxford, UK/New York: Oxford University Press, 1999), 162–63, 205; Hertz, *How Jews Became Germans*, 72, 79–80, 145.

5. S.[oma] Varga, "Egy keresztény zsidónak levele X**-hez," *Regélő*, November 21, 1839, 744.

6. Mária R. Hoffmann, "Egressy Gábor levele Hugó Károlyról," *Irodalomtörténeti Közlemények* 41, no. 3 (1931): 335.

7. Zsigmond Czakó, "A könnyelműek" (1847), in *Összes művei*, vol. 1, ed. József Ferenczy (Budapest: Aigner Lajos, [1883/1884]), 326.

8. Iczig Spitzigfalvy Spitzig, "Az uy nemesekrül és a régi góleszrül," *Borsszem Jankó*, May 1, 1870, 187.

9. Rf. [Reif], *Kosmopolitismus és nationalismus*, 22.

10. Ken Koltun-Fromm, *Moses Hess and Modern Jewish Identity* (Bloomington/Indianapolis: Indiana University Press, 2001), 86.

11. "Filozófia," *Fidibusz*, December 15, 1905, 8.

12. Szép, *Lila ákác*, 56.

13. See Ignotus' letter of October 20, 1895 and his subsequent undated letter in Veigelsberg Hugó levelei Tóth Bélához [Hugó Veigelsberg's letters to Béla Tóth]. OSZK Kt. Fond 129/387.

14. "Bánóczi József, a legidősebb zsidó akadémikus," *Remény*, December, 1925, 6. I would like to thank Michael Silber for bringing this article to my attention.

15. Jacob Katz, *Exclusiveness and Tolerance: Studies in Jewish-Gentile Relations in Medieval and Modern Times* (London: Oxford University Press, 1961), 140–42, 146–47.

16. [Ferenc Molnár], "Tarka krónika: Faji tulajdonság," *Pesti Napló*, September 24, 1907, 14.

17. Lajos Gáspár, *Nézetek az izraëliták felszabadításáról* (Pest: Engel és Mandello, 1861), 12.

18. *Képviselőházi napló, 1881–1884*, vol. 9 (Budapest: Pesti Könyvnyomda, 1883), 177. Károly Ballagi converted to the Reformed faith at the Scottish Mission in 1843, at the age of nineteen. See Kovács, "Ballagi Mór és a Skót Misszió," 117.

19. János Koricsáner, *Kiáltó szó a pusztában, vagy pedig miképen mozdíthatjuk elő az emberi nemnek boldogságát?* (Pest: Gyurian József, 1862), 30.

20. Ibid., 11, 30.

21. Ibid., 43.

22. Sándor Iván Kovács, ed., *Batu kán pesti rokonai: Vámbéry Ármin és tatárja, Csagatai Izsák* (Pozsony: Kalligram, 2001), 293–94.

23. Ibid., 126, 295.

24. The date of Somló's conversion comes from Kovács, *Diszkrimináció, emancipáció*, 134.

25. Somló Bódog szüleihez, 1896. nov. 26 [Bódog Somló's letter to his parents, November 26, 1896]. OSZK Kt. Levelestár.

26. György Litván, "Egy magyar tudós tragikus pályája a század elején: Somló Bódog (1873–1920)," *Valóság* 16, no. 8 (1973): 33.

27. Pikler Gyula Somló Bódognak, 1898. okt. 12 [Gyula Pikler's letter to Bódog Somló, October 12, 1898]. OSZK Kt. Levelestár.

28. Somló Bódog naplójegyzetei, 1898 [Bódog Somló's diaries, 1898]. OSZK Kt. Quart. Hung. 3038/1–2.

29. Litván, "Egy magyar tudós tragikus pályája," 34; Kovács, *Diszkrimináció, emancipáció*, 134–35.

30. Weisz, *A zsidók és a nemzetiségek*, 39.

31. Kayserling, "Mit kell tennünk," 1.

32. Secundus [József Patai], "Lapzárta előtt még zsidó volt," *Múlt és Jövő* 4, no. 2 (1914): 96.

33. Adler, "A kitérések," 5.

34. For a selection of Szegfi's Jewish short stories published before 1848, see Szalai, *Házalók, árendások, kocsmárosok, uzsorások*, 321–33, 365–69, 438–55.

35. Károly Vadnay, "Az első zsidó miniszteri fogalmazó" (1896), in *Irodalmi emlékek* (Budapest: Franklin-Társulat, 1905), 437–43; Emília Kánya, *Réges-régi időkről: Egy 19. századi írónő emlékiratai* (Budapest: Kortárs, 1998), 203–06. Emília Kánya's autobiography makes no mention of her husband's Jewish origins—nor, obviously, of his conversion.

36. Szegfi Mór Szász Károlyhoz, 1882. dec. 30 [Mór Szegfi's letter to Károly Szász, December 30, 1882]. OSZK Kt. Levelestár.

37. Lajos Hentaller, *Politikusaink pongyolában: Tollrajzok a képviselőházból* (Budapest: Kókai Lajos, 1886), 66.

38. [Szentiványi], *Századunk névváltoztatásai*, 229.

39. Andor Nagy, "Biharország," *Világ*, April 12, 1914, 35.

40. Sándor Halász, ed., *Országgyűlési almanach 1886: Képviselőház* (Budapest: Athenaeum, 1886), 54.

41. György Gracza, *A nevető Magyarország*, vol. 2 (Budapest: Lampel Róbert, 1901), 216.

42. Katalin Forró, "Kortesnóták szerepe a dualizmuskori választási kampányokban," in *Studia Comitatensia 29: Néprajzi, történeti tanulmányok*, ed. Rozália Farkas (Szentendre, Hungary: Pest Megyei Múzeumok Igazgatósága, 2004), 134.

43. Waktor, "A XIX. századi családmodell működése és változásai a Ballagi család levelezésének tükrében," 71.

AFTER CONVERSION

44. Károly Csemegi, "Nagy férfiak méltatása; az egyéni érték elismerése," in *Művei*, vol. 1, ed. Károly Edvi Illés and Zsigmond Gyomai (Budapest: Franklin-Társulat, 1904), 385. Csemegi's younger brother Ignác was baptized Catholic by his parents in 1829, when he was two; Károly was probably baptized at that same time. Their father, Móric Nasch, changed his name to Csemeghy in 1844. Gábor Bona, *Századosok az 1848/49. évi szabadságharcban*, vol. 1 (Budapest: Heraldika, 2008), 245; [Szentiványi], *Századunk névváltoztatásai*, 53.

45. Károly Eötvös, "Csemegi Károlyról" (1899), in *Magyar alakok* (Budapest: Révai Testvérek, 1901), 174–86; Jenő Molnár, "A mi nagyjaink: Vázsonyi Vilmos (Második közlemény)," *Egyenlőség*, August 4, 1923, 10–11.

46. "Csemegi Károly," *Budapesti Hírlap*, March 19, 1899, 2; Károly Edvi Illés, "Csemegi Károly élete és kora," in Csemegi, *Művei*, 1: XVII–XVIII.

47. "Az országgyűlési képviselők betűsorozatos névlajstroma," in *Az 1861-ik évi magyar országgyűlés*, vol. 3/6 (Pest: Osterlamm Károly, 1861), 464, 470, 473; Endre Bojthor, *Az 1865-dik évi dec. hó 10-dikére összehívott országgyűlés képviselőháza tagjainak betűsoros név- és lakjegyzéke* (Pest: Emich Gusztáv, 1866), 19, 29, 33; Béla Pálmány, ed., *Az 1848–1849. évi első népképviseleti országgyűlés történeti almanachja* (Budapest: Magyar Országgyűlés, 2002), 930–31.

48. Endre Bojthor, *Az 1869-ik évi april 20-ára összehívott országgyűlés képviselőháza tagjainak betűsoros név- és lakjegyzéke* (Pest: Eggenberger, 1869); id., *Az 1872-dik évi sept. hó 1-ső napjára összehívott országgyűlés képviselőháza tagjainak betűsoros név-, lak- és törvényhatóságok szerinti névjegyzéke* (Budapest: Eggenberger, 1875).

49. Falk converted in Vienna, most likely in order to marry Ernestine Cäcilia Ludowika von Lachmayer. Staudacher, *Jüdische Konvertiten in Wien 1782–1868*, 2: 109.

50. *A budapesti társaság*, 159.

51. *A nemzeti kaszinó évkönyve 1873*, 17; *Az Országos Kaszinó évi jelentése az 1899-ik évről* ([Budapest]: Werbőczy Könyvnyomda, [1900]), 33; *A Park Club évkönyve 1900*; "Falk Miksa," *Budapesti Hírlap*, September 11, 1908, 1–2.

52. "Arczképek és életrajzok: Szitányi Bernát," in *Szabadelvűpárti naptár az 1884. szökő évre*, vol. 1, ed. György Szathmáry (Budapest: Athenaeum, n.d.), 132; *A nemzeti kaszinó évkönyve 1847*, 53; *1853dik évi jelentés a pesti lovaregylet munkálódásairól* (n.p.: n.p., n.d.), 7.

53. "Arczképek és életrajzok: Szitányi Bernát," 132–33.

54. Károly Eötvös, "Szitányi Bernát halálára (1889)," in *Magyar alakok*, 126–30.

55. Zsuzsa Török, "A Wohl nővérek keresztvíz alatt: Két protestáns zsidó írói életpálya kezdete," *Századvég*, no. 2 (2013): 43–47.

56. Kánya, *Réges-régi időkről*, 48.

57. Klára Csapodiné Gárdonyi, "Wohl Janka emlékalbuma," in *Országos Széchényi Könyvtár Évkönyve 1958* (Budapest: Országos Széchényi Könyvtár, 1959), 247–57.

58. *A budapesti társaság*, 512; Angelo de Gubernatis, *La Hongrie politique et sociale* (Florence: Joseph Pellas, 1885), 340–42; Fanni Borbíró, "'Csevegés, zene és egy csésze tea': A Wohl-nővérek a pesti társaséletben," *Budapesti Negyed* 12, no. 4 (2004): 350–76.

59. "Wohl Stefanie," *Budapesti Hírlap*, October 17, 1889, 4; "Wohl Janka meghalt," *Budapesti Hírlap*, May 24, 1901, 5; Géza Zichy, "Wohl Janka," *Budapesti Hírlap*, May 25, 1901, 1.

60. [Koricsáner], *Kiáltó szó a pusztában*, 40–42.

61. Kecskeméti, "A 'zsidó' a magyar színműirodalomban," 216.

62. Zoltán Thury, "A rossz Gold és a jó Kapornay," in *Az ember, aki hazaballagott: Elbeszélések* (Budapest: Singer és Wolfner, 1907), 30–31.

63. Bródy, "Tímár Liza," 354.

64. The paper published this letter to the editor, which had been signed *A Hungarian woman*, under the title *Letter from a Jewish Lady*. *Fővárosi Lapok* 21, no. 16 (1884): 100–01.

65. Zay, "Zsidók a társadalomban," 961.

66. For a discussion of the near impossibility of German Jewish converts marrying members of the traditional elite, see Werner E. Mosse, "Problems and Limits of Assimilation. Hermann and Paul Wallich 1833–1938," *Leo Baeck Institute Year Book* 33 (1988): 43–65.

67. OSZK, obituaries, FM8/35797/569: Baron Mór Wodianer de Kapriora.

68. Duplicate of the civil marriage records of the ninth district of Budapest, March 14, 1900; Duplicate of the civil marriage records of the sixth district of Budapest, July 6, 1903; Duplicate of the civil marriage records of the second district of Budapest, October 8, 1908; János Szerencs, ed., *A főrendiház évkönyve*, vol. 3 (Budapest: Pesti Könyvnyomda, 1907), 528.

69. Bácskai, *A vállalkozók előfutárai*, 80–81; Kempelen, *Magyar zsidó családok*, 1: 51–52.

70. In 1877, Róbert Simon Biedermann (who would be granted an Austrian barony in 1903) married Adolfine Amalie Popper, the converted daughter of the unconverted industrialist Lipót Popper. In 1889, Rudolf Biedermann (who would be granted a Hungarian barony in 1902) married Elsa von Bleichröder (the only daughter of the still-Jewish Gerson Bleichröder of Berlin, a banker known throughout Europe), who had divorced her first husband, a Silesian aristocrat, the year before. Kempelen, *Magyar zsidó családok*, 1: 52–55; William D. Godsey Jr., "The Nobility, Jewish Assimilation, and the Austro-Hungarian Foreign Service in the Late Imperial Era," in *Austrian History Yearbook* 27 (1996): 178–79; Fritz Stern, *Gold*

AFTER CONVERSION 367

and Iron: Bismarck, Bleichröder and the Building of the German Empire (New York: Alfred A. Knopf, 1977), 492.

71. "Házasság," *Pesti Napló,* January 4, 1906, 12; "Bárósítás," *Egyenlőség,* October 12, 1913, 11; Kempelen, *Magyar zsidó családok,* 1: 104–05.

72. "A Park-Club és a Lipótváros," *Az Est,* May 4, 1910, 3; "A Park-Club mozgalma," *Az Est,* May 5, 1910, 6.

73. Paul Ignotus, *Hungary* (London: Ernest Benn Limited, 1972), 97–98.

74. Godsey Jr., "The Nobility, Jewish Assimilation, and the Austro-Hungarian Foreign Service in the Late Imperial Era," 161.

75. *A nemzeti kaszinó évkönyve 1845,* 56.

76. OSZK, obituaries, FM8/35797/569: Baron Albert Wodianer de Kapriora Sr.

77. Sándor Gyömrei, "A kereskedelmi tőke kialakulása és szerepe Pest-Budán 1849-ig," in *Tanulmányok Budapest múltjából,* vol. 12 (Budapest: Akadémiai, 1957), 253.

78. Veronika Tóth-Barbalics, "Vigyázó, Harkányi, Żeleński és társaik—1885 után örökös főrendiházi tagságot nyert családok," in *Vázlatok két évszázad magyar történelméből: Tanulmányok,* ed. Jenő Gergely (Budapest: ELTE BTK Új- és Jelenkori Magyar Történeti Tanszék, 2010), 80.

79. Mislovics, "A magyarországi zsidóság áttérési gyakorlata," 55; *A nemzeti kaszinó évkönyve 1850,* 14; Kempelen, *Magyar zsidó családok,* 1: 144; Székács József emlékiratai [Memoirs of József Székács], 99. F. MTA KIK Kt. Ms 10.653/1.

80. Dániel Szabó, "Országgyűlési választások az egyesítés előestéjén," in *Az egyesített főváros: Pest, Buda, Óbuda,* ed. Gábor Gyáni (Budapest: Városháza, 1998), 48.

81. *A budapesti társaság,* 450.

82. *Az Országos Kaszinó évi jelentése az 1890-ik évről* (Budapest: Athenaeum, 1891), 27; *A Park Club évkönyve 1900,* 14–15.

83. D'Artagnan [Sarolta Vay], "Válópörök hajdan és most," *Szalon Újság,* December, 1900, 13–14.

84. "Krónika," *Szalon Újság,* January 10, 1901, 16; "A táplányi kastély: Báró Lévay Henrik," *Szalon Újság,* June 30, 1901, 8–10.

85. Litván, "Zsidók a huszadik századi magyar modernizációban és progresszív mozgalmakban," 313.

86. Kovács, *Diszkrimináció, emancipáció,* 53–55.

87. Sámuel Radó, "Két levél," *Pesti Napló,* December 31, 1910, 1–2.

88. Bertalan Ormody, "Zsidó aristokrátia," *Regélő,* July 15, 1866, 43.

89. Rutilus [Szigetvári], A mi szabadelvűségünk, 238.

90. Andor Kozma, "Az antisemitismus lényege," *Budapesti Szemle* 108, no. 299 (1901): 186.

91. Molnár, *Az éhes város,* 165–66; Zoltán Ambrus, *Berzsenyi báró és családja: Tollrajzok a mai Budapestről* (1902) (Budapest: Révai Testvérek, 1906), 85, 192; [Pál

Farkas], *Egy önkéntes naplója: Második félév: Az üteg* (Budapest: Singer és Wolfner, 1911), 39–47.

92. Róbert Tábori, *Megfagyott pezsgő* (Budapest: Singer és Wolfner, [1899]), 118.

93. Bródy, "Tímár Liza," 357, 365, 371.

94. Szabolcsi, "A hitehagyás és a nevelőnőképző," 2.

95. Szabolcsi, "Téma: Levél egy íróbarátomhoz," 4–5.

96. Ivri, "'Liga a renegátok ellen,'" *Egyenlőség*, February 5, 1911, supplement, 1.

97. Szabolcsi, "A hitehagyás és a nevelőnőképző," 2.

98. There were instances in which individuals succeeded in hiding their origins—at least until 1939, when the so-called Second Jewish Law was passed and some Hungarian families discovered that a parent or a spouse was a Jewish convert. See Balázs Ablonczy, "Átok és könyörgés: Levelek Teleki Pál miniszterelnökhöz a második zsidótörvény időszakában," in *Kisebbség és többség között: A magyar és a zsidó/izraeli etnikai és kulturális tapasztalatok az elmúlt századokban*, ed. Pál Hatos and Attila Novák (Budapest: L'Harmattan/Balassi Intézet, 2014), 12.

99. Yohanan Petrovsky-Shtern, "Brafman, Iakov Aleksandrovich," in Hundert, *The YIVO Encyclopedia of Jews in Eastern Europe*, http://www.yivoencyclopedia .org/article.aspx/Brafman_Iakov_Aleksandrovich; Brigitte Hamann, *Hitler's Vienna: A Dictator's Apprenticeship*, trans. Thomas Thornton (New York: Oxford University Press, 1999), 230–33.

100. For discussions of Jaszi's attitude toward his Jewish origins and his position on the "Jewish question," see Gyurgyák, *A zsidókérdés Magyarországon*, 482–508; Litván, *A Twentieth-Century Prophet: Oscar Jászi 1875–1957*, 3–4, 84–86, 115–18; id., "Jászi Oszkár és a zsidókérdés," in Molnár, *A holokauszt Magyarországon európai perspektívában*, 45–53.

101. Jakubovits Ferenc névmagyarosítási kérelme [Jakubovits Ferenc's name change request]. MNL OL, K 150 BM 32 522–81.

102. Tamás Repiszky, "Ágas-bogas családfa: Adalékok Jászi Oszkár családtörténetéhez," in Farkas, *Studia Comitatensia 29*, 172.

103. Jászi, "Emlékeimből: Szülőföldemen," 547.

104. Ibid., 547–48.

105. Ibid., 545, 547–49.

106. Ibid., 547.

107. Litván, *A Twentieth-Century Prophet: Oscar Jászi 1875–1957*, 4.

108. Repiszky, "Ágas-bogas családfa," 173.

109. Jászi, "Emlékeimből: Szülőföldemen," 547–48.

110. Ibid., 555–57.

111. Oszkár Jászi, *Válogatott levelei*, comp. György Litván and János F. Varga (Budapest: Magvető, 1991), 370.

AFTER CONVERSION 369

112. X. [Ignotus], "Antisémitaság," *A Hét* 6, no. 5 (1895): 70.

113. György Litván, *"Magyar gondolat—szabad gondolat": Nacionalizmus és progresszió a század eleji Magyarországon* (Budapest: Magvető, 1978), 53–69.

114. Szabó, *Levelezése*, 1: 607.

115. Oszkár Jászi, "Kulturális elmaradottságunk okairól," *Huszadik Század* 6, no. 7 (1905): 23, 25.

116. Oszkár Jászi, "Zsidó-politika," *Világ*, April 30, 1911, 1–2.

117. Ibid., 2.

118. Oszkár Jászi, "A radikalizmus és a zsidók," *Világ*, June 15, 1912, 8.

119. Oszkár Jászi, *Miért léptem ki a "Világ" szerkesztőségéből?* (Budapest: Világosság, 1911), 32.

120. Oszkár Jászi, "A magyarországi reakció szervezkedése," *Huszadik Század* 11, no. 3 (1910): 372; id., "Zsidó-politika," 2.

121. Oszkár Jászi, "1912. május 23.," *Huszadik Század* 13, no. 6 (1912): 737–40.

122. Egy zsidó, "A radikalizmus ellenségei," *Világ*, June 14, 1912, 8; Litván, *A Twentieth-Century Prophet: Oscar Jászi 1875–1957*, 85.

123. Jászi, "A radikalizmus és a zsidók," 8.

124. Egy zsidó, "A radikalizmus és a zsidók," *Világ*, June 16, 1912, 10.

125. Kati Vörös, "The 'Jewish Question,' Hungarian Sociology and the Normalization of Antisemitism," *Patterns of Prejudice* 44, no. 2 (2010): 137–60.

126. *A zsidókérdés Magyarországon: A Huszadik Század körkérdése*, 97, 100.

127. Oszkár Jászi, *A nemzeti államok kialakulása és a nemzetiségi kérdés* (Budapest: Grill Károly, 1912), 228–29.

128. Gyurgyák, *A zsidókérdés Magyarországon*, 509.

129. See, for instance, Bartolo [Imre Décsi], "Lengyel zsidók," *Világ*, July 10, 1910, 8; Florestan [Imre Décsi], "A csodarabbi," *Világ*, May 28, 1911, 12; Zoltán Szász, "A bankfiú," *Világ*, December 17, 1911, 33; Elem, "Magyar Zsidó Múzeum," *Világ*, January 3, 1913, 10; Pál Relle, "A Hatvanyiak," *Világ*, July 6, 1913, 33; "A chéderek," *Világ*, August 2, 1913, 7; István Sárközy, "Antiszemitizmus," *Világ*, December 28, 1913, 8; "Egy orosz gettó-író: Beszélgetés Schalom Asch-sal," *Világ*, January 29, 1914, 9.

130. Mandl, "Két tragikus zsidó asszony," 11.

131. Tibor Darvas, "Az iskolai oktatás története Gyomán," in *Gyomai tanulmányok*, ed. Ferenc Szabó (Gyoma, Hungary: Gyoma Nagyközség Tanácsa, 1977), 276–77, 282.

132. Büchler, *A zsidók története Budapesten*, 387–88; Mandl, "A pesti izr. hitközségi fiúiskola monográfiája," 15.

133. Károly Ballagi, *Magyarország és Erdély története kapcsolatban az egyetemes történelem legfőbb vonásaival: Izraelita népiskolák számára* (Pest: Heckenast Gusztáv, 1868), 3.

134. Miksa Falk, "A pálya kezdetén (1888)," in *Kor- és jellemrajzok*, ed. Ernő Falk (Budapest: Révai Testvérek, 1903), 1–23; Ó. [Zsigmond Ózer], "Tisztelgés dr. Falk Miksánál," *Izr. Tanügyi Értesítő* 16, no. 5 (1891): 75–76.

135. "Tisztelgés," *Egyenlőség*, November 22, 1895, 12; "Zsinagógaavatás," *Egyenlőség*, March 28, 1897, 10.

136. Simonyi Zsigmond Concilia Emilnek, 1908. okt. 19 [Zsigmond Simonyi's letter to Emil Concilia, October 19, 1908]. OSZK Kt. Levelestár. I would like to thank Michael Silber for bringing this letter to my attention.

137. "Simonyi Zsigmond meghalt," *Egyenlőség*, November 29, 1919, 3.

138. Mór Kármán, *Löw Lipót emlékezete: Alkalmi beszédek* (Budapest: Singer és Wolfner, 1911), 10.

139. Márton Diósy, "A honi izraeliták között magyar nyelvet terjesztő pesti egylet; röviden: a magyarító egylet," in *Első magyar zsidó naptár és évkönyv 1848-ik szökőévre*, 92.

140. Vámbéry, *Küzdelmeim*, 106.

141. Goldziher, *Napló*, 36.

142. Kovács, *Diszkrimináció, emancipáció*, 60–61; Aladár Ballagi, "Emlékezés Goldziher Ignácra," *Vasárnapi Újság* 68, no. 23 (1921) 268–69.

143. Mór Ballagi, "Vallásügy az országgyűlésen," *Protestáns Egyházi és Iskolai Lap* 10, no. 49 (1867): 1558–64.

144. Hajehudi Mardochái [Miksa Szabolcsi], "Igazolásul egy reminiszcencia," *Egyenlőség*, October 23, 1904, 8.

145. Aladár Ballagi, "Zsidó-égetés Magyarországon 1529-ben," *Vasárnapi Újság* 29, no. 40 (1882): 637–40.

146. "Delitzsch Ferenc," *Egyenlőség*, March 9, 1890, 5; Mardochái [Szabolcsi], "Igazolásul egy reminiszcencia," 8–9; Miksa Szabolcsi, "Meturgeman: Ballagi Aladár," *Egyenlőség*, January 22, 1905, 4–5.

147. Mór Ballagi, "A kánon," in *Bibliai tanulmányok* (Pest: Engel és Mandello, 1865), 82–83.

148. "Egy volt bachurról," *Egyenlőség*, March 1, 1895, 9–10; M. Sz. [Miksa Szabolcsi], "Helfy Ignácz," *Egyenlőség*, October 17, 1897, 7; Dániel Varga, "Az öreg Kossuth Lajos 'palatinusa': Helfy Ignác (1830–1897)," *Polymatheia* 18, no. 1–2 (2021): 201.

149. *Képviselőházi napló, 1872–1875*, vol. 11 (Buda: Magyar Királyi Államnyomda, 1874), 261.

150. *Képviselőházi napló, 1881–1884*, 13: 206.

151. Ibid.

152. In his letter to Helfy, Kossuth had written, "On the 'Jewish question' (it is a shame and a scandal that this is even possible in Hungary), I receive letters by the hundred." Lajos Kossuth, *Iratai*, vol. 9, ed. Ferencz Kossuth (Budapest: Athenaeum, 1902), 525.

AFTER CONVERSION 371

153. *Képviselőházi napló, 1881–1884,* vol. 14 (Budapest: Pesti Könyvnyomda, 1884), 355–57.

154. Sz. [Szabolcsi], "Helfy Ignácz," 7.

155. Fürst, "Dóczi Lajos báró zsidósága eddig ismeretlen leveleiben," 119.

156. Ibid., 118.

157. Hegyesi Spitzné, "A Dóczi-lázról," *Kakas Márton,* April 20, 1902, 6.

158. Lajos Dóczi to Viktor Rákosi, April 25, 1902. Kónyi–Lónyay Papers, Library of the School of Slavonic and East European Studies [SSEES], University College of London.

159. Oszkár Kútfalvi, *Újságpaloták* (Budapest: Akadémiai, 1991), 11.

160. Fürst, "Dóczi Lajos báró zsidósága eddig ismeretlen leveleiben," 119. The piece in question: Tobias [Lajos Dóczi], "Deutsch-Kreutz: Gruß an meinem Landsmann Karl Goldmark," *Neues Pester Journal,* February 15, 1895, 1–3.

161. Lajos Dóczi, "Goldmark," *Egyenlőség,* March 8, 1895, 4–6.

162. Fürst, "Dóczi Lajos báró zsidósága eddig ismeretlen leveleiben," 120.

163. Komlós, *A magyar zsidóság irodalmi tevékenysége a XIX. században,* 242.

164. Fürst, *Dóczi Lajos mint német író,* 94.

165. Fürst, "Dóczi Lajos báró zsidósága eddig ismeretlen leveleiben," 120.

166. Ignác Peisner, "Dóczy Lajos báró," *Múlt és Jövő,* January 2, 1920, 11.

167. Kovács, *Batu kán pesti rokonai,* 305–06, 310.

168. Eötvös, *Levelek,* 568–69; "Vegyesek," *Izraelita Közlöny,* October 11, 1868, 382.

169. Vámbéry, "Egy tatár emlékirataiból," 8.

170. Vámbéry, *Küzdelmeim,* 482.

171. Max Nordau, "My Recollections of Vambéry," in *The Life and Adventures of Arminius Vambéry* (London: T. Fisher Unwin, 1914), XXI. Thirty-five of Vámbéry's letters to Herzl have been preserved at the Central Zionist Archives in Jerusalem; the last of these letters is dated January 30, 1902. They are also available on microfilm at the National Archives of Hungary. Vámbéry Ármin levelei Theodor Herzlnek [Ármin Vámbéry's letters to Theodor Herzl], 1898–1901 [correctly 1902]. MNL OL, X1184.4769.

172. Raphael Patai, ed., *The Complete Diaries of Theodor Herzl,* vol. 3, trans. Harry Zohn (New York/London: The Herzl Press/Thomas Yoseloff, 1960), 961.

173. Ibid., 962–63.

174. Herzl's account of this meeting appears in ibid., 1110–20.

175. Nordau, "My Recollections of Vambéry," XXI; Patai, *The Complete Diaries of Theodor Herzl,* 3: 1093.

176. "Vámbéry Ármin a czionismusról," *Ungarische Wochenschrift,* May 30, 1902, 1.

177. Meri-Jane Rochelson, *The Career of Israel Zangwill: A Jew in the Public Arena* (Detroit, MI: Wayne State University Press, 2008), 160.

178. "Vámbéry Ármin a cionistákról," *Egyenlőség,* July 22, 1906, 8.

179. "Vámbéry Ármin ünneplése," *Hitközségi Szemle* 3, no. 4 (1912): 95–96. The original interview appeared in the *Jewish Chronicle* on March 22, 1912.

180. For a discussion of racial discourse among Neolog intellectuals, see Miklós Konrád, "Vallásváltás és identitás: A kitért zsidók megítélésének változásai a dualizmus korában," *Századok* 144, no. 1 (2010): 41–42.

181. "Vámbéry Ármin halála," *Egyenlőség*, October 12, 1913, first supplement, 6. Emphasis in the original.

182. Pál Berend, "Beszélgetés a kortárssal, Vámbéry Rusztem dr-ral Herzl Tivadarról," *Múlt és Jövő* 25, no. 5 (1935): 155.

183. M. Sz. [Miksa Szabolcsi], "Dr. Falk Miksa szerkesztői jubileuma," *Egyenlőség*, December 16, 1892, 8; József Vészi, "Falk Miksa," *Magyar Géniusz*, December 25, 1892, 404; Antal Deutsch, *A Pesti Lloyd-Társulat 1853–1903* (Budapest: Pesti Lloyd-Társulat, 1903), 197–98.

184. Ballagi, *Magyarország és Erdély története*, 3.

185. *Jelentés a budapesti Lipótvárosi Casinó 25 éves fennállása alkalmából* (Budapest: Löbl Nyomda, 1907).

186. Carlebach, *Divided Souls*, 125–27; Hertz, *How Jews Became Germans*, 32.

187. Katz, *Exclusiveness and Tolerance*, 71.

188. Carlebach, *Divided Souls*, 14, 24–26, 111, 127; Dov Noy, "[Apostasy] In Jewish Law," in *Encyclopaedia Judaica*, Second Edition, vol. 2. Ed. Fred Skolnik (Detroit, MI: Thomson Gale, 2007), 276–77.

189. Michael A. Meyer, *The Origins of the Modern Jew: Jewish Identities and European Culture in Germany, 1749–1824* (Detroit, MI: Wayne State University Press, 1967), 98; Katz, *Out of the Ghetto*, 12–113; Lowenstein, *The Berlin Jewish Community*, 129–32; Deborah Hertz, "The Lives, Loves, and Novels of August and Fanny Lewald, the Converted Cousins from Königsberg," *Leo Baeck Institute Year Book* 46 (2001): 106–07.

190. Staudacher, *Jüdische Konvertiten in Wien 1782–1868*, 2: 239; Gusztáv Heinrich, *Emlékbeszéd Klein Lipót Gyula kültag felett* (Budapest: M. T. Akadémia, 1882), 9–10.

191. "Egyházi tudósítások," *Religio és Nevelés*, no. 15 (1st Half 1844): 118.

192. Lajos Arányi, *Rudnó és lelkésze 1844 és 1845ben, meg még valami, többi közt a mai magyar zsidó is* (Pest: Emich Gusztáv, 1846), 151–52.

193. Árpád Tóth, "Asszimilációs utak a késő-rendi társadalomban: A zsidóság szerepvállalásáról a reformkori pesti egyesületekben," in *Léptékváltó társadalomtörténet: Tanulmányok a 60 éves Benda Gyula tiszteletére*, ed. Zsolt K. Horváth, András Lugosi, and Ferenc Sohajda (Budapest: Hermész Kör/Osiris, 2003), 171; Tóth, *Önszervező polgárok*, 157, 252; *A Pesti Műegyesület részvényeseinek névsora 1846*, 8–9, 15–17.

194. Sára Friedländer, *Saphir Móric Gottlieb: Tanulmány a zsidó asszimilációs törekvések kezdeteiről* (Budapest: Minerva-Könyvtár, 1939), 33.

AFTER CONVERSION 373

195. Bácskai, *A vállalkozók előfutárai*, 148, 150; Mandl, "Két tragikus zsidó asszony," 11.

196. "Egyházi tudósítások," *Religio*, no. 6 (2nd Half 1854): 46; no. 6 (1st Half 1858): 50.

197. Deutsch, *A Pesti Lloyd-Társulat 1853–1903*, 239; Busbach, *Egy viharos emberöltő*, 111; "A 'Pannónia' czímű magyar viszontbiztosító-társaság," *Vasárnapi Újság* 8, no. 38 (1861): 452; "Napi hírek," *Szépirodalmi Közlöny*, May 6, 1858, 1490.

198. "Szerkesztői üzenetek," *Pesti Hírlap*, October 12, 1893, 20.

199. [Ferenc Herczeg], "Horkayné a kaszinóban," *Új Idők* 6, no. 10 (1900): 216–17.

200. Szabolcsi, "Téma: Levél egy íróbarátomhoz," 4.

201. Miksa Szabolcsi, *Az áldozat: Kor- és jellemkép* (Budapest: "Jókai" Könyvnyomdai Műintézet, 1908), 56.

202. Kayserling, "Mit kell tennünk," 1.

203. [Miksa Szabolcsi], "Meturgeman: Új társadalmi osztály," *Egyenlőség*, July 9, 1899, 7.

204. Ernő Mezei, "Programm," *Egyenlőség*, March 27, 1904, 1–2.

205. Simon Hevesi, "Gondolatok a hitcseréről," *Egyenlőség*, January 28, 1906, supplement, 2.

206. Samu Bleuer, *Mozgalmak a zsidóságban* (Budapest: n.p., 1904), 8; Szabolcsi, "Téma: Levél egy íróbarátomhoz," 4.

207. Ármin Perls, "Nemzet és felekezet," in *Szónoklatok*, vol. 4 (Pécs, Hungary: Pécsi Irodalmi és Könyvnyomdai R.-T., [1912]), 24.

208. Bánóczi, "A zsidó tanárok," 511; Kóbor, "Modern makabeusok," 1–2; Sándor Fleischmann, "Ismét kitért egy zsidó professor," *Egyenlőség*, November 12, 1911, 1–2.

209. Singer, "A kitérések, II," 4.

210. Miksa Szabolcsi, "Meturgeman: Megjegyzések egy lemondó levélre," *Egyenlőség*, February 15, 1903, 4.

211. Arnold Kiss, "Hitehagyottak," *Egyenlőség*, October 19, 1902, supplement, 1–3.

212. Ibid., 2.

213. Miksa Szabolcsi, "Meturgeman: Vallással csereberélő művészek," *Egyenlőség*, August 2, 1908, 5.

214. Szabolcsi, "Téma: Levél egy íróbarátomhoz," 5.

215. Szabolcsi, "Hívek egylete," 1; Pártközi [Mór Fényes], "Még egyszer az orthodox-neológ kérdéshez," *Hitközségi Szemle* 3, no. 6 (1911): 215.

216. "Elszakadók és renegátok-toborzók," *Egyenlőség*, March 7, 1909, 1, 3.

217. "Izraelita ultramontanizmus: Dr. Erasmus levele," *Pesti Hírlap*, December 17, 1895, 3.

218. "Zsidó klerikalizmus," *Népszava*, October 7, 1908, 9.

219. Balázs, *Napló 1903–1914*, 602.

374   JEWISHNESS AND BEYOND

220. Miksa Szabolcsi, "A tápió-szelei rabbi," *Egyenlőség*, September 11, 1891, 5–6; id., "A tápió-szelei rabbi és az ő hitközsége," *Egyenlőség*, October 23, 1891, 4–8; "Tápió-Szeléről," *Egyenlőség*, October 30, 1891, 13; "Tápió-szelei dolgok," *Egyenlőség*, November 27, 1891, 10; "A tápió-szelei rabbi egy ténye, melyet mi is helyeselünk," *Egyenlőség*, September 9, 1892, 10; Miksa Szabolcsi, "Üzenet Tápió-Szelére," *Egyenlőség*, April 28, 1893, supplement, 2–3. After losing his job, Lichteinstein converted and continued his proselytizing as a Christian. See J. Lichtenstein, *Zsidók tükre* (Budapest: Feinsilber Róbert, 1908).

221. "Házasságok," *Pesti Hírlap*, July 4, 1882, 5; Sándor Nagy, "Schosberger Ilona különös házassága," in *A felhalmozás míve: Történeti tanulmányok Kövér György tiszteletére*, ed. Károly Halmos, Judit Klement, Ágnes Pogány, and Béla Tomka (Budapest: Századvég, 2009), 48–57; OSZK, obituaries, FM8/35797/443: Henrik Schosberger; Gábor Forrai, *A Pesti Izraelita Nőegylet 1866–1891* (Budapest: Hungária, 1891), 70–73.

222. "Az Orsz. Magyar Izr. Közművelődési Egyesület felhívása," *Múlt és Jövő* 2, no. 1 (1912): 37–38; *A Pesti Izr. Hitközség elöljáróságának jelentése az 1914. közigazgatási évről*, 31; "Felhívás a magyar zsidósághoz," *Egyenlőség*, March 12, 1916, 1.

223. *A pesti izr. hitközség elöljáróságának jelentése az 1913-iki közigazgatási évről* (Budapest: n.p., 1914), 28–29; "Felhívás a magyar zsidósághoz," 1.

224. Miksa Szabolcsi, "Meturgeman: Vidéki nőegylet," *Egyenlőség*, October 18, 1903, 7.

225. M. Sz. [Miksa Szabolcsi], "Botrány," *Egyenlőség*, February 12, 1911, 9.

226. Práger Miklós emlékei [Memoirs of Miklós Práger]. MZsML, XIX: Hagyaték.

227. "A főünnepek," *Egyenlőség*, September 25, 1904, 8.

228. Vázsonyi, *Beszédei és írásai*, 1: 466–71.

229. Körmendi [Kulcsár], *Zsidó gyónás*, 77–78.

230. Halász, *Országgyűlési almanach 1886: Képviselőház*, 48.

231. Pál Tenczer, "Emlékezés Szilágyi Dezsőre," *Egyenlőség*, August 4, 1901, 4.

232. Kovács, *Diszkrimináció, emancipáció*, 127.

233. Morgó [László Gyöngyösy], "Csata után," *Pesti Hírlap*, October 28, 1885, 3.

234. *Jelentés a budapesti Lipótvárosi Casinó 25 éves fennállása alkalmából*.

235. "'Kár volt kikeresztelkedni,'" *Zsidó Szemle*, March 15, 1914, 3; "A fővárosi ügyvédi kamara tisztújító közgyűlése," *Autonómia*, March 21, 1914, 13.

236. "Elszakadók és renegátok-toborzók," 1.

237. Ibid.

238. For discussions of the salons hosted by Géza Moscovitz and the Polányi family, see Jászi, "Emlékeimből: Szülőföldemen," 557–59; Litván, *A Twentieth-Century Prophet: Oscar Jászi 1875–1957*, 8–9.

239. Szabolcsi, "Meturgeman: Megjegyzések egy lemondó levélre," 4; id., "Egy esküvő alkalmából," *Egyenlőség*, May 20, 1906, 1–2.

AFTER CONVERSION 375

240. Krausz, *A pénzember*, 83–84.

241. Shulamit S. Magnus, "Good Bad Jews: Converts, Conversion, and Boundary Redrawing in Modern Russian Jewry: Notes toward a New Category," in *Boundaries of Jewish Identity*, ed, Susan A. Glenn and Naomi B. Sokoloff (Seattle/London: University of Washington Press, 2010), 132–60.

242. Haber, "Wahrmann Mórról," 4.

243. Ágai Adolf levele Falk Miksához, 1886. febr. 1 [Adolf Ágai's letter to Miksa Falk, February 1, 1886]. OSZK Kt. Fond IV/9; Kiss József levele Falk Miksához, 1891. szept. 7 [József Kiss' letter to Miksa Falk, September 7, 1891]. OSZK Kt. Fond IV/478; Mezei Mór levele Falk Miksához, 1900. dec. 14 [Mór Mezei's letter to Miksa Falk, December 14, 1900]. OSZK Kt. Fond IV/583; Mezei Ernő levele Falk Miksához, [1897.] dec. 14 [Ernő Mezei's letter to Miksa Falk, December 14, 1897]. OSZK Kt. Fond IV/581; Fleischmann Sándor levele Falk Miksához, 1901. okt. 19 [Sándor Fleischmann's letter to Miksa Falk, October 19, 1901]. OSZK Kt. Fond IV/264.

244. "Hymen," *Egyenlőség*, May 15, 1898, 12.

245. Franz Alexander, *The Western Mind in Transition: An Eyewitness Story* (New York: Random House, 1960), 9.

246. Póli Marczali, *Apám pályája, barátai: Emlékek Marczali Henrikről* (München, Germany: Aurora Kiskönyvek, 1973), 29, 44–45; Marczali, *Emlékeim*, 270–85.

247. Sz. [Szabolcsi], "Helfy Ignácz," 7.

248. "Falk," *Egyenlőség*, September 13, 1908, 9. Emphasis mine.

249. "Vámbéri Ármin," *Egyenlőség*, September 21, 1913, 9.

250. "Simonyi Zsigmond meghalt," 3.

251. "Esküvő," *Fővárosi Lapok* 19, no. 150 (1882): 946.

252. Bendl, *Lukács György élete a századfordulótól 1918-ig*, 156–57, 165–66, 169–71, 173–74.

253. Bánóczi József hagyatéka [Bequest of József Bánóczi], MZsML, XIX-5.

254. *Boëthius boldog fiatalsága*, 372.

255. Miksa Fenyő, *Önéletrajzom* (1964–1968) (Budapest: Argumentum, 1994), 49, 94–95, 98.

256. Litván, *Szabó Ervin*, 24.

257. Körmendi [Kulcsár], *Zsidó gyónás*, 89–90.

258. Weiser Károly közjegyző iratai: 1893, Wahrmann Sándor végrendelete [Károly Weiser's notarial documents: Sándor Wahrmann's will, 1893]. BFL, VII.185.—1893—1648.

259. György Kövér, "Liedemann és Wahrmann: 19. századi kereskedő-bankár családi stratégiák," in *A felhalmozás íve: Társadalom- és gazdaságtörténeti tanulmányok* (Budapest: Új Mandátum, 2002), 42.

260. Hajehudi Mardochái [Miksa Szabolcsi], "A szeretet jegyében," *Egyenlőség*, January 16, 1910, 10.

261. Kóbor, *Ki a ghettóból*, 1: 22–26, 132–34.

262. Hegedüs, *Előjátékok egy önéletrajzhoz*, 70–72.

263. Hoffmann, *Ködkárpit*, 111.

264. "Dombóvár," *Zsidó Szemle*, December 28, 1917, 7.

265. Istvánné Takács, *A dombóvári zsidóság története* (Dombóvár, Hungary: Dombóvári Városszépítő és Városvédő Egyesület, 2007), 80, 105.

266. Irén Sas, "Néhány vonal Bródy Sándor portréjához," *Múlt és Jövő* 14, no. 10 (1924): 302–04.

Afterword

From the Reform Era up to the First World War, most Hungarian Jews who converted to Christianity were motivated by worldly concerns. Some converted because the law—until October 1, 1895—prevented a Jew from marrying a Christian partner; after that date, some Jews converted as a result of the intolerance of a future Christian spouse or that spouse's family. Many abandoned their faith to liberate themselves from a restraint that limited their professional opportunities, even though this sort of discrimination was theoretically outlawed in 1867; many others did so seeking the acceptance of a Christian Hungarian society that theoretically embraced them even as Jews.

The story of the conversion of Hungarian Jews is the history of an unkept promise. In principle, the liberal nationalism that evolved in the Reform Era and dominated Hungarian political and cultural life throughout the age of the Dual Monarchy was fully in favor of accepting the country's Jews, partly because the Hungarian population's numerical superiority over the kingdom's other nationalities depended in part on its willingness to integrate its Jews. As prime minister Kálmán Tisza put it in reflecting on a speech by an antisemitic representative in 1887, "Hungary's Israelite citizens must not be pushed away; let us instead remove the obstacles that keep them from blending in."[1] Despite the prevalence of such declarations, the traditional elites who controlled the state apparatus were more than reluctant to hire their Jewish compatriots for jobs at public offices, only exceptionally admitted them into their social clubs, and never allowed them into their family circles. Though emancipation made Hungary's Jewish inhabitants the legal equals of their Christian countrymen and "reception" made Judaism the legal equal of Christian denominations, the spirit of these laws had little effect on the legislators who wrote them or on the overwhelming majority of Christian Hungarian society.

Most of the insurmountable barriers that confronted Hungarian Jews collapsed when they converted, and one might justifiably consider this as proof that the liberal promise of acceptance for Hungary's "Israelite citizens" was a lie. For faithful Jews who ran up against such barriers, it must have seemed so. At the same time, families, social organizations, and public offices whose doors were closed to Jews opened them for converts, indicating that the exclusionary impulses of the era were not yet fed primarily by racial theories. Converted Jews' origins were not forgotten, but the symbolic gesture of baptism was appreciated and generally rewarded. Jews who remained in the fold and suffered disadvantages because of it hardly appreciated the situation, but it was still considerably better than what was to come. In 1939, the lord-lieutenant of Hajdú-Bihar County ordered the chief of the Debrecen police to investigate whether any of the wives (!) of any of the applicants for a departmental chairmanship at the University of Debrecen had any "Jewish blood." As a result of this investigation, Bálint Hóman, minister of religion and public education, was advised to reject an otherwise "pure-bred Hungarian" candidate on the grounds that his wife, "reckoned by blood . . . is 25 percent Jewish."[2] Nothing of this sort took place in the Dualist era, which might be called the golden age of Hungarian Jewry—though only in comparison with what was to come.

Statistically speaking, the approximately 9,475 Hungarian Jews who converted to Christianity between 1896 and 1914 made up a vanishingly small proportion of the country's Jewish population, which numbered 911,227 in 1910. Even the 6,915 Jews who were baptized in the capital during the conversion fever of 1918–20 constituted only 3.21 percent of Budapest's 1920 Jewish population of 215,560. In other words, even in this calamitous period, in the city where a Hungarian Jew was most likely to convert, close to 97 percent of Budapest's Jews remained loyal to their faith.[3] If, on the other hand, we look at Hungarian Jews who distinguished themselves in various spheres, particularly cultural figures who achieved fame in their era and/or whose memory has lived on, the list of converts among them is decidedly long—a significant proportion of the total.

Neolog intellectuals believed that the best way to combat conversion was to develop cultural institutions capable of fostering a sense of Jewish belonging, inspiring greater attentiveness to religious life and making religious education

AFTERWORD 379

more effective by emphasizing the cultural values of Judaism.[4] However, most Hungarian Jews who converted did so not because they were indifferent to Judaism or ignorant of the beauty of its rituals or the greatness of Maimonides but because they wanted to liberate themselves from the social disadvantages of Jewishness. In an article published in *Egyenlőség* in December of 1900, Tamás Kóbor advised facing this temptation with patience and self-denial. The role model he cited was "the wretched peddler" who would sacrifice anything for his faith.[5] The intellectuals Kóbor was chastising did not possess any such piety. The reason, according to Miksa Szabolcsi, was not merely the influence of the zeitgeist but also Jewish parents' failures to instill in their children the commitment to Jewry and Judaism they had inherited from their own parents.[6] There is no doubt that a large majority of these Hungarian Jews passed on less than they received, yet we have no reason to assume they passed on less than their similarly acculturated and secularized coreligionists in England and France, whose rates of conversion remained significantly lower.

In a society more open to the integration of Jews, even a fragmented, lukewarm bourgeois Jewish identity was enough to keep conversion a sporadic phenomenon—even among individuals who aspired to the summits of society. As was the case elsewhere in Central Europe, in Hungary, where the Christian elite and middle class's tolerance of Jews' religious otherness was inversely proportional to Jews' efforts to integrate, this sort of lukewarm Jewishness was often insufficient inducement to remain in the Jewish fold.

Notes

1. *Képviselőházi napló, 1884–1887*, vol. 14 (Budapest: Pesti Könyvnyomda, 1887), 258.

2. Lajos Timár, *Vidéki városlakók: Debrecen társadalma 1920–1944* (Budapest: Magvető, 1993), 202.

3. Kovács, *A zsidóság térfoglalása Magyarországon*, 25.

4. Szabolcsi, "Apák vétke," 6; [id.], "Egy áttérés alkalmából," 3; "Hulló levelek," *Magyar-Zsidó Szemle* 16, no. 1 (1899): 2; Strausz, "A guvernántok," 6; Kayserling, "Mit kell tennünk," 1–2; Singer, "A kitérések, IX," 1–2; "A hatodik községkerület gyűlése," 240; "Zsidó egyházpolitika," *Egyenlőség*, May 10, 1903, supplement, 3.

5. Kóbor, "Modern makabeusok," 2.

6. M. Sz. [Miksa Szabolcsi], "A 'haladó' vidék, IV," *Egyenlőség*, August 15, 1890, 3.

BIBLIOGRAPHY

Archival Sources and Manuscript Collections

Budapest Főváros Levéltára (BFL, Budapest City Archives)
  Holitscher Szigfrid közjegyző iratai: 1912, Hatvany-Deutsch Sándor báró há-
    zassági szerződése [Szigfrid Holitscher's notarial documents: Baron Sándor
    Hatvany-Deutsch's marriage contract, 1912]. BFL, VII.187. – 1912 – 1940.
  Weiser Károly közjegyző iratai: 1893, Wahrmann Sándor végrendelete [Károly
    Weiser's notarial documents: Sándor Wahrmann's will, 1893]. VII.185. – 1893
    – 1648.
Budapest Történeti Múzeum (BTM, Budapest History Museum), Kiscelli
  Múzeum (Kiscell Museum), Térkép-, kézirat- és nyomtatványtár (Collection
  of Maps, Manuscripts and Prints)
  Vidor Tekla visszaemlékezései [Tekla Vidor's memoirs]. Gépirat. Ltsz. 87.40.1.
Library of the School of Slavonic and East European Studies (SSEES), University
  College of London
  Kónyi–Lónyay Papers
Magyar Nemzeti Levéltár Országos Levéltára (MNL OL, National Archives of
  Hungary, Budapest)
  Budapest – Neológ (Pesti Izraelita Hitközség) születési anyakönyvei [Buda-
    pest – Neolog birth records (of the Israelite Congregation of Pest)], A3562
    tekercs
  Jakubovits Ferenc névmagyarosítási kérelme [Jakubovits Ferenc's name
    change request]. K 150 BM 32 522–81.
  Kálvin téri református gyülekezet, keresztelési anyakönyvek [Baptismal re-
    cords of the Reformed congregation of Kálvin Square], A620. tekercs

382   BIBLIOGRAPHY

Szentistvánvárosi (Lipótvárosi) r. kath. plébánia, kereszteltek anyakönyve [Baptismal records of the Roman Catholic parish of Szentistvánváros (Lipótváros)], A60–A65. tekercs

Vámbéry Ármin levelei Theodor Herzlnek [Ármin Vámbéry's letters to Theodor Herzl], 1898–1901 [correctly: 1902]. X1184.4769.

Magyar Tudományos Akadémia Könyvtár és Információs Központ (MTA KIK, Library and Information Centre of the Hungarian Academy of Sciences, Budapest), Kézirattár (Department of Manuscripts)

Székács József emlékiratai [Memoirs of József Székács], 99. f. Ms 10.653/1.

Waldapfel János: Hatvany Lajosról [János Waldapfel: concerning Lajos Hatvany], 3. f. Ms 5371/116.

Magyar Zsidó Múzeum és Levéltár (MZsML, Hungarian Jewish Museum and Archives, Budapest)

Balázs Béla naplója [The Diary of Béla Balázs]. XIX: Hagyaték.

Bánóczi József hagyatéka [Bequest of József Bánóczi]. XIX-5.

Chevra-tagok névjegyzéke, 1804–1882 [List of Chevra members, 1804–1882].

Kitérési és prozelita jegyzőkönyvek [Records of converts and proselytes]. TB. B/67.

A Pesti izr. hitközség teljes képviseletének tagjai [Complete membership list of the board of the Israelite Congregation of Pest], 1910. PIH, I-C-1.

Práger Miklós emlékei [Memoirs of Miklós Práger]. XIX: Hagyaték.

Országos Széchényi Könyvtár (OSZK, National Széchényi Library, Budapest), Kézirattár (The Manuscripts Archive)

Ágai Adolf levele Falk Miksához, 1886. febr. 1 [Adolf Ágai's letter to Miksa Falk, Feb. 1st, 1886]. Fond IV/9.

Az Ellenzéki Kör pénztári könyve [Treasurer's Ledgers of the Opposition Circle], 1847–1849. Fol. Hung. 980.

Fleischmann Sándor levele Falk Miksához, 1901. okt. 19 [Sándor Fleischmann's letter to Miksa Falk, Oct. 19th, 1901]. Fond IV/264.

Jakab István miszteři tanácsos naplója 1848–1849-ből [Diary of the ministerial counselor Jakab István, 1848–1849]. Quart. Hung. 1315, 6.

Kiss József levele Falk Miksához, 1891. szept. 7 [József Kiss' letter to Miksa Falk, Sep. 7th, 1891]. Fond IV/478.

Mezei Ernő levele Falk Miksához, [1897.] dec. 14 [Ernő Mezei's letter to Miksa Falk, Dec. 14th (1897)]. Fond IV/581.

Mezei Mór levele Falk Miksához, 1900. dec. 14 [Mór Mezei's letter to Miksa Falk, Dec. 14th, 1900]. Fond IV/583.

Pikler Gyula Somló Bódognak, 1898. okt. 12 [Gyula Pikler's letter to Bódog Somló, Oct. 12th, 1898]. Levelestár.

Simonyi Zsigmond Concilia Emilnek, 1908. okt. 19 [Zsigmond Simonyi's letter to Emil Concilia, Oct. 19th, 1908]. Levelestár.

BIBLIOGRAPHY   383

Somló Bódog naplójegyzetei, 1898 [Bódog Somló's diaries, 1898]. Quart. Hung.
3038/1–2.

Somló Bódog szüleihez, 1896. nov. 26 [Bódog Somló's letter to his parents,
Nov. 26th, 1896]. Levelestár.

Szegfi Mór Szász Károlyhoz, 1882. dec. 30 [Mór Szegfi's letter to Károly Szász,
Dec. 30th, 1882]. Levelestár.

Veigelsberg Hugó levelei Tóth Bélához [Hugó Veigelsberg's letters to Béla
Tóth]. Fond 129/387.

Országos Széchényi Könyvtár (OSZK, National Széchényi Library, Budapest),
Plakát- és Kisnyomtatványtár (PK, Map, Poster and Small Print Collection)

Kunewalder Jónás: *Moses vallású magyarokhoz: Tisztelt testvérek! An die
Ungarn mosaischer Confession: Geehrte Brüder!* [Esztergom]: Beimel. Kny.
1848.2°/49.

A Pesti Műegyesület részvényeseinek névsora 1846. Pest: Landerer és Heckenast,
[1846], 9., Kny. 1846. 8°/22.

Petőfi Irodalmi Múzeum (PIM, Petőfi Literary Museum, Budapest), Kézirattár
(Manuscript Collection)

Biró Lajos vegyes feljegyzései [Lajos Biró's miscellaneous notes] I. V. 5586/48/17.

Print Sources

Periodicals

Akadémiai Értesítő (1899, 1906)
Alkotmány (1896, 1898, 1902, 1906–07, 1909–11, 1914)
Allgemeine Zeitung des Judenthums (1843–44)
Aradi Híradó (1902)
Aradi Közlöny (1902)
Autonómia (1914)
Ben Chananja (1862)
Borsszem Jankó (1870)
A Budai Izraelita Hitközség Értesítője (1911, 1913–14)
Budapesti Hírlap (1884–85, 1887, 1889–91, 1894–98, 1900–03, 1905–09, 1912–13)
Budapesti Közlöny (1901, 1907)
Budapesti Szemle (1862, 1893, 1901, 1910)
Délmagyarország (1913)
Der Ungar (1848)
Dunántúli Protestáns Lap (1896)
Egyenlőség (1882–86, 1888–1917, 1919, 1922–23, 1926–27, 1935, 1938)
Élet (1894, 1911)
Az Est (1910)

384 BIBLIOGRAPHY

Esztergom (1908)
Esztergom és Vidéke (1889)
Fehér Könyv (1915)
Fidibusz (1905)
Fővárosi Lapok (1871, 1875, 1878–84, 1889)
A Hét (1895, 1906)
Hevesvármegyei Hírlap (1894)
Hitközségi Szemle (1910–12)
Hivatalos Közlöny (1896, 1898)
Huszadik Század 11 (1903, 1905, 1908, 1910, 1912–14)
Igazságügyi Közlöny (1897)
Ismertető Összművészetben, Gazdaságban és Kereskedésben (1840)
Izr. Tanügyi Értesítő (1891, 1897, 1925)
Izraelita Hitközségi és Iskolai Lap (1873)
Izraelita Közlöny (1868)
Izraelita Lapok (1874)
Jelenkor (1841, 1843, 1848)
Jövendő (1903)
A Jövő (1897–98)
Jövőnk (1919)
Kakas Márton (1902)
Korunk (1927)
Magyar Géniusz (1892)
Magyar Hírlap (1917)
Magyar Izrael (1909, 1911)
Magyar Izraelita (1861–64, 1867)
Magyar Nap (1937)
Magyar Nyelvőr (1919)
Magyar Szemle (1895)
Magyar Zsidó (1909)
A Magyar Zsinagóga (1847)
Magyarország (1928)
A Magyar-Zsidó Ifjúság Lapja (1885–86)
Magyar-Zsidó Szemle (1884–85, 1887–92, 1896, 1899–1900, 1903, 1907, 1912, 1917)
Magyar-Zsidó Tanítók Lapja (1903)
Múlt és Jövő (1912–14, 1919–20, 1922, 1924, 1926, 1930, 1934–35)
Nemzeti Iskola (1900)
Népszava (1908)
Neues Pester Journal (1895)
Országos Gentry-Közlöny (1889)
Országos Hírlap (1897–98)

Országos Pályázati Közlöny (1902, 1906)

Pápai Lapok (1876)

Pesti Hírlap (1841–42, 1844, 1848, 1880, 1882, 1885, 1890–91, 1893, 1895–96, 1899–1900, 1905, 1912, 1913, 1917)

Pesti Napló (1880, 1882, 1894–96, 1905–07, 1910, 1917, 1928)

Protestáns Egyházi és Iskolai Lap (1844, 1867, 1891)

Reform (1848)

Regélő (1839, 1866)

Religio (before 1849 *Religio és Nevelés*) (1843–46, 1854–55, 1858, 1862, 1866, 1881)

Remény (1925)

Somogy (1882)

The Sunday At Home (1866)

Szalon Újság (1900–01, 1905–06)

Szegedi Napló (1880)

Szépirodalmi Közlöny (1858)

Szombat (1934)

Szombati Újság (1882–83)

Szombati Újság (1906)

Themis (1839)

Új Idők (1900)

Az Újság (1910)

Ungarische Wochenschrift (1902)

Vasárnapi Újság (1861, 1868, 1882, 1905, 1921)

Világ (1910–14)

Zsidó Híradó (1895, 1899–1900)

Zsidó Szemle (1914, 1917–18)

Yearbooks, Monographs, Essays, and Pamphlets

Ábrányi, Kornél, Jr. *Nemzeti ideál*. Budapest: Légrády Testvérek, 1898.

A budapesti társaság. Budapest: Pallas, 1886.

Ady, Endre. *Összes prózai művei*. Vol. 1. Compiled by Gyula Földessy. Budapest: Akadémiai, 1955.

——. *Összes prózai művei*. Vol. 10. Edited by József Láng and Erzsébet Vezér. Budapest: Akadémiai, 1973.

Ágoston, Péter. *A zsidók útja*. Nagyvárad: Nagyváradi Társadalomtudományi Társaság, 1917.

A Katholikus Népszövetség tíz éve, 1908–1918: A Katholikus Népszövetség elnökségének jelentése. Budapest: Katholikus Népszövetség Kiadása, 1918.

A katholikusok vagyoni helyzete Magyarországon. Budapest: Katholikus Népszövetség, [1914].

BIBLIOGRAPHY

Alexander, Bernát. "Bánóczi József." In *Emlékkönyv Bánóczi Józsefnek születése hetvenedik évfordulójára, 1919. július 4.*, 1–38. Budapest: Franklin-Társulat nyomdája, 1919.

———. "Zsidó problémák." In *Magyar zsidó almanach*, vol. 1, edited by József Patai, 185–89. Budapest: Magyar Zsidó Almanach, 1911.

Alfonz szerzetes. *Tévelygő Izráel vagy a zsidók felvilágosítása a szentírás alapján.* Szatmár: A "Pázmány-sajtó" nyomása, 1904.

A magyar és erdélyhoni izraelitáknak 1868–69-dik évi egyetemes gyűlésén alkotott szabályzatok és hozott határozatok. Pest: Pesti Könyvnyomda, 1869.

A magyar országgyűlés: A főrendiház és képviselőház tagjainak életrajzi adatai. Budapest: Magyar Tudósító, 1906.

A magyar szent korona országainak 1900. évi népszámlálása: A népszámlálási mű VII. kötetének kiegészítő része. Budapest: Athenaeum, 1906.

A Nemzeti Casinó szabályai és tagjainak névsora 1901. Budapest: Franklin-Társulat Nyomdája, 1902.

A nemzeti kaszinó évkönyve (1829, 1841, 1844–45, 1847–48, 1850, 1852, 1860, 1862, 1873, 1878, 1898)

A Park Club évkönyve (1900, 1912, 1914).

A Pesti Chevra Kadisa választóképes tagjainak névjegyzéke. [Budapest]: n.p., 1914.

A Pesti izr. hitközség elöljáróságának jelentése az . . . -iki közigazgatási évről (1901, 1907, 1910, 1913, 1914).

A Pesti Izr. Hitközség elöljáróságának jelentése az. közigazgatási évről. Budapest: n.p., 1915.

Arányi, Lajos. *Rudnó és lelkésze 1844 és 1845ben, meg még valami, többi közt a mai magyar zsidó is.* Pest: Emich Gusztáv, 1846.

"Arczképek és életrajzok: Szitányi Bernát." In *Szabadelvűpárti naptár az 1884. szökő évre*, vol. 1, edited by György Szathmáry, 132–33. Budapest: Athenaeum, n.d.

Asbóth, János. *Társadalom-politikai beszédei.* Budapest: Szent-Gellért-Nyomda, 1898.

Az 1861-ik évi magyar országgyűlés. Vol. 3/6. Pest: Osterlamm Károly, 1861.

Az Országos Kaszinó évi jelentése (1883, 1890, 1899)

Az Országos Kaszinó évkönyve 1913. Budapest: n.p., 1914.

A zsidókérdés Magyarországon: A Huszadik Század körkérdése. Budapest: A Társadalomtudományi Társaság Kiadása, 1917.

Ballagi, Aladár. "Ballagi Mór." In *Protestáns Új Képes Naptár 1879. évre*, edited by Sándor Dúzs, 17–25. Budapest: Franklin-Társulat, 1879.

Ballagi, Károly. *Magyarország és Erdély története kapcsolatban az egyetemes történelem legfőbb vonásaival: Izraelita népiskolák számára.* Pest: Heckenast Gusztáv, 1868.

Ballagi, Mór. "A kánon." In *Bibliai tanulmányok*, 8–85. Pest: Engel és Mandello, 1865.

BIBLIOGRAPHY 387

Bánffy, Dezső. *Magyar nemzetiségi politika*. Budapest: Légrády Testvérek, 1903.

Bangha, Béla. *A kereszténység és a zsidók*. Budapest: Mária Kongregáció, 1912.

Báttaszéki, Lajos. *A vérvád*. Budapest: Orsz. Központi Községi Nyomda, 1900.

Bergl, Joseph. *Geschichte der ungarischen Juden*. Leipzig: Wilhelm Friedrich, 1879.

Bernstein, Béla. *A negyvennyolcas magyar szabadságharc és a zsidók* (1898). Budapest: Múlt és Jövő, 1998.

———. "A zsidók története Vasmegyében (1912–1915)." In *Bernstein Béla emlékkönyv*, edited by Ibolya Mózer, 25–214. Szombathely: BDTF Történelem Tanszéke, 1998.

———. *Jókai és a zsidók: Zsidó vonatkozások és alakok összes műveiből*. Budapest: "Garai" Irodalmi és Nyomdai R.–T., 1925.

Birányi, Ákos. *Pesti forradalom (Martius 15–18.): Hiteles adatok nyomán*. Pest: Trattner Károly, 1848.

Blau, Lajos. "Vallásunk jelenéről és jövőjéről." In *Évkönyv 1900*, edited by József Bánóczi, 166–79. Budapest: IMIT, 1900.

Bleuer, Samu. *Mozgalmak a zsidóságban*. Budapest: n.p., 1904.

[Bloch, Móricz]. *Mózes öt könyve*. Vols. 1–5. Translated and notes by Móricz Bloch. Buda: Magyar Kir. Egyetem, 1840–41.

Bloch, Móritz. *A zsidókról*. Pest: Trattner-Károlyi, 1840.

Bojthor, Endre. *Az 1865-dik évi dec. hó 10-dikére összehívott országgyűlés képviselőháza tagjainak betűsoros név- és lakjegyzéke*. Pest: Emich Gusztáv, 1866.

———. *Az 1869-ik évi april 20-ára összehívott országgyűlés képviselőháza tagjainak betűsoros név- és lakjegyzéke*. Pest: Eggenberger, 1869.

———. *Az 1872-dik évi sept. hó 1-ső napjára összehívott országgyűlés képviselőháza tagjainak betűsoros név-, lak- és törvényhatóságok szerinti névjegyzéke*. Budapest: Eggenberger, 1875.

Budapest Székesfőváros Statisztikai és Közigazgatási Évkönyve. Vol. 11, 1909–1912. Budapest: Budapest Székesfőváros Statisztikai Hivatala, 1914.

Budapest Székesfőváros Statisztikai Évkönyve. Vol. 1, 1894. Budapest: Grill Károly, 1896.

Budapest Székesfőváros Statisztikai Évkönyve. Vol. 4, 1899–1901. Budapest: Grill Károly, 1904.

Buday, László. *A m. kir. központi statisztikai hivatal adatgyűjtéseinek magyarázata*. Budapest: Országos Központi Községi Nyomda, 1901.

Büchler, Sándor. *A zsidók története Budapesten a legrégibb időktől 1867-ig*. Budapest: Izraelita Magyar Irodalmi Társulat, 1901.

———. "De Judaeis." In *Évkönyv 1900*, edited by József Bánóczi, 286–304. Budapest: IMIT, 1900.

Büchler, Zsigmond. *Gondolatok és ötletek*. Kunszentmiklós: Schwarcz Lipót, 1910.

Carlyle, Gavin. *"Mighty in the Scriptures": A Memoir of Adolph Saphir, D. D.* London: John F. Shaw & Co., 1893.

388   BIBLIOGRAPHY

Csemegi, Károly. "Nagy férfiak méltatása; az egyéni érték elismerése." In *Művei*, vol. 1, edited by Károly Edvi Illés and Zsigmond Gyomai, 385–86. Budapest: Franklin-Társulat, 1904.

Csergő, Hugó. "A magyar zsidóság szerepe a századforduló szellemi életében." In *Zsidó írások . . . 5701 szivanra*, comp. Sándor Wasserstrom, 11–15. Budapest: Wasserstrom Sándor, 1941.

Csetényi, Imre. "A hatvanas évek és a zsidóság." In *Tanulmányok a zsidó tudomány köréből Dr. Guttmann Mihály emlékére*, edited by Sámuel Lőwinger, 98–114. Budapest: Neuwald Illés, 1946.

———. "Az ötvenes évek sajtója és a zsidókérdés." In *Emlékkönyv néhai dr. Kohn Sámuel pesti főrabbi születésének századik évfordulójára*, edited by Sámuel Lőwinger, 83–112. Budapest: Neuwald Illés, 1941.

Czirbusz, Géza. *Magyarország a XX. évszáz [sic] elején: Föld- és néprajzi, nemzetgazdasági és társadalomtudományi szempontból*. Temesvár: Pollatsek, 1902.

De le Roi, Joh. *Judentaufen im 19. Jahrhundert: Ein statistischer Versuch*. Leipzig, Germany: J. C. Hinrichs'sche Buchhandlung, 1899.

Deutsch, Antal. *A Pesti Lloyd-Társulat 1853–1903*. Budapest: Pesti Lloyd-Társulat, 1903.

Diósy, Márton. "A honi izraeliták között magyar nyelvet terjesztő pesti egylet; röviden: a magyarító egylet." In *Első magyar zsidó naptár és évkönyv 1848-ik szökőévre*, 81–93. Pest: Landerer és Heckenast, 1848.

Dohm, Christian Wilhelm. *Über die bürgerliche Verbesserung der Juden*. Berlin und Stettin: bei Friedrich Nicolai, 1781.

Dolányi (Kovács), Alajos. "A keresztény vallású, de zsidó származású népesség a népszámlálás szerint." *Magyar Statisztikai Szemle* 22, no. 4–5 (1944): 95–103.

Éber, Ábrahám. *A zsidó nép és a sionizmus*. Győr, Hungary: Gross Testvérek, 1900.

Edelstein, Bertalan. "Áldás és átok: Próbabeszéd, 1901. augusztus 10." In *Zsinagógai beszédek*, 1–8. Budapest: Szerző kiadása, 1906.

———. "Kétség és remény." In *Zsinagógai beszédek*, 19–26. Budapest: Szerző kiadása, 1906.

Edvi Illés, Károly. "Csemegi Károly élete és kora." In Károly Csemegi. *Művei*, vol. 1, edited by Károly Edvi Illés and Zsigmond Gyomai, VII–XXIII. Budapest: Franklin-Társulat, 1904.

Egy hitrokon. *A zsidók reformátiója*. Pest: Heckenast Gusztáv, 1867.

Egy jogász és egy bölcsész. *Kereszt, zsidó, vallás*. Budapest: Stephaneum, 1900.

Egy szabadelvű. *A zsidókérdés Magyarországon: Röpirat, melyben megbizonyíttatik, hogy a művelt zsidóknak áttérése valamelyik protestáns vallásra erkölcsileg igazolt és nagy politikai érdekek által sürgetett eljárás*. Budapest: Kókai Lajos, 1882.

BIBLIOGRAPHY 389

[Egy zsidó]. *A zsidókérdés.* Budapest: Wilckens és Waidl, [1884/1885].

Ehrlich, Gusztáv G. "Ötven éve dolgozom." In *Zsidó évkönyv az 5688. bibliai évre,* edited by Vilmos Kecskeméti, 245–46. Budapest: n.p., 1927–28.

Einhorn, I[gnaz]. *Die Revolution und die Juden in Ungarn.* Leipzig: Carl Geibel, 1851.

Eisler, Mátyás. "A magyar zsidók emancipációja." In *Évkönyv 1908,* edited by József Bánóczi, 304–14. Budapest: IMIT, 1908.

Ellrich, August. *Die Ungarn wie sie sind.* Berlin: Vereins-Buchhandlung, 1831.

Előadási anyagok gyűjteménye: Katholikus körök, egyesületek és szervezetek vezetőinek használatára. Vol. 1. Budapest: Katholikus Népszövetség, 1912.

Első jósok. Translated and notes by Móritz Bloch. Buda: Magyar Kir. Egyetem, 1841.

Első magyar zsidó naptár és évkönyv 1848-ik szökőévre. Pest: Landerer és Heckenast, 1848.

Eötvös, József. *A zsidók emancipációja* (1841). Budapest: Magvető, 1981.

———. *Vallomások és gondolatok.* Budapest: Magyar Helikon, 1977.

… *évi jelentés a pesti lovaregylet munkálódásairól* (1845, 1852–53, 1865).

Falk, Miksa. "A pálya kezdetén (1888)." In *Kor- és jellemrajzok,* edited by Ernő Falk, 1–23. Budapest: Révai Testvérek, 1903.

Farkas, Ödön. *A zsidó kérdés Magyarországon.* Budapest: Aigner Lajos, 1881.

Fischer, Gyula, and Gábor Weisz. *Rachel: Imák zsidó nők számára.* Budapest: Schwarz Ignácz, 1908.

Forgács, Gyula. *A százéves skót misszió.* Budapest: Szerző kiadása, 1941.

Forrai, Gábor. *A Pesti Izraelita Nőegylet 1866–1891.* Budapest: Hungária, 1891.

Főrendiházi napló, 1881–1884. Vol. 2. Budapest: Pesti Könyvnyomda, 1884.

Főrendiházi napló, 1892–1897. Vol. 4. Budapest: Pesti Könyvnyomda, 1895.

Frieder, Mór. *A magyar zsidók egyenjogosítása 1867-dik évben.* Pest: Hornyánszky és Träger, 1868.

Frisch, Ármin. "Az egyházpolitika jegyében." In *Évkönyv 1899,* edited by Vilmos Bacher and József Bánóczi, 200–15. Budapest: IMIT, 1899.

Gáspár, Lajos. *Nézetek az izraëliták felszabadításáról.* Pest: Engel és Mandello, 1861.

Gedeon [Kupár, Rezső]. "Keresztény hegemónia." In *A zsidókérdés Magyarországon,* 5–8. Budapest: Szent Gellért Könyvnyomda, 1898.

Gracza, György. *Az 1848–49-iki magyar szabadságharcz története.* Vol. 1. Budapest: Lampel Róbert, [1895].

Groszmann, Zsigmond. *A magyar zsidók a XIX. század közepén (1849–1870).* Budapest: Egyenlőség, 1917.

———. *A magyar zsidók V. Ferdinánd alatt (1835–1848).* Budapest: Egyenlőség, 1916.

———. "A pesti zsidó gyülekezet alkotmányának története." In *Emlékkönyv dr. Hevesi Simon pesti vezető főrabbinak, papi működése negyvenedik évfordulójára,* edited by Mihály Guttmann, Sámuel Lőwinger, Ferenc Hevesi, and Dénes Friedmann, 126–72. Budapest: Neuwald Illés, 1934.

———. "A pesti zsidóság vezetői." In *Emlékkönyv dr. Kiss Arnold budai vezető főrabbi hetvenedik születésnapjára*, edited by Mihály Guttmann, Simon Hevesi, and Sámuel Lőwinger, 51–57. Budapest: Lőwinger, 1939.

———. "Vallásoktatásunk." In *Tanulmányok a zsidó tudomány köréből Dr. Guttmann Mihály emlékére*, edited by Sámuel Lőwinger, 273–82. Budapest: Neuwald Illés, 1946.

Gubernatis, Angelo de. *La Hongrie politique et sociale*. Florence: Joseph Pellas, 1885.

Hajdu, Miklós. *Konfesszionális vizeken*. Budapest: A Páholy sajátja, 1912.

Halász, Sándor, ed. *Országgyűlési almanach 1886: Képviselőház*. Budapest: Athenaeum, 1886.

Handler, Márk. *A nő áldásdús befolyása: Szónoklat*. Budapest: Burián Mór, 1881.

———. "Szónoklat." In *Jubiláris emlékmű Handler Márk tatai rabbi 40 éves hivatali jubileuma alkalmából*, edited by Simon Hevesi (Handler) lugosi rabbi, 19–28. Lugos, Hungary: Handler Rudolf, 1904.

Hanuy, Ferencz. *A vallásváltoztatás az egyházjog és a magyar államjog szerint*. Pécs, Hungary: Taisz József, 1905.

Hartmán, Lipót. *Magyar zsidó, vagy: zsidó magyar?* Pécs, Hungary: Lyceumi nyomda, 1848.

Hatvany, Lajos. "Magyar írók száműzetésben" (1924). In *Utak, sorsok, emberek*, 439–46. Budapest: Szépirodalmi, 1973.

Heinrich, Gusztáv. *Emlékbeszéd Klein Lipót Gyula kültag felett*. Budapest: M. T. Akadémia, 1882.

Heller, Bernát. "Kármán Mór, 1843–1915." In *Évkönyv 1916*, edited József Bánóczi, 251–84. Budapest: IMIT, 1916.

Hentaller, Lajos. *Politikusaink pongyolában: Tollrajzok a képviselőházból*. Budapest: Kókai Lajos, 1886.

Herczeg, Ferencz. "Zsúrok és zsúr-látogatók." In *A mulató Budapest*, edited by Henrik Lenkei, 145–52. Budapest: Singer és Wolfner, 1896.

Herczfeld, Sándor. *Mi nem megyünk Amerikába, hanem itt fogunk maradni!* Pest: Trattner-Károlyi, 1848.

Hevesi, Simon. *Vallástani előkészítő a konfirmáns leányok számára*. Budapest: Lampel R., 1914.

Hoffmann, Mór. *A nemzetiség és a nemzeti nyelv*. Nagykanizsa: Fischel Fülöp, 1877.

———. *A sémiták és antisemiták*. Budapest: Franklin, 1883.

———. *Zsidóinkról! Igaza van-e Csernátony Lajos úrnak vagy nincs?* Nagykanizsa: Fischel Fülöp, 1874.

Hoitsy, Pál. *Régi magyar alakok: A letűnt nemzedék férfiai*. Budapest: Légrády Testvérek Kiadása, [1923].

BIBLIOGRAPHY 391

Horovicz, Jenő. *A zsidók mint választók, vagy: a zsidók a politikában*. Besztercze, Hungary: Szerző kiadása, 1892.

Horváth, János. *A magyar királyság közjoga*. Budapest: Dobrowsky és Franke, 1894.

Huszár, Károly. *A keresztények legyenek-e zsidók?* Budapest: Bagó Márton és Fia, 1884.

Imre, Sándor. *Emlékbeszéd Ballagi Mór M. T. Akad. r. tagról*. Budapest: Akadémiai, 1893.

Istóczy, Győző. *Országgyűlési beszédei, indítványai és törvényjavaslatai, 1872–1896*. Budapest: Buschmann F., 1904.

J., G. *Némelly igénytelen nézetek, vallásilag véve, a magyarhoni zsidók meghonosítása ügyében*. Kőszeg: Reichard Károly, 1843.

Jászi, Oszkár. *A nemzeti államok kialakulása és a nemzetiségi kérdés*. Budapest: Grill Károly, 1912.

———. *Miért léptem ki a "Világ" szerkesztőségéből?* Budapest: Világosság, 1911.

Jelentés a budapesti Lipótvárosi Casinó 25 éves fennállása alkalmából. Budapest: Löbl Nyomda, 1907.

Jiszrael könyörgései egész évre. Translated by Móricz Rosenthal. Edited by Móricz Bloch. Pozsony, Hungary: Korn Fülöp, 1841.

Kais. Königl. Militär-Schematismus für 1885. Wien: K. K. Hof- und Staatsdruckerei, 1884.

Kais. Königl. Militär-Schematismus für 1888. Wien: K. K. Hof- und Staatsdruckerei, 1887.

Kármán, Mór. *Löw Lipót emlékezete: Alkalmi beszédek*. Budapest: Singer és Wolfner, 1911.

Kayserling, M. *Zsidó nők a történelem, az irodalom és a művészet terén*. Vols. 1–2. Budapest: Révai Testvérek, 1883.

Kellér, Andor. *Mayer Wolf fia (Wahrmann Mór életregénye)*. [Budapest]: Hungária, [1941].

Kempelen, Béla. *Magyar zsidó családok*. Vols. 1–3. Budapest: Makkabi, 1999.

Képviselőházi irományok, 1892–1897. Vol. 10. Budapest: Pesti Könyvnyomda, 1893.

Képviselőházi napló, 1869–1872. Vol. 5. Pest: Légrády Testvérek, 1870.

Képviselőházi napló, 1872–1875. Vol. 11. Buda: Magyar Királyi Államnyomda, 1874.

Képviselőházi napló, 1878–1881. Vol. 10. Budapest: Pesti Könyvnyomda, 1880.

Képviselőházi napló, 1881–1884. Vol. 6. Budapest: Pesti Könyvnyomda, 1882.

Képviselőházi napló, 1881–1884. Vol. 9. Budapest: Pesti Könyvnyomda, 1883.

Képviselőházi napló, 1881–1884. Vol. 13. Budapest: Pesti Könyvnyomda, 1883.

Képviselőházi napló, 1881–1884. Vol. 14. Budapest: Pesti Könyvnyomda, 1884.

Képviselőházi napló, 1884–1887. Vol. 14. Budapest: Pesti Könyvnyomda, 1887.

Képviselőházi napló, 1887–1892. Vol. 20. Budapest: Pesti Könyvnyomda, 1890.

Képviselőházi napló, 1892–1897. Vol. 3. Budapest: Pesti Könyvnyomda, 1892.

Képviselőházi napló, 1892–1897. Vol. 20. Budapest: Pesti Könyvnyomda, 1894.

Képviselőházi napló, 1892–1897. Vol. 25. Budapest: Pesti Könyvnyomda, 1895.

Képviselőházi napló, 1906–1911. Vol. 1. Budapest: Athenaeum, 1906.

Kiss, Arnold. *Mirjam: Imádságok zsidó nők számára.* Veszprém: Köves és Boros kiadása, [1898].

Kiss, Jenő Sándor. "Bevezetés." In József Kiss, *Legendák a nagyapámról,* 7–16. Budapest: Kiadják Kiss József gyermekei, 1916.

Kiss, József (Szentesi, Rudolf), ed. *Zsidó évkönyv.* Vol. 1, *5636 (1875–1876).* Budapest: Franklin-Társulat, 1875.

Kohn, Sámuel. "Az Istenben való öröm a mi erősségünk." In *Zsinagógai szónoklatok,* 18–24. Budapest: Rosenberg Testvérek, 1875.

———. "Újévünk intése." In *Zsinagógai szónoklatok,* 1–9. Budapest: Rosenberg Testvérek, 1875.

Koricsáner, János. *Kiáltó szó a pusztában, vagy pedig miképen mozdíthatjuk elő az emberi nemnek boldogságát?* Pest: Gyurian József, 1862.

Kossuth, Lajos. *Iratai.* Vol. 9. Edited by Ferencz Kossuth. Budapest: Athenaeum, 1902.

Kovács, Alajos. *A zsidóság térfoglalása Magyarországon.* Budapest: Szerző kiadása, 1922.

Kovács, Ferencz, ed. *Az 1843/44-ik évi magyar országgyűlési alsó tábla kerületi üléseinek naplója.* Vols. 1–6. Budapest: Franklin-Társulat, 1894.

Kőhalmi, Béla. *Könyvek könyve.* Budapest: Lantos, [1918].

Kőrösi, József. "Buda és Ó-buda városa népességének évenkénti kimutatása 1813-tól 1857-ig." *Statisztikai Havi Füzetek* 9, no. 5 (1881): 131–37.

Krausz, Bernát. *A zsidóság egyesülése: Két felekezet-e a zsidóság?* Gyöngyös, Hungary: Szerző kiadása, 1908.

Lichtenstein, J. *Zsidók tükre.* Budapest: Feinsilber Róbert, 1908.

Ligeti, Ernő. "Emőd Tamás." In *Ararát: Magyar zsidó évkönyv az 1944. évre,* edited by Aladár Komlós, 55–65. Budapest: Országos Izr. Leányárvaház, 1944.

Linzbauer, Franciscus Xav. *Codex sanitario-medicinalis Hungariae.* Vol. 2. Budae: Typis Caesareo-Regiae Scientiarum Universitatis, 1852.

———. *Codex sanitario-medicinalis Hungariae.* Vol. 3, sectio 1. Budae: Typis Caesareo-Regiae Scientiarum Universitatis, 1853.

Lőrintei, István. *Magyarország nagybirtokosai.* Szatmár: "Szabad Sajtó" Könyvnyomda, 1893.

Löw, Immánuel. *Beszédei 1874–1899.* Szeged: Traub B. és Társa, 1900.

Löw, Immánuel and Zsigmond Kulinyi. *A szegedi zsidók 1785-től 1885-ig.* Szeged, Hungary: Szegedi Zsidó Hitközség, 1885.

Löw, Leopold. *Der jüdische Kongress in Ungarn, historisch beleuchtet: Beitrag zur Rechts-, Religions- und Kulturgeschichte.* Pest: Verlag von L. Aigner, 1871.

Löw, Leopold. *Gesammelte Schriften.* Vol. 4. Edtied by Immanuel Löw. Szegedin, Hungary: Ludwig Engel, 1898.

BIBLIOGRAPHY 393

Lukács, György. "Előszó." In *Magyar irodalom—magyar kultúra: Válogatott tanulmányok*, 5–21. Budapest: Gondolat, 1970.

Madarász, István. *A vallásváltoztatás magyar közjogi szempontból*. Budapest: Szerző kiadása, 1938.

Magyar Statisztikai Évkönyv. New series, vol. 15, *1907*. Budapest: Athenaeum, 1909.

Magyar Statisztikai Évkönyv. New series, vol. 18, *1910*. Budapest: Athenaeum, 1911.

Magyar Statisztikai Közlemények. New series, vol. 1. Budapest: Pesti Könyvnyomda, 1893.

Magyar Statisztikai Közlemények. New series, vol. 16. Budapest: Athenaeum, 1906.

Magyar Statisztikai Közlemények. New series, vol. 27. Budapest: Athenaeum, 1909.

Magyar Statisztikai Közlemények. New series, vol. 36. Budapest: Pesti Könyvnyomda, 1911.

Magyar Statisztikai Közlemények. New series, vol. 56. Budapest: Pesti Könyvnyomda, 1915.

Magyar Statisztikai Közlemények. New series, vol. 64. Budapest: Athenaeum, 1920.

Magyarországi rendeletek tára 1878. Budapest: M. Kir. Belügyministerium, 1878.

Mandl, Bernát. "A pesti izr. hitközségi fiúiskola monográfiája." In *A magyar-zsidó felekezet elemi és polgári iskoláinak monográfiája*, vol. 1, edited by Jónás Barna and Fülöp Csukási, 1–112. Budapest: Corvina, 1896.

Matók, Béla. *A Zsidó Kérdés, Nro. 2*. Budapest: Kocsi Sándor, 1881.

Melichár, Kálmán. *Egyházi szervezet és vallásügyi igazgatás Magyarországon*. Budapest: Pallas, 1902.

Mikszáth, Kálmán. *Cikkek és karcolatok*. Vol. 7, *1879*. Edited by József Nacsády. Budapest: Akadémiai, 1968.

———. *Cikkek és karcolatok*. Vol. 10, *1880–1881*. Edited by József Nacsády and Gyula Bisztray. Budapest: Akadémiai, 1970.

———. *Cikkek és karcolatok*. Vol. 12, *1881. augusztus–december*. Edited by Gyula Bisztray. Budapest: Akadémiai, 1971.

Mit akar a néppárt? Budapest: Szent Gellért Könyvnyomda, 1895.

Mócsy, Antal. "A zsidó-kérdésről." In *A zsidókérdés Magyarországon*, 9–12. Budapest: Szent Gellért Könyvnyomda, 1898.

Munkácsi, Bernát. *A Pesti Izraelita Hitközség oktatásügyének értesítője az 1904/905. iskolaévre*. Budapest: Kállai Ármin, 1904.

———. *A Pesti Izraelita Hitközség oktatásügyének értesítője az 1912–13. iskolaévre*. Budapest: Breitner Károly, 1912.

Münstermann, Győző. *A középosztály önvédelme*. Kolozsvár: Ajtai K. Albert, 1904.

Neumann, Ede. *A nagykanizsai izr. hitközség hitoktatási intézményei az 1909–1910. tanévben*. Nagykanizsa: Krausz és Farkas, 1910.

———. *A nagykanizsai izr. hitközség hitoktatási intézményei az 1912–1913. tanévben*. Nagykanizsa: Gutenberg-Nyomda, 1913.

BIBLIOGRAPHY

Nordau, Max. "My Recollections of Vambéry." In *The Life and Adventures of Arminius Vambéry*, XV–XXIV. London: T. Fisher Unwin, 1914.

Oesterreicher, Elias. *Der Jude in Ungarn wie er war, wie er ist und wie er seyn wird*. Pesth: Trattner-Károlyi, 1842.

Pardoe, Miss. *The City of the Magyar, or Hungary and Her Institutions in 1839–40*. Vols. 1–3. London: George Virtue, 1840.

Pásztor, Mihály. *Cifra nyomorúság: Adatok a modern Budapestről*. Budapest: Nap Nyomda RT., [1909].

Patai, József. *Herzl*. Budapest: A »Pro Palesztina« kiadása, [1932].

Perls, Ármin. "Nemzet és felekezet." In *Szónoklatok*, vol. 4, 19–25. Pécs, Hungary: Pécsi Irodalmi és Könyvnyomdai R.-T., [1912].

Petrássevich, Géza. *Magyarország és a zsidóság*. Budapest: Szent Gellért Könyvnyomda, 1899.

Platz, Bonifácz. *Katholikus levelek egy megtérő nőhöz*. Budapest: Szent-István-Társulat, 1902.

Pollák, Miksa. *A zsidók története Sopronban: A legrégibb időktől a mai napig*. Budapest: IMIT, 1896.

Radnóti, József. *Kornfeld Zsigmond*. Budapest: Szerző kiadása, [1931].

Rákosi, Jenő. "Budapest városrészei." In *Az Osztrák–Magyar Monarchia írásban és képben*, vol. 9, *Magyarország III. kötete*, 169–92. Budapest: Magyar Királyi Állami Nyomda, 1893.

Recouly, Raymond. *Le pays magyar*. Paris: Félix Alcan, 1903.

Révész, György. *A zsidó Jókai regényeiben*. Nyíregyháza, Hungary: Szerző kiadása, 1940.

Rf., J. [Reif, Jakab]. *Kosmopolitismus és nationalismus, különös tekintettel a zsidóság jelenkori állására*. Budapest: Reach Zs. kiadása, 1875.

Richtmann, Mózes. *Landau Ezekiel prágai rabbi (1713–1793) és a magyar zsidók*. Budapest: Athenaeum, 1905.

Ruppin, Arthur. *The Jews of To-Day*. Translated by Margery Bentwich. New York: Henry Holt and Company, 1913.

S., A. *Zsidó vagyok-e én? Párbeszéd egy névleges és egy tényleges zsidó között*. Budapest: Vallásos Iratokat Terjesztő Társulat, 1901.

Samter, N. *Judentaufen im neunzehnten Jahrhundert: Mit besonderer Berücksichtigung Preußens*. Berlin: M. Poppelauer, 1906.

Schächter, Miksa. "Az assimilatióról." In *Évkönyv 1905*, edited by József Bánóczi, 265–83. Budapest: IMIT, 1905.

Schmittely, József, ed. *Pesti Hírlap naptára az 1919. közönséges évre*. Budapest: Légrády Testvérek, n.d.

Schwab, Arszlán. *A zsidók: Fölvilágosító értekezés*. Edited and notes by Móritz Bloch. Buda: Magyar Kir. Egyetem, 1840.

———. *Emlékeztetés a vallásban nyert oktatásra*. Buda: Magyar Kir. Egyetem, 1846.

BIBLIOGRAPHY

Singer, Izrael. *Emlék-könyv 50 éves néptanítói és hittanári működésemből*. Sátoral-jaújhely, Hungary: Alexander Vilmos, 1904.

———. *Vallástan az izraelita ifjúság számára*. Budapest/Sátoraljaújhely, Hungary: Klein Alfréd Könyvkiadása, 1876.

Steed, Henry Wickham. *The Habsburg Monarchy*. London: Constable, 1913.

Sturm, Albert, ed. *Új országgyűlési almanach 1887–1892: Rövid életrajzi adatok a főrendiház és a képviselőház tagjairól*. Budapest: Ifjabb Nagel Ottó, 1888.

Szabó, Imre. "A budapesti reformátusság lelki rajza." In *Íme, a magvető kiméne vetni*, 3–14. Budapest: n.p., 1928.

Szabolcsi, Miksa. *Az áldozat: Kor- és jellemkép*. Budapest: "Jókai" Könyvnyomdai Műintézet, 1908.

Szatmári, Mór. *Közszellemünk fogyatkozásai*. Budapest: Werbőczy Nyomda, 1898.

Székely, Ferenc. "Két levél." In *Évkönyv 1897*, edited by Vilmos Bacher and József Bánóczi, 79–85. Budapest: IMIT, 1897.

Szendrey, Gerzson, and József Gareis, eds. *A függetlenségi és 48-as antiszemitapárt alapja és létjoga Magyarországon*. Budapest: Buschmann F., 1887.

[Szentiványi, Zoltán]. *Századunk névváltoztatásai 1800–1893*. Budapest: Hornyánszky Viktor, 1895.

Szerencs, János, ed. *A főrendiház évkönyve*. Vol. 3. Budapest: Pesti Könyvnyomda, 1907.

Szűcs, István. *Szabad királyi Debreczen város történelme*. Vol. 3. Debreczen, Hungary: A Város Könyvnyomdája, 1871.

Theilhaber, Felix. A. *Der Untergang der deutschen Juden: Eine volkswirtschaftliche Studie*. München, Germany: Ernst Reinhardt Verlag, 1911.

Tomcsányi, Lajos. *Báró Barkóczy Sándor D^R*. Budapest: n.p., 1925.

Tóthfalussy, Béla. *A keresztény és a zsidó vallás összehasonlítása*. Budapest: Athenaeum, 1900.

Trefort, Ágoston. "A pozsonyi I. választókerületben 1884. június 22. tartott beszéd." In *Beszédek és levelek*, 141–56. Budapest: Méhner Vilmos, 1888.

Új kormány. Budapest: Singer és Wolfner, 1894.

Ujvári, Péter, ed. *Zsidó Lexikon*. Budapest: A Zsidó Lexikon kiadása, 1929.

Vajda, Béla. "Szabolcsi Miksa, 1857–1915." In *Évkönyv 1916*, edited by József Bánóczi, 208–13. Budapest: IMIT, 1916.

Vambéry, Hermann. *Deutsch-Türkisches Taschen-Woertebuch*. Constantinopel: Gebrüder Koehler, 1858.

Vázsonyi, Vilmos. *Beszédei és írásai*. Vols. 1–2. Edited by Hugó Csergő and József Balassa. Budapest: Az Országos Vázsonyi-Emlékbizottság kiadása, 1927.

Venetianer, Lajos. *A magyar zsidóság története a honfoglalástól a világháború kitöréséig*. Budapest: Fővárosi Nyomda, 1922.

Vereby, Soma. *A zsidókról és ezeréves szenvedéseikről*. Bécs: Manz Nyomda, 1858.

Vigyázó, Gyula. *A magyar zsidóság és a keresztény társadalom.* N.p.: Szerző kiadása, 1908.

Weiller, Ernő. "Jelentés." In *Cultur-Almanach,* vol. 2, 1911–12, edited by Simon Hevesi, 108–19. Budapest: OMIKE, 1912.

Weisz, Ignácz. *A zsidók és a nemzetiségek.* Brassó, Hungary: A "Brassó" Könyvnyomdája, 1894.

Weisz, Sámuel. *A Budapest-Lipótvárosi imaházegyesület (előbb Lipótvárosi Talmudtóra-Egyesület) 25 éves története.* Budapest: Jakab-Nyomda, 1930.

Weszprémy, Kálmán, Jr. *A Magyarországi zsidók statisztikája.* Debreczen, Hungary: Debreczen Sz. Kir. Város Könyvnyomda-Vállalata, 1907.

Zboray, Miklós. "Tanuljunk összetartást." In *A Katholikus Népszövetség naptára 1911-re,* 67–70. Budapest: Katholikus Népszövetség, 1910.

Zeller, Árpád. *A magyar egyházpolitika 1847–1894.* Vols. 1–2. Budapest: Boruth E., 1894.

[Zimándy, Ignác]. *Mi tett engem antiszemitává?* Budapest: "Hunyadi Mátyás" Könyvnyomdai Intézet, 1886.

Memoirs, Diaries, Correspondence, Literary Fiction, Jokebooks

Ábrányi, Kornél, Jr. *Régi és új nemesek.* Budapest: Athenaeum, 1881.

Acsády, Ignác. "Áttérések a múltban." In *Évkönyv 1905,* edited by József Bánóczi, 75–84. Budapest: IMIT, 1905.

[Ágai, Adolf]. *Abrincs! 150 jordány vicz Seiffensteiner Salamontul.* Budapest: Athenaeum, 1879.

Alexander, Franz. *The Western Mind in Transition: An Eyewitness Story.* New York: Random House, 1960.

Ambrus, Zoltán. *Berzsenyi báró és családja: Tollrajzok a mai Budapestről* (1902). Budapest: Révai Testvérek, 1906.

Angyal, Dávid. *Emlékezések* (1943). Edited by Lóránt Czigány. London: Szepsi Csombor Kör, 1971.

Balázs, Béla. *Álmodó ifjúság* (1946). Budapest: Magvető/Szépirodalmi, 1976.

———. *Levelei Lukács Györgyhöz: Egy szövetség dokumentumai.* Edited by Júlia Lenkei. [Budapest]: MTA Filozófiai Intézet/Lukács Archívum, 1982.

———. *Napló 1903–1914.* Budapest: Magvető, 1982.

———. *Napló 1914–1922.* Budapest: Magvető, 1982.

Bartók, Béla. *Családi levelei.* Edited by Béla Bartók Jr. Budapest: Zeneműkiadó, 1981.

Bauer, Hilda. *Emlékeim: Levelek Lukácshoz.* Budapest: MTA Filozófiai Intézet/Lukács Archívum, 1985.

Benedek, Elek. *Édes anyaföldem! Egy nép s egy ember története.* Vols. 1–2. Budapest: Pantheon, 1920.

BIBLIOGRAPHY

————. *Katalin*. Budapest: Athenaeum, 1896.

Benedek, Marcell. *Naplómat olvasom*. Budapest: Szépirodalmi, 1965.

Boëthius boldog fiatalsága: Demény János válogatása Molnár Antal leveleiből és írásaiból. Budapest: Magvető, 1989.

Boros, Géza. *"Folik vagy nem folik?" Egy kupléénekes emlékei*. Budapest: Szerző kiadása, 1942.

Brámer, Frigyes. "Zsidó élet Pesten a század elején." In *Évkönyv 1977/78*, edited by Sándor Scheiber, 91–95. Budapest: MIOK, 1978.

Bródy, István. *Régi pesti dáridók: Egy letűnt világ regénye*. Budapest: Szerző kiadása, 1940.

Bródy, Miksa, Kornél Tábori, and Szomaházy István. *Börzehumor*. Budapest: Vidám Könyvtár, [1912].

Brody, Samu. "A zsidó hitközség élete." In *Emlékezések*, 9–18. Gyula, Hungary: Corvina nyomda, 1903.

Bródy, Sándor. "Oroszlánszívű Richárd utolsó órája." In *Elmélkedések*, 3–10. Budapest: Lampel R., [1914].

————. "Tímár Liza" (1914). In *Színház*, 351–430. Budapest: Szépirodalmi, 1964.

Busbach, Péter. *Egy viharos emberöltő. Korrajz*. Vol. 2. Budapest: Kilián Frigyes, 1899.

Csiky, Gergely. "Az Atlasz család (1890)." In *Századvég*, vol. 1., edited by Anna Szalai, 361–560. Budapest: Szépirodalmi, 1984.

Czakó, Zsigmond. "A könnyelműek" (1847). In *Összes művei*, vol. 1, edited by József Ferenczy, 313–403. Budapest: Aigner Lajos, [1883/1884].

Dóczi, Lajos. "Hogy tanultam magyarul." In *Magyar szellemi élet: Elbeszélések és rajzok a magyar írók és művészek életéből*, edited by Mihály Igmándi, 8–9. Budapest: Hornyánszky Viktor, 1892.

————. *Vegyes párok*. Budapest: Ráth Mór, 1889.

Drukk! Humorisztikus naptár az 1882-ik ordenáré esztendőre. Budapest: Athenaeum, [1882].

Eötvös, József. *Levelek*. [Budapest]: Magyar Helikon, 1976.

Eötvös, Károly. "Csemegi Károlyról" (1899). In *Magyar alakok*, 174–86. Budapest: Révai Testvérek, 1901.

————. "Szitányi Bernát halálára" (1889). In *Magyar alakok*, 126–30. Budapest: Révai Testvérek, 1901.

[Farkas, Pál]. *Egy önkéntes naplója: Második félév: Az üteg*. Budapest: Singer és Wolfner, 1911.

Fenyő, Miksa. *Önéletrajzom* (1964–1968). Budapest: Argumentum, 1994.

Förster, Aurél. *Anekdoták*. Vol. 1. Budapest: "Stádium" Sajtóvállalat RT. Kiadása, 1925.

Gábor, Andor. "A Zsazsa." In *Erélyes elégia*, 37. Budapest: Szépirodalmi, 1967.

————. *Doktor Senki* (1918). Budapest: Szépirodalmi, 1982.

Gelléri, Andor Endre. *Egy önérzet története* (1957). Budapest: Szépirodalmi, 1966.

Goldziher, Ignác. *Napló.* Budapest: Magvető, 1984.

Gömöry, János. *Emlékeim egy letűnt világról.* Budapest: Szépirodalmi, 1964.

Gracza, György. *A nevető Magyarország.* Vol. 2. Budapest: Lampel Róbert, 1901.

Grósz, Emil. *Ötven év munkában.* Budapest: Királyi Magyar Egyetemi Nyomda, 1939.

Gyergyai, Albert. "Egy barátságos ház története." In *Magyar zenetörténeti tanulmányok Kodály Zoltán emlékére,* edited by Ferenc Bónis, 411–25. Budapest: Zeneműkiadó, 1977.

Hatvany, Lajos. *Levelei.* Selected and edited by Lajosné Hatvany and István Rozsics. Budapest: Szépirodalmi, 1985.

———. *Zsiga a családban.* Budapest: Genius, [1927].

Hatvany, Ludwig. *Bondy Jr.* Translated by Hannah Waller. London: Hutchinson, 1931.

———. *Bondy Jr.: Ein Roman.* München, Germany: Drei Masken, 1929.

Hegedüs, Géza. *Előjátékok egy önéletrajzhoz.* Budapest: Szépirodalmi, 1982.

Herczeg, Ferenc. *Andor és András* (1903). Budapest: Singer és Wolfner, 1925.

Hevesi, Sándor. "Egy magyar író konverziójának története" (1930s). *Vigilia* 13, no. 4 (1948): 203–10.

Hirschler, Ignaz. (*Autobiographisches Fragment*). Budapest: Druck von Max M. Pollak & Comp., 1891.

Hoffmann, János. *Ködkárpit: Egy zsidó polgár feljegyzései 1940–1944.* Szombathely, Hungary: Szombathely Megyei Jogú Város, 2001.

Jászi, Oszkár. "Emlékeimből: Szülőföldemen" (1953–1955). In *Publicisztikája: Válogatás,* edited by György Litván and János F. Varga, 542–91. Budapest: Magvető, 1982.

———. *Válogatott levelei.* Compiled by György Litván and János F. Varga. Budapest: Magvető, 1991.

Jókai, Mór. *A mi lengyelünk* (1903). Budapest: Akadémiai, 1969.

Kánya, Emília. *Réges-régi időkről: Egy 19. századi írónő emlékiratai.* Budapest: Kortárs, 1998.

Károlyi, Mihály. *Hit, illúziók nélkül.* Budapest: Magvető/Szépirodalmi, 1977.

Károlyi, Mihályné. *Együtt a forradalomban.* Budapest: Európa, 1978.

Katz, Jacob. *With My Own Eyes: The Autobiography of an Historian.* Hanover, NH/London: University Press of New England, 1995.

Keresztury, Dezső. *Emlékezéseim: Szülőföldeim.* Budapest: Argumentum, 1993.

Kóbor, Tamás. *Ki a ghettóból.* Vols. 1–2. Budapest: Franklin-Társulat, 1911.

Kodolányi, János. *Süllyedő világ.* Vols. 1–2. Budapest: Athenaeum, [1940].

Kóhn, Dávid. *Hatvan év múltán: Visszaemlékezések.* Gyula: Dobay János, 1936.

Körmendi, Balázs [Kulcsár, István]. *Zsidó gyónás* (1942–1943). Budapest: Interart, 1990.

BIBLIOGRAPHY 399

Kosztolányi, Dezsőné Harmos Ilona. "Burokban születtem: Ifjúkori memoár."
In *Burokban születtem: Memoár, novellák, portrék*, 19–185. Budapest: Noran,
2003.

Krausz, Simon. *A pénzember: Egy magyar bankár élettörténete* (1937). Budapest:
Kossuth, 1991.

Kubán, Endre. *Kósere Snókesz: Zsidó adomák*. Budapest: Biró Albert, [1912].

Láng, József. "Jókai Mórné Nagy Bella emlékirata." *Irodalomtörténeti Közlemények* 79, no. 3 (1975): 355–77.

Lesznai, Anna. *Kezdetben volt a kert*. Vols. 1–2. Budapest: Szépirodalmi, 1966.

Linksz, Arthur. *Harc a harmadik halállal: Ifjúkorom Magyarországon*. Budapest:
Magvető, 1990.

Lukács, György. *Levelezése (1902–1917)*. Edited by Éva Fekete and Éva Karádi.
Budapest: Magvető, 1981.

———. "Megélt gondolkodás" (1971). In *Curriculum vitae*, 9–39. Budapest:
Magvető, 1982.

———. *Megélt gondolkodás: Életrajz magnószalagon*. Budapest: Magvető, 1989.

Márai, Sándor. *Egy polgár vallomásai (1934–1935/1940)*. [Budapest]: Helikon, 2013.

Marczali, Henrik. *Emlékeim*. Budapest: Múlt és Jövő, 2000.

———. "Hogy lettem én egyetemi tanár." In *Zsidó évkönyv az 5689. bibliai évre*,
edited by Vilmos Kecskeméti, 129–30. Budapest: n.p., 1928–29.

[———]. "Marczali Henrik." In [Sándor Nádas], *Ki volt mi volt: 99 önéletrajz:
Magyar selfmademanek*, 78–79. Budapest: Pesti Futár Kiadása, 1928.

Marczali, Póli. *Apám pályája, barátai: Emlékek Marczali Henrikről*. München,
Germany: Aurora Kiskönyvek, 1973.

Molnár, Ferenc. "A modern: Egy új pesti típus természetrajza." In *Hétágú síp:
Tréfák, karcolatok, tárcák*, 34–50. Budapest: Franklin-Társulat, 1911.

———. *Az éhes város* (1901). Budapest: Pesti Szalon Könyvek, 1993.

Nagy, Lajos. *A lázadó ember* (1948). Budapest: Magvető/Szépirodalmi, 1977.

Návay, Lajos. *Politikai jegyzetei (1910–1912)*. Edited by János Gilicze and Zoltán
Vígh. Békéscsaba/Szeged: Csongrád Megyei Levéltár, 1988.

Patai, Raphael, ed. *The Complete Diaries of Theodor Herzl*. Vols. 1–5. Translated by
Harry Zohn. New York/London: The Herzl Press/Thomas Yoseloff, 1960.

Popperné Lukács, Mici. "Emlékeim Bartókról, Lukács Györgyről és a régi
Budapestről." In *Magyar zenetörténeti tanulmányok Kodály Zoltán emlékére*,
edited by Ferenc Bónis, 379–410. Budapest: Zeneműkiadó, 1977.

Preisich, Kornél. "Önéletrajzi jegyzeteiből." In *Évkönyv 1983/84*, edited by Sándor
Scheiber, 260–74. Budapest: MIOK, 1984.

Pulszky, Ferenc. *Életem és korom* (1880–1882). Vols. 1–2. Budapest: Franklin-
Társulat, 1884.

R. Hoffmann, Mária. "Egressy Gábor levele Hugó Károlyról." *Irodalomtörténeti
Közlemények* 41, no. 3 (1931): 333–35.

Sorsával tetováltan önmaga: Válogatás Lesznai Anna naplójegyzeteiből. Selected by Petra Török. Budapest: Petőfi Irodalmi Múzeum/Hatvany Lajos Múzeum, 2010.

Stancsics, Mihál. *Pazardi.* Kolozsvár: Barra Gábor, 1836.

Strasserné Chorin, Daisy, and András D. Bán. *Az Andrássy úttól a Park Avenue-ig: Fejezetek Chorin Ferenc életéből (1879–1964).* Budapest: Osiris, 1999.

Szabó, Ervin. *Levelezése.* Vol. 1, *1893–1904.* Edited by György Litván and László Szűcs. Budapest: Kossuth, 1977.

Széchenyi, István. *Naplói.* Vol. 4, *(1830–1836).* Edited by Gyula Viszota. Budapest: Magyar Történelmi Társulat, 1934.

———. *Naplói.* Vol. 5, *(1836–1843).* Edited by Gyula Viszota. Budapest: Magyar Történelmi Társulat, 1937.

Székács-Schönberger, István. *Egy zsidó polgár gyermekkora: Analitikus háttérrel.* Budapest: Múlt és Jövő, [2007].

Szentkirályi, István. *A zsidók Magyarhonban.* Pest: Gyurian József, 1861.

Szép, Ernő. *Lila ákác* (1919). Budapest: Szépirodalmi, 1976.

Tábori, Róbert. *Megfagyott pezsgő.* Budapest: Singer és Wolfner, [1899].

Thury, Zoltán. "A rossz Gold és a jó Kapornay." In *Az ember, aki hazaballagott: Elbeszélések,* 30–37. Budapest: Singer és Wolfner, 1907.

Timár, Kálmán. "Simonyi Zsigmond levele Haynald érsekhez." *Irodalomtörténeti Közlemények* 41, no. 3 (1931): 332–33.

Vadnay, Károly. "Az első zsidó miniszteri fogalmazó" (1896). In *Irodalmi emlékek,* 437–43. Budapest: Franklin-Társulat, 1905.

Vámbéry, Ármin. *Küzdelmeim.* Budapest: Franklin-Társulat, 1905.

Vambéry, Arminius. *His Life and Adventures Written by Himself.* London: T. Fisher Unwin, 1884.

———. *The Story of My Struggles.* Vols. 1–2. London: T. Fisher Unwin, 1904.

Vázsonyi, Vilmosné. *Az én uram.* Budapest: Genius, [1931].

Vezér, Erzsébet. "A mindennapi élet története: Beszélgetés Popperné Lukács Máriával." *Kritika,* no. 6 (1985): 25–31.

Weltner, Jakab. *Milljók egy miatt: Emlékek.* Budapest: Szerző kiadása, 1927.

Zsolt, Béla. *Villámcsapás (Schwarz András önéletrajza).* Budapest: Pantheon, [1937].

Secondary Sources

Ablonczy, Balázs. "Átok és könyörgés: Levelek Teleki Pál miniszterelnökhöz a második zsidótörvény időszakában." In *Kisebbség és többség között: A magyar és a zsidó/izraeli etnikai és kulturális tapasztalatok az elmúlt századokban,* edited by Pál Hatos and Attila Novák, 9–20. Budapest: L'Harmattan/Balassi Intézet, 2014.

BIBLIOGRAPHY 401

Albert, Phyllis Cohen. "Ethnicity and Jewish Solidarity in Nineteenth-Century France." In *Mystics, Philosophers, and Politicians: Essays in Jewish Intellectual History in Honor of Alexander Altmann*, edited by Jehuda Reinharz and Daniel Swetschinski, 221–43. Durham, NC: Duke University Press, 1982.

Alpár, Ágnes. *A fővárosi kabarék műsora 1901–1944*. Budapest: Magyar Színházi Intézet, 1979.

Bácskai, Vera. "A pesti zsidóság a 19. század első felében." *Budapesti Negyed* 3, no. 2 (1995): 5–21.

———. *A vállalkozók előfutárai: Nagykereskedők a reformkori Pesten*. Budapest: Magvető, 1989.

Baiersdorf, Kristóf. "A jánosi Engel családról: Adatok és kérdőjelek, III. rész." *Pécsi Szemle* 12, no. 4 (2009): 72–87.

Balogh, Margit, and Jenő Gergely. *Egyházak az újkori Magyarországon 1790–1992: Kronológia*. Budapest: História/MTA Történettudományi Intézete, 1993.

Barta, István, ed. *Kossuth Lajos 1848/49-ben*. Vol. 1, *Kossuth Lajos az utolsó rendi országgyűlésen 1847/48*. Budapest: Akadémiai, 1951.

Belia, György. "Utószó." In Lajos Hatvany, *Urak és emberek*, 727–29. Budapest: Szépirodalmi, 1980.

Bendl, Júlia. *Lukács György élete a századfordulótól 1918-ig*. Budapest: Scientia Humana, 1994.

Benoschofsky, Ilona. "Bánóczi József—levelezése tükrében." In *Évkönyv 1977/78*, edited by Sándor Scheiber, 18–48. Budapest: MIOK, 1978.

B. Horváth, Csilla. "A pécsi kereskedők szerepe a helyi polgári társas élet szervezésében." In *Struktúra és városkép: A polgári társadalom a Dunántúlon a dualizmus korában*, edited by Péter G. Tóth, 441–51. Veszprém: Laczkó Dezső Múzeum, 2002.

Birnbaum, Pierre. *Les fous de la République: Histoire politique des Juifs d'État de Gambetta à Vichy*. Paris: Seuil, 2000.

Blumenberg, Hans. *Säkularisierung und Selbstbehauptung*. Frankfurt am Main, Germany: Suhrkamp, 1974.

Bódy, Zsombor. *Egy társadalmi osztály születése: A magántisztviselők társadalomtörténete 1890–1938*. Budapest: L'Harmattan, 2003.

Bölöny, József. "Klubélet a magyar fővárosban, 1827–1944." *História* 15, no. 2 (1993): 10–12.

Bona, Gábor. *Századosok az 1848/49. évi szabadságharcban*. Vols. 1–2. Budapest: Heraldika, 2008.

Borbíró, Fanni. "'Csevegés, zene és egy csésze tea': A Wohl-nővérek a pesti társaséletben." *Budapesti Negyed* 12, no. 4 (2004): 350–76.

Boronkai, Szabolcs. "Német–magyar kétnyelvűség: Ludwig Dux—Báró Dóczi Lajos (1845–1919)." *Irodalomtörténeti Közlemények* 105, no. 1–2 (2001): 71–83.

BIBLIOGRAPHY

Boyer, John W. "Karl Lueger and the Viennese Jews." *Leo Baeck Institute Year Book* 26 (1981): 125–41.

Breuer, Mordechai. *Jüdische Orthodoxie im Deutschen Reich 1871–1918: Die Sozial-geschichte einer religiösen Minderheit.* Frankfurt am Main: Jüdischer Verlag bei Athenäum, 1986.

———. "The Early Modern Period." In *German-Jewish History in Modern Times*, vol. 1, *Tradition and Enlightenment 1600–1780*, edited by Michael A. Meyer, 79–260. New York: Columbia University Press, 1996.

Bucsay, Mihály. *A protestantizmus története Magyarországon 1521–1945.* Budapest: Gondolat, 1985.

Carlebach, Elisheva. *Divided Souls: Converts from Judaism in Germany, 1500–1750.* New Haven, CT/London: Yale University Press, 2001.

Clark, Chris. "The 'Christian' State and the 'Jewish Citizen' in Nineteenth-Century Prussia." In *Protestants, Catholics and Jews in Germany, 1800–1914*, edited by Helmut Walser Smith, 67–93. Oxford, UK/New York: Berg, 2001.

Cohen, Carl. "The Road to Conversion." *Leo Baeck Institute Year Book* 6 (1961): 279.

Csapodiné Gárdonyi, Klára. "Wohl Janka emlékalbuma." In *Országos Széchényi Könyvtár Évkönyve 1958*, 247–257. Budapest: Országos Széchényi Könyvtár, 1959.

Csekő, Ernő. "Pályatöredékek a századfordulóról: Leopold Samu és Guttmann Irén (Lys-Noir)." *Múlt és Jövő*, new series, 22, no. 2 (2011): 69–91.

Darvas, Tibor. "Az iskolai oktatás története Gyomán." In *Gyomai tanulmányok*, edited by Ferenc Szabó, 255–323. Gyoma, Hungary: Gyoma Nagyközség Tanácsa, 1977.

Deák, George. *The Economy and Polity in Early Twentieth Century Hungary: The Role of the National Association of Industrialists.* Boulder, CO: Westview, 1990.

———. "The Search for an Urban Alliance: The Politics of the National Association of Hungarian Industrialists [GYOSZ] before the First World War." In Michael K. Silber, *Jews in the Hungarian Economy 1760–1945: Studies Dedicated to Moshe Carmilly-Weinberger on his Eightieth Birthday*, 210–24. Jerusalem: The Magnet Press/The Hebrew University, 1992.

Deáky, Zita. "Falusi és mezővárosi zsidó bábák Magyarországon (18–19. sz.)." In . . . *és hol a vidék zsidósága? . . . Történeti és néprajzi tanulmányok a falusi, mezővárosi zsidók és nemzsidók együttéléséről*, edited by Zita Deáky, Zsigmond Csoma, and Éva Vörös, 145–56. Budapest: Centrál-Európa Alapítvány, 1994.

Dénes, Zsófia. *Akkor a hársak épp szerettek . . . Legendaoszlató emlékezések és dokumentumok Ady Endre váradi életéről.* Budapest: Gondolat, 1983.

Dezsényi, Béla. "A Nemzeti Kör a negyvenes évek irodalmi és hírlapi mozgalmaiban." *Irodalomtörténeti Közlemények* 57, no. 1–4 (1953): 172–73.

Dobszay, Tamás, and Zoltán Fónagy. "A rendi társadalom utolsó évtizedei." In *Magyarország története a 19. században*, edited by András Gergely, 57–124. Budapest: Osiris, 2003.

BIBLIOGRAPHY

———. "Magyarország társadalma a 19. század második felében." In *Magyarország története a 19. században*, edited by András Gergely, 397–459. Budapest: Osiris, 2003.

Don, Yehuda, and George Magos. "The Demographic Development of Hungarian Jewry." *Jewish Social Studies* 45, no. 3–4 (1983): 189–216.

Duczynska Polanyi, Ilona. "'I first met Karl Polanyi in 1920 . . . .'" In *Karl Polanyi in Vienna: The Contemporary Significance of the Great Transformation*, edited by Kenneth McRobbie and Kari Polanyi Levitt, 302–15. Montréal: Black Rose, 2006.

Ellenson, David. "German Jewish Orthodoxy: Tradition in the Context of Culture." In *After Emancipation: Jewish Religious Responses to Modernity*, 237–56. Cincinnati, OH: Hebrew Union College Press, 2004.

———. "On Conversion and Intermarriage: The Evidence of Nineteenth-Century Hungarian Orthodox Rabbinic Writings." In *Text and Context: Essays in Modern Jewish History and Historiography in Honor of Ismar Schorsch*, edited by Eli Lederhendler and Jack Wertheimer, 321–46. [New York]: Jewish Theological Seminary, 2005.

Elon, Amos. *The Pity of it All: A Portrait of German Jews*. London: Allen Lane, 2003.

Endelman, Todd M. "Anti-Semitism and Apostasy in Nineteenth-Century France: A Response to Jonathan Helfand." *Jewish History* 5, no. 2 (1991): 57–64.

———. "Conversion as a Response to Antisemitism in Modern Jewish History." In : *Modern Jewish Responses*, edited by Jehuda Reinharz, 59–83. Hanover, NH/London: University Press of New England, 1987.

———. "Gender and Conversion Revisited." In *Gender and Jewish History*, edited by Marion A. Kaplan and Deborah Dash Moore, 170–86. Bloomington/Indianapolis: Indiana University Press, 2011.

———. "Introduction." In *Jewish Apostasy in the Modern World*, edited by id., 1–19. New York/London: Holmes & Meier, 1987.

———. "Jewish Converts in Nineteenth-Century Warsaw: A Quantitative Analysis." *Jewish Social Studies* 4, no. 1 (1997): 28–59.

———. "Jewish Self-Identification and West European Categories of Belonging." In *Religion or Ethnicity? Jewish Identities in Evolution*, edited by Zvi Gitelman, 104–30. New Brunswick, NJ/London: Rutgers University Press, 2009.

———. *The Jews of Britain, 1656 to 2000*. Berkeley/Los Angeles/London: University of California Press, 2002.

———. *Leaving the Jewish Fold: Conversion and Radical Assimilation in Modern Jewish History*. Princeton, NJ/Oxford, UK: Princeton University Press, 2015.

———. "Memories of Jewishness: Jewish Converts and their Jewish Pasts." In *Jewish History and Jewish Memory: Essays in Honor of Yosef Hayim Yerushalmi*, edited by Elisheva Carlebach, John M. Efron, and David N. Myers, 311–29. Hanover, NH: University Press of New England/Brandeis University Press, 1998.

———. *Radical Assimilation in English Jewish History, 1656–1945.* Bloomington/Indianapolis: Indiana University Press, 1990.

———. "Response." In *The State of Jewish Studies,* edited by Shaye J. D. Cohen and Edward L. Greenstein, 158–64. Detroit, MI: Wayne State University Press, 1990.

———. "The Legitimization of the Diaspora Experience in Recent Jewish Historiography." *Modern Judaism* 11, no. 2 (1991): 195–209.

———. "The Social and Political Context of Conversion in Germany and England, 1870–1914." In *Jewish Apostasy in the Modern World,* edited by id., 83–107. New York/London: Holmes & Meier, 1987.

Eőry, Gabriella. "Az Országos Kaszinó és a középosztály." In *Zsombékok: Középosztályok és iskoláztatás Magyarországon a 19. század elejétől a 20. század közepéig,* edited by György Kövér, 321–49. Budapest: Századvég, 2006.

Eperjessy, Géza. "Városi kereskedők a reformkorban." In *A polgárosodás útján: Tanulmányok Magyarország társadalmának átrétegződéséhez a polgári átalakulás korában,* edited by György Szabad, 57–100. Budapest: Tankönyvkiadó, 1990.

Feiner, Shmuel. *The Origins of Jewish Secularization in Eighteenth-Century Europe.* Translated by Chaya Naor. Philadelphia/Oxford, UK: University of Pennsylvania Press, 2011.

Fejtö, François. *Hongrois et Juifs: Histoire millénaire d'un couple singulier (1000–1997).* Paris: Éditions Balland, 1997.

Fenyves, Katalin. "Jákob háza Magyarországon: A zsidó női vallásosság alakulása a 19. Században." In *Hagyományláncolat és modernitás,* edited by Norbert Glässer and András Zima, 259–74. Szeged, Hungary: Néprajzi és Kulturális Antropológiai Tanszék, 2014.

Fischer, Rolf. "Anti-Semitism in Hungary 1882–1932." In *Hostages of Modernization: Studies on Modern Antisemitism 1870–1933/39,* vol. 2, *Austria—Hungary—Poland—Russia,* edited by Herbert A. Strauss, 863–92. Berlin/New York: Walter de Gruyter, 1993.

———. *Entwicklungsstufen des Antisemitismus in Ungarn, 1867–1939: Die Zerstörung der magyarisch-jüdischen Symbiose.* München, Germany: Oldenbourg, 1988.

Fogle, Lauren. "Between Christianity and Judaism: The Identity of Converted Jews in Medieval London." *Essays in Medieval Studies* 22, no. 1 (2006): 107–16.

Forró, Katalin. "Kortesnóták szerepe a dualizmuskori választási kampányokban." In *Studia Comitatensia 29: Néprajzi, történeti tanulmányok,* edited by Rozália Farkas, 125–38. Szentendre, Hungary: Pest Megyei Múzeumok Igazgatósága, 2004.

Frank, Tibor. "Magyar és zsidó: A Wahrmann-életrajz kérdései." In *Honszeretet és felekezeti hűség: Wahrmann Mór, 1831–1892,* edited by id., 11–37. Budapest: Argumentum, 2006.

BIBLIOGRAPHY

Friedländer, Sára. *Saphir Móric Gottlieb: Tanulmány a zsidó asszimilációs törekvések kezdeteiről*. Budapest: Minerva-Könyvtár, 1939.

Frigyesi, Judit. *Béla Bartók and Turn-of-the-Century Budapest*. Berkeley/Los Angeles/London: University of California Press, 1998.

Frojimovics, Kinga, Géza Komoróczy, Viktória Pusztai, and Strbik Andrea. *A zsidó Budapest: Emlékek, szertartások, történelem*. Vols. 1–2. Budapest: Városháza/MTA Judaisztikai Kutatócsoport, 1995.

Fürst, Ilona. *Dóczi Lajos mint német író: Egy zsidó írói nemzedék típusa*. Budapest: Pfeifer Ferdinánd, 1932.

Gémes, István. *Hungari et Transylvani: Kárpát-medencei egyetemjárók Tübingenben (1523–1918)*. Budapest: Luther, 2003.

Gergely, András. *Az Eötvös Loránd Tudományegyetem filozófiai tanszékének története 1867–1918*. Budapest: n.p., 1976.

Gluck, Mary. *Georg Lukács and his Generation 1900–1918*. Cambridge, MA/London: Harvard University Press, 1985.

Godsey, William D., Jr. "The Nobility, Jewish Assimilation, and the Austro-Hungarian Foreign Service in the Late Imperial Era." *Austrian History Yearbook* 27 (1996): 155–80.

Gunst, Péter. "A polgári társadalom kiformálódása." In *Polgárosodás és szabadság: Magyarország a XIX. században*, edited by János Veliky, 236–61. Budapest: Nemzeti Tankönyvkiadó, 1999.

———. "Marczali Henrik (ami az emlékezésekből kimaradt)." In Henrik Marczali. *Emlékeim*, 317–43. Budapest: Múlt és Jövő, 2000.

———. *Marczali Henrik*. Budapest: Akadémiai, 1983.

Gyáni, Gábor. "Budapest története 1873–1945." In Vera Bácskai, Gábor Gyáni, and András Kubinyi, *Budapest története a kezdetektől 1945-ig*, 127–249. Budapest: Budapest Főváros Levéltára, 2000.

———. "Etnicitás és akkulturáció a századfordulós Budapesten." *Regio* 6, no. 1–2 (1995): 101–13.

———. "Magyarország társadalomtörténete a Horthy-korban." In Gábor Gyáni and György Kövér, *Magyarország társadalomtörténete a reformkortól a második világháborúig*, 187–389. Budapest: Osiris, 2006.

———. "Polgárosodás mint zsidó identitás." *BUKSZ* 9, no. 3 (1997): 266–76.

Gyömrei, Sándor. "A kereskedelmi tőke kialakulása és szerepe Pest-Budán 1849-ig." In *Tanulmányok Budapest múltjából*, vol. 12, 197–278. Budapest: Akadémiai, 1957.

György, József. *Dóczi Lajos*. Budapest: Pécsi Egyetemi Könyvkiadó, 1932.

Gyurgyák, János. *A zsidókérdés Magyarországon: Politikai eszmetörténet*. Budapest: Osiris, 2001.

Hajdu, Tibor. "A diplomások létszámnövekedésének szerepe az antiszemitizmus alakulásában." In *A holokauszt Magyarországon európai perspektívában*, edited by Judit Molnár, 54–66. Budapest: Balassi, 2005.

406 BIBLIOGRAPHY

———. "Az értelmiség számszerű gyarapodásának következményei az első világháború előtt és után." *Valóság* 23, no. 7 (1980): 21–34.

Halmos, Károly. "A Hatvany-Deutsch dinasztia." In *Sokszínű kapitalizmus: Pályaképek a magyar tőkés fejlődés aranykorából*, edited by Marcell Sebők, 84–97. Budapest: HVG Könyvek, 2004.

———. "Két építési nagyvállalkozó a századfordulón." In *Gazdaság—Politika— Kultúra: Tanulmányok Kelet-Közép-Európa történetéből*, edited by Sándor Gyimesi, 41–62. Budapest: Aula, 1992.

———. "Kornfeld Zsigmond, az emancipált 'állambankár.'" In *Sokszínű kapitalizmus: Pályaképek a magyar tőkés fejlődés aranykorából*, edited by Marcell Sebők, 155–65. Budapest: HVG Könyvek, 2004.

———. "Lánczy Leó: Hagyomány és nonkonformizmus egy bankvezér történetében." In *Sokszínű kapitalizmus: Pályaképek a magyar tőkés fejlődés aranykorából*, edited by Marcell Sebők, 180–95. Budapest: HVG Könyvek, 2004.

Halpern, Ben. "Reactions to Antisemitism in Modern Jewish History." In *Living with Antisemitism: Modern Jewish Responses*, edited by Jehuda Reinharz, 3–15. Hanover, NH/London: University Press of New England, 1987.

Hamann, Brigitte. *Hitler's Vienna: A Dictator's Apprenticeship*. Translated by Thomas Thornton. New York: Oxford University Press, 1999.

Hamburger, Ernest. "Jews in Public Service under the German Monarchy." *Leo Baeck Institute Year Book* 9 (1964): 206–38.

———. *Juden im öffentlichen Leben Deutschlands: Regierungsmitglieder, Beamte und Parlamentarier in der monarchischen Zeit, 1848–1914*. Tübingen, Germany: Mohr Siebeck, 1968.

Hanák, Péter "Magyarország társadalma a századforduló idején." In *Magyarország története 1890–1918*, vol. 1, edited by id., 403–515. Budapest: Akadémiai, 1978.

———. "Vázlatok a századelő magyar társadalmáról." In *Magyarország a Monarchiában: Tanulmányok*, 341–404. Budapest: Gondolat, 1975.

Handler, Andrew. *Blood Libel at Tiszaeszlár*. Boulder, CO: East European Monographs, 1980.

Haraszti, György. "Az 1848. évi magyarországi zsidóösszeírás háttere és mozgatórugói." In *Két világ határán*, 185–219. Budapest: Múlt és Jövő, 1999.

Harsányi, László. *A szentesi izraelita hitközség története*. Budapest: MIOK, 1970.

Hertz, Deborah. *How Jews Became Germans: The History of Conversion and Assimilation in Berlin*. New Haven, CT/London: Yale University Press, 2007.

———. *Jewish High Society in Old Regime Berlin*. New Haven, CT/London: Yale University Press, 1988.

———. "Seductive Conversion in Berlin, 1770–1809." In *Jewish Apostasy in the Modern World*, edited by Todd M. Endelman, 48–82. New York/London: Holmes & Meier, 1987.

———. "The Lives, Loves, and Novels of August and Fanny Lewald, the Converted Cousins from Königsberg." *Leo Baeck Institute Year Book* 46 (2001): 95–112.

———. "The Troubling Dialectic Between Reform and Conversion in Biedermeier Berlin." In *Towards Normality? Acculturation and Modern German Jews*, edited by Rainer Liedtke and David Rechter, 103–26. Tübingen, Germany: Mohr Siebeck, 2003.

Honigmann, Peter. *Die Austritte aus der Jüdischen Gemeinde Berlin 1873–1941: Statistische Auswertung und historische Interpretation*. Frankfurt am Main, Germany: Peter Lang, 1988.

———. "Jewish Conversions—A Measure of Assimilation? A Discussion of the Berlin Secession Statistics of 1770–1941." *Leo Baeck Institute Year Book* 34 (1989): 3–39.

Hyman, Paula E. *Gender and Assimilation in Modern Jewish History: The Roles and Representation of Women*. Seattle/London: University of Washington Press, 1995.

———. "The Ideological Transformation of Modern Jewish Historiography." In *The State of Jewish Studies*, edited by Shaye J. D. Cohen and Edward L. Greenstein, 143–57. Detroit, MI: Wayne State University Press, 1990.

———. *The Jews of Modern France*. Berkeley/Los Angeles/London: University of California Press, 1998.

———. "The Modern Jewish Family: Image and Reality." In *The Jewish Family: Metaphor and Memory*, edited by David Kraemer, 179–93. New York/Oxford, UK: Oxford University Press, 1989.

Ignotus, Paul. *Hungary*. London: Ernest Benn Limited, 1972.

Janos, Andrew C. *The Politics of Backwardness in Hungary, 1825–1945*. Princeton, NJ.: Princeton University Press, 1982.

Jersch-Wenzel, Stefi. "Population Shifts and Occupational Structure." In *German-Jewish History in Modern Times*, vol. 2, *Emancipation and Acculturation 1780–1871*, edited by Michael A. Meyer, 50–89. New York: Columbia University Press, 1997.

Kádár, Gábor, and Zoltán Vági. "Hosszú évszázad: Antiszemita erőszak Magyarországon, 1848–1956." In *A holokauszt Magyarországon hetven év múltán*, edited by Randolph L. Braham and András Kovács, 76–110. Budapest: Múlt és Jövő, 2015.

Kaplan, Marion. *The Making of the Jewish Middle Class: Women, Family, and Identity in Imperial Germany*. New York/Oxford, UK: Oxford University Press, 1991.

———. "Tradition and Transition: The Acculturation, Assimilation and Integration of Jews in Imperial Germany—A Gender Analysis." *Leo Baeck Institute Year Book* 27 (1982): 3–35.

Karady, Victor, and István Kemény. "Les Juifs dans la structure des classes en Hongrie." *Actes de la Recherche en Sciences Sociales* 22, no. 1 (1978): 25–59.

408   BIBLIOGRAPHY

Karady, Victor. "Assimilation and Schooling: National and Denominational
Minorities in the Universities of Budapest around 1900." In *Hungary and Euro-
pean Civilization*, edited by György Ránki and Attila Pók, 285–319. Budapest:
Akadémiai, 1989.

Karády, Viktor. "A felekezetek közötti házasságok általános szociológiája a
régi rendszer idején." In *Zsidóság, modernizáció, polgárosodás: Tanulmányok*,
196–248. [Budapest]: Cserépfalvi, 1997.

———. "Asszimiláció és társadalmi krízis." In *Zsidóság, modernizáció, polgárosodás: Tanulmányok*, 114–50. [Budapest]: Cserépfalvi, 1997.

———. "Felekezeti státusz és iskolázási egyenlőtlenségek." In *A tudománytól a
tömegkultúráig: Művelődéstörténeti tanulmányok 1890–1945*, edited by Miklós
Lackó, 125–68. Budapest: MTA Történettudományi Intézete, 1994.

———. "'Magyar, zsidó és katolikus': Egy kitérési jegyzőkönyv margójára."
Korunk 10, no. 7 (1999): 25–31.

———. "Zsidó identitás és asszimiláció Magyarországon." In *Zsidóság, modernizáció, polgárosodás: Tanulmányok*, 11–77. [Budapest]: Cserépfalvi, 1997.

Katus, László. "The Occupational Structure of Hungarian Jewry in the Eighteenth and Twentieth Centuries." In Michael K. Silber, *Jews in the Hungarian Economy 1760–1945: Studies Dedicated to Moshe Carmilly-Weinberger on his Eightieth
Birthday*, 92–105. Jerusalem: The Magnet Press/The Hebrew University, 1992.

Katz, Jacob. *A House Divided: Orthodoxy and Schism in Nineteenth-Century
Central European Jewry*. Translated by Ziporah Brody. Hanover, NH/London:
University Press of New England, 1998.

———. *Exclusiveness and Tolerance: Studies in Jewish-Gentile Relations in Medieval and Modern Times*. London: Oxford University Press, 1961.

———. "Judaism and Christianity Against the Background of Modern Secularism." In *Jewish Emancipation and Self-Emancipation*, 34–48. Philadelphia/New
York/Jerusalem: The Jewish Publication Society, 1986.

———. *Out of the Ghetto: The Social Background of Jewish Emancipation, 1770–
1870*. Cambridge, MA: Harvard University Press, 1973.

———. "The Identity of Post-Emancipatory Hungarian Jewry." In *A Social and
Economic History of Central European Jewry*, edited by Yehuda Don and Victor
Karady, 13–31. New Brunswick, NJ/London: Transaction, 1990.

———. *Tradition and Crisis: Jewish Society at the End of the Middle Ages*. Translated by Bernard Dov Cooperman. Syracuse, NY: Syracuse University Press,
2000.

Katzburg, Nathaniel. "Assimilation in Hungary During the Nineteenth Century:
Orthodox Positions." In *Jewish Assimilation in Modern Times*, edited by Bela
Vago, 49–55. Boulder, CO: Westview Press, 1981.

———. *Fejezetek az újkori zsidó történelemből Magyarországon*. Budapest: MTA
Judaisztikai Kutatócsoport/Osiris, 1999.

———. *Hungary and the Jews: Policy and Legislation 1920–1943.* Ramat-Gan, Israel: Bar-Ilan University Press, 1981.

———. "Problems of Organization within the Hungarian-Jewish Community during the Inter-War Period." In *Occident and Orient: A Tribute to the Memory of Alexander Scheiber,* edited by Robert Dán, 261–72. Budapest/Leiden, Netherlands: Akadémiai/E. J. Brill, 1988.

———. "The Jewish Congress of Hungary, 1868–1869." In *Hungarian-Jewish Studies,* vol. 2, edited by Randolph L. Braham, 1–33. New York: World Federation of Hungarian Jews, 1969.

Kecskeméti, Károly. *Magyar liberalizmus 1790–1848.* [Budapest]: Argumentum/Bibó István Szellemi Műhely, 2008.

Kerecsényi, Edit. "Nagykanizsa társadalma és egyleti élete 1900 táján." In *Zalai Gyűjtemény 21: Közlemények Zala megye közgyűjteményeinek kutatásaiból 1984–1985,* edited by Alajos Degré and Imre Halász, 105–20. Zalaegerszeg, Hungary: Zala Megyei Levéltár, 1985.

Kieval, Hillel J. "The Importance of Place: Comparative Aspects of the Ritual Murder Trial in Modern Central Europe." In *Comparing Jewish Societies,* edited by Todd M. Endelman, 135–65. Ann Arbor: University of Michigan Press, 1997.

K. Nagy, Magda. *Balázs Béla világa.* Budapest: Kossuth, 1973.

Kókai, Károly. "A fiatal Lukács György és a zsidóság." *Szombat* 12, no. 2 (2000): 20–23.

Koltun-Fromm, Ken. *Moses Hess and Modern Jewish Identity.* Bloomington/Indianapolis: Indiana University Press, 2001.

Komlós, Aladár. *A magyar zsidóság irodalmi tevékenysége a XIX. században* (1940–1942). Budapest/Jerusalem: Múlt és Jövő, 2008.

Komoróczy, Géza. *A zsidók története Magyarországon.* Vols. 1–2. Pozsony, Slovakia: Kalligram, 2012.

Konrád, Miklós. "Egyenjogúsítás feltételekkel: A feltételes zsidóemancipáció eszméjének diadala és bukása." *Múlt és Jövő* 28, no. 3 (2017): 28–35.

———. "Jewish Emancipation as a Compromise." In *The Creation of the Austro-Hungarian Monarchy: A Hungarian Perspective,* edited by Gábor Gyáni, 229–56. New York/London: Routledge, 2022.

———. "Jewish Perception of Antisemitism in Hungary before World War I." In *Jewish Studies at the Central European University,* vol. 4, 2003–2005, edited by András Kovács and Michael L. Miller, 177–90. Budapest: Central European University, 2006.

———. "Vallásváltás és identitás: A kitért zsidók megítélésének változásai a dualizmus korában." *Századok* 144, no. 1 (2010): 3–46.

———. "Vegyes házasság és asszimiláció: Érvek a keresztény-zsidó házasság bevezetése mellett." *Történelmi Szemle* 63, no. 3 (2021): 483–94.

————. "Wahrmann Mór és gyermekei: Adalék a dualizmus kori zsidó nagypolgárság történetéhez." *Történelmi Szemle* 54, no. 3 (2012): 441–68.

Kósa, László. "Felekezeti és nemzeti azonosságtudat kapcsolódása: A magyar protestáns példa." In *Bennünk élő múltjaink: Történelmi tudat—Kulturális emlékezet*, edited by Richárd Papp and László Szarka, 391–400. Zenta, Serbia: Vajdasági Magyar Művelődési Intézet, 2008.

Kovács, Ábrahám. "Ballagi Mór és a Skót Misszió: megtérés, áttérés vagy kitérés? Egy liberális protestáns zsidó életútjának kezdete." *Confessio* 31, no. 3 (2007): 109–25.

————. *The History of the Free Church of Scotland's Mission to the Jews in Budapest and its Impact on the Reformed Church of Hungary 1841–1914*. Frankfurt am Main, Germany: Peter Lang, 2006.

Kovács, András. "Az asszimilációs dilemma." *Világosság* 29, no. 8–9 (1988): 605–12.

Kovács, Gábor I., ed. *Diszkrimináció, emancipáció—asszimiláció, diszkrimináció: Magyarországi egyetemi tanárok életrajzi adattára 1848–1944*. Vol. 1, *Zsidó és zsidó származású egyetemi tanárok*. Budapest: ELTE Eötvös, 2012.

Kovács, Sándor Iván, ed. *Batu kán pesti rokonai: Vámbéry Ármin és tatárja, Csagatai Izsák*. Pozsony, Slovakia: Kalligram, 2001.

Kövér, György. *A tiszaeszlári dráma: Társadalomtörténeti látószögek*. Budapest: Osiris, 2011.

————. "'Deutsch Ig. és fia.'" In *A Hatvanyak emlékezete*, edited by László Horváth, 13–21. Hatvan, Hungary: Hatvany Lajos Múzeum, 2003.

————. "Liedemann és Wahrmann: 19. századi kereskedő-bankár családi stratégiák." In *A felhalmozás íve: Társadalom- és gazdaságtörténeti tanulmányok*, 31–46. Budapest: Új Mandátum, 2002.

————. "Magyarország társadalomtörténete a reformkortól az első világháborúig." In Gábor Gyáni and György Kövér, *Magyarország társadalomtörténete a reformkortól a második világháborúig*, 9–186. Budapest: Osiris, 2006.

————. "'Wahrmann és fia.'" In *Honszeretet és felekezeti hűség: Wahrmann Mór, 1831–1892*, edited by Tibor Frank, 79–90. Budapest: Argumentum, 2006.

Kubinszky, Judit. *A politikai antiszemitizmus Magyarországon 1875–1890*. Budapest: Kossuth, 1976.

Kútfalvi, Oszkár. *Újságpaloták*. Budapest: Akadémiai, 1991.

Lakatos, Ernő. *A magyar politikai vezetőréteg 1848–1918*. Budapest: Szerző kiadása, 1942.

Landau, Philippe-Éfraïm. "Se convertir à Paris au XIXᵉ siècle." *Archives Juives* 35, no. 1 (2002): 27–43.

László, Anna. *Hevesi Sándor*. Budapest: Gondolat, 1960.

Lederer, Emma. *A magyar társadalom kialakulása a honfoglalástól 1918-ig*. [Budapest]: Népszava, [1947].

BIBLIOGRAPHY   411

Lengyel, Dénes. *Benedek Elek*. Budapest: Gondolat, 1974.

Litván, György. *A Twentieth-Century Prophet: Oscar Jászi 1875–1957*. Budapest/ New York: Central European University Press, 2006.

———. "Egy magyar tudós tragikus pályája a század elején: Somló Bódog (1873–1920)." *Valóság* 16, no. 8 (1973): 32–42.

———. "Jászi Oszkár és a zsidókérdés." In *A holokauszt Magyarországon európai perspektívában*, edited by Judit Molnár, 45–53. Budapest: Balassi, 2005.

———. *"Magyar gondolat—szabad gondolat": Nacionalizmus és progresszió a század eleji Magyarországon*. Budapest: Magvető, 1978.

———. *Szabó Ervin, a szocializmus moralistája*. Budapest: Századvég, 1993.

———. "Szellemi progresszió a századelőn." In *A zsidókérdésről*, edited by Balázs Fűzfa and Gábor Szabó, 11–27. Szombathely, Hungary: Németh László Szakkollégium, 1989.

———. "Zsidók a huszadik századi magyar modernizációban és progresszív mozgalmakban." In *1100 éves együttélés: A magyar és magyarországi zsidóság a haza és a fejlődés szolgálatában*, edited by Péter Püspöki Nagy, 308–16. Budapest: Magyarországi Holocaust Emlékalapítvány, 2001.

Lowenstein, Steven M. "Jewish Intermarriage and Conversion in Germany and Austria." *Modern Judaism* 25, no. 1 (2005): 23–61.

———. *The Berlin Jewish Community: Enlightenment, Family, and Crisis, 1770–1830*. New York/Oxford, UK: Oxford University Press, 1994.

———. "Was Urbanization Harmful to Jewish Tradition and Identity in Germany?" In *People of the City: Jews and Urban* Challenge, edited by Ezra Mendelsohn, 80–106. New York/Oxford, UK: Oxford University Press, 1999.

Lupovitch, Howard. "Ordinary People, Ordinary Jews: Mór Jókai as Magyar Philosemite." In *Philosemitism in History*, edited by Jonathan Karp and Adam Sutcliffe, 128–45. Cambridge: Cambridge University Press, 2011.

Magnus, Shulamit S. "Good Bad Jews: Converts, Conversion, and Boundary Redrawing in Modern Russian Jewry: Notes toward a New Category." In *Boundaries of Jewish Identity*, edited by Susan A. Glenn and Naomi B. Sokoloff, 132–60. Seattle/London: University of Washington Press, 2010.

Majoros, Judit. "Egy elfeledett irodalmi emlékhely Zemplénben: Az alsókörtvélyesi kúria." *Enigma* 14, no. 51 (2007): 25–41.

Marjanucz, László. *A szegedi zsidó családok a 19. században*. Szeged, Hungary: Móra Ferenc Múzeum, 1988.

Marrus, Michael R. *Les Juifs de France à l'époque de l'affaire Dreyfus*. Bruxelles, Belgium: Editions Complexe, 1985.

McCagg, William O., Jr. *A History of Habsburg Jews, 1670–1918*. Bloomington/ Indianapolis: Indiana University Press, 1989.

———. "Austria's Jewish Nobles, 1740–1918." *Leo Baeck Institute Year Book* 34 (1989): 163–83.

————. "Jewish Conversion in Hungary in Modern Times." In *Jewish Apostasy in the Modern World*, edited by Todd M. Endelman, 142–64. New York/London: Holmes & Meier, 1987.

————. *Jewish Nobles and Geniuses in Modern Hungary*. Boulder, CO: East European Quarterly, 1972.

McLeod, Hugh. *Secularisation in Western Europe, 1848–1914*. Basingstoke, UK: Macmillan Press, 2000.

Mendelsohn, Ezra. *The Jews of East Central Europe between the World Wars*. Bloomington: Indiana University Press, 1983.

Menes, A. "The Conversion Movement in Prussia During the First Half of the 19th Century" (1939). In *YIVO Annual of Jewish Social Science*, vol. 6, edited by Koppel S. Pinson, 187–205. New York: Yiddish Scientific Institute/YIVO, 1951.

Mérei, Gyula, and Ferenc Pölöskei. *Magyarországi pártprogramok 1867–1919*. Budapest: ELTE Eötvös, 2003.

Merényi-Metzger, Gábor. "Karinthy Frigyes származásának anyakönyvi forrásai." *Irodalomtörténeti Közlemények* 107, no. 4–5 (2003): 535–44.

Mészáros, Judit, ed. *In memoriam Ferenczi Sándor*. Budapest: Jószöveg Műhely, [2000].

Meyer, Michael A. *Response to Modernity: A History of the Reform Movement in Judaism*. Detroit, MI: Wayne State University Press, 1995.

————. *The Origins of the Modern Jew: Jewish Identities and European Culture in Germany, 1749–1824*. Detroit, MI: Wayne State University Press, 1967.

Miskolczy, Ambrus. *A zsidóemancipáció Magyarországon 1849-ben*. Budapest: Múlt és Jövő, 1999.

Mislovics, Erzsébet. "A magyarországi zsidóság áttérési gyakorlata Buda, Óbuda, Pest településeken és Bécsben 1746 és 1850 között." *Aetas* 30, no. 1 (2015): 31–58.

Mosse, Werner E. "Problems and Limits of Assimilation. Hermann and Paul Wallich 1833–1938." *Leo Baeck Institute Year Book* 33 (1988): 43–65.

Nagy, Beáta. "Az elit társasélete a klubok, kaszinók keretében." In *Rendi társadalom—Polgári társadalom 1: Társadalomtörténeti módszerek és forrástípusok*, edited by László Á. Varga, 69–76. Salgótarján, Hungary: Nógrád Megyei Levéltár, 1987.

Nagy, Péter. *Szabó Dezső*. Budapest: Akadémiai, 1964.

Nagy, Sándor. "Schosberger Ilona különös házassága." In *A felhalmozás míve: Történeti tanulmányok Kövér György tiszteletére*, edited by Károly Halmos, Judit Klement, Ágnes Pogány, and Béla Tomka, 48–57. Budapest: Századvég, 2009.

Nagy, Sz. Péter. *Hatvany Lajos*. Budapest: Balassi, 1993.

Németh, József. "Hoffmann Mór." In *Zalai Múzeum 12*, edited by László Horváth, 255–66. Zalaegerszeg, Hungary: Zala Megyei Múzeumok Igazgatósága, 2003.

Németh, László, ed. *A Zala megyei zsidóság történetének levéltári forrásai, 1716–1849*. Zalaegerszeg, Hungary: Zala Megyei Levéltár, 2002.

BIBLIOGRAPHY 413

Novák, Béla. "Fővárosi kaszinók a 19. században." *Budapesti Negyed* 12, no. 4 (2004): 90–114.

Oxaal, Ivar, and Walter R. Weitzmann. "The Jews of Pre-1914 Vienna: An Exploration of Basic Sociological Dimensions." *Leo Baeck Institute Year Book* 30 (1985): 416–17.

Paksy, Zoltán. *Istóczy Győző és a magyar antiszemita mozgalom (1875–1892)*. Budapest: L'Harmattan, 2018.

Pálmány, Béla, ed. *Az 1848–1849. évi első népképviseleti országgyűlés történeti almanachja*. Budapest: Magyar Országgyűlés, 2002.

Patai, Raphael. *The Jews of Hungary: History, Culture, Psychology*. Detroit, MI: Wayne State University Press, 1996.

Péter, László. "Lukács György apja." In *A szerette város: Írások Szegedről*, 426–29. Budapest: Szépirodalmi, 1986.

Petrovsky-Shtern, Yohanan. "Brafman, Iakov Aleksandrovich." In *The YIVO Encyclopedia of Jews in Eastern Europe*, edited by Gershon David Hundert, http://www.yivoencyclopedia.org/article.aspx/Brafman_Iakov_Aleksandrovich.

Prepuk, Anikó. "A területi átrétegződés vizsgálata Pest ortodox zsidó kereskedői között (1873–1895)." *Magyar Történeti Tanulmányok*, 21 (1988): 41–55.

———. "Az izraelita hírlapirodalom kezdetei Magyarországon." In *Emlékkönyv ifj. Barta János 70. születésnapjára*, edited by Imre Papp, János Angi, and László Pallai, 311–28. Debrecen, Hungary: Debreceni Egyetem Történeti Intézete, 2010.

———. "Kísérletek az izraeliták felekezeti jogainak szélesítésére az emancipáció után (1867–1892)." In *Zsidóság—tradicionalitás és modernitás: Tisztelgő kötet Karády Viktor 75. Születésnapja alkalmából*, edited by Zsuzsanna Hanna Biró and Péter Tibor Nagy, 45–66. Budapest: Wesley János Lelkészképző Főiskola, 2012.

———. "Miért éppen a recepció? Az izraelita vallás egyenjogúsítása az 1890-es években." In *Emlékkönyv L. Nagy Zsuzsa 70. születésnapjára*, edited by János Angi and János Barta, 263–81. Debrecen, Hungary: Multiplex Media/DUP, 2000.

Pulzer, Peter. *Jews and the German State: The Political History of a Minority, 1848–1933*. Detroit, MI: Wayne State University Press, 2003.

———. "Legal Equality and Public Life." In *German-Jewish History in Modern Times*, vol. 3, *Integration in Dispute 1871–1918*, edited by Michael A. Meyer, 153–95. New York: Columbia University Press, 1997.

———. *The Rise of Political Anti-Semitism in Germany and Austria: Revised Edition*. Cambridge, MA: Harvard University Press, 1988.

Ránki, György. "The Development of the Hungarian Middle Class: Some East-West Comparisons." In *Bourgeois Society in Nineteenth-Century Europe*, edited by Jürgen Kocka and Allen Mitchell, 439–55. Oxford, UK/Providence, RI: Berg, 1993.

Repiszky, Tamás. "Ágas-bogas családfa: Adalékok Jászi Oszkár családtörténetéhez." In *Studia Comitatensia 29: Néprajzi, történeti tanulmányok*, edited by Rozália Farkas, 153–232. Szentendre, Hungary: Pest Megyei Múzeumok Igazgatósága, 2004.

———. "Emlékkép-foszlányok: Adalékok Lesznai Anna családtörténetéhez." *Enigma* 14, no. 52 (2007): 9–36.

Richarz, Monika. "Demographic Developments." In *German-Jewish History in Modern Times*, vol. 3, *Integration in Dispute 1871–1918*, edited by Michael A. Meyer, 7–34. New York: Columbia University Press, 1997.

———. "Jewish Women in the Family and Public Sphere." In *German-Jewish History in Modern Times*, vol. 3, *Integration in Dispute 1871–1918*, edited by Michael A. Meyer, 68–102. New York: Columbia University Press, 1997.

Riff, Michael Anthony. "Assimilation and Conversion in Bohemia: Secession from the Jewish Community in Prague 1868–1917." *Leo Baeck Institute Year Book* 26 (1981): 73–88.

Robertson, Ritchie. *The "Jewish Question" in German Literature 1749–1939: Emancipation and Its Discontents*. Oxford, UK/New York: Oxford University Press, 1999.

Rochelson, Meri-Jane. *The Career of Israel Zangwill: A Jew in the Public Arena*. Detroit, MI: Wayne State University Press, 2008.

Romsics, Ignác. "Nemzet és állam a modern magyar történelemben." In *Magyarország helye a 20. századi Európában*, edited by Pál Pritz, 7–25. Budapest: Magyar Történelmi Társulat, 2002.

Rozenblit, Marsha L. *Reconstructing a National Identity: The Jews of Habsburg Austria during World War I*. Oxford, UK/New York: Oxford University Press, 2001.

———. "The Jews of Germany and Austria: A Comparative Perspective." In *Austrians and Jews in the Twentieth Century: From Franz Joseph to Waldheim*, edited by Robert S. Wistrich, 1–18. New York: St. Martin's Press, 1992.

———. *The Jews of Vienna, 1867–1914: Assimilation and Identity*. Albany: State University of New York Press, 1983.

Schmidt, H. D. "The Terms of Emancipation 1781–1812: The Public Debate in Germany and Its Effect on the Mentality and Ideas of German Jewry." *Leo Baeck Institute Year Book* 1 (1956): 28–47.

Schorsch, Ismar. *Jewish Reactions to German Anti-Semitism, 1870–1914*. New York: Columbia University Press; Philadelphia: Jewish Publication Society of America, 1972.

Schweitzer, Gábor. "Reflexiók a 'zsidókérdés'-ről: Két magyar történész memoárjai: Angyal Dávid és Marczali Henrik." *Budapesti Negyed* 16, no. 1 (2008): 174–83.

Schweitzer, József. *A pécsi izraelita hitközség története*. Budapest: A Magyar Izraeliták Országos Képviseletének Kiadása, 1966.

Sebők, László, ed. *Az 1869. évi népszámlálás vallási adatai*. [Budapest]: TLA Teleki László Intézet/KSH Népszámlálás/KSH Levéltár, 2005.

BIBLIOGRAPHY   415

Silber, Michael K. "Budapest." In *The YIVO Encyclopedia of Jews in Eastern Europe*, edited by Gershon David Hundert, http://www.yivoencyclopedia.org/article.aspx/Budapest.

———. "Hungary before 1918." In *The YIVO Encyclopedia of Jews in Eastern Europe*, vol. 1, edited by Gershon David Hundert, 770–82. New Haven, CT/London: Yale University Press, 2008.

———. "The Entrance of Jews into Hungarian Society in the *Vormärz*: The Case of the 'Casinos.'" In *Assimilation and Community: The Jews in Nineteenth-Century Europe*, edited by Jonathan Frankel and Steven J. Zipperstein, 284–323. Cambridge, UK/New York: Cambridge University Press, 1992.

———. "The Historical Experience of German Jewry and Its Impact on Haskalah and Reform in Hungary." In *Toward Modernity: The European Jewish Model*, edited by Jacob Katz, 107–57. New Brunswick, NJ/Oxford, UK: Transaction Books, 1987.

———. "The Social Composition of the Pest Radical Reform Society (Genossenschaft für Reform im Judenthum), 1848–1852." *Jewish Social Studies* 1, no. 3 (1995): 99–128.

———. "Ullmann Family." In *The YIVO Encyclopedia of Jews in Eastern Europe*, edited by Gershon David Hundert, http://www.yivoencyclopedia.org/article.aspx/Ullmann_Family.

———. "Wodianer Family." In *The YIVO Encyclopedia of Jews in Eastern Europe*, edited by Gershon David Hundert, http://www.yivoencyclopedia.org/article.aspx/Wodianer_Family.

Simon, Róbert. *Goldziher Ignác: Vázlatok az emberről és a tudósról*. Budapest: Osiris, 2000.

Sipos, András. *Várospolitika és városigazgatás Budapesten 1890–1914*. Budapest: Budapest Főváros Levéltára, [1996].

Skolnik, Fred, ed. *Encyclopaedia Judaica*. Second Edition. Vol. 2. Detroit, MI: Thomson Gale, 2007.

Somogyi, Éva. "Egy magyar hivatalnok a bécsi külügyminisztérium szolgálatában: Báró Dóczy Lajos." In *Hagyomány és átalakulás: Állam és bürokrácia a dualista Habsburg Monarchiában*, 120–36. Budapest: L'Harmattan, 2006.

Sorkin, David. *Jewish Emancipation: A History Across Five Centuries*. Princeton, NJ/Oxford, UK: Princeton University Press, 2019.

———. *The Transformation of German Jewry, 1780–1840*. Oxford, UK/New York: Oxford University Press, 1987.

Spira, György. *A pestiek Petőfi és Haynau között*. Budapest: Enciklopédia, 1998.

Stanislawski, Michael. "Jewish Apostasy in Russia: A Tentative Typology." In *Jewish Apostasy in the Modern World*, edited by Todd M. Endelman, 189–205. New York/London: Holmes & Meier, 1987.

Staudacher, Anna L. *Jüdische Konvertiten in Wien 1782–1868*. Vols. 1–2. Frankfurt am Main, Germany: Peter Lang, 2002.

Stern, Fritz. *Gold and Iron: Bismarck, Bleichröder and the Building of the German Empire*. New York: Alfred A. Knopf, 1977.

Stourzh, Gerald. "An Apogee of Conversions: Gustav Mahler, Karl Kraus, and fin de siècle Vienna." In *From Vienna to Chicago and Back: Essays on Intellectual History and Political Thought in Europe and America*, 224–47. Chicago/London: University of Chicago Press, 2007.

Szabó, Dániel. "A magyar társadalom politikai szerveződése a dualizmus korában." *Történelmi Szemle* 34, no. 3–4 (1992): 199–230.

———. *A Néppárt 1895–1914*. PhD dissertation, Budapest: 1983.

———. "Kortesdalok (avagy a választás, mint a poéták paradicsoma)." In *Polgárosodás Közép-Európában: Tanulmányok Hanák Péter 70. születésnapjára*, edited by Éva Somogyi, 229–41. Budapest: MTA Történettudományi Intézet, 1991.

———. "Országgyűlési választások az egyesítés előestéjén." In *Az egyesített főváros: Pest, Buda, Óbuda*, edited by Gábor Gyáni, 31–59. Budapest: Városháza, 1998.

Szabó, Miklós. *Az újkonzervativizmus és a jobboldali radikalizmus története (1867–1918)*. Budapest: Új Mandátum, 2003.

———. "Középosztály és új konzervativizmus." In *Politikai kultúra Magyarországon 1896–1986: Válogatott tanulmányok*, 177–90. Budapest: Medvetánc, 1989.

———. "Nemesi és polgári liberalizmus." In *Filozófia és kultúra: Írások a modern magyar művelődéstörténet köréből*, edited by Miklós Lackó, 113–64. Budapest: MTA Történettudományi Intézete, 2001.

Szabolcsi, Lajos. *Két emberöltő: Az Egyenlőség évtizedei (1881–1931): Emlékezések, dokumentumok*. Budapest: MTA Judaisztikai Kutatócsoport, 1993.

Szalai, Anna. "Bevezető." In *Házalók, árendások, kocsmárosok, uzsorások: Zsidóábrázolás a reformkori prózában*, edited by id., 7–97. Budapest: Osiris, 2002.

Széchenyi, Ágnes. "Vészi József, a műhelyteremtő és dinasztiaalapító (1858–1940)." *Budapesti Negyed* 16, no. 2 (2008): 243–71.

Szögi, László. *Magyarországi diákok németországi egyetemeken és főiskolákon 1789–1919*. Budapest: Eötvös Loránd Tudományegyetem Levéltára, 2001.

Takács, Istvánné. *A dombóvári zsidóság története*. Dombóvár, Hungary: Dombóvári Városszépítő és Városvédő Egyesület, 2007.

Takáts, Sándor. "A Kör és a Gyülde." In *Hangok a múltból*, 251–67. Budapest: Athenaeum, [1930].

Tal, Uriel. *Christians and Jews in Germany: Religion, Politics, and Ideology in the Second Reich, 1870–1914*. Ithaca, NY/London: Cornell University Press, 1975.

Timár, Lajos. *Vidéki városlakók: Debrecen társadalma 1920–1944*. Budapest: Magvető, 1993.

BIBLIOGRAPHY 417

Toronyi, Zsuzsanna. "A zsidó asszimiláció a Pesti Chevra Kadisa elöljáróinak társadalmi pozíciói alapján." In *Otthonkeresők, otthonteremtők: Zsidó társadalomtörténeti tanulmányok*, edited by György Gábor, Piroska Hajnal, and Gábor Schweitzer, 81–114. [Budapest]: Universitas/Judaica Alapítvány, 2001.

Tóth, Árpád. "Asszimilációs utak a késő-rendi társadalomban: A zsidóság szerepvállalásáról a reformkori pesti egyesületekben." In *Léptékváltó társadalomtörténet: Tanulmányok a 60 éves Benda Gyula tiszteletére*, edited by Zsolt K. Horváth, András Lugosi, and Ferenc Sohajda, 156–85. Budapest: Hermész Kör/Osiris, 2003.

———. *Önszervező polgárok: A pesti egyesületek társadalomtörténete a reformkorban*. Budapest: L'Harmattan, 2005.

Török, Petra. "'Gránit a siratófalban, ütem magyar ajkú dalban.'" *Múlt és Jövő*, new series, 12, no. 1 (2001): 59–73.

Török, Zsuzsa. "A Wohl nővérek keresztvíz alatt: Két protestáns zsidó írói életpálya kezdete." *Századvég*, no. 2 (2013): 41–58.

Tóth-Barbalics, Veronika. "A 'korona védpajzsa' vagy 'észarisztokrácia'? A magyar főrendiház élethossziglan kinevezett tagjai." *Századok* 145, no. 3 (2011): 723–52.

———. "Vigyázó, Harkányi, Żeleński és társaik—1885 után örökös főrendiházi tagságot nyert családok." In *Vázlatok két évszázad magyar történelméből: Tanulmányok*, edited by Jenő Gergely, 67–83. Budapest: ELTE BTK Új- és Jelenkori Magyar Történeti Tanszék, 2010.

Urbancsok, Zsolt. "A Pulitzer család stratégiái a 18–19. században." In *Hagyományláncolat és modernitás*, edited by Norbert Glässer and András Zima, 121–36. Szeged, Hungary: Néprajzi és Kulturális Antropológiai Tanszék, 2014.

Varga, Dániel. "Az öreg Kossuth Lajos 'palatinusa': Helfy Ignác (1830–1897)." *Polymatheia* 18, no. 1–2 (2021): 198–219.

Varga, László. "A hazai nagyburzsoázia történetéből." *Valóság* 26, no. 3 (1983): 75–88.

———. "Egy pénzcsőkés karrier: A Weiss-család és Weiss Manfréd." *Történelmi Szemle* 26, no. 1 (1983): 36–66.

———. "Zsidó bevándorlás Magyarországon." In *Zsidóság a dualizmus kori Magyarországon: Siker és válság*, edited by id., 11–30. Budapest: Pannonica Kiadó/Habsburg Történeti Intézet, 2005.

Vezér, Erzsébet. *Lesznai Anna élete*. Budapest: Kossuth, 1979.

Vital, David. *A People Apart: A Political History of the Jews in Europe 1789–1939*. Oxford, UK/New York: Oxford University Press, 1999.

Vörös, Károly. "A budapesti zsidóság két forradalom között, 1849–1918." *Kortárs* 30, no. 12 (1986): 100–17.

———. "A világváros útján, 1896–1918." In *Budapest története a márciusi forradalomtól az őszirózsás forradalomig*, edited by id., 525–771. Budapest: Akadémiai, 1978.

―――. *Budapest legnagyobb adófizetői 1873–1917*. Budapest: Akadémiai, 1979.

―――. "Pest-Budától Budapestig 1849–1873." In *Budapest története a márciusi forradalomtól az őszirózsás forradalomig*, edited by id., 117–320. Budapest: Akadémiai, 1978.

―――. "Wahrmann Mór: egy zsidó politikus a dualizmus korában." In *Honszeretet és felekezeti hűség: Wahrmann Mór, 1831–1892*, edited by Tibor Frank, 71–78. Budapest: Argumentum, 2006.

Vörös, Kati. "The 'Jewish Question,' Hungarian Sociology and the Normalization of Antisemitism." *Patterns of Prejudice* 44, no. 2 (2010): 137–60.

Waktor, Andrea. "A XIX. századi családmodell működése és változásai a Ballagi család levelezésének tükrében." *Sic Itur ad Astra* 9, no. 1–2 (1995): 43–92.

Welker, Árpád. "Vegyes házasságok és vallásváltások a Kálvin téri gyülekezetben a 19. században." In *Reformátusok Budapesten: Tanulmányok a magyar főváros reformátusságáról*, vol. 1, edited by László Kósa, 147–71. Budapest: Argumentum/ELTE BTK Művelődéstörténeti Tanszék, 2006.

―――. "Wahrmann a magyar országgyűlésben." In *Honszeretet és felekezeti hűség: Wahrmann Mór, 1831–1892*, edited by Tibor Frank, 111–70. Budapest: Argumentum, 2006.

―――. "Zsidó betérések a protestáns felekezetekbe Pesten, 1895 előtt." *Korall* 8, no. 27 (May 2007): 94–109.

Wistrich, Robert S. "Dilemmas of Assimilation in Central Europe." In *Between Redemption and Perdition: Modern Antisemitism and Jewish Identity*, 86–101. London/New York: Routledge, 1990.

―――. *The Jews of Vienna in the Age of Franz Joseph*. Oxford, UK: Oxford University Press, 1989.

Yerushalmi, Yosef Hayim. *Assimilation and Racial Anti-Semitism: The Iberian and the German Models (The Leo Baeck Memorial Lecture 26)*. New York: Leo Baeck Institute, 1982.

Zeke, Gyula. "Statisztikai mellékletek." In *Hét évtized a hazai zsidóság életében*, vol. 1, edited by Ferenc L. Lendvai, Anikó Sohár, and Pál Horváth, 185–99. Budapest: MTA Filozófiai Intézet, 1990.

―――. "Szakadás után … Adalékok a magyarországi zsidóság felekezeti irányzatainak társadalomtörténetéhez (1868–1949)." In *Hét évtized a hazai zsidóság életében*, vol. 1, edited by Ferenc L. Lendvai, Anikó Sohár, and Pál Horváth, 145–61. Budapest: MTA Filozófiai Intézet, 1990.

Zsoldos, Jenő, ed. *1848–1849 a magyar zsidóság életében*. Budapest: Múlt és Jövő, 1998.

INDEX

Page numbers in italics refer to figures.

Abdul-Hamid II, Ottoman sultan, 342
acculturation, Jewish: and conversion, 4, 10–11, 82, 122, 134, 143, 182, 362; progress of, 76, 124, 233, 334. *See also* Magyarization
Acsády, Ignác, 141
Adler, Illés, 308
Ady, Endre, 243, 262, 264, 267
Ágai, Adolf, 303, 356
Ágoston, Péter, 43
Alexander, Bernát, 56–57, 60, 356
Amberg, Ottilia (Tilly), 265
Ambrus, Zoltán, 324
Andrássy, Gyula, Jr., 241, 245, 310
Andrássy, Gyula, Sr., 37, 48, 74, 241, 245–47
Andrássy, Katinka, 339
Andrássy, Maricza, 72
Angyal, Dávid, 38, 52, 222, 229–33, *230*, 286
Angyal, Paula, 233
antisemitism: and Hungarian political elite, 48, 51, 54, 65, 207, 337, 377; and Jewish conversion, 10, 30–31, 121–22, 134, 137–38, 144, 165, 222; in political and social life, 70, 121–22, 135–37, 221–22, 308–10, 332; Jewish perception of, 1, 48, 55, 66, 70–71, 122, 125, 128, 137–38, 216, 233, 329; level of in various countries, 30–31, 134; psychological vulnerability to, 81–83, 138
Apponyi, Albert, 36, 58
Apponyi, Rudolf, 306
Arany, János, 315
Arányi, Lajos, 347
assimilation. *See* acculturation, emancipation, Magyarization
Asztalos, György, 327
Atzél, Béla, 75
Atzél, Zsófia, 320

Bácskai, Vera, 210, 213
Bak, Hirs, 12
Balázs, Béla, 239, 243, 257–60, *261*, 262–64, 286, 302, 352
Ballagi, Aladár, 198, 201–02, 335
Ballagi, Géza, 310

420 INDEX

Ballagi, Károly, 305, 333, 345
Ballagi, Mór (Móric Bloch), 126,
198–99, *200*, 201–03, 285–86, 305, 310,
312, 333–35, 341, 345
Bánffy, Dezső, 33, 171, 276
Bangha, Béla, 47
Bánóczi, József, 28, 53, 56, 222–24, 304,
357
Bánóczi, Margit, 357
baptism of children, 111, 113–15,
117–18, 130–31, 145n20, 161, 268,
312, 327–38
Barabás, Miklós, 211
Bárczy, István, 57
Barkóczy, Sándor, 58–59
Barnay, Ignác, 69
Bartók, Béla, 76
Bauer, Ervin, 257, 352
Bauer, Hilda, 243, 257
Bauer, Simon, 257–58
Belia, György, 265
Benedek, Elek, 44–45, 56, 58, 127,
238–39
Benedek, Marcell, 58, 239
Beretvás, Endre, 277
Bergl, József, 208
Bernstein, Béla, 22, 207
Berzeviczy, Albert, 56
Biedermann, Leontine, 319
Biedermann, Michael Lazar, 319
Biedermann, Ottó, 319
Biedermann, Rudolf, 164
Biedermann, Simon, 319
Biró, Lajos, 162
Blaskovich, Melánia, 68, 271, 321
Blau, Lajos, 1, 4, 17, 20
Bloch, Móric. *See* Ballagi, Mór
Bonaventura, Mayer, 13
Boncz, Ödön, 58
Boncza, Berta (Csinszka), 267
Bornemisza, Lipót, 243, 285

Bornemisza, Pál, 357
Borovszky, Samu, 274
Boscovitz/Boskovitz, Amália, 241
Botfai Hűvös, József, 165
Börne, Ludwig, 229
Brafman, Iakov (Jacob), 327
Bródy, Samu, 24
Bródy, Sándor, 29, 73, 279, 318, 325, 362
Bródy, Zsigmond, 340
Brunswick, Teréz, 315
Brüll, Adél, 72
Brüll, Alfréd, 232
Brüll, Erzsébet (Lili, Lily), 243, 285
Brüll, Henrik, 232
Brüll, Ignác, 243
Buday, Dezső, 43
Büchler, Zsigmond, 24

casinos and clubs, 12, 33, 69–70, 73–76,
138, 212–13, 241, 272–73, 285, 312, 314,
318–21, 339, 345, 347, 354, 377
Chorin, Ferenc, Jr., 165
Chorin, Ferenc, Sr., 165, 312, 352
Christian intellectuals: and
expectations of conversion, 34,
38–45, 47–48
Chwolson, Daniel, 348
Concha, Győző, 42–43
Concilia, Emil, 333
conversion to Christianity: and
antisemites' perception of, 46–47,
139; and career choice, 9, 50, 53, 57,
59, 181–82, 197, 236, 285, 308; and
Christian clergymen, 31, 36, 45–47,
113, 115–18, 126, 130, 158, 162, 242,
327–28, 347; and Neolog rabbis'
views on, 1, 55, 117, 126, 140–42, 159,
163, 201, 302, 308, 348–50, 352; and
Orthodox Jews, 10, 132, 143–44,
172–73, 353; and the 1848 revolution,
121, 206–08; efficacy of, 305–23;

INDEX

sincerity of, 31, 35, 45–47, 162, 254–57; statistics on, 110, 119, 129–35, 157n165, 168–74, 176–77, 378; waves of, 5, 120–23, 125–26, 129, 142, 144, 157n165, 165–66, 348–49. *See also* antisemitism, baptism of children, political elite, marriages between unconverted/converted Jews and Christians

Czigány, Dezső, 180

Cziráky, János, 319

Csáky, Albin, 53, 80–81, 111–13, 115, 319

Csáky, Mária Iphigénia, 319

Csemegi, Károly, 310, 312, 313

Csukási, Fülöp, 18

Dániel, Tibor, 320

Dassl-Rosenberg, Paula, 248, 338

De le Roi, Johann, 110

Deák, Ferenc, 282, 312

Dessewffy, Arisztid, 73

Dessewffy, Emil, 217

Deutsch, Bernát, 267

Deutsch, Emma, 265

Deutsch, Ignác, 267

Deutsch, Janka, 166

Deutsch, Johanna, 227

Deutsch, József, 67, 241, 267

Diamant, Johanna, 227

Dickens, Charles, 234

Diósy, Márton, 334

discrimination, anti-Jewish: in the public sector, 48–62; in the private sector, 62–64; in social life, 68–80

Disraeli, Benjamin, 348

Ditrichstein, Ilka, 162

Dóczi (Dóczy), Lajos, 37, 164, 245–48, 249, 334, 338–41, 345, 348

Dóczi, Péter, 250

Dohm, Christian Wilhelm, 35

Domony, Móricz, 165

Don, Jehuda, 49, 131

Dux, Móric, 245

Edelstein, Bertalan, 28

Edward, Prince of Wales (King Edward VII), 71

Egressy, Gábor, 303

Egyedi, Lajos, 181

Ehrenfeld, Antal, 68

Ehrenfeld, Ilka, 68

Ehrenfeld, Irma, 162

Ehrlich, Gusztáv G., 143

Einhorn, Ignác. *See* Horn, Ede

Eisler (Enyedi), Mátyás, 19, 55

Elek, Pál, 181, 184, 330, 356

Ellrich, August, 68

emancipation: of Hungarian Jews, 3, 15–16, 30, 35, 47, 49, 110–11, 121, 123, 126, 199, 202, 205–07, 212, 282, 285, 304, 335, 377; terms of, 31–32, 39–40, 43, 47, 51

Endelman, Todd, 4, 10, 31, 131, 169

Engel de Jánosi family, 165

Engel, Márton, 231

Enyedi, Mátyás. *See* Eisler, Mátyás

Eörsi, István, 239–40

Eőry, Gabriella, 74

Eötvös, József, 15, 35, 51, 54, 56, 199, 216–17, 315, 334, 341, 344

Eötvös, Károly, 315

Eötvös, Loránd, 54

Eperjessy, Géza, 158

Equality Circle, 69, 246

essentialist perception of Jewishness, 139, 303–04

Esterházy, Móric, 61

Fábián, Gábor, 40

Falk, Miksa, 312, 314, 333, 339, 345, 348, 354, 356–57

Farkas, Pál, 324

INDEX

Fáy, Béla, 277
Fehér, Mrs. Dezső, 72
Fekete, Gyula, 128, 220
Feldmann, Mózes, 117
Fellner, Henrik, 163
Fényes, Mór, 117, 142
Fenyő, Miksa, 358
Ferdinand V, emperor of Austria
  (Ferdinand I) and king of Hungary,
  205
Ferri, Lipót, 319
Feuchtmann, Simon, 210
Fischel, Hermina, 187
Fischer, Mirjám, 45
Fleischmann, Sándor, 54
Földes, Béla, 322–23, 323
Földváry, Mihály, 166
Fraknói, Vilmos, 54
Franz Joseph I, emperor of Austria and
  king of Hungary, 15, 54, 272, 277
Frieder, Mór, 77
Friedländer, Sára, 347
Fuchs, Mrs. Mór (née Malvin Kohn),
  184
Fürst, Ilona, 247, 341

Gábel, Gyula, 342–43
Gábor, Andor, 80
Gajári, Ödön, 309–10
Gajáry, Géza, 310
Garay, Károly, 253
Gáspár, Lajos, 304
Glass, Izor, 19
Glück, Adolf, 176
Goethe, Johann Wolfgang von, 257
Gold, Lujza, 275
Goldmark, Károly (Karl), 340
Goldschmied, Ede, 361
Goldschmied, Izrael, 361
Goldschmied, József, 361
Goldschmied, Lipót, 361

Goldziher, Ignác, 18, 51–52, 56–57, 224,
  334–35, 341, 345
Goldziher, Ilona, 18
Gömöry, Ilona, 78
Gömöry, János, 78
Göndöcs, Benedek, 36
Gratze, Amália, 319
Gróf, Berta, 161
Groszmann, Zsigmond, 115–16, 175, 210
Gunst, Péter, 77–78
Gutmann, Arthur, 166
Gutmann, Stefánia, 166
Gyáni, Gábor, 49, 78
Gyergyai, Albert, 237
Gyulai, Pál, 38, 229, 232, 269
Gyurgyák, János, 34, 333

Haber, Samu. See Komáromi, Sándor
Hajdu, Miklós, 24
Hajdu, Tibor, 49
Hajós, Edit, 262
Halász, Lajos, 166
Halász, Mór, 344
Hammersberg, Miklós, 310
Hamvassy, Anna, 239
Handler, Márk, 16, 238
Hanuy, Ferenc, 46
Harden, Maximilian, 268, 270
Harkányi (Koppély), Frigyes, 321, 333,
  354
Harkányi (Koppély), Fülöp, 163, 319, 321
Harkányi, András (Andor), 319
Harkányi, Béla, 319
Harkányi, Ferenc, 273
Harkányi, Károly, 273, 319, 321
Harkányi, Mária, 319
Harmos, Ilona (Mrs. Dezső
  Kosztolányi), 79
Hartmán, Lipót, 126
Hatala, Péter, 56
Hatvany, Bertalan, 264

INDEX

Hatvany, Ferenc, 264–65
Hatvany, Lajos, 165, 264–65, 266, 267–70
Hatvany, Lili, 264
Hatvany-Deutsch, Hermina, 241, 242
Hatvany-Deutsch, József, 163, 264, 267
Hatvany-Deutsch, Károly, 359
Hatvany-Deutsch, Sándor, 163, 241, 264–65, 267
Havas, Ármin, 175
Haynald, Lajos, 54, 224–25, 276
Hazai, Samu, 164
Hegedüs, Andor, 144, 359–60
Hegedüs, Arnold, 360–61
Hegedüs, Géza, 144, 359
Hegedüs, Miksa, 359–60
Hegedüs, Sándor, 276
Heidelberg, Lipót, 143
Heine, Henrik, 331, 348
Heinrich, Gusztáv, 61
Helfy, Ignác, 53, 334–39, 336, 345, 357
Heltai, Ferenc, 61
Helvey, Tivadar, 143
Hensel, Luise, 255
Hentaller, Lajos, 309
Hercz, Zsigmond, 181, 184
Herczeg, Ferenc, 72, 348
Herczel, Manó, 164
Herczfeld, Sándor, 126
Herschkovits, Mór, 187
Herschkovits, Regina, 187
Herzl, Theodor, 134, 342
Herzog, Mór Lipót, 166
Hess, Moses, 303
Heves, Kornél, 356
Hevesi, Sándor, 254–57, 256
Hevesi, Simon, 349
Hieronymi, Blanka, 319
Hieronymi, Károly, 319
Hirsch, Sámuel, 234
Hirschl, Frumet (Szidónia, Veronika), 209, 285, 313

Hirschler, Ignác, 74, 272
Hirschler, Ödön, 187
Hochmuth, Ábrahám, 224
Hódoly, László, 235
Hoffmann, Henrik, 361
Hoffmann, Ignác, 361
Hoffmann, János, 361
Hoffmann, Lajos, 361
Hoffmann, Mór, 254–55
Holländer, Leó, 69
Holló, Andor, 175
Hóman, Bálint, 378
Honigmann, Peter, 134
Horn, Ede (Ignác Einhorn), 61, 167, 312
Horthy, Miklós, 269
Horvát, Boldizsár, 51
Horváth, Géza, 161
Hugó, Károly, 303
Hyman, Paula, 27–28

Ignotus (Hugó Veigelsberg), 304, 329
Ignotus, Pál, 320
illegal baptisms, 111, 117, 130, 174
Istóczy, Győző, 46, 122, 135, 222, 282

Jászi, Alice, 327, 331
Jászi, Ferenc, 327–28
Jászi, Oszkár, 43, 241, 243, 250, 253, 327–33, 331
Jászi, Viktor, 327
Jeiteles, János, 309
Jekelfalussy, József, 33
Jewish converts: age of, 177–78; among political elite, 166–67; among university professors and members of the Hungarian Academy of Sciences, 167; antisemitism of, 324–27, 357; converting back to Judaism, 352, 355; gender distribution of, 168–70, 177–78; occupation of, 178–84

424 INDEX

Jókai, Mór, 43–44, 282, 304–05
jokes about Jewish conversions, 139,
162, 303–04, 339, 351, 353
Joseph II, emperor of Austria and king
of Hungary, 111, 124

Kaffka, Margit, 257
Kallós, Ede, 350
Kálmán, Jenő, 177
Kanitz, Manó, 163
Kann, Gyula, 350
Kánya, Emília, 308, 315
Kaplan, Marion, 27
Karády, Viktor, 49, 67, 131, 161, 171
Karinthy, Frigyes, 161
Kármán, Mór, 334
Károlyi, Mihály, 71
Katz, Jacob, 14, 131–32, 159, 161, 198
Katzburg, Nathaniel, 49, 161
Kayserling, Meyer, 140, 348
Kelemen, Gyula, 181, 184
Kempelen, Béla, 110, 166, 210
Kenedi, Géza, 348
Kepes, Samu, 72
Keresztessy, József, 355
Keresztury, Dezső, 78
Keresztury, József, 78
Khuen-Héderváry, Károly, 48
Kiss, Arnold, 20, 27–28, 61, 117, 349
Kiss, József, 29, 356
Klapka, György, 69, 78
Klein, Francziska, 160, 347
Klein, Gyula Lipót, 346
Kóbor, Anna, 359
Kóbor, Noémi, 358
Kóbor, Tamás, 16, 23, 55, 279, 284,
357–59, 360, 379
Kodolányi, János, 79
Kohlmann, Károly, 210, 333
Kóhn, Dávid, 69
Kohn, Ferdinand, 305–06

Kohn, Hermann, 187
Kohn, Jozefin, 187
Kohn, Oszkár, 187
Kohn, Sámuel, 16, 127, 175, 276, 302, 335
Kohner family, 166, 232
Komáromi, Sándor, 20, 63–64
Komlós, Aladár, 220
Kont, Ignác, 61
Kónyi, Manó, 246, 248, 339–40, 345
Koppély, Frigyes. See Harkányi,
Frigyes
Koppély, Fülöp. See Harkányi, Fülöp
Koralek, Emil, 352
Korányi, Frigyes, 164
Koricsáner, János, 305–06, 315–16
Kornfeld, Mária, 165
Kornfeld, Zsigmond, 21–22, 163, 165
Kossuth, Ferenc, 36
Kossuth, Lajos, 36, 40, 207, 248, 337
Kovács, Alajos, 172–73
Kovács, István, 187
Kozma, Andor, 324
Kozma, Sándor, 38, 75
Königswarter, Hermann, 68, 271–73,
321
Königswarter, János, 271
Königswarter, Jonas von, 271
Königswarter, Moritz von, 68, 271
Krausz, Amália Lujza, 276–77
Krausz, Izidor, 276, 359
Krausz, Lajos, 359
Krausz, Simon, 38, 356
Kulcsár, István, 80, 353, 358
Kunewalder, Fülöp, 203
Kunewalder, Jónás, 203, 204, 205–08,
286
Kürschner, Adolf, 164

Lánczy, Leó, 163
Láng, Fülöp, 180
Lassalle, Ferdinand, 234, 331

Lederer, Béla, 37
Légrády, Károly, 309–10
Lehoczky, Ida, 310
Leibniz, Gottfried Wilhelm, 257
Leopold, Samu, Jr., 78
Lesznai, Anna, 67, 241, 243, 245, 250–51, 252, 253–54, 331
Léva, Izor, 18
Lévai, Aladár, 177
Lévay, Henrik, 272–73, 274, 321–22
Levy, Eugénia (Jenny), 257
Lichtenstein, Ignác, 352
Liebermann, Pál, 329
Liebermann, Róza, 327
Liechtenstein, János, 72
Ligeti, Ernő, 72, 137
Linksz, Arthur, 24
Liszt, Franz, 315
Litván, György, 234–36, 322, 329, 358
Lowenstein, Steven, 172
Löw, Immánuel, 127
Löw, Lipót, 12, 126, 201–02, 210, 231
Löwinger, Jakab, 236
Lőwy, Anna, 24
Löwy, Herman, 205
Löwy, Johanna, 315
Ludasi (Ludassy), Mór, 48, 273
Lukács, György, 22, 67, 233, 236–40, 239, 257, 260, 262, 286, 308, 357
Lukács, János, 237
Lukács, József, 67, 236–38, 357
Lukács, Mária, 236–38
Lukács, Pál, 237
Lukácsy, Sándor, 44, 318

Madarassy-Beck, Gyula, 165
Madarassy-Beck, Marcell, 165
Máday, Lajos, 312
Magos, George, 49, 131
Magyarization, 3, 14, 16, 33–34, 36, 40, 44, 124, 197, 199, 201–02, 228, 255, 282, 285, 334, 336–38; of names, 38, 41, 186–87, 224, 227, 231, 233–34, 236, 245, 254, 262, 309, 327, 334. *See also* acculturation
Maimonides, 338, 379
Mandl, Alice, 233
Mandl, Bernát, 209–10
Mann, Thomas, 237
Márai, Sándor, 63–64, 76–77, 79, 303
Marczali, Henrik, 37, 54, 60, 356
Maria Theresa, archduchess of Austria and queen of Hungary, 111
Marjanucz, László, 119
Márk, Lajos, 350
marriages between unconverted/ converted Jews and Christians, 30, 40, 44–45, 66–68, 77, 112, 123, 131, 133, 162, 165, 169, 185–86, 243, 247–48, 267–69, 277, 285, 318–21, 337, 339, 352
Marx, Karl, 331
Matók, Béla, 41
Mauthner, Alfréd, 166
Mauthner, Ödön, 165
Mayer, Helene, 250
Mayer, Móric, 161
McCagg, William, 210, 213
Mendelssohn, Moses, 209
Mezei (Mezey), Sándor, 59
Mezei, Mór, 138, 345, 356
Mezey, Ferenc, 275
Miklós, Gyula, 319
Mikszáth, Kálmán, 40–41, 64
Miskolczi, Ferenc, 72
missionizing. *See* Scottish Mission
Molière, 257
Molnár, Aladár, 36
Molnár, Antal, 302, 358
Molnár, Ferenc, 66, 76, 138–39, 324, 351
Montesquieu, Charles-Louis de Secondat, 220
Móricz, Zsigmond, 262

426 INDEX

Morin de Banneville, Gaston, 319
Morin de Banneville, Guillaume, 319
Moscovitz, Géza (Geyza), 70–72, 75,
  241–42, 242, 316, 355
Moscovitz, Iván, 240, 242--43, 244,
  245, 250
Moscovitz, Mór, 69, 74–75, 241, 319
Munkácsi, Bernát, 23, 38, 117, 304

Nagy, Beáta, 74
Nagy, Bella, 44
Nemes, Albert, 320
Nemes, Vince, 319–20
Neolog intelligentsia, 4, 17–21, 31, 59,
  62, 66, 81, 127–29, 140, 142, 162, 222,
  255, 348–49, 351, 378
Neuman, Dániel, 320
Neuman, Margit (Mrs. Tibor Dániel),
  320
Neumann, Ede, 24–25
Neuschlosz family, 165
Nordau, Max, 342
Nyáry, Pál, 303
Nyegre, László, 243
Nyegre, Róza, 243

Oesterreicher, Elias, 13
Ónody, Géza, 75, 282
Oppenheimer, Simon, 12
Ordódy, Pál, Jr., 68
Ordódy, Pál, Sr., 68
Ormody, Bertalan, 66, 324
Ormody, Rose, 352
Ormody, Vilmos, 165, 352
Orthodox–Neolog schism, 15

Palágyi, Lajos, 129
Palágyi, Menyhért, 27
Pálffy, Miklós, 72
Pap, Géza, 35
Pardoe, Julia, 125

Pásztor, Mihály, 50
Patai, József, 308
Pauler, Tivadar, 15, 51–52
Pázmándy, Dénes, 279
Perls, Ármin, 349
Pikler, Gyula, 306
Podmaniczky, Zsuzsanna, 321
Polányi family, 355
Polányi, Károly, 262
political elite: and assimilationist
  expectations, 32–33; and
  expectations of conversion, 34–38,
  47–48, 52; integrationist policy of, 3,
  33. See also antisemitism
Pollacsek, Lujza, 234
Pollák, Antal, 161
Pollák, Mózes, 227
Pollák, Samu, 161
Pólya, Jakab, 222, 225, 226, 227–29, 285
Pólya, Jenő, 225, 227
Porzsolt, Kálmán, 43
Práger, Miklós, 353
Preisich, Adolf, 19, 76
Preisich, Kornél, 19, 76
Prohászka, Ottokár, 47
Pserhofer, Samu, 12–13
Pulszky, Ferenc, 69, 70, 112

Radó, Sámuel, 324
Radó, Vilmos, 18
Rákosi, Jenő, 72
Rapoch, Arje Löb, 11–12
Recouly, Raymond, 23
Reif, Jakab, 303
Reinhard, Károly, 350
Reinmann, Lázár, 356
Repiszky, Tamás, 328
Révész, Irma, 187
Richtmann, Mózes, 22, 159
Riff, Michael Anthony, 178
Ripp, Júlia, 177

INDEX

Romsics, Ignác, 33
Rosenberg, Oskar Adolf, 164
Rosenberg, Róza, 245
Rosenberg, Sámuel, 22
Rosenberg, Sándor, 253
Rosenthal, Izsák, 209
Rosenthal, Naftali, 209
Róth, Miksa, 180
Rothschild, Alfonso, 75

Sachs, Henrik, 352–53
Salamon, József, 160
Saphir, Izrael, 125–26, 160
Saphir, Moritz Gottlieb, 347
Sas, Irén, 362
Schächter, Miksa, 141
Schick, Lavoslav, 25
Schiller, Friedrich, 234, 257
Schlauch, Lőrinc, 271
Schlesinger, Gyula, 234
Schlesinger, Vilmos, 79
Schosberger, Henrik, 352
Schosberger, Ilona, 352
Schosberger, Lajos, 165
Schosberger, Ottilia, 352, 357
Schosberger, Zsigmond, 273
Schwab, Löw, 126, 201
Schwarcz, Gyula, 166
Schwartz, Jakab, 70
Schwarz, Gusztáv, 54
Schwarz, Szerén, 187
Schweitzer, József, 13
Schwimmer, Ernő, 354
Scottish Mission, 120, 125–26, 160, 203
Sebestyén, Károly, 27
secession from the Jewish community
    (*Konfessionslosigkeit*), 114, 132, 135,
    171–75, 262
secularization: among acculturating
    Jews, 11–26; and gender differences,
    26–28

secular Jewish identity, 17, 28–29
Silber, Michael, 13, 69, 131, 161, 203
Simonyi, Iván, 75
Simonyi, Zsigmond, 222–25, 223, 232,
    304, 308, 333, 356–57
Simor, János, 162
Singer, Bernát, 55, 140–41, 163, 349
Singer, Izrael, 17
Soltész, Adolf, 62
Somló, Bódog, 306–08, 307, 357
Somló, Felix, 307
Spinoza, Baruch, 331
Steed, Wickham, 23
Steiner, Simon, 224
Stern, Pál, 160
Stourzh, Gerald, 133
Strausz, Adolf, 162
Sturm, Albert, 51–52
Sváb, Károly, 272
Szabó, Adolf, 234
Szabó, Alfréd, 234
Szabó, Ervin, 233–36, 235, 243, 285, 330,
    331, 358
Szabó, Ottó, 234
Szabolcsi, Miksa, 28, 116–17, 140, 171,
    275, 278–80, 283–84, 325–26, 335, 338,
    345, 348–50, 379
Szalkay, Margit, 70
Szász, Károly, 276, 308
Szász, Zoltán, 42, 64
Széchenyi, István, 33, 73, 202, 312, 329
Szegfi, Mór, 308–09, 311
Székács, József, 126
Szekfű, Gyula, 231
Széll, Kálmán, 54, 136
Szentiványi, Borbála, 210, 285
Szentkirályi, István, 44
Szentkirályi, Móric, 206
Szép, Ernő, 82–83, 304
Szigetvári, Iván, 37, 324
Szilády, Áron, 306

INDEX

Szilágyi, Dezső, 75
Szitányi (Ullmann), Bernát, 74, 312–15
Szterényi, József, 164
Szűcs, István, 34

Tábori, Róbert, 325
Táncsics, Mihály, 38–39, 43
Teleki, Blanka, 315
Teleszky, István, 309, 312
Teleszky, János, 309
Tenczer, Pál, 246, 354
Thun-Hohenstein, Leo, 14
Thury, Zoltán, 318
Tisza, István, 59, 61, 136, 237, 330, 332
Tisza, Kálmán, 65, 123, 312, 321, 337, 354, 377
Toronyi, Zsuzsanna, 175
Tóth, Béla, 34, 304
Tóthfalussy, Béla, 116–17
Töreky, Géza, 269
Trebitsch, Arthur, 327
Trefort, Ágoston, 35, 37–38, 51–52, 54, 56, 60, 224
Tüköry, Margit, 319

Udvardy Cserna, János, 39
Ullmann, Ábrahám, 208
Ullmann, Adolf, 163
Ullmann, Bernát. See Szitányi, Bernát
Ullmann, Gábriel (Gábor), 9
Ullmann, István, 165
Ullmann, László, 312
Ullmann, Mór János (Mózes), 9, 74, 163, 208–13, 211, 285, 312–13, 319, 333, 345, 347
Ullmann, Mózes. See Ullmann, Mór János
Ullmann, Ödön, 165
Ullmann, Sándor, 53

Vadász, Lipót, 61, 167
Vajay, István, 36
Vajda, Péter, 33
Vámbéry, Ármin, 215–17, 218, 219–21, 231, 285, 306, 334, 341–44, 348, 357
Vámbéry, Rusztem, 344
Varga, László, 66–67, 163
Varga, Soma, 303
Vargha, Gyula, 225, 227–28
Vargha, Katalin, 160
Vázsonyi, Jenő, 129
Vázsonyi, Vilmos, 61, 66, 70, 129, 167, 353
Vereby, Soma, 40
Verhovay, Gyula, 46
Vészi, József, 28
Vezér, Erzsébet, 239–40, 243
Vidor, Tekla, 19
Víg, Emil, 177
Vörös, Emília, 319
Vörös, Károly, 49, 124, 181
Vörös, Kati, 332
Vukovics, Sebő, 35

Wachtler, Géza, 319
Wahrmann, Amália (Mrs. Bernát Pollák), 358
Wahrmann, Ernő, 275–79, 283–85, 359
Wahrmann, Mór, 70, 248, 271, 273, 275–80, 281, 282–84, 312, 345, 356, 358–59
Wahrmann, Renée, 275–78, 285, 359
Wahrmann, Richard, 275–79, 283–85, 359
Wahrmann, Sándor, 358–59
Waldapfel, János, 265
Weber, Max, 237
Weil, Fülöp, 347
Weiss, Elza, 165
Weiss, Manfréd, 21–22, 163, 165
Weisz, Bernát Ferenc, 74

INDEX

Weiszburg, Gyula, 48, 81, 344
Wekerle, Sándor, 61, 71, 136, 243
Welker, Árpád, 119–20, 123, 185
Wertheimer, Adél, 237
Wertheimstein, Charlotte von, 271
Wesel, Wilhelmina (Anna), 254
Weszprémy, Kálmán, 23, 139
Wingate, William, 203
Winsloe, Christa, 269
Wlassics, Gyula, 54, 307
Wodianer, Albert, Jr., 213, 312, 319
Wodianer, Albert, Sr., 74, 163, 213, 273, 320–21
Wodianer, Anna, 319
Wodianer, Borbála, 319

Wodianer, Gabriella, 319–20
Wodianer, Mór, 163, 208, 211, 213, *214*, 273, 312, 319–20
Wodianer, Sámuel, 74, 125, 163, 201, 208, 211–13, 320, 333
Wohl, Antal, 315
Wohl, Janka, 315, *316*
Wohl, Stefánia, 315, *317*

Zalka, János, 273
Zangwill, Israel, 343
Zay, Miklós, 31, 42, 73, 318
Zichy, Nándor, 36
Zimándy, Ignác, 47
Zsolt, Béla, 24, 78

MIKLÓS KONRÁD is Senior Research Fellow at the Institute of History of the Research Centre for the Humanities and at the Ignác Goldziher Jewish Historical and Cultural Research Institute (Budapest, Hungary).

For Indiana University Press

Lesley Bolton, Project Manager/Editor
Sophia Hebert, Assistant Acquisitions Editor
Samantha Heffner, Marketing and Publicity Manager
Brenna Hosman, Production Coordinator
Katie Huggins, Production Manager
Bethany Mowry, Acquisitions Editor
Dan Pyle, Online Publishing Manager
Pamela Rude, Senior Artist and Book Designer